Birds
of the Pacific Northwest

Northern Spotted Owl, a rare inhabitant of the dense spruce and fir forests. (From a painting by Olaus J. Murie.)

Birds
of the Pacific Northwest

WITH SPECIAL REFERENCE TO OREGON

[*formerly titled: Birds of Oregon*]

BY

Ira N. Gabrielson
and Stanley G. Jewett

Dover Publications, Inc.
New York

Published in Canada by General Publishing Company, Ltd., 30 Lesmill Road, Don Mills, Toronto, Ontario.

Published in the United Kingdom by Constable and Company, Ltd., 10 Orange Street, London WC 2.

This Dover edition, first published in 1970, is an unabridged republication of the work originally published by Oregon State College in 1940 under the title *Birds of Oregon*. The work is reprinted by special arrangement with Oregon State University.

In the original edition the frontispiece and map of the life zones of Oregon were reproduced in color.

Standard Book Number: 486-22346-9
Library of Congress Catalog Card Number: 72-106489

Manufactured in the United States of America
Dover Publications, Inc.
180 Varick Street
New York, N.Y. 10014

Foreword

Lovers of the great out-of-doors, as well as those scientifically inclined, are to be felicitated upon the publication of *The Birds of Oregon* by Gabrielson and Jewett. For forty years these men patiently and painstakingly assembled the material for this imposing and delightful book. They brought to the task a wealth of experience and of scientific knowledge. They covered the state from the Columbia to Goose Lake and from the Pacific Ocean to the Snake River. By personal contact they know Oregon from sea level to the summit of Mt. Hood. They transferred from nature's book to the printed page some of nature's most interesting and beautiful expressions. Dr. Ira N. Gabrielson, Chief of the United States Biological Survey, and Mr. Stanley G. Jewett, Regional Biologist of the Biological Survey, have done exceptionally well something they particularly desired to do. It is significant that the results of their labor are preserved, a work of art, for the pleasure and profit of all of us.

The authors, for years, have cooperated with Oregon State College in the promotion of plans for the preservation of the wild life of the region. They have visioned the time when leisure hours would be more plentiful and when the wild things of field and forest would contribute greatly to the recreational features of the Northwest.

Oregon has wonderful recreational possibilities. When one knows the birds, their habits and their value, his interest in them is stimulated and his joy in seeing them is increased. In the accomplishment of these things, the book fulfills its mission.

George W. Peavy
President, Oregon State College
Corvallis, Oregon

Preface

As THEY undertook to write this record of the birds found in Oregon, the authors were quickly impressed with the scarcity of published notes on the avifauna of this State, which ornithologically is one of the richest and most interesting areas in the West. The more important ornithological papers that have been published about this fascinating territory since Lewis and Clark made the first recorded notes in 1805 could be counted on the fingers of two hands.

The task of gathering the literature and tabulating the records, an enormous though enjoyable one that has occupied the authors' spare time for many years, would have been insurmountable without the kindness of hosts of friends who have saved specimens and forwarded notes that have been freely drawn upon. Attempt has been made to give due credit in the text to all these friends, and the authors wish here to express their appreciation to them collectively and individually for the very great help extended.

The State Game Commission and the State Fish Commission of Oregon have been very generous in helping the authors obtain data, often even having detailed the services of staff members; and the Fish Commission has given financial aid as well in carrying out some of the investigations. All field notes and specimens of the Bureau of Biological Survey have been made available, and every possible help has been extended by numerous members of the Bureau. The same holds true for the National Museum, where Dr. Alexander Wetmore, Assistant Secretary of the Smithsonian Institution, has examined many old specimens and verified records. Among the Oregon students of birds, Dr. William L. Finley, Dr. A. G. Prill, Alex Walker, W. E. Sherwood (now deceased), J. C. Braly, and Ed. S. Currier have furnished many valuable records and notes. Among later students, Reed Ferris, H. M. Dubois, Overton Dowell, Jr., John Carter, and J. E. Patterson have furnished specimens and notes that have contributed to the book materially. Many others, too numerous to mention here, have been helpful, and due credit has been given to each.

Every effort has been made to go over the literature and to make this volume, the first comprehensive bird book for the State, a condensed summary of the existing knowledge of Oregon birds. It is impossible that the effort has been fully successful. Oregon is far distant from the larger scientific libraries, so that for information concerning many of the older and rarer works it has been necessary to depend on sources other than the original. A few of the older journals were checked by Gabrielson on several trips east, but the limited time available has permitted examination of only the most important ones.

As it seemed desirable to have brief understandable descriptions of the birds, the authors have used extensively, with her permission, the descriptions written by Florence Merriam Bailey in her *Handbook of Birds of the Western United States* (1921 edition), either verbatim or modified as necessary to meet more recent subspecific descriptions. Bent's descriptions of downy young birds have also been drawn upon. The first of these two features has been incorporated because of the need of younger students to have convenient descriptions available in one book; the second, in answer to many queries and in view of the authors' own difficulties in finding descriptions of downy young birds before Bent's studies were published.

In addition to this literature, the authors have had their own notes and specimens, collected whenever opportunity offered as they traveled over the State on other work and during vacation periods that for many years were devoted to filling in the gaps in their knowledge. Jewett has been engaged in collecting and observing birds in Oregon since 1902, with only comparatively brief absences from the State; and Gabrielson, since 1918. Since 1930 both authors have given time and such funds as they could spare to a study of the offshore bird population, about which little has been known. There is still a great deal to learn, but much information has been acquired, the essentials of which have been incorporated in this book. The tabulation and classification of these personal records has been in itself a huge task that has taken many years.

The mass of available data seemed appalling when the compilation started, and except for the efficient help of Miss Adelaide G. King, who tabulated most of the card records and typed almost all the manuscript, the book would still be far from finished. Notwithstanding this wealth of material, as the work drew to a close, great gaps had a way of showing up in the most unexpected places, partly because of the hit-and-miss type of collecting necessarily practiced and partly because the territory is so large and so varied in topography and faunal conditions that two men could not fill in all of the detail even were they free to devote their entire lifetimes to the task. The authors feel that they have merely laid the groundwork on which others can build intelligently. Existing published records and the unpublished work of the few present-day bird students in the State have been tabulated and brought down to 1935 and thus made accessible for future workers. It is hoped that the book will provide an incentive for many others to take up this fascinating study and carry it much further than the authors have been able to do. The manuscript was completed in June 1935, but a few important records made since that date have been added. Additional distribution data would have been included if time had permitted. The outlook for some of the birds, particularly the migratory waterfowl, is now more hopeful than at that time.

The book has been written entirely by Gabrielson, but a large part of the endless task of checking records and literature has been assumed by Jewett. For the identifications and for distribution data, the authors are jointly responsible, except that in some of the more difficult groups the specimens have been submitted to others. To these men, especially to Dr. H. C. Oberholser, Dr. Joseph Grinnell, Harry S. Swarth, and George Willett, the authors are particularly grateful for their patience in helping with knotty problems and answering inquiries.

It would be grossly unfair not to acknowledge the constant encouragement that has been received from Dr. A. K. Fisher, Dr. W. B. Bell, and Stanley P. Young, under whose direction the authors have at various times been engaged in rodent and predatory animal control work. Recognizing the importance of the research work necessary, Mr. Young not only allowed ample time to work out special problems and to prepare this book, but also furnished clerical help when it could be spared from regular duties.

To the State College Committee in charge of the publication of the Oregon State Monographs, a research series in which this study has been assigned a place, grateful acknowledgment is extended for their efficient service in arranging for the publication of the book and for valuable editorial assistance.

The work has thus become a joint enterprise of the Bureau of Biological Survey and the Oregon State College, the College having handled the publication of the report.

IRA N. GABRIELSON,
Chief, Bureau of Biological Survey.

Contents

CONTENTS—Continued

List of Illustrations

Plates from Photographs

List of Illustrations—Continued

List of Illustrations—Continued

Text Figures

List of Illustrations—Continued

Check-List of the Birds of Oregon

Order ANSERIFORMES: Ducks, Geese, and Swans

Check-List of the Birds of Oregon—Continued

Order Falconiformes: Birds of Prey

Order Galliformes: Gallinaceous Birds

Order Gruiformes: Cranes, Rails, and Allies

Check-List of the Birds of Oregon—Continued

Order Charadriiformes: Shore Birds, Gulls, Auks, and Allies

CHECK-LIST OF THE BIRDS OF OREGON—Continued

Order COLUMBIFORMES: Pigeons and Doves

Order CUCULIFORMES: Cuckoos

Order STRIGIFORMES: Owls

Order CAPRIMULGIFORMES: Goatsuckers

Order MICROPODIFORMES: Swifts and Hummingbirds

Order CORACIIFORMES: Kingfishers

Order PICIFORMES: Woodpeckers

Order Passeriformes: Perching Birds

CHECK-LIST OF THE BIRDS OF OREGON—Continued

Check-List of the Birds of Oregon—Continued

Check-List of the Birds of Oregon—Continued

Hypothetical List

Check-List of the Birds of Oregon—Continued

Birds
of the Pacific Northwest

Something About Birds as a Group

No form of wildlife has such a popular appeal to the general public as birds, and none a greater fascination. This is due to the combination of characters that make them spectacular, noticed even by those who are not particularly interested in the out-of-doors. The activity, color, song, nest building, care of the young, and migration of birds all combine to bring them to popular attention.

Birds are easily characterized, the old definition that "A bird is an animal with feathers" being still perfectly sound biologically and more easily remembered than more involved statements of structural differences.

In comparison with other groups, birds are remarkably homogenous—a fact that for taxonomic purposes has led to comparative exaggeration of the differentiating characters present—and any who doubt it have only to pluck a few birds and view them without their feathered coverings. "Fine feathers" do "make fine birds," for without the feathers the brilliant orioles have a remarkable superficial resemblance to the dull-colored sparrows. Examining plucked birds and forgetting skeletal and internal characters, we see that aside from feathers the chief differences are those of size, length of neck, and length, size, and shape of bills, legs, and feet. Differences in the abundance, color, structure, size, and shape of the feathers, particularly those of the head, wings, and tail, combined with the structural variations just mentioned give us the remarkable variety of birds with which we are privileged to be acquainted.

Aside from these differences in superficial appearance, birds have certain common characters that set them apart from other groups. All the well-known birds have skeletons of strong, light bones with the forelimbs modified into organs of flight. Examining the skeleton, we find that the bones in the fingers and wrists are more or less fused to form at the extremity of the wing a single strong bone that supports the primaries, the feathers chiefly used in flight. The rest of the wing is composed of the secondaries, which are on the forearm, and the tertials, inserted in the upper arm. These three groups of feathers compose the fan, or wing, surface that makes flight possible. The smaller feathers at the base of the wing are chiefly valuable for form and covering. The great differences in wing shape, from the shortly rounded wings of the rails, which are scarcely able to sustain the flight of the birds, to the enormously elongated flight organs of the albatross, are produced by the variation in number, shape, and comparative length of the flight feathers.

The bills also are variable, according to the feeding needs and feeding habits of the species. Some striking examples of this variation may be noted in the following forms: Swallows have an exceedingly weak bill with an enormous gape that allows them to scoop up small insects while in full flight. Nighthawks' bills are quite similar. Warblers are equipped with slender, comparatively weak bills with which they pick small insects from foliage and flowers. Sparrows, which are generally seed eaters, possess powerful, cone-shaped beaks that are used in cracking hard seeds and obtaining the meat from within. Hawks and owls are provided with powerful hooked upper mandibles for tearing the flesh of their prey. Ducks have wide, shovellike bills for scooping seeds, plant parts, and small animal life out of the mud. Sometimes these bills are still further adapted to this particular work by the presence of strainers and combs that sift out and retain insects and other food when mud and water are forced through them. The Shoveller, or Spoonbill, is a conspicuous example of this type. Herons have long, sharp javelins with which they stab their prey with lightninglike thrusts. Anyone who has watched a Great Blue Heron impale an incautious fish will appreciate the power of this equipment. The beak, which is long and needle sharp, is driven forward by the long neck as if unleashed from a spring. Seldom does the luckless fish, frog, or crustacean manage to move fast enough to escape the deadly thrust. These examples indicate generally a wide adaptation in birds' bills for the particular use to which they are put. Instances of special adaptation could be cited almost indefinitely to further elaborate this point.

Feet and legs also are modified according to the needs of the different species. Those of the swallows, swifts, and nighthawks are small and weak, as these birds are constantly on the wing and do all their feeding in the air. Obviously they do not need the strength in these organs that is necessary in those of other species with different feeding habits. Most of the sparrows, which feed on the ground, have rather stout legs and feet equipped with powerful and elongated claws for use in scratching seeds from the earth. Herons, ibises, and many of the shore birds have long legs and elongated toes with which they can wade in the water and readily walk in the soft mud. Rails have exceedingly long toes to enable them to run about on the floating vegetation of the marshes. Ducks, cormorants, loons, and other water birds have webs between the toes, which provide efficient paddles for swimming and diving. Coots have a curious adaptation of this webbed-foot principle: instead of the webs extending from toe to toe, as in most other swimming birds of Oregon, the webs are flaps on each side of the toe that close as the foot is drawn forward and open as it is pushed back. Hawks and owls, as a group, have strong feet armed with powerful talons for striking and carrying their prey. In this group the Osprey, which lives largely on fish, has a further curious adaptation of the foot. On the inner side of the toes and on the sole of the foot there are knoblike protuberances that assist in catching and holding the prey.

Activity

Any living, moving thing is of interest to children. If the activity is correlated with brilliant color, the activity itself attracts old as well as young. When, in addition to the movement and coloration of birds, we consider their home life, their courting, and their feeding habits, often carried on close to human habitations, we can understand in some measure the strength of their appeal to popular imagination. Some species have so adapted themselves to human dwellings and other buildings that they readily avail themselves of artificial facilities provided intentionally or otherwise for their use. Martins, Tree Swallows, and Violet-green Swallows frequently occupy nest boxes placed for them. Bluebirds and House Wrens do so regularly. Robins, Phoebes, Starlings, and English Sparrows avail themselves of crevices or projections about buildings as nesting places. The Barn Swallow has so adapted itself to human habitations that it commonly makes its cup-shaped nest about outbuildings. Many birds will use material, such as string, wool, cotton, and rags, that is provided them for nest building; and a wide variety of species will visit feeding stations where suet, fruit, and seeds are available. This has led many friends of the birds to erect more or less elaborate feeding stations for attracting them to window ledges or nearby points where their daily activities can be watched.

Coloration

The colors of birds, particularly those of brilliant hues, have long excited interest. Although the dull-colored species far outnumber the bright ones, the latter arouse popular interest. The bright hues and intricate patterns of many of the warblers always attract attention, as do the flaming colors of the orioles. The Scarlet Tanager and the flame-crested Cardinal are ever conspicuous, whereas the myriad dull-colored sparrows pass almost entirely unnoticed. Many birds of somber color, however, have intricate patterns and delicate shadings that are beautiful in themselves. The modestly colored Pintail drake, for example, when observed closely, is seen to be marked with delicate lines and vermiculations in a complicated pattern that becomes more appealing as one studies it. Similarly, the soft browns of the Bohemian Waxwing, contrasted only with the yellow bar on the tail and the brilliant red wax tips on the wing feathers, shade almost imperceptibly from one soft pastel tint into another in one of the most beautiful color combinations to be found in an American bird. The brilliant markings of the drake Wood Duck always excite interest, but few notice the intricate patterns in soft grays and whites that decorate a male Gadwall's breast.

Since Darwin propounded his theories of protective coloration and sexual selection many other theories have been advanced to account for the remarkable color patterns and plumage variations to be found in birds. In a book of this kind there can be little more than mention of those theories more commonly considered as accounting for these color patterns. They are all interesting, but no one theory has been accepted in its entirety by all biologists.

The theory of protective coloration assumes that a bird or other animal may be colored so like the background against which it habitually lives that it escapes detection as long as it remains motionless. Striking examples are seen in grouse and prairie chickens, which flatten themselves into invisibility against the ground as long as they do not move. The longitudinal brown and yellow stripes of bitterns strikingly simulate the light and shadows of the reed patches in which they habitually live. Even brilliantly colored birds may be protected by the breaking-up of the pattern. For example, a White-headed Woodpecker might be a conspicuous bird, but in many situations the striking contrast between the black body and white head actually seems to behead the bird and make it appear a black or white spot against the background. Even such brilliantly colored birds as the tanagers and the warblers may be concealed by their pattern as long as they remain motionless in the treetops, the contrasting colors having the effect of breaking up the outline and rendering the bird more difficult to see. The art of camouflage, developed to a considerable degree in military and naval operations in the Great War, is recognition of this fact.

The theory of sexual selection was advanced to account for the brilliant colors of the male birds. The theory presupposes that by conscious or unconscious selection of the more strikingly marked males, special characters or brilliant colors have been gradually developed over a long time. This might account for the crests of some species of birds, the aigrettes and plumes of some of the herons, the wattles and combs of the turkeys, and the brilliantly colored air sacs of the grouse. The same theory also has been used to account for the development of highly colored beaks and varied feathers in many species.

The latest theory, advanced by Abbott H. Thayer, is that of counter shading. Thayer, artist and demonstrator, pointed out the prevalence of dark backs and light under parts in the animal world and demonstrated that such a pattern had some concealing value against almost any background in comparison with a solid-colored body of the same size and shape.

Many marks in birds may not be accounted for by any of the above theories, and for these, the theory of recognition marks or revealing characters has been advanced. The white tail feathers of juncos and meadowlarks and the conspicuous rump patches of many birds when taking flight, for example, are supposed to be of value in directing birds of similar species or in affording recognition marks to guide others of the same species.

Physically, color is produced in bird feathers by two methods: first, by pigmentation, in which color pigments are actually deposited in the feathers as they grow; and second, by feather structure, in which the feather is so developed as to produce myriads of tiny prisms that break up and reflect the light beams. These prisms against a background of dark-colored pigments produce the ever-changing iridescent gorgets of the hummers and the evanescent purple, bronze, and green reflections in some of the blackbirds, ducks, and other species.

Song

One of the chief interests in birds is afforded by their songs. Many species, in addition to call and alarm notes, have developed songs of varied length, intensity, and complexity. These are a study in themselves, and many books and articles have been written about different methods of recording and studying them. Those interested in following this subject further should consult Saunder's books on bird song (cited in Bibliography).

It is widely believed that there are not so many song birds present in the western as in the eastern part of the country. It is true that Cardinals, Eastern Mockingbirds, Brown Thrashers, Catbirds, Carolina Wrens, and others that make up the great bird choruses in towns and about homes in eastern states are absent on the Pacific Coast. About most of the towns are found only the Northwestern and Western Robins, Bullock's Orioles, Black-headed Grosbeaks, Western House Wrens, Western Meadowlarks, and similar species; but in the mountains there are songsters equal to any to be found elsewhere. Along mountain streams, the beautiful song of the Dipper, or Water Ouzel, may be heard above the noise of the tumbling waters; and in the Cascades and the ranges in eastern Oregon the loud, clear song of the Fox Sparrow rings from every thicket. Townsend's Solitaire, a slim, trim, shy, gray bird of the mountain tops and juniper thickets, has a song that cannot be excelled by any other bird in America; and the second-growth thickets of spruce and fir along the summit of the Cascades and the tangled jungles of salmonberry in the stream bottoms ring with the weird minor melodies of the Hermit and Russet-backed Thrushes, premier songsters of the American woodlands.

Other bird voices are attractive, although they may not be called songs. The wild, free call of the Olive-sided Flycatcher, flung from a lofty perch on the top of a dead snag on a mountain slope, or that of the Pileated

Woodpecker, expresses the very spirit of the untamed mountains; and the ringing laugh of the loon, still heard on some coastal and mountain lakes, is one of the most thrilling sounds in the Oregon out-of-doors. There are few whose imagination is not stimulated by the strident cries of the V-shaped flocks of wild geese passing far overhead or by the trumpet calls of the Sandhill Cranes that continue to float back to earth long after the circling flocks have passed from sight into the heavens.

Nest Building

The nest-building habit of birds still arouses a great deal of popular interest. The nests may vary from none at all to the complicated apartment-house structures built by the weaver finches of Africa. Among the birds that build no nests are many shore birds that lay their eggs on the open ground or in shallow depressions, possibly lined with a few bits of vegetation or small pebbles; the nighthawks that deposit their two eggs either on the ground or on the roofs of buildings in cities; and the seafowl, such as murres, that select bare ledges of rock on precipitous cliffs for their eggs, which, sharply pointed at one end, roll around and around on the sharp point and thus often are prevented from being blown or knocked from the cliffs.

Many nesting habits have been developed apparently independently in many sections of bird families. Birds from such widely separated families as kingfishers, petrels, auklets, puffins, and Bank and Rough-winged Swallows nest in burrows in the ground, while in North Portland and a few other localities in Oregon the Red-shafted Flickers, despite the abundance of trees to furnish normal nesting sites, have abandoned their traditional wooden apartment houses for holes excavated in clay banks.

Holes in trees are popular nesting sites with birds. Birds of the woodpecker and nuthatch families do their own construction work, the woodpeckers being equipped with up-to-date wood-working tools that are especially developed for collecting wood-boring insects and excavating holes for nest sites. Many other species of birds later appropriate the abandoned woodpecker holes or make use of natural cavities in the trees. In Oregon, such widely varied species as owls, hawks, chickadees, bluebirds, tree swallows, and wood ducks are regular tenants of such structures.

Many small birds nest on the ground, building more or less complicated structures in which to lay their eggs. Numerous sparrows and warblers belong in this class, weaving cup-shaped nests in shallow depressions in the ground. Many ducks do likewise, covering the eggs with down plucked from their own breasts. A great variety of other birds occasionally or habitually build ground nests.

Most of the more familiar birds, however, build structures of one kind or another, in trees, in bushes, or even in herbaceous plants. They may vary in design from the Mourning Dove's flimsy platform of twigs, which in some miraculous manner holds the eggs and the young squabs, to the neatly woven pensile nests of the orioles. There are many different types of tree nests. Doves and herons build flimsy platforms of twigs. Crows, jays, and hawks build substantial nests of sticks that are more or less completely lined with vegetable fibers, leaves, or rootlets. Sparrows, vireos, and warblers build neat nests of finer vegetation, often mixed with wool, hair, cotton, string, or other similar material. The Chipping Sparrow, for example, is widely known among small boys as the "horse-hair bird" because it lines its nest with horsehair, while the small fly-catchers' nests are frequently so covered with lichen as to resemble from below a lichen-clad knot. Others, including robins and the varied thrushes, build nests of vegetable matter lined with mud. These structures are described in more detail under each species. The object of this short discussion is to call attention to the great variation in nesting habits and behavior of the common birds of the State.

Care of the Young

Young birds are generally divided into two classes: precocial, those with the ability to feed and care for themselves from the time of hatching; and altricial, those requiring feeding by the parents.

Precocial birds, represented by the grouse, shore birds, and waterfowl, are able to run about and gather their own food within a few hours after kicking themselves from the shell. In proportion to the size of the bird, the eggs in this group are large and the period of incubation long, so that the young are comparatively well developed when they emerge from the shells. Young waterfowl and shore birds immediately take to the water or the water's edge. Those that swim are very skillful in concealing themselves in the aquatic vegetation or by submerging with just the tip of the bill showing. Small sandpipers match so perfectly the surroundings of their shore-line habitat that as long as they remain motionless they are invisible to human eyes. Young grouse have the same advantage, but in addition their wing quills grow with such amazing rapidity that they are able to fly by the time they are ten days old.

Altricial birds, born helpless and unable to move about, are fed for varying periods of time by the parents. Small songbirds are normally fed in the nest for approximately two weeks and are frequently provided for by the parents for a few days after they begin to try their wings. Many varied groups of birds carry food to their young. Among songbirds it is the common practice of the parents to gather insects or seeds and feed them directly to the young birds by inserting them into the open mouths and pushing them well down the throat, so that the nestlings swallow them almost automatically. Young of this class are helpless, homely bits of flesh scantily decorated with a little fuzz or down and at hatching capable only of raising their heads and opening their mouths at the slightest sound. They grow rapidly, however, and in a few days are scrambling about the nest competing with each other for the food supply. The quantity of food collected and brought to the young is astonishing. To some nests that have been watched, the adults have been observed to make as many as 344 feeding visits a day. Usually both parents take part in this arduous duty, although there is considerable temperamental and individual variation. In the majority of cases the female is the more active at this task, although at individual nests males have been observed carrying the heavy end of the job.

In addition to direct feeding, which occurs with the majority of songbirds, the helplessness of young birds and the type of feeding activity have brought the development of a number of peculiar methods of transferring the food from the parents to the young. In the pelican family, for example, fishes are swallowed by the adult bird, which returns to the nest heavily laden. On arriving, the huge bill is opened and the one or two homely, fuzzy youngsters insert their heads far down the throat of the parent to obtain the partly digested food. Adult herons partly digest frogs, crustaceans, and small fishes before arrival at the nest. There the youngsters seize the parent's bill crosswise, exactly as if they were attempting to cut it off with a pair of scissors. When the two birds are locked together, the parent goes through a series of contortions and pumping motions that eventually result in bringing up a mass of partly digested food that is transferred to the mouth of the young bird as its bill slides along that of the adult towards the tip. The hummers expertly feed their young by thrusting their long beaks far down the throats of the babies. The nestlings are so tiny and the bill is so sharp and long that an observer seeing a performance for the first time half fearfully expects to see the baby bird completely impaled. Many sparrows carry seeds in their throats and gullets, bringing the softened material up into their mouths to feed the young birds on their return to the nest. Hawks and owls tear up their prey for the younger birds, feeding them small bits of flesh at a time, although these ferocious and stoutly built youngsters soon learn to do their own carving.

There are many interesting things going on about the nest of any bird; the individual reactions of the parents, their battles with real or potential enemies, the feeding of the young, and the sanitation of the nest make up a kaleidoscopic picture that is intensely fascinating to an observer. In the past few years a great deal has been accomplished by erecting blinds close to nests and watching at short range the varied activities. Occasionally a pair of birds refuses to become reconciled to the presence of such a blind, but in the majority of cases they quickly become accustomed to it and in some instances show an astonishing indifference. An observer who watches from one of these blinds soon learns that each adult has built up a stereotyped behavior. It habitually forages in the same area and comes to and leaves the nest by the same route, even alighting on the same twigs each time. In some individuals, this response becomes almost automatic and very firmly fixed. Gabrielson, in preparing to watch a House Wren, inadvertently placed his blind across the out-bound path of one of the parents. This disconcerted the bird for a time and resulted in a lot of scolding. It eventually solved the problem, not by changing its route, but by varying the steps. From the nest it flew directly to the opening of the blind, lit on the cloth in the opening, hopped from that to the observer's knee, then onto his shoulder, and out through the entrance opening on the opposite side of the tent. After this routine was established, the bird became reconciled to the tent and made the trips through it in the fashion indicated many times that day.

Migration

From the early dawn of history, the migratory movements of birds have excited curiosity and speculation among the peoples of the world. This interest has resulted in the development of curious legends and beliefs, some of which still persist strongly in many countries. For example, at one time it was widely accepted that when all the clan of swallows and swifts that gathered in the large autumnal companies that are such familiar late-summer sights over the marshlands were assembled, all the birds took wing at once, dived into the water, swam to the bottom and buried themselves in the mud, to emerge the following spring after the cold weather had passed. In other lands, barnacles were supposed to change into geese, and fruits or seeds of certain trees that grew along the seashore and dropped into the water were supposed, by some mysterious alchemy of the deep, to be transformed into waterfowl of various types.

Study of Migration Routes

In modern times, with modern facilities of travel and methods of communication, bird migrations are much better understood, and we now know in a great measure the summer and winter homes of our common birds and the routes traveled. The first systematic study of migrations of North American birds on a large scale was undertaken by the Biological Survey and was carried on for many years by Professor Wells W. Cooke. By using hundreds of volunteers, acquainted at least with the common birds scattered over the United States, and getting these observers to record the first spring and fall appearances of the birds and other data, he soon began to accumulate an immense volume of information. True, there were probably many individual errors of observation and identification, but by taking averages and placing them on maps, Professor Cooke was able to forecast with remarkable accuracy the date of probable first arrival of the birds in a given locality and to plot their migration routes. This work is still going on, and the records from individual observers in the same locality, sometimes running back for many years, furnish a remarkable picture of the ebb and flow of the migratory movements at that particular point.

Birdbanding a Factor in Plotting Routes

More recently, the work of banding birds, started many years ago by individuals, has been systematized and greatly extended by the Biological Survey, until now the country is covered with a network of stations. The Survey acts as a clearing house for information, furnishes bands to cooperators, and develops traps of various kinds. Many individuals have also developed traps for special uses. The work is carried out entirely on a cooperative basis, volunteer workers doing the banding solely to assist in getting vital information. Banding stations are maintained on many of the migratory waterfowl refuges. To date (1940), more than three million birds have been banded, and the returns have been great enough to allow the plotting of migration routes with remarkable accuracy.

As a result of this work, two facts stand forth increasingly clear. First, the normal behavior of migratory birds traveling hundreds or thousands of miles is exceedingly stereotyped. Banded birds are retrapped in the same breeding location year after year, and wintering birds return for many seasons to the same locality and even to the same field to spend that season. For example, White-throated Sparrows and juncos, two birds that winter commonly and widely over the eastern United States, are caught season after season in the same stationary trap. The bands furnish an invaluable means of identification and have revealed some remarkable histories of movements and behavior of individual birds. For example, one much-publicized Common Mallard hen has returned for eight consecutive seasons to build her nest on the same shed roof in northern Nebraska.

The second fact brought out by birdbanding is that, although the normal behavior of birds, as stated, is apparently to follow the same line of travel and to spend the summer and winter in the same localities each year, there are many interesting cases of birds that have wandered far afield. Two Black-headed Gulls, banded on July 18, 1911, at Rossitten, Germany, were recaptured, one at Bridgetown, in the Barbadoes, in November 1911, and the second at Vera Cruz, Mexico, in February 1912. Two kittiwakes were banded at the Farne Islands, England, on June 28, 1923, and June 30, 1924. The first was killed in Newfoundland on August 12, 1924, and the second in Labrador on October 28, 1925. An American

Common Tern, banded on the coast of Maine on July 3, 1913, was found dead four years later, in August 1917, at the mouth of the Niger River in British West Africa.

A number of banding stations have been operating in Oregon more or less sporadically. Until 1935, the station at the great Malheur Migratory Bird Refuge, in charge of George M. Benson, had banded the greatest number of birds and had had the greatest number of recoveries reported. Table 1 shows the number of waterfowl banded at this and other Oregon stations and the number and percentage of banded birds recovered to July 1, 1935. Table 2 shows these returns by localities.

TABLE 1.—Returns of Waterfowl Banded in Oregon, to July 1, 1935.

Species	Banded at Malheur	Recovered		Banded at other Oregon stations	Recovered	
	Number	*Number*	*Per cent*	*Number*	*Number*	*Per cent*
Mallard	4,145	889	21.4	1,279	84	6.5
Baldpate	2,788	692	25.0	50	2	4.0
Pintail	2,211	457	20.6	1,535	174	11.3
Gadwall	921	227	24.6	6	1	16.6
Green-winged Teal	955	180	18.8	79	7	8.8
Canvas-back	83	17	20.4	553	39	7.0
Cinnamon Teal	38	2	5.2	....	....	....
Redhead	53	17	32.0	41	6	14.6
Scaups	16	3	18.7	1,370	160	11.6
Shoveller	14	1	7.1	20	5	25.0
Golden-eye	2	....	....	....	....	....
Wood Duck	2	....	....	....	....	....
Total	11,228	2,484	22.1	4,933	478	9.68

One of the interesting things shown in Table 1 is that a return of approximately 20 per cent of the ducks banded may be expected. Other species than game birds show far lower returns, although the percentage tends to mount on all birds as the years pass and more of the birds banded in earlier years are recovered.

Table 2 and the accompanying map (Figure 1) indicate how widely the ducks bred or captured in migration at Malheur spread over the country. It will be noted that the great majority of returns of Malheur-banded birds are from California, Oregon, and Idaho. This is entirely to be expected and confirms popular belief that the great Malheur marshes furnish a large percentage of their birds to California sportsmen.

The banding records show migration routes clearly. Malheur-raised birds are shot regularly in western Oregon but not in great numbers. On the other hand, great numbers of mallards banded at the National Bison

TABLE 2.—Returns of Waterfowl Banded in Oregon, by Localities, to July 1, 1935.[1]
[M=Lake Malheur; O=Other points]

Recovery localities	Mallard		Baldpate		Pintail		Gadwall		Green-winged Teal		Canvas-back		Scaups	
	M	O	M	O	M	O	M	O	M	O	M	O	M	O
	No.	*No.*	*No.*	*No.*	*No.*	*No.*	*No.*	*No.*	*No.*	*No.*	*No.*	*No.*	*No.*	*No.*
Northwest Territory			1											
Alaska			8		10	5						1		9
Yukon Territory			1						1					
British Columbia	17	6			2				2					9
Mackenzie					1									
Alberta	27	5	13		4				1			3		1
Saskatchewan	3				1		2					6		
Manitoba	1				1							1		
Washington	37	15	28		14	5	2		4			3		18
Oregon	179	46	90	1	39	87	24		12	6	7	19	1	105
California	453	8	512	1	343	68	153		154	1	10	4	2	17
Baja California					1									
Idaho	110	3	10		7	1	14		3					
Nevada	28		26		4	1	21		2					
Montana	13	1	1		3	1	1		1			1		1
Wyoming					1									
Utah	4				4	1	5							
Arizona			1		1		3							
Colorado	4													
Mexico	2				6	1	2	1						
British Honduras						1								
North Dakota	2				1	1						1		
South Dakota					1									
Nebraska	2				2									
Oklahoma	1				2									
Texas	2				6	2								
Minnesota			1											
Iowa	2													
Missouri	2				1									
Louisiana					1									
Illinois					1									
Total	889	84	692	2	457	174	227	1	180	7	17	39	3	160

Range at Moiese in northwestern Montana are recovered in Idaho, Washington, and Oregon. These birds gather in Montana on their southward movement from the Alberta and Saskatchewan country, travel from there to the headwaters of either the Columbia or Snake Rivers and down these rivers to western Oregon, and then turn south. Returns from this banding station illustrate vividly the fact that Oregon sportsmen are vitally interested in the welfare of the birds in the Canadian plains section.

[1] As indicated in Table 1 there are a few other species of ducks of which small numbers have been banded in Oregon, but the returns are too few to be of importance and so are omitted in this table.

Another interesting map (Figure 2) shows the returns of Cackling Geese banded near the mouth of the Yukon River, Alaska, chiefly in the vicinity of Hooper Bay. These birds have a very restricted breeding area and migration route. Captured birds bearing these bands have come from the coasts of Alaska, British Columbia, and Washington. The birds follow the coast to the mouth of the Columbia River or to Tillamook Bay and there turn inland, heading directly for Tule Lake on the Oregon-California border east of the Cascades. They remain at this favored spot until freezing weather forces them south into the Sacramento Valley, where they spend the rest of the winter. In spring the route is reversed.

There have been many explanations advanced to account for the fixed migratory habits of so many species of birds. Those interested will find the various theories outlined and discussed in ornithological literature.

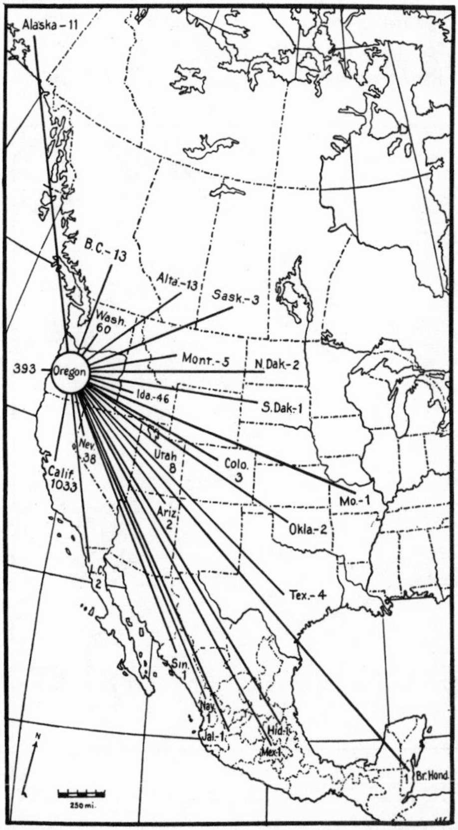

FIGURE 1.—Distribution of returns from ducks banded in Oregon.

We can do no more than mention them here. Among those most prominently advanced have been the following: (1) seasonal shift of food supply; (2) response to changes in temperature—birds are supposed to have originated in the north and to have traveled south during the ice ages; (3) population pressure—birds are assumed to have arisen in the south and moved northward because of population pressure; (4) phototropism—birds are assumed to have moved to the regions of greatest light; and (5) physiological changes in the sex organs—such changes are assumed to be correlated with these great mass movements. No one of these theories has been entirely accepted, and it does not seem necessary to assume that any one of them may entirely account for migration habits.

Mortality among Migrants

The loss of life among migratory hosts is sometimes enormous, and ornithological literature contains many stories of bird tragedies. Small birds are often blown to sea. Some of them come aboard steamships in

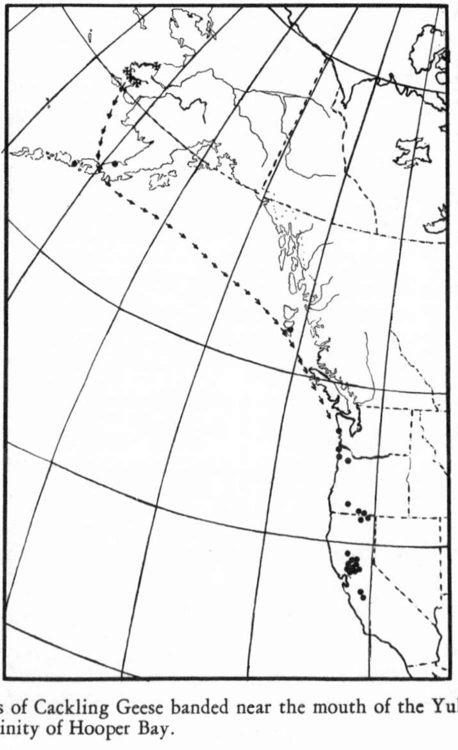

Figure 2.—Returns of Cackling Geese banded near the mouth of the Yukon River, Alaska, chiefly in the vicinity of Hooper Bay.

an exhausted condition, but those not fortunate enough to find a ship inevitably perish, although we get only an occasional hint of such occurrences.

In Oregon, some of the losses that have come under our observation are as follows: In December 1912 and early January 1913, Jewett and Murie found many dead birds at Netarts Bay, among them many common and semirare species of seafowl. In November 1921, following one of the most severe storms in a decade, Gabrielson found thousands of live but exceedingly emaciated Red Phalaropes and many dead ones on the beach along the coast of Tillamook County. With them were hundreds of Pacific Fulmars and a miscellaneous collection of other birds. In the winter of 1932–33, in a period from Christmas to early March, tens of thousands of birds were washed dead and dying onto the Oregon beaches. Horned Puffins, for which previously there had been only two records in the State, were found by the hundreds. Ancient Murrelets were abundant, although we had previously considered them a rather infrequent bird along our coast. With them were many Tufted Puffins, hundreds of California Murres, gulls of several species, including the rather rare Pacific Kittiwakes, the various species of loons and grebes wintering on the coast, and a few Paroquet Auklets.

Late in October 1934 there occurred the greatest disaster to migratory birds that either of us has ever seen. The great southward movement of Red Phalaropes was caught off the Oregon coast by the worst storm in many years. Before the three-day blow was over, phalaropes had been blown inland for a hundred miles, carcasses lay in windrows on the beaches, and dead and dying birds were found along the highways and in every pool of water along the coast. Total casualties must have run into tens of thousands in Oregon alone, and reports indicated that the destruction extended along the entire Washington coast, as well as far south into California. In January 1935, there was evidently a considerable casualty list among the Pacific Kittiwakes and Slender-billed Shearwaters, as many dead birds were found between Astoria and Newport.

Mortality among birds during migration may be due to various agencies. Some birds die as a result of being oil-soaked from wastes dumped by offshore ships. Other deaths, as in the Red Phalarope disaster of 1934, are clearly the effect of violent storms. We are not able, however, to correlate the tremendous destruction of birds that took place in 1932 and 1933 with any particular cause. It is quite evident that there was an above-normal southward movement of birds that normally winter on the Alaska and British Columbia coasts. Horned Puffins, Paroquet Auklets, Ancient Murrelets, and Pacific Kittiwakes were present far more abundantly than in any previous year of which we have any record. At the same time, Tufted Puffins wintered in Oregon more commonly than usual. The winter was not exceptionally stormy. Perhaps there were some unfavorable food conditions on the Alaska coast that drove the birds away and especially favorable conditions on the Oregon coast that not only held an abnormal number of the Tufted Puffins and similar birds there but also attracted a greater number of birds of the more northern species. The fact that more records of kills appear in the past three or four winters is not to be taken to indicate a higher mortality than in previous years but rather reflects the fact that we have been in position to make more extensive observations on the coasts.

Speed of Flight

The speed of flight of birds in their great migratory movements has long been a cause of speculation. Gätke, a German observer on the Island of Helgoland, became obsessed with the idea, induced perhaps by his isolated home, that most birds pass the greatest part of their migratory flight in a single night. On this basis, he estimated that small birds flew 180 to 240 miles an hour and various shore birds, 212 to 240. The development of the automobile and the airplane have given us improved methods of measuring the speed of birds. It is apparent from figures thus obtained that the speed of birds in flight has been generally overestimated, although some birds are capable of high speed for at least short distances.

Wetmore has published records made by timing birds as they flew parallel to automobile roads. He found that such diverse species as herons, hawks, Horned Larks, ravens, and shrikes covered 22 to 28 miles an hour in ordinary flight. H. B. Wood found that the rate of speed of the Arkansas Kingbird and the Scissor-tailed Flycatcher varied between 10 and 17 miles an hour. All these birds are capable of greater speed in emergencies. Records in England and Europe, obtained in the same manner, show the speed of small birds to be 20 to 25 miles an hour. Colonel R. Meinertzhagen, from figures obtained from observations with theodolites (instruments also used to estimate the speed of airplanes), stop watches on measured courses, and readings from airplanes, gave the following numbers of miles an hour for common groups of birds: crow family, 31 to 45; small birds, 20 to 37; starlings, 38 to 49; geese, 42 to 55; ducks, 44 to 59; falcons, 40 to 48; and sand grouse, 43 to 47. Swifts in Mesopotamia are reported to have circled a plane when it was traveling at 68 miles an hour; and E. C. Stuart Baker timed swifts with stop watches over a course known to be 2 miles long and found that they covered this distance in 36 to 42 seconds, or at the rate of 171 to 200 miles an hour. This is by far the highest estimated speed that we have found in modern literature. Various American species of ducks, timed by airplane and by automobile, have been found traveling at 42 to 72 miles an hour.

Economic Status

No country in the world has a better understanding of the food habits of birds and their interrelationships to agriculture than the United States. This is due to the economic studies that have been carried on by the Biological Survey for more than 50 years and to the subsequent publication of the information acquired. The major groups of birds have been covered in these publications, and the bird-protection laws have been largely based on the data obtained from this source. Most biologists agree that in general birds have a tendency to be economically beneficial rather than harmful. There are times and places, however, where some species become destructive to special agricultural interests, and there are a few birds, including crows and magpies, that often are considered injurious over wide areas.

There is a great deal of honest difference of opinion between groups as to the exact value of birds as weed-seed and insect destroyers. The earlier students of bird interrelationships considered birds valuable as weed-seed destroyers, a view that has been largely abandoned in more recent years. It is now recognized that birds feeding on weed seed do not usually destroy enough of the total production on a given area to make any appreciable difference in the next year's crop of weeds. It is also recognized that birds act as spreaders of weeds of many kinds. Economic entomologists generally feel that the value of birds as insect checks has been greatly exaggerated, and there is little doubt that statements sometimes made by enthusiastic bird lovers to the effect that the country would become a vegetationless desert were it not for the insect-eating birds are far beyond the truth. Such birds destroy, of course, not only insects that are pests, but also valuable predatory and parasitic species that do have a recognizable repressive effect upon destructive insects.

Our own opinion is that the great congregations of birds sometimes appearing at scenes of insect outbreaks are not always of real use in controlling insects. In such cases the birds and other predators feed upon enormous insect surpluses built up by particularly favorable conditions, and though such activity may tend to shorten the duration or restrict the area of local outbreaks, it may have little or no measurable effect upon the permanent insect population of the area. The greatest value of birds as insect destroyers lies in the steady toll they exact when insects are present in normal or less than normal numbers. Such repressive effects may go far toward preventing the building up of great surpluses but are exceedingly difficult to measure in mathematical terms. Ornithologists generally are agreed, however, that there is a large, if uncertain, value in such activities.

A consideration of the activities of birds will reveal that every ecological condition finds species that are especially adapted to feeding under that condition. Birds police the air by day and night and search the treetops, the surface of the ground, and even the water. Swallows and swifts, for example, feed entirely on the wing and are equipped with small beaks and wide gapes that allow them literally to scoop their food from the air as they dart back and forth through swarms of small insects. Flycatchers dart into the air from sentinel positions, pick large and small insects from the air, and return to the perch. At times late in summer and in fall, they are joined by other widely dissimilar species. During those seasons, Lewis's Woodpecker and bluebirds habitually feed in this manner, and flickers, blackbirds, several species of sparrows, and some of the warblers have been noted occasionally gathering food in this spectacular way. Their place is taken at night by nighthawks and poor-wills. Nighthawks feed high in the air and are literally open-ended projectiles that dart back and forth through the air on long, powerful wings, scooping up small insects by the hundreds. Poor-wills feed closer to the ground, behaving much more like the flycatchers.

Coursing through the treetops are myriads of small birds, headed by the warblers and vireos, that spend their waking hours gathering small insects from the foliage, flowers, and buds of the trees. Chickadees, kinglets, and other small treetop inhabitants join them regularly. The branches and trunks of the trees are policed by woodpeckers, creepers, nuthatches, kinglets, and chickadees. Throughout the year these small birds search the tree crevices and crannies for insects, eggs, and larvae. The woodpeckers are especially equipped with drilling tools that allow them to search out and obtain wood-boring insect larvae from their homes within the tree, but the other birds of these small groups work more on the surface of the bark. Winter and summer alike, they are at it, and because of their numbers and the fact that they are present throughout the year, it seems probable that the entire surface of many of the trees is searched again and again for luckless insects. On the ground, sparrows, thrushes, and some of the warblers, together with a sprinkling of birds from other families, work through the woodlands and brush patches searching among leaves and accumulated debris for insects and seeds, while meadowlarks, blackbirds, crows, magpies, robins, and hosts of sparrows police the grasslands and open country. Fruit-eating sparrows, thrushes, mockers, and thrashers feed alike on the ground or in the bushes and treetops—wherever their favorite food may be available.

The abundant food supplies of the shore lines of the larger lakes and bays, as well as of the ocean beaches, are harvested periodically by migrating shore birds, gulls, and a scattering of other birds. Shore birds feed on living insects, crustaceans, and mollusks, while the gulls are scavengers but willing to take almost anything living or dead that comes their way. The open surfaces of the larger lakes and streams are policed by gulls and terns, and the open ocean has myriads of birds of the shearwater, petrel, and albatross tribes, as well as gulls and terns, that pick their food from its surface. The marshes and shallows grown to masses of vegetation furnish food and shelter for rails, herons, ducks, geese, cranes, ibises, and many shore birds. Such species as mergansers and the diving ducks feed under water in the fresh-water areas, and auks, auklets, murres, puffins, guillemots, and cormorants obtain their food from the depths of the open ocean and the larger bays.

Hawks and eagles by day and owls by night act as a check on the myriads of rodents in Oregon, and, because of the seriousness of the rodent problem in this and other Western States, these birds should be preserved, rather than persecuted, as at present. Some species, including the Prairie Falcon, the Duck Hawk, and the Goshawk, are universally condemned because they feed upon game birds, small songbirds, and poultry. There are so few of these raptors left, however, that their effect upon bird populations is negligible, and they should not be molested, as they are the most magnificent birds of prey in existence. No other birds are so swift, so fierce, and so untamable as are the Duck Hawks and the Prairie Falcons, and certainly something would be missing from the landscape for the nature lover if he knew that never again would he see these falcons strike with thunderbolt speed.

Buzzards are pre-eminently scavengers and are assisted by the gulls along the littoral, and by crows, magpies, and ravens everywhere. They clean up the carcasses of dead animals, dead and dying fish, and other things that would become excessively offensive if allowed to accumulate.

This brief review of some of the more spectacular and interesting phases of bird activity and behavior is not intended to be a complete treatise on any one subject, but simply to point out those of major interest. All these activities have been written up elsewhere at considerable length, and books and pamphlets concerning them are available in most libraries.

Plate 1, *A*. Coast Range in Coos County, Oregon. (Photo by Ira N. Gabrielson.)

Plate 1, *B*. Haystack Rock, Pacific City, Oregon, a great bird colony. (Photo by Reed Ferris.)

Topography and Life Zones of Oregon

Topography

Oregon has a varied topography, rich in plants, animals, and birds. In its approximately 96,000 square miles of land and water area it offers many fascinating problems to the biologist or geologist, no matter what particular group or specialty of behavior or distribution may absorb his attention. In order to present something of the picture of the State and give a basis for an understanding of the distribution of its bird life it will be necessary to discuss, in a general way, geological formation, present topography, and plant and animal distribution, as all of these factors play an important part in the distribution and abundance of the bird population.

The State is roughly a rectangle, approximately 350 miles east and west and 300 miles north and south. If the mountain peaks and ranges were graded down to fill the canyons and valleys, it would be found that generally the eastern edge would be tilted upward with the western rim at sea level on the shores of the Pacific. Topographically, Oregon is cut into sections by various mountain ranges, chief among which is the Cascade. Paralleling the coast, about 100 miles inland, from the Columbia River to the California line, this great range is the dominant physical feature of the State. In fact, it might with propriety be called the backbone of Oregon. It has the highest general elevation of all the mountains of the State, and its crest is dominated by a series of huge volcanic cones that rise along its summit in solitary cloud-piercing grandeur. This has a profound effect on climate and rainfall, a feature that will be discussed later.

The Coast Range (Plate 1, *A*), as the name implies, is never far from the Pacific Coast and in places even jut into the ocean itself in great headlands that have been beaten away by the ceaseless pounding of the waves to form groups of pinnacles and arched rocks. These are now the homes of myriads of sea birds that find secure nest sites on inaccessible spots (Plate 1, *B*). The general elevation of the summits is low, the highest point, Mt. Bolivar, southeast corner of Coos County, having an altitude of 4,297 feet. The formation, more ancient than that of the Cascades, is weathered down to rounded knobs and ridges that are now all clothed with dense vegetation. On the western slope are numerous small rivers and streams that empty either into small bays or directly into the Pacific. South of the Columbia River the range is cut only by the Umpqua and

Rogue Rivers in Oregon. Both these streams rise on the western slope of the Cascades and flow through the Coast Range in narrow rocky canyons.

At the northwest corner of the State is the mouth of the Columbia River, which is itself a huge bay. South along the coast are Nehalem Bay, at the mouth of the Nehalem River; Tillamook Bay, which receives the waters of five rivers (Miami, Kilchis, Wilson, Trask, and Tillamook) and which has about its shores one of the two large areas of agricultural land on the coastal slope; Netarts Bay, just south of Tillamook Bay, small but highly important for bird life; Siletz Bay, at the mouth of the Siletz River; Yaquina Bay; Alsea Bay; Coos Bay, the largest bay in the State, with hundreds of miles of inlets and channels extending in all directions from its central body; and the small bay found at the mouth of the Rogue River.

Inland about 100 miles from the mouth of the Columbia, which forms the northern boundary of the State except for a small section in the northeastern corner, the Willamette River empties into the mighty river. It rises in the central part of the State (north and south), where several branches that flow from the Coast and Cascade Ranges unite near Eugene to form the river. The valley formed by this stream is the largest area of agricultural land in the western part of the State. It is well watered and can be successfully farmed without irrigation. As a consequence it was the promised land of the early emigrants and is now the most heavily populated section of the State. Flowing northward from Eugene, the Willamette gathers up the many streams that flow from the western slope of the Cascades and the eastern slope of the Coast Range, making a regular network of small waterways that profoundly affect the bird population of the district.

Just south of Eugene the Calapooya Mountains, a low cross range between the Cascade and Coast Ranges, separate the headwaters of the Willamette from the drainage of the Umpqua River. This latter stream and its tributaries drain the western slope of the central Cascades from south of Diamond Peak to Diamond Lake. Many of the tributaries and much of the Umpqua itself are in narrow rocky canyons, but the valleys of the main branches widen out in the vicinity of Roseburg to form a considerable area of rich bottom land.

The western slope of the Cascades from Crater Lake National Park southward to the California line is drained by the Rogue, which is separated from the Umpqua on the north by the Umpqua Mountains and from the Klamath on the south by the Siskiyou Mountains that lie along the Oregon-California line between the two major north and south ranges. The valley of the Rogue also widens for a considerable distance to form an extensive area of flat land and rolling foothills, which, because of its similarity to California topography, furnishes many puzzling problems of distribution between northern and southern geographical forms.

East of the Cascades the general topography is that of a great inland plateau, rapidly rising from its lower edge along the Columbia to attain elevations of 2,000 to 9,000 feet.

In the extreme northeastern corner of Oregon is found some of the most spectacular scenery in the State. There a spur of the Rockies crosses into Oregon in a generally northeast to southwest direction, and through it, the Snake River, which forms the eastern boundary, has carved a gigantic canyon that in depth is equal to the Grand Canyon of the Colorado and is bordered by perpetually snow-capped mountains in both Oregon and Idaho. Those on the Oregon side, known as the Wallowas, are a miniature Glacier Park and contain almost innumerable icy lakes, often perched high on the precipitous slopes in little glacial cirques. To the south and west this spur, known generally as the Blue Mountains, extends to the vicinity of Prineville, where it is lost in the sage plains with a gap of only a few miles between it and the Cascades to the west. (See Plates 2 to 4.)

The two major streams in Oregon that flow into the Columbia River east of the Cascades are the Deschutes and the John Day. The Deschutes rises in the central Cascades, gathers the waters of the lakes about Bachelor Butte, Diamond Peak, and the Three Sisters, and, flowing almost straight north after it emerges from the mountains, receives additional water from the eastern slope of the Cascades, and finally reaches the Columbia a few miles east of The Dalles. (See Plate 5.) The John Day rises well in the eastern part of the State, draining many of the spurs of the Blue Mountains before it enters its rocky gorge and turns north to join the Columbia not many miles east of the Deschutes.

In the south, all of Klamath County and the western edge of Lake County are drained by many small streams that finally empty into the Klamath Lakes. From Upper Klamath Lake, the Klamath River flows south and west to carve a gorge through both the Cascade and Coast Ranges before it empties into the Pacific in northern California. The Klamath and the mighty Columbia are the only rivers that have succeeded in cutting through the Cascade-Sierra Nevada Range, which, except for these two gaps, extends unbroken by rivers from the Canadian border to Mexico.

The great shallow alkaline lakes of Harney and Lake Counties—remnants of vastly greater bodies of water of bygone ages—are highly important physical features from the biologist's point of view. They are created by the waters draining from the slopes of the Blue, Warner, and Steens Mountains and other smaller ranges. Some of these lakes occasionally evaporate completely in dry cycles, a condition that has been distressingly acute during the past few years, but several times within historic ages they have filled again, following increased rainfall, and have become a haven for myriads of migratory waterfowl and other birds.

Plate 2, *A*. John Henrys Lake, Wallowa Mountains, Oregon. (Photo by S. G. Jewett.)

Plate 2, *B*. Kamela to Meacham, Oregon Trail on summit of Blue Mountains. (Photo by S. G. Jewett.)

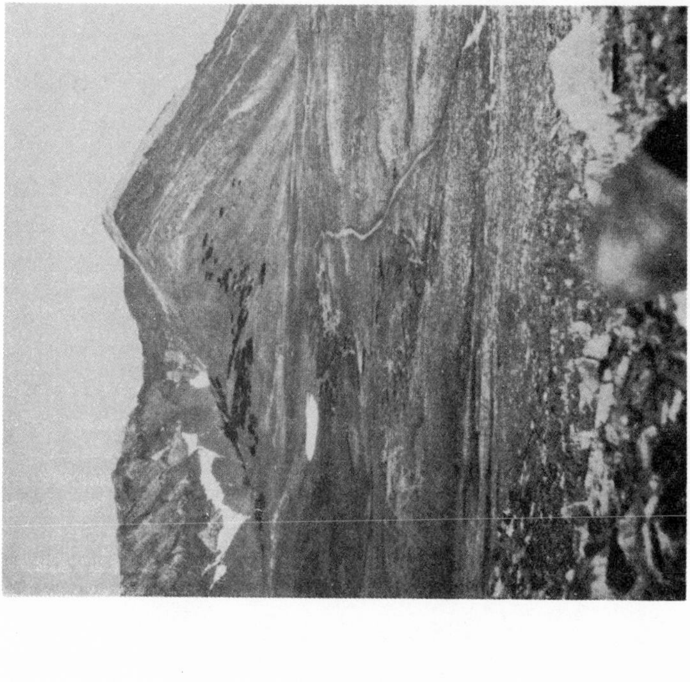

Plate 3, *A*. Trail, Aneroid Lake to Tenderfoot Basin, Wallowa Mountains, Oregon. (Photo by S. G. Jewett.)

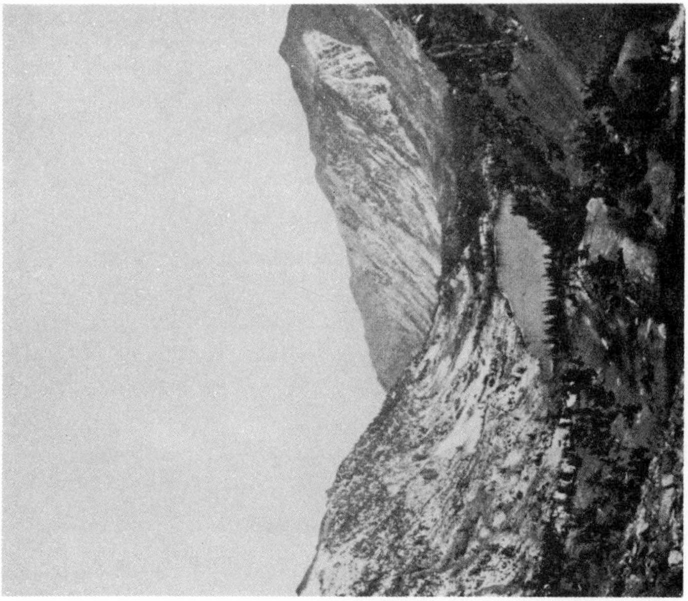

Plate 3, *B*. Aneroid Lake, from Pete's Point, Wallowa County, Oregon. (Photo by S. G. Jewett.)

Plate 4, *A*. Steamboat Lake, in the Wallowa Mountains, Oregon. (Photo by Ira N. Gabrielson.)

Plate 4, *B*. Winter in the Blue Mountains, Oregon. (Photo by Ira N. Gabrielson.)

Plate 5, *A*. Wapinitia Canyon, Wasco County, Oregon. (Photo by S. G. Jewett.)

Plate 5, *B*. Waterfalls between Sparks Lake and Green Lake, central Oregon Cascades, the haunt of the water ouzel, or dipper. (Photo by Ira N. Gabrielson.)

Other than this basin drainage and the drainage from the Klamath Basin southward into the Klamath River, all the innumerable streams rising in the Blue Mountains are gathered up by the Columbia-Snake system.

Geologically, the Siskiyou and Blue Mountains are the most ancient areas in the State. Both are composed of sedimentary rocks of many kinds, and geologists say that in some prehistoric time they stood as two islands in a stormy sea. The Blue Mountains area is particularly rich in fossils, the great John Day beds being part of this formation.

The Coast Range is adjudged to be the next oldest land, probably rising at one time to greater heights than at present and more or less completely closing off from the open ocean a shallow inland sea.

The Cascades are the youngest and greatest of the major ranges and are largely volcanic in character. The great sage plains that stretch from their eastern base to the Blue Mountains and on into southern Idaho and northern Nevada were built up by a succession of vast flows of basaltic lavas. These lavas surged up against the Blue Mountains, burying the foothills under a lava cap that, superimposed on the older rocks, is now plainly visible where the rivers have carved their canyons. Much of the basic rock of the Cascades, particularly northward, is of this type. Later came another volcanic period during which the lighter-colored lavas and cinders that form the great series of cones along the backbone of the range were thrust upward through this dark-colored lava. Beginning at the north, those of major importance are Mount Hood, Olallie Butte, Mount Jefferson (Plate 6, *A*), Three Fingered Jack, Mount Washington, Belknap Crater, The Three Sisters (Plate 6, *B*), Broken Top, Bachelor Butte, Diamond Peak, Mount Thielsen, old Mount Mazama—the great caldera that is Crater Lake—and Mount McLoughlin (Mount Pitt). In addition, there are innumerable cinder cones and lesser craters where dying volcanic fires dissipated their last energies.

Sometime later the basaltic lavas were broken by great earth convulsions into a series of north-and-south faults that extend for miles. Each of these has a steep face, which is almost sheer precipice, and a gentler slope, up which a car may be driven with ease (Plate 7, *A*). So far as their effect on fauna and flora is concerned, the most important of the faults are the Warner Mountains just east of Lakeview, the fault line of which is most perfectly preserved as the Abert Lake rim; Hart Mountain (Plate 7, *B*) to the east of Warner Valley in eastern Lake County; and the Steens Mountains, which extend from just south of Malheur Lake almost to the Nevada line.

Life Zones

Field workers in biology have long known that plants, birds, mammals, and other living forms are to be found grouped in more or less characteristic fashion into communities and associations. Some of these groups and

Plate 6, *A*. Mount Jefferson, Cascade Range, Oregon. (Photo by Ira N. Gabrielson.)

Plate 6, *B*. Three Sisters, Cascade Range, Oregon. (Photo by S. G. Jewett.)

Plate 7, *A*. Basalt canyons of southeastern Oregon. (Photo by Ira N. Gabrielson.)

Plate 7, *B*. Hart Mountain, Lake County, Oregon. (Photo by S. G. Jewett.)

associations are strikingly obvious, while others are so intricate and obscured by other phenomena that recognition is difficult and in some instances almost impossible. Differences of opinion and interpretation confuse the beginning student. It is not the intention here to go into detail concerning these biotic communities, but rather to paint a simple word picture that can be understood by those who are just beginning their study of Oregon's fascinating out-of-doors.

Broadly speaking, North America is divided into bands of characteristic associations of plants and animals that extend in a generally east-and-west direction across the continent. If the continent were perfectly flat, these bands would tend to lie in arcs with the ends on the oceans and the arc sprung northward toward the center of the land mass. A glance at the general life-zone map will show that this idealistic line is warped out of place by altitude, presence or absence of considerable bodies of water, mountain ranges, rainfall, temperature, and many other factors, with the result that, particularly in a mountainous State such as Oregon, these zones are broken up into irregular blocks, tongues, and islands that lie scattered among the mountains and along the rivers in apparent confusion. This lack of uniformity, when once understood, is not confusion, however, but rather conformity with the series of laws that are the basis of the science of ecology.

Plants are most frequently used as life-zone indicators, as they are available the year around and are not quite so flexible in their response to environmental change as are birds and mammals. Every species of plant and animal has a definite range within which one may confidently expect to find it. Some of these species have a range that is almost world-wide. A good example is the Short-eared Owl, which is found not only over much of North America but also over the northern part of the Old World. Such forms, which apparently are little affected by environmental differences, are useless for determining life zones. Others are so definitely limited by environment that their presence in any numbers is at once indicative of certain zones. Yellow pine, which characterizes the Transition Zone of eastern Oregon, is an excellent example.

The zone pattern of vegetation types is controlled by many factors, prominent among which are soil depth, fertility, acidity, alkalinity, water supply, temperature—both summer and winter—slope, exposure, altitude, and latitude. If there could be found an isolated mountain peak, such as Mount Hood, formed as a perfect cone, with slopes at equal angles in all directions, with no valleys or ridges, and with exactly similar soil, rainfall, and other conditions from sea level to the peak, the life zones would be arranged in the form of circular belts around the mountain. These belts would be tilted downward on the colder northern slope and upward on the warmer southern slope, due to the difference in exposure. This ideal arrangement is never found, however, for zones are disturbed by many local factors of configuration alone. The higher or colder zones tend to extend downward into the canyons with the flow of cold air, while the plants of the warmer zones tend to creep upward along the south side of the ridges and thus take advantage of the better air drainage and the southern exposure. This fact is regularly used to advantage by farmers in planting fruits and nuts in Oregon where, everything else being equal, air drainage is the factor that furnishes protection against innumerable frosts and determines success or failure of an orchard section.

This brief discussion of the zone concept as used by modern biologists must suffice here, without an attempt to go further into the many often obscure environmental factors that affect and disrupt the zones. The following life zones are recognized in North America:

1. Tropical
2. Austral, or Sonoran
   - Lower Austral, or Lower Sonoran
   - Upper Austral, or Upper Sonoran
3. Transition
4. Canadian
5. Hudsonian
6. Arctic-Alpine

All of the zones, except the Tropical and Lower Austral, or Lower Sonoran, are found in Oregon in varying extent, the Upper Sonoran and Transition including most of the land surface of the State. The areas are shown in color on the map of the Life Zones of Oregon, prepared by Vernon Bailey, formerly of the Bureau of Biological Survey, which is placed in an envelope at the end of this publication.

Since the Tropical Zone does not occur in the State, the Austral, or Sonoran, is considered first. So far as north or south zones are concerned the terms "Austral" and "Sonoran" are synonymous, representing as they do the subtropical fauna and flora of Mexico and the southern United States. There are such marked differences east and west, however, that Austral is now generally used to designate the eastern, or more humid part, of the zone; and Sonoran, the western, or arid section. The word "Sonoran" is therefore used to designate the arid part of the subtropical belt. This zone has been further divided into a lower, or southern, and an upper, or northern, section, and these sections represent almost as distinct differences as those found between zones. Only the Upper Sonoran part of the zone is represented in Oregon.

In "The Mammals and Life Zones of Oregon," *North American Fauna* No. 55, of the United States Biological Survey, Vernon Bailey (1936)[1] has

[1] Dates in parentheses following an author's name refer to Bibliography, p. 609.

recently published extensive lists of plants and animals characteristic of the life zones of the State, so that it seems useless to repeat them here in detail. Only a few of the more prominent and characteristic zonal indicators are listed, therefore, in the following discussion of the different zones.

Upper Sonoran Zone

Of the life zones present in Oregon, the Upper Sonoran is the first in the order presented above. The valleys of the Columbia and the Snake Rivers and the tongues of varying width and length along their tributaries are Upper Sonoran; likewise, that part (approximately half) of the great sage plateau that lies at an altitude of 4,500 feet or less. On cold northern exposures the upper edge of this zone may drop down to 3,500 feet or less and on hot dry southern slopes it may rise to 5,000 feet or more as tongues or islands surrounded by the Transition or even the Canadian Zones. West of the Cascades the upper valley of the Rogue River, particularly the flat lands and foothills about Medford and as far down the river as Hells Canyon below Grants Pass, and the valley of the Umpqua in the vicinity of Roseburg are both in this zone. The farthest northward extensions recognizable are along the Willamette River north of Eugene, where several patches of almost typical Upper Sonoran vegetation are to be found.

Specialists in ecology, as in other lines of scientific research, tend to draw finer and finer distinctions and break such concepts as the life zones into successively smaller and less recognizable units. Like some of our ultramodern subspecies of birds and mammals, they are unrecognizable without reference to notes and locality labels. Following this idea, the Upper Sonoran, which in itself is the arid subdivision of the Austral Zone, is again divided into extreme arid and semiarid zones as they apply to our State, and each of these in turn is capable of being still further divided, again and again.

Without considering these further, in the semiarid section of the Upper Sonoran that covers the Rogue and Umpqua sections of western Oregon are found certain plants that most conspicuously characterize this area. Some of these are the California lilacs (*Ceanothus cuneatus*, *C. integerrimus*, and *C. sanguineus*), manzanita (*Arctostaphylos viscida*), a tiny mariposa (*Calochortus uniflorus*), birchleaf mahogany (*Cercocarpus betulaefolius*), soaproot (*Chorogalum pomeridianum*), a rabbitbrush (*Chrysothamnus nauseosus*), a false buckwheat (*Eriogonum nudum*) growing two feet or more tall, alfileria (*Erodium cicutarium*), the striking red bells (*Fritillaria recurva*), two brodiaeas (*Brodiaea capitata* and *B. hendersoni*), bitterbush (*Purshia tridentata*), white pentstemon (*Pentstemon deustus*), a wild iris (*Iris chrysophylla*), chokecherry (*Prunus demissa*), and tasselbush (*Garrya fremonti*).

Among the characteristic mammals are the California jack rabbit (*Lepus californicus californicus*), a dark-colored kangaroo rat (*Dipodomys heermanni gabrielsoni*) that frequents the chaparral areas, and forms of the wood rat (*Neotoma*), meadow mouse (*Microtus*), pocket gopher (*Thomomys*), and white-footed mouse (*Peromyscus*) peculiar to the Upper Sonoran Zone. Here, too, that queer character, the ring-tailed cat (*Bassariscus astutus*), that appears to be part skunk and part raccoon, finds its northern limit.

Among the birds (scientific names are given in the individual accounts of each), the California Woodpecker, Oregon Brown Towhee, Sacramento Towhee, Ash-throated Flycatcher, Oregon Titmouse, California House Finch, Bendire's Screech Owl, and Valley Quail are characteristic. Long-tailed Jays and Long-tailed Chats are abundant, but these two and some others of their hardier brethren extend into the Transition Zone of the Columbia River bottoms at Portland, though in greatly diminished numbers.

East of the Cascades, the Upper Sonoran spreads out as a great irregular blotch on the map of north-central Oregon, with islands scattered all over the rest of the eastern half of the State. This more arid section does not have such a variety of characteristic plants. The most widely distributed and easily recognized is the common sagebrush (*Artemisia tridentata*), which is almost the universal ground cover in this gray landscape except for the stream bottoms. In good soil, it grows into miniature trees but on poor soil and in areas of scantier moisture is smaller and more widely spaced. Although this species extends upward into the Transition Zone, where it mingles with other hardier sages, it is neither so robust nor so abundant on the higher lands and is characteristically Upper Sonoran. On the lower, more alkaline areas, particularly the extensive flat playas of southeastern Oregon, is the greasewood (*Sarcobatus vermiculatus*), rabbit-brush (*Chrysothamnus nauseosus* and *C. viscidiflorus*), wild currant (*Ribes aureum*), and bitterbush (*Purshia tridentata*). Barely reaching into the State are a few of the saltbushes (*Atriplex*), which farther south become such a conspicuous part of the desert flora. Associated with these are other shrubs and a host of annual and perennial plants adapted to the difficult conditions of life on these semidesert areas.

Characteristic mammals of this arid Upper Sonoran are the black-tailed jack rabbits (*Lepus*), the Piute squirrel (*Citellus mollis mollis*), species of kangaroo rats (*Perodipus*) and pocket mice (*Perognathus*), a kangaroo mouse (*Microdipodops megacephalus oregonus*), and forms of the pocket gopher (*Thomomys*), wood rat (*Neotoma*), and white-footed mouse (*Peromyscus*) peculiar to the area. In extreme southeastern Oregon, the little antelope squirrel (*Ammospermophilus leucurus leucurus*) may be found running about the thickets of greasewood and rabbitbrush in such places as Warner Valley and the flat valley north of McDermitt, Nevada.

Breeding birds of the great alkaline lake areas that belong in the Upper Sonoran Zone include the Cinnamon Teal, White-faced Glossy Ibis, Black-necked Stilt, and American Egret. Thriving colonies of these are present in the Klamath Lake district, Warner Valley, and Harney Valley. In the sagebrush, the Burrowing Owl, Arkansas Kingbird, Gray Flycatcher, Merrill's Horned Lark, Sage Sparrow, Brewer's Sparrow, and Rock Wren are common, while along the river bottoms and open valleys Mourning Doves, Bullock's Oriole, the Western Lark Sparrow, and the Long-tailed Chickadee may be considered characteristic birds.

Some of these associations grow to be very real as one travels the country. For example, it was no greater shock to hear the cheerful little trill of Brewer's Sparrow at above 6,000 feet altitude on a hot slope in the Wallowa country than to find the two-acre growth of sagebrush that the bird frequented. Somehow, where one is found the other is expected also, although this tiny island of Upper Sonoran was many miles from the nearest extensive area of that zone.

Transition Zone

From a utilitarian standpoint, the Transition Zone, which covers broad areas of the State, is the most important. Except for irrigated valleys of the Upper Sonoran, most of the important agricultural areas and the bulk of the commercially important timber stands lie in this zone. Like the Sonoran, it is divided into humid and arid sections in Oregon, the former lying west of the summit of the Cascades and the latter east of that range.

The humid Transition Zone occupies all of western Oregon except the Sonoran valleys of the Rogue and Umpqua Rivers, a paper-thin area of Canadian near the coast, and a few islands of Canadian on the highest peaks of the Coast Range. It extends upward onto the flanks of the Cascades to an altitude that varies from 3,000 to 5,000 feet, according to slope and exposure. It is a region of heavy rainfall—the precipitation varying from 40 inches in the Willamette Valley to upward of 80 on the coast and the slopes of the Cascades. Much of the moisture of the Cascades comes in the form of heavy snow, which furnishes water through the summer to keep the cool trout streams flowing.

On the western slopes of the Cascades through much of the Willamette Valley magnificent virgin forests of Douglas fir (*Pseudotsuga taxifolia*) that often extend for miles are characteristic and dominant, while on the western slope of the Coast Range equally magnificent stands of Sitka spruce (*Picea sitchensis*) outline the zone. Mingled with these are many other coniferous trees, such as western hemlock (*Tsuga heterophylla*), sugar pine (*Pinus lambertiana*), white fir (*Abies grandis*), western arborvitae (*Thuja plicata*), and Oregon yew (*Taxus brevifolia*). Along the streams deciduous trees, such as Oregon maple (*Acer macrophyllum*), Oregon alder (*Alnus oregona*), Oregon ash (*Fraxinus oregona*), black cottonwood (*Populus *trichocarpa*), vine maple (*Acer circinatum*), cascara (*Rhamnus purshiana*), western dogwood (*Cornus occidentalis*), and Oregon crab apple (*Malus diversifolia*) are to be found in mixed stands. On the slopes, particularly on the foothills of the Willamette Valley, such trees as madrone (*Arbutus menziesii*), Garry oak (*Quercus garryana*), and Pacific dogwood (*Cornus nuttallii*) are found intermingled with the second growth of Douglas fir. Farther south, on the slopes above the Rogue and Umpqua, a live oak (*Quercus chrysolepis*), incense-cedar (*Libocedrus decurrens*), and the laurel or myrtlewood (*Umbellularia californica*) make their appearance, and madrone becomes much more conspicuous.

Among the legion of shrubs, which make impenetrable thickets in well-watered areas and more or less complete ground cover throughout the forests, are several species of California lilac (*Ceanothus*), hazel (*Corylus californica*), salal (*Gaultheria shallon*), Oregon grape (*Berberis aquifolium*), devilsclub (*Echinopanax horridum*), evergreen blueberry (*Vaccinium ovatum*), salmonberry (*Rubus spectabilis*), thimbleberry (*Rubus parviflorus*), pink spirea (*Spiraea douglasi*), and elderberries (*Sambucus glauca* and *S. callicarpa*). With these is a wealth of annual and perennial herbaceous plants, as one would expect in such a well-watered land. Among the more conspicuous may be mentioned some that are of striking beauty, as the camas (*Camassia esculenta* and *C. leichtlinii*), the Mount Hood lily (*Lilium washingtonianum*); troutlilies, or lamb's-tongues, in cream, lavender, and pink (*Erythronium giganteum*, *E. hendersoni*, and *E. revolutum*), which are the most brilliantly colored of their type in all the world; gorgeous silenes (*Silene hookeri* and *S. ingrami*); showy bird bills (*Dodecatheon latifolium*); a delphinium (*Delphinium trolliifolium*), which rivals in beauty the best creations of the plant breeders; and a gray-leafed, yellow-flowered composite (*Eriophyllum lanatum*), which has earned fame throughout the land under the poetic name of Oregon sunshine. A hundred others might be mentioned, but these are enough to designate this zone, which covers most of western Oregon like a blanket.

Conspicuous breeding birds of the humid section of the Transition Zone are the Sooty and Oregon Ruffed Grouse, Northern Spotted Owl, Pygmy Owl, Brewster's Screech Owl, Band-tailed Pigeon, Harris's and Gairdner's Woodpeckers, Northern Pileated Woodpecker, Vaux's Swift, Coast Jay, Western Winter Wren, California Creeper, Chestnut-backed and Oregon Chickadees, Coast Wren-tits, Western Golden-crowned Kinglet, and many others.

Some of the conspicuous mammals of this section are the black-tailed deer (*Odocoileus columbianus columbianus*), Roosevelt's elk (*Cervus canadensis roosevelti*), brush rabbit (*Sylvilagus bachmani ubericolor*), Washington rabbit (*Lepus americanus washingtonii*, the humid coast relative of the snowshoe), silver gray squirrel (*Sciurus griseus griseus*), Douglas's pine squirrel (*Sciurus *douglasii douglasii*), mountain beaver (*Aplodontia rufa rufa*), and numerous species of mice (*Microtus*) and pocket gophers (*Thomomys*).

In the arid Transition Zone, great open, parklike forests of yellow pine (*Pinus ponderosa*) cover the eastern slopes of the Cascades, the plateaus and lower slopes of the Blue Mountains, and the numerous little ranges that are found in the broad triangle that lies with its apex at Bend and its southern base along the California boundary from Klamath Falls to east of Lakeview. In this section, the Transition Zone varies from 1,000 to 5,000 or 6,000 feet in altitude, according to local conditions, although it descends almost to sea level in the Columbia gorge. So completely is this zone outlined by the yellow pine that no other plant need be mentioned as characteristic. Associated with it, however, are the western tamarack (*Larix occidentalis*), numerous species of willow (*Salix*), such shrubs as the low-growing species (*Berberis repens* and *B. nervosa*) that are related to the Oregon grape (*B. aquifolium*), bearberry or kinnikinnick (*Arctostaphylos uva-ursi*), snowberry (*Symphoricarpus albus*), bitterbush (*Purshia tridentata*), and a prostrate *Ceanothus* (*C. prostratus*), which grows like a holly-leafed carpet beneath the yellow pine and is known as mahala-mat or squawcarpet.

In southeastern Oregon, where the rainfall is too scanty to permit tree growth, the Transition Zone on the Steens Mountains and the high rough country to the south and east of that range, is not well marked vegetatively. On the eastern slope of Hart Mountain, a small patch of yellow pine is found; but to the east this indicator is absent and here it is difficult to distinguish this zone from the sage-clad areas of the Upper Sonoran. The sage (*Artemisia*) is not quite so rank and grows more widely scattered than in the bottoms of the Sonoran, while juniper (*Juniperus*) and mountain-mahogany (*Cercocarpus ledifolius*) are found scattered over the slopes. In this territory, Transition influence predominates up to 6,000 or 7,000 feet, but the boundaries are poorly defined, and the zones merge into one another almost imperceptibly. Such plants as *Balsamorhiza sagittata*, *Wyethia amplexicaulis*, *Paeonia brownii*, *Phlox rigida* and *P. viscida*, *Erigeron aureus* and *E. poliospermus*, *Eriogonum ovalifolium*, *Gaillardia aristata*, several species of wild parsnip (*Lomatium*), *Lewisia rediviva*, and *Pentstemon aridus* and *P. cusickii* become conspicuous members of the flora at proper seasons.

Few mammals are confined to the arid sections of the Transition Zone, though the rimrock sheep (*Ovis canadensis californiana*) were formerly present in some numbers. At present most of our remaining antelope (*Antilocapra americana oregona*) range in it; white-tailed jack rabbits (*Lepus townsendii townsendii*), pygmy rabbits (*Brachylagus idahoensis*), desert woodchucks (*Marmota*), chipmunks (*Eutamias*), and Oregon ground squirrels (*Citellus oregonus*) are found; and numerous species of mice and pocket gophers (*Thomomys*) overflow from other zones into its boundaries.

Among the characteristic birds one may look for in this section are the Sage Grouse, Brewer's Sparrow, Green-tailed Towhee, Sage Thrasher, Pygmy Nuthatch, MacFarlane's Screech Owl, and the Northern White-headed Woodpecker.

Canadian Zone

The Canadian Zone in Oregon is much smaller than the Transition or Sonoran. As the yellow pine and Douglas fir forests mark the Transition Zone, so the lodgepole pine and spruce forests mark the Canadian. Roughly, it is the zone of lodgepole pine (*Pinus murrayana*), western white pine (*Pinus monticola*), Engelmann spruce (*Picea engelmanni*), fir (*Abies amabilis*), Alaska cedar (*Chamaecyparis nootkatensis*), and quaking aspen (*Populus tremuloides*). It covers a comparatively narrow belt that includes the summit of the Cascades, except for a few of the highest peaks, most of the tops of the Blue Mountains, except in the Elkhorns and Wallowas, and a few other scattered peaks. Curiously enough, a thin strip of almost pure Canadian Zone is found along the coast as far south as Cape Blanco. At some places it disappears, at others it opens out to a width of a mile or more, though more frequently it is only a few rods wide.

The strip of Canadian, or almost pure Canadian, flora on the coast is a curious phenomenon. It is dominated by the lodgepole pine, about the bases of which thickets of *Vaccinium ovatum*, rhododendron (*Rhododendron californicum*), and less commonly Labrador tea (*Ledum groenlandicum* and *L. glandulosum*). Along exposed points on the coast are to be found such characteristic Canadian Zone indicators as the dwarf juniper (*Juniperus communis*) and crowberry (*Empetrum nigrum*), the latter not being found in abundance elsewhere in the State. Associated with these are Oregon Jays and Sitka Crossbills, which are to be found more consistently along this narrow coast strip than anywhere else in Oregon. In sharp contrast with this strong Canadian infusion, on the cliffs directly beneath some of these exposed points, southern plants, including *Cotyledon farinosa* and the curious figmarigold (*Mesembryanthemum equilaterale*), are to be found clinging to the face of the rocks barely above tide line.

Similarly on the eastern side of the Cascades, local conditions may cause an almost complete inversion of the zones. The best example of this is in the vicinity of Lapine along The Dalles-California highway. Here the combination of a poor pumice soil and cold-air drainage has pulled the lodgepole pine of the Canadian Zone below its normal level into this extensive enclosed basin, where it has prospered, frequently to the exclusion of other vegetation. It has brought such birds as Clarke's Crow, and the Arctic and Alaska Three-toed Woodpeckers with it. All around the sides of the basin the slopes are covered with yellow pine, in pure Transition type. Even a slight increase in elevation will change the balance, and consequently there are small knobs and ridges through the valley that scatter islands of yellow pine all through the lodgepole. Such anomalies as these confuse the beginner's efforts to understand life zones and make for the serious student a fascinating puzzle to fit together. Incidentally, studies of these unusual distributions often throw much light on the factors affecting distribution of species.

Red elder (*Sambucus callicarpa*), mountain-ash (*Pyrus sitchensis*), serviceberry (*Amelanchier*), mountain maple (*Acer douglasii*), and balsam poplar (*Populus balsamifera*) are commonly found in the zone. Among the characteristic herbaceous species of plants are beargrass (*Xerophyllum tenax*), Oregon box (*Pachistima myrsinites*), several low blueberries (*Vaccinium*), the dainty twinflower (*Linnaea borealis*), a low-growing manzanita (*Arctostaphylos nevadensis*), several species of *Arnica*, and *Clintonia uniflora*.

Mule deer (*Odocoileus*), snowshoe hares (*Lepus*), conies (*Ochotona*), flying squirrels (*Glaucomys*), martens (*Martes*), shrews (*Sorex*), chipmunks (*Eutamias*), pine squirrels (*Sciurus*), and many forms of mice are peculiar to this zone or have their greatest abundance here.

Among the most noticeable and characteristic breeding birds are the Harlequin Duck, Barrow's Golden-eye, Richardson's and Gray Ruffed Grouse, Williamson's, Red-naped, and Red-breasted Sapsuckers, Arctic and Alaska Three-toed Woodpeckers, Olive-sided Flycatchers, Rocky Mountain and Gray Jays, Cassin's Finch, White-crowned Sparrows, Juncos, Water Ouzel, Crossbills, and Evening Grosbeaks.

Hudsonian Zone

The Hudsonian is the timber-line zone surrounding the highest peaks in the State. In many ways it is poorly defined, and most of the species found in it overlap into the zones above and below. In reality it is an enchanted land where one may wander through clumps of grotesque misshapen trees and meadows bedecked with flowers of all the hues of the rainbow. The altitudinal range of the zone itself, which is generally 1,000 feet, or less, and does not exceed 1,500 feet, may occur anywhere between 6,000 and 9,000 feet, depending on slope and exposure. For example, on Mount Hood, at the northern end of the Cascades, timber line is at approximately 6,000 feet on the northern slope and 7,000 on the southern slope, whereas on Mount McLoughlin (Mount Pitt), at the southern end of the Range, it is at 7,000 feet or more. In the Wallowas, timber line is at approximately 8,000 feet on cold exposures and 9,000 feet on warmer exposures, whereas in the Steens Mountains, the corresponding figures are approximately 500 feet higher. There are no great areas of Hudsonian Zone anywhere in the State. The area about the bases of the Three Sisters and Broken Top forms the largest continuous mass in the Cascades. In the higher parts of the Wallowas there is also considerable Hudsonian. All other areas of this zone in the State are small bands on the slopes of the highest peaks and a few ill-defined areas on the summits of the Steens.

The characteristic trees are the white-barked pine (*Pinus albicaulis*), alpine fir (*Abies lasiocarpa*), alpine hemlock (*Tsuga mertensiana*), and creeping juniper (*Juniperus communis montana*). This is also the land of the little mat-forming willows (*Salix*) and the false heathers (*Phyllodoce empetriformis*, *P. glandulosa*, and *Cassiope mertensiana*), which sometimes make solid carpets of pink, yellow, or white, acres in extent.

A list of the herbaceous plants of the Hudsonian Zone form would fill a book, for in this zone are all the great alpine floral displays about which volumes have been written. Avalanche-lilies (*Erythronium montanum*) and glacierlilies (*E. parviflorum*) sometimes grow in such riotous abundance as to cover the ground for long distances, while the profusion of such striking species as the great hairy western anemone (*Pulsatilla occidentalis*), prickly phlox (*Phlox diffusa*), mountain mat (*Lutkea pectinata*), and *Dasiphora fruticosa* frequently becomes nationally known to alpine-plant enthusiasts. Along the streams and in the wet meadows great banners of vivid colors indicate the presence of both pink and yellow species of monkeyflowers (*Mimulus*), and about the shores of the little alpine lakes such rare beauties as the loveliest American gentian (*Gentiana calycosa*), the dwarfed little mountain-laurel (*Kalmia microphylla*), and the striking Dodecatheon (*Dodecatheon jeffreyi*) are found in abundance. The total list of species peculiar to this zone or having their greatest abundance here would run into the hundreds, if not thousands, and would be more appropriate in a botanical than in a bird book.

This zone has no value for agriculture and little for commercial lumbering. It is the summer playground not only for many of the inhabitants of the State, but for an increasing number of tourists who come to enjoy the pure mountain air, spectacular scenery, and marvelous floral displays. For this reason, if for no other, it should be zealously guarded as a priceless heritage, the value of which never can be entirely measured in dollars and cents.

In contrast with the floral richness of the zone no mammals and few birds are confined to it, although various meadow mice (*Microtus*), pine squirrels (*Sciurus*), chipmunks (*Eutamias*), and golden-mantled squirrels (*Callospermophilus*) extend up into and through the Hudsonian. Deer, bears, coyotes, and foxes, all wide-ranging species, on occasion are to be found in the timber-line parks.

The timber-line country is the chosen home of Clarke's Crow for most of the year, and Gray and Rocky Mountain Jays, Western Golden-crowned Kinglets, Townsend's Solitaires, Red-breasted Nuthatches, and Alaska Three-toed Woodpeckers are to be found more or less regularly throughout the breeding season. Late in summer their numbers are augmented by the advent of many other species that wander upward after their domestic duties are fulfilled.

Arctic-Alpine Zone

The Arctic-Alpine Zone is represented in Oregon only as a series of islands on the upper slopes of the higher peaks. It is entirely above timber line, and the scanty vegetation quickly gives way to permanent ice and snow where the altitude is great enough. Mount Hood, Mount Jefferson, Three Sisters, and the higher peaks of the Blue Mountains are the most important of these highest zone areas, and with the exception of the Three Sisters and the Wallowas the areas are not large. There are no trees and shrubs, the nearest approach to shrubs being the dwarfed forms of the false heathers (*Phyllodoce empetriformis*, *P. glandulosa*, and *Cassiope mertensiana*) and a little ground-hugging willow (*Salix nivalis*) that scarcely reaches two inches in height. The mountain-sorrel (*Oxyria digyna*), *Anemone drummondi*, *Lupinus lyalli*, *Saxifraga tolmiei* and *S. caespitosa*, *Pentstemon menziesii* and *P. tolmiei*, *Veronica alpina*, *Eriogonum umbellatum*, and *Potentilla flabellifolia* are showy species in the Cascades that spread out between timber line and the region of ice and snow. Most of these and many others likewise grow in the Wallowa Mountains and, together with such true Arctic species as *Silene acaulis*, *Eritrichium argentium*, dwarf daisies (*Erigeron aureus*, *E. compositus*, and *E. radicatus*), and *Saxifraga oppositifolia*, mark the zone.

No mammals in Oregon and only three breeding birds are confined to this zone. In the Cascades, Hepburn's Rosy Finch breeds in small numbers on Mount Hood, Mount Jefferson, and Three Sisters, while in the highest part of the Wallowa Mountains the Gray-crowned Rosy Finch and the American Pipit are regular summer residents and breeding birds.

Federal Bird Refuges in Oregon

On August 18, 1908, by order of President Theodore Roosevelt, Malheur Lake was made a Federal bird refuge. It was the third such refuge to be established as a direct result of the interest aroused by the studies of William Lovell Finley and Herman Theodore Bohlman in the spectacular bird-population areas along the Oregon coast and in the great interior marshes of the State. Ten days earlier, Klamath Lake Bird Refuge had been established by Executive order, and on October 14, 1907, Three Arch Rocks Bird Refuge was established. Since then, Cold Springs Bird Refuge (1909), McKay Creek Bird Refuge (1927), Upper Klamath Bird Refuge (1928), and more recently, Goat Island Migratory Bird Refuge have been established, and a tract in Blitzen Valley has been acquired to be combined with the Lake Malheur Bird Refuge, the combined areas to be known as Malheur Migratory Bird Refuge. The locations of these refuges are shown on the accompanying map (Figure 3).

Malheur Migratory Bird Refuge

The Malheur Migratory Bird Refuge awakens the imagination and kindles the vision of a naturalist. Before its possibilities all other Federal bird refuges in Oregon pale to insignificance. Located in Harney County, it was for many years the greatest waterfowl breeding ground in the West. It has been known to ornithologists from Captain Bendire's time and has had more written about it than any other spot in the State. As late as 1920, the magnitude of its bird populations stunned the observer who tried to classify the masses of birds into their component parts. Pelicans, cormorants, grebes, herons, ibises, shore birds, cranes, rails, and myriads of ducks and geese, gulls, terns, and swans made it their home. It held in its teeming fastnesses the farthest-north colonies of egrets, White-faced Glossy Ibises, and Black-necked Stilts. Dainty Wilson's Phalaropes trod the small animals from the mud in approved whirling dervish style; and long-legged Avocets scooped up the alkali flies with their upturned beaks. Red-winged and Yellow-headed Blackbirds drifted over the marsh, like clouds of gnats; while Caspian Terns, Forster's Terns, and California and Ring-billed Gulls added their raucous voices to the din that at times became deafening. The authors have stood late in August in helpless bewilderment watching the clattering, clucking hosts, entirely at sea as to how to estimate the numbers of birds and equally at a loss for words adequately to paint the picture.

After 1920, the effects of drought, additional irrigation, and deliberate diversion of water played havoc with this biological wonderland, until from 1930 to 1935 it was either entirely dry or contained so little water that by midsummer it became only a stinking remnant of its former grandeur. In 1935, the Biological Survey, almost miraculously it seemed to those who had watched the tragedy, became possessed of enough money to purchase the P Ranch, which not only is wonderful bird country itself but controls the precious water supply for Malheur. This added 64,717 acres to the original 95,155 acres. The Survey is now engaged in restoring the marshlands insofar as water supply will permit. With any sort of a break in the drought, the Malheur Migratory Bird Refuge can again take its place as one of the greatest waterfowl breeding areas south of the Canadian line.

Three Arch Rocks and Cape Meares Bird Refuges

Three Arch Rocks Bird Refuge has a spectacular colony of seafowl that nests on several enormous rocks, remnants of a rocky headland that once projected far out into the sea. The area comprises about 17 acres in Tillamook County. California Murres are the most abundant birds present, but Forked-tailed and Beal's Petrels, Farallon, Brandt's, and Baird's Cormorants, Western Gulls, and Tufted Puffins are also well represented. During the nesting season, birds constantly circle the rocks like swarms

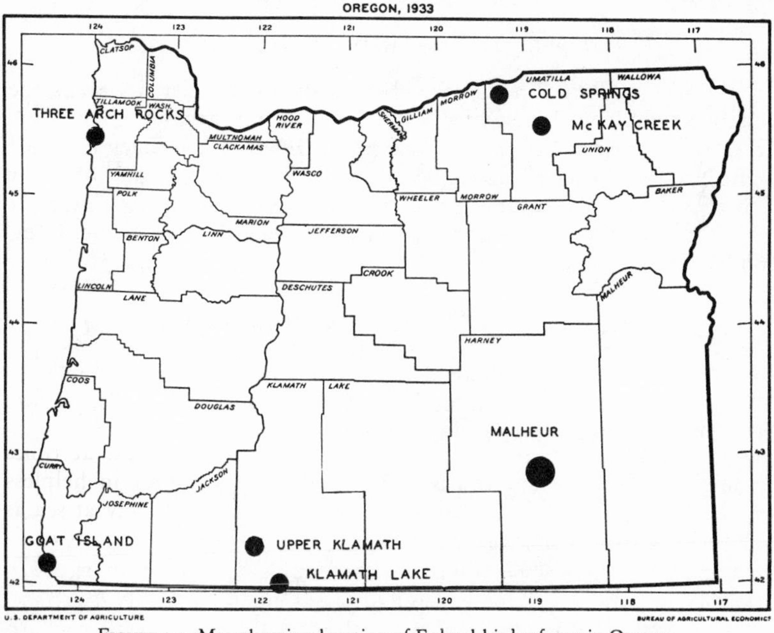

Figure 3.—Map showing location of Federal bird refuges in Oregon.

of bees, and it would be a rash person indeed who ventured a guess as to their numbers.

The Cape Meares Migratory Bird Refuge, about 1 mile north of Three Arch Rocks, was established in August 1938 to protect migratory birds, Band-tailed Pigeons, grouse, shore birds, black-tailed deer, and brown bears. It contains 139 acres.

Klamath Lake Bird Refuge

Klamath Lake Bird Refuge is an area of 81,619 acres on Lower Klamath Lake in Klamath County, Oregon, and Siskiyou County, California. It was frequented by American Coots and by a variety of gulls, ducks, geese, grebes, cormorants, pelicans, and shore birds. Because of an ill-advised drainage scheme it is now largely a dry alkaline lake bed.

Cold Springs and McKay Creek Bird Refuges

Cold Springs and McKay Creek Bird Refuges, situated in Umatilla County, embrace 2,677 and 1,813 acres espectively. They are fine nesting grounds and provide breeding grounds for geese, ducks, and other waterfowl in limited numbers, and feeding grounds for swans and herons during migrations.

Upper Klamath Bird Refuge

Upper Klamath Bird Refuge extends for only a short distance along the western side of Upper Klamath Lake in Klamath County but covers 8,140 acres. It has a wonderful mixed rookery of Blue Herons, Black-crowned Night Herons, American Egrets, and Farallon Cormorants, and, together with the adjoining lowlands, supports the largest nesting population of Redheads to be found in the State, as well as many Canada Geese, Common Mallards, Cinnamon Teals, and many other water birds.

Goat Island Migratory Bird Refuge

Goat Island Migratory Bird Refuge is an area of 21 acres in Curry County established for the protection of California Murres, gulls, puffins, geese, and other migratory and resident species.

Hart Mountain Antelope Refuge

The Hart Mountain Antelope Refuge, comprising 264,935 acres in historic southeastern Lake County, was established in December 1936 primarily for the protection of prong-horned antelopes, mule deer, and native fur and upland game species, but birds and other wildlife also are protected, as on all other national wildlife refuges administered by the Biological Survey. A recent (1939) publication of the Survey shows that the area is a haven for birds of 120 species, ranging from forms that inhabit the hot semideserts among the sagebrush at the base of Hart Mountain to those that live in the cool climate of the mountain top, 3,400 feet above Warner Valley. Among the birds on the refuge are Canada Geese, quails, hawks, owls, swallows, warblers, kinglets, and sparrows.

History of Oregon Ornithology

First Records by Lewis and Clark, 1805–06

The history of Oregon ornithology extends back one hundred and thirty-four years to the time when Meriwether Lewis and William Clark wintered at the mouth of the Columbia River in 1805–06. Their journals, a tale of hardships caused by a combination of stormy weather and hunger, contain only incidental references to birds that can be surely identified as Oregon records. A camp near the present site of Fort Vancouver was their natural stopping place below the Cascades, as it was for most of the other early visitors, and many of their scattered notes apply to Washington. Travel in those days was no easy matter, and on reading the record of their historic trip across the continent one marvels at the hardiness of the men in enduring all sorts of discomforts and hardships. As they came down the Columbia they were obliged to buy dogs and half-spoiled cured fish from the Indians for food, often living for several days on such scanty fare. After being forced to subsist on unappetizing fish for several successive meals, in fact, they came to regard dog meat as a delicacy.

These men, fighting weather, rapids, and hunger, had little time to write voluminous notes, and consequently many of their entries concerning birds are vague both as to locality and species. The first reference that seems to have a definite Oregon location was made on Saturday, November 2, 1805. It refers to a camp 27 miles below the Cascades on the "left side of the river opposite the point of a large meadow. . . . . We saw great numbers of water-fowl, such as swan, geese, ducks of various kinds, gulls, plover and the white and gray brant, of which last we killed eighteen." This "swan" might have been either the Trumpeter or Whistling Swan, both of which wintered on the Columbia in the early days; the "plover" was undoubtedly the Killdeer; and the "geese" were without doubt the Lesser Snow Goose and the Lesser Canada Goose, the latter form being the one that still frequents the river in numbers at that season.

No other mention of birds in the journals definitely referable to Oregon was made until Saturday, November 30, 1805, when, after having been soaked for days and having had their camp on the north bank of the Columbia flooded several times by huge tides that piled up before southwest gales, they crossed and made camp near Astoria. This crossing had been delayed by heavy storms and mountainous seas on the bay. The journal speaks several times of the dexterity of the Indians in handling their dugouts and their fearlessness in crossing the bay at times when the explorers themselves were afraid to attempt it. After they had crossed to the south bank of the river, hunting parties were immediately sent out to get meat, resulting in this entry:

> The hunters had seen three elk, but could not obtain any of them; they however brought in three hawks and a few black ducks, of a species common in the United States, living in large flocks, and feeding on grass; they are distinguished by a sharp white beak, toes separated, and by having no craw. Besides these wild fowl, there are in this neighbourhood a large kind of buzzard with white wings, the gray and the bald eagle, the large red-tailed hawk, the blue magpye, and great numbers of ravens and crows. We observe, however, few small birds, the one which has most attracted our attention being a small brown bird, which seems to frequent logs and the roots of trees.

This furnishes our first record of the American Coot, California Condor, Bald Eagle, Western Red-tailed Hawk, Coast Jay, American Raven, crow (probably Western, though it might include the Northwestern Crow), and the Western Winter Wren.

From that date the explorers were too busy hunting food, building a winter camp for shelter from the interminable rain, and making salt, to pay any attention to birds for a while. On Thursday, January 2, 1806, this entry was made:

> The birds which most strike our attention are the large as well as the small or whistling swan, the sandhill crane, the large and small geese, cormorants, brown and white brant, duckauinmallard, the canvass and several other species of ducks. There is also a small crow, the blue crested corvus, and the smaller corvus with a white breast, the little brown wren, a large brown sparrow, the bald eagle, and the beautiful buzzard of the Columbia.

Here we have definite records for the Trumpeter and Whistling Swan, Common Mallard, Canvas-back, Coast Jay, Oregon Jay, and Western Winter Wren. The "cormorants" might have been any one or all of the three coast species; the "sandhill crane" was possibly a Blue Heron; the "brown and white brant" and "large and small geese" probably included several species, though only the Lesser Snow Goose can be surely identified; and the "large brown sparrow" might be either a Rusty Song Sparrow or one of the wintering forms of Fox Sparrow, both of which are common winter residents of the district.

On Friday, March 28, 1806, the journal contained an account of Elalah, or Deer Island, visited on the up-river trip. It mentioned: ". . . great numbers of geese, ducks, large swan, sandhill cranes, a few canvass-backed ducks and particularly the duckinmallard, the most abundant of all."

On Friday, April 4, 1806, "Wappatoo island," now known as Sauvies Island, was visited and the "small speckled woodpecker, with a white back" was recorded from that point, which is still a favorite haunt of Gairdner's Woodpecker. One who is familiar with the present carp-infested waters of this area, barren of aquatic vegetation, will read with interest their account of the abundance of wapato (*Sagittaria*) and the

Indian methods of harvesting this important food and article of trade between the Indians of the neighborhood and less fortunately located villagers far and wide.

On Wednesday, April 9, 1806, is entered the last Oregon bird note, made from observations on the opposite side of the river from Beacon Rock, as follows: "We saw to-day some turkey-buzzards which are the first we have observed on this side of the Rocky Mountains."

David Douglas, 1825–26

With the foregoing note Lewis and Clark pass out of the Oregon ornithological picture, and a blank remains until the visit of David Douglas some twenty years later. This young botanist left England on July 25, 1824, on a sailing ship bound around Cape Horn. The vessel arrived off the Columbia on February 12, 1825, but terrific gales and mountainous seas forced it to lie off the mouth of the river until April 7 before finally crossing the bar and anchoring under the north shore. In his Journal, Douglas gives a vivid account of the weather experienced on the voyage and states finally: "Here we experienced the furious hurricanes of North-West America in the fullest extent a thousand times worse than Cape Horn." This should be an interesting statement to Oregonians who have often supposed that the South Seas storms are much more violent than anything ever experienced in this country.

Douglas actually landed on April 9, 1825, collected at the mouth of the river until the 17th, and arrived at Fort Vancouver on the 20th. From this point as headquarters he traveled over much of Oregon and Washington. Even a bare outline of his explorations is too long to be included here—the trips that most interest Oregonians being those of June 20 to July 19, 1825, when he visited the country east of the Cascades; August 19 to September 5, 1825, when he traveled up the Willamette Valley to the mouth of the Santiam and returned to Vancouver; March 20 to August 30, 1826, spent in eastern Washington, as far north as Kettle Falls, and in the Blue Mountains of eastern Oregon; and September 20 to November 20, 1826, when he journeyed up the Willamette and on to the Umpqua. He spent both winters at Vancouver and left March 20, 1827, traveling up the Columbia and overland to York Factory on Hudson Bay.

Although Douglas was primarily a botanist and devoted his efforts mainly to the science of plant life, he found time to interest himself in both birds and mammals. When one considers that all travel was by canoe, on horseback, and on foot, it is evident that Douglas covered an immense territory and accomplished a seemingly impossible amount of work during his visit to our country. The many plants and numerous birds and animals that bear the name of this untiring young collector are a lasting tribute to the laborious journeys he made in the pursuit of knowledge of this new country.

In his Journal, definite statements regarding birds are infrequent. On August 19, 1825, he "Killed 2 females and 3 males of a fine species of pigeon; feet, legs, and part of the beak yellow, a white ring round the neck." This was evidently near the mouth of the Santiam River and is our first definite record for the Band-tailed Pigeon. Various other references to eagles, blue jays, horned owls, geese, vultures, and crows occur but are always rather vague as to time and place. When it is considered that he traveled much of his time on foot with only such supplies and equipment as he and his companions could carry, the lack of detail in notes on birds—very definitely a side line with him—is understandable.

Douglas (1828) did find time to report on some of the most interesting birds. He described the California Condor and its nests and eggs (evidently from word of mouth reports rather than personal observation) and stated:

> I have met with them as far to the north as 49° N. Lat. in the summer and autumn months, but nowhere so abundantly as in the Columbian valley between the Grand Rapids and the sea. . . . Specimens, male and female, of this truly interesting bird, which I shot in lat. 45.30.15., long. 122.3.12., were lately presented by the Council of the Horticultural Society to the Zoological Society, in whose Museum they are now carefully deposited.

In a paper read before the Linnaean Society December 16, 1828, and later published in its *Transactions* (1829) he discussed the presence and enormous abundance of the Sage Hen and Columbian Sharp-tailed Grouse on the plains of the Columbia and reported the Oregon Ruffed Grouse as an inhabitant of the coast of Oregon and Washington. He also described from memory and notes the Plumed Quail—his specimens having been lost while crossing a tributary on the head of the Willamette in November, 1826.

Among the most interesting statements in this account of the grouse and quail is one Douglas made about *Tetrao* [=*Lagopus*] *lagopus:* "On the north-west coast it exists as low as 45° 7′, the position of Mount Hood. This is the same bird as the Scotch Ptarmigan." So far as we have been able to ascertain, this note is the basis for all subsequent designation of the ptarmigan as an Oregon species. No other ornithologist has noted it south of the Goat Rocks, some 50 to 70 miles north of the Oregon line in the wild jumble of peaks between Rainier, Adams, and St. Helens, Washington, and Douglas does not state that he actually observed the birds on Mount Hood. Certainly there have been no ptarmigan in Oregon for many years, if indeed they were ever present.

Townsend and Nuttall (1834–36) and Others

Following Douglas's departure nothing more was accomplished in the study of the ornithology of the Oregon country until 1834, when John Kirk Townsend and Thomas Nuttall started overland with a party from

St. Louis. Nuttall, primarily a botanist, had induced Townsend to join the party. The two men, traveling on foot, left St. Louis ahead of the main party on March 29, 1834, and spent their time collecting until they were overtaken by the rest of the adventurers. Townsend's *Narrative*, published in 1839, contains a vivid account of the trials and tribulations as well as the good fortunes of the journey. It is well written and entertaining now after almost a hundred years have elapsed. The party first arrived on what is now Oregon soil late in August (probably August 24), since on that date Townsend stated: "We passed, this morning, over a flat country, very similar to that along the Platte, abounding in wormwood bushes, the pulpy-leaved thorn, and others, and deep with sand, and at noon stopped on a small stream called *Malheur's creek.*"

Contrary to a somewhat popular belief, these early explorers did not find the enormous abundance of game that is supposed to have existed in this country before the white man destroyed it. Townsend's party, as well as many others, often went on scant rations for days at a time and rejoiced when they could purchase by barter dried salmon and dried chokecherries from the squalid Indian villagers. On August 28, on Powder River, the hunters killed an antelope and a deer fawn, the first game larger than a rabbit they had seen since leaving extreme eastern Idaho, where they killed their last buffalo.

In crossing the Blue Mountains from the Grande Ronde Valley toward Walla Walla the party suffered from both hunger and thirst. Townsend stated that at noon (September 2) he wandered out along the stream and made a meal of rosebuds. On his return to camp he—

> was surprised to find Mr. N[uttall] and Captain T[hing] picking the last bones of a bird which they had cooked. Upon inquiry, I ascertained that the subject was an unfortunate owl which I had killed in the morning, and had intended to preserve as a specimen. The temptation was too great to be resisted by the hungry Captain and naturalist, and the bird of wisdom lost the immortality which he might otherwise have acquired.

So much for the imaginary plenitude of game in the good old days and also for the fate of the bird that furnishes the first Oregon ornithological note in this interesting narrative.

On December 8, 1834, the two naturalists reached Fort George at the mouth of the Columbia, and one is interested to read Townsend's comments:

> This is the spot where once stood the fort established by the direction of our honored countryman John Jacob Astor. One of the chimneys of old Fort Astoria is still standing, a melancholy monument of American enterprise and domestic misrule. The spot where once this fine parterre overlooked the river, and the bold stoccade enclosed the neat and substantial fort, is now overgrown with weeds and bushes, and can scarce be distinguished from the primeval forest which surrounds it on every side.

Evidently there were troubles and disagreements in public policy even in those golden days. Following this visit the two men sailed to the Hawaiian Islands and returned to the mouth of the Columbia and the Oregon country on April 16, 1835. Townsend remained at Fort Vancouver, making excursions from there to the Blue Mountains and up the Willamette for short distances, until November 30, 1836, when he again crossed out over the Columbia bar, bound for his home in Philadelphia.

Townsend reaped a rich harvest of birds and mammals during his long visit to the Oregon territory, but his notes are so vague that many of the forms cannot be definitely localized. Much of his time was spent at Fort Vancouver, and many of the small western birds were described from specimens he collected there. Among them are two that have since been definitely ascribed to what is now Oregon. The type locality of the Black-throated Gray Warbler is old Fort William, which stood near the present site of the city of Portland; and that of Townsend's Solitaire is Astoria, which is a case of the first described specimen coming from a point distant from the normal range of the species.

The Reverend Samuel Parker in his *Journal of an Exploring Trip Beyond the Rocky Mountains*, a trip performed in the years 1835, 1836, and 1837 (revised ed. 1844) gives credit to Townsend for aid in the following interesting account of "the birds of Oregon:"

The birds of Oregon are not so numerous as those which inhabit civilized countries, probably because they have not access to the grain and fruit of cultivated fields, and the woods and groves are more widely dispersed. But they are sufficiently numerous to employ an ornithologist profitably, for a great length of time in collecting and preserving specimens. This region is particularly interesting from the fact, that . . . , it has hitherto been an unexplored field—no competent scientific person having visited this country to classify the different genera and species. Mr. J. K. Townsend, of Philadelphia, an ornithologist, has spent 2 years in examining scientifically this field, and will probably give to the public the result of his labors. I am indebted to him for assistance in the following summary.

The largest part of the feathered race are migratory, and are seen only a part of the year. There are many, however that reside here during the whole year. Among these are the majestic white-headed eagle, and the golden eagle, and 3 or 4 species of hawks, 2 species of jay, the magpie, *Corvus pica*, and thousands of ravens and crows; several species of small sparrows, and 2 or 3 species of grouse, the common partridge of the United States, and the dusky grouse of the Rocky Mountains; and also an interesting species of the dipper or water ousel. . . . The red-winged black-bird and the robin continue throughout the year. The notes of the latter are heard even in the chill of winter, though in feeble strains.

As the autumn advances, the number of swans, geese and ducks multiply. . . . The black cormorant is common upon the Columbia river, and there are other species of the same genus, seen about the shores of the Cape, which do not ascend the rivers. Among these is the violet green cormorant, the most splendid of all the known species of cormorants. The loon, or great northern diver, is very plentiful in this river. Gulls, terns, auks, and petrels, in great numbers, visit this river to seek shelter from the violent storms which agitate the ocean during the winter.

. . . Among these [that remain through the summer] are hundreds of warblers, wrens, titmice and nuthatches. Of the warblers there are 11 species, 6 of which are new; the other 5 are common to the States. Several of the species are but transient visitors, but most of them remain through the season. Of the wrens there are 6 species; three of the titmice, and 2 of the nuthatches. And in the train follow the thrushes, of which there are 7 species, 2 of which are new; of these Wilson's thrush is pre-eminent in sweetness of song. The fly-catchers number 8 species, 3 of which are new; and there are 13 species of finches, 3 of which are new.

. . . In no instance do we find more richness and delicacy of plumage, with the most sweet melody of voice, than in a new species of large bullfinch, which visits this section of country in the spring. If these were domesticated, they would form a most valuable addition to any aviary. There are 8 species of woodpeckers, 4 of which are new; and of the swallow tribe there are 5 species, one of which is new, and is the most beautiful of the family, characterized by a splendid changeable green plumage on the head and back, while the other parts are purple and white. About the middle of March the splendid little Nootka humming bird makes his appearance, coming so suddenly, that you wonder from whence he came . . . .; the neck of this beautiful bird presents fine variations of color; now it is ruby red, with a metallic lustre; turn it, and the tints vary from purple to violet and crimson, according as the light falls upon it.

I pass over the mention of many genera, and still more numerous species of the different birds of this region, as it is not my design to attempt a history of them, but only to give a succinct sketch, that some idea may be formed of the ornithological treasures of this interesting country.

Throughout the early years of Oregon's history, trappers and adventurers constantly passed through the country, but those men had scant inclination to put on paper their experiences and observations. The journals of General John Charles Frémont concerning his historic 1843 trip over the Blue Mountains, down the Columbia to The Dalles, up the Deschutes, thence into the Klamath Marsh (Summer Lake), and southeastward out of Oregon toward Pyramid Lake, Nevada, furnish practically no information about the bird life of the region, although they are filled with botanical and geological notes.

Government Surveys, 1855

The Pacific Railroad survey reports, based on the notes of many surveying parties in the West, contain the first definite papers of importance in Oregon ornithology. A surveying crew under Lieutenant R. S. Williamson entered Oregon on August 11, 1855, near Tule Lake (then known as Rhett Lake). This party was accompanied by Dr. John Strong Newberry, who published his notes made in California and Oregon on the zoology of the route in Volume VI (1857) of the ponderous survey tomes. After exploring the Klamath basin, the expedition worked north onto the headwaters of the Deschutes looking for a practical pass through the Cascades. At this point the party split for a time, Williamson remaining in the Cascades while a detachment under Lieutenant Henry L. Abbot made a trip to The Dalles and to the head of the Deschutes. After their return the party again separated, Williamson and his group crossing the Cascades south of Diamond Peak and following down the Willamette and thence northward to Vancouver, from which point Williamson sailed for San Francisco. Meanwhile, Abbot, accompanied by Newberry, worked north along the Deschutes, explored the country about Black Butte and Mount Jefferson, worked slowly northward to Tygh Valley, and then crossed the Cascades south of Mount Hood. They were one of the first groups, if not the very first, to use this particular route. After a brief stop at Vancouver they traveled south through the Willamette, Umpqua, and Rogue River Valleys, finally crossing out of the State on November 6, 1855.

During this trip Newberry collected voluminous notes, and his material is the most definite and important contribution to Oregon ornithology up to that date. First records for many of the species within the State limits were made, and this material, together with that collected privately by Dr. George Suckley at The Dalles in 1854–55 after he had completed his services with a northern survey, furnished most of the basis for Oregon records in Spencer Fullerton Baird's report (Baird, Cassin, and Lawrence 1858), which was the final ornithological result of all the surveys. When one considers the comparative isolation of Diamond Peak and Mount Jefferson, even up to the last few years, it is odd to read the records of Newberry and realize that at that early date scientific men were scouting the fastnesses of the Cascades looking for new information.

Bendire, Henshaw, Mearns, and Others, 1872 to 1902

The Civil War and its attendant tension apparently interrupted further work on birds in Oregon, for it was not until Captain Charles Bendire published his work on collections and observations in Harney Valley some twenty years later that the next noteworthy contribution was made. He spent the period from November 1875 to January 1877 in residence at Camp Harney. The results were published in two papers, the first in 1875 (Brewer 1875) and the second in 1877 (Bendire 1877). In addition his notes were amplified in many instances in his two volumes on *Life Histories of North American Birds*, published in 1892 and 1895. As Bendire was the first resident ornithologist in eastern Oregon, he is responsible for a long list of first records. These cover both breeding and occurrences of birds in this rich area and probably make the greatest individual contribution to the knowledge of the birds of the State. Most of the specimens he collected are deposited in the United States National Museum at Washington.

Henry Wetherbee Henshaw, who later become Chief of the Biological Survey, was ornithologist of the Wheeler Survey of the Territories from 1872 to 1879, in the course of which he collected many birds, 238 on a trip in 1878 from Carson, Nevada, to The Dalles and Portland, Oregon. In his autobiographical notes Henshaw related the following experience that befell him while collecting birds at Albany, Oregon, in 1881 (*Condor* 22: 55–56, 1920):

While in Oregon an amusing incident occurred by which I fell into the clutches of the law, the first and only time in my long experience as a bird collector. Being detained in Albany, Oregon, for a few days because of a flood which interfered with the operation of the stages and railroads to the south, I employed an hour's leisure in collecting a few birds on the outskirts of the town, by no means so large then as now. Fate played me a sorry trick by leading me to collect a number of curious looking Shore Larks directly in front of the house of the constable, who proceeded to instill the fear of the law into my heart by a fine of ten dollars. As, however, the birds subsequently proved to be the types of a new form (*Eremophila* [=*Otocoris*] *alpestris strigata*), I have always considered that I got the worth of my money.[1]

Almost contemporary with Bendire, Dr. Henry McElderry and Lt. Willis Wittich, stationed at Fort Klamath during the late seventies, had been collecting birds and making the notes that were compiled and published by Dr. Edgar Alexander Mearns in 1879. Following this, James Cushing Merrill, who was stationed at the same post from September 1886 to August 1887, published his own experiences in 1888. These notes from Harney and Klamath Counties were for many years the greatest contribution to Oregon ornithology and made the birds of these basins much better known to the ornithological world than those from other sections of the State.

While these men were making their studies east of the Cascades, O. B. Johnson's list of birds observed in Forest Grove, Portland, and East Salem appeared in 1880. Many of his specimens are still preserved at the University of Washington at Seattle. At about the same time Dr. Clinton T. Cooke did considerable bird collecting in the Willamette Valley. He wrote little, but his specimens have been available to the present authors and have been valuable aids in formulating the statements regarding the birds of western Oregon.

Alfred Webster Anthony collected for many years in the vicinity of Beaverton and in 1886 published a list of the birds of Washington County. Many of his specimens are now in the Carnegie Museum at Pittsburgh, Pennsylvania. He later contributed a special list of birds from Portland and vicinity for Mrs. Florence Merriam Bailey's use in her *Handbook of Birds of the Western United States*. Johnson's and Anthony's publications were the most important on western Oregon birds until 1902, when Arthur Roy Woodcock, then a student at Oregon Agricultural College, published the first real list of the birds of the State, which he had compiled from his own notes on the birds in the vicinity of Corvallis, from data obtained by correspondence with observers in various parts of the State, and from a partial check of the literature. Woodcock's own notes are authentic and valuable, and most of his skins are still available for study at Corvallis; but he was somewhat unfortunate in the selection of his observers and accepted many statements that, to say the least, are dubious. Some of these species are here assigned to the hypothetical list, and some of the distributional data are questioned in the present discussion of other species.

---

[1] Through some oversight, Henshaw has here considered Albany to be the type locality of *Otocoris a. strigata*, whereas the type specimen as now labeled in the National Museum is an adult male from Fort Steilacoom, Washington; in his original description, however, Henshaw did mention one of the adult females from Albany, Oregon.

Since 1891, Dr. Albert Gregory Prill has been publishing notes from Linn County and other parts of the State. He has contributed several new species to the Oregon list. His collection at Scio and his many nesting records have been available in compiling the present distributional data. Many of his specimens are deposited in the United States National Museum at Washington, at the California Academy of Sciences, and at the University of Oregon.

Recent Ornithological Investigations

In 1902, William Lovell Finley's first notes on Oregon birds appeared. His photographic studies of the birds on Three Arch Rocks, Lower Klamath Lake, and Malheur Lake, published in numerous books and magazine articles—some of them in collaboration with Herman Theodore Bohlman—have become classics in American ornithological literature. As a direct result of these studies all three areas mentioned have been set aside as Federal bird refuges. The work has been continued by both Mr. and Mrs. Finley until now their wildlife pictures and stories are familiar throughout this country and Canada.

Alex Walker collected for years in Tillamook County and at various places in eastern Oregon for the Oregon Game Commission, during the time Finley was State game warden, and for the Cleveland [Ohio] Museum of Natural History. He has published a number of short articles, and Dr. Harry Church Oberholser has published descriptions of several new subspecies of birds that are based largely on his collections.

Alfred Cooper Shelton, while at the University of Oregon, worked out a distributional list of the birds of west-central Oregon, based largely on his own field work in Lane County. This was published in 1917 and is one of the outstanding works on Oregon birds to date.

George Willett's notes on his experiences and observations at Malheur Lake appeared in 1919. These included important nesting data that have filled in many missing details regarding this area.

Since that time many short notes on Oregon birds have appeared from various sources, but no papers of outstanding importance have been printed.

Since 1925, John Claude Braly, an active bird collector throughout Oregon, has contributed much information on nesting dates. These notes are included in the present account for the proper species. They have been taken from his field notes and egg catalog, since few of the data have been published.

Edward Samuel Currier, who has been collecting in Oregon since 1903, has accumulated much information on Oregon birds, particularly on nesting dates, that has been available for the present work.

Finley, when State game warden, employed Jewett, beginning July 1, 1912, to build up a State collection of birds and mammals. Olaus Johan

Murie joined Jewett in September and worked with him about a year. Until June 1916, Jewett put in parts of each year collecting and was assisted by various wardens and temporary employees. A total of about 2,000 bird and 1,000 mammal skins were collected and are still the property of the State Game Commission. This work, so well started, was abandoned by Finley's successors, but the material has been available for the present writers.

Overton Dowell, Jr., has for many years carried on a limited amount of collecting, largely in the vicinity of Mercer Lake in western Lane County. The astonishing number of new distributional records that have resulted from his persistent efforts are only an indication of what can be expected from intensive work in other parts of this practically virgin State.

Since 1931, H. M. Dubois and John A. Carter, both of Portland, have worked in the vicinity of that city, and Reed Ferris has been active in Tillamook County. Their material and that of J. E. Patterson, who has collected eggs for several years in Klamath and Jackson Counties, have been incorporated in this book. Patterson has kindly loaned his manuscript notes to the Biological Survey, and from these the present writers have obtained much valuable information.

Willard Ayres Eliot, an enthusiastic bird observer, incorporated his own notes from the vicinity of Portland in his *Birds of the Pacific Coast* (1923). This book, intended primarily for popular use, has furnished valuable information and has stimulated an intensified public interest in things ornithological, particularly in the vicinity of Portland.

This completes the record of the more important workers in this field of bird study, though a glance at the Bibliography (p. 609) will show contributions from many other sources.

Work by the United States Biological Survey

In addition to the foregoing publications, specimens, and manuscript notes on Oregon ornithology, the writers have had access to a vast mass of unpublished data in the files of the Biological Survey, including reports made and specimens collected in Oregon at various times for nearly 50 years by the many field workers and cooperators of that organization.

Dr. Clinton Hart Merriam, first chief of the Bureau, visited parts of Oregon in 1888, chiefly to study losses occasioned by rodents, and in 1896 he led the first exploration undertaken by the Biological Survey in Oregon, with Vernon Bailey, E. A. Preble, and Cleveland Allen as assistants. The party collected specimens of mammals and birds as a basis for life-zone determinations in the Blue, Steens, and Warner Mountains, and in the Cascades from the Klamath region north to Mount Hood. About a month, from August 12 to September 15, was spent in the vicinity of Crater Lake and the region between Crater Lake and Fort Klamath. In the Cascade region between Crater Lake and Fort Klamath, collections were made at the following localities: Williamson River, near Fort Klamath; Anna Creek Canyon; Pole Bridge Creek; Crater Lake; Diamond Lake; Western Sink Creek, between Diamond Lake and Klamath Marsh; and Prospect in the Rogue River Valley. Both the birds and the mammals collected are now in the Biological Survey collection of the United States National Museum.

The Bureau's biological survey of Oregon was furthered by later chiefs, particularly Henry Wetherbee Henshaw (who had collected earlier in the State) and Dr. Edward William Nelson. As a result, representative collections of birds and other forms of wildlife from virtually every part of the State have been assembled. Throughout these surveys local cooperation was extended by the University of Oregon at Eugene, the Willamette University at Salem, the Oregon State College at Corvallis, Reed College at Portland, and the State Fish and Game Department. In addition, the work was furthered by close and cordial cooperation of the Forest Service, the National Park Service, and the Geological Survey.

Among other field naturalists of the Survey who have made important natural history observations and collections of birds and mammals at various times and localities in Oregon are the following: Dr. Theodore Sherman Palmer, in 1889; Clark P. Streator, from 1890 to 1896; J. E. McLellan, in 1894; Vernon Bailey, in 1895 and in many subsequent years; Arthur Holmes Howell, in 1895; Edward Alexander Preble, in 1896 and 1915; Dr. Albert Kenrick Fisher and J. Alden Loring, in 1897; Ned Hollister, in 1904; D. D. Streeter, Jr., in 1909; Luther J. Goldman and Harry Telford, in 1914; Professor Morton Eaton Peck, beginning in 1915; and Robert H. Becker and Harry H. Sheldon, beginning in 1916. Other Survey students of Oregon bird life have been Dr. Walter Kenrick Fisher, Edwin Richard Kalmbach, Olaus Johan Murie, Professor Robert T. Young, George G. Cantwell, Alex Walker, and the present writers, Gabrielson and Jewett. Although in many instances the work of these men was largely in the then almost virgin mammalian field, many of them paid considerable attention to birds. The notes and specimens collected, as well as the other available information previously referred to, have been freely used in preparing this report on the birds of the State, with a view to making it as nearly complete as is possible at this time.

Although this is by no means the complete list of Survey workers in Oregon, it includes the most important field efforts of the Survey. The localities covered by some of the investigations are presented briefly as follows:

Palmer, in 1889, made collections in western Oregon, including the Grants Pass section in the southwest and Astoria and other parts of Clatsop County in the northwest.

Streator also collected in western Oregon at various localities, in 1890, 1891, and 1893, and in the eastern part of the State in 1896. In each instance his work was primarily on mammals, but he also collected some birds.

McLellan spent the summer and fall of 1894 collecting in the coast sections.

Bailey began his collections at Burns, Strawberry Mountain, the Warner Mountains, and Wallowa Mountains and other parts of eastern Oregon in 1895. He was accompanied at times during this and subsequent years by Merriam, Howell, Preble, and Jewett. In 1920, he again furnished some bird notes while engaged in mammal work in the vicinity of Malheur Lake.

In 1896, Preble collected extensively in southeastern Oregon, spending some time also in the Wallowas, as did Howell the previous year. He made a second trip through the same general territory in 1915, collecting at numerous localities in southern Malheur County.

Fisher collected a number of birds in 1897 in Tillamook, Clatsop, Washington, and Douglas Counties, and during the same year Loring worked in the vicinity of The Dalles and southward, while Young collected a number of birds near Wallowa Lake.

From 1914 to 1917, Cantwell worked at Malheur Lake as reservation warden and furnished many valuable notes and specimens. In 1919 he collected in Wallowa County, in various localities in Hood River County, and in western Oregon at Philomath, in Benton County.

In 1914, Goldman did rather intensive work in central Oregon in Deschutes, northern Lake, and northern Klamath Counties.

In 1916, Shelton worked the Snake River Canyon in Baker County and the Steens Mountains in Harney County; Becker did similar work in Malheur County; and Peck in western Oregon, particularly Douglas County, after having spent the previous summer season in the Blue Mountains in Umatilla, Union, Baker, and Grant Counties.

Kalmbach spent the late summer and the fall of 1920 near Ontario, working on crow problems, and the three seasons of 1929–1931 at Klamath Falls, working on the duck sickness and contributing incidental notes and specimens on these and other groups of birds.

Jewett was engaged by the Survey from 1916 to 1935 in predatory animal control work; Gabrielson, from 1918 to 1935 in rodent control and supervisory work, both largely in Oregon. Their duties required constant travel that carried them into every section of the State and furnished an opportunity for observation of bird life over a long period of years. The notes and specimens collected have been made the basis for this book, and the appended bibliography carries a list of papers and notes published thereon from time to time.

List of Birds Originally Described From Oregon

Species	Type Locality
Falco communis var. *Pealei* Ridgway (=*Falco peregrinus pealei*). Bull. Essex Inst. 5: 201, December 1873.	Sitka [Alaska]=Oregon.
Canace obscura var. *fuliginosa* Ridgway (=*Dendragapus fuliginosus fuliginosus*). Bull. Essex Inst. 5: 199, December 1873.	Cascade Mountains, Chiloweyuck Depot, Washington Territory, foot of Mount Hood, Oregon=Mount Hood.
Phasianus Columbianus Ord (=*Pedioecetes phasianellus columbianus*). In Guthrie, Geog., 2d Am. ed., 1815, 317. Based on the Prairie Hen, Lewis and Clark, Exped. Rocky Mts., II, 180–182.	Great plains of the Columbia River, Oregon, between mouths of Deschutes and Snake Rivers.
Oreortyx picta palmeri Oberholser. Auk 40: 34, January 10, 1923.	Yaquina.
Lophortyx californica orecta Oberholser. Cleveland Mus. Nat. Hist. Sci. Pubs. 4(1): 2, September 19, 1932.	Mouth of Twenty Mile Creek, Warner Valley, 9 miles south of Adel.
Zenaidura macroura caurina Ridgway. U. S. Nat. Mus. Bull. No. 50, Part VII: 348, May 5, 1916.	Oregon.
Otus asio brewsteri Ridgway. U. S. Nat. Mus. Bull No. 50, Part VI: 700, 1914.	Salem.
Phalaenoptilus nuttallii nyctophilus Oberholser. Cleveland Mus. Nat. Hist. Sci. Pubs. 4(1): 2, 3, September 19, 1932.	Hart Mountain, near site of old Fort Warner, northern end of Warner Valley, 20 miles northeast of Adel.
Tyrannus tyrannus hespericola Oberholser. Cleveland Mus. Nat. Hist. Sci. Pubs. 4(1): 3, 4, September 19, 1932.	Mouth of Twenty Mile Creek, Warner Valley, 9 miles south of Adel.
Empidonax traillii adastus Oberholser. Cleveland Mus. Nat. Hist. Sci. Pubs. 4(1): 3, September 19, 1932.	Hart Mountain, northern end of Warner Valley, 20 miles northeast of Adel.
Otocoris alpestris lamprochroma Oberholser. Cleveland Mus. Nat. Hist. Sci. Pubs. 4(1): 4, 5, September 19, 1932.	Spanish Lake, east base of Hart Mountain, northern end of Warner Valley, 20 miles northeast of Adel.
Otocoris alpestris merrilli Dwight. Auk 7: 153, April 1890.	Fort Klamath.

Species	Type Locality
Stelgidopteryx ruficollis aphractus Oberholser. Cleveland Mus. Nat. Hist. Sci. Pubs. 4(1): 5, 6, September 19, 1932.	Twenty Mile Creek, Warner Valley, 9 miles south of Adel.
Petrochelidon albifrons aprophata Oberholser. Cleveland Mus. Nat. Hist. Sci. Pubs. 4(1): 6, September 19, 1932.	Mouth of Twenty Mile Creek, Warner Valley, 9 miles south of Adel.
Cyanocitta stelleri syncolla Oberholser. Cleveland Mus. Nat. Hist. Sci. Pubs. 4(1): 6, 7, September 19, 1932.	Barley Camp, Warner Mountains, 14 miles southwest of Adel.
Cyanocitta stelleri paralia Oberholser. Cleveland Mus. Nat. Hist. Sci. Pubs. 4(1): 7, September 19, 1932.	Pleasant Valley, 9 miles southeast of Tillamook.
Aphelocoma californica immanis Grinnell. Auk 18: 188, April 1901.	Scio.
Corvus americanus hesperis Ridgway (=*Corvus brachyrhynchos hesperis*). Manual North Amer. Birds: 362, 1887.	Western United States north to Washington Territory, Idaho, Montana, etc., south to northern Mexico=Fort Klamath.
Baeolophus inornatus sequestratus Grinnell and Swarth. Calif. Univ. Pubs. Zool. 30: 166, September 16, 1926.	Eagle Point, Jackson County.
Baeolophus inornatus zaleptus Oberholser. Cleveland Mus. Nat. Hist. Sci. Pubs. 4(1): 7, 8, September 19, 1932.	Rim of Warner Valley, northwest of the Jacobs Ranch, Twenty Mile Creek, 9 miles south of Adel.
Chamaea fasciata phaea Osgood. Biol. Soc. Wash. Proc. 13: 42, May 29, 1899.	Newport, Yaquina Bay.
Thryomanes bewickii atrestus Oberholser. Cleveland Mus. Nat. Hist. Sci. Pubs. 4(1): 8, September 19, 1932.	Mouth of Twenty Mile Creek, Warner Valley, 9 miles south of Adel.
Hylocichla guttata oromela Oberholser. Cleveland Mus. Nat. Hist. Sci. Pubs. 4(1): 8, 9, September 19, 1932.	North base of Crook Peak, Warner Mountains, 15 miles northeast of Lakeview.
Ptilogonys [sic] *Townsendi* Audubon (=*Myadestes townsendi*). Birds Amer. (folio), IV, pl. 419, fig. 2, 1838 (Orn. Biog., V, 1839, 206).	Columbia River=near Astoria.
Vireosylva gilva leucopolia Oberholser. Cleveland Mus. Nat. Hist. Sci. Pubs. 4(1): 9, September 19, 1932.	Barley Camp, Warner Mountains, 14 miles southwest of Adel.
Sylvia nigrescens J. K. Townsend (=*Dendroica nigrescens*). Journ. Acad. Nat. Sci. Phila., vol. 7, Part II, p. 191 [November 21, 1837].	Vicinity of Columbia River=near Fort William [Portland].

Species	Type Locality
Euphagus cyanocephalus aliastus Oberholser Cleveland Mus. Nat. Hist. Sci. Pubs. 4(1): 9, 10, 1932.	Twenty Mile Creek, Warner Valley, 9 miles south of Adel.
Loxia curvirostra bendirei Ridgway Biol. Soc. Wash. Proc. 2: 101, April 28, 1884.	Fort Klamath.
Oberholseria chlorura zapolia Oberholser Cleveland Mus. Nat. Hist. Sci. Pubs. 4(1): 10, 11, September 19, 1932.	Hart Mountain, northern end of Warner Valley, 20 miles northeast of Adel.
Pipilo fuscus bullatus Grinnell and Swarth Calif. Univ. Pubs. Zool. 21: 431, April 6, 1926.	Eagle Point, Jackson County.
Poocaetes gramineus affinis G. S. Miller (= *Pooecetes gramineus affinis*) Auk 5: 404, October 1888.	Salem.
Pooecetes gramineus definitus Oberholser Cleveland Mus. Nat. Hist. Sci. Pubs. 4(1): 11, September 19, 1932.	Twenty Mile Creek, Warner Valley, 9 miles south of Adel.
Chondestes grammacus actitus Oberholser Cleveland Mus. Nat. Hist. Sci. Pubs. 4(1): 12, September 19, 1932.	Mouth of Twenty Mile Creek, Warner Valley, 9 miles south of Adel.
Zonotrichia leucophrys oriantha Oberholser Cleveland Mus. Nat. Hist. Sci. Pubs. 4(1): 12, September 19, 1932.	Barley Camp, Warner Mountains, 14 miles southwest of Adel.
Melospiza cinerea phaea Fisher Condor 4: 36, 37, January-February 1902.	Gardiner, mouth of Umpqua River.

Annotated List of the Birds of Oregon

Order Gaviiformes

Loons: *Family Gaviidae*

Lesser Loon:
Gavia immer elasson Bishop

Description.—"*Adults in summer plumage:* Head and neck velvety black, glossed with green; throat and sides of neck crossed by series of white streaks; breast white; back black, spotted with white. *Winter plumage and young:* back slaty, without white spots; throat white." (Bailey) *Downy young:* "The young loon when first hatched is completely covered with soft, thick, short down; the entire upper parts, including the head, neck, chest, and sides, are dark colored, 'fuscous black' on crown and back, 'fuscous' on throat and sides; only the central belly portion is white, tinged laterally with grayish." (Bent) *Size:* Length 28–36, wing 13.55–13.90, bill 2.90–3.19. *Nest:* Sometimes the hollowed-out top of an old muskrat house or a mass of soggy half-rotten vegetable matter heaped up in shallow water or on the shore. *Eggs:* 1 to 3, usually 2, dark olive gray, spotted with black and more or less stained with brown.

Distribution.—*General:* Breeds from northern California, North Dakota, and Wisconsin north to British Columbia and probably Manitoba. Winters on Pacific Coast. *In Oregon:* Likely to be seen on any larger lake or stream, although far more abundant on salt-water bays and inlets of coast.

Townsend's Narrative (1839)[1] first recorded the Lesser Loon for Oregon; Newberry (1857) listed it as found on the lakes of the Cascades; Bendire (1877) stated it was a probable breeder at Malheur Lake; Mearns (1879) and Merrill (1888) both recorded it from Fort Klamath; Johnson (1880) gave it as a casual visitor to the Willamette Valley (Multnomah, Marion, and Washington Counties); and Woodcock (1902) listed it from various points in the State as a migrant and winter resident.

Our own notes record the species from Wallowa (October 27), Lake (November 20), Wasco (Columbia River, October 15), Klamath (several records between September 22 and November 15), Deschutes (North Twin Lake, April 29, one in full plumage), and Multnomah (October 17) Counties inland, and from Tillamook and Lincoln (every month in the year), Coos (May 5 and October 29), and Curry (November 18) Counties on the coast. A pair remained at Devils Lake, Lincoln County, throughout the summers of 1931 to 1934, inclusive, where Gabrielson observed them at frequent intervals. It is probable that the species breeds in that and other coastal lakes, although as yet no nests have been reported from

---

[1] Dates in parentheses following an author's name refer to Bibliography, p. 609.

the State, and it is as a fall migrant and winter resident of the coast that we have the best opportunity to know this fine bird.

The wild cry of the loon has long furnished a theme for poets and writers, and when heard in the misty light of early dawn on some lonely little mountain lake, it thrills one as do few other wilderness sounds. The pair of Lesser Loons at Devils Lake called most fiercely and continuously in the early mornings of foggy or rainy days, at which time the wild ringing laugh echoed and reechoed from shore to shore. Despite the fact that this lake is a somewhat popular summer resort, these birds were not particularly shy and often allowed a boat to come within easy gunshot range. Several times, as Gabrielson sat quietly in a boat, both birds approached within thirty yards, making a wonderful picture as they floated gracefully on the lake's surface with their black and white checkered backs showing conspicuously against the water. At the slightest movement of the boat's occupants they disappeared almost instantaneously beneath the water, usually to reappear above the surface at an astonishing distance. On several occasions, when they were being watched from the shore, one bird, for no apparent reason, took suddenly to the air and swung in great circles about the lake before alighting again.

Rising from the water on a still morning is a laborious task for these heavy-bodied birds, and they cause almost as much commotion as would coots under similar circumstances. When the wind is blowing briskly they can rise from the surface much more easily. Once in the air, their flight is strong, rapid, and direct, the short, powerful wings beating the air rapidly to thrust the long neck, extended bill, and plump body on an arrowlike line of flight. They are much more at home in the water than in the air, however, and few birds are able to outswim or outdive them. In diving, the wings are usually held close to the body, while the big feet drive the birds through the water at a rate of speed more than sufficient to overtake the small fish on which they feed.

Two Oregon stomachs have been examined. One, collected by Jewett at Netarts Bay (November 9, 1915), contained one fish, *Leptocottus armatus;* the other, taken by J. W. Fry at Klamath Falls (November 16, 1912), contained two *Leuciscus* and fragments of another fish. Curiously enough, both stomachs were examined by Gabrielson while a member of the Biological Survey Division of Food Habits Research, long before he became a resident of Oregon. These data are insufficient to serve as a basis for judging the food habits of the Lesser Loon in relation to food and game species of fish. Loons are too uncommon in Oregon, however, to be any factor in the abundance or scarcity of game fish, even though they subsisted entirely on such forms, and their wild cries, wonderful diving performance, and general appeal are more than enough to pay for any fish they may consume.

Plate 8. Pacific Loon. (Photo by Wm. L. and Irene Finley.)

Pacific Loon:
Gavia arctica pacifica (Lawrence)

Description.—"*Breeding plumage:* Back of head and neck smoky gray or whitish; throat black, glossed with greenish or purplish and crossed by transverse bar of white streaks; sides of neck with series of longitudinal white streaks; back black, with four series of white bars; lower parts white. *Winter plumage and young:* back without white markings; throat white." (Bailey) *Downy young:* "The downy young is plainly colored; the short, thick down, with which it is covered is 'light seal brown' on the back, 'clove brown' on the sides, head, and neck, and 'light drab' on the breast and belly." (Bent) *Size:* Length 24, wing 11, bill 2.25. *Nest:* A heap of half-rotten vegetation on the shore, very similar to that of the Lesser Loon. *Eggs:* 2, much like those of other loons, only smaller. "The ground color is 'Prouts' brown,' 'Saccardo's umber,' 'cinnamon brown,' 'dark olive buff,' or 'Isabella color,' very rarely 'pale olive buff.' The egg is usually sparsely covered with small spots, but often there are a few scattering larger spots, of the darkest shades of brown or nearly black; some eggs show underlying spots or pale shades of lavender or drab." (Bent)

Distribution.—*General:* Breeds in northern part of North America. Winters mainly along Pacific Coast south to Lower California. *In Oregon:* More or less common winter resident along coast.

The Pacific Loon (Plate 8) should be watched for on the Oregon coast by all bird students, as it is almost certainly a regular winter resident there. The development of many of the bays and beaches into resorts—frequented to a considerable extent during the winter months by fishermen, clam diggers, and others—has made the birds more scarce or at least has driven them to the larger bays and the open ocean where they are more difficult to observe. This loon is recorded by Mearns (1879) from Fort Klamath and included by Woodcock (1902), without annotations, in his Oregon list, on the authority of A. W. Anthony. These are the only references to it in the literature of Oregon bird life, and we can add only our own notes.

Most of our winter specimens are either the Lesser or Red-throated Loons, but we have two male winter birds of this species in the Gabrielson collection, one taken at Netarts (December 27, 1932) and the other at Barview (January 10, 1934). We have four spring and summer specimens. Jewett has three from Netarts, an adult female in full breeding plumage found dead on the beach (August 14, 1914), an immature male (May 1, 1915), and an adult male (May 3, 1915); and Gabrielson collected an adult male in high plumage at the mouth of Pistol River (August 6, 1932). The extreme ossification of the skull of Gabrielson's specimen indicated that it was a very old individual. It showed no signs of having bred that summer. There was an old leg-bone break that had entirely healed, and the stomach was absolutely empty. When first observed, the bird was resting on the water's edge, and a Western Gull stood beside it. It allowed a close approach behind a flimsy screen of bushes and remained on the bank after the gull took wing. When disturbed it slid into a deep pool in the stream, and Gabrielson, standing on a 10- or 12-foot bank, could see every movement in the clear water. The wings were held closely pressed to the sides, and the two powerful feet struck out straight backward, furnishing all the motive power. The bill, head, and neck were extended straight ahead as in flight, and the bird moved through the water with remarkable swiftness. Gabrielson watched it swim the length of the pool possibly a dozen times. Judging by its actions and the somewhat emaciated condition of the body, it was assumed that the bird was sick or injured.

No Oregon stomachs containing food are available, but those from other localities examined by the Biological Survey contained remains of fish, small gasteropods, and caddisfly larvae.

Red-throated Loon:
Gavia stellata (Pontoppidan)

Description.—"*Adults in summer plumage:* Head and neck plumbeous gray; throat with a wedge-shaped patch of rich chestnut; back sooty; top of head and back of neck streaked and back specked with white; under parts white. *Winter plumage and young:* throat and fore neck white." (Bailey) *Downy young:* "The young loon when first hatched is completely covered with short, thick, dark brown down, 'seal brown' above, shading gradually to 'drab' below." (Bent) *Size:* "Length 24–27, wing 10–11.50, bill 2.25." (Bailey) *Nest:* Usually like those of other loons, although sometimes eggs are laid directly on wet muddy ground. *Eggs:* Usually 2, ground color from "sepia" to "deep olive buff," usually irregularly spotted with small spots or scattering larger spots.

Distribution.—*General:* Breeds in Alaska and northern Canada. Winters southward, chiefly along coast to Florida and California. *In Oregon:* Winter resident along coast, more commonly found on larger bays. Straggles inland occasionally.

While in Oregon, the Red-throated Loons stick very close to salt water, and as they are wild and suspicious—in common with most of our other bay-frequenting birds—observation is not easy. Considerable field work needs to be carried out in the coastal waters to fill in the huge gaps in our knowledge of this and other wintering waterfowl. The only inland records are Suckley's (1860) report of one at The Dalles, March 20, 1855, and a male (Gabrielson Coll. No. 2465) taken by John Carter on the Columbia River near Portland, February 7, 1933. Woodcock (1902) reported the species as a common coastal winter resident on the authority of A. W. Anthony. Overton Dowell, Jr., took a specimen at Mercer Lake, March 5, 1922.

Our own records are from Netarts and Tillamook Bays in Tillamook County, Coos Bay in Coos County, and Yaquina Bay in Lincoln County. Doubtless the species would be found on the mouths of the Columbia, Umpqua, Siuslaw, and Rogue Rivers, too, if enough field work were carried on at those points. Most of our specimens are in winter plumage with the red throat entirely absent. Jewett has one bird (Coll. No. 2028), taken January 1, 1913, that is in partial breeding plumage. Our earliest fall record is November 4; our latest spring record, April 30.

A single stomach taken by Alex Walker at Netarts, December 12, 1921, containing two *Leptocottus armatus*, furnishes the only record we have of the food of this loon in Oregon. The bird is too scarce, anyway, to be of any particular importance economically, whatever its food habits may be.

Order Colymbiformes

Grebes: *Family Colymbidae*

Holboell's Grebe:
Colymbus grisegena holboelli (Reinhardt)

DESCRIPTION.—"Bill nearly as long as head; crests inconspicuous or wanting. *Breeding plumage:* Top of head greenish black; back blackish, with brown on wings; sides of head and throat patch white or grayish; neck rufous; lower parts washed with white over gray. *Winter plumage:* neck brownish. *Young:* neck rufous." (Bailey) *Downy young:* ". . . black above when first hatched, fading to blackish brown or seal brown as the chick increases in size; this color includes the sides and crissum, leaving only the belly pure white; the head and neck are broadly and clearly striped, longitudinally, with black and white; the chin and throat are often spotted with black but are sometimes clear white. There is usually a distinct white V on the top of the head, starting on the forehead, above a superciliary black stripe which usually includes the eyes, and terminating in broad white stripes in the sides of the neck; there is also a medium white stripe or spot on the crown and the back is, more or less distinctly, marked with four long stripes of dull white or grayish. The lighter stripes, especially on the head and neck are often tinged with buffy pink." (Bent) *Size:* "Length 18–20.50, wing 7.30–8.10, bill 1.65–2.40." (Bailey) *Nest:* A floating platform of dead and rotten reeds and drift, usually built in thick vegetation in water up to 3 or 4 feet deep. *Eggs:* Usually 4 or 5, occasionally 6 or, rarely, 8, pale bluish white to "cartridge buff," usually dirty and nest-stained.

DISTRIBUTION.—*General:* Breeds from arctic North America south to Minnesota, North Dakota, Montana, and Washington. Winters principally on coasts south to North Carolina and southern California. *In Oregon:* Recorded from Lake, Tillamook, Lincoln, Curry, Douglas, and Multnomah Counties in fall and winter.

HOLBOELL'S GREBE, which is next in size to the Western Grebe, can be classed as a fairly common winter resident in the State. Townsend (1839) listed it as found in the territory of Oregon, the only record of it in Oregon literature except for our own notes and specimens. The writers saw and took a single individual at Summer Lake, October 25, 1926 (Jewett, orig. No. 5002), our only definite record for eastern Oregon, where it should appear, in migration at least, as a casual visitor to the larger lakes and rivers. It is evident that it has never been a very common bird there, or some one of the numerous ornithologists who have worked eastern Oregon would have mentioned it.

For western Oregon we have a number of records in Tillamook and Lincoln Counties, where it frequents the salt-water bays and rivers during the winter months; and Jewett took one August 5, 1931, at Diamond Lake, in Douglas County. In addition there are two specimens from Multnomah County in the Oregon State Game Commission collection, one from Sauvies Island taken October 5, 1915, and the other from the Willamette River near Portland collected November 9, 1913. As it is recorded as a winter resident from far south along the California coast, it can be looked for in all the small bays on our coast as well as in the larger rivers. The earliest date of arrival noted is August 5 (Douglas County); the latest date in spring, March 6.

Like the others of its family, this grebe is very awkward in rising from the water but is capable of strong, direct, and sustained flight. In the water it is as graceful as the Western Grebe and makes the same effortless speed under water. It is master of the art of diving, either by the forward plunge or by lowering the body vertically into the water until completely submerged. It is able to regulate its floating powers, so that it rides high on the water or swims with only the head above water. Altogether, it is an interesting citizen that we would be glad to have with us more commonly.

Little is known about the food habits of Holboell's Grebe in Oregon. Of two stomachs examined, one, from Multnomah County, contained the usual ball of partly digested grebe feathers, water striders, fragments of water beetles and of a bee or wasp, and a scarabid beetle; the other, from Tillamook County, was empty except for the feathers.

Horned Grebe:
Colymbus auritus Linnaeus

Description.—One of the smaller grebes that in the adult has crests or ruffs on the cheeks and sides of the head. "*Breeding plumage:* Sides of head with yellow tufts of silky feathers, rest of head and throat black; upper parts dusky; lower neck, chest, and sides rufous; breast silvery white. *Winter adults and young:* Crests scant or wanting; throat white; sides with little or no rufous." (Bailey) *Downy young:* "The downy young is almost black above, striped and spotted with grayish white; there is a median white stripe on the occiput and a white V on the forehead, extending down the sides of the neck in broad irregular stripes; the sides of the head, neck, and throat are white tinged with 'salmon buff' and spotted with dusky; the under parts are white and the sides dusky." (Bent) *Size:* "Length 12.50–15.25, wing about 5.75, bill about .85–1.00." (Bailey) *Nest:* A floating platform of soft vegetation, mixed with mud, usually among tules or other swamp vegetation. *Eggs:* Usually 3 to 5, sometimes 9 or 10 in one nest, dull bluish white or pale olive white, more or less concealed by nest stains that cannot be entirely removed by washing.

Distribution.—*General:* Breeds in North America from Arctic south to northern United States. Winters in United States, principally along coasts. *In Oregon:* Winters on coast and along larger streams west of Cascades.

The Horned Grebe, a common winter resident of the salt-water bays and inlets along the Oregon coast, is the most abundant of all wintering grebes in the coastal waters and one of the most regularly found of all water birds. It is a less common species on the larger rivers of western Oregon also. From September to May it may be found—a miniature

Western Grebe dressed in shining white and black plumage—displaying its silky white breast as it disports itself after the manner of its larger and more imposing relatives. It is capable of strong, direct flight and is a finished performer at swimming and diving.

Although the breeding plumage of the Horned Grebe differs greatly from that of the Eared Grebe, its winter plumage is very similar to that of the young Eared Grebe. The shapes of the bills are the best distinguishing characters. The bill of the Horned Grebe is compressed from side to side and is distinctly higher than wide at the nostril, whereas the bill of the Eared Grebe is the reverse of this, being flattened to such an extent that it is wider at the nostril than it is high.

Jewett (1914b) published the first Oregon record for the species when he listed six specimens taken at Netarts Bay between December 26 and March 21. Willett (1919) listed May and June birds at Malheur Lake, the only eastern Oregon record known to us. Perhaps they were stragglers, as so good an observer as Willett could scarcely have confused these birds, so remarkably different at that season, with another species. We have coastal records from Curry, Coos, Lincoln, Tillamook, and Clatsop Counties, and Jewett has a skin (Coll. No. 1689) seized by game warden Ed Clark on November 9, 1913, at Portland, Multnomah County. Our earliest date of arrival in fall is September 15; our latest spring record, May 5.

Food of the Horned Grebe in Oregon consists of water insects, shrimps, small crustaceans, small fish, and remains of land insects that presumably have fallen into the water and have been picked from the surface. The species also has the usual grebe appetite for its own feathers. The purpose or meaning of this feather-eating habit is yet to be satisfactorily explained.

Eared Grebe:
Colymbus nigricollis californicus (Heermann)

Description.—"*Breeding plumage:* A fan-shaped tuft of tawny silky feathers on each side of head; rest of head, neck, and chest black; back blackish; sides brown; breast silvery white. *Winter plumage and young:* Upper parts and sides dusky; throat and ear patch white or grayish; bill slender, wider than deep at base; crests wanting." (Bailey) "*Downy young:* The downy young is glossy black on the back with a few brownish or grayish longitudinal stripes anteriorly; the head is dusky, more or less striped or spotted with whitish; the under parts are white, becoming dusky on the sides and tinged with pinkish buff on the breast and throat." (Bent) *Size:* "Length 12–14, wing 5.30, bill 1." (Bailey) *Nest:* A floating platform of green vegetation and rotting debris, with the eggs sometimes partially covered with water; compared to other grebe nests, very flimsy and unsubstantial. *Eggs:* 3 to 9, usually 4 or 5, the larger sets being possibly the work of more than one bird; bluish or greenish white, soon becoming permanently nest-stained with browns and buffs, indistinguishable from eggs of the other small grebes (Plate 9, *A*).

Distribution.—*General:* Western North America east to Mississippi, north to Great Slave Lake, south to Central America, breeding throughout most of its range. *In Oregon:* Common breeding bird in tule-grown marshes of Malheur, Crook, Harney, Lake, and Klamath Counties, wandering to other lakes and streams after breeding season.

The dainty and beautiful little Eared Grebe (Plate 9, *B*), able to dive like a flash or to sink slowly out of sight as fancy dictates, is very much at home in the great tule-grown marshes of eastern Oregon. Newberry (1857) reported it as common on the Oregon coast, a statement that is somewhat doubtful in the light of present-day knowledge. Bendire (1877) found it breeding on Malheur Lake, that unrivaled bird-producing area that always had a colony of these beautiful little water sprites until the lake entirely dried up. Finley (1912) reported 2,465 nests there on July 4, 1912, of which 2,000 were destroyed by a terrific wind storm on July 15, according to L. A. Lewis, who was reservation warden at that time.

Since Malheur Lake dried up, this grebe has been reported frequently by visitors to the eastern Oregon lake region. Lower Klamath Lake, before it was destroyed, and Silver Lake, before it dried up, contained great colonies in 1912, 1913, and 1914, reported in manuscript to the Biological Survey by L. A. Lewis and J. J. Furber. The Warner Lakes, particularly Crump Lake, have had flourishing colonies for many years. The authors have records of this species from Deschutes, Malheur, Wallowa, Lane, Douglas, Lincoln, and Multnomah Counties, and doubtless it will be found in late summer on mountain lakes of many other counties. Fresh-egg dates vary from May 12 to July 4.

From their great colonies, the birds move out in August over the surrounding country, at which time almost any open water is likely to accommodate a few of them. Diamond Lake, Douglas County, is a favorite rendezvous for them at this season when several dozen, or even hundreds, may be seen swimming about erratically, picking insects from the surface of the water in immediate competition with the trout. Wind-blown insects at times almost cover the waters of this lake and are present in abundance, not only for the fish and grebes, but also for the gulls and other miscellaneous water birds that gather to take advantage of this abundant food supply. Crescent and Odell Lakes to the north along the summit of the Cascades are also regularly visited by these little grebes at this season, and there is no doubt that many others of these lakes would be recognized as the summer homes of the Eared Grebes, if only there were enough bird watchers to visit them at the proper season.

The status of this species as a winter resident is not so clear. Notes from J. J. Furber show it present in January 1915, at Klamath Falls, and there is a skin in the Biological Survey collection taken November 15, 1917, at Jordan Valley. On the coast, where it is to be expected during

Plate 9, *A*. Nest and eggs of Eared Grebe. (Photo by Alex Walker.)

Plate 9, *B*. Eared Grebe. (Photo by Wm. L. Finley and H. T. Bohlman.)

the winter, the abundance of the very similar Horned Grebe has added uncertainty to such records as we have. There is a skin in the Finley collection, taken in June 1908, at Portland, that is evidently a straggler. Woodcock (1902) recorded it from Dayton as a common resident on the statements of Ellis F. Hadley. Gabrielson noted a few on Siltcoos Lake, western Lane County, on March 20, 1921, that may have been wintering birds. Braly has collected a few skins on the coast, and Gabrielson has one or two taken at Devils Lake, Lincoln County, in November and December, and there is some basis in these records for the belief that the Horned Grebe is the more common form on salt water, and the Eared Grebe, when present, on the fresh-water lakes along the coast. Most of the small grebes of this type collected by the writers on the coast during the winter months have been Horned Grebes. This of course does not preclude the possibility of the Eared Grebe being present in greater numbers than we have yet detected, but on the basis of the available evidence it is far the more uncommon of the two. Stopping the traffic in the plumage of native birds has been a great boon to this bird, whose silky white breast was once in great demand for millinery purposes, and it has prospered since the plumage laws were passed and enforced.

Like the Horned Grebe, this species feeds on a variety of small fish, shrimps, and insects, many of the latter land forms picked from the surface of the lakes and bays. It has no appreciable economic importance.

Western Grebe:
Aechmophorus occidentalis (Lawrence)

Description.—Largest Oregon grebe. "Head without side crests; bill slender; neck nearly as long as body. *Adults* [sexes alike]: Top of head and line down back of neck, blackish; back slaty gray; throat and under parts silvery white." (Bailey) *Downy young:* "Upper parts are 'light mouse gray' in color, darkest on the back, lighter on the crown and shading off to 'pallid mouse gray' on the neck and sides and almost to pure white on the belly; there is a triangular naked spot on the crown." (Bent) *Size:* "*Male*, length 24–29, wing 7.45–8.50, bill 2.60–3.05. *Female*, smaller, bill 2.10–2.48." (Bailey) *Nest:* Floating platform of dead and rotten reeds, mixed with a few green flags and plastered with stringy vegetable matter. *Eggs:* 3 to 10, usually 3 to 5, dull bluish white or cream color to various shades of dirty buff or olive buff, generally more or less nest-stained.

Distribution.—*General:* From central Mexico to British Columbia and Alberta and along Pacific to Manitoba. *In Oregon:* Nests in Klamath (Upper Klamath Lake) and Lake (Warner Lakes) Counties, often in great colonies. Winters on rivers and bays of western Oregon (Multnomah, Clatsop, Tillamook, Lincoln, Lane, Douglas, Coos, Curry, and Benton Counties). Casual in Umatilla County (June 11).

The Western Grebe (Plate 10, *A*) is the largest of the grebes in Oregon and has been known as one of Oregon's common winter birds since Newberry (1857) first recorded it from the mouth of the Columbia, where it still winters in fair numbers. Goss (1889) reported two sets of eggs taken by Bendire in Klamath County, May 28, 1883, and since then numerous observers have recorded the species either from the three great lake counties or from the coast. During the winter months, from mid-September to early May, it is abundant on all the bays of the Oregon coast and can frequently be seen displaying its silvery white breast beyond the breakers in the open ocean. It is also found in winter, though less commonly, on the larger rivers and streams inland. Its earliest date of arrival on the coast is September 14; latest date of departure, May 5. It spends the summer months, from early May to late September, in the great tule marshes and alkaline lakes of interior Oregon. Our earliest date for its arrival on the nesting ground is March 19; latest date of departure, November 15. Egg dates extend from May 10 to 23.

Whether riding the Pacific breakers in midwinter or diving about in the dense tule marshes of central Oregon during the nesting season, the beautiful Western, or "Swan," Grebe is one of the most graceful of all water birds. No Oregon bird is more specialized for living in the water. It is so thoroughly at home in this, its natural element, that it swims with scarcely a ripple, and so effortless is its dive that it appears to slide into the water. Its flight is rapid and direct, the rather short wings driving the long, slim, almost arrowlike body at surprising speed, once the bird is successfully launched in the air.

For many years plume hunters killed Western Grebes by the thousands for their beautiful satiny white breasts, until they were practically exterminated; but the better protection afforded them in recent years has brought them back in greater numbers. The colony on Upper Klamath is a thriving one. There, during June, it is possible to find hundreds of the floating platforms that serve as nests. Placed usually in the thick tule growth, they are kept by the dense vegetation from drifting about. Crump Lake, in the Warner chain, also supports a fair population. The drying up of Malheur Lake in recent years has scattered its once fine colony.

Very little is known about the food of this species. It has the curious grebe habit of swallowing its own feathers, and nearly every stomach examined contained a closely packed wad of feathers. A stomach from Silver Lake contained only unidentified fish bones and grebe feathers. Two stomachs from Netarts Bay contained small fish, fish eyes, remains of a ground beetle, and water-plant seeds. This grebe has no economic status, as the fish it eats are largely trash and scrap fish. It more than pays for its keep in the pleasure its graceful actions and beautiful plumage give to observers.

Pied-billed Grebe:
Podilymbus podiceps podiceps (Linnaeus)

Description.—"Bill short and stout, head not crested. *Breeding plumage:* Bill whitish, crossed by a black band; upper parts blackish; chin and throat black; breast mottled silvery gray. *Winter plumage:* Bill brownish, with paler lower mandible; chin, throat, and breast whitish." (Bailey) *Downy young:* "The downy young is prettily and quite strikingly marked with black and white; it is mainly glossy black above, with longitudinal stripes of grayish white on the neck and back; the crown is black, more or less variegated with 'walnut brown' or 'burnt umber,' sometimes in the form of a central patch, and with two broad superciliary stripes of white meeting on the forehead and two white stripes above them; the sides of the neck and throat are variegated with black and white and the sides of the body are more or less washed with dusky; the under parts are grayish white, lightest on the belly." (Bent) *Size:* "Length 12–15, wing 4.50–5.00, bill about .87." (Bailey) *Nest:* A floating platform of rotting vegetation, anchored to or built around green or dead reeds or tules; not in colonies as with other grebes, but few at most, in a place. Eggs usually covered by nest material during absence of owners. *Eggs:* 3 to 10, usually 5 to 7, very similar to the dull bluish white of other grebes and badly nest-stained with browns or buffs.

Distribution.—*General:* Over North America, except extreme north, nesting throughout most of this territory. *In Oregon:* Permanent resident throughout State wherever suitable pond and water conditions are present.

The Pied-billed Grebe, or "dabchick," with its drab color and heavy bill, is undoubtedly better known to the farmer boys of Oregon than is any other water bird, unless it is the Mud Hen, or American Coot. Townsend (1839) first reported it from Oregon. His notes were followed by those of Suckley (1860), Bendire (1877), and Merrill (1888), among the earlier naturalists, of whom Bendire was the first to report it breeding. Johnson (1880) recorded it from Multnomah, Washington, and Marion Counties; Woodcock (1902) from Yamhill, Lincoln, Linn, and Benton Counties; Merrill (1888), from Klamath County; Walker (1917b), from Lake County; and Finley (1908b) and Willett (1919), from Malheur County. Our own records are from Multnomah, Polk, Tillamook, Lincoln, Lane, Coos, Douglas, Jackson, Klamath, Lake, Harney, Malheur, Deschutes, Umatilla, and Wallowa Counties. It can be looked for in small tule-bordered ponds in any part of the State during breeding season and on unfrozen and sluggish rivers everywhere during the fall, winter, and early spring.

Unlike the other grebes that breed in Oregon, it prefers to nest alone rather than in colonies, and any tule-lined pond, however small, is likely to harbor a pair of these small waterfowl. They nest most commonly in Klamath, Lake, and Harney Counties, where the almost innumerable tiny ponds and swamps furnish ideal conditions for them. They have been found breeding in western Oregon also, on Sauvies Island in Multnomah County, Gales Creek in Washington County, and Devils Lake in Lincoln County, where at least two pairs have bred each year since 1929. They

Plate 10, *A*. Western Grebe. (Photo by Wm. L. Finley and H. T. Bohlman.)

Plate 10, *B*. Nest and eggs of Pied-billed Grebe. (Photo by Ira N. Gabrielson.)

occur regularly in summer along the Columbia River. Undoubtedly they breed in other coastal lakes to the south, though we have no definite records of our own.

The nest (Plate 10, *B*) is a pile of decaying vegetation, the heat of which undoubtedly assists in incubating the eggs, which the parent birds leave covered with damp rotting material during their absence. Gabrielson witnessed this performance once. The parent bird stood on the nest drawing the wet material over the eggs with the bill. When the eggs were thoroughly covered, two or three green reeds were seized in the bill and broken with a jerk and twist of the head so that they bent over the nest. The adult then slipped into the water and swam quietly away. The eggs are laid from late April to early June. Normal dates extend from May 9 to June 6, but there is one manuscript record in the Biological Survey files of a nest at Malheur containing five newly hatched young on April 27, 1914 (Fawcett).

Although clumsier than its near relatives, the Pied-billed Grebe is nevertheless an accomplished diver, able to perform all the feats credited to others of the family. The newly hatched babies can swim and dive almost as soon as they leave the egg, their prettily streaked heads and soft, colored down harmonizing astonishingly well with the water vegetation in which they hide when alarmed. After the young are feathered out, these grebes congregate in little flocks in the larger ponds and swamps and feed on the abundant aquatic life found there during the summer months. During the fall and winter they scatter somewhat and at that time may be found in any open water. There is a noticeable increase in the numbers present on the coast in October, and most of our birds evidently spend the winter there or south of our borders.

Like the other grebes, the "dabchick" feeds on fish, frogs, water insects, and various other insects largely gleaned from the surface of the water. Two stomachs, taken at Mulino in October 1913, each contained bits of various water insects, fragments of fish, and a ball of grebe feathers that comprised 50 per cent of the stomach contents in one case and 85 per cent in the other.

Order Procellariiformes

Albatrosses: *Family Diomedeidae*

Black-footed Albatross:
Diomedea nigripes Audubon

Description.—"*Adults:* Face and chin whitish, top of head and rest of upper parts blackish, except for whitish tail coverts and base of tail; under parts sooty gray; bill dusky, feet black. *Young:* Face with less white, and upper tail coverts dusky. *Length:* 28.50–36.00, wing 18.50–20.50, bill 4.00–4.25." (Bailey) *Nest:* On the ground. *Eggs:* 1, white.

Distribution.—*General:* Breeds on many islands in north Pacific, including some in Hawaiian group, and wanders to North American coast from Alaska to Lower California. *In Oregon:* Of casual occurrence on coast, usually well offshore, though we have seen it within 10 miles of land.

Black-footed Albatrosses are not abundant off the Oregon coast but are apparently regular visitors in small numbers during the summer months. Woodcock (1902) recorded Anthony's statement that both this species and the next are found off the Oregon coast in winter. Jewett reported seeing four, just off the Oregon coast, from his steamer as he came up the coast on May 5, 1927, and Gabrielson, Jewett, and Braly saw two about 9 miles off Newport Bar on August 30, 1930. These are our only records for the State, and they are all sight records. This big, striking albatross, however, with its dark plumage, dark bill, and dark feet, cannot readily be confused with any other species likely to be found in this territory.

It is a wonderful spectacle to watch one of these birds on the wing during windy or stormy weather. Its almost miraculous ability to sail across, into, or with the wind without moving its great wings perceptibly and its uncanny skill in turning even the breakers and swells to its own advantage as it skims the surface of the water like a great plane are a never-ending source of wonder to the observer. No bird known to us can compare in powers of flight with this master of the air, and after watching it for a time, we conclude that the flight of even such an aerial expert as the Turkey Buzzard seems that of a novice.

Short-tailed Albatross:
Diomedea albatrus Pallas

Description.—"*Adults:* Mainly white, but head and neck washed with yellowish, tail and most of wings dusky, primaries with yellow shafts; bill and feet yellowish. *Young:* Plumage sooty brown, darker on head and neck; primary shafts yellowish.

Length: 33–37, wing 22–23, bill 5.50–5.60." (Bailey) *Eggs:* 1, white, laid on ground.

DISTRIBUTION.—*General:* Breeds in western Pacific on Wake and Bonin Islands. Wanders eastward to North American coast from Alaska to southern Lower California. *In Oregon:* Rare visitor to coast; two definite records.

THE SHORT-TAILED ALBATROSS was reported by Suckley (1860) and Anthony (Woodcock 1902) as having been found on the Oregon coast. We have never seen it there, but we have two definite records for the State, both supported by identifiable remains of bones. The first were collected by Jewett from shell mounds on the Tillamook County coast and identified by Dr. Alex. Wetmore (1928), of the National Museum, who recorded it in the *Condor* as an Oregon species. The other bones were taken by Jewett from shell mounds near Yachats in August 1934.

The adult of this species is the only white-plumaged albatross reported from this coast. The dark-colored, immature birds can be distinguished from the Black-footed Albatross by their light-colored bills and feet. This is one of the species that has suffered so heavily from plumage hunters on the islands of the Pacific that it is probably near extermination, if not already extinct.

Shearwaters and Fulmars: *Family Procellariidae*

Slender-billed Shearwater:
Puffinus tenuirostris (Temminck)

DESCRIPTION.—"Size small; bill relatively small and slender; plumage sooty or blackish except for paler throat and white under wing coverts; bill and feet dusky. *Wing:* 10.00–11.10, tail 3.20–3.60, bill 1.20–1.28, depth at base .35–.50, tarsus 1.90–2.00." (Bailey) *Eggs:* 1, white.

DISTRIBUTION.—*General:* Breeds on islands near New Zealand and southern Australia and migrates northward to Bering Sea. *In Oregon:* Casual straggler to coast in September, December, January, and May.

THE SLENDER-BILLED SHEARWATER, the small companion of the Sooty Shearwater, distinguished chiefly by its smaller size and smaller, more slender bill, is undoubtedly more common on the Oregon coast than records indicate. It is almost impossible to pick individuals out of the great swarms of shearwaters present, but there are several records for the State. There are three specimens in the Jewett collection, one found dead on the beach at Netarts by Mrs. Iva Neilsen (May 11, 1916), one found at Seaside (September 29, 1930), and the third killed just south of the Columbia River on one of our offshore trips (September 23, 1932). Gabrielson also has three skins, one found dead on the beach at Netarts by Iris Gabrielson (December 27, 1932), one from Depoe Bay, taken by Braly (January 1, 1935), and one from Clatsop Beach (January 12, 1935).

In December 1934 and January 1935, Slender-billed Shearwaters and Pacific Kittiwakes seem to have been on the coast in considerable numbers, as dead birds were found repeatedly by Braly and the authors along the entire northern coast. Many of those found were not saved because of the condition in which they were discovered, but the evidence points to an unusual abundance of the two species. The original type of this bird was described from Townsend's collection as near the mouth of the Columbia River. In view of our present knowledge, it is possible that the specimen was obtained in that vicinity, although some of Townsend's other records of birds taken off the mouth of the Columbia River have never been confirmed.

Sooty Shearwater:
Puffinus griseus (Gmelin)

Description.—"Entire plumage sooty gray except for white under wing coverts, which are mottled with gray at tips; bill and feet dusky or black. *Wing:* 11.15–12.00, bill 1.55–1.70, depth of bill at base .45–.55, tarsus 2.12–2.35." (Bailey) *Eggs:* 1, white.

Distribution.—*General:* Breeds on many islands near New Zealand and also Cape Horn and ranges north to Aleutians and Greenland. *In Oregon:* Appears on coast first in May and is present in great numbers during August and September, dwindling after October 1 to a few individuals that may remain as late as November.

The graceful Sooty Shearwater, known to the fishermen on the coast as the "Whale Bird," is the most abundant seafowl present. It was first definitely recorded from Oregon by Loomis (1901), who found it off the mouth of the Rogue River. Woodcock (1902) listed it for Yaquina Bay. These are the only written records of its occurrence in the State prior to our own work. Breeding on the islands in the vicinity of New Zealand and also near Cape Horn, these shearwaters swarm northward across the equator in incredible numbers on both the Atlantic and Pacific Oceans. We have found them to be regular summer visitors to the Oregon coast from May until November (our earliest date, May 5; our latest, November 27), sometimes prevalent in unbelievable numbers. They can be found in some numbers in every month of this period, but most of them pass to the northward, possibly far offshore, and swing south again in August and September, the months when they appear off the Oregon coast in numbers not computable, the great flocks sometimes taking hours to pass a given point. They fly either in a steady column, or, after stopping to feed off the surface of the water, the birds in the rear rise and fly over those ahead.

They are expert fishermen and often follow great schools of anchovies close inshore, congregating in great screaming, struggling, fighting masses as the fishes come close to the surface. When full fed they frequently rest on the water in extended companies, being at such times often so loath to move that a boat can enter the resting swarms before they take wing ahead of the bow. In common with other birds of their class, they pick most of their food from the surface of the sea and seem to be particularly fond of squid. We have had examinations of three stomachs, collected at various times, that bear out claims of various writers that these birds subsist to a large extent on squid. One stomach was empty except for about 60 pebbles that weighed about 3 ounces; the second contained squids' eyes, bills, and fragments representing about 25 individuals; and the third contained 32 squids' mandibles.

Pink-footed Shearwater:
Puffinus creatopus Coues

DESCRIPTION.—"Breast and throat white, shading into brownish gray of upper parts and under tail coverts; bill yellowish, feet flesh color. *Length:* 19, wing 12.50–13.25, bill 1.60–1.70." (Bailey) *Eggs:* 1, white.

DISTRIBUTION.—*General:* Breeds in December and January on Juan Fernandez and Santa Clara Islands off coast of Chile and wanders north to southern Alaska. *In Oregon:* Regular August and September visitor to coast.

THE PINK-FOOTED SHEARWATER is the largest of the white-breasted shearwaters that we have so far discovered on the Oregon coast, where it occurs in August and September (our earliest record, July 20, latest, September 23) in company with great swarms of Sooty Shearwaters. It is a fairly common species and is seen both as single individuals mixed in the great swarms and as smaller separate flocks of three or four to a dozen birds. It is one of the comparatively few species that breed south of the equator and migrate across it to winter in the northern hemisphere. We have taken numerous specimens since beginning the offshore work in 1930, and our publication in the *Murrelet* (Gabrielson, Jewett, and Braly 1930) is the first definite record for the State. We have taken specimens off Newport and Depoe Bay and have observed individuals off the Clatsop beaches on various occasions. Our experience off the coast has been rather meager so far, and it is probable that whenever sufficient work is done there, many of these species will be found to be much more abundant than our present knowledge indicates.

In our experience the Pink-footed Shearwater is wilder and more difficult to approach than the Sooty. Its flight is very similar to that of the much more common dusky-colored species, but the wing beat is a trifle slower and more deliberate, somewhat after the fashion of the fulmars. Like all masters of the air, it is able to sail either into or across the wind, apparently for long distances, without any visible alteration in the position of its wings.

New Zealand Shearwater:
Thyellodroma bulleri (Salvin)

Description.—"*Adults:* Mantle gray, in striking contrast to black on head, tail, and lesser wing coverts; greater coverts gray, tipped with white; outer primaries black, with two thirds of inner webs white; cheeks mottled grayish white; lower parts and under wing coverts white. *Length:* 16.50, wing 11.30, tail 5.20, bill 2.60." (Bailey) *Eggs:* 1, white.

Distribution.—*General:* Breeds on Mokohinu Island, New Zealand, and migrates across south Pacific to Chile and north along shore to coast of Oregon and Washington. *In Oregon:* Rare visitor to Oregon waters, seen only once when two specimens were taken.

The New Zealand Shearwater, one of the rarest and least known of all the shearwaters, is a rare bird anywhere in the north Pacific. It is known from Oregon from two specimens taken by Jewett and Gabrielson (September 22, 1932) just south of the mouth of the Columbia River (Jewett Coll. No. 7262, Gabrielson Coll. No. 1732) from a flock of five that flew past the boat at long range. So far as known, the only specimens taken previously to these are from Monterey Bay, California. These are beautiful shearwaters, the sharp contrast between the pure white under parts and the black cap and slaty back being most striking when viewed from the side. The wings seem narrower, longer, and more pointed than those of other whale birds, and the flight is more deliberate and direct than that of the Sooty Shearwaters. We were able to watch them for some time on the wing, and this was the impression of both observers.

Apparently little is known regarding the migrations or behavior of this bird, the only other specimen known from the north Pacific being one taken by Gabrielson (October 30, 1932, Coll. No. 1823), at Grays Harbor, Washington, where he collected a single bird out of a great flock of Sooty Shearwaters. This record is only an indication of what might be done. If someone had the time and opportunity thoroughly to work Oregon's offshore waters, undoubtedly there would be found many regular visitors and many more stragglers of which we now know nothing.

Pacific Fulmar:
Fulmarus glacialis rodgersi Cassin

Description.—"Bill short and stout, wider than deep at base, nasal tubes occupying about half the length of bill and opening as one tube; nasal tubes and tip of bill yellow. *Light phase:* head, neck, and under parts white; upper parts bluish gray, with quills darker. *Dark phase:* whole plumage deep plumbeous. *Length:* 17–19, wing 11.90–12.35, bill 1.35–1.65." (Bailey) *Eggs:* 1, white, deposited in a shallow burrow.

Distribution.—*General:* Breeds on islands of Bering Sea and on adjacent coast of

Asia. Winters over north Pacific as far south as Lower California on American side. *In Oregon:* Quite common and regular winter resident off coast from September to February.

UNDER THE HEADING "Pacific Fulmar" are now included both the Pacific Fulmar and the bird reported in Woodcock's *Annotated List of the Birds of Oregon* (1902) as Rodgers Fulmar. It was formerly believed that the Pacific Fulmar had both a gray and a light phase and that there was another very similar light fulmar called Rodgers Fulmar, but the two are now generally regarded as one species and are so placed in the last *A. O. U. Check-List*. Therefore, both the light and dark fulmars found off the Oregon coast are included herewith. Woodcock (1902) and Bailey (1917) are the only ones except ourselves who have mentioned the Pacific Fulmar as an Oregon bird. Woodcock listed it on the authority of B. J. Bretherton, and Mrs. Bailey stated she found it dead on the beaches following severe storms.

It is a common and regular winter resident off the Oregon coast, and we have found it in every coastal county. It arrives in September and remains until well toward the first of March (our earliest date, September 19; our latest, February 26). Undoubtedly it is present later in the spring, as it is known to occur on the California coast as late as mid-April, but the small amount of work done off the Oregon coast in the spring months —because of the usual stormy conditions prevailing at that time—has prevented our records from being anything more than fragmentary.

We have known the Pacific Fulmar largely from dead birds picked up on the beach through the winter, usually a single bird or a few. It is evident that even these masters of the air have their troubles in the wild storms that occasionally lash our coast and are either weather killed or find it impossible to obtain sufficient food. On November 20 and 21, 1921, during and following a terrific southwester, Gabrielson found many hundreds of them dead on the Tillamook beaches. On the 20th, during the same storm, numbers of them were dead on the beach between Netarts and Three Arch Rocks. On the 22d, at Barview, which is just at the north entrance of Tillamook Bay, the combination of tide and wind had thrown ashore, just north of the jetty, many thousands of birds, the great bulk of which were Pacific Fulmars, but which included ducks of several species, scoters, loons, grebes, and even ravens. The beach for a mile or more north of the jetty was covered with dead birds, and scattered individuals were visible beyond the point where Gabrielson turned back.

These beautiful sea birds in their soft gray or gray and snow-white plumage are one of the offshore attractions of the fall and winter months. Like the shearwaters, they are masters of the air, capable of sailing for long distances on set wings and at the same time being able to turn and wheel by dipping the wing on the inside of the circle. They are adept at rising over breakers or dipping down into the troughs as the vagrant air currents permit. When the wings are used in flying, the beat is somewhat slower and more deliberate than that of the shearwaters but carries the same impression of power and expertness found in the more slender-bodied birds.

We have only one stomach examination of this bird taken off the Oregon coast. This stomach contained bits of beaks and eye lenses of three squids, feathers, lining of eggshell, and coniferous needles, the latter two obviously debris, as the bird was collected on December 29.

Storm Petrels: *Family Hydrobatidae*

Forked-tailed Petrel:
Oceanodroma furcata (Gmelin)

Description.—"Body light bluish gray, fading to white on chin, throat, and under tail coverts; bend of wing, quills, and space around eye, dusky." (Bailey) *Downy young:* "The downy young when first hatched is covered with long, soft, thick down foreshadowing the color of the parent, except on the chin and throat, which are naked. The color varies from 'deep mouse gray' or 'light mouse gray' above to 'pale mouse gray' below." (Bent) (See Plate 11, *A.*) *Size:* "Length 8.00–9.20, wing 5.90–6.40, bill .60, tail 3.75–4.00 forked for about 1." (Bailey) *Nest:* A small enlargement of an underground burrow, sometimes lined with a little dried grass. *Eggs:* 1, dull white, with a cloud of faint minute dark specks forming a wreath or patch on the large end.

Distribution.—*General:* Breeds on north Pacific from Kurile and Aleutian Islands south to northern California. Winters over north Pacific as far south as southern California. *In Oregon:* Breeds on Three Arch Rocks and possibly other offshore islands. Probably winters sparingly.

The only definitely known breeding place of the little Forked-tailed Petrel in Oregon is on Three Arch Rocks, where it is much the less common of the two breeding petrels. Like others of its race, it excavates burrows in the earth on the upper parts of the rock and lays a single dull white egg that is more or less wreathed at the upper end with minute dark spots. In the colonies, these burrows sometimes intersect each other until it is almost impossible to form any idea of the extent of a single excavation. Finley, first in 1902 and later in subsequent publications, wrote of this petrel as an Oregon bird. Numerous specimens have been collected on Three Arch Rocks and on the beaches, and Jewett had one bird brought to him alive that was captured on the Columbia above Astoria on January 30, 1916. This is the only winter specimen, but winter collecting conditions off the Oregon coast are not the best.

These petrels are beautiful birds, with soft gray plumage and forked tails, reminding one very much of small dainty terns in shape and general appearance. As they are almost entirely nocturnal in their habits while

Plate 11, *A*. Downy young Forked-tailed Petrel, removed from nest burrow. (Photo by Alex Walker.)

Plate 11, *B*. Young White Pelicans. (Photo by Ira N. Gabrielson.)

in the State, few people have seen them alive on the wing. They are present on the Oregon coast from May to November (earliest date, May 9; latest, November 25) and possibly through the winter, although we have no direct evidence on this point and little is known of their whereabouts or migrations. Occasionally, at least, in common with the other sea birds, they suffer from severe storms. Between May 9 and 11, 1916, Mrs. R. C. Neilson found numbers of them dead on the ocean beach of the Netarts Sand Spit, and Gabrielson found remains of 21 on the beach between Netarts and Three Arch Rocks on November 19 and 20, 1921, during the same big storm that was responsible for the destruction of so many Pacific Fulmars on the Oregon coast.

Beal's Petrel:
Oceanodroma leucorhoa beali Emerson

Description.—"Uniform sooty brown, washed with a bluish slate-gray on head, throat, chest and back, the gray most pronounced on head and chest; forehead, chin and upper throat decidedly ashy; greater and median wing-coverts edged with ashy; upper tail coverts white with black shafts; lateral lower coverts edged with whitish; rectrices black with white at base." (Emerson, 1906) *Downy young:* "When first hatched it is covered with long, soft, thick down varying from 'hair brown' at the base to 'smoke gray' at the tips." (Bent, in describing the young of Leach's Petrel, which applies equally well to this subspecies.) "*Size: Male*, wing 5.90, tail 3.10, forking of tail 0.80, tarsus 0.87. *Female*, wing 5.75, tail 3.10, forking of tail 0.70, tarsus 0.90." (Emerson, 1906) *Nest:* A slight enlargement of an underground burrow, sometimes lined with a little dried grass. *Eggs:* 1, dull to pure white, sometimes wreathed on the larger end with faint spots or other markings.

Distribution.—*General:* Breeds on islands from southern Alaska to central California. *In Oregon:* Breeds on Three Arch Rocks, Island Rock off Port Orford, the rocks near Brookings, and possibly on other islands off coast.

Beal's Petrel is present on the Oregon coast probably all through the year in small numbers, but it is most abundant between May and August (our earliest date, May 9; our latest, August 18). It is much the more common of the two species on the coast and breeds abundantly on Three Arch Rocks. The colony there has long been famous, owing largely to the writings of Finley, Jewett, and others who have visited it. Finley's (1902) explorations of the bird rocks of the Oregon coast first made this species and others definitely a part of the State fauna, and since this time little has been added to our knowledge of the bird. In 1930, Braly found it nesting on Island Rock off Port Orford, where, on June 15, he obtained downy young birds and eggs. We have several times found wings and feathers about excavated nest burrows on the inshore rocks near Port Orford. Small predators, principally skunks, have access to these islands at extreme low tides and quickly take advantage of that occasion to get a meal of petrel eggs and young, or adults even. Jewett has one skin in his collection (No. 2860) taken July 10, 1923, in the Willamette River near Portland, certainly an odd place for a petrel.

As in the case of other petrels, little is known of the migratory movements of Beal's Petrels, although presumably they spend the period when not breeding in wandering over the ocean. They are frequently reported by travelers, but the difficulty of distinguishing the numerous species that occur on the oceans of the world has prevented definite knowledge of their movements. Like the less common Forked-tailed Petrel, they are nocturnal, and few persons have seen them in life. With the coming of dusk, they leave their nesting rocks for their feeding grounds at sea, and fishermen report having heard their twittering as they traveled back and forth at night.

Order Pelecaniformes

Pelicans: *Family Pelecanidae*

White Pelican:
Pelecanus erythrorhynchos Gmelin

Description.—"Tail feathers 24. *Breeding plumage:* mainly white, primaries and most of secondaries black; back of head with thin white or yellowish crest, breast and lesser wing coverts with narrow lanceolate yellowish feathers; upper mandible with upright horn. *Post-breeding plumage:* crest replaced by short grayish feathers, upper mandible without horny excrescence. *Adults in winter plumage:* back of head white; bill pouch and feet pale yellow instead of orange. *Young:* white, with gray on top of head and lesser wing coverts." (Bailey) *Downy young:* Born naked but soon covered with soft pure white down. *Size:* "Length 4½ to nearly 6 feet, extent 8½ to nearly 10 feet, wing 20.00–25.25, bill 11.05–15.00; weight about 17 pounds." (Bailey) *Nest:* Often only a depression in the ground, sometimes a structure built up above ground with almost any available material. In the tule marshes often trampled masses of tule that form great floating platforms. *Eggs:* 1 to 3, with 2 the usual number, dull white, with usually more or less of a calcareous deposit (Plate 12, *A*).

Distribution.—*General:* Breeds from Manitoba and North Dakota west and south to British Columbia and Pyramid Lake, Nevada, to Salton Sea, California. Winters along southern coasts southward. *In Oregon:* Breeds, or formerly bred, in Klamath, Lake, and Harney Counties. Now much reduced in numbers.

The White Pelican, one of the largest and most majestic birds of Oregon, arrives in March and remains until November (earliest date, March 11; latest, November 13, both Klamath County). Formerly very abundant in the State, it has been very greatly reduced in numbers in recent years. Before this reduction occurred, practically every naturalist who visited Oregon after Townsend's time (1839) found opportunity to visit the great pelican colonies and comment at length upon them, so that more has been written about this species than about most other water birds. The colonies were usually located on great masses of floating tules that had been trampled down by the birds until they formed floating platforms, often firm enough to support a grown person. There the birds laid their eggs, usually two (egg dates from May 10 to June 15), and reared their young.

Drainage and unprecedented drought conditions combined seemed to doom the species as a nesting bird in Oregon, and in 1932 there was not a single known nesting colony in the State. In 1934, however, there was a small colony on Upper Klamath Lake, although its location was known to few. No one who has read the descriptions of the great nesting colonies of lower Klamath and Malheur Lakes by Bendire (1877), Finley (1907b), and others can view the present plight of the species with anything but a feeling of sadness, and it is to be hoped that when the drought is finally broken and the lakes reflooded this magnificent bird will return in numbers to its old nesting grounds.

Clear Lake, California, just across the Oregon line, still supports a colony. It furnishes the pelicans that attract so much attention at Klamath Falls, where naturalists and other out-of-door visitors are greatly interested in the pelicans that inhabit Link River and gratefully catch the fish that spectators throw to them from the bridge. One thrifty citizen has made quite an income by keeping on hand quantities of minnows that he sells to those who wish to feed the white giants.

Pelicans, like cormorants, are born naked and ugly (Plate 11, *B*), but the young soon acquire a coating of pure white down that remains with them until fully grown. The flight feathers of the wings appear first, and the body feathers come only after the entire development of the wing quills. The feeding of the young by the parents is a unique performance, matched only by that of the cormorants. The parent, carrying food in its throat, returns to the nest and opens its big bill. The young bird thrusts its head far down the parent's throat and feeds greedily on the mass of material carried therein.

After the young can fly, the birds gather in huge flocks on the marshes and lakes until they resemble great snow banks in the rays of the sun (Plate 12, *A*). One of the most unique spectacles in the bird world is to see a group of these pelicans standing on a bank sunning themselves, with their necks extended to the limit and their enormous bills pointing straight to the zenith. If the observer happens to be on the water and the birds upon even a slight elevation, they seem gigantic as viewed through the openings in the tules. On shore, they are rather clumsy and awkward-looking; but once launched in the air, there are few more magnificent spectacles than these great birds in flight, circling about on widespread pinions (Plate 12, *B*). The ease with which they soar upward is something never to be forgotten, and the contrast furnished by their white plumage, black wing tips, and yellow bills and feet is most striking. On the water, they are equally graceful and loom up among the hordes of other waterfowl like great white battleships amid a fleet of motorboats.

Pelicans feed almost entirely from the water, scooping up fish and other food in their capacious beaks and allowing the water to drain out. When a school of small fish appears, the excitement is intense as dozens of these feathered fishermen engage busily in operating their dredging equipment. Because of their fishing habits they have been subjected to a great deal of senseless persecution. It is possible that they catch some trout, but stomach examinations indicate that they—like all other fish-eating birds

Plate 12, *A*. White Pelicans, with eggs in left foreground. (Photo by Ira N. Gabrielson.)

Plate 12, *B*. White Pelicans taking off. (Photo by Ira N. Gabrielson.)

—are willing to take the food that is most easily obtained and that in most of the great shallow lakes frequented by them suckers and other trash fish answer the purpose. We have no stomach examinations of Oregon birds, but the remains about colonies are seldom those of game fish. The authors feel strongly that many fish-eating birds are persecuted at every turn by people who simply desire to kill anything as magnificent in appearance as this bird, working great harm thereby, as the birds certainly do no wrong in destroying spawn-eating fish. Where carp are present in numbers, game fish suffer correspondingly. As carp are slower than game fish, they are much more easily caught by pelicans than the latter, and it is inevitable that they furnish a much larger per cent of the pelican's diet than the swiftly moving trout and other game fish.

California Brown Pelican:
Pelecanus occidentalis californicus Ridgway

DESCRIPTION.—"Tail feathers 22. *Breeding plumage:* pouch reddish; head, and feathers next to pouch, white; crown tinged with yellow; neck, including manelike crest, rich velvety brown; upper parts silvery gray, streaked with brownish; under parts brownish, streaked on sides with white. *Winter plumage:* head and neck white, tinged with yellowish on throat and crown. *Young:* upper parts grayish brown, darker on back; under parts white, tinged on sides with brownish." (Bailey) *Downy young:* Born naked with a dull red skin that changes to black but soon covered with white down. *Size:* "Length 4½ feet or more, wing 20.50–23.25, bill 12.25–14.75." (Bailey) *Nest:* A bulky structure of sticks, grass, and rubbish, usually on rocky islands, often used year after year with fresh material added. *Eggs:* 1 to 3, usually 3, dull, dirty white with a rough granular surface.

DISTRIBUTION.—*General:* Breeds on islands off coast from Santa Barbara Islands southward to the Galapagos Islands and ranges northward between breeding seasons to British Columbia. *In Oregon:* Off coast, from June to December, most abundant in August and September.

THE CALIFORNIA BROWN PELICAN is a breeding bird of the southern part of the United States and is known as an Oregon bird only when it makes its appearance on the coast between breeding seasons. The number making the flight to the coastal bays has decreased markedly in recent years, a statement true of most of the larger birds. The northward flight apparently occurs in July, as the birds are most abundant in August and September (our earliest date, June 22, Curry County), and there are usually few present after the first of November (our latest date, December 27, Tillamook County). Townsend (1839) recorded seeing one on December 11, 1834, off the mouth of the Columbia—certainly the first Oregon record and also one of the latest winter dates yet noted. Woodcock (1902) listed it from Yaquina Bay. Subsequent to these records our own notes and publications are all that are available. We have seen the birds along every coastal county and on all the larger bays. Most of them are immature, although adults with the distinctly marked heads are not uncommon.

They are usually seen in solemn flight, singly or with a few others, on the larger bays. They are smaller than their white relatives but have the same powerful flight and carry themselves with the same absurd dignity.

Unlike the White Pelican, which does its fishing while sitting on the water, these birds fish from the air, circling over the water and dropping like giant kingfishers after their prey. When fish are caught, the birds usually remain sitting on the water until they have swallowed them, when they again take flight and resume fishing operations. These pelicans certainly do no harm whatever while off the Oregon coast. Their numbers are usually not sufficient to make any appreciable difference, even should they feed entirely on valuable fish, which is not the case, however, as all available evidence indicates that they—like many other fish-eating birds—feed very largely on small trash fish of no commercial value. One Oregon stomach from Sand Lake (November 5) contained two *Amphistichus argenteus*, entire save for heads.

Cormorants: *Family Phalacrocoracidae*

Farallon Cormorant:
Phalacrocorax auritus albociliatus Ridgway

Description.—"*Adults in breeding plumage:* Throat pouch orange, a narrow crest of curved black feathers above and back of each eye; back and wings slaty, feathers bordered with black; rest of plumage glossy greenish black. *Post-breeding plumage:* Head without crest. *Young:* Plumage brownish becoming grayish brown on head and neck; throat and breast lighter, sometimes white before the first moult." (Bailey) Young, when first hatched, are black, naked, and helpless. *Size:* Length 29.0–33.5, "wing 11.75–13.00, bill 1.90–2.35." (Bailey) *Nest:* On the coast, usually of weeds, grasses, or sticks on the bare rock on offshore islands or precipitous headlands; in the interior, crudely made of sticks—in trees or sometimes on the ground—of tules or weeds, or in masses of broken-down tules. *Eggs:* 3 to 5, occasionally more, very pale blue to bluish white, more or less concealed by a white calcareous covering and frequently badly nest-stained.

Distribution.—*General:* Breeds on offshore islands and rocky headlands from Three Arch Rocks, Oregon, south to Mexico and inland through eastern Oregon (Snake River, Malheur Lake, etc.) south to southern California. Winters over much of breeding territory except where all water freezes up entirely. *In Oregon:* Breeds on almost all offshore rocks and in various places in Klamath, Lake, and Harney Counties, occasionally at least along Snake River (usually in Idaho), and perhaps other places.

The Farallon Cormorant (Plate 13, *A*), in common with all the great colony-nesting birds of the interior basin, has attracted much attention from ornithologists and consequently enjoys a place of prominence in Oregon bird literature somewhat greater than its actual importance would seem to warrant. It is the largest and by far the most numerous of the three shags that occur regularly in the State and can readily be distinguished from the two smaller species by its bright yellow pouch and bill. It nests on the offshore rocks and rocky headlands of the coast and abundantly in eastern Oregon, where there are usually great colonies (Plate 13, *B*) in the Klamath country and also in Lake, Harney, and Malheur Counties. Bendire (1875, 1877, 1882c), Merrill (1888), Finley (1907b, 1912, 1915b), and Willett (1919), among others, have written of the huge nesting colonies of the lake counties, and since Lewis and Clark (1814) reported "cormorants" from the mouth of the Columbia in 1805, nearly every bird writer has mentioned them. Townsend (1839) reported the species from the Columbia River. His is the first definite record, although Lewis and Clark undoubtedly saw this species among other cormorants, as it is still a regular inhabitant of the Astoria district. Outside of the breeding season, it is likely to be found on any of the larger bodies of water, particularly in eastern Oregon and along the coast. It remains the year around on open water, except where solid ice forms.

On the coast the eggs are laid in nests composed of seaweed and various other bits of vegetation arranged on the surface of the bare rock. On Upper Klamath Lake there is a large colony that builds crude nests of sticks in the low-growing willow trees bordering some of the channels in the swampy section of the lake (Plate 13, *B*). This colony contains a mixture of Farallon Cormorants, Black-crowned Night Herons, American Egrets, and Blue Herons. At Malheur Lake, Willett (1919) reported them nesting in clumps of broken-down tules. In the Drews Creek Reservoir, Lake County, on a point where a few old giant yellow pines have been killed by the raising of the water level of the lake, some dozen nests of a cormorant colony are saddled on the dead limbs of these huge old pines, some of them at least 50 feet above the water. A cormorant colony is usually a rather smelly place. The nests are filthy, and the trees that support them are liberally white-washed with excrement. As if this were not enough, bits of decaying fish or other food and dead birds, both old and young, add to the stench.

Nest building commences in April, and the three to five pale bluish-white eggs, somewhat covered with a peculiar limy deposit and very frequently nest-stained, are usually laid in April or early May. Egg dates extend from April 6 to June 15. Nesting is somewhat irregular, and in mid-June it is generally possible to find nests in all stages from those containing newly laid eggs to those containing well-developed youngsters. When first hatched, the young are repulsive looking, with wrinkled faces and naked jet-black skin. They are blind and helpless but grow very rapidly and by early June are well developed and some of them are ready to fly. The parents make little effort to defend the young and either sit off at some distance and watch an intruder or circle about over his head.

Just prior to the breeding season, the Farallon Cormorants sometimes develop white head plumes that are very ephemeral and generally lost by

Plate 13, *A*. Farallon Cormorants. (Photo by Reed Ferris.)

Plate 13, *B*. Farallon Cormorant colony at Klamath Lake. (Photo by Ira N. Gabrielson.)

the time the nesting is started. During the remainder of the year the adults are plain iridescent green-black; the young, dull brownish-black. Their plumage does not seem to be as well waterproofed as that of the ducks, and the birds regularly drape themselves over the bare branches about the nest or sprawl with extended wings over the rocks to dry out, looking most bedraggled and forlorn. Their flight is strong, direct, and rapid, with steady wing beats, although occasionally they sail much as buzzards and pelicans do.

Food of this cormorant consists very largely of fish and other aquatic life that it catches by swimming under water, where its snakelike form and powerful feet enable it to outswim the minnows, carp, suckers, and other fish. The bird is not generally regarded as detrimental to any economic interests of man, and although fishermen sometimes claim that it destroys large numbers of commercially valuable fish, examinations of some Oregon stomachs confirm our belief that trash fish comprise a large percentage of its diet. Two stomachs from Warner Valley each contained remains of one sucker (*Catostomus warnerensis*). One stomach from Tillamook Bay (taken May 20) contained seven or more *Chitonotus pugetensis* and remains of a few shrimp. Three stomachs contained pieces of two species of crustaceans, bits of grass, and a mass of fish remains, so digested as to be unidentifiable, that comprised 95 per cent of the entire contents. Another stomach taken at the same time in Tillamook Bay contained the remains of six sculpins (*Cottus asper*), and another (taken January 1) contained remains of one *Chitonotus pugetensis*. Two other stomachs were practically empty and contained only tiny bits of fish bones and crustaceans.

Brandt's Cormorant:
Phalacrocorax penicillatus (Brandt)

Description.—"Bill slender, nearly straight; tail short, with narrow, rigid feathers; head without crests or elongated tufts. *Adults:* head and neck glossy blue black, except for light brownish patch next to gular sac; under parts glossy greenish black; scapulars and wing coverts dull greenish black. *Breeding plumage:* sides of neck and shoulders with long white or yellowish filaments; throat pouch blue. *Young:* plumage brown, throat and under parts paler; upper parts darker, becoming blackish on back of neck." (Bailey) (See Plate 14.) *Downy young:* Born naked with greasy black skin but soon covered with a "clove brown" down, "paler below, mottled with white on the under parts and wings." (Adapted from Bent.) *Size:* Length 28-33, "wing 10.50-11.75, bill 2.60-2.95, tail 5.50-6.50." (Bailey) *Nest:* Of seaweeds and mosses on offshore rocks or inaccessible headlands along coast (Plate 14). *Eggs:* 3 to 6, usually 4, pale bluish or white, more or less concealed by a white coating.

Distribution.—*General:* Breeds from southern Alaska southward along coast to Lower California. Winters over approximately same range. *In Oregon:* Common all along coast on suitable offshore rocks and headlands. Winters on all bays along coast.

Brandt's Cormorant (Plates 14 and 15) is one of the common permanent residents of the Oregon coast and winters regularly on the open ocean about the breeding rocks, bays, and inlets, taking refuge in the latter in stormy periods, in common with many of the pelagic waterfowl. Very little smaller than the huge Farallon Cormorant, it may readily be distinguished as it has a dark-colored bill and a blue or black pouch instead of a yellow or orange one. It has the same slow, clumsy, but strongly sustained flight as its larger relative. Despite its present abundance, it was evidently overlooked by early ornithologists, as no one actually recorded it until Finley (1902) first visited Three Arch Rocks and began to write about the great Oregon bird colonies. It is most abundant in Clatsop, Tillamook, and Lincoln Counties, where the rocky islands or precipitous headlands furnish it with the nesting sites it prefers (Plates 14 and 15).

This cormorant is one of the birds that one may expect to see on any trip to the rocky sections of the Oregon coast at any season of the year. Once at Depoe Bay, Gabrielson had a unique opportunity to watch one fishing. From the float at the landing where he was sitting, little schools of a small anchovy type of fish appeared to be moving through the water much as swarms of gnats travel in the air. A Brandt's Cormorant appearing on the scene put on an interesting performance. Locating one of these schools of fish by the broken surface of the water, the bird dove some distance away and came up through the swarm of fish, driving them to the surface. To the observer on the dock, he appeared first far below the fish as a formless black shadow, then rapidly assumed size and form as he swiftly glided toward the surface. The fish in panicky confusion bolted to the surface making the water fairly boil with their struggles. The dark fisherman, darting up from below, almost invariably succeeded in catching two or three fish before they scattered and regained the depths. The successful catcher crushed its prey in its bill—sometimes dropping one or two fish in the water—swallowed the fish head first, and then, locating another swarm, repeated the performance. Several times, when it was not possible for the observer to locate any fish from the surface, the cormorant dove and reappeared again from far below with a swarm of fish ahead of him. This was repeated until the bird could not eat another fish, when he hauled out on the rocks and spread himself out in the sunshine for his feathers to dry. During the performance the wings were not used at all under the water, the motive power being supplied solely by the huge feet and legs. This point was carefully noted because of Gabrielson's special interest in the method of progression of various kinds of diving birds while under the water.

Cormorants of all kinds on the Oregon coast are subjected generally to a continual persecution on the part of sportsmen and commercial fishermen who assert that the birds are terrific destroyers of commercial and game

Plate 14. Brandt's Cormorant at nest with young. (Photo by Wm. L. Finley and H. T. Bohlman.)

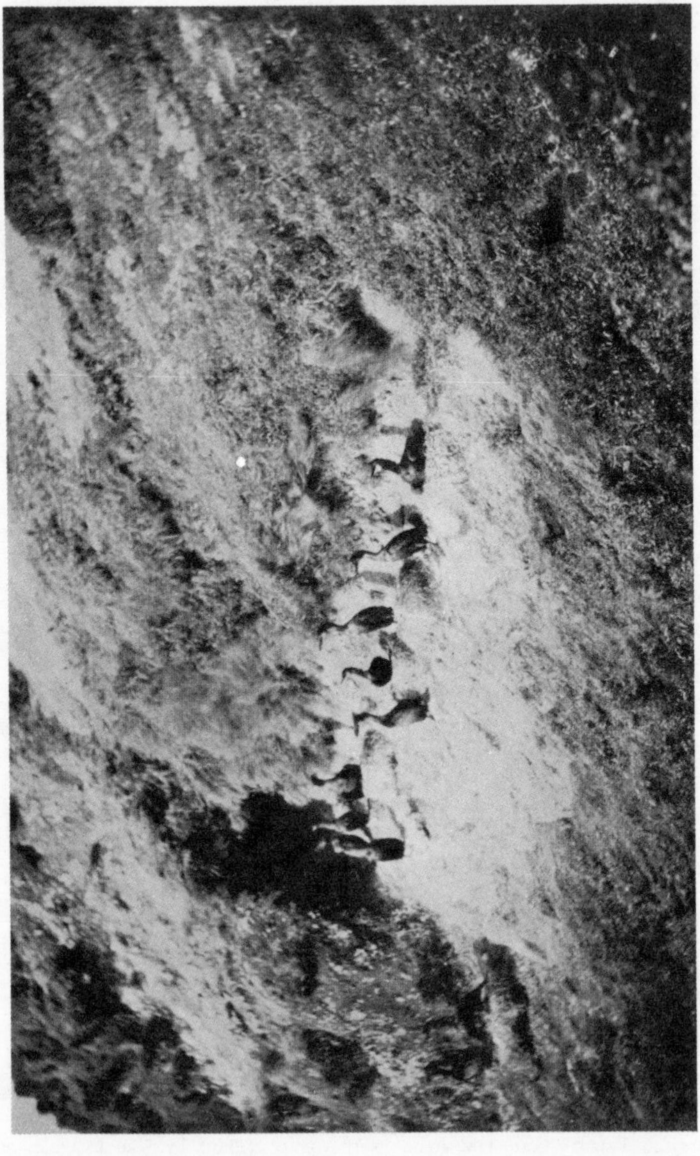

Plate 15. Nesting colony of Brandt's Cormorants. (Photo by Alex Walker.)

fish. No evidence has ever been produced to substantiate this accusation against any of our three species. Stomach contents invariably show that they feed largely on anchovies, sculpins, stickleback, and other trash fish and consume a very small proportion of edible food fish. Only three stomachs of Brandt's Cormorant have been examined from the Oregon coast. One was empty; one contained remains of four or more *Spirontocaris*, one hermit crab, and one shrimp; and the third showed remains of four or more *Spirontocaris* and a few bones of small minnows. There is no evidence whatever on which to justify persecution of this species, and as the great bird rookeries of the Oregon coast add a great deal to the attractiveness of the coast for tourists and nature lovers, there seems to be no good reason why these colonies should not remain undisturbed.

Baird's Cormorant:
Phalacrocorax pelagicus resplendens Audubon

Description.—"*Breeding plumage:* Throat pouch dull coral red; crown and back of head with purplish green crests; neck with loose white filaments; flank with large circular white patch; head and body dark glossy green, changing to rich purple on neck and purplish green on wings; quills and tail black. *Post-breeding plumage:* crests, white filaments, and white flank patch wanting. *Young:* dusky brown, lighter on head; upper parts darker, with a tinge of green." (Bailey) *Downy young:* Born naked with black skin but soon covered with a short, thick down, sooty gray in color. *Size:* "Wing 9.30–10.50, tail 5.80–7.00, bill 1.65–2.00." (Bailey) *Nest:* Usually of kelp and seaweed, placed on the most inaccessible cliffs and rocks. *Eggs:* 3 to 7, usually 3 to 5, much like those of other cormorants, pale blue or white, coated with a white calcareous material.

Distribution.—*General:* Breeds from southern British Columbia to Mexico. Winters in approximately same territory. *In Oregon:* Permanent resident of coast. Breeds on suitable rocks and cliffs from Three Arch Rocks southward. Winters on open ocean and salt-water bays.

Under the title "Baird's Cormorant" will be found both the bird known as "Baird's" and records and literature of the "Violet-green Cormorant," which is a northern form of this species. There is no evidence to indicate that the Violet-green Cormorant has ever actually been taken on the Oregon coast, but Baird's Cormorant is a permanent resident, breeding on suitable rocks and cliffs from at least Three Arch Rocks south to the California line and wintering all along our coast, both on the open ocean and on the salt-water bays and inlets. It has been known as an Oregon bird since Townsend (1839) listed it from the mouth of the Columbia, but little attention was given it until Finley's work on the coastal bird rookeries in 1901 and thereafter.

In the hand, it is one of the most beautifully feathered of all Oregon water birds with its resplendent iridescent plumage of shining greens and purples. It is the smallest cormorant in the State, but its flight is much more graceful and rapid than that of its two larger relatives. It builds its nest of seaweed and other vegetable matter on shelves and ledges of the most precipitous rocks and cliffs. There it lays its three to five eggs in early June, and there are hatched its homely, naked, black youngsters, which are soon covered with a peculiar sooty-gray down. The latest definite dates on which eggs have been collected are June 28 and 29, 1899 (Prill 1901). The young remain in the nest for a number of weeks and require constant attention from the parents until they are able to fly.

This beautiful bird is subjected to the same tireless persecution by fishermen as every other species of cormorant. Two stomachs collected at Netarts were both practically empty. One contained a few bones of a small fish; the other, a few fragments of a crustacean. Stomach examinations from other localities show that this species, like other cormorants, feeds on the teeming millions of trash fish that are found in salt waters. It has less tendency to go inland than either of its relatives, and it is entirely unlikely that it can do any real harm to the commercial fishing interests of the coast.

Man-o'-war-bird: *Family Fregatidae*

Man-o'-war-bird:
Fregata magnificens Matthews

Description.—"Wings very long; tail deeply forked; feet small, half webbed. *Adult male:* plumage black, base of wings glossed with greenish or purplish. *Adult female:* plumage dull black, wings with grayish patch; sides and breast white. *Young:* head, neck, and under parts white; upper parts dull brownish black. *Size:* Length 37.50–41.00, wing 22.00–27.10, tail 14.25–19.25, forked for about 9, bill 4.25–5.15." (Bailey) *Nest:* A crude structure of sticks, placed in tops of low bushes or trees. *Eggs:* 1, white.

Distribution.—*General:* Breeds in West Indies, Bahamas, on islands off coast of Venezuela, and on islands along west coast of Mexico. Winters in adjacent seas, ranging north more or less regularly to Florida, Louisiana, and northern California. *In Oregon:* Rare straggler. Only one record.

The only Oregon record of the Man-o'-war-bird is of one that appeared at Tillamook Rock Light, which is located on a tiny rock just off the coast of Clatsop county. This bird was first noticed soaring over the rock on the morning of February 18, 1935. It swung slowly from side to side until sundown, when after several attempts to find a roosting place it settled on a small iron tripod. During the night it moved, and the keeper on watch noticed it perched on a cable. In the morning it was found dead. Realizing that it was a stranger, Mr. Hugo Hansen skinned it out and later presented the bird to Jewett. It was not sexed.

Order Ciconiiformes

Herons, Egrets, and Bitterns: *Family Ardeidae*

Treganza's Heron:
Ardea herodias treganzai Court

Description.—Much like the California Heron, but upper parts and neck paler in color. *Size:* Wing 17.50, tarsus 5.30, bill 5.90. *Nest:* In trees, bushes, or on the ground; the first two types made of sticks, the latter, sometimes of tules. *Eggs:* 3 to 6, dull greenish blue (Plate 16, *A*).

Distribution.—*General:* Breeds from southern Wyoming, southern Idaho, and eastern Washington south to southern California, southern New Mexico, and western Texas. Winters south into Mexico. *In Oregon:* Permanent resident of eastern Oregon. Breeds in suitable areas throughout territory. Winters in small numbers along streams that remain unfrozen, such as the Columbia, Snake, Deschutes, John Day, Malheur, and Klamath Rivers.

Treganza's Heron, which differs from the western Oregon form only in being somewhat paler in color, is as common and widely distributed in eastern Oregon as the California Heron is in the western part of the State. It is found at times in every county east of the Cascades and has been reported by every ornithologist since Bendire (1877) found it breeding at Malheur Lake, in April. There are thriving colonies at Malheur Lake, in the Warner Basin, and on Upper Klamath Lake, and numerous smaller ones along the streams of the State. After the young are able to fly, these herons wander widely, often being found most unexpectedly at the smallest water holes in the arid country. We have found it wintering regularly in Deschutes, Malheur, Klamath, Wasco, and Umatilla Counties along streams that do not freeze during the winter and have casual winter records for Crook (February 10), Grant (December 12 and February 16), Union (January 12), Baker (December 12), Wallowa (December 28), and Morrow (December 3) Counties. In fact, it may be expected to appear in winter wherever there is open water.

In wooded country this subspecies builds bulky nests of sticks in the treetops, but in the great open marsh country it must resort to different locations. Nests in Harney Valley and the Warner Lakes districts are placed on low bushes, on the rocks, or even on the ground, where there is no other recourse. They are often handsomely built of sagebrush (Plate 16, *A*), and where the birds are undisturbed the nests are apparently used for many years, a slight addition being made to the mass each season. Egg dates are from April 11 to May 28.

Plate 16, *A*. Nest and eggs of Treganza's Heron. (Photo by Alex Walker.)

Plate 16, *B*. Nests and eggs of California Heron in the treetops. (Photo by J. C. Braly.)

Wherever it occurs in Oregon, this gaunt fisherman suffers much at the hands of sportsmen who persecute the entire tribe out of a feeling of resentment toward any competition, real or imaginary, for the supply of fish. As a matter of fact, there is little scientific basis for their belief in this bird's enormous destruction of game fish. Stomach examinations show that an overwhelming percentage of the food is trash fish, such as suckers, carp, and chubs, together with frogs, crayfish, and other aquatic forms of life. A little careful thinking would show without question that this is logical. With the heron, it is not a question of selecting a certain type of fish because of its sporting proclivities but rather entirely a question of procuring a meal. It is therefore to be expected that in a stream containing slow-moving fish, often in numbers greater than the game fish, the heron would find it much easier and just as satisfactory to take the former. This is exactly what happens over the greater part of the State, although around a trout or salmon hatchery our elongated subjects are not at all averse to helping themselves to the fish so conveniently confined for them. Not only do they eat fish, but they can often be found far from water successfully hunting such tidbits as snakes, meadow mice, and other small mammals.

California Heron; Blue Heron; Blue Crane: *Ardea herodias hyperonca* Oberholser

Description.—"*Adults:* Upper parts bluish gray; top of head white, bordered by black and with black occipital crest; shoulders black, striped with white; under parts heavily streaked with black and white; thighs and edge of wings cinnamon brown. *In breeding season:* crest with two or more slender white plumes. *Young:* whole crown and crest black; wing coverts without white or rufous spots." (Bailey) *Size:* Wing 18.62–19.5, bill 5.42–5.70, tarsus 6.70–7.41. *Nest:* In western Oregon, usually a bulky mass of sticks in tall trees, the eggs being laid in a hollow in the platform. *Eggs:* 3 to 6, dull greenish blue (Plates 16, *B*, and 17, *A*).

Distribution.—*General:* Breeds on Pacific Coast from western Oregon to San Diego, California. Winters in about same territory. *In Oregon:* Permanent resident west of Cascades. Recorded in every county in that section, either in our own notes or published literature.

This elongated blue-gray fisherman—4 feet of legs, slender body, and long neck terminating in a javelinlike beak—is without doubt the most widely known water bird in Oregon. Every creek, however small, and every pond, however well hidden, are likely to be visited at intervals either by this form or the preceding one found east of the Cascades. The ungainly appearance of the California Heron in the air and its large size combine to call it to the attention of the least observant. Townsend (1839) and Newberry (1857) both recorded it, and almost all ornithologists since have noted its presence. Numerous breeding colonies have been reported—the best known in western Oregon undoubtedly being the

Plate 17, *A*. Nests of California Heron, up 150 feet. (Photo by J. C. Braly.)

Plate 17, *B*. Young American Egret. (Photo by Wm. L. and Irene Finley.)

one that was located for many years at Linnton (Plate 16, *B*) near the city limits of Portland—and the bulky nests in tall trees are a familiar sight to many Oregonians.

The eggs are laid through the spring, usually in March and April, and the summer is well advanced before the ungainly youngsters are able to leave the nests to fish for themselves along the streams and ponds. The parents feed them during the long nestling period in exactly the same manner as described for the American Bittern, and the sight of a half-grown youngster grimly following the contortions of its ungainly parent is one never to be forgotten.

Birds from the Portland colony are intermediates between this form and the darker *A. h. fannini* but are somewhat closer to the latter in coloration. Doubtless occasional wintering birds might well be typical of the latter race, but to date we have not collected enough material to determine this point with certainty. We both feel that Columbia River birds are closer to such Puget Sound birds as we have had available for comparison, but the material is not complete enough to warrant a final statement.

American Egret:
Casmerodius albus egretta (Gmelin)

Description.—"Plumage always pure white. *Adult in nuptial plumage:* scapular plumes of dissected filamentose feathers covering back and reaching well beyond end of tail; head and neck without crests or long feathers; feet and legs black; bill yellow; usually blackish near tip. *Post-breeding plumage and young:* back without plumes. *Length:* 37–41, wing 14.10–16.80, bill 4.20–4.90, tarsus 5.50–6.80." (Bailey) *Nest:* Sometimes a loose platform of sticks in trees, at other times built on platforms of bent-down tules. *Eggs:* 3 to 6, usually 4 or 5, pale bluish green.

Distribution.—*General:* Breeds in Oregon and California and from Arkansas, Tennessee, North Carolina, and Florida far south into South America. Winters over most of breeding ground. *In Oregon:* Summer resident and breeding species of Harney and Klamath Counties. Casual records in Lake County. Record of a single bird in Multnomah County.

The American Egret (Plate 17, *B*), one of the showiest species found in Oregon, arrives in April (earliest date, April 11) and remains until late October (latest date, November 19). The only breeding colonies now known in the State are in Harney Valley and Upper Klamath Lake, and if the birds are seen away from these areas, it is largely in late summer during the postbreeding wanderings. The Harney Valley colony, the northernmost known one of the species, was first reported by Bendire (Brewer 1875), who found "at least 300 nests," and has been an attraction to ornithologists ever since. For years it was the only known breeding colony of these pure white herons in Oregon. The activities of plume hunters and possibly other factors caused a gradual reduction in the thriving colony until Finley (1908b) was able to report only two birds in the valley. That was apparently the low ebb, however, for in 1911 Finley found 61 birds and in 1912, 23 adult birds and 11 nests. Willett (1919) found 20 pairs nesting in the Malheur Lake Reservation, the only colony he could locate. Even though so greatly diminished in numbers, the birds still return each year to the valley to nest, shifting the location of their breeding colony from year to year.

Our own notes on the varying fortunes of this colony began in 1912 when Jewett first visited it and found 16 pairs breeding on the Double O Ranch. In 1919, Gabrielson saw a few nests still containing well-grown young on the Island Ranch. There were numerous other nests that may have been occupied, but the visit was too late to determine accurately the number breeding. In 1922, Jewett and Dr. L. E. Hibbard visited the colony, which was again located in willows on the Island Ranch, found about 40 nests with young or eggs, and counted 80 adults. Some nests contained as many as 10 eggs, and numbers of dead young were on the ground. Dr. W. B. Bell, Jewett, and Gabrielson next visited the colony in 1926, again on the Island Ranch. They found about 25 nests containing eggs or young and counted 40 adults. In 1930, the colony was near Burns in a clump of willows at Potter Swamp. There were only 10 or 12 nests with young, but whether this was the entire population is not known.

The nests are usually built of sticks and are located in the tops of the stunted willows, generally not more than 10 to 15 feet from the ground, so that the great white herons are visible for a long distance. When the birds locate in the marshes, however, as occasionally happens, the nests are more or less carefully made structures of tule stems woven into bent-over tules. The colonies, like those of all other herons, are interesting, if smelly places. The willows and the ground beneath are more or less whitewashed and strewn with rotting remains of fish, frogs, small animals, and other food brought to the young. There are also usually a number of dead young, adding to the stench. These rookeries have a magnetic attraction for crows, magpies, and ravens that hover about or perch in nearby trees awaiting a chance to snatch the unguarded eggs or young. Coyote tracks and telltale prints of any other four-footed predator that happens to be in the vicinity are usually in evidence on the ground beneath the trees. The adults are not particularly wild, sailing back and forth over the colony during our visits or standing in a loose company approximately 100 yards away.

Mearns (1879), in his report on Lieutenant Wittich's collection at Fort Klamath, reported one egret collected there on January 8, 1878. Merrill (1888) reported that a few were seen at Fort Klamath during the summer and that a single bird passed the winter on Wood River. These two are the only winter records for the State. J. J. Furber, when warden, frequently reported one or two birds seen usually in October or November, although he reported two on June 8, 1913. Jewett saw a single bird at Agency Lake, October 7, 1932. On May 30, 1934, H. M. Worcester, then warden on Upper Klamath Lake Reservation, and the writers found at least three pairs of American Egrets in the Blue Heron and Farallon Cormorant colony on that refuge. High water prevented entry into the willows, but from their actions we were certain the birds were nesting. Later Worcester returned and found several nests, the first known with certainty in the Klamath basin.

Henshaw (1880) reported this egret as a common breeding species at the Warner Lakes, but no nesting colony has been known there for many years, the only recent record being a single bird reported by M. E. Jacobs, May 25, 1925, as staying several days on a small lake at the Guano Ranch. This ranch lies east of the Warner Lakes near the south end of Hart Mountain.

Our only record for western Oregon is of a single bird, first reported by local residents to W. A. Eliot as a "white crane," staying on the river bottoms near the Swan Island airport in Portland. The two writers upon hearing of it immediately visited the place (September 11, 1933), in company with C. A. Leichhardt, and found a single egret that remained several days.

We have had no Oregon stomachs to examine, but in general the food consists of small aquatic forms, with seldom any fish of food value included. Baynard (1912), who forced 50 young egrets in Florida to disgorge their meals immediately after they had eaten, found the items of the 50 meals to total as follows: "297 small frogs, 49 small snakes, mostly the water moccasin, 61 young fish, suckers, not edible, 176 crayfish."

Brewster's Egret:
Egretta thula brewsteri Thayer and Bangs

Description.—"Plumage always pure white. *Adults in nuptial plumage:* scapulars with long plumes of dissected filamentose feathers reaching beyond tail and recurved at tip; head and throat crested; feet yellow, legs black; bill black, with yellow base. *Post-breeding plumage and young:* back without plumes." (Bailey) *Size:* Wing 10.46–10.79, culmen 3.42–3.72, tarsus 4.05–4.43. *Nest:* Either a loose platform of sticks in a tree or, more commonly in the West, tule stems supported by a mass of bent-over and broken-down tules. *Eggs:* 3 to 6, usually 4 or 5, pale green.

Distribution.—*General:* Breeds from Utah, Nevada, and California south to Lower California. Wanders north to British Columbia and Alberta after breeding season. *In Oregon:* Formerly bred in Harney County.

Brewster's Egret, a dainty little snow white bird, with blacklegs and yellow feet, can now be considered only as a rare straggler in Oregon. Bendire (1877) recorded the "Great White Egret" as: "a moderately common summer resident, breeding in the thick willows on the lower Sylvies River, in company with other species of herons," and then for the "Little White Egret," stated: "The same remarks apply to this species, which is found in the same locality." This is the only record we have found of its breeding within our State. Fawcett, when warden at Malheur, reported a few between May 24 and 26, 1914, and Vernon Bailey saw a dozen on Aspen Lake, August 24, 1916. On November 3, 1934, Alex Walker took a specimen at Tillamook, the only specimen we have of this beautiful little heron, which, however, may wander into the State almost any fall.

Anthony's Green Heron:
Butorides virescens anthonyi (Mearns)

Description.—Bill longer than tarsus, crown and back with long, lanceolate, but not dissected plumes. *Adults:* Crown and crest, tail, and most of wings dark green; scapular plumes bluish green; sides of neck bright yellowish chestnut; belly dusky. *Young:* Similar to adults, but with scapular plumes shorter and darker green; most of quills tipped with white and under parts coarsely streaked. (Adapted from Bailey.) *Size:* "Length 19.10, wing 8.20, bill 2.35." (Bailey) *Nest:* Woven of sticks and often lined with smaller twigs. *Eggs:* 3 to 6, usually 4 or 5, pale bluish green.

Distribution.—*General:* Breeds from Oregon south to Lower California and northern Mexico. Winters south to Central America. *In Oregon:* Rare summer resident from Portland south to west side of Cascades and in Klamath County east of mountains.

Anthony's Green Heron, the paler western form of the Green Heron, can be considered as an uncommon summer resident in Oregon. It was first reported by Merrill (1888), who saw one on Crooked Creek, Klamath County, May 4, 1887. Woodcock (1902) listed it as a common resident on Yaquina Bay on reports from Bretherton and at Dayton on information from Hadley. These are the only definite statements we have found in literature, although there are many general references to it as an Oregon species.

In the experience of the authors, the bird has been a decided rarity. Our notes contain six definite records of its occurrence in the State. Jewett saw one near the Oakes Slough in South Portland, June 7, 1927, and took an adult male, June 22, 1934, and Gabrielson watched one at close range on the bank of a small pond on Sauvies Island, August 11, 1932, all from Multnomah County. Jewett saw a single bird near Olene, Klamath County, June 19, 1928, and he and Vernon Bailey saw two at Grants Pass, Josephine County, August 26, 1927. Aside from these there are seven skins available. Overton Dowell, Jr., took a male, July 11, 1923, and a female, August 27, 1932, both at Mercer Lake, western Lane County, and Prill collected five skins in Linn County during the summers of 1933 and 1934. Evidently in recent years the bird has become more regular in western Oregon.

Black-crowned Night Heron:
Nycticorax nycticorax hoactli (Gmelin)

DESCRIPTION.—"Bill about as long as tarsus. *Adults:* crown and back black; wings and tail ashy gray; forehead and throat creamy white, shading into light gray of sides and under parts. *Young:* crown blackish, streaked with buff; back dusky gray, spotted and striped, and quills tipped with buff; neck and under parts coarsely striped with buff and dusky. *Length:* 23–26, wing 11.00–12.80, bill 2.80–3.10, tarsus 3.10–3.40." (Bailey) *Nest:* A rough structure of sticks, reeds, and grass, built on the ground, in tules, or in trees. *Eggs:* 3 to 7, usually 3 to 5, pale bluish green.

DISTRIBUTION.—*General:* Breeds from northern Oregon, southern Manitoba, and southern Quebec south to Paraguay and winters from northern California and Oregon, Nevada, Utah, Colorado, Illinois, Michigan, and New York, south. *In Oregon:* Common summer resident and breeder from about May 10 to October 1. Uncommon winter resident in areas where open water remains.

THE BLACK-CROWNED NIGHT HERON (Plate 18, *A*), or "quawk," is a widely distributed bird in Oregon. It is most abundant in Klamath, Lake, Harney, and Baker Counties, but is found at least occasionally along any of the waterways of that part of the State. Our own records and field notes of other members of the Biological Survey show winter specimens and records from Malheur (December 14), Klamath (December 14, January 26, February 17 and 28), Harney (December 20, January 15, March 11), Umatilla (January 15), and Multnomah (December 15, January 14 and 15) Counties. In western Oregon it is a fairly common resident at Portland, where it was formerly more abundant, and a less common resident elsewhere. We have no records from Douglas, Jackson, or Josephine Counties, and our only coastal record is from Lincoln County, where Gabrielson saw a single individual, August 11, 1930. Straggling individuals are to be expected along the coast, particularly in the lake area of Lane and Douglas Counties.

Townsend (1839) first recorded this species from the State, and practically all of the literature since his time refers to the colonies in Harney, Klamath, and Lake Counties. Nesting colonies have been definitely recorded from Malheur Lake, Harney County (Bendire 1877; Willett 1919), Klamath County (Allen 1909; Walker 1917), Warner Valley, Lake County (Prill 1922a, 1924), and Portland, Multnomah County (Finley 1906a). The birds in Harney County have shifted location several times in recent years, but the colony still persists in somewhat diminished numbers. The rookery on Upper Klamath Lake, which contained a mixture of Farallon Cormorants, Treganza's Herons, and Black-crowned Night Herons, was in a thriving condition in 1934, the last year in which either of us visited it. We have not visited the Lake County colony, but the herons are still common in Warner Valley, so without doubt it is still in existence. We do not know the present location of the Portland rookery, but the birds still frequent the vicinity in small numbers. Finley, in 1906, reported 200

Plate 18, *A*. Black-crowned Night Heron. (Photo by Wm. L. Finley and H. T. Bohlman.)

Plate 18, *B*. Nest and eggs of American Bittern. (Photo by Ira N. Gabrielson.)

nests, but the numbers have greatly diminished in recent years. In addition to these well-known rookeries, there is a thriving colony a few miles from Baker in a dense willow thicket. The writers together visited it first on May 25, 1924, and found about 100 pairs of birds nesting. There are doubtless other small groups nesting in eastern Oregon that have not been located, due to the comparatively small amount of intensive field work in that area.

The nests, when built in trees, are more or less loosely constructed platforms of sticks, whereas those in the great marshes are composed of sticks or tule stalks and are sometimes built on the water and anchored to living tules. The nesting behavior, including feeding of the young, is quite similar to that practiced by other herons. Available notes show egg dates extending from April 11 to May 28.

The Black-crowned Night Heron is a shorter and more heavily built bird than any other species in Oregon in this group. The adults, with the long white crest plumes contrasted against the black crown and back, cannot be confused with any other Oregon bird. The striped and spotted young are sometimes confused with the American Bittern, but are easily distinguished by the following differences: They are much more heavily built than the bitterns; the general color tone is gray brown, quite different from the bright-brown, buff, and black pattern of the bittern; and the backs of the young are spotted with buff on a dusky-gray background, whereas the bittern has no such markings in any plumage.

American Bittern:
Botaurus lentiginosus (Montagu)

Description.—"Sexes alike, except for white or buffy nuptial ruffs on sides of breast of adult male in breeding season; feathers lax and coarse; upper parts broadly striped with dusky on buff; crown and streak along jaw blackish; throat and under parts creamy buff, striped with brown. Young similar to adults. *Length:* 24–34, wing 9.80–12.00, bill 2.50–3.20, tarsus 3.10–3.85." (Bailey) *Nest:* On the ground, usually near the water, a trampled flat mass of grass, weeds, or rubbish. *Eggs:* 3 to 7, buff to buffy brown.

Distribution.—*General:* Breeds from central British Columbia, northern Manitoba, southern Ungava, and Newfoundland south to southern California, central Arizona, Utah, Colorado, Kansas, Ohio Valley, and southern New Jersey. Winters south to West Indies and Panama. *In Oregon:* Common summer resident in eastern Oregon from April to October. Less common in western Oregon but found in Willamette Valley (Multnomah, Washington, Marion, Lane, and Polk Counties), in southwestern Oregon (Jackson County), and on coast (Coos, Lane, Tillamook, and Lincoln Counties, and probably others). Casual winter resident in Klamath and Harney Counties.

The American Bittern is easily recognized by its brown, buff, and black plumage, green legs, and medium size. Its weird love song is responsible for many vernacular names applied to it, as "Thunder Pumper" and

"Stake Driver." The noise, produced by pumping the gullet full of air by convulsive movements, is at times likened to the sound of an old squeaky wooden pump and again to the sound produced by the driving of a stake. The weird notes, however interpreted, are the voice of the marshlands themselves echoing above the gabbling of the coots and the noisy clatter of the swamp blackbirds. The species is widely distributed and is one of the best known American marsh birds. It was first found in the State by Newberry (1857), who called it common. Bendire (Brewer 1875) reported it from Harney County, and both Mearns (1879) and Merrill (1888) found it in Klamath County. It was reported as a casual winter resident in Klamath County by Cantwell (January 27 and February 5, 1915), and Furber (December 30, 1910, and January 18 and 19, 1913) and in Harney County by Cantwell (December 1 and 20, 1914). We have found it to be a common summer resident of eastern Oregon, particularly in Klamath, Lake, and Harney Counties, the great water-bird breeding grounds of the State, and have noted it in Baker (August 25), Malheur (June 17), and Crook (June 7) Counties. Doubtless with more field work it will be found in many others.

Johnson (1880) was the first to report it from western Oregon, stating it was a common resident at East Portland, Salem, and Forest Grove. Jewett has recorded it from Tillamook and Coos Counties, and Gabrielson has observed it on several occasions about Devils Lake, Lincoln County, and once or twice on Sauvies Island, Multnomah County. Migration observers have reported it to the Biological Survey from the following localities: Aumsville, Marion County (Matteson); Mercer, Lane County (O. Dowell, Jr.); and Rickreall, Polk County (Oliver).

The nest (Plate 18, *B*) is usually an unpretentious trampled mass of vegetation on the edge of the marsh, although occasionally it is a floating platform of broken reeds. Two or more well-defined trails lead away from it, and the parents seldom light directly at the nest, preferring to drop into the rank vegetation some distance away and stalk quietly to it along one of these paths. The few egg dates available extend from May 12 to May 24, obviously an incomplete record.

The babies hatched from the dull, buffy-colored eggs are not beautiful in any sense of the word. The long, thin, yellowish down does not conceal their angular forms. In fact the down on the head and neck stands stiffly erect as if a constant succession of "hair-raising" experiences had finally resulted in fixing the thin covering in a permanent pompadour effect. The young are fed partially digested food from the parent's gullet. As the parent approaches the nest each youngster commences to jump upward, striving to seize the beak of the parent. When successful, the young bittern clamps its beak firmly across the base of that of the parent exactly as if the intention were to shear it off. Locked together in this fashion, the adult goes through a weird series of contortions while the offspring hangs on grimly. Eventually a lump of food travels up the parent's throat to be disgorged into the mouth of the baby, who allows the parent's beak to slip through its own until the morsel falls into its open mouth. Frequently the food falls to the nest, and a wild and clumsy scramble to get the scattered lunch ensues, often resulting in a tug of war as two of the nestlings try to grab the same frog leg or other dainty.

When flushed, the bittern jumps from the grass with a startled squawk, legs dangling loosely and wings flapping wildly; but when once safely launched the flight is strong and steady. In the grass it is a master in the art of concealment. Its brown and buff stripes blend well with the sunlight and shadow in the grass, and the blending is often accentuated by the action of the bird. It will draw itself fully erect until the extended neck is little larger than a blade of the luxuriant swamp grass and, with the bill pointing skyward, will stand motionless for many minutes until the observer's neck begins to ache in sympathy with the "crick" he is sure must be present in that of the bird.

Western Least Bittern:
Ixobrychus exilis hesperis Dickey and Van Rossem

Description.—"Size very small, sexes and young different. *Adult male:* back, crown, rump, and tail greenish black; back of neck and patch on wing chestnut; throat and under parts light buff, with two dusky spots on breast. *Adult female:* back mainly chestnut, and buff of under parts striped with dusky. *Young:* like female, but brown feathers of back tipped with buff." (Bailey) *Size: Male,* wing 4.80–5.25, tail 1.67–1.82, exposed culmen 1.75–2.05, tarsus 1.55–1.70. *Female,* wing 4.50–5.10, tail 1.62–1.80, exposed culmen 1.70–1.97, tarsus 1.55–1.65. *Nest:* A loosely woven platform of grass or reeds, attached to the swamp vegetation a few inches to several feet above the water. *Eggs:* 4 to 7, usually 4 or 5, bluish white or greenish white.

Distribution.—*General:* Breeds from southern Oregon to central Lower California. Winters from southern California southward. *In Oregon:* Summer resident and breeding species of Harney, Klamath, and probably Lake Counties.

The beautifully marked Western Least Bittern, the smallest North American member of the heron family, is perhaps more abundant in Oregon than our rather scanty information would imply. Its small size and secretive ways render it difficult to observe, and it might be present in considerable numbers without being detected by a casual visitor. In behavior and actions it is much like its larger cousin, the American Bittern.

Bendire (1877) reported that he had seen it twice at Malheur Lake, and Willett (1919) found it a rather common breeder at the same lake, building its nests (Plates 19, *A* and *B*) in the tall tules well out toward the open water. Jewett saw two birds in Klamath Falls on November 11, 1912, taken in and near Klamath Falls during the preceding summer, but

Plate 19, *A*. Nest and eggs of Least Bittern. (Photo by Ira N. Gabrielson.)

Plate 19, *B*. Young Least Bitterns. (Photo by Ira N. Gabrielson.)

without data. There is a specimen in the Biological Survey collection taken by Vernon Bailey on July 5, 1899, at Tule Lake, Oregon, long before Tule Lake had been reduced in size and confined to California, as at present. Wardens stationed at Malheur and Lower Klamath Lakes reported it as a rare summer visitor, most of the records being in May and June (Malheur: Rare, one record between July 1 and 15, 1912, Lewis; and rare, only one bird seen in 1920, Benson. Klamath: Rare, Lewis; and rare, May 21, 1913, one June 21, and two June 26, 1914, Furber). E. S. Currier (1929a) reported it from Blue Lake, Multnomah County, on August 7, 1927, but no specimens were taken.

Ibises: *Family Threskiornithidae*

White-faced Glossy Ibis: *Plegadis guarauna* (Linnaeus)

Description.—"Lores and eyelids naked, rest of head well feathered; bill long and narrow, gently curved downward, grooved from nostril to tip. *Adults:* lores red; face whitish; head, neck, shoulders, and under parts dark rich chestnut; crown and wings glossed with iridescent purplish and greenish. *Young:* head and neck streaked with white and dusky, and under parts grayish brown. *Length:* 19–26, wing 9.30–10.80, bill 3.75–6.00, tarsus 3.00–4.40." (Bailey) *Nest:* Sometimes a floating platform, attached to the tules, and at other times well woven into the tules a foot or more above the water. *Eggs:* 3 to 7, usually 3 or 4, pale green.

Distribution.—*General:* Nests from Oregon and Utah to southern Texas and southern Mexico. Winters from extreme southern United States to South America. *In Oregon:* Known only from Malheur Lake and surrounding territory where northernmost breeding colony is found. Straggler anywhere else.

The handsome White-faced Glossy Ibis (Plate 20) is the only representative of the family found in the State. Its bronzed iridescent plumage and heavy decurved bill serve to distinguish it from any other Oregon bird with which it might possibly be confused. It arrives in May and leaves in September (earliest date, May 15; latest, October 4, both Harney County), and can be looked for regularly in the vicinity of Malheur, where a small colony has bred for many years. Coues (1876) reported it as a breeding bird at Camp Harney. Willett (1919) reported a colony of about 100 nesting pairs in the tules along the west side of Malheur Lake that began to deposit eggs about June 1. Despite the long-continued drought and consequent shrinking of water areas, the birds still remained about the lake in small numbers in 1933, but we cannot say whether or not they nested that year.

Aside from these Malheur Lake birds there is a specimen in the Henshaw collection taken at Warner Lakes, September 6, 1877, and last known to be in the British Museum (Sharpe 1898). So far as we know this is the

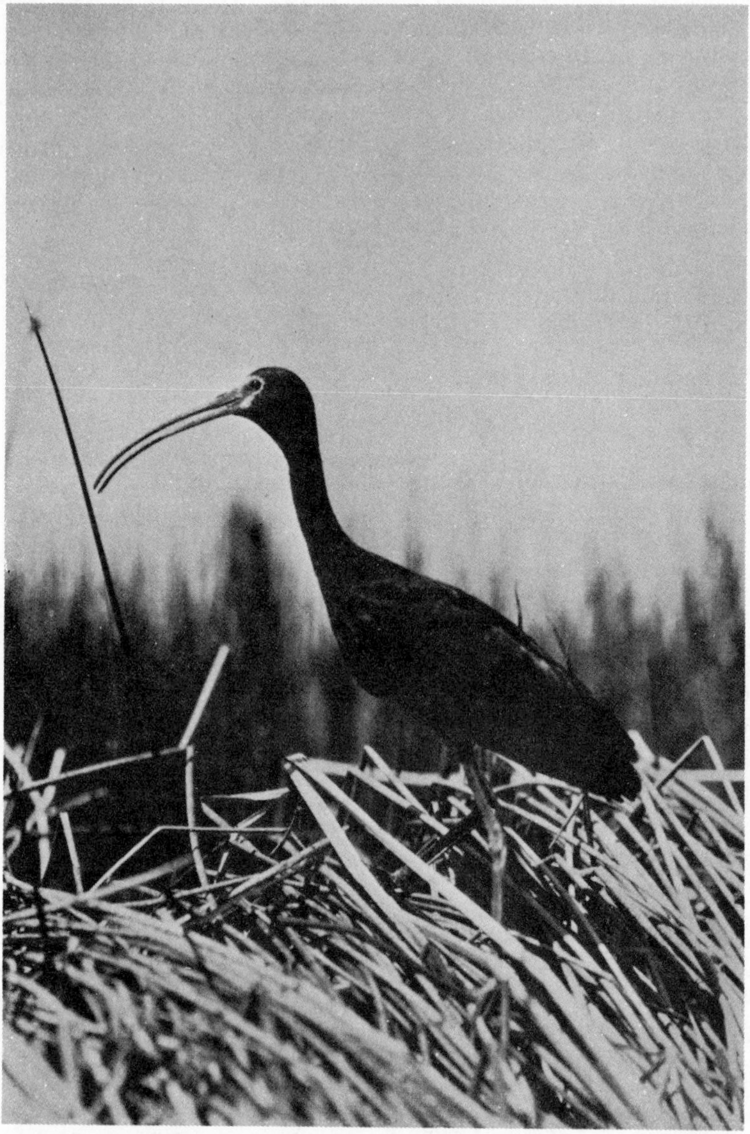

Plate 20. White-faced Glossy Ibis. (Photo by Wm. L. Finley and H. T. Bohlman.)

only definite Oregon record outside of Harney County. There is an old dismounted bird in the National Museum (Cat. No. 12630) from the "Columbia River Oregon" taken on the T. R. Peale U. S. Exploring Expedition. Nothing further is known about it. If it is actually an Oregon specimen, it probably came from the vicinity of Portland, but the record is not definite enough for a locality record.

The young in the nest are unlovely creatures, being awkward, angular, and scantily covered with dull black down, relieved only by a white patch on the crown. In August, after the young are able to fly, these ibises are to be found in the wet meadows or shallow ponds in Harney Valley, feeding on the small aquatic life—crustaceans, water insects, frogs, and the like—the dull black youngsters and ragged molting adults being but poor caricatures of the brilliant spring adults. Their movements and flight are much like those of the curlew—strong and rapid—the flocks sometimes indulging in swift aerial evolutions as perfectly synchronized as those of some sandpipers.

Plate 21, *A*. Whistling Swan. (Photo by Wm. L. Finley and H. T. Bohlman.)

Plate 21, *B*. Young Canada Goose. (Photo by Wm. L. Finley and H. T. Bohlman.)

Order Anseriformes

Ducks, Geese, and Swans: *Family Anatidae*

Whistling Swan:
Cygnus columbianus (Ord)

Description.—*Adults:* Plumage pure white, bill black, large, and high at the base, with a naked space reaching the eyes. Lores usually with a small yellow spot. Distance from the eye to the back of the nostril greater than the rest of the bill. Young birds ashy or tinted with brownish. (Adapted from Bailey.) *Downy young:* "The downy young is described by Dr. D. G. Elliott (1898) as 'pure white, bill, legs, and feet yellow'; but the young of European swans are all either pale grayish-white or grayish-brown." (Bent) *Size:* Length about 54.00, wing 21.00–22.00, bill 3.80–4.20. *Nest:* Mound of moss, grass, and other vegetable matter. *Eggs:* 2 to 7, usually 4 or 5, creamy white to dull white.

Distribution.—*General:* Breeds north of Arctic Circle from northern Alaska to Baffin Island south to St. Lawrence Island and Alaska Peninsula. Winters on Atlantic Coast from Massachusetts to Florida and on Pacific Coast from southern Alaska to Lower California. *In Oregon:* Migrant and winter resident, most abundant in October, November, February, and March in migration, but present from September to May.

Lewis and Clark (1814) first reported the magnificent Whistling Swan (Plate 21, *A*)—the largest wild fowl that can still be found in Oregon—from the mouth of the Columbia River on January 2, 1806, and a few of the snowy birds still winter along that stream from Portland westward. Nearly every writer since has mentioned it, and it is still fairly common within the State. It is most abundant of course during the migratory movement of the swans from their Arctic breeding grounds to their winter home in California, but it is present from September to May (earliest date, August 20, Klamath County; latest, June 13, Malheur County). Two stragglers were observed on September 20 and May 26, the earliest and latest dates, respectively, on which more than a single bird was seen. During February, March, and early April, and again in October and November, the birds can be seen by the hundreds, if not by the thousands. As late as 1912, the wardens at Malheur Lake estimated from 10,000 to 20,000 at one time on the lake; and Gabrielson counted more than 900 on February 24, 1928, and 565 on March 11, 1929, on Spring Lake, a small body of water in Klamath County. Jewett's notes, covering Klamath, Harney, and Lake Counties particularly, contain many references to a hundred or more birds or to their great abundance.

The main stopping places for the Whistling Swan in Oregon are the great shallow lakes of Klamath, Lake, and Harney Counties, although it is found in smaller numbers on the Snake and Malheur Rivers (occasionally wintering on the latter), on the Columbia River throughout its course along the Oregon border, and on the smaller lakes in Wallowa County (Wallowa Lake), and in the Cascades (Davis Lake). Jewett found four swans wintering in 1913–14 on Davis Creek, the outlet of the above lake. He saw the birds twice in late January. They have been reported by many observers from the Willamette Valley and the Lower Columbia River. In fact our records and those published by others cover the entire State, with the exception of the coast counties south of Clatsop, of Jackson and Josephine Counties in southern Oregon (and we believe that more opportunity for observation would result in finding them occasionally in that territory), and of a few interior counties of eastern Oregon, such as Grant, Wheeler, Union, and Jefferson, where, however, we may expect to find them during migration on any sufficient body of water.

It would be a curious individual, indeed, who would not thrill to the musical bugling of these huge white birds and to the sight of them resting gracefully on the water or beating their way against the wind with slow but powerful thrusts of their wide pinions. Their calls are the very voice of the wild untamed north itself, and we rejoice exceedingly that these swans seem to be holding their own during the last few years, since absolute protection has been afforded them.

Trumpeter Swan:
Cygnus buccinator Richardson

Description.—Exactly like the Whistling Swan except for its larger size and differences as follows: Bill and lores entirely black, lacking the yellow spot usually present in the former species, and the distance from the eye to the back of the nostril less than the rest of the bill. *Downy young:* (Not known.) *Size:* Length 60–66, wing 21.00–27.50, bill 4.30–4.70. *Nest:* A mass of grass, intermingled with feathers and down. *Eggs:* 2 to 8, usually 4 to 6, creamy white to dull white.

Distribution.—*General:* Bred formerly from Alaska, northern Mackenzie, and James Bay south to British Columbia, Alberta, Montana, Wyoming, Nebraska, and Missouri and wintered south to Gulf of Mexico to California. *In Oregon:* Formerly reported by many observers but no authentic records for many years.

The Trumpeter Swan, the largest and most magnificent North American waterfowl, is practically extinct and has been for many years. A few are known to breed in British Columbia, Alberta, Montana, and Yellowstone Park and, because of the careful protection afforded them, may now be holding their own. Whether or not these few remaining birds are enough to increase their numbers remains to be seen.

The first Oregon report of the Trumpeter Swan was made by Lewis and Clark (1814) from the mouth of the Columbia River (January 2, 1806), and they reported it again, from Deer Island (March 28, 1806), on their return trip. Townsend listed it in 1839; Newberry (1857) considered it not rare in early November on the Columbia River; Bendire (1877) reported collecting a single specimen at Malheur Lake, March 24, 1877; Mearns (1879) listed it from Fort Klamath on the authority of Dr. McElderry, the post surgeon; Johnson (1880) stated that it was a common migrant in the Willamette Valley; Anthony (1886) considered it common on the Columbia River; Woodcock (1902) reported it from only two localities, one a single bird in the winter of 1894–95 that stayed for several days on a small lake near McMinnville (Pope) and one a rare migrant in October and May at Dayton (Hadley). Allan Brooks (1926b) stated that at least 18 birds crossed from British Columbia, at Okanogan, to winter in Washington, Oregon, or Idaho, which indicated that there might still be a possibility of finding Trumpeter Swans in our State. On September 7, 1929, Oberholser, Gabrielson, and Jewett saw a single swan at Davis Lake that, judging from its huge size, might have been this species. This is the only recent record of even its hypothetical occurrence within the State. So far as we can learn, the only Oregon specimen of this noble bird in existence is one in the Chicago Academy of Science collection that was taken three miles west of Portland in the Columbia River on April 8, 1881.

Common Canada Goose:
Branta canadensis canadensis (Linnaeus)

Description.—"Head and neck black except for broad white band across throat and cheeks; body deep gray, feathers tipped with lighter; rump, tail, and quills black; upper and lower tail coverts, and ventral region, white. *Length:* 35–43, wing 15.60–21.00, bill 1.55–2.70." (Bailey) *Downy young:* "The downy young when recently hatched is brightly colored and very pretty. The entire back, rump, wings, and flanks are 'yellowish olive,' with a bright, greenish-yellow sheen; a large central crown patch is lustrous 'olive'; the remainder of the head and neck is bright yellowish, deepening to 'olive ocher' on the cheeks and sides of the neck and paling to 'primrose yellow' on the throat; the under parts shade from 'deep colonial buff' on the breast to 'primrose yellow' on the belly; the bill is entirely black." (Bent) *Nest:* Built-up mound of grass, rushes, leaves, or other vegetation, lined with down. *Eggs:* 4 to 10, usually 5 or 6, creamy white to dull white.

Distribution.—*General:* Breeds from Mackenzie, northern Quebec, and Labrador south to Gulf of St. Lawrence, James Bay, South Dakota, Colorado, Utah, Nevada, and northern California. Winters south to Gulf of Mexico and to southern California. *In Oregon:* Common permanent resident, breeding in suitable areas in eastern Oregon and wintering throughout State wherever open water is found.

There are few persons who have not thrilled to the strident voices of the Common Canada Geese (Plate 21, *B*), or "Honkers," as the great gray-breasted squadrons travel the air lanes in their annual migrations. Spring is in the air, and even the staid business man, who never gives the out-of-door world a thought at any other time, pauses to look with an appreciative eye as the wild music warns of the great V's of huge birds moving over the city. Sadly reduced in numbers, as compared to former years, these geese are still the greatest prize that can possibly fall to the gun of a wild-fowler. Townsend first reported them from Oregon in 1839, and ever since that time much has been written regarding their presence here.

Unlike all other geese and many ducks that breed entirely outside of the State, this great bird still breeds in numbers in eastern Oregon, in the great marshy areas of Harney and Warner Valleys, in Summer Lake, Klamath County, and less frequently in smaller swampy areas or along the larger streams. We have notes on eggs and newly hatched goslings from Klamath, Lake, Harney, and Deschutes Counties. It also breeds in small numbers on an island in the Columbia River east of The Dalles, along the John Day River, and along the Snake River and its tributaries near Ontario. We have frequently seen pairs of birds along these streams through the summer but have not been able to approach their nests. It is evident, therefore, that if we are so inclined, we can do something ourselves to see that these wonderful wild fowl are protected and given a chance to perpetuate themselves within the State borders.

The birds mate for life, and nesting begins early. The nests are bulky affairs of weeds, grass, or other vegetation with a slight depression in the center to receive the big white eggs, most of which are laid in late March and early April and vary in number from two to eight, usually three to five. Furber, who was warden for years at Lower Klamath Lake, reported newly hatched young on April 17, 1914, and April 20, 1915, and Gabrielson saw newly hatched young in Klamath County on April 19, 1924, the earliest dates on which young have been noted. As the period of incubation in this species is 28 to 30 days, this would place the period of laying in mid-March. Jewett found a female sitting on seven eggs at Silver Lake, April 8, 1919, and blew two sets of three and five eggs respectively, taken at Adel, April 17, 1927, in which incubation had just started. The latest date is that of Prill, who collected a set of two half-incubated eggs in Warner Valley on June 5, 1922.

During July, the adults lose all the wing quills in the annual molt and are unable to fly until the new feathers grow. At this time they seek the thick tules and other vegetation in which to hide, although if pressed on open ground they are able to run with amazing speed. When both young and old are able to fly, the birds begin to gather into flocks that wander over the adjacent country, feeding in the grainfields or pastures and frequently doing considerable damage in the former. By September, the exodus from the breeding grounds begins, the first flocks appearing in western Oregon by mid-September and remaining until May (our earliest date, September 4; latest, May 20). Most of the birds return to the breeding grounds in March, only stragglers remaining later than mid-

April. While in western Oregon, the species frequents the lakes on Government and Sauvies Islands in the Columbia River as well as the grainfields of the Willamette Valley. It also occurs to some extent on the coast, though sight records might easily be confused with the White-cheeked Goose, to which form at least part of the early coastal records undoubtedly apply.

White-cheeked Goose:
Branta canadensis occidentalis (Baird)

Description.—"Like *canadensis*, but under parts darker, white cheek patches usually separated by black on throat; lower part of neck with a more or less distinct collar." (Bailey) *Downy young:* "The central crown patch and the upper parts of the body are lustrous 'brownish olive,' darkest on the head and rump; the lores are washed or striped with the same dark color, which surrounds the eye and extends in a post-ocular stripe down the neck; the under parts, including the forehead and the sides of the head and the neck, are dull yellowish or 'colonial buff,' washed on the sides of the head and neck with 'honey yellow' or 'yellow ocher,' paling on the belly and flanks to 'ivory yellow' and deepening on the breast to 'deep colonial buff'." (Bent) *Size:* "Length 35, wing 16.25–18.00, bill 1.40–1.65." (Bailey) *Nest:* A depression, lined with moss and down. *Eggs:* About 5, dull white, almost exactly like those of the Common Canada Goose.

Distribution.—*General:* Breeds along Alaska coast from Prince William Sound to Queen Charlotte Island and British Columbia. *In Oregon:* Winter visitor along coast, straggling inland, at least occasionally, to Willamette Valley.

The big dark-colored White-cheeked Goose breeds on the coast of Alaska and British Columbia and remains there through the winter to a large extent. There are two Oregon skins in the Jewett collection—the first taken at Netarts Bay (November 27, 1914), the second at McMinnville (November 15, 1931)—that match breeding birds from the Alaska coast, and we have occasionally seen big, dark geese, particularly in Tillamook and Lincoln Counties, that most probably are this form. Every winter on the Oregon coast as far south as Curry County, small flocks of geese appear that show a decided fondness for the offshore rocks, alighting on them and staying well out to sea, except during severe storms. The gunners along the coast know them as "honkers," but all that we have seen or had described to us have been much too dark for *canadensis* and are most probably this subspecies.

Lesser Canada Goose:
Branta canadensis leucopareia (Brandt)

Description.—A medium-sized goose, with a light breast and underbody, bill shorter for its depth and feet smaller in proportion to the tarsus than in *canadensis*. *Size:* Wing 14.90–17.45, bill 1.40–1.69, tarsus 3.06. *Nest and eggs:* As in *canadensis*.

Distribution.—*General:* Breeds on Arctic Coast from Alaska to Southampton Island. Winters from Washington to northern Mexico. *In Oregon:* Migrant and winter resident, appearing in October and remaining until April.

The Lesser Canada Goose, a smaller edition of the Common Canada Goose, has been reported in Oregon by various ornithologists, the first of whom was Townsend (1839). Johnson (1880), Anthony (1886), and Woodcock (1902) all recorded it as a common or abundant species in western Oregon, and Merrill (1888) listed it likewise for Klamath County. All of these records were for Hutchins's Goose but are now to be referred to the above subspecies, as in the latest revision of this puzzling group the name *hutchinsi* has been restricted to the form breeding in eastern Arctic America and migrating through the Mississippi Valley. This is the medium-sized goose of the *canadensis* group that migrates commonly through eastern Oregon. It is one of the most abundant species on the Columbia River near Arlington and an important part of the great goose flocks in Harney, Lake, and Klamath Counties (earliest date, October 16, Multnomah County; latest, April 19, Klamath County). Comparatively few geese have been killed in western Oregon in recent years, and therefore its present status in that territory is somewhat doubtful, but it undoubtedly still occurs in small numbers among the wintering bands of geese there. Walker collected one at Blaine, Tillamook County, April 16, 1923, and Jewett, one at Netarts, December 29, 1929. It usually winters on the Columbia River above The Dalles, feeding out over the wheatfields in the morning and evening and resting on the gravel bars during the day.

One of the impressive waterfowl spectacles still left to us is the sight of great bands of these and other geese leaving their resting grounds on the river. In the early morning light, one flock leads the way, and then for many minutes flock after flock takes wing, rising in great circles until sufficient altitude is attained to cross over the bluffs to the stubble fields. In a short time the shrill clamor of the circling flocks dies away and the river is deserted. Later in the day the geese drift back, a flock at a time, to sit on the gravel bars preening their feathers or to float lazily in the slack water close inshore. In the late afternoon the process is repeated, the feeding birds sometimes returning long after sunset. From October to April it is often possible to count many thousands of these great birds from the Columbia Highway—anywhere from The Dalles to Umatilla—all the equipment necessary being a pair of good binoculars and the will to stop the car at points commanding a view of the stream.

Cackling Goose:
Branta canadensis minima Ridgway

Description.—A small dark form of the *canadensis* group, very similar to *B. c. occidentalis*. *Downy young:* "Exactly like that of *occidentalis*." (Bent) *Size:* "Length 23–25, wing 13.60–14.50, bill .95–1.15." (Bailey) *Nest:* A depression, lined with grass and down. *Eggs:* 4 to 7, dull white to cream white.

Distribution.—*General:* Breeds on coast of northwestern Alaska. Winters mainly in Sacramento and San Joaquin Valleys of California. *In Oregon:* Abundant migrant with perhaps occasional wintering flocks.

THE CACKLING GOOSE, the smallest of the *canadensis* group, is an abundant migrant, particularly in Klamath County and the adjoining area about Tule Lake, California, a great goose concentration area, where at times it equals in numbers any other species present. Merrill (1888) listed it as an abundant migrant at Fort Klamath, which is the first record of it as an Oregon bird, and Willett (1919) reported it as a common spring migrant at Malheur Lake. None of the numerous men who have worked the State in recent years mention it. Woodcock, Anthony, and Johnson overlooked it entirely in western Oregon, though at present it is a regular migrant there and has been noted by Jewett (1914b) as wintering on Netarts Bay. Our earliest date is October 24 (Washington County); our latest, April 30 (Jackson County).

In addition to its small size and dark color, this species has a distinctive high-pitched call, resembling the syllables *luk-luk*, many times repeated, that is recognized by many hunters who, in various localities, call it "China Goose," "Cackler," "Cack," or "Squealer." The birds fly swiftly and often heedlessly, frequently diving headlong into decoys without the precautionary circling indulged in by the larger and more wary geese.

One of the most interesting papers yet published concerning this species and one that contains information of particular value to Oregon students is a report by Lincoln (1926b) on the banding of a great number of Cackling Geese on the Yukon Delta, Alaska, between July 14 and 31, 1924, and the record of the subsequent recapture of some of the banded individuals during the fall of 1924 and spring of 1925. (See Figure 2, p. 14.) Briefly, these recaptures indicate a migratory flight closely paralleling the coast line from the nesting grounds to the mouth of the Columbia River. From there the flight turns inland toward Tule Lake and the Sacramento Valley, which proved to be the wintering ground of these birds breeding in this area. Four of the banded birds were reported from Oregon during the first season as follows: Fort Stevens (October 28), Hillsboro (October 24), Tillamook (October 27), all in 1924, and Evans Creek, Jackson County (April 30) in 1925.

On April 27, 1933, at Grays Harbor, Washington, Gabrielson watched a great flight of dark *canadensis* type geese moving northward in a constant succession of good-sized flocks. Subsequent inquiries indicated that this same flight passed along the Columbia River between Portland, Oregon, and Kelso, Washington, on April 26 and 27. This flight was undoubtedly the main body of these and possibly other geese moving northward from Tule Lake, where this species finds a regular stopping point in both the spring and fall migrations, and where some of these geese winter, unless the water freezes solid, undoubtedly spreading out at times into the adjoining areas. It is strange that we have not detected this form at Arlington, where the Lesser Canada Goose is the chief species present. Neither of us has hunted in this area, but we have examined numerous geese killed there without finding a single "Cackler." At present we know it chiefly as a western Oregon bird that, curiously enough, is most abundant in the State in the Klamath area on the east side of the Cascades.

Black Brant:
Branta nigricans (Lawrence)

Description.—"*Adults:* Head entirely black, neck almost encircled by a broad white collar open behind; upper parts dark sooty brown; breast black, shading to dark slaty; anal region white. *Young:* white collar indistinct or wanting; larger wing coverts and secondaries broadly tipped with white." (Bailey) *Downy young:* "The downy young black brant is thickly covered with soft down in dark colors; the upper half of the head, including the lores, to a point a little below the eyes is 'fuscous' or 'benzo brown'; the chin is white; the back varies from 'benzo brown' to 'hair brown,' darkest on the rump; the flanks and chest shade from 'hair brown' to 'light drab,' fading off nearly to white on the belly and throat." (Bent) *Size:* "Length 22–29, wing 12.70–13.50, bill 1.20–1.35." (Bailey) *Nest:* A depression in the moss and grass of the tundra, lined with down. *Eggs:* 4 to 8, buff to cream.

Distribution.—*General:* Breeds on Arctic Coast and Islands of Siberia and Alaska to Coronation Gulf. Winters on Pacific Coast from Vancouver to Lower California. *In Oregon:* Common winter resident of coast. Appears inland as a straggler, if at all.

There has been a great deal of confusion in the minds of early observers as to the Black Brant on the inland waters of Oregon. Bendire (1877) reported it as an uncommon migrant seen several times in the hands of the Indians; Mearns (1879) recorded it from Fort Klamath on the authority of Dr. Henry McElderry, the post surgeon; Anthony (1886) considered it as occasional in spring and fall in Washington County; and Woodcock (1902) listed it as found inland at Dayton, Scio, and Elkton, on the authority of various observers; but so far as we can find, not one of these records is supported by a specimen. It is possible, of course, that in the earlier days of more water and a greater flight of waterfowl this maritime species did occasionally drift inland. Yet the confusion that exists throughout the country in inland records of the Black Brant leads us to seek another explanation.

The Little Cackling Goose (*Branta minima*), smallest and darkest member of the *canadensis* group, was not recognized as distinct until Ridgway described it in 1885. Inasmuch as it is much darker and quite distinct from either of the other two representatives of the group found inland, it is quite possible that these early records refer to that dark race rather than to the present species. This theory seems strengthened by the fact that Merrill in 1888 reported *B. c. minima* as a common species at Fort Klamath but made no mention of *B. nigricans*. However this may be, the facts today are that the Little Cackling Goose is still a common bird inland, whereas the Black Brant, known also as "China Goose," is strictly a maritime species that remains on the ocean and the salt-water bays.

The Black Brant, a late migrant, seldom appears in numbers on the Oregon coast until December or January. From then on, its numbers increase up to the time of its departure for the north in April. Our earliest record is November 25 (Tillamook County); latest, May 2 (Coos County). During its stay it remains at sea or in the bays that contain an abundance of eelgrass (*Zostera marina*), which makes up a large percentage of its diet. Yaquina, Netarts, and Tillamook are the favorite bays with the Black Brant, so far as our personal experience goes, and in the late winter great rafts of these geese can be seen congregated about the eelgrass patches in those waters.

Emperor Goose:
Philacte canagica (Sevastianoff)

DESCRIPTION.—"Bill small and not much elevated at base, mainly light colored, bluish or pinkish white above; pit of nostrils reaching feathers of forehead; feet orange. *Adults:* head and back of neck white or stained with rusty orange; chin and throat dusky or brownish black; rest of plumage, except white tail, bluish gray, each feather with a black bar and white tip. *Young:* similar to adult, but whole head dusky, specked with white on top." (Bailey) *Downy young:* "Mr. Blaauw (1916) says: 'The chick in down is of a beautiful pearl-gray, darkest on the head and upper side and lighter below. The legs and bill are black.' A larger downy young, about the size of a teal, in the United States National Museum, has probably faded some; the upper parts vary in color from 'bister' to 'buffy brown' and the under parts from 'smoke gray' to 'olive buff'." (Bent) *Size:* Length 26, wing 14.30–15.75, bill 1.40–1.65." (Bailey) *Nest:* On the ground. *Eggs:* About 5, white with fine pale-brown dots.

DISTRIBUTION.—*General:* Breeds on northwest coast of Alaska. Winters primarily in Aleutian Islands, straggling southward to California. *In Oregon:* More or less regular straggler to coast and inland points between October and mid-February.

THE BEAUTIFULLY marked Emperor Goose, the most striking of all the species that visit the State, was first found by Alex Walker, who took a specimen on December 31, 1920, at Netarts Bay. The second specimen was reported by Steele (1924) as taken near Eugene, October 7, 1923. Jewett has the third, which was obtained by C. E. Edner near Netarts on December 3, 1923. Since that time there have been a number of specimens from Lane, Lincoln, Multnomah, and Tillamook Counties. It has also been taken frequently in the Sacramento Valley and at Tule Lake. The number that drift south to Oregon seems to be increasing in recent years, at least more of them are being reported (earliest date, October 3; latest, February 17). The Emperor Geese usually arrive here as single birds mingling with other species or in small bands of three to six. The general bluish color and whitish head distinguish them from other geese, and they are consequently quickly noticed by any one who happens to kill one.

White-fronted Goose; Speckle Breast; Gray Goose: *Anser albifrons albifrons* (Scopoli)

DESCRIPTION.—"Bill comparatively low at base, yellow or orange; feet orange or reddish. *Adults:* face white, bordered with dusky; rest of head and neck, also shoulders and chest, dark gray; belly and sides black or spotted with black, becoming white posteriorly and on under tail coverts; back dusky gray. *Young:* without white face or black on belly." (Bailey) *Downy young:* "The colors of the upper parts, including the central crown, back, wings, rump, and flanks, vary from 'buffy olive' to 'ecru olive,' darkest on the crown and rump and palest on the upper back, with a yellowish sheen; there is a faint loral and postocular stripe of olive; on the remainder of the head and neck the colors shade from 'olive ocher' on the forehead, cheeks, and neck to 'colonial buff' on the throat; the colors on the under parts shade from 'mustard yellow' on the breast to 'citron yellow' on the belly." (Bent) *Size:* Length 27, wing 14.25–17.50, bill 1.80–2.35. (Bailey) *Nest:* A shallow depression, lined with grass, feathers, and down. *Eggs:* 4 to 7, light buff to pale pinkish white.

DISTRIBUTION.—*General:* Breeds from Yukon Valley east to Anderson River and also in Greenland, Iceland, and Siberia. Winters in United States from southern British Columbia and southern Illinois south to the Gulf and central Mexico. *In Oregon:* Common migrant and less abundant winter resident that arrives in September and remains until late April.

THE FIRST RECORDED occurrence of the White-fronted Goose in Oregon is Lewis and Clark's note (1814) that a few wintered in 1805–06 at the mouth of the Columbia. Newberry (1857), Kerry (1874), and Woodcock (1902) are among those who reported it as a wintering species within the State. It formerly remained in numbers in the Willamette Valley through the winter; but in recent years it has decreased and at present stays sporadically in small numbers during that season in the Willamette Valley and along the Columbia River near Portland. It is most abundant in October, November, March, and April (earliest date, September 2, Multnomah County; latest, May 18, Klamath County). It is now apparently rare on the coast, the only recent record being that of Alex Walker, who collected one in Tillamook County, September 15, 1921.

Most of the published records of this species refer to migrant birds in the four months mentioned above, although Merrill (1888) stated that 20 birds remained at Fort Klamath until June 3, 1887. Perhaps no better evidence of the former abundance of these and other waterfowl can be given than to quote Merrill's statement regarding the flight:

Very common in April, the main flight occurring between the 20th and the 30th, and many flocks stopping to feed in the grassy meadows bordering the marsh. The upper part of the valley is enclosed on the west and north by the main divide of the Cascade Mountains, and on the east by a spur from the same range, all averaging a height of over 6,500 feet. On stormy days, if the wind was not blowing from the south, Geese flying low up the valley had great difficulty in rising sufficiently to cross the abrupt divide, and most of them would return to the marsh and its vicinity to wait for a more favorable opportunity. At such times Geese of this and the next species [Canada Geese] gathered by thousands and afforded great sport. The immense numbers of these birds that migrate through Western Oregon cannot be appreciated until one has seen their spring flight, which, I am informed, extends in width from the coast inland about two hundred and fifty or three hundred miles. About fifty of this species were seen on the Marsh on May 23, and twenty on May 27 and June 3, after which none were observed; their remaining so late excited general remark among the settlers.

The Speckle Breast, or Gray Goose, is ardently sought by hunters of wild fowl, many of whom will let a shot at Snow or Cackling Geese pass if there is a possibility of a flock of "Specks" approaching their shooting blinds. These geese are usually fat while in Oregon and are ranked next to the Canada Goose, by discriminating hunters.

Lesser Snow Goose:
Chen hyperborea hyperborea (Pallas)

Description.—"*Adults:* A conspicuous hard, black plate along side of lower mandible; plumage pure white except for wing, which has black tip and gray patch; white of head and sometimes neck and breast washed or stained with rusty orange." (Bailey) *Downy young:* "In the small downy young snow goose, recently hatched, the color of the head shades from 'olive buff' above to 'pale olive buff' below, suffused with 'colonial buff' or pale yellow on the throat, forehead, and cheeks; the down on the back is quite glossy and appears 'hair brown,' 'light drab,' or 'light grayish olive' in different lights; the under parts are 'pale olive buff,' suffused on the breast and sides with pale yellow shades." (Bent) *Size:* "Length 23–28, wing 14.50–17.00, bill 1.95–2.30." (Bailey) *Nest:* A depression in the ground, lined with down. *Eggs:* 5 to 7, dull white or creamy white.

Distribution.—*General:* Breeds on Arctic Coast and islands to north. Winters from Mississippi Valley west and British Columbia south into Mexico. *In Oregon:* Migrant only, most abundant in October and November and again in March and April.

The Lesser Snow Goose is most abundant in Oregon east of the Cascades, but it appears also in numbers in the Willamette Valley and less commonly on the coast. It is not particularly sought by hunters in Oregon, as the meat is dark and the birds are usually thin when they arrive. Lewis and Clark (1814) first recorded it for the State, their expedition having found it at the mouth of the Columbia on January 2, 1806, and it has been noticed by practically every working ornithologist since. Johnson (1880) reported it as a common migrant in the Willamette Valley, and Woodcock (1902) as a rare migrant at Dayton.

Great flocks of these White, or Snow, Geese are familiar sights in eastern Oregon, where they are particularly abundant in Klamath, Lake, and Harney Counties. On the coast, several specimens are available from Tillamook and Lincoln Counties, and the birds are seen each season in those and other coastal counties. The main concentration areas in Oregon are Malheur, Warner, Abert, and Summer Lakes; and in California, Tule Lake (just across the State line). Our earliest fall date is October 17 (Multnomah County), but Dr. Hibbard has reported their arrival at

Burns as early as September 27; and our latest fall record is December 10 (Klamath County). Our earliest spring date is February 10 (Klamath County); our latest, April 27 (Multnomah County).

With the advent of freezing weather, if not before, the snowy clans move south into California, a few perhaps occasionally remaining in Oregon through the winter. Our latest fall date of December 10 and our earliest spring date of February 10 leave a comparatively short interval during which the birds might easily remain through mild winters. They winter in small numbers about Netarts, Tillamook, and Coos Bays and are also occasionally seen in migration over the Willamette Valley, seldom having stopped there in recent years. Jewett saw them on Government Island in April 1902, and Gabrielson several times noted them in the same month flying over his home east of Portland.

Ross's Goose:
Chen rossi (Cassin)

Description.—"*Adults:* Base of upper mandible often rough and warty; bill comparatively small and without black stripe along side; plumage as in *hyperborea*." (Bailey) *Downy young* [from birds raised in captivity]: "Mr. Blaauw (1903) describes the downy young as follows: 'The chicks are of a yellowish gray, darker on the upper side and lighter below, and have, what makes them most conspicuously beautiful, bright canary-yellow heads, with the most delicate grayish sheen over them, caused by the extremity of the longer down hairs being of that color. The bill is black, with a flesh-colored tip. A little spot in front of each eye is also blackish. The legs are olive green.' " (Bent) *Size:* "Length 20–26, wing 13.75–15.50, bill 1.50–1.70." (Bailey) *Nest:* Unknown. *Eggs:* Number unknown, those laid by captive birds 3 to 5, pure white.

Distribution.—*General:* Breeding range unknown. Winters in Sacramento and San Joaquin Valleys. *In Oregon:* Known only as rare straggler.

Ross's Goose, which is easily distinguished from the Lesser Snow Goose by its small size and the roughened warty area at the base of the bill, is listed in this State on the basis of two specimens. The first was reported by Bendire (1877), as follows:

> A single specimen obtained on Silvies River, Oregon, April 12, 1876. It appears to be a rare species, was shot out of a flock of twelve by Sergt. Kennedy of my company, and is now in the collection of the Museum of Comparative Zoology, Cambridge, Mass.

The second, from Adel, Lake County, was killed November 6, 1921, by Mr. W. S. Wyble, of that place, and presented to Jewett. It is evident that Oregon lies to the west of the main flight line of this little goose. It stops regularly at Great Falls, Montana, and winters in the northern Sacramento Valley, most of the records of its occurrence being in a direct line between these two points.

Common Mallard:
Anas platyrhynchos platyrhynchos (Linnaeus)

Description.—"*Male in winter and breeding plumage:* Four of the black upper tail coverts recurved; head and neck, down to white collar, rich iridescent green; chest dark chestnut brown; belly and sides gray; wing with iridescent violet green speculum bordered by black and white bars; rump and upper and lower tail coverts black. *Male in summer plumage:* Like female. *Female and immature:* Entire plumage variously mottled, scalloped, and streaked with dusky and buff, except for plain buffy chin and white under surface of wing; buff predominating on belly; wing as in male." (Bailey) *Downy young:* "The downy young mallard when first hatched, is richly colored; the upper parts, the crown and back, are 'sepia' or 'clove brown,' darkest on the crown; the under parts, including the sides of the head and a broad superciliary stripe, are napthalene yellow' more or less clouded, especially on the cheeks with 'honey yellow' or intermediate shades; there is a loral and postocular stripe and an auricular spot of 'clove brown'; four yellowish spots, two on the scapulars and two on the rump, relieve the color of the back." (Bent) *Size:* "Length 20–25, wing 10.25–12.00, bill 2.00–2.40." (Bailey) *Nest:* Usually on the ground near the edge of a slough or lake but occasionally at least in the timber some distance from the water; sometimes in trees, usually in a huge old crotch near the ground; generally well lined with down. *Eggs:* 8 to 12, occasionally more, greenish buff to nearly white.

Distribution.—*General:* In North America south to Virginia, Missouri, Kansas, New Mexico, and Lower California. Winters over practically entire continent. *In Oregon:* Permanent resident over entire State.

Of all the waterfowl native to North America, the Common Mallard (Plate 22, *A*), or "Greenhead," is undoubtedly our best known and most desirable game bird. Found over the entire northern hemisphere, it is universally distributed in North America from the Arctic southward to Virginia and Missouri during the breeding season, and over the entire continent where there is open water during the winter months. It is an exceedingly adaptable bird, accommodating itself to conditions found in almost any territory, so long as there is some water present. It breeds in tiny pot holes and swamps in the Mississippi Valley, in and about the great tule marshes of eastern Oregon, and along streams anywhere in the State. It has been recorded by practically every worker in our territory since Lewis and Clark (1814) noted it January 2, 1806, at the mouth of the Columbia.

In the eastern part of the State, as a usual thing, the Common Mallard builds an orthodox and regulation mallard nest on the ground, usually quite close to water, and lines the nest and covers the eggs carefully with the soft fluffy down from the female's breast. Egg dates vary from May 6 to June 10. In western Oregon, it accommodates itself to the timbered conditions and often builds its nest at the base of a huge tree, or even in the big crotch of an old Oregon maple, up to 10 or 12 feet from the ground. Despite this most unducklike behavior the mallard thrives under almost all conditions. During the summer, one is likely to run across a female with her little fleet of ducklings on any body of water, and in the winter,

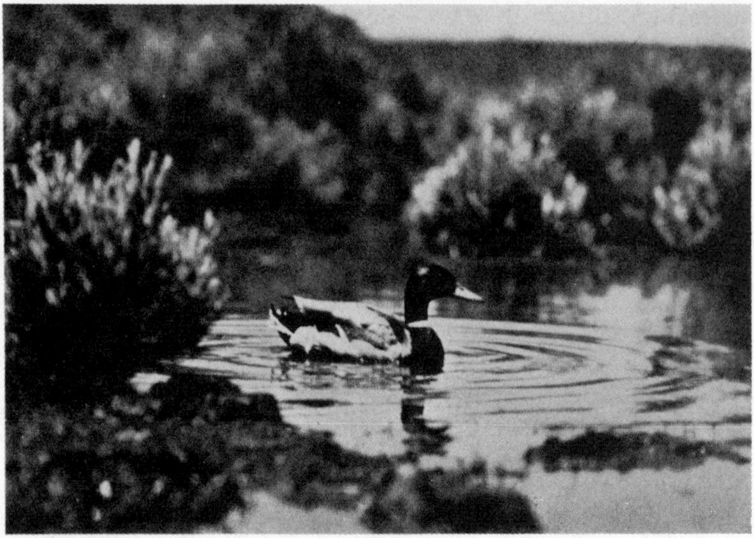

Plate 22, *A*. Mallard drake. (Photo by Wm. L. Finley and H. T. Bohlman.)

Plate 22, *B*. Baldpate. (Photo by Wm. L. Finley and H. T. Bohlman.)

wherever open water prevails, either from warm springs or from swiftly running water that prevents freezing. They often winter in numbers along the little willow-bordered streams of the eastern part of the State and can also be found on the streams in western Oregon, many of which are mere silvery threads through heavily timbered country.

One of the greatest game birds—wise, wary of decoys as a usual thing, unless on baited ground, swift of wing, and quick to take alarm—the mallard is the peer of any bird that flies. It can leap from the water straight into the air and get under way with a swiftness that entirely belies its weight. Despite the fact that it is usually picked by gunners to the exclusion of many other birds, its wariness and adaptability have enabled it to hold its own as well as any other species of waterfowl, and it is still one of the most abundant ducks. Whether it is the soft nasal *quank* of the male or the vigorous *quack*, *quack* of the female, its voice is better known and brings a greater thrill to wild-fowl hunters than the voice of any other duck.

A shallow-water feeder by preference, it gains most of its food by tipping up so that only the tail and feet project above the water, with its broad heavy bill scooping vegetable matter from the bottom. It makes a most excellent table bird, as it feeds almost entirely on vegetable matter, its food consisting of grain, which it has learned to glean expertly from wheatfields, and seeds, leaves, bulbs, bulblets, and roots of a great variety of water plants. The seeds and bulblets of various sedges and the seeds of pondweeds (*Potamogeton*) are particularly favored in Oregon. Insects also are taken but usually to a minor degree. Examination of many stomachs from various parts of the State indicates a very decided preference for seeds and other parts of aquatic plants.

Gadwall:
Chaulelasmus streperus (Linnaeus)

DESCRIPTION.—"*Adult male:* top of head with wide low crest; head and body gray, crossed with wavy lines of black and white; rump and upper and lower tail coverts black; wing marked with black, white, and bright brown; belly white. *Post-breeding plumage:* duller and more spotted below. *Adult female:* head without crest; head and neck finely specked with dusky on a buffy or whitish ground; chin and belly white; rest of body with feathers dusky, bordered with buff." (Bailey) *Downy young:* "The downy young of the gadwall is very much like that of the mallard, except that it is decidedly paler and less richly colored; the pale yellow of the under parts is more extensive on the sides and head extending nearly around the neck where it is separated by a narrow dark stripe on the nape, the light superciliary stripe is broader; the dark loral and postocular stripe is narrower and the auricular spot is hardly noticeable. The upper parts are 'bister,' deepening on the crown to 'bone brown'; the under parts are 'cartridge buff,' paler on the belly and deepening to 'cream buff' or 'Naples yellow' on the neck and sides of the head; the light patches on the scapulars and sides of the rump are buffy white." (Bent) *Size: Male,* length 19.25–21.75, wing 10.25–11.00, bill 1.60–1.75. *Female,* length 18, wing 10.00–10.25, bill 1.55–1.65." (Bailey) *Nest:* On the ground, well lined with dried vegetation and down. *Eggs:* 7 to 13, usually 10 to 12, dull creamy white.

Distribution.—*General:* In North America breeds from Hudson Bay west to Alberta and northern Saskatchewan south through Washington and Oregon to southern California, New Mexico, Kansas, northern Iowa, and Wisconsin. Winters west to Pacific Coast, east to Atlantic, and south to Mexico. *In Oregon:* Breeds commonly in the big tule marshes of Klamath, Lake, and Harney Counties. Winters somewhat sparingly on Snake River and other open waters of eastern Oregon, and on coast in limited numbers.

Although the Gadwall, or Gray Duck, as it is known locally in many places, is one of the most inconspicuously colored ducks, its wonderful feather patterns and soft gray tints make it a very beautiful bird in the hand. Bendire (1877) first recorded it for Oregon from Malheur Lake, where he found it breeding abundantly, and Merrill (1888) considered it not common at Fort Klamath. It is still a common breeding bird in the great tule marshes of eastern Oregon, particularly in Malheur, Harney, and Lake Counties. It also appears regularly in the Willamette Valley and on the coast in small numbers, where it can be found occasionally in the winter months.

The nest is a shallow hollow in the ground, lined with bits of weeds, sticks, grass, or any other vegetable debris that may be available, together with down from the breast of the female bird, and concealed as best it may be in the grass, tules, and other vegetation. The eggs are usually deposited in May (May 13) or June (June 1), together with those of the other nesting species of ducks, and the young are able to swim as soon as hatched.

The Gadwall, like the other species of ducks that generally nest in this territory, has a flightless season during the time the quill feathers are growing out after having been shed. It is one of nature's curious facts that ducks, among the speediest of all birds in the air, should have a period of 6 weeks to 2 months in which they lose entirely the power of flight. During this time they live in the tules and other vegetation, employing remarkable powers of concealing themselves and escaping observation by swimming under water. Following the nesting season, they disperse from the nesting grounds in little flocks, either composed entirely of Gadwalls or mixed with other species. It is a comparatively common sight to see a flock of several dozen Cinnamon Teal with two or three Gadwalls conspicuous in the group because of their larger size.

Despite its abundance in Oregon the Gadwall is one of the least known ducks to the average sportsman and gunner. Gunners in western Oregon do not know it at all, and we frequently receive specimens from them for identification. This may be accounted for by the facts that Gadwalls are often confused with the females and young of Pintail or Sprig ducks and that they are one of the earliest ducks to leave their nesting grounds and go south. There need be no confusion if the following distinctions are kept in mind: In the Pintail, the color patch on the wing, or speculum, is a bright green, whereas in the Gadwall it is snow white. The only other species of duck with a white speculum commonly found in Oregon is the Baldpate, or Widgeon, which might be confused with the Gadwall on this account. Both birds are about the same size and have about the same habits of flight, but the male Baldpate has a white crown and greenish sides to the head and fine speckling and dotting of the plumage. It is also more reddish on the back and lacks the beautiful gray and white pattern found on the neck and breast of the Gadwall.

Like the Common Mallard, the Gadwall is a lover of the shallows, where it also feeds by the tipping-up process, during which the heavy bill is vigorously engaged in sifting edible morsels from the debris on the bottom and gathering succulent bulblets or roots of water plants. These bottom-feeding ducks are all equipped with strainers on the side of the bill through which the mud of the bottom may be forced out and in which the seeds, bulblets, and other vegetable matter on which they feed may be retained. Foliage of many kinds of aquatic plants, small snails, seeds of many kinds, grain, acorns, and other vegetable matter make up their food supply. Numerous stomachs taken in Oregon and examined by the Biological Survey reveal a great preponderance of leaves, stems, and seeds of aquatic plants, such as pondweeds (*Potamogeton*), parrot-feathers (*Myriophyllum*), sedges, and smaller plants.

European Widgeon:
Mareca penelope (Linnaeus)

Description.—"*Adult male:* Bill blue with black tip; crown white or creamy; rest of head and neck rich russet brown, more or less specked with black; chest light vinaceous brown; back, rump, and sides gray crossed by fine wavy black and white lines; wing with green speculum framed in black, and bordered above by large white patch; under, and sides of upper, tail coverts, black. *Adult female:* head and neck thickly specked all over with dusky on buff; breast, sides, and back mottled with dusky and buff; speculum grayish, bordered above and below by narrow white tips to feathers. *Young male:* head and neck brown, thickly specked with black; breast and sides dull brown, back mottled dusky and brown. Length: 18–20, wing 10–11, bill 1.35–1.45." (Bailey)

Distribution.—Breeds entirely in Old World and appears on this continent only as irregular straggler.

The European Widgeon is a straggler in Oregon, as it is in other parts of North America. There are a number of records of it for the State. One, taken in Lane County, December 17, 1926, was seen by Jewett in a taxidermist's shop in Eugene. Three were obtained in Multnomah County: one on Government Island, January 18, 1903, and two on Sauvies Island December 22, 1918, and December 12, 1926. Alex Walker (1923) reported taking one on Netarts Bay, November 22, 1922. One bird was reported on several occasions on the little lake in Eastmoreland Golf Course at Portland during the winter, where Gabrielson saw it on December 27, 1931. It is possible that this species is more common than our records indicate, as it is only the most observant gunners who pick out these strange-looking birds.

Gunners should be on the watch for this rare bird. It can be distinguished from the American Widgeon, or Baldpate, as it is more commonly known on the west coast, by the russet-brown sides of the head of the male in contrast to the white crown and green sides of the American bird. Females are more difficult to distinguish but may be told by the fact that in the American bird the background is white, heavily streaked with a gray or grayish-brown color, whereas in the female of the European bird the streaking is on a buff background.

Baldpate:
Mareca americana (Gmelin)

Description.—"*Adult male:* Bill blue with black tip; crown white, bordered on sides and back with wide patch of metallic green; rest of head and neck finely specked with dusky over buffy; chest and sides grayish lavender or vinaceous, often barred and specked with dusky; belly white; back dark gray crossed with wavy lines of black, white, and lavender; speculum green, framed in velvety black; bordered above by large white patch; lower, and sides of upper, tail coverts, black. *Adult female:* head and neck finely specked with dusky on whitish ground, the dusky predominating on top of head; chest, sides, and back dull brown, mottled with blackish; belly white; wing with dull-black speculum bordered above and below by white." (Bailey) *Downy young:* "Above dark olive-brown, relieved by a spot of greenish buff on posterior border of each wing, one on each side of back, and one on each side of rump; top of head and hind-neck, dark olive, like back; rest of head and neck, with lower parts, pale olive-buff or fulvous, the side of the head with a dusky streak, extending from bill, through eye, to occiput." (Ridgway 1887) *Size:* "Length 18–22, wing 10.25–11.00, bill 1.30–1.50." (Bailey) *Nest:* Much like that of Gadwall, a slight depression in the ground, thickly lined with down. *Eggs:* 6 to 12, usually 9 to 11, pure creamy white.

Distribution.—*General:* Breeds in northwestern America from Alaska to Hudson Bay, south to northern California, Nevada, and Utah. Winters from northern States southward to Central America. *In Oregon:* Rather uncommon breeding species in eastern Oregon, being most abundant at Malheur. Common fall and spring migrant in eastern Oregon, with some scattered winter records in Klamath, Malheur, and Lake Counties. Abundant migrant and winter resident on coast and in Willamette Valley.

Although it is a breeding bird in eastern Oregon, the Baldpate, or American Widgeon (Plate 22, *B*), is best known to Oregonians as a spring and fall migrant throughout the State and as an abundant wintering species on the coast and in the valleys of coastal streams, where it congregates in huge flocks, occasionally doing some damage in grainfields or to newly seeded crops and to pastures, both by puddling the wet soil and by destroying the young vegetation. This has been particularly noticeable around Tillamook Bay, where the species at times becomes exceedingly abundant.

In eastern Oregon, it nests on Malheur Lake and possibly in other areas. Bendire (1877) first listed it as a breeding bird in Oregon when he was stationed in the Malheur Lake country in the seventies, and nests have occasionally been reported there since, notably by Cantwell when he was reservation warden at Malheur. He also reported it as nesting in Cold Springs Reservoir. It is most common in the great fall flights that appear on the coast from early October on, depending somewhat on the season. Our earliest date of arrival in the coast country is August 18, but as a usual thing it is well into October before numbers are present. It remains until mid-March, our latest date being April 24.

The Baldpate is a handsome bird with ruddy plumage checked with black lines, conspicuous white and green wings, and a head bordered with shiny green on the sides. Its call is a softly whistled *wheuw* repeated three times, somewhat similar to that of the Green-winged Teal. It is very swift of wing and behaves much like the teal. The wings, in flight, make a characteristic whistling sound that gunners soon learn to recognize. As a usual thing Baldpates are good table birds, but occasionally on the coastal lakes and bays the flesh becomes tainted or strong from some food that they get in abundance there.

Food of the Baldpate in Oregon is somewhat like that of other shallow-water ducks. The greater proportion of it is vegetable matter, composed largely of the seeds of water plants. Among the favorites found in stomachs taken at Klamath Falls are seeds of parrotfeather (*Myriophyllum*), pondweeds (*Potamogeton*), smartweed (*Polygonum amphibium*), and sedges (*Zannichellia palustris* and *Scirpus americanus*). A few water insects and remains of various kinds of snails and other small mollusks constitute most of the animal matter. The stomach of a bird taken on the Columbia River contained 2,800 seeds of a grass (*Eragrostis hypnoides*), 1,200 seeds of another grass (*Panicum*), and 750 seeds of a sedge (*Eleocharis*), which constituted 93 per cent of the stomach contents. The balance consisted of seeds of the buttercup (*Ranunculus*), and 80 seeds of the smartweed (*Polygonum lapathifolium*).

American Pintail:
Dafila acuta tzitzihoa (Linnaeus)

Description.—"A large duck, with long neck and long, sharp tail of 16 feathers; head not crested. *Adult male:* sides of head snuff brown, with a purple gloss; crown darker, back of neck blackish, a white stripe down side of neck; throat and under parts white; sides and upper parts gray crossed by wavy lines; wing slaty, with purple speculum bordered above by a line of buff, and below by white; tertials with broad stripes of velvety black and white; under tail coverts black. *Adult female:* gray, with head and neck finely specked, and under parts, including under surface of wing, finely mottled with dusky; back and wings more heavily mottled with black, brown, and buffy; wing without speculum, but greater coverts tipped with white." (Bailey) *Downy young:* "The downy young is grayer and browner than other young surface-feeding ducks and thus easily recognized. The crown is dark, rich 'clove brown'; a broad superciliary stripe of grayish white extends from the lores to the occiput; below this the side of the head is mainly grayish white, fading to pure white on the throat and chin, with a narrow postocular stripe of 'clove brown' and a paler and broader stripe of the same below it. The back is 'clove brown' darkest on the rump, with grayish or buffy tips on the down of the upper back; the rump and scapular spots are white, the latter sometimes elongated into stripes. The lower parts are grayish white, palest in the center. The chest, and sometimes the sides of the head, are suffused with pinkish buff, but never with yellow. The colors become duller and paler as the bird grows older." (Bent) *Size:* "*Male*, length 26–30, wing 10.25–11.20, bill 1.85–2.15, tail 7.25–9.50. *Female*, smaller, length 21.00–23.50, wing 9.60–10.10, bill 1.80, tail 4.50–5.00." (Bailey) *Nest:* Very similar to that of other ducks, a depression in the ground, lined with grass and feathers (Plate 23, *A*). *Eggs:* 6 to 12, pale greenish to olive buff, well covered with down as incubation proceeds.

DISTRIBUTION.—*General:* Found throughout most of northern hemisphere. In North America, breeds from Hudson Bay west to Pacific and south to Wisconsin, Iowa, Nebraska, Colorado, and southern California. *In Oregon:* Breeds regularly in eastern Oregon, abundant particularly in Klamath, Lake, and Harney Counties. Found throughout year.

THE SLIM, ELEGANT silhouettes of the American Pintails (Plate 23) are familiar figures of the air lanes wherever wild ducks congregate in Oregon. The long necks and elongated tail feathers of the males combine to form a distinctive outline that makes identification of the species possible at a distance. Added to this trimness of build are the soft grays, whites, and blacks in an intricate pattern delicately traced against contrasting background that make this one of the most beautiful ducks, though many are more brilliantly colored. Seen on the water, it has an elegance of carriage and movement—lacking in many waterfowl—comparable to the aristocratic lines and actions of a thoroughbred horse. It is hardy, alert, and shy, and because of its wide breeding range it has withstood the vicissitudes of agricultural development, drought, and overshooting better than any species, except the Common Mallard. It ranks next to the Common Mallard in importance as a game bird in the eyes of many sportsmen.

First recorded for Oregon by Townsend (1839) and noted by numerous observers since, it is one of the most abundant ducks found in the State. We have records for practically every county. Wherever there are suitable feeding grounds and open water in eastern Oregon a few will be found, and it is one of the first migrants to appear with the break-up of the ice in the frost-bound portions of the State. In eastern Oregon, most of the spring migrants arrive in March to remain until freezing weather in the

Plate 23, *A*. Female American Pintail on nest. (Photo by Wm. L. Finley and H. T. Bohlman.)

Plate 23, *B*. American Pintail drake. (Photo by Wm. L. Finley and H. T. Bohlman.)

fall, usually in November. It winters as far north as weather permits. It has been an abundant breeding species in the great alkaline marshes of southeastern Oregon and is still a regular nesting species in the remnants of those marshes.

It builds its nest beneath some small shrub or grassy tuft and deposits its 6 to 10 eggs. The female often sits exceedingly close, allowing an intruder to all but step on her before taking alarm. Typical nesting data are as follows: "Sycan Marsh, June 12, 1927, nest with seven eggs under a sage brush 300 yards from water" (Jewett); "Warner Lakes, May 21, 1932, nest with three eggs" (Jewett); "May 14, 1919, Round Lake, Klamath County, nest with six eggs" (Gabrielson); "June 16, 1926, several broods of young seen on Island Ranch, Harney County" (Gabrielson); "June 13, 1926, parents and young near Midland, Klamath County" (Gabrielson).

As soon as the young are able to fly, there is a marked movement among these ducks, and great bands appear on the high mountain lakes in early August (Minam Lake, Wallowa County, August 20, 1923; Kinney Lake, Wallowa County, August 21, 1930; and Diamond Lake, Douglas County, several August dates, Gabrielson). This dispersion of local ducks apparently coincides with or slightly precedes the first flight of northern birds, which is composed largely of this species. At least by mid-August, Pintails have become common birds, not only in the great breeding marshes and the mountain lakes, but on the bays and inlets on the coast.

The American Pintail feeds by tipping up, and it is an amusing spectacle to watch a group of them standing on their heads in shallow water, with the sharp tails pointing straight toward the zenith as they work the bottoms with their bills, searching out the seeds and tubers of the aquatic plants that furnish the bulk of their food.

A series of 14 stomachs collected in September, October, November, and December, at Klamath Falls, were filled mainly with seeds of *Hippuris vulgaris*, *Myriophyllum*, *Polygonum amphibium* and *P. aviculare*, *Scirpus americanus*, *Potamogeton* sp., *Eleocharis* sp., *Ranunculus* sp., *Cicuta* sp., *Portulaca*, *Menyanthes trifoliata*, *Amaranthus* sp., *Zannichellia palustris*, *Ruppia maritima*, *Naias flexilis*, and vegetative parts of the duckweed (*Lemna*), algae, *Chara* and *Potamogeton*. The animal matter consisted of fragments of various mollusks, crustaceans, beetles, and a variety of water insects, chiefly important as showing that such food is entirely acceptable. Only one stomach contained more than fragments of animal matter. It was filled with small mollusks, including 260 *Pisidium occidentale*, 19 *Pompholyx effusa*, 700 *Planorbis parvus*, 2 *Fluminicola Nuttaliana*, and fragments of *Valvata vireus*. In addition to this animal food, a few fragments of seeds of several plants had been taken, surely a full meal.

From west of the Cascades, one stomach from Sauvies Island and five from Netarts Bay were examined and found to be entirely or largely filled with animal matter. The Sauvies Island stomach was one-third filled with wheat, the balance of the food consisting of crane-fly and chironomid larvae, small crustaceans, snails, and dragonfly nymphs. The Netarts birds had taken snails and other mollusks as their main article of food, although one had fed heavily on eelgrass and another on clover (*Trifolium* sp.) and sedge (*Scirpus*) seeds. Caddisfly larvae also had been taken.

Green-winged Teal: *Nettion carolinense* (Gmelin)

Description.—"*Adult male:* Head light chestnut, forehead and chin blackish; a wide crescent of green and black inclosing eye and reaching to base of crest; breast buffy, spotted with black; back gray, shoulders crossed by white bar; shoulders and sides finely cross-lined with black and white; wing with green and black speculum, bordered above by buff and below by white; under tail coverts black, bordered by rich buff. *Adult female:* back, sides, and breast dusky, scalloped and mottled with buff; throat and belly whitish; base of wing slaty; wing with speculum as in male. *Young male:* belly white." (Bailey) *Downy young:* "The upper parts are mummy brown' or 'Prout's brown,' darkest on the crown and rump; the under parts shade from 'buckthorn brown' or 'clay color,' on the side of the head and throat, to 'cinnamon buff' or 'light buff,' on the breast and belly; the side of the head is distinctly marked by a broad loral and postocular stripe of dark brown and a similar auricular stripe below it, from the eye to the occiput; a broad superciliary stripe of buff extends from the bill to the occiput, but it is interrupted by an extension of the dark crown nearly or quite down to the eye; the color of the back is relieved by buffy spots on the thighs, scapulars, and wings." (Bent) *Size:* "Length 12.50–15.00, wing 6.25–7.40, bill 1.40–1.60." (Bailey) *Nest:* A shallow depression, usually well concealed in the grass, well lined with grass and weeds and protected with a cover of down. *Eggs:* 6 to 18, usually 10 to 12, dull white or cream colored.

Distribution.—*General:* Breeds over northern part of continent south to Gulf of St. Lawrence, southern Ontario, Wisconsin, northern Iowa, Nebraska, southern Colorado, New Mexico, Nevada, and central California. Winters in southern part of continent, most abundantly in southwestern United States and Mexico. *In Oregon:* Reported as breeding in Klamath Lake, Harney, and Washington Counties by early observers but known to us only as a migrant. In migration, one of the common ducks on all waters of State. Winters regularly and commonly on coast and on Columbia River, at least as far as Portland, and occasionally on open waters in eastern part of State.

The Green-winged Teal, the smallest of the ducks that visit Oregon, is popularly reported to be the fastest on the wing, and many are the stories told around duck clubs of the speed these birds are able to attain when really in a hurry. Townsend (1839) included it in his list of birds for this area. Anthony (1886) stated in his paper on the birds of Washington County that a few bred in that territory in the eighties. Bendire (1877) reported it as breeding in the Harney Valley. It has also been reported as breeding in the Klamath country by J. J. Furber, formerly warden of the Lower Klamath Bird Reservation, and as nesting near the

Warner Lakes region, by Prill, but we have not found it breeding during our years in the State.

This beautiful little bird appears in abundance in late September or early October in many sections of the State and remains to winter wherever there is open water available. It is one of the common wintering ducks on the Columbia River about Portland and is regularly found on all the larger bays and lakes of the coast. We have records for Umatilla and Klamath Counties, December 10, and for Wallowa County, near Enterprise, February 20. It remains well into the spring, although most of the flocks have departed by mid-April. Our earliest record of its fall appearance in numbers is August 18 (Klamath County); and the latest record on the west side of the Cascades, April 21 (Multnomah County). Our earliest fall record is August 17; our latest spring date, May 13 (both Lake County).

Although teal are not as noisy as some ducks, one of the characteristic sounds of the willow-grown lakes and ponds of the Columbia River bottoms is the soft throaty whistle of the little males that are quite talkative at times. Usually, however, they are rather quiet birds, spending hours at a time sitting motionless on the water or standing statuelike on some little point. They walk better than most ducks and can run quite rapidly. Like others of their immediate relatives, they can spring straight into the air from water or land for a surprising height and, when once launched, carry out aerial evolutions that are equaled only by those of some of the sandpipers. With bewildering speed they turn at right angles in full flight, dip straight down, or rise straight into the air. At such times they are as difficult to shoot as jacksnipes and for this reason are great favorites with many sportsmen. The sight of a small flock of these birds darting, swinging, and turning suddenly downward at almost right angles to drop into the water is one never to be forgotten by an out-of-doors enthusiast. Words cannot adequately describe the suddenness of their flight-direction changes or their swift downward rocketing, throwing their wings first to one side and then the other.

Their food is like that of most other shallow-water ducks. More than 90 per cent of it is vegetable matter, most of which, according to Biological Survey records, is comprised of seeds of sedges, pondweeds (*Potamogetons*), grass, smartweeds (*Polygonum*), duckweeds, and various other water plants.

Blue-winged Teal:

Querquedula discors (Linnaeus)

Description.—"*Adult male:* Sides of head slaty gray, with purple gloss; white crescent in front of eye bordered by black; under parts vinaceous, finely spotted with dusky; back scalloped and streaked with dusky and vinaceous; wing bright blue at base, middle coverts tipped with white and buffy, speculum iridescent green; under tail coverts black, base of tail with white patch on either side. *Adult female:* Crown mainly dusky, rest of head and neck speckled and streaked with dusky; back dusky; under parts gray, mottled with dusky; wing with lesser coverts blue, greater [coverts] tipped with white, speculum greenish. *Young:* Belly white, wing without green." (Bailey) *Downy young:* "In the downy young the colors of the upper parts vary from 'mummy brown' to 'Dresden brown,' darker on the crown and rump, lighter elsewhere, the down being much darker basally; the under parts are 'maize yellow,' shaded locally with 'buff yellow,' due to the darker tips of the down; the sides of the head are 'yellow ocher' or pale 'buckthorn brown' in young birds, but these colors soon fade and all the colors grow paler as the young bird increases in size. The color pattern of the head consists of a dark-brown central crown bordered on each side by a broad superciliary stripe of yellow ocher, below which is a narrow postocular stripe, a loral patch, and an auricular spot of dusky. On the back the brown is broken by four large spots of yellowish, one on each side of the rump and one on each scapular region." (Bent) *Size:* "Length 14.50–16.00, wing 7.00–7.50, bill 1.40–1.65." (Bailey) *Nest:* A shallow depression in the ground or in the reeds, well lined with fine grasses and down. More down is added as incubation advances until eggs are well concealed when female leaves the nest. *Eggs:* 6 to 15, usually 10 to 12, dull white to creamy white.

DISTRIBUTION.—*General:* Breeds mainly in central North America from central British Columbia, Great Slave Lake, northern Saskatchewan and Ontario south to Louisiana, Oklahoma, Texas, and New Mexico. Winters in southern States south to South America. *In Oregon:* Regular but not common visitor to eastern Oregon; probably breeds each year in small numbers.

THE STRIKINGLY marked little Blue-winged Teal is primarily a bird of the great interior section of the continent, being the most abundant breeding duck of the upper Mississppi Valley. It is a beautiful and showy little species, and it is to be regretted that it is not more common in the State. It is a regular, but not common, summer resident of eastern Oregon and has been listed from there in small numbers by most observers. It is probable that many of the records given by casual observers for eastern Oregon in reality referred to the Cinnamon Teal, as the conspicuous light-blue patch on the wings is common to both species and not diagnostic for the Blue-winged Teal, as is frequently assumed.

Newberry (1857) credited it with being a common species in Oregon. Bendire (1877) reported it from Camp Harney as a rare species, nonbreeding. Various other early travelers listed it as found in eastern Oregon. Willett (1919), while warden at Malheur Lake, reported it on June 13; and various men stationed as wardens at Malheur and Klamath Lakes have listed occasional individuals. Prill (1922a) reported one nest with eggs found May 25 in the Warner Valley. We have seen it in Lake, Harney, and Klamath Counties more or less regularly during April, May, and June. Our earliest record is April 18 (Klamath County); our latest, June 16 (Harney County). Records for later dates would be difficult to substantiate unless birds were taken, as in the eclipse plumage it is very difficult to distinguish these birds in the field. There is one specimen in the Gabrielson collection taken at Klamath Falls April 18, 1924, and

Plate 24, *A.* Nest and eggs of Cinnamon Teal. (Photo by Alex Walker.)

Plate 24, *B.* Nest and eggs of Redhead. (Photo by Alex Walker.)

George Tonkin, who was familiar with the species in eastern United States, reported a pair seen at Baldock Slough, near Baker, on May 19, 1924. Woodcock (1902) reported it as found near Dayton and Scio; Prill (1895a) listed it as wintering near Sweet Home, Linn County; and Overton Dowell, Jr., saw five on Mercer Lake, Lane County, June 29, 1931, and collected specimens to confirm the record, the only western Oregon skins known to us.

It would be well for sportsmen, particularly in western Oregon, where Cinnamon Teal, both males and females, are killed frequently, to be on the lookout for the beautiful little Blue-winged Teal. We know of no way in which the females of the two species may be distinguished by gunners, as they are inseparable in the field and can only with difficulty be distinguished in the hand; the only differences being comparative ones of shade. The male Blue-winged Teal are well marked, however, and could be readily picked out by any one at all familiar with the other species of teal. The adult males are easily distinguished from the adult Cinnamon Teal males by their much paler coloration—the breast in particular being a bright, buffy brown marked with round black polkadots instead of the bright cinnamon red—and by the conspicuous white crescent on the side of the head that distinguishes this duck from all others.

We have no Oregon food notes, but the general feeding habits are similar to those of the Cinnamon Teal.

Cinnamon Teal:
Querquedula cyanoptera (Vieillot)

Description.—"*Adult male:* Head, neck, breast, and sides bright cinnamon brown, fading to dull brown on belly and becoming blackish on chin and crown; back dusky, shoulders spotted and barred with dusky and brown; wing with lesser coverts light blue, middle coverts tipped with white, speculum green, tertials broadly striped with blue, greenish black, and rich buff. *Adult female:* crown dusky, rest of head and neck finely specked and streaked with dusky on buffy ground; rest of upper parts dusky scalloped with buff; wing with large blue patch; under parts brownish, mottled with dusky. *Young:* like female, but more streaked below." (Bailey) *Downy young:* "The downy young of the Cinnamon Teal is 'mummy brown' above, darkest on the crown, and the tips of the down are 'buffy citrine,' producing a golden olivaceous appearance on the back; the forehead, the sides of the head, including a broad superciliary stripe, and the under parts vary from 'mustard yellow' on the head to 'amber yellow' on the breast and 'napthaline yellow' on the belly; there is a narrow stripe of dark brown on the side of the head; and the color of the back is relieved by a yellowish spot on each side of the rump, scapular region, and edge of the wing." (Bent) *Size:* "Length 15.50–17.00, wing 7.20–7.25, bill 1.65–1.85." (Bailey) *Nest:* A shallow depression in the ground, often at considerable distance from the water, lined with grass and vegetable debris and quantities of dark-colored down. *Eggs:* 6 to 14, usually 10 to 12, pale buff to pure white (Plate 24, *A*).

Distribution.—*General:* Breeds in western North America from western Montana, eastern Wyoming, western Kansas, and central Texas west to southern British Columbia, northwestern Washington, central Oregon, and central California.

Winters in southwestern United States and Mexico. *In Oregon:* Breeds commonly in great marshes of Klamath, Lake, and Harney Counties and more sparingly in marshes of Malheur, Union, Umatilla, Crook, and probably other counties of eastern Oregon.

THE BRIGHTLY marked and showy little Cinnamon Teal is as common in eastern Oregon as the preceding species is rare. Townsend (1839) first noted it in Oregon, and since his time nearly every ornithologist who has visited the eastern part of the State has reported it as a nesting species (Plate 24, *A*). Walker (1917b) found it breeding in Paulina Marsh in northern Klamath County. It is an abundant summer resident that nests in May and June, our earliest date of arrival being April 2 (Lake County). Stragglers and small flocks remain until November, or occasionally even into the winter, our latest record being December 15 (Malheur County).

In May, June, and early July every roadside pond and water-filled ditch in eastern Oregon is likely to display some of these very beautiful ducks. In districts where not molested at this season they become very tame and frequently allow a car to drive past without disturbing them in their feeding in roadside ditches. Most of the eggs are laid in May or early June, and fleets of infant ducklings are common sights on all of the ponds, large or small, during July and early August. When the young are first able to fly they are exceedingly reckless in their behavior and easily killed by out-of-season gunners along the roadside. As these birds leave comparatively early in the season, most of them being gone within a few days after October 1, they do not suffer greatly from hunters in this State, and any decrease in the numbers of breeding birds, except that caused by destruction of their nesting grounds, must be laid to gunners farther south.

Cinnamon Teal, like the Green-winged Teal, are surprisingly swift on the wing and are exceeded only by that species in their ability to maneuver in the air. They are very quiet, the only note reported by most observers being a very matter of fact *quack* given by the female. The males are among the most brilliantly colored of all our ducks, and the females, in their demure gray plumage and showy blue-tinted wings, furnish effective foils for their brilliant mates.

Food of the Cinnamon Teal, like that of related species, is largely vegetable matter. Various species of pondweeds, sedges, grass, and smartweeds and other miscellaneous water and land plants furnish the bulk of it. Such animal matter as is taken consists of insects, mollusks, and miscellaneous items.

Shoveller:
Spatula clypeata (Linnaeus)

DESCRIPTION.—"Bill long, much widened toward end; the long, fine comb-like teeth conspicuous along side of closed bill. *Adult male:* head and neck black, glossed on sides and back with green; wing coverts light blue with a white bar; scapulars streaked with blue, white, and black; speculum green; chest white, belly chestnut; bill black, feet orange. *Adult female:* plumage mainly spotted and streaked with dusky and brown; wing as in the male but duller." (Bailey) *Downy young:* "Even when first hatched the young shoveller's bill is decidedly longer and more spatulate than that of the young mallard, and it grows amazingly fast, so that when two weeks old there is no difficulty in identifying the species. The color of the downy young above varies from 'olive brown,' or 'sepia,' to 'buffy brown,' darker on the crown, which is 'clove brown' or 'olive brown'; the color of the back extends far down onto the sides of the chest and on the flanks. The under parts vary from 'maize yellow' or 'cream buff' to 'cartridge buff' or 'ivory yellow'; this color deepens to 'chamois' on the cheeks. There is a stripe of 'olive brown' through the eye, including the loral and postocular region, also an auricular spot of the same. There is a light buffy spot on each side of the back, behind the wings, and one on each side of the rump. The buffy or chamois colored stripes above the eyes are well marked and often confluent on the forehead." (Bent) *Size:* "Length 17–21, wing 9–10, bill 2.60–2.90, width of bill at the base .60, near end 1.10–1.20." (Bailey) *Nest:* Like that of other ducks of its kind, on the ground in grass or under bushes or trees, made of grass or other vegetation and lined and covered with down. *Eggs:* 9 to 14, olive greenish to buff.

Distribution.—*General:* Breeds from Alaska to west coast of Hudson Bay and central New York, south to Indiana, northern Iowa, Kansas, New Mexico, Arizona, and southern California. Winters from British Columbia on coast and in interior from southern California, Arizona, New Mexico, central Texas, and southern Mississippi Valley to South America. *In Oregon:* Breeds regularly in eastern Oregon, mostly in Klamath, Lake, and Harney Counties. Appears on west side of Cascades during migrations.

The Shoveller, or "Spoonbill" or "Spoony," as it is known among lovers of the duck marshes, is, in the male, one of our most brilliantly colored native ducks and at the same time one of our most grotesque looking. The striking markings of the male, with white and chestnut red and bright blue in the plumage, are all obscured by the huge spoon bill, which is almost twice as wide at the upper end as at the base. In watching their flight, an observer constantly expects to see these birds tipped downward, head over heels, by the weight of the huge bills, and one wonders how they manage to keep their feet down and their heads up when in the water. Awkward as the bill appears, however, it is a very useful implement, as it is edged with fine, comblike teeth that act as a strainer for sifting out the mud from the seeds and bulblets on which this duck delights to feed.

The Spoonbill is an abundant summer resident of the great eastern Oregon marshes. As it loves warm weather, it is one of the later ducks to arrive, usually appearing in numbers in April or early May. Our earliest record is March 22 (Lake County); and our latest, December 10 (Klamath County). The Shoveller population is not at its height, however, until well into April, and it becomes increasingly scanty after mid-September. Townsend (1839) first listed the species for the State, and every ornithological observer who has visited eastern Oregon since has commented on its presence. It is a regular nesting species on the Malheur

Lake Refuge, on Klamath and Warner Lakes, and possibly on many other small swamps east of the Cascades. Its nest, similar to other duck nests, is made on the ground, frequently at some distance from the water's edge, and is well concealed by the grass or low bushes. The 10 or 12 pale buff to pale-greenish eggs are laid in the shallow depression, which is lined with vegetable matter and with down from the mother's breast. As incubation progresses, the amount of down is increased until the eggs are well covered and concealed by it during the parent bird's absence from the nest.

In western Oregon, where the Shoveller appears in migration, it is most common in November, so far as our own rather deficient records go, and occasionally at least spends the winter on the Columbia River or the larger bays of the coast. It is fairly common in the vicinity of Portland during the fall hunting season and has wintered there on Reed College Lake in the Eastmoreland Golf Course.

Although this species feeds by tipping up, it can, on occasion, swim well under water. A wounded female observed by Gabrielson in a small, clear pond repeatedly crossed the pond under water and several times endeavored to conceal herself in the vegetable matter at the bottom by grasping a stem with her bill. When compelled to rise to the surface for air, only the tip of the bill was protruded. Gabrielson concealed himself and watched for some time; when the bird thought herself unobserved, she swam away down stream so low in the water that only the very top of the back and the end of the bill projected above the surface.

Shovellers are not generally regarded as good table birds in this territory, as they are frequently in poor flesh during the hunting season. In other sections of the country they are rated much higher. Their food consists of buds and shoots of young water plants, species of other vegetable matter, and a great variety of small aquatic worms, insects, snails, tadpoles, and other animal matter frequently strained from the mud and debris of the bottom by their specially adapted big bills.

Wood Duck:
Aix sponsa (Linnaeus)

Description.—"Bill narrow, higher than wide at base. Both sexes with drooping crests. *Adult male:* bill marked with black, white, red, and yellow; head and crest brilliant purple and green, with white stripes; throat white; chest rich chestnut, with rows of white triangles; sides gray, with black and white bars and crescents; shoulder crossed by black and white bars; rest of upper parts black, varied with rich iridescent colors. *Adult female:* head dull grayish, glossed with green on crest and crown; sides of head and throat white; chest brown, belly white; back richly glossed grayish brown." (Bailey) *Downy young:* "Much darker above and paler below than the young mallard; the lower mandible and the smaller tip of the upper mandible are of a rich yellowish shade, which will serve to distinguish it from other ducks. The crown is a very deep rich 'seal brown' or 'bone brown,' or halfway between these colors and black; a stripe of the same color extends from the eye to the dark color of the occiput and there is a lighter auricular spot; the back shades from 'bister' anteriorly to the same color as the crown posteriorly, the hind neck is of a darker shade of 'bister'; the sides of the head and neck, including a superciliary stripe and the lores are 'cream color' shaded locally with 'Naples yellow'; the throat and under parts are 'ivory yellow' to 'Marguerite yellow,' the colors of the upper and under parts mingling on the sides; there is a pale yellowish spot on each wing and on each side of the rump." (Bent) *Size:* "*Male*, length 19.00–20.50; wing 9.00–9.50; bill 1.40." (Bailey) *Nest:* A natural cavity in a tree, lined with down. *Eggs:* 8 to 14, creamy white.

Distribution.—*General:* Breeds from British Columbia, northern Montana, Manitoba, Ontario, and Labrador south to West Indies and southern United States. Winters largely in southern part of range. *In Oregon:* Mainly west of Cascades where it is abundant summer resident and common winter species. Much less common in eastern Oregon, but found at least in John Day Valley and Klamath Basin at present and formerly in Harney Valley.

Every student of ornithology in this State since Townsend published his observations in 1839 has noted the strikingly colored Wood Duck. Bendire (1877) reported it as a rare resident of the Harney Valley in 1876, and both Mearns (1879) and Merrill (1888) reported it from the Klamath Valley. Baird (1858) reported it from The Dalles in February 1855. This and Merrill's report (1888) of a flock of six that frequented the head of Squaw Creek just outside the fort and of a specimen shot at Fort Klamath on January 29 are the only winter records of this species in eastern Oregon, although it is a permanent resident west of the Cascades.

We have records extending from Curry to Multnomah County and including every month. According to Jewett's records, by 1912 the Wood Duck had become a rare species along the Columbia River, but since that time it has increased until it is today an exceedingly common species not only along that river but in the other wooded river bottoms of the State. It has become so numerous, in fact, that some gunners complain bitterly about the amount of wheat eaten by the "woodies" in their baiting grounds. Although the species is found throughout the wooded areas of the State, in our experience Sauvies Island and Carleton Lake are the two great concentration points. There these ducks frequently may be seen by the hundreds, and one seldom visits either area without listing them.

During the summer, although common, these ducks do not attract a great deal of attention from the average observer, as they stay in scattered pairs along the brush-grown streams and ponds where it is easy to escape detection. In fact, if it were not for their funny high-pitched squeals as they dart through the trees or circle over the treetops, they would be noticed very infrequently by most observers. In the fall and winter months, they gather in small bands that frequent the more open ponds, where the gaudy drakes and their softly beautiful mates become a conspicuous element in the waterfowl population.

Probably no single feature of bird life has provoked more discussion than this duck's habit of nesting in trees, sometimes 30 or 40 feet above the ground. How does it get the young down? Various observers have reported seeing them carried down in the parent's bill or on her back. Others report that the young flutter down to the water or ground, as the case may be, using their wings to break the force of the descent. Bent (1923), who has spent a great deal of time investigating the habits and behavior of waterfowl, believes the latter to be the usual method and that carrying is resorted to only in unusual cases. Gabrielson knows of a pair of Wood Ducks that has nested for several years in an Oregon ash on Sauvies Island but he has never been fortunate enough to witness the ceremony of getting the young to the water. As the tree in question is on the water's edge and the cavity not more than 15 feet above the surface, it probably presents no special problem to an anxious mother.

Studies by the Biological Survey show that this duck feeds on a great variety of vegetable food. It not only takes the seeds and vegetative parts of many water plants commonly eaten by other ducks but shows a fondness for acorns, beechnuts, pecans, and other nuts. It also takes a small proportion (less than 10 per cent) of animal food, consisting chiefly of dragonflies, damsel flies, grasshoppers, crickets, beetles, flies, and other miscellaneous matter. One Oregon stomach from Klamath Falls was filled with seeds of *Myriophyllum* and seeds and vegetative parts of *Hippuris vulgaris*, two common water plants of this region. A second stomach, from Portland, contained seeds of smartweed (*Polygonum hydropiper*), *Triglochin maritima*, snowberry (*Symphoricarpos*), and fragments of several insects.

Redhead:
Nyroca americana (Eyton)

Description.—"Bill little more than twice as long as wide. *Adult male:* whole head and neck bright reddish chestnut; shoulders and chest black; belly white; sides and back uniform gray, with fine lines of black and ashy; tail and feathers around base black. *Adult female:* plumage dull grayish brown except for whitish chin, throat, and belly." (Bailey) *Downy young:* "The downy young is quite different from other ducklings, being more uniformly colored with less contrast between the light and dark areas. The upper parts, including the crown, back, rump, and tail are 'light brownish olive,' but the deep color of the basal portion of the down is much concealed by the light yellowish tips; the side of the head and neck, including the forehead and a broad stripe above the eye, are 'olive-ocher' paling to 'colonial buff' on the throat and chin; the remainder of the under parts is 'colonial buff' with deeper shadings; there are shadings of 'chamois' on the sides of the head and neck, but no conspicuous dark markings; in some specimens there are suffusions of brighter yellow in all of the lighter-colored parts, such as amber-yellow' or 'citron yellow'; there is a yellowish spot on each of the scapulars and on each side of the rump. All of the colors become paler and duller as the duckling increases in size." (Bent) *Size:* "Length 17–21, wing 8.50–9.25, bill 2.05–2.25, width of bill .75–.85." (Bailey) *Nest:* On marshy ground or on floating platforms of reeds in shallow water, built of grasses and weeds and lined with down. *Eggs:* From 6 to 22, usually between 10 and 15, grayish white or pale olive (Plate 24, *B*).

DISTRIBUTION.—*General:* Breeds from central British Columbia, central Alberta, central Saskatchewan, and central Manitoba south to southern Michigan, Wisconsin, southern Minnesota, central Nebraska, southern Colorado, New Mexico, and southern California. Winters mainly in southern United States. *In Oregon:* Present breeding range restricted to Malheur, Harney, Lake, and Klamath Counties, much less common there than formerly. Formerly reported an abundant migrant and winter resident of western Oregon, now of only local occurrence west of Cascades.

THE REDHEAD, once one of the common breeding ducks of Oregon, particularly in the ponds of Klamath County, has suffered as much from the combination of long-continued drought and agricultural development of its summer home as any species found in the State and must now be ranked as one of our rapidly vanishing species of waterfowl. Baird (1858) first recorded it for Oregon at The Dalles, January 7, 1885. Every ornithologist who has since visited the great interior country has commented on its presence either as a nesting or migrant species. Anthony (Bailey 1902) reported it as wintering on the Columbia. Bohlman (Woodcock 1902) reported a specimen taken at Ross Island in the Willamette, November 28, 1897, and there is a specimen in the University of Washington collection taken by Rev. P. S. Knight at Salem, April 16, 1874.

The species was formerly common from April to September, breeding in numbers in the shallow ponds and lakes of Klamath and Malheur Counties, and it still breeds in much reduced numbers in the fresh-water ponds and lakes of the southern half of the State east of the Cascades, where water conditions are favorable, being somewhat more abundant in Klamath than in Lake and Harney Counties and relatively scarce in Malheur, where it is a comparatively rare summer resident of the Cow Lakes district. In Klamath, Lake, and Harney Counties it has been regularly found on the deeper ponds. The earliest date we have is March 11; the latest, October 7, both Klamath County. Jewett found a nest containing 10 eggs on Miller Island in Klamath County, June 27, 1925, and reported one containing 6 eggs at Malheur Lake, June 10, 1922, and one with 9 eggs, June 4, 1926. Prill recorded sets of from 8 to 10 eggs at Pelican Lake, Lake County, in May and June 1922. Visitors to these ponds in July and August are almost invariably rewarded by the sight of fleets of sooty-looking ducklings accompanied by an equally sooty, anxious mother. By mid-August, the young are well feathered and able to fly but, where unmolested, remain tame and unsuspicious up to the opening of the shooting season. We have no winter records from eastern Oregon in our own notes, but in the Biological Survey notes Furber reported the species at Klamath, December 18, 1910, and January 14, 1913, and Cantwell, at Malheur, December 8, 1914.

In western Oregon, this duck is seldom reported by present-day sportsmen, and although Johnson (1880) formerly recorded it as an abundant migrant and winter resident of western Oregon, it is now of only local occurrence west of the Cascades. Milton Furness found a few wintering near Scappoose in January 1935. He saw them on several dates, and on January 30, 1935, Gabrielson visited the area with him, on which occasion four adult males were seen at close range. It is painfully apparent that so far as Oregon is concerned this species is rapidly declining in numbers and may soon be classed as one of our rarer waterfowl.

All the three Oregon stomachs available for examination were from Klamath Falls, and they reveal that this diving duck feeds on much the same plants in this immediate vicinity as do the shallow-water ducks. It is probable that in so acting the Redhead makes a virtue of necessity, as no other food supply is easily available. The stomachs, all taken in late October and early November, contained 97 per cent vegetable matter and only 3 per cent animal matter. Seeds of pondweed (*Potamogeton*), sedge (*Scirpus americanus*), parrotfeather (*Myriophyllum spicatum*), and marestail (*Hippuris vulgaris*) were the principal foods.

Ring-necked Duck; Black-Jack; Black Duck:
Nyroca collaris (Donovan)

Description.—"Bill narrower than in *Nyroca*[1] *marila*, black, crossed by blue band near end. *Adult male:* head, except small white triangle on chin, black, glossed with rich purple; neck encircled by narrow chestnut collar; chest and back black, back glossed with greenish; wings blackish, with blue gray speculum; middle of belly buffy white; sides finely vermiculated gray; crissum black. *Adult female:* throat and face whitish, rest of head, neck, and upper parts dull brown; wing with blue gray speculum as in male; chest and sides fulvous, belly white." (Bailey) *Downy young:* "The whole head, except the posterior half of the crown, is yellowish, shading from 'chamois' or 'cream buff' on the cheeks and auriculars to 'colonial buff' on the throat; the posterior half of the crown and the occiput are 'bister,' nearly separated by points of yellow from a broad band of 'bister' which extends down the hind neck to the back; narrow dusky postocular streaks are faintly suggested; the dark color of the back changes gradually from 'sepia' anteriorly to 'bister' posteriorly; the under parts are 'ivory yellow' tinged with 'cream buff'; there are two large scapular patches, two narrow wing stripes and two small rump patches of 'cream buff'; there is also a narrow streak of the same color in the center of the upper back." (Bent) *Size:* "Length 15.50–18.00, wing 8.00, bill 1.75–2.00." (Bailey) *Nest:* Usually on a mass of dead rushes in shallow water, lined with down. *Eggs:* 8 to 12, dark olive drab and indistinguishable from those of the Lesser Scaup.

Distribution.—*General:* Breeds from northern Saskatchewan, western Ontario, and southern Wisconsin west to northeastern California, eastern Oregon, and southern British Columbia and north to Mackenzie Valley and Athabaska Lake. *In Oregon:* In winter found regularly in western Oregon and in Klamath and Malheur Counties in eastern Oregon, at least where open water is found.

The Ring-necked Duck is a squarely built, short-necked species, similar in appearance and habits to the scaups, with which it frequently associates. Many observers have failed to differentiate the three species, so that our knowledge of the relative abundance of each is meager. Some

[1] *Nyroca*=*Aythya*.

gunners group all three under the name "Bluebill." More discriminating sportsmen, particularly those who have shot in the Middle West, use the name "Black-jack" for this species, the name commonly given it along the Mississippi. In life it is distinguishable in any plumage by the gray speculum, or wing patch, which contrasts with the dead-white speculum of the scaups. In any ordinary light, this character usually shows up surprisingly well either when the bird is on the water or on the wing.

The first record of this duck in Oregon is of one killed on Deer Island near the mouth of the Willamette River, March 28, 1806, by members of the Lewis and Clark expedition (Lewis and Clark 1814). Although the species was described in England in 1809 from a straggler there, this Deer Island bird was in reality the first of its kind to be obtained and described from America by any scientific expedition. Practically all naturalists who have visited the State since 1806 have noted the species in small numbers. Merrill (1888) stated that a few pairs remained to breed in Klamath marsh, but we have no recent records of its nesting in Oregon, and its present status, so far as known, is that of a regular migrant and winter resident that is widely distributed and of regular occurrence on the open waters of the State. In Klamath County, it occurs regularly on the Klamath River about Keno. Along the coast, it is regularly found on Siltcoos, Tahkenitch, and Devils Lakes and is probably regularly present on many others. At Portland, it not only frequents the Columbia River but is a regular visitor to Reed College Lake on the Eastmoreland Golf Course. Jewett believes that the species has become relatively more common in recent years. Since about 1920, we have taken numerous specimens and have seen it regularly. We have specimens from Lane, Klamath, and Malheur Counties and from the Columbia River, near The Dalles and below Portland, and numerous sight records and notes on birds seen in hunters' bags, from Crook, Harney, Klamath, Lincoln, and Multnomah Counties. Our earliest fall date is September 23 (Crook County); latest spring date, April (Klamath County).

The feeding habits of the species differ little from those of the scaups, and the food of the three species is undoubtedly the same in the same localities. The single Oregon stomach available for examination, from Klamath Falls, was filled with fragments of mollusk shells and seeds of *Potamogeton*, *Scirpus*, and *Hippuris*.

Canvas-back:
Nyroca valisineria (Wilson)

Description.—"Bill three times as long as wide. *Adult male:* head and neck rich chestnut brown, becoming dusky on crown and face; shoulders and chest black; sides and back light gray; belly white or grayish; tail and quills dark gray; feathers around base of tail black. *Adult female:* plumage mainly umber brown, becoming whitish around face and chin." (Bailey) *Downy young:* "The downy young show their aristocratic parentage as soon as they are hatched in the peculiar wedge-shaped bill and head. The color of the upper parts—crown, hind neck, and back—varies from 'sepia' to 'buffy olive.' The under parts are yellowish, deepening to 'amber yellow' on the cheeks and lores, brightening to 'citron yellow' on the breast, fading out to 'napthalene yellow' on the belly and to almost white on the throat. The markings on the side of the head are but faintly indicated; below the broad yellow superciliary stripe is a narrow brown postocular stripe and below that an indistinct auricular stripe of light brown. The yellow scapular patches are quite conspicuous, but the rump spots are hardly noticeable. The colors become duller and browner as the young bird increases in size." (Bent) *Size:* "Length 20.00–23.50, wing 8.75–9.25, bill 2.10–2.50." (Bailey) *Nest:* Usually a bulky mass of reeds in shallow water with a shallow depression in the top, lined with small bits of vegetable matter and down. *Eggs:* 7 to 9, pale olive green.

DISTRIBUTION.—*General:* Breeds in western North America from central Alaska; Anderson River, Great Slave Lake, east and south to central Manitoba and Wisconsin and south to central Nebraska, northern New Mexico, northern Utah, and western Nevada. *In Oregon:* Formerly an abundant and still a regular migrant in Klamath, Harney, and Lake Counties. A few remain during summer in those counties and breed sparingly.

THE GLISTENING white back and dark head of the Canvas-back, taken in conjunction with the long neck and low-brow effect of the bill and head, make this an easy duck to identify, either on the water or in the air. Its flight is swift and direct, and the long neck and bill extended to the utmost give it a trimness of outline in the air equalled only by the male Pintail. It was first definitely recorded from Oregon by Lewis and Clark (1814), who recorded it from the coast of Oregon, probably near the mouth of the Columbia River, on January 2, 1806, and also a few, March 28, 1806, at Deer Island. Townsend (1839) found it common off the mouth of the Columbia on April 15, 1835, and Baird (1858) recorded it at The Dalles in January 1855. Newberry (1857) listed it as a breeder in Oregon and common on the Columbia in November. He stated:

During the summer we found them more numerous than any other duck in the lakes and streams of the Cascade mountains. In those solitudes they nest and rear their young, as we frequently saw broods of young there, though the period of incubation had passed.

This statement is curiously interesting in view of the fact that the Canvas-back does not at present frequent these high lakes during the summer. The only breeding species we now find regularly there is Barrow's Golden-eye, one or two pairs of which may be expected on each of the larger lakes. Bendire (1877) said:

Equally common during the migrations, and breeding in the higher mountain valleys in the Blue Mountains, where I found them nesting on Bear Creek, at an altitude of six thousand feet.

These are the only definite nesting records we have found for the Canvas-backs in the State. They still remain through the summer in limited numbers in the alkaline lake country of eastern Oregon, particularly in Klamath, Lake, and Harney Counties, and are frequently found in pairs. Until 1936 neither of the authors had ever found a nest. Since that time a number of pairs have nested each year at Malheur Lake.

Our records indicate that the vanguard of the Canvas-backs arrives in September (earliest dates, September 20, Multnomah County, and September 25, Harney County), but the species does not become common until November. These ducks remain on the Columbia River and on the coastal bays and lakes through the winter until early May (latest record is May 5, Tillamook County). We have found the greatest concentrations on Tillamook Bay, where in January and February we have frequently seen rafts estimated to contain more than 5,000 birds.

It seems evident that most of the Canvas-backs come down the Columbia River from the great midcontinent nesting grounds rather than down the coast. All observers report the species as decidedly uncommon on Puget Sound, which would not be the case if there were a coastal flight line. On the contrary, it is regularly and commonly found on the Columbia River and on the Oregon coast. There is no doubt whatever that the flight has greatly decreased in the past 10 years and that this magnificent waterfowl annually is becoming progressively scarcer.

The lordly Canvas-back is stamped by gourmets and epicures as the finest of American waterfowl. Perhaps its reputation as a table bird has had something to do with its great decrease in numbers, although we can say frankly that, in common with other species of diving ducks that frequent the bays and lakes of the Oregon coast, it is frequently of very inferior table quality. When it is able to feast on ample quantities of its favorite eelgrass or on grain, it lives up to its reputation; but when, as frequently occurs, it feeds on the abundant snails and other small mollusks of those waters, it becomes so strong that only those with defective olfactory organs are able to remain in the house while one is being cooked.

Nine stomachs from Klamath Falls showed that the Canvas-backs in that area had taken the same type of food as other ducks frequenting the district. Five stomachs were filled with seeds and tubers of a pondweed (*Potamogeton pectinatus*), and three others contained pondweed to the extent of more than 50 per cent of the meal, the balance being made up of seeds of a sedge, *Scirpus*, a smartweed (*Polygonum muhlenbergii*), *Hippuris vulgaris*, *Myriophyllum*, *Brasenia schreberi*, and *Menyanthes trifoliata*. One nearly empty stomach contained a few insects, including a water beetle and two flies. Of three stomachs taken at intervals in the salt-water bays of Tillamook County, two were filled with the remains of mollusk shells and the third contained remains of four small crabs, bits of mollusk shells and rootstalks, and leaves and seeds of eelgrass (*Zostera marina*), a favorite food of this duck as well as of the brant in many western bays.

Greater Scaup Duck: *Nyroca marila* (Linnaeus)

DESCRIPTION.—"Bill short and wide, bluish with black tip. *Male in breeding plumage:* head black, glossed with green; shoulders, rump, and chest black; belly white, margined along sides with light grayish; crissum black. *Post-breeding plumage:* similar to female but darker brown. *Adult female:* head, neck, chest, and sides brownish; region around base of bill, and belly, whitish." (Bailey) *Downy young:* "The downy young scaup duck is a swarthy duckling, deeply and richly colored with dark brown on the upper parts. The crown, hind neck, and entire back are a deep rich 'raw umber,' darker than any color in Ridgway's standards, with glossy reflections of bright 'argus brown'; this color invades the lores and cheeks and shades off gradually on the neck and sides into the color of the under parts; the sides of the head and neck are 'old gold' or 'olive ocher,' shading off to 'colonial buff' on the throat and to 'cream buff' and 'cartridge buff' on the belly; an area of darker color, approaching that of the upper parts, encircles the lower neck and fore breast and invades the posterior under parts, restricting the light-colored belly." (Bent) *Size:* "Length 18–20, wing about 8.50, bill 2.03." (Bailey) *Nest:* Usually a tuft of grass near the water, lined to some extent with fine grass and down. *Eggs:* Usually from 7 to 10, sometimes more, dark olive buff.

DISTRIBUTION.—*General:* Breeds from southern Michigan, northern Iowa (formerly), central Manitoba, central Alberta, and central British Columbia, east of Cascades northward and westward from Hudson Bay to Aleutian Islands and Bering Sea and Arctic Coast. In winter southward throughout United States. *In Oregon:* Appears on coast in winter from October to February, perhaps later. We have seen specimens from Lane, Douglas, Lincoln, Tillamook, and Benton Counties and from Columbia River below Portland but have not been fortunate enough to find specimens from east of the Cascades.

THE GREATER SCAUP DUCK, or Big Blue-bill, has been reported in Oregon by many observers, but from all the evidence available it seems it has been hopelessly confused with the next species. Townsend (1839) stated it was found in the territory of Oregon. Bendire (1877) reported it as a common migrant at Camp Harney, and Merrill (1888) said:

> Abundant from autumn till spring. On June 15 I watched a pair of this species—although it has not been recognized as breeding so far south, their size was certainly too great for *affinis*—for some time in the marsh, and from their actions am confident that they were breeding and had a nest or young close at hand.

Woodcock (1902) recorded one specimen shot south of Corvallis on December 27, 1899, and Walker (1926) reported one taken at Netarts on December 21, 1920. In the Jewett collection, there are two from western Lane County taken November 20, 1924, one from Siltcoos Lake shot January 12, 1925, and one from the Columbia River just below Portland taken October 17, 1926. Gabrielson collected one in Tillamook County, November 5, 1932, and one at Devils Lake, Lincoln County, December 3, 1932. In addition he has seen a few birds in hunters' bags about Devils Lake, most commonly in November 1930.

From the above, it will be seen that definite information concerning this duck in Oregon is meager. The difficulty of separating the two species of scaups in the field except under particularly favorable conditions makes it hard to determine their relative abundance. Aside from the larger size and heavier bill, the chief distinction, found only in adult males, is in the color of the iridescent reflection on the head. In *marila* this is green, while in *affinis* it is purple. Both writers have consistently examined hunters' bags whenever it was possible to do so. Despite what Bendire and Merrill have said, we have never had an actual specimen in hand in eastern Oregon and, as will be noted by checking the above records, have found this duck regularly only on the coast and as a straggler inland. It possibly occurs in small numbers more or less regularly on the Columbia and should be found at least casually on the Snake River, Upper Klamath Lake, and similar situations in eastern Oregon. To date, however, we have failed to detect it.

No Oregon stomachs of this duck have been examined, but there is no reason to believe that the food differs materially from that of the Lesser Scaup.

Lesser Scaup Duck:
Nyroca affinis (Eyton)

Description.—"Like *Nyroca*[1] *marila*, but smaller, with black of head glossed with purple instead of green, and sides more heavily lined with gray." (Bailey) *Downy young:* "The downy young is darkly and richly colored. The upper parts are dark, lustrous 'mummy brown' or 'sepia,' shaded with 'brownish olive'; these colors are darkest and most lustrous on the posterior half of the back and lightest on the shoulders; the dark colors cover the upper half of the head and neck, the back and the flanks, fading off gradually into a dusky bank around the lower neck and encroaching on the ventral region posteriorly. The color of the under parts, which covers the lower half of the head, throat, breast, and belly, varies in different individuals; in some it runs from 'olive ocher' to 'primrose yellow'; but in most specimens from 'chamois' to 'cream buff'; these colors are brightest and richest on the cheeks and on the breast. The markings on the head are usually indistinct, but a superciliary buff stripe, a loral dusky stripe and a postocular dusky stripe are discernible in the majority of a series of 11 specimens in my collection. There is also an indistinct yellowish spot on each scapular region, but none on the rump." (Bent) *Size:* "Length 15.00–16.50, wing 7.50–8.25, bill 1.58–1.90, width of bill .80–.95." (Bailey) *Nest:* A hollow in the ground, lined with a little dry grass and down, usually in a tuft of grass or beneath a bush near the water. *Eggs:* 6 to 15, usually 9 to 12, dark olive buff in color.

Distribution.—*General:* Breeds from northern limit of timber west of Hudson Bay south to northern Ohio, southern Wisconsin, southeastern Iowa, northwestern Colorado, and central British Columbia. Winters from southern United States south to Central America. *In Oregon:* Abundant winter resident from September to about May 1. Stragglers remain throughout summer but are nonbreeding birds so far as we know.

Our own experience, as well as a check of many hunters' kills, demonstrates that in Oregon the Lesser Scaup Duck is much the more abundant

[1] *Nyroca=Aythya.*

of the two scaups, or blue bills, as it is found wherever open water occurs. It usually keeps away from the shore in much the same manner as the Canvas-back. Bendire (1877) reported it from Camp Harney as an abundant migrant and as a possible breeder "in upper Sylvies Valley in the Blue Mountains, where I noticed several specimens June 8, 1876." It is not mentioned by the earlier naturalists who may have confused it with the Greater Scaup.

Throughout the winter it is found on any available open water in Klamath (Link River and Upper Klamath Lake), Deschutes (Deschutes River), Harney, and Malheur (Snake River) Counties and may be expected on any considerable body of open water. Our earliest date is September 25 (Harney County); our latest when numbers were seen, May 12 (Klamath County). In western Oregon, it may be found anytime from October to April. It is a common winter resident of the coastal bays, such as the mouth of the Columbia River, and Tillamook, Siletz, Yaquina, and Coos Bays, and of many smaller bodies of water. It is common on the Columbia River also, at least from Portland westward, and on Tahkenitch, Siltcoos, Devils, and many other lakes along the coast. Occasionally great rafts containing many Lesser Scaups and a scattering of other ducks are observed over favorite feeding grounds on Tillamook and other bays.

Stragglers remain through the summer, particularly in Klamath and Harney Counties, but so far as we know these are nonbreeding birds. There is one summer record for Portland (August 10), when Jewett saw a few birds on the Eastmoreland Golf Course on Reed College Lake, a small pond that is a regular resort for waterfowl.

This species, in common with other diving ducks, feeds in deeper water than do the river ducks, such as Mallards and Pintails. Eleven Lesser Scaup stomachs from Klamath Falls have been examined by the Biological Survey. The vegetable food taken in this locality is much the same as that eaten by other species of ducks. It consists of seeds and vegetative parts of such plants as pondweeds (*Potamogeton*), sedges (*Scirpus*), water milfoil (*Myriophyllum*), and *Hippuris*. Four stomachs were filled with vegetable matter as above, while seven contained animal material almost entirely—save for fragments of vegetable matter—being filled with shells of mollusks, badly broken up, among which were individuals of *Fluminicola Nuttaliana*, a *Planorbis*, and a species of *Lymnaea*. This is a greater amount of animal matter than has been taken by any species of ducks so far discussed for this locality. Two taken at Netarts likewise had partaken liberally of mollusks and a mass of ground-up vegetable matter. Lesser Scaups on the coast frequently become so strongly flavored as to become inedible, probably due to their habit of feeding heavily on the abundant small mollusks of that area.

American Golden-eye:
Glaucionetta clangula americana (Bonaparte)

Description.—"*Adult male:* Head and crest rich dark green, a round white patch at base of bill; neck and under parts white; back black, shoulders white; wing with white central patch and white stripes on scapulars. *Adult female:* head and upper neck light snuff brown, neck with wide white or gray collar; belly white; chest, sides, and shoulders gray; wing dusky, with white on coverts and secondaries, the white greater coverts not tipped with dusky. Nail of bill not over .20 wide. *Young male:* like female, but sometimes with a suggestion of the white patch at base of bill, and less gray on chest." (Bailey) *Downy young:* "The upper part of the head, down to a line running straight back from the commissure to the nape, is deep, rich, glossy 'bone brown'; the throat and cheeks are pure white, the white spaces nearly meeting on the hind neck; the upper parts vary from pale 'clove brown' on the upper back to deep 'bone brown' on the rump; these colors shade off to 'hair brown' on the sides and form a ring of the same around the neck; the posterior edges of the wings are white, and there is a white spot on each scapular region and one on each side of the rump; the belly is white." (Bent) *Size:* "*Male*, length 18.50–23.00, wing 9.18, bill 1.95. *Female*, 16.50, wing 8.14, bill 1.64." (Bailey) *Nest:* A cavity in a tree, usually over the water, the nest itself hollowed out in a mass of rotten wood and lined with down. *Eggs:* 8 to 12, although occasionally up to 19, clear pale green in color.

Distribution.—*General:* Breeds from central Maine, northern New Hampshire, and Vermont, northern Michigan, northern Minnesota, northern North Dakota, northwestern Montana, and central interior British Columbia north to the limit of large trees. Winters on coasts from Maine and the Aleutian Islands southward and in interior wherever there is open water on larger lakes and streams from Canada to Gulf coast. *In Oregon:* Common winter resident on all coastal bays and lakes, and also on Snake, Columbia, Deschutes, Klamath, Umatilla, Wallowa, and other similar streams that remain unfrozen through the winter.

For some reason, the American Golden-eye appears neither in Lewis and Clark's nor in Douglas' records for this district. Townsend (1839) reported it for Oregon, however, and nearly every ornithologist who has visited the State since has had some comment to make about it. The beautiful black and white males and the demure brownish and gray females are now equally familiar winter residents of the open waters of the State. The name "American Golden-eye" is given to distinguish the species from similar Old World forms, but because of the peculiar whistling noise produced by the rapid beat of its powerful wings it is known to most Oregonians as "Whistler," which is the name used widely by gunners in distinguishing it. Its squarely built, heavy body and striking black and white coloration combine to make it an easily recognized species either in flight or on the water. Its flight is strong and direct, the weighty body hurtling through the air at a surprisingly fast rate.

This showy whistler is a hardy species and frequents the swift waters of the mountain streams which, with their tumbling rapids, churned into white foam, remain unfrozen through the coldest weather. It is very common on the Snake River and furnishes one of the attractions of a midwinter ride up the Wallowa Canyon. It occurs regularly and commonly on the Columbia throughout its entire course along the northern boundary of the State and on the Deschutes and Klamath Rivers also, and it may be expected on any of the streams and lakes of western Oregon from November to March. We have winter records for Malheur, Wallowa, Grant, Baker, Umatilla, Morrow, Wasco, Deschutes, Klamath, and Harney Counties, and it undoubtedly occurs in all other eastern counties wherever there is open water. It is one of the latest ducks to arrive. Our earliest date is November 14 (Harney County); our latest spring date, May 17 (Klamath County), although its numbers diminish rapidly after March 1.

The American Golden-eye is an expert diver and feeds extensively on animal matter obtained from the icy waters. The percentage of animal food eaten while in Oregon is much larger than for most ducks, so that its flesh is frequently strong and unpalatable. Perhaps this accounts for the fact that it is not particularly sought by gunners and therefore remains comparatively common. Seven stomachs, five from Klamath County, one from Deschutes County, and one from Tillamook County, were examined by the Biological Survey. Five contained mostly animal matter, consisting of amphipods, crustaceans, mollusks, and insects, the latter being chiefly larvae of aquatic forms. One of the birds from Klamath County, however, had made almost a full meal on seeds of *Hippuris*, *Scirpus*, and *Myriophyllum*, and a finely ground mass of vegetable debris, and the Tillamook bird had fed chiefly on a similar unrecognizable mass of vegetable debris.

Barrow's Golden-eye:
Glaucionetta islandica (Gmelin)

Description.—"Similar to *americana*, but male with glossy blue black head, and triangular or crescent-shaped spot at base of bill; female with head and neck dark umber brown, white collar narrower, and white greater wing coverts tipped with dusky; nail of bill over .23 wide." (Bailey) *Downy young:* "The downy young of the Barrow goldeneye is very much like that of the common goldeneye. The upper half of the head, from below the eyes, and the hind neck are deep 'bone brown' or 'seal brown'; the upper parts are 'bone brown,' relieved by white on the edge of the wing and by scapular and rump spots of white; the lower half of the head and the under parts are white; there is a brownish gray band around the lower neck." (Bent) *Size:* "*Male*, length 21–23, wing 9.17, bill 1.75. *Female*, wing 8.46, bill 1.56." (Bailey) *Nest:* In hollow trees, lined with down. *Eggs:* 6 to 15, pale green, almost indistinguishable from those of the American Golden-eye.

Distribution.—*General:* Breeds in Greenland, Iceland, and Labrador; also from Alaska, British Columbia, Oregon, and California east to Colorado and Montana and north into Alberta and Mackenzie. Winters south on coasts to southern New England and San Francisco Bay. *In Oregon:* Breeds regularly in higher Cascade Lakes and possibly Wallowas and may be found sparingly in winter on coast.

Barrow's Golden-eye, except in adult male plumage, is so easily confused with the more common American Golden-eye that our records of its occurrence in Oregon are probably much more meager than its actual numbers warrant. Mearns (1879) first reported it from Fort Klamath, and Merrill (1888) later found it a common wintering species in the same locality. We know very little about its present winter distribution, as we have only two winter records, both of them adult males, one, a mounted specimen seen by Jewett in Hermiston on January 13, 1917, but reported to have been killed earlier in the winter, and the other, a bird taken by him at Klamath Falls on January 1, 1929. The species may be expected in the State wherever there is open water, however, and hunters should carefully examine their game bags in an effort to detect it.

We know it best as a summer resident of the high Cascade lakes and it may be expected on any of the larger lakes there during that season. There is an adult female (No. 3511) in Jewett's collection taken at Frog Lake, Lane County, on July 19, 1914, and we have both seen the species frequently on Diamond, Sparks, Elk, Paulina, and East Lakes. On Sparks Lake, Gabrielson saw a female with 10 to 12 young on July 27, 1929; and on Diamond Lake, he saw a female with 6 young on July 30, 1930, and two broods of partly grown birds on August 8, 1932.

The only stomach examined was that of Jewett's Frog Lake bird. It contained fragments of diving beetles, dragonfly and other insect remains, and finely divided vegetable matter. There is no reason to believe that its food differs materially from that of the American Golden-eye.

Buffle-head; Butterball:
Charitonetta albeola (Linnaeus)

Description.—"A plump little duck with short, pointed bill and round, crested head. *Adult male:* head, except white patch, rich iridescent purple, violet, and green; back and part of wings black; rump and tail gray; rest of plumage white. *Adult female:* mainly grayish or dusky, with a large white spot on ear coverts and white patch on middle of wing; belly white." (Bailey) *Downy young:* "As might be expected, the downy young buffle-head closely resembles the young goldeneye in color pattern. The upper parts, including the upper half of the head from below the lores and eyes, the hind neck, the back and the rump, are deep rich 'bone brown,' with a lighter gloss on the forehead and mantle; the inner edge of the wing is pure white; there is a large white spot on each side of the scapular region and on each side of the rump; and an indistinct whitish spot on each flank. The under parts, including the chin, throat, cheeks, breast, and belly are pure white, shading off gradually into the darker color on the sides of the body and with an indistinct brownish collar around the lower neck." (Bent) *Size:* "*Male,* length 14.25–15.25, wing 6.75–6.90, bill 1.10–1.15." (Bailey) *Nest:* In hole in a tree or a bank, lined with down. *Eggs:* 6 to 14, usually 10 to 12, varying from ivory yellow to pale olive buff.

Distribution.—*General:* Breeds from British Columbia, central Alaska, northern Mackenzie, and Great Slave Lake south to northern Montana. Winters from Aleutians, Great Lakes, and coast of Maine southward to Mexico and Lower California. *In Oregon:* Formerly an abundant migrant and winter resident of Oregon, arriving in numbers in mid-October and remaining until mid-April.

THE SPRIGHTLY little Buffle-head, or Butterball, is one of our widely distributed wintering species and is found wherever there is open water. It appears most frequently in our records in the coast district, along the Columbia and Snake Rivers, and in the big duck counties, Harney, Lake, and Klamath. Our earliest date is September 20 (Lake County); our latest, May 15 (Tillamook County). It is rather remarkable that none of the earlier naturalists mentioned the species in their writings. The first record we find for Oregon is Bendire's report (1877) of it as a common migrant at Camp Harney, but there is an unrecorded specimen in the University of Washington Museum, taken by O. B. Johnson at Forest Grove, January 6, 1876. Since that time it has been reported by many naturalists.

In our experience, this beautiful little waterfowl was one of the most abundant and widely distributed winter ducks up to about 1930. Since then there has been a very noticeable reduction in the numbers that visit the State. Allen (1909) once reported the Buffle-head as breeding in Klamath Lake but later wrote the Biological Survey that this record was not to be used, and as there is no other evidence of its nesting within our limits, its status remains that of a migrant and winter resident.

Few waterfowl that visit Oregon are more conspicuous than the little black and white male Buffle-head, either in the air or riding high on the water to best display its strikingly contrasted color pattern. The flight is exceedingly swift, and this, combined with its small size, makes it a difficult target. The bird is so small that it has little food value, even if the meat were of the finest quality. Frequently the meat is strong and unpalatable, however, particularly in our coastal waters, and consequently the bird is comparatively little sought by local gunners.

Old-squaw:
Clangula hyemalis (Linnaeus)

DESCRIPTION.—"A trim little duck with short bill; male with long slender tail; head not crested. *Adult male in winter:* head and fore parts to shoulders and breast white, except for patches of ashy and dusky on side of head; back middle tail feathers, and breast black; belly white posteriorly, shading into pearl gray on sides. *Adult male in summer:* sooty, except for white belly, ash gray face, and white eyelids; back and scapulars streaked with chestnut. *Adult female in winter:* tail not lengthened; head, neck, and under parts mainly white; chest grayish; crown dusky, rest of upper parts dusky brown, the scapulars bordered with lighter brown. *Adult female in summer:* head and neck grayish brown, with whitish spaces around eye and on side of neck. *Young:* similar to female in summer." (Bailey) *Downy young:* "The downy young old-squaw is very dark-colored above, very deep, rich 'clove brown,' becoming almost black on the crown and rump, and paler 'clove brown' in a band across the chest. This dark color covers more than half of the head, including the crown, hind neck, and cheeks; it is relieved, however, by a large spot below the eye and a smaller one above it of whitish, also an indistinct loral spot and postocular streak of the same.

The throat is white and the sides of the neck and auricular region are grayish white. The belly is white. Both the dark and the light brown areas become duller and grayer with age." (Bent) *Size:* "*Male*, length 20.75–23.00, wing 8.50–9.00, middle tail feathers 8.00–8.50. *Female*, length 15–16, wing 8–9, tail 8." (Bailey) *Nest:* Usually in the grass or beneath bushes near the water, lined with down. *Eggs:* Usually 5 to 9, "deep olive buff to yellowish glaucous."

DISTRIBUTION.—*General:* Breeds on Arctic coast and barren grounds of Canada and Alaska south to Aleutian Islands and shores of Hudson Bay. Winters south to North Carolina, Great Lakes, and California. *In Oregon:* Irregular winter visitor to the coast.

THE OLD-SQUAW was first reported from Oregon by Townsend (1839). Newberry (1857) listed it as common at the mouth of the Columbia River in winter, and Woodcock (1902) recorded it as wintering on Yaquina Bay, on the report of B. J. Bretherton. At present it can be regarded only as an irregular winter visitor to the coast. T. T. Craig, of the Oregon Game Commission, shot one on Tillamook Bay, November 16, 1913 (now in Jewett Coll.). A female, killed on Depoe Bay, December 27, 1933, and skinned and salted by Roy Kerr, was presented to Gabrielson through Braly and is now in his collection; and Jewett has a bird that was taken on Nehalem Bay, February 23, 1935. So far as we know these are the only existing specimens from the State. Gabrielson saw two birds at Tillamook Bay, December 29, 1931, that were almost certainly this species. They were at quite a distance but were observed for a long time through 8-power binoculars. Gabrielson also saw a total of perhaps 50 individuals at sea off Depoe Bay, May 7, 1932. All were flying northward in small groups or as individuals except one flock of 20.

Western Harlequin Duck:
Histrionicus histrionicus pacificus Brooks

DESCRIPTION.—"A small duck with moderate crest, short bill, and long sharp tail. *Adult male in winter and spring:* head and neck bluish black, with white patches; collar white; shoulder bar black and white; middle of crown black, bordered behind by chestnut; chest and shoulders dark plumbeous; belly sooty, sides bright rufous; wing with steel blue speculum and four white spots; rump black, with white spot on each side. *Adult male in summer:* colors much duller than in winter. *Adult female:* head, neck, and upper parts sooty, with a white spot on ear coverts and a large white patch on sides of face; belly mottled grayish." (Bailey) *Downy young:* (From three specimens in Jewett's collection taken in Wallowa County, two July 21, 1925, and one July 29, 1929.) These downy young are all a dark brown ("bister") on the back, top, and sides of head. In all three there are white spots above and in front of the eyes, an indistinct whitish streak in the scapular region, a white margin on the wings, and an indistinct yellowish brown spot on either side of the rump. A small area directly above the base of the bill varies from almost pure white to a yellowish brown in one specimen, spreading until it almost merges with the white spot in front of the eye. The under parts are white with more or less of the dark brown base of the down showing through, particularly on the throat and sides. *Size:* "Length 15.00–17.50, wing 7.40–8.00, bill 1.05–1.10." (Bailey) *Nest:* In hollow tree or stump or

Plate 25. Western Harlequin Duck and young. (Photo by Major John D. Guthrie.)

under rocks or drift wood. *Eggs:* 5 to 10, varying from "light buff" or "cream color" to pale tints of same color.

Distribution.—*General:* Breeds from Alaska, British Columbia, and Mackenzie southward in mountains to Colorado and central California. Winters on coast from Pribilof Islands to central California. *In Oregon:* Permanent resident breeding along swift mountain streams of Wallowas and Cascades. Winters on coast.

The Western Harlequin Duck (Plate 25) was first reported from what is now Oregon territory by Townsend (1839). Woodcock (1902) listed it on the basis of Bretherton's statement of "two or three pairs seen on the ocean in March of each year," the only other reference to it in Oregon ornithological literature aside from notes on the species in two short *Condor* articles by Jewett (1925, 1931c). We have found it to be a regular and fairly common resident of the State that winters regularly on the coast from Curry to Tillamook County from August to May (earliest date, August 8; latest, May 18; both Tillamook County). We have specimens and records from Curry, Lane, Lincoln, and Tillamook Counties and feel sure it will be found in other coast counties whenever adequate field work is done.

We have three definite breeding records in Oregon, all of them made by Jewett. An adult female and two downy young were taken from the swift waters of the Wallowa River near Frazier Lake, July 21, 1925, and on July 28, 1929, a female and six downy young (one collected) were seen in the Imnaha River near the spot where Cliff River empties into it. Both of these localities are high in the Wallowa Mountains. The third record was made in the Cascades on Zigzag River in the Mount Hood National Forest where, on May 31, 1931, Jewett collected a set of six eggs, the first ever taken within the State and one of the few sets known. These eggs are now in the Braly collection. Jewett's notes on that occasion were as follows:

May 30–31, 1931. Arrah Wauna, Wemme P. O., a female seen in front of the Fred Meyer cottage, feeding among the rocks in the swift waters of the Salmon River between nine and ten in the morning of May 30 and again on May 31. A female seen near Mossy Rocks cottage, a few miles above Rhododendron postoffice, and just out of Tollgate on Zig Zag River. The small son (Donald) of Herbert Cook showed me a nest containing six eggs which he had found the day before (May 30). The nest was located in debris on an overturned stump of Oregon alder, washed out in mid-stream during a recent flood. The nest was composed of dry rootlets well rimmed with dark down from the parent's breast. Donald told me that he had caught the female on the nest and handled her.

Undoubtedly this beautiful little inhabitant of the mountain streams nests through the Cascades in suitable localities and more records will be procured as the number of bird students increases.

While on the coast, Western Harlequin Ducks frequent the rocky promontories and capes, where they are often found resting on the rocks at high tide and feeding about the exposed rocks at low tide (Plate 25).

At such times they are quite tame and unsuspicious and allow a reasonably close approach if sudden movements are avoided. The gaudily marked drakes and more demure females are usually found together, sometimes in pairs, but more often in small groups of three or four up to a dozen or more. As spring approaches, they are frequently found in trios of two males and one female, each of the former undoubtedly trying to win the demure female as a mate. Little has been written about the courtship of these birds. Bent (1925) stated that B. J. Bretherton in 1896 had written the best account, as follows:

> The writer has often watched the males in spring, calling, and the actions of these birds may justly be said to resemble the crowing of a rooster. In giving forth their call the head is thrown far back with the bill pointed directly upward and widely open; then with a jerk the head is thrown forward and downward as the cry is uttered, and at the same time the wings are slightly expanded and drooped. Afterwards they will rise in the water and flap their wings.

White-winged Scoter; Sea Coot:
Melanitta deglandi (Bonaparte)

DESCRIPTION.—"Bill swollen at base over nostrils and on sides; tip orange in male; feathers of lores coming close to nostrils, as far forward as those of forehead. *Adult male:* eyes white; plumage black or sooty, with white eye patch and wing speculum. *Adult female:* eyes brown; plumage sooty gray, darker above; wing speculum white." (Bailey) *Downy young:* "The downy young of the white-winged scoter is thickly covered with soft, silky down. The upper parts, including the upper half of the head, down to the base of the lower mandible and a space below the eye, are uniform 'clove brown,' shading off to 'hair brown' on the flanks and into a broad collar of 'hair brown' which encircles the lower neck. The chin and throat are pure white, which shades off to grayish white on the lower cheeks and the sides of the neck. The under parts are silvery white, and there is an indistinct, tiny white spot under the eye." (Bent) *Size:* "Length 19.75–23.00, wing 10.65–11.40, bill 1.40–1.70." (Bailey) *Nest:* Usually a depression in the ground, lined with grass, moss, and down and concealed beneath some small shrub. *Eggs:* 9 to 14, "sea-shell pink."

DISTRIBUTION.—*General:* Breeds from northwestern Alaska, Hudson Bay, and Gulf of St. Lawrence to southern Manitoba, central North Dakota, and northeastern Washington. Winters south to South Carolina, Great Lakes, and Lower California. *In Oregon:* Abundant winter and fairly common summer resident of coast. Appears only casually in interior.

THE BIG, clumsy, heavy-bodied White-winged Scoter, or Sea Coot, is the most abundant of the three species represented in the great rafts found along the Oregon coast, our records showing it to be present every month. Its flight is somewhat labored but swift and straight once it leaves the water. It is one of the most abundant seafowl, constituting a large part of the V- or U-shaped flocks seen flying up and down the coast or crossing into the bays and lakes to feed in their winter waters. It is common on the ocean and also on the bays and big fresh-water lakes adjacent to the coast. When its present abundance is considered, it is remarkable that none of the early naturalists mentioned its presence in the State. So far we have found that Woodcock's list (1902) contained the first published reference to it as an Oregon bird. The numerous individuals that remain with us through the summer are nonbreeding birds, as there is no evidence whatever to indicate that they nest in the State.

Inland, we have only a few records. Woodcock (1902) reported a specimen received from a hunter near Corvallis on November 4, 1900. Jewett has a specimen from the Columbia River below Portland, collected January 2, 1927. There have been at least two birds taken near Klamath Falls. One, a female (Game Commission Coll. No. 480), was obtained on November 20, 1912, and the second, reported by Telford (1916), was killed November 11, 1915. Almost certainly ducks of this species have been noted on the Snake River near Ontario on one or two occasions, but conditions prevented positive identification. Since this species nests abundantly in the interior of Canada and must reach the Oregon coast by an overland flight, it may be expected on any large body of water in eastern Oregon.

In common with other scoters the White-winged Scoters display an uncanny power to handle themselves even in the heaviest surf. They habitually feed among the breakers, diving through them just in time to avoid the smother of foam or riding buoyantly over the crests if there is even a slight gap of solid water where the wave has not broken. It is a fascinating sight to watch them under such conditions. An observer momentarily expects to see them tumbled end over end in the breaking waters, but always at the last possible moment they dive into the solid water to appear behind the crest or an unbroken bit of crest will appear to allow them to ride triumphantly over. Never have we seen a case of misjudgment on the part of one of these ducks, so much at home in the rough waters of our coasts.

These sea ducks feed on shellfish and are often accused of destroying quantities of oysters. They swallow shellfish of almost unbelievable size, and their economic status has been the subject of recent studies by the Biological Survey, the results of which are not yet available for publication.

Surf Scoter; Sea Coot; Skunk Duck:
Melanitta perspicillata (Linnaeus)

Description.—"Bill with swollen sides of base naked; feathers of forehead reaching to near nostril, of lores only to corner of mouth; bill black and less swollen in female; red, orange, yellow, and white in male, with large black spot on side of base. *Adult male:* entire plumage velvety black except for triangular white patch on forehead and another on back of head; eyes white. *Adult female:* upper parts sooty brown, under parts silver gray, usually with white patch at corner of mouth. *Young:* like female, but with whitish patches at base of bill and back of ear." (Bailey)

Downy young: No specimens, the youngest known being two half-grown young, described as follows: "Although as large as teal, these birds are still wholly downy, with no trace of appearing plumage. The smaller, a female, has the crown, down to and including the eyes, a deep glossy 'clove brown' in color; the color of the back varies from 'olive brown' anteriorly to 'clove brown' on the rump; the sides of the head and throat are grayish white, mottled with 'clove brown'; the entire neck is pale 'clove brown'; the colors of the upper parts shade off gradually into paler sides and a whitish belly. In younger birds these colors would probably be darker, brighter, and more contrasted, as they are in other species." (Bent) *Size:* "Length 20–22, wing 9.25–9.75, bill 1.30–1.60." (Bailey) *Nest:* Of plant stems, lined with down, usually concealed beneath a bush near the water. *Eggs:* 5 to 9, cartridge buff.

Distribution.—*General:* Breeds far north in northwestern Alaska and northern Canada south to Mackenzie, James Bay, and Gulf of St. Lawrence. Winters south to Florida, Great Lakes (occasionally to Louisiana), and Lower California. *In Oregon:* Abundant permanent resident on coastal waters. Found only casually inland.

The Surf Scoter, or Skunk Duck, is a very common species on the Oregon coast, where it is a familiar inhabitant of the bays and lakes. It ranks second only to its white-winged cousin and at times exceeds it in numbers, often being present in immense numbers from August to May and in smaller numbers during June and July. These latter individuals are undoubtedly nonbreeding birds, possibly recovered cripples as yet unable to endure the long northward flight to the breeding grounds. We have coastal records for every month, but our only inland record is of a bird killed on the Columbia River at Portland, October 8, 1928, and given to Jewett. Little has appeared in Oregon literature regarding this abundant species. It is curious that Townsend (1839) mentioned it as present but omitted any reference to the White-winged Scoter, which at present is equally abundant.

The conspicuous head markings distinguish the male Surf Scoters, either in the air or on the water. The females are more difficult to identify, although they do show some traces of the head markings. The flight is direct and much less labored than that of the White-winged Scoter, and everything said about the skill of the latter in the surf applies equally to this closely related species. While in Oregon, the feeding habits and behavior of these two scoters are much the same, and the two are often intermingled in great flocks, or rafts, just outside the breakers.

American Scoter:
Oidemia americana Swainson

Description.—"Plumage dark without white markings; eyes always brown. *Adult male:* bill swollen back of nostrils, with a large yellow and red spot at base, including nostrils; plumage black or sooty. *Adult female:* bill black, with a trace of yellow at base in breeding plumage, not swollen at base; upper parts dusky brown, under parts grayish brown. *Young:* like female but lighter and indistinctly barred below." (Bailey) *Downy young:* "The downy young, when first hatched, is dark colored above, varying from 'Prout's brown' or 'verona brown' to 'bister,' darkest on the crown and rump; the throat and cheeks, below the lores and the eyes, are white; the under parts are grayish white centrally, shading off on the flanks into the color of the upper parts; the bill is broadly tipped with dull yellow." (Bent) *Size:* "Length 17.00–21.50, wing 8.75–9.50, bill 1.65–1.80." (Bailey) *Nest:* "The nest is described as made of down in a tussock of grass." (Bent) *Eggs:* 6 to 10, varying from "light buff" to "cartridge buff." (Bent)

Distribution.—*General:* Breeds from Bering Sea and Aleutian Islands to James Bay and Newfoundland. Winters south to New Jersey, Great Lakes, and California. *In Oregon:* Regular but uncommon visitor to coast, most frequently found in winter. Occasional individuals remain throughout summer.

The American Scoter is much the rarest species in the great rafts of scoters found off the Oregon coast throughout the year. It is difficult to identify as there are no distinctive field marks whatever. The lack of white head or wing markings would seem to make it easy to distinguish the adult males, but the White-winged Scoter frequently folds its wings in such a manner as to render its white spots invisible. Newberry (1857) reported the American Scoter as common on the Oregon coast, the first published reference to the species for the State. Bendire (1877) recorded it as not uncommon at Malheur Lake, surely a confusion with some other species, as no other observer has found this seafowl in Oregon inland waters. Woodcock (1902) listed it as a rare winter visitor to Yaquina Bay, a statement that correctly describes its present status on the Oregon coast. There are two specimens in the University of Oregon collection (from the coast of Lane County), four in the Jewett collection (one from Tillamook, one from Lincoln, and two from Curry Counties), and two in the Gabrielson collection (from Lincoln County). All of these specimens were taken between November 24 and February 23. In addition, we both have a number of winter sight records taken when favorable conditions allowed positive identification, and we believe the species to be a regular but not common winter visitor. A single adult male was noted by Gabrielson off Depoe Bay on May 7, 1932. It flew by the boat at close range, permitting certain identification. We have only one summer specimen, a dead bird found at Newport on July 21, 1922. On the same day, three other scoters that were feeding on the Newport sewer outlet on Yaquina Bay were under observation for an hour at a distance of a few feet.

Ruddy Duck; Wire-Tail; Pintail:
Erismatura jamaicensis rubida (Wilson)

Description.—"Bill short and widest near end, bright blue in adult male. *Adult male:* top and back of head black; neck and rest of upper parts chestnut; cheeks and chin white; belly gray, washed with silvery white, or sometimes rusty. *Female and immature:* upper parts plain grayish brown; sides of head whitish with a dusky streak from corner of mouth to back of ear; under parts gray, washed with silvery white or rusty." (Bailey) *Downy young:* "The downy young, when first hatched, is a large, fat, awkward, and helpless looking creature, covered with long coarse down, which on the upper parts is mixed with long hair-like filaments, longest and coarsest on the rump and thighs. The upper parts are 'drab' or 'hair brown,' deepening to 'Prout's brown' or 'mummy brown' on the crown and rump, with two whitish rump patches, one above each thigh; the brown of the head extends below the eyes to the lores and auriculars, a broad band of grayish white separating this from a poorly defined malar stripe of 'drab'; the under parts are mostly grayish white, shading into the darker colors on the sides and into an indistinct collar of 'drab' on the lower neck." (Bent) *Size:* "Length 13.50–16.00, wing 5.75–6.00, bill 1.50–1.60." (Bailey) *Nest:* A mass of reeds built well on, but above the water level, usually concealed in thick masses of tules or other aquatic vegetation. *Eggs:* Up to 19 or 20, usually 6 to 10, large for size of bird, dull white or creamy white.

Distribution.—*General:* Breeds from central British Columbia, Alberta, and northern Manitoba south to Michigan, Wisconsin, Iowa, Texas, New Mexico, Arizona, and Lower California. Winters south to West Indies and Central America. *In Oregon:* Permanent resident. Breeds in Klamath, Lake, and Harney Counties (perhaps others). Winters on coast and wherever open water is found inland.

The squarely built, heavy-bodied little Ruddy Duck, with the absurd habit of carrying its stubby tail cocked over its back in a wrenlike manner, was first recorded from the State by Mearns (1879), from Fort Klamath, and since then it has been recorded by most naturalists who have written about Oregon birds. It was formerly a common summer resident and breeder in the inland lake country of southern Oregon, where numerous observers have reported it breeding (Furber, Fawcett, Lewis, Prill, Gabrielson, and Jewett), but in common with other inland nesting species it has decreased alarmingly since 1930. It is still fairly common in the coastal waters, where it is frequently known as "Pintail," to the confusion of the hunters who have applied that name to *Dafila acuta* away from the coast. We find it common on the coast from September to March (earliest date, September 16, Douglas County; latest, March 2, Lincoln County). It frequents not only the salt-water bays but the coastal lakes as well, being the most abundant species found on Devils Lake. It is also found more or less regularly in the Willamette Valley wherever suitable water occurs. We have numerous winter records for Klamath County.

Many times during the fall, usually in November, when they are present on Devils Lake in little flocks of from 4 to 12, Gabrielson has watched these ducks apparently playing a game. When the lake is like a mirror, its surface broken only by the wakes of the waterfowl, one of these little flocks will arrange itself in single file—each tail perfectly cocked forward over each back and each head thrown back—and the entire file will swim sedately on until suddenly the leader dives, to be followed down by each succeeding individual as it reaches the spot. They reappear in the same fashion, the leader breaking water and swimming onward at the same speed as before, to be followed single file by the others at regular intervals as they emerge from the water. The entire performance has a mechanical air about it, as if they were all on a string manipulated by some unseen power.

While on the coast, the birds often feed on mollusks and other aquatic life until their flesh becomes strong and unpalatable. Consequently, they are not sought as game as ardently as are some of the more palatable species.

Hooded Merganser:
Lophodytes cucullatus (Linnaeus)

Description.—"Bill narrow, slender, and with terminal part cylindrical, armed along edges of mandibles with blunt, scarcely inclined teeth; head with high thin, wheel-shaped crest, less prominent in female. *Adult male:* Head, neck, and back black; middle of crest and under parts, white; sides light brown, finely cross-lined with black. *Adult female:* upper parts grayish brown, browner on crest; patch on wing, throat, and belly white. *Young:* similar to female, but with little or no crest." (Bailey) *Downy young:* "The downy young is thickly and warmly clothed with soft down in deep, rich shades of 'bister' or 'sepia' above, including the upper half of the head, the hind neck, and the flanks; the sides of the head, neck, and cheeks, up to the eyes, are 'buff pink' or 'light vinaceous cinnamon,' the chin, throat, and underparts are pure white; and there is an obscure dusky band across the chest and an indistinct white spot on each side of the scapular region and rump." (Bent) *Size:* "Length 17.25–19.25, wing 7.50–7.90, bill 1.50." (Bailey) *Nest:* In hollow trees, lined with grass and down. *Eggs:* 6 to 18, usually 10 to 12, pure white.

Distribution.—*General:* Temperate North America from southeastern Alaska, British Columbia, northern Manitoba, Ontario, and Labrador south to Oregon, Nevada, northern New Mexico, Arkansas, Tennessee, and central Florida. Winters from northern States to Cuba and Mexico. *In Oregon:* Year-around resident, most abundant west of Cascades.

The little Hooded Merganser, or "Fish Duck," ranks with the Wood Duck and the Western Harlequin Duck in sheer beauty. The lovely black and white crest and dainty shape of the male make an exceedingly beautiful display, and the females have the same soft beauty as the hens of the other two species mentioned. The species was first recorded for the State by Townsend (1839). Bendire (1877) listed it from Malheur, and Mearns (1879) from Fort Klamath. Johnson (1880) and Anthony (1886) both found it in the Willamette Valley. Although found over a wide territory in Oregon, it is not seen as frequently as is either of the other two species, and we do not regard it as quite as abundant. It remains as a year-around resident and is most common west of the Cascades, where it is found along the smaller streams, near which it nests in hollow trees. The nest is lined with grass, and the eggs are covered with soft down. We have no actual egg dates from Oregon, a gap that must be filled by later workers.

Many observers have written of seeing this and other tree-nesting ducks bring their young to the water, and it is quite generally agreed that the young flutter down from their lofty perches without injury. The young birds are light, fluffy, and exceedingly elastic, and even when coming down from a tree 40 or 50 feet high apparently suffer no harm. Occasionally observers have reported seeing the young carried to the water in the beak of the parent birds, but this is certainly not the usual practice. Perhaps such a means of transportation is reserved for those living in the topmost stories and apartments.

We have no data on the food of this species while in Oregon waters, but data from other territories do not indicate that its diet is greatly different from that of other mergansers. It feeds on small fish, crustaceans, and water insects and is not abundant enough to have any appreciable effect on any valuable aquatic forms.

American Merganser:
Mergus merganser americanus Cassin

Description.—"*Adult male:* Head and short crest black glossed with green; shoulders black; wing black, with white in middle; rump and tail gray; neck and sides white; breast creamy white or pale salmon. *Adult female:* head, neck, and long thin crest light brown; rest of upper parts bluish gray, except white patch on middle of wing; chin and breast white." (Bailey) *Downy young:* "Downy young mergansers are beautiful creatures; the upper parts, including the crown, down to the lores and eyes, hind neck, and back, are rich, deep 'bister' or 'warm sepia,' relieved by the white edging of the wing and a large white spot on each side of the rump; the sides of the head and neck are 'mikado brown' or 'pecan brown,' shading off on the neck to 'light vinaceous cinnamon' or 'buff pink'; a pure white stripe extends from the lores to a point below the eyes and it is bordered above and below by dark brown stripes; the rest of the lower parts are pure white." (Bent) *Size:* "*Male,* length 25–27, wing 10.50–11.25, bill 1.90–2.20. *Female:* length 21–24, wing 9.60–9.75, bill 1.80–2.00." (Bailey) *Nest:* In hollow trees or on the ground, eggs protected in either case with down from the female's breast. *Eggs:* 6 to 17, usually 9 to 12, pale buffy.

Distribution.—*General:* Breeds in Canada and northern States south to central Vermont, New Hampshire, New York, Wisconsin, Minnesota, South Dakota, and in western mountain ranges south to northern New Mexico, Arizona, and central California. *In Oregon:* Breeds on all larger streams. Winters throughout State on all open waters.

The American Merganser, or Goosander, widely known to sportsmen and out-of-door people in Oregon as the "Fish Duck," or "Sawbill," was first listed from Oregon by Townsend (1839) and since then has often been mentioned from one part of the State or another. It is among the most beautiful of Oregon waterfowl, and the big, handsomely marked males, with their green heads and brilliant scarlet bills, are very conspicuous in comparison with the much smaller, trimly built females, with their dainty brownish-red crests. It is a permanent resident throughout the State on all the larger lakes and streams that do not freeze over during the winter.

It is much more common on the fresh waters than on salt water, and the similar-appearing females found on the bays and salt waters are largely of the species next discussed. One of the spots in Oregon where we have enjoyed seeing these birds, either from the train or from the highway, is along the Wallowa River. This river is a famous resort for mergansers, particularly during the winter, and one seldom makes a trip through the river canyon without seeing numbers of them.

These mergansers are among the most interesting of all Oregon waterfowl. Wonderfully skilled in the water, their big powerful paddles drive them through the waters of the swift streams with speed enough to catch any of the finny denizens. They are rather clumsy on land and usually do not venture far from the water's edge. They are also rather heavy of body, and the large males frequently have difficulty in launching themselves into the air, pattering along the surface much after the manner of coots until they obtain momentum enough to rise. Once in the air, they are strong, rapid flyers.

During March and April, observers are occasionally fortunate enough to see the courtship antics when two or more of the brilliantly colored males display to the best advantage their various plumage markings for the benefit of the female, who usually appears entirely indifferent until she selects the favored suitor. After the young are grown it is quite common to see family parties consisting of 1 to 10 females, or young in the female plumage, to every adult male.

The species nests along the swifter streams and about the shores of the larger lakes throughout the State, building its nest either in a hollow tree or on the ground. In the latter case, the nest is usually well hidden in grass or other debris or placed under the sheltering boughs of some bush or tree. The eggs, pale buff in color, usually number about 10 or 12. Like many other ducks, this one protects and shields its eggs with down plucked from the breast of the female. In late June or early July, the female can be seen leading her little fleet of downy chicks along the shores of the home body of water. These chicks are among the most beautiful of all waterfowl, the dark biscuit brown of their backs contrasting beautifully with the pure white under parts.

Fishermen and sportsmen frequently condemn these birds as voracious destroyers of trout and other game fish. When they get into hatchery ponds or into shallow pools where game fish are confined, the mergansers undoubtedly do considerable damage to the fish. At other times they feed largely on trash or slow-moving fish, crustaceans, and other aquatic life. There is at present no evidence to show that this species greatly harms the food or game fish of this State. It is not an abundant bird, although widely distributed. A few are usually to be found on each stream, and it is very questionable whether they do not do more good by eating spawn-eating fish than harm by any incidental destruction of game fish. We have very few data on Oregon stomachs on which to base an estimate, and stomach examinations by the Biological Survey over the entire area of the United States show that this species is not particularly destructive to game fish.

Red-breasted Merganser:
Mergus serrator Linnaeus

Description.—"*Adult male:* Head and crest black, glossed with green; neck white; back black; middle of wings white; rump gray; chest buffy brown, streaked with blackish; belly white or creamy; sides gray. *Adult female:* head and neck brown, darker and duller on crown and crest; rest of upper parts and tail slaty gray, except for white patch on wings; under parts white." (Bailey) *Downy young:* "The downy young red-breasted merganser is exactly like the young American merganser except for two very slight differences in the head; the nostrils in the red-breasted are in the basal third of the bill, whereas in the American they are in the central third; and the white loral stripe is tinged with brownish or buffy, but with a more or less distinct white spot under the eye." (Bent) *Size:* "Length 20–25, wing 8.60–9.00, bill about 2.50." (Bailey) *Nest:* On the ground, usually near the water, well concealed by weeds, shrubs, or trees, and lined with down. *Eggs:* 8 to 10, olive buff.

Distribution.—*General:* Breeds in northern portion of northern hemisphere south in North America to Newfoundland, northern New York, central Michigan, Wisconsin, and Minnesota, southern Manitoba, and southern British Columbia. Winters mainly on coasts of United States. *In Oregon:* Abundant winter resident on all coastal bays and river mouths from November until May.

First reported by Lewis and Clark (1814) from the mouth of the Columbia on March 27, 1806, the Red-breasted Merganser is now known as a winter bird on all the larger bays and river mouths along the coast, where it replaces the American Merganser, which is abundant over the fresh waters of the State. It arrives in November and remains until early May (our earliest date, November 22; latest, May 23, both Tillamook County), during which time it may be seen either as single birds or in little flocks. All Oregon specimens that we have been able to obtain have come from the coastal district, and so far as we know the species is at best only a casual visitor to the interior. Bendire (1877) and Merrill (1888) recorded it from Fort Klamath, and Bendire (1877) from the Blue Mountains. Although the adult males can be distinguished easily in life, it is possible to tell the young males and all females only by specimens in hand. We feel, therefore, that many of the Red-breasted Mergansers reported on sight observation from Malheur and Klamath basins are in reality the American Merganser.

Like its larger relative, previously discussed, the Red-breasted Merganser, is rather clumsy on land and in launching itself into the air, but once aloft is a swift, strong flyer. Either in or under the water, it is an expert of the first rank, being able to pursue and capture small fish and other aquatic life with ease. The strikingly marked males, with their red breasts and brilliant green crests, contrasting beautifully with their brilliant red bills, are among the handsomest of American birds. The females are very much like those of the American Merganser and can be distinguished from them only by the position of the nostril on the bill. In this species, the nostril is in the basal third of the bill, close to the feathering, whereas in the American Merganser it is in the central third of the bill, approximately halfway between the feathering and the tip. This characteristic will distinguish the bird in any plumage.

This species, like the preceding, is able to capture almost any kind of fish present in the waters that it frequents. Stomach examinations show, however, that trash fish make up a large percentage of the diet in other sections of the United States, and we have no reason to believe that it would be different in this territory. In any event, the birds are so few in numbers in Oregon that they can have little effect on the abundance of valuable fish, and we can well afford to contribute the few fish that they take in return for the pleasure that many persons get from seeing them.

Plate 26. Young Turkey Vulture. (Photo by Wm. L. Finley and H. T. Bohlman.)

Order Falconiformes

Vultures: *Family Cathartidae*

Turkey Vulture:
Cathartes aura septentrionalis Wied

Description.—"Whole head and upper part of neck naked, the skin corrugated and sparingly bristled; nostrils large, elliptical; wings long, pointed, folding to or beyond the short round tail. *Adults: head bare and crimson* in life, bill white; lores and top of head sometimes with wart-like papillae; neck and under parts dull black; upper parts blackish glossed with green and purple, feathers broadly edged with grayish brown, secondaries edged with gray; shafts of quills and tail feathers varying from pale brown to yellowish white. *Young:* like adults, but bill and naked skin blackish, brownish margins to wing coverts less distinct [Plate 26]. *Length:* 26–32, extent about 6 feet, wing 20–23, tail 11–12, bill 1." (Bailey) *Nest:* None, eggs laid in a cave, old stump, or hollow log. *Eggs:* Usually 2, white to greenish white, or buff, splotched and speckled with brown and gray.

Distribution.—*General:* From southern British Columbia, central Alberta, Saskatchewan, Manitoba, Minnesota, Michigan, Ontario, New York, and Connecticut south to Gulf coast and northern Mexico. Winters from Connecticut, Ohio Valley, Nebraska, and California. *In Oregon:* Common summer resident and breeding bird throughout State except in highest parts of mountains. Arrives in March and remains until late September.

The Turkey Vulture, or Turkey Buzzard, master of the airways, is a familiar sight almost everywhere in Oregon as it sails and glides on effortless pinions, taking advantage of every variation of wind and air currents to sustain itself in the air. On still days it can be seen making use of rising columns of air, swinging about in steadily mounting circles until the desired altitude is reached and then gliding away like a dark airplane. It can be distinguished from all other Raptores in the State by its naked head and neck, uniform dark color, and the silvery lining of its wings conspicuously displayed in flight.

Townsend (1839) first listed it from territory that is now Oregon, and Bendire (1877) found it breeding in Harney County. From April to September, it is the most commonly seen bird of prey in the State, though it may not be more abundant than some that do not so persistently advertise their presence. Our earliest record is February 16, Coos County; our latest, October 7, Polk County. Prill (1891b and 1895a) stated that it wintered in Linn County, but no other observers have reported it in the winter. Eggs are laid from May to July in caves, old stumps, hollow logs, and similar places. Jewett found a nest in Harney County, May 12,

1923, containing two fresh eggs, and Patterson reported egg dates from May 2 to June 10 in Klamath and Jackson Counties.

The Turkey Buzzard lives on carrion that it finds by searching the landscape from a vantage point high in the air. There has been a great deal of controversy as to whether sight alone is used in locating the food supply or sight aided by a keen sense of smell.

California Condor:
Gymnogyps californianus (Shaw)

Description.—"Wing 30 or more; head and entire neck bare, skin smooth; plumage of under parts lanceolate or pencillate; head much elongated, forehead flattened; nostril small, its anterior end acute; bill small, mandibles broader than deep; wings folding to or beyond end of square tail. *Adults:* head and neck bare, yellow, or orange in life; bill whitish or pale yellowish, plumage sooty blackish; outer webs of greater wing coverts and secondaries grayish, wing coverts tipped with white and outer secondaries edged with white; axillars and under wing coverts pure white. *Young:* like adults, but neck more or less covered with sooty grayish down, bill and naked skin blackish; brown edgings of feathers of upper parts producing a scaled effect; white of under wings and gray webbing of coverts and secondaries wanting. *Length:* 44–55, extent 8½ to nearly 11 feet; weight 20–25 pounds, wing 30–35, tail 15–18, bill 1.50." (Bailey) *Nest:* None, eggs laid in rocky caves or in decaying stumps or logs. *Eggs:* 1 or 2, greenish white.

Distribution.—*General:* At present restricted to Coast Ranges from San Benito County, California, to Los Angeles County and northern Lower California. Formerly reported to Columbia River. *In Oregon:* Extinct, but reported by early ornithologists.

Lewis and Clark (1814) wrote that the California Condor (Plate 27, *A*) was "not rare" near the mouth of the Columbia, November 30, 1805, and January 2, 1806; that it was abundant at Deer Island, March 28, 1806; and that it was seen again in Oregon, April 4, 1806. Douglas (1828) shot a male and female "in latitude 45.30.15., longitude 122.3.12.," which is near Multnomah Falls. Townsend (1839) listed it for the territory. Newberry (1857) reported it as "rare and not seen by us." Suckley did not see it, although on a constant lookout for it; but Cooper reported that in January 1854 he saw a bird that he was certain was this species (Cooper and Suckley 1860). He made a number of trips up and down the Columbia in the 50's but found only the one bird. Cooper stated:

> The Californian Vulture visits the Columbia river in fall, when its shores are lined with great numbers of dead salmon, on which this and other vultures, besides crows, ravens, and many quadrupeds, feast for a couple of months.

Barnston (1860) gave a detailed account of the capture of a California Vulture at Fort Vancouver in the spring of 1827 and told of the great joy with which Douglas received it. This interesting bit of early history was later quoted by Fleming (1924).

All the numerous subsequent references to the California Vulture as an

Oregon species rest on the observations of those quoted above, except the account of Finley (1908a), who referred to two at Drain about July 4, 1903, and four in March 1904. These birds were observed by George and Henry Peck, both familiar with the condor in California and both good ornithologists, who further stated that one was killed on the coast of southern Oregon. It is impossible that these observers, all keen and experienced naturalists, could have been mistaken, but the condor, if ever common in this State, seems to have become rare or almost completely extinct between Douglas' visit and the time of the Pacific Railway Surveys. Jewett has talked to several well-informed woodsmen who described accurately to him condors seen in southern Oregon at about the time of the Peck observation, and it seems highly probable that two or more of these big birds strayed into southern Oregon, perhaps to remain for some time.

Kites, Hawks, and Eagles: *Family Accipitriidae*

White-tailed Kite:
Elanus leucurus majusculus Bangs and Penard

Description.—"Bill rather weak and compressed; feet very small; tarsus feathered half way down in front, and below covered with minute roundish scales; claws not grooved beneath; hind toe very short, claws all small and little curved; wings nearly or about twice as long as tail, pointed, first and second quills emarginate, the feathers broad, obtuse at tips. *Adults:* under parts white, upper parts plain bluish gray, except for *white top of head and tail*, and *black patches around eye and on shoulders*. *Young:* resembling adults, but tinged with rusty, extensively on under parts; upper parts indistinctly streaked; wing feathers tipped with white; tail with an indistinct subterminal band. *Length:* 15.15–16.75, wing 11.50–13.30, tail 5.90–7.40, bill .65–.80." (Bailey) *Nest:* Of twigs, lined with grasses and other dried vegetation. *Eggs:* 3 to 5, white, heavily marked with red and brown.

Distribution.—*General:* Breeding bird in California valleys, Texas, Oklahoma, and Florida. *In Oregon:* Rare straggler, on basis of statements below.

Jewett (1933), who spent his boyhood years in California and who at that time was thoroughly familiar with the White-tailed Kite, has published a note in the *Murrelet* that reads as follows:

Some eight or ten years ago, Mr. Ben Hur Lampman, editorial writer of the Portland Oregonian, while fishing at Blue Lake in the Columbia River flats a few miles east of Portland, Oregon, saw a bird which he described accurately, and it could be none other than the White-tailed Kite (*Elanus leucurus*). Mr. Lampman was positive of this at the time and his description certainly verified his identification of the bird in life. No mention of this incident appeared in any of the ornithological journals.

On February 23, 1933, while I was on the Honeyman estate near Scappoose, Oregon, on the Columbia River bottoms some 20 miles west of Portland, with Game Protector Chester Leichhardt, one of these birds was seen at close range by both of us. We made careful obser-

Plate 27, *A*. California Condor. (Photo by Wm. L. Finley and H. T. Bohlman.)

Plate 27, *B*. Cooper's Hawk. (Photo by Wm. L. and Irene Finley.)

vations, both with and without eight-power binoculars, at a distance as close as 30 yards. The bird was kept under observation for at least half an hour.

Although I am opposed to publishing sight records under ordinary circumstances, I feel justified in recording the occurrence of this bird, as I am thoroughly familiar with the species in life from my boyhood experiences in California and have had opportunity to handle many skins and mounted specimens of the White-tailed Kite.

Under these circumstances, I do not hesitate to place on record the occurrence of this Kite in Oregon.

We have known Ben Hur Lampman for many years as a keen and accurate observer and have no reason to doubt that he actually saw a White-tailed Kite on Blue Lake. Jewett's thorough field knowledge of western birds makes it impossible that he could have been mistaken in his identification of so conspicuous a bird. On the basis of these incidents, we are therefore admitting the species to the Oregon list, although we are ordinarily opposed to such additions on the basis of sight records.

Goshawk:
Astur atricapillus (Wilson)

Description.—"Bare portion of leg in front shorter than middle toe; wing more than 12 inches. *Adults:* under parts with whitish ground, uniformly covered with *finely penciled gray zigzags*, touched up with dark shaft streaks; upper parts *dark bluish gray*, with black shaft streaks, and becoming black on head; tail bluish gray, more or less tipped with white and crossed by about four dusky bands, sometimes obsolete on the upper surface. *Young:* upper parts dull brown, head and neck streaked with buffy salmon, and rest of upper parts spotted and edged with pale buffy and whitish; under parts bright buffy, broadly streaked with dark brown. *Male:* Length 22.00, wing 12.00–13.25, tail 9.50–10.50. *Female:* Length 24.50, wing 13.50–14.25, tail 11.50–12.75." (Bailey) *Nest:* A bulky mass of twigs, placed well up in a tall tree, usually lined with finer grass and vegetable fibers. *Eggs:* 2 to 5, pale bluish white.

Distribution.—*General:* Breeds in boreal zones from Alaska, Mackenzie, Manitoba, Ontario, northern Quebec, and Newfoundland south to northern United States and southward along Allegheny Mountains to Pennsylvania and Maryland and in western ranges to central California, Arizona, and New Mexico. *In Oregon:* Permanent resident of Cascades and Blue Mountains. Apt to be found anywhere in State in fall and winter.

The first Oregon record of the striking Goshawk is that of Cassin (Baird, Cassin, and Lawrence 1858) at The Dalles, March 8, 1854. Newberry (1857) also found it, Mearns (1879) mentioned one taken by Henshaw at Fort Klamath on August 31, 1878, and Brewster and Merrill recorded a specimen from the same point, March 11, 1887 (Merrill 1888). Woodcock (1902) listed it from Scio, Beaverton, and Corvallis, the first western Oregon localities reported.

Bendire (1892) listed four nests found by him. One taken May 26, 1875, in the vicinity of Camp Harney contained two newly hatched young and an egg already chipped. Two others, taken April 18, 1876, and April 9, 1877, contained eggs, as did the fourth, taken April 17, 1881, in a canyon of the Blue Mountains. Dr. W. B. Bell, while with the writers, shot a female on Hart Mountain, June 15, 1926, that had a well-developed incubation patch, and Gabrielson found a nest with young on the Klamath Indian Reservation in June 1933.

We had numbers of skins collected at all seasons of the year, including several breeding birds from both eastern and western Oregon, and we had also a number of eastern birds with which to compare them. The characters supposed to separate the two subspecies were present in individual skins, but after long study we were not able to correlate such variations with any geographical range. Rather, they seemed distinctly to be correlated with age. In order to check our conclusions, we sent about a dozen of our birds to the National Museum in Washington for comparison. We then learned that Dr. Friedmann of that institution had already reached the same conclusion; namely, that there were not two geographical races of Goshawk. Our specimens only added further evidence to what he already possessed. His conclusions, based on much more material than ours, will undoubtedly appear in print before our statement does, so it seems unnecessary to elaborate further on the point.

The Goshawk is the largest and fiercest of the hawks of its group, which includes those other bird killers, the Sharp-shinned and Cooper's Hawks. It lives largely on birds, being a persistent enemy of grouse and pheasants. When the Blue and Ruffed Grouse take their broods to the ridges in the late summer it is often possible to find a Goshawk sitting on an inconspicuous perch in the thickest part of a tree waiting to take advantage of the slightest let-down in the vigilance of the feeding covey. If the Goshawk were more abundant, it might be to some limited extent the factor in holding down grouse populations for which it receives the blame among sportsmen. It is one of the rarer hawks of the State, however, and if the few breeding pairs remaining were to live throughout the year on grouse, quail, and pheasants, the effect would not be noticeable.

Sharp-shinned Hawk:
Accipiter velox velox (Wilson)

Description.—"*Adult male:* Under parts white, heavily barred and spotted with reddish brown; *upper parts nearly uniform* bluish gray; tail *even or slightly notched* with three or four narrow blackish bands, and narrow white tip. *Adult female:* similar, but duller, less blue above, less reddish below. *Young:* upper parts dark brown, edged with rusty and with hints of white spotting; under parts white, often tinged with buffy, streaked vertically with brown; sides and flanks barred with reddish brown. *Male:* length 10.00–11.50, wing 6.10–7.10, tail 5.80–6.10. *Female:* length 12.50–14.00, wing 7.80–8.80, tail 6.60–8.20." (Bailey) *Nest:* Usually an old crow's, magpie's, or squirrel's nest. *Eggs:* 4 to 5, greenish or grayish white, heavily blotched and spotted with brown.

Distribution.—*General:* Breeds from Alaska, Mackenzie, Manitoba, Ontario, Quebec, and Labrador south to northern Florida, Gulf coast, and central California.

Winters from southern Alaska, British Columbia, Montana, Minnesota, Great Lakes, New York, and central New England south to Central America. *In Oregon:* Common permanent resident in all parts.

The speedy little Sharp-shinned Hawk is much more abundant than most casual observers suspect, as its habit of doing its hunting by short dashes from a concealed perch in a tree often allows it to escape observation. It was first recorded for the State by Bendire (1877) from Camp Harney, and both Mearns (1879) and Merrill (1888) listed it from Fort Klamath. Anthony (1886) considered it common in Washington County, and Woodcock (1902) listed it from various localities in western Oregon. In our records it appears to be of equal abundance throughout the wooded areas. It undoubtedly nests throughout the State, although records of the actual finding of nests are rare. Bendire (1892) obtained a set of five eggs on May 18, 1883, near Fort Klamath; Jewett found a completed nest and collected the female with a fully developed egg in an ovary on May 16, 1914, at Vida (Lane County); and Gripentrog (1929) collected a set of eggs near Salem on May 22, 1928.

The resemblance of this hawk to the larger Cooper's Hawk is very close in comparable plumages, and a large female Sharp-shinned Hawk might easily be confused with a male Cooper's Hawk in either immature or adult plumage. If a clear view can be obtained in flight, the shape of the tail furnishes a good field identification mark. In this species, the outer tail feathers are about the same length as the central ones, so that the tail has a square appearance, while the tail of Cooper's Hawk looks rounded when spread enough to show the shorter outer feathers.

The Sharp-shinned Hawk is one of the few really destructive species. It feeds habitually on small birds, young chickens, and probably young game birds and because of its comparative abundance is undoubtedly the most destructive hawk in the State.

Cooper's Hawk:
Accipiter cooperi (Bonaparte)

Description.—"*Adult male:* Under parts white, heavily spotted and barred with reddish brown; *top of head black* contrasted with bluish gray of back; *tail rounded,* with 3 or 4 black bands and narrow white tip. *Adult female:* upper parts duller and less bluish than in male; top of head more brownish black; hind neck and sides of head washed with dull rusty. *Young:* upper parts dark brown, with rusty edgings and suggestion of white spotting; under parts streaked vertically. *Male:* length 14–17, wing 8.85–9.40, tail 7.80–8.30. *Female:* length 18–20, wing 10.10–11.00, tail 9.00–10.50." (Bailey) *Nest:* Usually an old crow's, hawk's, or squirrel's nest. *Eggs:* 4 to 5, bluish or greenish white, either with or without scrawls of brown or buff.

Distribution.—*General:* Breeds from southern Canada to northern Mexico. Winters from British Columbia, Colorado, Nebraska, Ohio Valley, and New England south to Central America. *In Oregon:* Regular permanent resident throughout State.

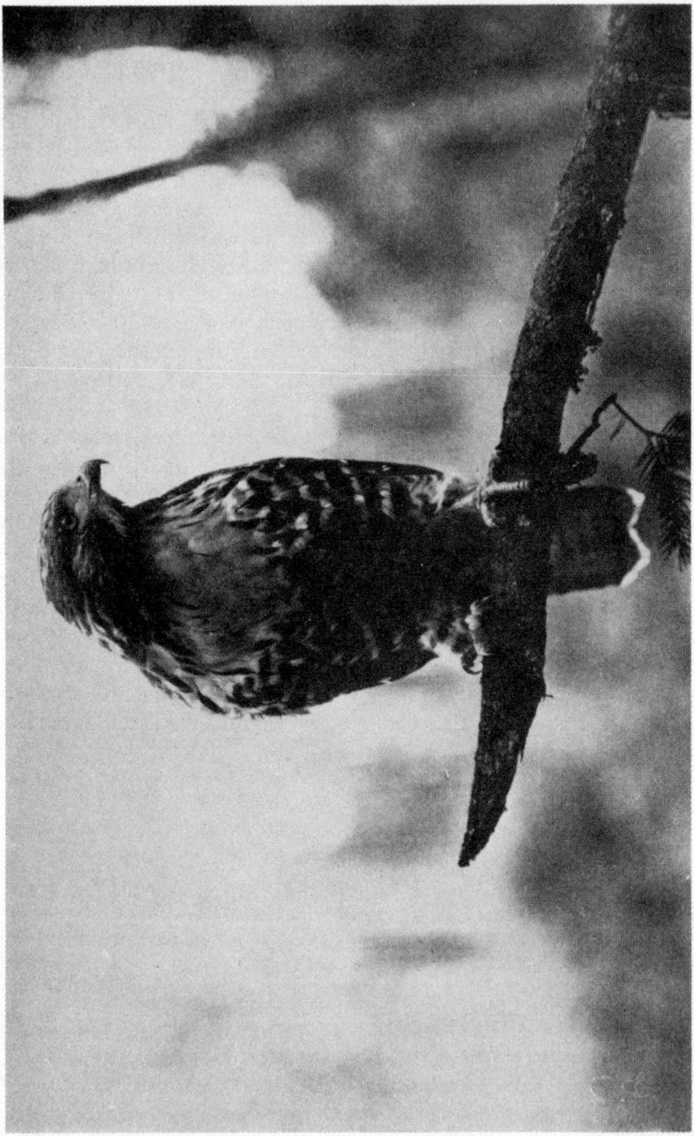

Plate 28. Young Western Red-tailed Hawk. (Photo by Wm. L. and Irene Finley.)

Cooper's Hawk (Plate 27, *B*), the larger cousin of the Sharp-shinned Hawk, is not quite so abundant in Oregon as that species but, like it, can be found throughout the wooded sections. This little falcon has a different flight than other hawks. It is able to move rapidly and turn quickly with its short, blunt wings. Although it does not appear to be traveling fast, the quick flaps of the powerful wings, alternating with short periods of soaring, really carry it through the air at an exceedingly rapid rate of speed. It was first listed by Townsend (1839) and was recorded by Newberry (1857), Heermann (1859), and Suckley (1860), who were connected with the Pacific Railway Surveys in this territory. As noted for the preceding species, nests are rarely reported, as it is difficult to find them in the huge firs and spruces that comprise so much of the forests, particularly in western Oregon. Hadley (Woodcock 1902) found eggs near Dayton in an old crow's nest 85 feet up in a fir tree, and Jewett discovered a nest near Minthorn (Milwaukie), Clackamas County, May 21, 1909, containing 4 eggs. Patterson collected eggs near Pinehurst, Jackson County, on May 10, and June 2, 1921.

This bird-killing hawk, known as the "Blue Darter" and "Chicken Hawk," is another of the few species in the State that is almost consistently destructive, living to a large extent on poultry, game, and insectivorous birds. In hunting, it selects as vantage point a low perch, frequently on a limb near the center of the tree. There it waits patiently until a bird comes within striking distance and then captures it by a short, quick dash. Gabrielson, when living on Powell Valley Road, lost some thirty baby chickens to a Cooper's Hawk that would sit concealed in a thick growth of firs until a chick came close. Then the marauder would dash out, seize its prey, and swing out of sight around the trees so quickly that unless one had been looking closely it would never have been seen. These raids took place at irregular intervals, and it required several mornings of lying in ambush to dispose of the killer.

Western Red-tailed Hawk:
Buteo borealis calurus Cassin

Description.—"*Adults:* Varying greatly in plumage—*Light extreme:* under parts white or buffy, with broad reddish brown streakings on throat, belly, and sides; *tail bright reddish brown*, with one or more subterminal blackish bars; rest of upper parts dark brown, more or less marked with yellowish brown and whitish. *Dark extreme:* uniform dark sooty brown except for rufous tail. *Intermediates:* reddish brown underneath, and with more or less reddish brown wash on upper parts. There are also all grades of plumage in this form between the light and dark extremes. *Young:* tail grayish brown varying to dull yellowish brown, crossed by 9 to 10 blackish bands; rest of plumage dark brown heavily spotted beneath, sometimes wholly dusky [Plate 28]. *Male:* length 19.00–22.50, extent of wings 49–53, wing 13.50–16.50, tail 8.50–10.00, bill .95–1.08. *Female:* length 23–25, extent 54.00–57.50, wing 15.25–17.75, tail 9.50–10.50, bill 1.00–1.15." (Bailey) *Nest:* A bulky mass of sticks, lined with roots or shredded bark and usually placed high up in a huge tree. Often used for years and gradually enlarged each year. *Eggs:* 2 or 3, creamy white, either unspotted or blotched and spotted with irregular marks of yellowish and reddish brown.

DISTRIBUTION.—*General:* Breeds from southern Alaska and central Mackenzie south to Lower California and east to Great Plains. Winters from southern Canada to Central America. *In Oregon:* Common permanent resident in every part.

THE WESTERN RED-TAILED HAWK was first found in Oregon by Lewis and Clark (1814), who listed it from the mouth of the Columbia on November 30, 1805, and it has been reported by every observer since. It is the only large *Buteo* found regularly in western Oregon, although some of the others may occasionally straggle into that part of the State. It is equally common in eastern Oregon but must share that country with the Ferruginous Rough-legged and Swainson's Hawks in summer and with the American Rough-legged Hawk in winter. In western Oregon, almost all of the large hawks seen sailing on set wings in ever-widening circles are this species, but in eastern Oregon careful identification is necessary. The best field mark, of course, is the red tail, which is often distinctly visible as the bird wheels and turns high overhead. The Red-tail has also a somewhat distinctive outline and a peculiar combination of black and white on the under side of the wings, but both of these characters can be learned only by long-continued field observation. Like all hawks of this genus, this species is quite variable in color, as it is particularly subject to melanism; that is, a darkening of the plumage throughout, which in extreme cases produces a dull black hawk with a red tail. The streaked young (Plate 28) also are exceedingly variable and are sometimes affected with this same darkening.

The Red-tail begins nesting operations early, having been seen engaged in repairing nests in late March and early April. Our earliest date for eggs is March 15 (Wasco County); our latest, June 23 (Klamath County), most of the fresh or nearly fresh sets having been taken in late April and early May. Braly has taken many sets between March 31 and April 30 in eastern Oregon, and Patterson found three fresh eggs in a nest near Spring Lake, Klamath County, on June 23, 1929.

Even though this hawk is largely a rodent eater, it is relentlessly persecuted by farmers and sportsmen, the former because of its supposed prowess as a "chicken hawk" and the latter out of the unreasoning belief that exists generally that all hawks spend their lives maliciously destroying game birds that should exist only for the benefit of those who hunt. In Oregon, there is little evidence to support such actions and much to the contrary. Three Western Red-tailed Hawks collected in Wallowa County in April and May 1928 by George Rodgers, a State game warden, in the belief that the hawks were killing Hungarian Partridges, quail, and pheasants, were examined by the Biological Survey, which found that two had fed exclusively on meadow mice (*Microtus nanus canescens*) and one on Columbian ground squirrels (*Citellus columbianus*). This is the usual result of such examinations.

Swainson's Hawk:
Buteo swainsoni Bonaparte

Description.—"*Adult male in normal plumage:* throat and belly white, *white of throat sharply contrasted with reddish brown chest band;* upper parts nearly uniform dark grayish brown; tail crossed by about 9 or 10 narrow blackish bands. *Adult female in normal plumage:* like male, but chest patch grayish brown instead of rufous. *Melanistic phase, both sexes:* whole plumage uniform sooty brown, under tail coverts sometimes spotted or barred with rusty or whitish. Every possible gradation is shown by different individuals between this black phase and the light colored normal plumage. *Young:* upper parts blackish brown varied with buffy or yellowish brown, head, neck, and under parts buffy brown, head and neck streaked with blackish; under parts usually more or less blotched with blackish. *Male:* length 19.50–20.00, extent 48.00–50.50, wing 14.40–16.00, tail 8–9, bill .80–.90. *Female:* length 21–22, extent 50.50–56.00, wing 14.75–17.25, tail 9–10, bill .80–.90." (Bailey) *Nest:* A bulky mass of sticks, lined with leaves and bark, usually in cottonwood or juniper. *Eggs:* 1 to 4, greenish white, sparingly spotted with brown.

Distribution.—*General:* Breeds from British Columbia (east of Cascades), Fort Yukon, Great Slave Lake, and Manitoba south to Mexico. Winters in southern South America. *In Oregon:* Common summer resident in all counties east of Cascades. Arrives in March and remains until September. Occurs in western Oregon only as a straggler.

Swainson's Hawk was described from a specimen taken near Fort Vancouver, Washington, but at present is only a straggler anywhere west of the Cascades. There is a specimen in the Biological Survey collection, taken at Corvallis in 1899 by A. H. Higginson, and there is one in the University of Oregon collection from Lane County. The species was first reported from Oregon by Cassin (Baird, Cassin, and Lawrence 1858) as found in 1854, and Bendire (Brewer 1875) collected eggs in Harney Valley. Shelton (1917) considered it a breeding bird in the Willamette Valley, but we have no evidence to substantiate this statement. In eastern Oregon, where it has been one of the most abundant nesting raptorial birds, it can still be considered a common summer resident, despite a noticeable decrease in its numbers in recent years. Our earliest record is March 11 (Wasco County); and our latest, October 25 (Harney County). Like other hawks, this one has a marked variation of plumage. Melanism is quite common, and all variations of darkness are found, some of them being a curious chocolate color. The young birds are a peculiar buff tone beneath with longitudinal brown stripes—quite unlike their parents.

The favorite nesting site is one of the gnarled twisted junipers growing in the sagebrush. There a bulky mass of sticks is built, sometimes close to the ground and usually not over 20 feet up. The nests are used for years if the birds are not molested, and the gradual accumulation of material frequently results in a huge structure. Eggs have been found by various collectors from April 21 to June 14. These include many records by Jewett and Braly.

This big squirrel hawk is one of the most beneficial species in the State as it lives almost entirely on ground squirrels, mice, rabbits, and other rodents. The hawks often congregate about a squirrel-infested meadow, as many as 27 having been noted about a single small field (Gabrielson 1922c). Despite convincing evidence published and republished over a long period of time showing it to be preeminently a rodent destroyer, Swainson's Hawk is still subjected to the persistent persecution of every man and boy who carries a gun, the excuse being that it is a "chicken hawk." Two birds killed in Wallowa County in 1928 by George Rodgers, the stomachs of which were examined by the Biological Survey, had eaten only rodents and insects. One stomach contained two meadow mice (*Microtus nanus canescens*) and one white-footed mouse (*Peromyscus maniculatus*); and the second stomach, one young Columbian ground squirrel (*Citellus columbianus*) and a number of stone flies (*Plecoptera*).

American Rough-legged Hawk: *Buteo lagopus sanctijohannis* (Gmelin)

Description.—"*Adults, normal phase:* Under parts varying from whitish to yellowish brown, more or less spotted with blackish, most heavily on breast; upper parts grayish brown or dark brown, streaked with white and reddish brown; *tail with base and upper coverts white* and end with subterminal dusky band; wing quills with *outer webs silvery gray*. *Young, normal plumage:* similar to adults, but end of tail plain grayish brown, the basal part plain whitish; under parts whitish or buffy, crossed on belly by a broad belt of uniform dark brown. *Melanistic phase* in both young and old—connected with normal plumage by every variety of intermediate character—entirely deep black except for white forehead, white on inner webs of quills above emargination, and narrow broken bands across base of tail. *Male:* length 19.50–22.00, wing 15.75–16.80, tail 9–10. *Female:* length 21.50–23.50, wing 16.15–18.00, tail 9–11." (Bailey) *Nest:* A bulky structure of sticks, lined with grass, leaves, or feathers. *Eggs:* 2 to 5, greenish white, irregularly blotched with brown and lavender.

Distribution.—*General:* Breeds from Aleutian Islands, Arctic Coast of Alaska, and Arctic islands south to Labrador, Quebec, and northern Alberta. Winters from southern Canada south to southern California, New Mexico, Texas, Louisiana, and North Carolina. *In Oregon:* Regular and at times abundant migrant and somewhat less common winter resident of eastern Oregon that appears in October and remains until April. Rare straggler in western Oregon.

The American Rough-legged Hawk is easily distinguished in normal plumage by the dark band across the belly. Like many other hawks, it is exceedingly variable in plumage, and melanism of varying degrees is quite common. Townsend (1839) first reported it from Oregon, and Bendire (Brewer 1875) and Merrill (1888) both reported it as a common winter resident. It has since been recorded by other observers from various parts of eastern Oregon. It is most abundant in October, November, March, and April, but it is a particularly common winter resident of Harney Valley and of the irrigated areas along the Snake and Columbia Rivers. Our earliest record is September 24 (Harney County); and our latest, May 9 (Lake County). West of the Cascades it is a rare straggler, being known from two specimens only, one taken at Seaside, October 13, 1925 (Jewett 1926a), and the second, at Netarts Bay, October 25, 1925 (Walker 1926).

While in the State as a migrant, as well as during the winter months, this hawk's favorite haunts are the irrigated meadows where an abundance of mice are normally available. These birds also show a marked tendency to congregate in areas where jack rabbits are numerous, among which are the sagebrush district of northern Morrow and Umatilla Counties and the rolling sage-covered hills of northern Malheur and Harney Valleys. The hawks habitually sit on available telephone poles or fence posts and are so tame and unsuspicious that they are easily approached and many are killed by farmer boys or hunters after other game. In the meadows, they are found on similar perches or on the haystacks, from which vantage point they watch for some luckless rodent to come into view.

Until about 1930, this was an exceedingly common winter resident in the eastern part of the State. Since that date there has been a great decrease in numbers. Coincident with this decrease has been an organized antihawk campaign by sportsmen in British Columbia, in which thousands of these harmless rodent-eating hawks have been slaughtered. Although no connection between these two events has been or can be demonstrated, they come suspiciously close together.

Ferruginous Rough-leg:
Buteo regalis (Gray)

Description.—"*Adults, normal phase:* Under parts white, sometimes slightly streaked with brown; *upper parts and flanks reddish brown;* tail white, more or less stained with reddish brown, and sometimes marked with a subterminal band. *Adults, melanistic phase:* tail normal; upper parts chocolate brown, marked with rusty; under parts rusty and chocolate. *Young:* upper parts grayish brown, feathers edged with rusty or yellowish brown; flanks white, more or less spotted with dusky; tail whitish for basal third, the rest brownish gray, usually with several more or less distinct dark bands. *Male:* length 22.50, wing 15.90–17.00, tail 9.50–10.50. *Female:* length 24, wing 17.00–18.80, tail 10.50–11.00." (Bailey) *Nest:* Bulky mass of sticks, lined with dry vegetation, bark, and feathers (Plate 29, *A*). *Eggs:* 2 to 5, creamy or greenish white, irregularly marked with brown and lavender.

Distribution.—*General:* Breeds from southern Alberta and Manitoba south to northeastern California, Utah, southern Arizona, New Mexico, and Kansas. Winters from Montana and Oregon to Lower California and northern Mexico. *In Oregon:* Regular summer resident and breeding species in eastern Oregon. Much less common in winter.

Plate 29, *A*. Nest of Ferruginous Rough-leg. (Photo by S. G. Jewett.)

Plate 29, *B*. Nest of Golden Eagle. (Photo by S. G. Jewett.)

Suckley (1860) reported the Ferruginous Rough-leg from Fort Dalles in December 1854. Bendire (1877) reported it from Camp Harney as rare. Woodcock (1902) listed these two records but gave no additional information, though curiously enough he took a specimen ten miles south of Corvallis, November 22, 1902, just a few months after publishing his list. This specimen and a single bird by Jewett seen near Independence, January 15, 1919, are the only two records for western Oregon. There are no other published references to it as an Oregon species prior to our own. We have found it to be a regular resident of eastern Oregon, most common along the Columbia. We have summer records for Jefferson, Deschutes, Malheur, and Wallowa Counties, and the species would probably be found in Grant, Wheeler, Union, and Baker Counties, if sufficient field work could be carried out. It is the largest and most striking *Buteo* known in the State and can be distinguished by the white tail and very light under parts, which stand in decided contrast to the reddish legs and lower belly. It flies more than the American Rough-legged Hawk and resembles the Western Red-tailed Hawk in its flight and hunting habits.

In northern Morrow and Umatilla Counties, by year-to-year additions, these birds build huge nests of sticks and sagebrush, some of which will support a man. The nests are usually located in the low junipers that are characteristic of that area and are seldom more than 20 feet from the ground (Plate 29, *A*). Twenty-eight nests inspected in that territory and two in Harney County between April 3 and May 13 were found to contain from one to five eggs (mostly three to five).

The Ferruginous Rough-leg is a persistent hunter of ground squirrels and rabbits and is known by a few farmers as the "Squirrel Hawk." In common with other large hawks of this group, it should be rigorously protected and not subjected to persecution.

Golden Eagle:
Aquila chrysaëtos canadensis (Linnaeus)

Description.—"A bird of great size, robust form, and powerful physique. Tarsus closely feathered all around to the toes, outer and middle toes webbed at base; bill large, long; wings long, pointed; tail moderate, rounded, or graduated; feathers of occiput and nape lanceolate. Sexes alike. *Adults:* whole bird dark brown, lanceolate feathers of hind neck and those on legs lighter brown; wing quills black; tail blackish, more or less clouded or irregularly banded with grayish. *Young:* like adult, but basal part of tail plain white, under parts white beneath the surface [Plate 30]. *Male:* length 30–35, extent about 6½ to 7 feet, wing 23.00–24.70, tail 14–15, bill 1.50–1.62. *Female:* length 35–40, extent about 7 to 7½ feet, wing 25–27, tail 15.16, bill 1.68–1.85." (Bailey) *Nest:* A bulky platform of sticks, lined with softer material, such as grass, feathers, or moss, usually (in Oregon) on a cliff, although occasionally in a big tree (Plate 29, *B*). *Eggs:* 2, white or irregularly marked with brown.

Distribution.—*General:* Breeds from northern Alaska and northwestern Mackenzie south to Lower California, central Mexico, and Texas. *In Oregon:* Permanent resi-

Plate 30. Young Golden Eagle. (Photo by Wm. L. Finley and H. T. Bohlman.)

dent of eastern Oregon, most abundant in the big sparsely settled counties of Malheur, Harney, and Lake, and in northern Morrow County. Only a straggler to western part of State.

Townsend (1839) first included the Golden Eagle, the most majestic of Oregon's raptorial birds, in a list applicable to the State. Cassin (1856) recorded it, and Bendire took eggs in 1877 and 1878 in Harney Valley. Since that time it has been mentioned by many observers. Woodcock (1902) listed one specimen from Scio and two from Corvallis, Johnson (1880) stated that it occurred at East Portland, Forest Grove, and Salem, and Walker (1924) reported one from near Tillamook on November 22, 1914. Jewett saw one shot near Tillamook, January 10, 1916, and saw another bird near Gold Hill, May 17, 1916. It is rare now west of the Cascades, however, and to be sure of seeing this regal bird, one must go to the great rim-rock country of eastern Oregon, where it is still a common breeding species and permanent resident. There it builds its nest on the inaccessible cliffs and soars far and wide over the surrounding country in search of food. We have recorded it in our notes from every county in eastern Oregon except Jefferson and Sherman, and for every month.

The eggs are usually laid in April, and the young birds remain in the nest until well into June. We have seen numerous nests in inaccessible places in many parts of eastern Oregon. One nest visited by the writers near Voltage on June 23, 1930, contained a young eagle that took off on unsteady pinions as we scrambled up the rocks below the nest. There are eggs in the United States National Museum taken by Bendire on April 9, 1877, and April 4, 1878, and there is a set from Harney Valley in the Braly collection taken April 8, 1931.

The Golden Eagle feeds largely on jack rabbits in Oregon but also takes waterfowl and other birds, all kinds of rodents, and possibly occasionally lambs and fawns.

Northern Bald Eagle:
Haliaeetus leucocephalus alascanus Townsend

Description.—"Tarsus feathered only half way down, middle and outer toes without web; wing pointed, secondaries much shorter than primaries; tail less than two thirds as long as wing, rounded. *Adults:* Head, neck, tail, and tail coverts snowy white; rest of plumage blackish or dark brownish, feathers edged with brown. *Young:* first year wholly black except for white bases of feathers showing through; second or third year under parts mixed black and white; head and neck black, rest of upper parts mixed gray, brown, black, and white." (Bailey) *Size:* Length (skins) 34.50–43.00, wing 22.44–26.97, tail 11.42–14.37, culmen from cere 1.50–1.65. *Nest:* A huge mass of sticks, lined with various plant materials and placed on high cliffs or in huge trees. *Eggs:* Usually 2, white.

Distribution.—*General:* From northwestern Alaska, northern Mackenzie, and northern Quebec south to Oregon and Great Lakes. Winters about in its breeding range. *In Oregon:* Uncommon resident along larger waterways and about high Cascade lakes. More common along coast.

THE NORTHERN BALD EAGLE was first recorded from Oregon in the report of the Lewis and Clark expedition (Lewis and Clark 1814), which mentioned that it had been seen about the mouth of the Columbia on November 30, 1805, and again on January 2, 1806. Townsend (1839) listed it, and Newberry (1857) found it common along the Columbia and Willamette Rivers and abundant about the Klamath Lakes. Heermann (1859) recorded it as common at the falls of the Columbia, and Suckley (1860) considered it abundant. Bendire (Brewer 1875) reported it from Camp Harney, and both Mearns (1879) and Merrill (1888) considered it a common breeding species about Fort Klamath. Applegate (1905b) stated it was common about Klamath, and this district is still one of the areas in which it is most regularly found.

Examining our own notes, we find that it has become rather an uncommon bird in Oregon, except along the coast where a number of pairs still breed. It also occurs fairly regularly along the Columbia River and in the Klamath Lake country. Aside from these areas, our records show recent reports of scattered individuals from the lakes of the Wallowa Mountains, the Deschutes River and lakes about its headwaters, Harney Valley, Lake County, and the headwaters of the Umpqua River.

Of the several pairs that still nest along the coast, all but two known to us built their nests on inaccessible cliffs. Those two chose sites high in old spruce trees near salt water. Patterson reported eggs taken in western Klamath County on April 6 and 22, 1922.

Marsh Hawk:
Circus hudsonius (Linnaeus)

DESCRIPTION.—"Bill with conspicuous bristles; face encircled by an owl-like ruff of short feathers; tarsus slender, much longer than middle toe and claw; a basal web between middle and outer toes; claws large and sharp, much curved; four outer primaries cut out on inner webs, second to fifth on outer webs. *Adult male:* body bluish slate, streaked with white and becoming *pure white on rump* and belly; under parts lightly specked with reddish brown; tail with 6 or 8 bands, on nearest end widest and blackest; tips of wing black. *Adult female and young:* brown or rusty, more or less streaked. *Length:* 19.50–24.00, wing 12.90–16.00, tail 8.80–10.50." (Bailey) *Nest:* On the ground, usually of grass and lined somewhac with feathers (Plate 31, *A*). *Eggs:* 4 to 6, pale greenish, either with or without blotches and spots of brown and buff.

DISTRIBUTION.—*General:* Breeds from Alaska, Mackenzie, Manitoba, Ontario, Quebec, and Newfoundland south to Lower California, Arizona, Texas, southern Illinois, Indiana, Maryland, and Virginia. Winters over most of United States and south to Columbia. *In Oregon:* Permanent resident, much more common east than west of Cascades. Least common on coast.

THE MARSH HAWK (Plate 31, *A*) is easily distinguished from all other hawks by its trim shape, its comparatively long tail, and the square white patch at the upper base of its tail. It was first listed by Townsend

Plate 31, *A*. Young Marsh Hawks in nest. (Photo by Ira N. Gabrielson.)

Plate 31, *B*. Osprey. (Photo by Wm. L. Finley and H. T. Bohlman.)

(1839) and has been reported as common in eastern Oregon by Newberry (1857), Suckley (1860), Bendire (1877), Mearns (1879), and Merrill (1888), as well as numerous later observers. Johnson (1880) reported it from East Portland, Forest Grove, and Salem; Anthony (Bailey 1902) thought it rare at Portland; Woodcock (1902) stated it was uncommon at Corvallis; and Shelton (1917) considered it of irregular occurrence in Lane County. In eastern Oregon, it is an exceedingly common species about the irrigated areas and the hayfields of the big stock ranches and is regularly found in the grain-growing sections. Patterson took eggs in Klamath County, May 1 and 6, 1922, and Jewett found a nest at Malheur Lake, May 19, 1924, with three well-incubated eggs. He also found a nest near Malheur Caves on June 29 containing young. The species is uncommon but occasionally seen in all parts of the Willamette Valley. It is a rarity on the coast, where our only records are of those seen by Jewett at Tillamook, November 9, 1915, and at Brookings, Curry County, March 14, 1933. It has not been noted in either the Rogue or Umpqua Valleys.

The Marsh Hawk habitually feeds by circling and swinging low over the marshes and pasture lands, seldom being seen high in the air. It is and has been the subject of much debate. Sportsmen, seeing it quartering the marshes, immediately visualize it as spending its entire time feeding on ducks. We feel that it seldom kills a healthy adult duck, although it may capture wounded birds and feed to a limited extent on young ducklings. Meadow mice, which usually are abundant in the surrounding hay lands, are its staple article of diet, whereas its depredations on ducks are limited to a few weeks during the summer when the downy young are present in numbers.

Osprey:
Pandion haliaetus carolinensis (Gmelin)

Description.—"Plumage close, firm, imbricated, oily; feet large and strong, roughly granular; toes all free to the base, outer toe reversible; claws all the same length; wings long, pointed; tail short. *Adult male:* Head, neck, and under parts white, head more or less streaked with blackish, broad dark streak on side of head; breast sometimes slightly blotched with brown; tail narrowly tipped with white and crossed by 6 or 7 narrow blackish bands. *Adult female:* similar, but chest heavily spotted with brown. *Young:* sexes similar to adults, but upper parts blackish brown, feathers tipped with white or buffy. *Length:* 20.75–25.00, extent about 65, wing 17–21, tail 7–10, bill 1.20–1.45." (Bailey) *Nest:* A mass of sticks, weed stalks, and similar material, lined with softer material and placed almost anywhere, on the ground, on old buildings, cliffs, or in trees. In Oregon, almost invariably in tall trees. *Eggs:* Usually 3, variable in color, generally white overlaid with buffy and frequently heavily blotched with browns of various shades.

Distribution.—*General:* Breeds from Alaska, Mackenzie, Hudson Bay, Labrador, and Newfoundland south to Gulf coast, Mexico, and Lower California. Winters from Gulf States, Mexico, and Lower California south to Central America. *In Oregon:* Uncommon summer resident throughout State. Arrives in April and remains until October.

The Osprey, or Fish Hawk (Plate 31, *B*), formerly common along the Columbia and Willamette Rivers, in the Klamath basin, and about the larger Cascade lakes, must now be considered one of the rarer Oregon hawks. It is still present in the Klamath basin but in sadly diminished numbers. A few are found along the coast, and scattered pairs occur along the larger streams, such as the Rogue, the Umpqua, the Deschutes, the John Day, and the Columbia Rivers. Throughout the State, however, it is now an uncommon summer resident that arrives in April and remains until October (earliest date, March 30, Deschutes County; latest, October 25, Union County).

Townsend (1839) included it in his list of birds found in the "Territory of Oregon." Newberry (1857) found it common in all parts of the State visited by him, including the Cascades, the Klamath Lakes, the Willamette Valley, and the Columbia River. Bendire (1877) reported it as a rare breeder in Harney Valley, and both Mearns (1879) and Merrill (1888) considered it common about Fort Klamath. Many years later Applegate (1905b) found it still common in the same territory, a condition that unfortunately no longer exists.

In many sections of the Atlantic Coast, Ospreys are protected and even provided with nest sites by the farmers, but in Oregon, like all other hawks, they are killed at every opportunity, both by farmer boys and those sportsmen who begrudge them the few fish they consume. These birds do feed on fish obtained by diving into the lakes and streams, but needless to say, such species as suckers and carp are captured much more frequently than more valuable fish. Certainly, the few trout or game fish they take in no wise justify the persecution to which the birds are subjected in the State.

Falcons: *Family Falconidae*

Gyrfalcon:
Falco rusticolus obsoletus Gmelin

Description.—"*Adults:* Top of head largely streaked with white; anterior upper parts barred with grayish or whitish and darker; tail strongly banded; flanks and thighs more or less marked with slaty. *Young:* upper parts much spotted with white or buffy; under parts with dark stripes usually narrower than white interspaces. *Male:* length 20–21, wing 14.10, tail 8.51, bill .90, tarsus 2.40. *Female:* length 22.00–24.50, wing 15.76, tail 9.72, bill 1.01, tarsus 2.46." (Bailey)
Distribution.—*General:* Breeds in northern North America from Point Barrow to Labrador and wanders south to northern States in winter. *In Oregon:* Rare straggler known from three records only.

THIS GRAY TERROR from the north, the Gyrfalcon, is one of Oregon's rarest birds. It is known from three skins only. The first was taken at Hermiston, Umatilla County, November 17, 1916, and is now in the Jewett collection (Jewett 1919); the second was obtained at Scio, Linn County, in May 1925 (Prill 1928); and the third, a female, now in Dr. Prill's collection, was killed in the St. Helens district in 1927 by a duck hunter.

There has been much confusion in the classification of these birds. It has been generally assumed that three or four races occurred in North America. These races have been based largely on variations in winter birds with all too few breeding birds available for study. Friedmann has only recently come to the conclusion, after careful study of all available skins, that there is only one Gyrfalcon in North America and this he calls *obsoletus*. We are following his ideas, but in calling these birds *obsoletus* the name is not restricted as it is in the 1931 Check-List but applies generally to the birds that breed from Point Barrow across the Arctic wastes to Labrador.

Prairie Falcon:
Falco mexicanus Schlegel

DESCRIPTION.—"*Adult male:* Under parts and nuchal collar *white*, sides of head with dark patches; median under parts lightly streaked or spotted, and flanks heavily spotted or blotched with dusky; *upper parts pale clay brown*, usually tinged with rusty and indistinctly but broadly barred with pale clay color or dull buffy anteriorly, and with pale bluish gray posteriorly. *Adult female:* upper parts dull clay brown, feathers edged with rusty brown or dull whitish, paler toward tail; tail tipped with whitish and lighter on outer edges of feathers. *Young:* upper parts grayish brown, feathers edged with light rusty; under parts buffy with broader dusky streaks; dark flank patch larger and more uniform than in the adult, and axillars unbroken dusky [Plate 32, *A*]. *Male:* length 17–18, wing 11.60–12.50, tail 6.40–7.50, bill .70–.75. *Female:* length 18.50–20.00, wing 13.25–14.30, tail 8–9, bill .85–.90." (Bailey) *Nest:* Built of sticks, usually on a ledge of a high cliff or rim. *Eggs:* 3 to 5, creamy white, blotched and spotted with reddish brown.

DISTRIBUTION.—*General:* From southern British Columbia, southern Alberta, and southeastern Saskatchewan to southern Lower California and southern Mexico. *In Oregon:* Common permanent resident of eastern Oregon. Straggles occasionally to western Oregon.

THE PRAIRIE FALCON is the most abundant representative of the larger falcons found in Oregon. Cassin (Baird, Cassin, and Lawrence 1858) first listed it, from Fort Dalles, and Suckley (1860) found it not rare at the same point. Bendire (1877) found it common in the Harney Valley, and Mearns (1879) reported it from Fort Klamath. There is no bird whose power of flight commands more admiration than that of this falcon, the aerial abilities of which enable it to overtake such speed artists as the

Plate 32, *A*. Young Prairie Falcon. (Photo by S. G. Jewett.)

Plate 32, *B*. Eastern Sparrow Hawk. (Photo by Wm. L. Finley and H. T. Bohlman.)

Mourning Dove and teal. About the nests one usually finds a wide assortment of feathers of the above birds and of meadowlarks, flickers, Sage Thrashers, and robins, although there is often a liberal sprinkling of smaller species also. Because of its wariness and speed it has held its own in eastern Oregon better than many of the other hawks and is still a common permanent resident of the towering rims of most of that part of the State, where it can be seen flying along at tremendous speed on effortless wings. It nests about the rims and lays its eggs in April. The dates of five sets taken by Braly in the past few years, mostly along the Columbia River, vary from April 6 to 20, although Patterson took eggs in the Klamath country on May 5 and 8, 1928.

In western Oregon it occurs only as an irregular straggler. Johnson (1880) reported one specimen from the Willamette Valley; Jewett (Gabrielson 1931) saw one near Medford, Jackson County (March 1, 1924), and received one taken at Portland (November 27, 1934); and Gabrielson (1931) took one at Eagle Point, Jackson County (November 8, 1926). There is also a specimen in the Jewett collection taken at the game farm at Corvallis (November 26, 1925), and Walker (1927) reported three in the Griepentrog collection taken at Salem (November 16, 1924, December 25, 1925, and November 10, 1926).

Of two stomachs collected in winter in eastern Oregon, one taken at Arlington contained a domestic pigeon, and one from Pilot Rock, a white-footed mouse (*Peromyscus maniculatus gambelii*).

Duck Hawk:
Falco peregrinus anatum Bonaparte

Description.—"*Adults:* Sides of head and neck black, in striking contrast to white or buffy of throat and breast; rest of under parts deeper colored and spotted or barred with blackish; *top of head sooty black, rest of upper parts slaty blue*, lighter on rump, indistinctly barred with dusky; wing quills blackish, inner webs of quills spotted regularly with buffy or yellowish brown; tail blackish, crossed by 8 to 10 light grayish bars, and with narrow white tip. *Young:* under parts yellowish, brown or reddish brown, heavily streaked with dark brown; upper parts blackish, feathers edged with rusty; tail spotted with reddish brown and conspicuously tipped with buffy. *Male:* length 15.50–18.00, wing 11.30–13.00, tail 6.00–7.50, bill .75–.80. *Female:* length 18.20, wing 13.00–14.75, tail 6.90–9.00, bill .85–1.00." (Bailey) *Nest:* Usually on a ledge of rock or in old hawks' nests in trees. *Eggs:* 4, creamy white, spotted with brown or brick red.

Distribution.—*General:* Breeds from Alaska, northern Mackenzie, Baffin Island, and west coast of Greenland south to Lower California, central Mexico, Kansas, Missouri, Tennessee, and Connecticut. Winters from Vancouver Island, Colorado, Nebraska, Ohio River, New Jersey, and Massachusetts south to West Indies and Panama. *In Oregon:* Rare permanent resident, likely to be noted in any part of State during migration, but most frequently seen in eastern Oregon.

Townsend (1839) first listed the Duck Hawk from our territory, and Bendire (1877) listed it as rare in Harney Valley, though he took a set of three eggs from a basaltic cliff near Malheur Lake on April 24, 1877 (Bendire 1892). Merrill (1888) reported it as common at Fort Klamath, and Anthony (Woodcock 1902) stated that a few were seen in Portland and vicinity.

We consider it a comparatively rare bird in Oregon, where it is usually to be found following the migrating waterfowl or near wintering flocks of the same birds. We have noted it in Klamath, Lake, Harney, Malheur, Crook, Douglas (Diamond Lake), Lincoln, Multnomah, and Curry Counties and have known of one pair nesting in Lake County since 1920. Curiously enough this nesting pair, the only one known definitely to us in recent years, is on an isolated rock far from water, where Mourning Doves, meadowlarks, Sage Thrashers, and similar birds usually preyed upon by the Prairie Falcons must of necessity furnish their food supply.

The Duck Hawk, like the Prairie Falcon, has remarkable powers of flight. Flying with steady, apparently easy wing beats, it is yet able to overtake the swiftest waterfowl. Gabrielson (1922) saw one overtake a flock of teal in full flight and strike one down. The Duck Hawk was traveling much faster than the teal, whose frantic wing beats made a haze beside their bodies, and yet the hawk gave the very definite impression that he had unused speed in reserve.

Peale's Falcon:
Falco peregrinus peali Ridgway

Description.—"*Adults:* Like *F. p. anatum*, but ***head and upper parts uniform dark slate blue;*** barred on back of wings and tail; chest marked with tear-shaped blackish spots, and rest of under parts broadly barred with blackish. *Young:* under parts sooty black, streaked with buffy or buffy white; upper parts with only faint traces of rusty feather margins. *Male:* wing 12.95, tail 6.75, bill .84. *Female:* wing 14.66, tail 7.84, bill .96." (Bailey) *Nest and eggs:* Same as those of *F. p. anatum*.

Distribution.—*General:* Breeds on Aleutian, Commander, and possibly Queen Charlotte Islands. Winters south to Oregon. *In Oregon:* Regular winter resident of coast. Usually appears in late August and remains until March.

Peale's Falcon, or Black Duck Hawk, is strictly a bird of the coast in Oregon, the only inland record being one of a bird found dead in Portland on October 25, 1927 (Gabrielson Coll.). It is a regular winter resident that ordinarily begins to appear in late August and remains until March (earliest date, July 5, Tillamook County; latest, May 3, Clatsop County). It is most abundant from September to January. Our earliest specimen is from Waldport, Lincoln County, August 31, 1923 (Gabrielson Coll.), and our latest spring record is the one taken May 3, 1931, at Seaside, Clatsop County.

Little has been written about this species as an Oregon bird. Gurney

(1882) credited it to the State, and Woodcock (1902) listed it as a breeding bird at Newport on B. J. Bretherton's report. Walker (1926) listed it from Netarts, and various general ornithologists have credited it to Oregon. In our experience it is a regular but not common winter resident on the coast, occasionally as far south as Curry County, frequenting the offshore rocks and rocky promontories where it makes life exciting for the Black Turnstones, scoters, murres, and other wintering water birds. Occasionally one takes up a winter residence on the wind-carved timber that adorns the long sand spits across the mouths of many Oregon bays. There this speedy killer will be found perched on a dead snag that affords a clear view of the open spit in a fine strategic position to observe and attack any of the constant procession of water birds that cross the spit. Its speed enables it to overtake the swiftest, and its boldness often leads it to attack birds larger than itself. The bird collected at Waldport by Gabrielson had just killed and was tearing apart an adult California Gull.

Black Pigeon Hawk:
Falco columbarius suckleyi Ridgway

DESCRIPTION.—"*Adult male:* Upper parts blackish brown, wing coverts and tertials slaty, tail coverts bluish slate; tail black, with three slaty whitish bars, and tip marked with whitish; throat white streaked with black; rest of under parts blackish brown with whitish and tawny markings. *Adult female and young:* under parts heavily marked with dusky; upper parts blackish brown, wing coverts and tertials slaty; tail coverts bluish slate; inner webs of quills not distinctly spotted or barred; tail bands, except for whitish tip, indistinct or obsolete. *Male:* wing 8, tail 4.90, tarsus 1.40, bill .70. *Female:* wing 8.25–8.50, tail 5.70–5.80, bill .55–.60." (Bailey)

DISTRIBUTION.—*General:* Breeds apparently in western British Columbia and perhaps on Vancouver Island. Winters south along coast to southern California. *In Oregon:* Rare winter resident of coast. Only of casual occurrence inland.

LITTLE has been written regarding the status of the Black Pigeon Hawk in Oregon. Bendire (1892) recorded a pair at Fort Klamath, May 9, 1883, and Eckstrom (1902) listed a specimen for the same locality and date. Evidently these two records refer to the same bird or birds. Anthony (Bailey 1902) considered it a common winter visitor in the vicinity of Portland, but no other observer has ever regarded it as anything except a rare species. Woodcock (1902) stated it was not common at Yaquina Bay and Corvallis. Walker (1924) took a specimen October 1, 1921, at Netarts Bay, and Prill (1928) one from Scio, November 1, 1922. In addition to these, there are four specimens from Oregon. The first two are in the Jewett collection, one from Seaside, taken October 18, 1927, and the second, a most remarkable record, procured by Harold Dobyns at Heppner, July 31, 1929. The third is in the Gabrielson collection, and was taken at Modoc Point, Klamath County, October 9, 1934. The fourth was taken by Alex Walker, in Tillamook County, May 5, 1934.

We have noted this hawk also in Portland, where, for several winters, one harassed the pigeons and English Sparrows about the Post Office Building at Broadway and Glisan Streets, and we have seen it in Coos, Tillamook, and Lincoln Counties under exceptionally favorable opportunities for observation.

Western Pigeon Hawk:
Falco columbarius bendirei Swann

Description.—"Middle tail feathers crossed by not more than four blackish or five lighter bands. *Adult male:* under parts heavily striped on whitish, buffy, or rusty ground, striping lightest or wanting on throat; upper parts bluish gray, with black shaft streaks, hind neck mixed with whitish, buffy, or yellowish brown; wing quills blackish, inner webs distinctly barred or spotted. *Adult female:* upper parts brownish, top and sides of head streaked with blackish; under parts whitish or buffy, without rusty tinge. *Young:* like female but darker, or tinged with rusty or yellowish brown above, and whitish or buffy below. *Size: Male*, length 10–11, wing 7.40–7.80, tail 4.65–5.20, bill .48–.50. *Female*, length 12.50–13.25, wing 8.35–8.60, tail 5.30–5.50, bill .55–.60." (Bailey) *Nest:* On cliffs or in trees, those in the latter situations built of sticks and lined with feathers, shredded bark, or moss. *Eggs:* 4 or 5, ground color white, usually suffused with reddish brown.

Distribution.—*General:* Breeds from Alaska, Yukon, and northwestern Mackenzie to British Columbia, Alberta, and Saskatchewan, and south in mountains to California. *In Oregon:* Very rare breeding bird and uncommon migrant and winter resident in eastern Oregon. Very rare straggler west of Cascades.

The Pigeon Hawk was first recorded from Oregon by Townsend (1839). Newberry (1857) reported it as paired and nesting about Klamath Lake. Bendire (1877), under the name *F. c. richardsoni*, reported a nest containing young in May 1876, which he stated was the only nest he had seen, although later he listed eggs taken at Camp Harney, April 20, 1876 (Bendire 1892). Merrill (1888) reported it from Fort Klamath and Diamond Lake, and Anthony (1886) regarded it as rare in Washington County. Willett (1919) listed two taken in August near Malheur Lake, and there are scattered references to it in Biological Survey field notes for Oregon, including two specimens taken in August 1914, in Lake County, by L. J. Goldman and a record of the bird at Empire, Coos County, in October, by D. D. Streeter, Jr.

In our own experience, this little falcon is an uncommon bird in Oregon except in late August and September, the period in which most of our records fall. We have specimens taken in Wallowa (April 11), Harney (September 16), Gilliam (December 22), Malheur (December 5), and Klamath (January 22) Counties and sight records under favorable conditions in Grant, Klamath, Lake, Washington, and Jackson Counties, all in eastern Oregon except the last two. The species is perhaps more common than these records indicate, but except under favorable observational conditions it can easily be confused with the more plentiful young

Sharp-shinned Hawk. It is a rather tame and unsuspicious little falcon, often allowing an observer to walk directly beneath its perch on a telephone pole or small tree. Several of our specimens and records have been obtained in such situations.

One bird taken by Harold Dobyns near Arlington on December 22, 1927, had eaten a Horned Lark.

Eastern Sparrow Hawk:
Falco sparverius sparverius Linnaeus

Description.—"*Adult male:* Top of head bluish or slaty, with or without rufous crown patch; cheeks with two black stripes; back rufous, with or without black bars or spots; wings bluish gray; tail rufous, with black subterminal band; under parts varying from white to rufous, with or without black spots. *Adult female:* similar, but back, wings, and tail barred with dusky. *Young:* similar to adults, but colors more blended and—in male—feathers of upper parts edged with whitish. *Male:* length 8.75–10.60, wing 7.16, tail 4.73, bill .50. *Female:* length 9.50–12.00, wing 7.57, tail 5.14, bill .50–.55." (Bailey) *Nest:* In old woodpecker holes or natural cavities in trees. *Eggs:* 2 to 5, from pure white, faintly marked, to deep buff, spotted and blotched with brown.

Distribution.—*General:* Breeds from Upper Yukon, British Columbia, northwestern Mackenzie, Alberta, Saskatchewan, Manitoba, northern Ontario, Quebec, and Newfoundland south to northwestern California, Colorado, Texas, and Gulf States. Winters from southern British Columbia, Kansas, Indiana, central Illinois, Ohio, Ontario, and Massachusetts, south to Panama. *In Oregon:* Very common permanent resident throughout State.

Since Newberry (1857) first listed the Eastern Sparrow Hawk (Plate 32, *B*) as an abundant Oregon species, many ornithologists have commented on its presence. This handsome little falcon is without doubt the most abundant raptorial bird found in the State and is a familiar sight to most travelers as it perches on the telephone poles along the highways, now and then darting to the ground to get a mouse, a beetle, or a grasshopper detected by its keen eyes. In addition to hunting for its prey in this fashion, it often hovers over a field on rapidly beating wings while carefully scanning the area below for some evidence of an edible tidbit. It is most abundant from March to September but remains commonly through the winter in all parts of the State except the higher mountains. It has been noted in every county.

The nests are built in holes in trees, often in old excavations made by the flicker. Egg dates vary from April 26 to June 20, most of those taken being from eastern Oregon where it is easier for the collector to find nesting sites than in the dense timber of western Oregon.

Order Galliformes

Grouse: *Family Tetraonidae*

Richardson's Grouse: *Dendragapus obscurus richardsoni* (Douglas)

DESCRIPTION—"Similar to *D. obscurus*, but tail without distinct terminal gray band, and tail feathers more truncated at tip." (Bailey) *Downy young:* Similar to Sooty Grouse. *Size: Male*, length 20–23, wing 9.40–10.00, tail 8. *Female*, length 17.50–19.00, wing 8.70–9.00, tail 6. *Nest and eggs:* Similar to Sooty Grouse.

DISTRIBUTION—*General:* Resident in Rocky Mountains from central British Columbia and western Alberta to northeastern Oregon, central Idaho, and Wyoming. *In Oregon:* Permanent resident. All Blue Grouse records from Wallowa, Baker, Union, northern Malheur and Harney, eastern Crook, Grant, Wheeler, southern Morrow, and southern and eastern Umatilla Counties are properly referred to this form. (See Figure 4.)

THE MALE Richardson's Grouse is distinguished in life from the Sooty and Sierra Grouse by the following salient differences. It is a somewhat larger bird with a noticeably longer and squarer tail, and it lacks entirely the terminal band found in the other two. Its *hoot* is much the same as that of the others but lacks volume and carrying power. Its air sacs are much smaller than the huge affairs of the others and are red purple instead of orange yellow. The females and young are quite similar to those of the other species.

Early records of Blue Grouse were badly confused, so that we find Richardson's Grouse reported on the coast and breeding records for the Sooty Grouse in the Blue Mountains. All records of Blue Grouse in the Blue Mountain area refer to Richardson's Grouse, whereas those from the Warner Mountains, Cascades, and Coast Ranges refer to the Sooty and Sierra Grouse. So far as we can tell the earliest definite reference to this species as an Oregon bird was by Audubon (1838), who listed it from the Blue Mountains of Oregon. Bendire (1877) found the first nest reported from the state on June 7, 1876, near the summit of Canyon City Mountain. It contained 9 eggs. He reported both this species and *fuliginosus* abundant in this territory; this was surely a mistake, as there is no evidence of an overlapping of ranges of these forms in this area.

In habits and behavior Richardson's Grouse are quite similar to other Blue Grouse and gather on the higher open ridges in August to feed. At this season the currant patches of the Wallowas are a favorite rendezvous of this species and the Gray Ruffed Grouse, which feed together, each going its separate way when alarmed, the Ruffed Grouse usually making for the aspen and lodgepole thickets, and their larger cousins seeking the shelter of the higher trees. They remain on the high ridges until the available food supply is exhausted and then take to the timber to feed on buds and needles till spring.

Richardson's Grouse, when feeding on the ground, frequently leave a single bird on guard in the branches of a nearby tree. The whirr of the lookout's wings as he takes alarm seems to serve as a warning signal to the birds below. This species when feeding on the currants or other berries, almost invariably stands on the ground, reaching up to get the fruit or picking up fallen berries. In the same patches, the Ruffed Grouse likewise may be found on the ground but often are perched in the bushes competing with the robins and Varied Thrushes for the fast-vanishing crop.

Sooty Grouse:
Dendragapus fuliginosus fuliginosus (Ridgway)

Description—*Adult male:* Upper parts sooty blackish, finely mottled with gray and brown, buffy brown on wings; hinder scapulars usually with distinct shaft streaks and terminal spots of white; tail blackish with a narrow bluish gray band; under parts slaty, marked with white on side of neck and flanks. *Adult female:* Similar to male, but decidedly smaller, and upper parts, chest, and sides barred and mottled with dark brown and buffy. *Young:* upper parts yellowish brown, with irregular barring or mottling, and black spots and white or buff shaft streaks widening at tip; under parts dull whitish, chest and sides spotted with black. (Adapted from Bailey.) *Downy young:* "In the downy chick the head and under parts vary from 'cream color' to 'ivory yellow'; the crown is mottled with black and a little 'hazel,' and the auriculars are spotted with black; the upper parts are variegated with 'hazel,' 'chestnut,' dusky, and pale buff. The wings begin to grow soon after the chick is hatched; in a chick 3 inches long they already reach beyond the tail. These first wing feathers

Figure 4.—Distribution of three forms of grouse in Oregon: 1, Richardson's Grouse (*Dendragapus obscurus richardsoni*); 2, Sooty Grouse (*D. fuliginosus fuliginosus*); 3, Sierra Grouse (*D. f. sierrae*).

Plate 33, *A*. Downy Young Sooty Grouse. (Photo by Alex Walker.)

Plate 33, *B*. Nest and eggs of Sooty Grouse. (Photo by Alex Walker.)

and their greater coverts are broadly tipped with white and have white shaft streaks." (Bent) (See Plate 33, *A*.) *Size: Male*, length 20–23, wing 9.40–10.00, tail 8. *Female*, length 17.50–19.00, wing 8.70, tail 6. *Nest:* A slight depression, lined with dead leaves, ferns, and other dry vegetable matter. *Eggs:* 6 to 10, usually 6 or 7, pale cream to light buff, more or less spotted with fine dots of dark brown (Plate 33, *B*).

Distribution—*General:* Northwest coast mountains from Alaska to northwestern California. *In Oregon:* Permanent resident of Coast Ranges, Willamette Valley, Cascade Mountains, and intervening ranges to Siskiyous. (See Figure 4.)

The Sooty Grouse, or "Hooter" (Plate 34, *A*), was first listed for this State by Townsend (1839), and since that time it has been in practically every list for the territory in which it is found. It is still a fairly common resident of the wooded areas, including the isolated buttes and wooded hills of the Willamette Valley, though much diminished in numbers in recent years. Mount Hood is the type locality of this subspecies, and from here it is found along the Cascades south to about the California line. Specimens from the southern Cascades, particularly from the vicinity of Keno and Fort Klamath, show intergradation with *D. f. sierrae*, some being quite like specimens from the Warner Mountains and Sierra Nevadas. All the Blue Grouse in the territory to the north and west including the east slope of the Cascades can be considered to be this subspecies.

Early in the spring, in late February or March, the males of the Sooty Grouse begin their curious love song, the low-pitched *hoot-hoot-hoot*, repeated from four to six times and audible for amazing distances. It has a curious ventriloquial quality that makes the "singer" difficult to locate. When finally discovered, he usually will be found perched high in a giant fir, close to the trunk. The call is uttered with a slightly opened bill and is accompanied by an inflating of the throat that continues until the brilliant-yellow air sacs are on full display.

The nests (Plate 33, *B*) are usually built beneath a small tree or shrub. They may or may not be concealed and usually contain six or seven eggs. Nests with fresh eggs have been found from April 14 (Hadley 1899) to June 4 (Prill 1893). In addition to these published records, Alex Walker has three Tillamook County nests taken April 10 and 30, 1933, and May 14, 1929, each with eight eggs. He also has records of one nest near Mulino, Clackamas County, on May 11, 1912, containing eight eggs, a second with ten eggs on May 22, 1913, and a third with eight eggs on April 27, 1914. Jewett found nests in Clackamas County, on April 28, 1903, May 3, 1908, and June 2, 1921, each containing six eggs.

The Sooty Grouse reverses the usual bird migration procedure. Although it does not migrate in the commonly accepted sense of the term, there is a seasonal altitudinal movement. In the spring the birds come down to the lower edge of the timber or to the openings about meadows to nest. As soon as the young are able to fly well the parents lead them into the mountains. There they spend the summer and fall months on

Plate 34, *A*. Sooty Grouse. (Photo by Wm. L. Finley.)

Plate 34, *B*. Nest and eggs of Oregon Ruffed Grouse. (Photo by Reed Ferris.)

the more open ridges, feeding on ripening berries and insects, particularly grasshoppers, which are abundant at times. With the coming of winter, the grouse take to the heavy timber, feeding on the buds and needles of coniferous trees and remaining hidden in the thick tops of the trees.

When flushed from the ground, the Sooty Grouse leaves with a startling whirr of wings, making straight for the nearest timber and swerving sharply upward to land in a tree where it is expert in concealing itself either by remaining motionless or crouching lengthways on a heavy limb. When flushed from the trees on a ridge, the bird pitches straight downward out of the tree at almost bullet speed, to land in another tree far below.

Sierra Grouse:
Dendragapus fuliginosus sierrae Chapman

DESCRIPTION.—Similar to Sooty Grouse but paler and with a heavier vermiculation above. It has a whiter throat and paler under parts and practically lacks neck tufts. *Downy young, size, nest, and eggs:* About same as those of Sooty Grouse.

DISTRIBUTION.—*General:* Southern Cascades and Warner Mountains of Oregon south into California to southern Sierras. *In Oregon:* Permanent resident of mountains of Lake and Klamath Counties. (See Figure 4.)

IN HABITS and behavior, the Sierra Grouse is entirely like the Sooty Grouse. Typical birds of this subspecies are found in Oregon, so far as we have been able to ascertain from a careful examination of numerous specimens, only in Lake County. There in the Warner Mountains these grouse match very closely birds from the central Sierras. From the extreme southern end of the Cascades, our specimens are somewhat intermediate but most of them are closer to birds from Mount Hood, which is the type locality of the Sooty Grouse, than they are to those of the Sierras. We have one bird from Keno, Klamath County, that is intermediate but closer to the Warner Mountain birds, while others might be placed in either form. Chapman (1904), in naming this form, commented on this intergradation on this area as follows:

Several of the specimens, in an admirable series collected by Major Bendire, at Fort Klamath, are referable to *sierrae* rather than to *fuliginosus*, though not typical of the former. Other examples in this series, however, are much nearer to *fuliginosus*.

Despite the fact that the 1931 Check-List states that this subspecies is found north to Washington, we have been unable, even with careful collecting, to obtain a single specimen nearer to *sierrae* anywhere north of Fort Klamath. Although we have few specimens from the Siskiyous south of the Rogue River, it would not be surprising to find some evidence of intergradation in an extensive series. Those that we have are closer to *fuliginosus*.

Patterson took eggs of Blue Grouse in the area of intergradation on May 10, 1931, in southern Klamath and Jackson Counties.

Franklin's Grouse:
Canachites franklini (Douglas)

Description.—"Similar to *Dendragapus*, but tail with sixteen feathers, which are more truncated at tip. *Adult male:* orange comb over eye; upper parts dark, broadly marked with black bands and narrower bars of gray and brown; tail feathers black to tip, or narrowly edged with white; *upper tail coverts mottled and strikingly banded with white;* throat and chest black, with white band between; belly banded with white; flanks mottled and banded with brown and streaked with white. *Adult female:* upper parts blackish, irregularly banded, barred, and mottled with rusty brown and ash; white bands of tail narrower than in male; under parts uniformly banded with black, white, and rusty brown." (Bailey) *Downy young:* "The Franklin's Grouse chick is beautifully colored. The central crown patch, which is bordered with black, and the upper parts in general are rich brown, from 'Sanford's brown' to 'amber brown'; the colors of the forehead, sides of the head, and under parts vary from 'mustard yellow' to 'Naples yellow,' deepest and tinged with brownish on the forehead and flanks, and palest on the sides of the head and belly; there are black spots below the eyes, on the lores and auriculars, on the lower forehead, and on the rump; and there is a black ring around the neck." (Bent) *Size:* "Length 14.70–16.20, wing about 6.50–7.35, tail 5.00–5.75." (Bailey) *Nest:* A depression in the ground, lined with pine needles, grass, and other dry matter. *Eggs:* Buff to pale brown, spotted with small spots of dark brown.

Distribution.—*General:* Southeastern Alaska, British Columbia, and Washington, Cascades east and south to Alberta, western Montana, central Idaho, and northeastern Oregon. *In Oregon:* Known only as rare and local resident in a few spots in Wallowa Mountains, mostly in Wallowa County, with a few in extreme northern Baker County.

The beautifully marked Franklin's Grouse is Oregon's rarest and most local species of upland game bird, being found only in a few very restricted spots in eastern Wallowa County and northeastern Baker County in the lodgepole pine forests adjacent to and on the slopes of the highest part of the Wallowa Range. There is a single specimen in the Biological Survey collection taken at the junction of Cliff and Imnaha Rivers, September 9, 1915, by Jewett, and there are specimens in our collections from the same general territory. The birds are occasionally seen in this vicinity about Lick Creek Ranger Station and on the ridge between the Imnaha and Snake Canyons but can by no means be considered common We know of no actual nesting records, although various rangers at Lick Creek Ranger Station have reported coveys of partly grown young. So far as we can learn, there are no specimens in existence from Oregon taken outside the territory indicated above, although this grouse has been credited occasionally to the Oregon Cascades, particularly about Mount Hood. The Mount Hood records should be eliminated, however, as we have found no definite records of the species from the parts of this range now included in the State. Suckley (1860) reported it from the vicinity of The Dalles, but a careful reading of the text indicates that this reference is entirely to the present State of Washington, probably in the vicinity of Mount Adams.

Gray Ruffed Grouse:
Bonasa umbellus umbelloides (Douglas)

Description.—"*Adult male:* Ruffs black, with bluish green gloss to tips; upper parts gray, whole surface finely mottled gray and black, more or less washed with rufous, blotched with black, and streaked with white; tail always gray, with broad black subterminal band; under parts white and buffy, barred with brown. *Adult female:* similar but smaller, with neck tufts rudimentary or obsolete. *Young:* similar to adult female, but browner, barring paler, less distinct, dim white and neck tufts wanting." (Bailey) *Downy young:* Bent describes the plumage of the eastern Ruffed Grouse chick, which is very similar to this species, as follows: "In the ruffed grouse chick the entire crown and back are 'tawny' or 'russet,' darkest on the back and rump, shading off to 'pale ochraceous-buff' on the sides of the head, chest, and flanks; the underparts are pale yellow, shading off to yellowish white on the chin and belly; there is a black auricular patch, but no other spotting on the head." *Size:* "Length 15.50–19.00, wing 7.00–7.50, tail 5.50–7.00." (Bailey) *Nest:* A shallow depression, usually at the foot of a tree, lined with leaves or other convenient dry vegetation. *Eggs:* 9 to 14, buff to cinnamon buff, sometimes spotted with dots of dull clay color or buff.

Distribution.—*General:* Ranges from Alberta and Mackenzie south to northeastern Oregon, northern Utah, northern Colorado, and South Dakota. *In Oregon:* Resident of Blue Mountain area, including all Ruffed Grouse of Wallowa, Union, Baker, Malheur, Harney, Crook, Grant, Wheeler, Morrow, and Umatilla Counties. (See Figure 5.)

The Gray Ruffed Grouse is the pale-gray form of the Blue Mountain section of Oregon, where it is quite common during the breeding season

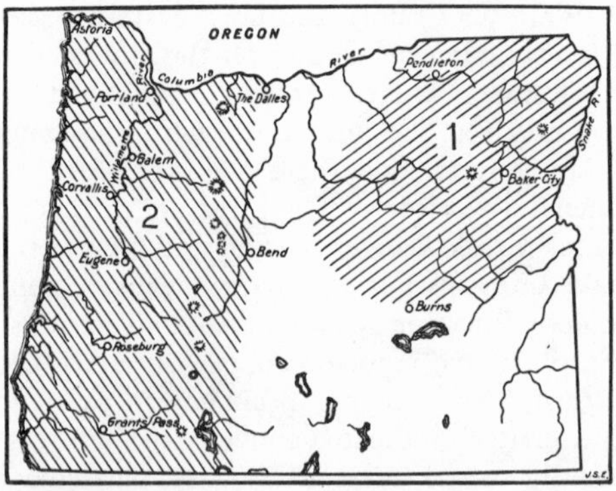

Figure 5.—Distribution of Ruffed Grouse in Oregon: 1, Gray Ruffed Grouse (*Bonasa umbellus umbelloides*); 2, Oregon Ruffed Grouse (*B. u. sabini*).

in the willow and alder bottoms. The earliest Oregon record that we can refer definitely to this form is that of Bendire (1875), who reported it as rare near Camp Harney. References in literature to the Canada Ruffed Grouse as an Oregon bird all belong to this race as at present defined. Our only actual nesting record is a nest found by Jewett on Beech Creek, Grant County, July 2, 1915, containing six eggs. When he visited it on July 5 he saw two young birds. The families stay together well into the fall, during which season they can be found feeding in the berry patches, sometimes in company with Richardson's Grouse, or foraging through the thickets of lodgepole pine gathering the berries of the kinnikinnick or the seed pods of pipsissewa. The birds are subject to a variety of diseases, some of which possibly account for cycles of abundance and scarcity that appear in the species.

The drumming produced by this grouse when the wings are beating rapidly has caused a great deal of discussion among naturalists as to whether the booming sound is made by the wings alone or by clapping them together over the back, striking the strutting leg or the sides of the body. The controversy seems finally to have been definitely settled by the use of motion pictures that show distinctly that the sound is produced by the wings alone.

The Gray Ruffed Grouse is one of the best known and best loved of upland game birds. Where it is persistently hunted, it soon develops an almost uncanny knack of bursting into full flight at the most inopportune moments; that is, from the hunter's point of view. It seems always to launch into the air behind a tree or to dodge quickly behind one, or else to choose the moment when the hunter is entangled in a fence. These tricks make wing shooting of Ruffed Grouse the highest test of a hunter's skill and give the bird its reputation as one of the sportiest of game birds.

Oregon Ruffed Grouse: *Bonasa umbellus sabini* (Douglas)

Description.—"Like *B. u. umbelloides*, but much darker; upper parts black and dark rusty or reddish brown, rarely with any gray; tail usually deep rusty, rarely grayish; under parts heavily marked with blackish and washed with buffy brown." (Bailey) *Downy young:* Similar to Canada Ruffed Grouse and Gray Ruffed Grouse. *Nest and eggs:* Similar to those of Gray Ruffed Grouse (Plate 34, *B*).

Distribution.—*General:* Vancouver Island and British Columbia south on coast to central California. *In Oregon:* Resident of coast counties, Willamette, Umpqua, and Rogue River Valleys, and Cascades, at least south to Mount McLoughlin, Jackson County, including east slope of this range. (See Figure 5.)

The Oregon Ruffed Grouse is the brown, strikingly marked Ruffed Grouse of the Northwest. Its habits and behavior are identical with those described for the Gray Ruffed Grouse, of which it is a darker and handsomer blood relative. It is a fairly common resident of the alder and willow bottoms of the State, although it has decreased much in numbers in recent years. This form was originally described by Douglas (1829) from specimens collected on the Oregon coast, and it has been listed by practically every ornithologist since that time. All of the specimens available from the Cascades and the country to the west of the range clearly belong to this form, except for a single female (Gabrielson Coll. No. 2160) taken at Rustler Peak, November 6, 1926, on the west slope of the Cascades in Jackson County that is apparently an eastern Oregon bird. It closely matches our series of gray birds from the Blue Mountains and lacks entirely the browns of the western Oregon bird, except for a slight brown tinting on the base of the tail and a few brown feathers on the back of the neck.

The species nests throughout its range, and eggs have been found by various observers from April 23 to May 29. In addition to our own and published records, Alex Walker has furnished three nesting records for Clackamas County: Mulino, May 18, 1912, 10 eggs, and May 4, 1913, 11 eggs; and Canby, May 3, 1913, 8 eggs.

Columbian Sharp-tailed Grouse: *Pedioecetes phasianellus columbianus* (Ord)

Description.—"*Adults:* Upper parts grayish brown, with black and buffy markings; under parts buffy or clear whitish, white or buffy prevailing in feathers with V-shaped markings. *Young:* similar to adult female but grayer, and throat white." (Bailey) *Downy young:* "Downy young sharp-tails are decidedly yellowish; the general color varies from 'mustard yellow' above to 'straw yellow' below, washed on the crown and back with 'ochraceous-tawny'; they are spotted on the crown and blotched or streaked on the back with black; there is a black spot at the base of the culmen and a black spot on the auriculars." (Bent) *Size:* "Length 15–19, wing 8.50–9.00, tail 4.00–5.50." (Bailey) *Nest:* A hollow in the ground, lined with dried grass, weeds, and feathers. *Eggs:* 10 to 15, buff or olive buff, sometimes spotted with small dots of dark brown.

Distribution.—*General:* Interior of British Columbia to northeastern California (formerly), Utah, Colorado, and northern Mexico. *In Oregon:* Formerly found over most of eastern Oregon but now, greatly reduced in numbers, an uncommon resident of a few counties. Recorded in recent years in Wasco, Sherman, Morrow, Umatilla, Wallowa, Union, Baker, and Harney Counties.

The Columbian Sharp-tailed Grouse, palest and grayest of the three recognized races, was described by Ord in 1815 from specimens collected by the Lewis and Clark expedition on the "great plains of the Columbia River." In view of the fact that it is now a scarce bird and one apparently headed for early extinction, it seems advisable to outline something of the ornithological record available at this time. Douglas (1829) recorded it from the Plains of the Columbia, and Townsend (1839) credited it to

Oregon. Newberry (1857) reported it from Klamath and from the Deschutes to The Dalles. Suckley (1860) reported young birds near The Dalles as early as April 1, 1855, and Elliot (1865) said it was exceedingly abundant. Bendire (1877) reported it from Camp Harney, and both Mearns (1879) and Merrill (1888) listed it from Fort Klamath. Miller (1904) noted it in Wheeler County. By 1905, Applegate (1905b) considered it rare in the Klamath country. Walker (1917b) reported it from Wasco, Sherman, and Gilliam Counties. Since that date the only record published is Gabrielson's (1924a) from Wallowa County.

We see it occasionally in small flocks, most frequently in the grain country along the north-central boundary of the State. There the wide fields of grain, broken and interrupted by canyons and scab-rock patches grown to bunchgrass, and the original vegetation of the territory provide conditions that permit the species to persist in limited numbers, but continual persecution and shooting, combined with human encroachment on its breeding grounds, have so reduced it in numbers that its future as an Oregon bird is precarious.

Alex Walker has records of two nests, both taken near Miller, at the mouth of the Deschutes River, on April 19, 1935. One contained 13 eggs; the data are missing on the other. The nests were slight hollows in a grainfield and were lined with grasses, grains, stems, and feathers.

Sage Hen:
Centrocercus urophasianus (Bonaparte)

Description.—Tail longer than the wings, graduated, feathers pointed, neck with distensible air sacs surmounted by hairlike filaments and erect feathers; tarsus feathered to the toes. *Adult male:* "Upper parts mottled gray or buffy, irregularly spotted or barred with black or brownish; in breeding season tufts of white downy feathers, mixed with black egret-like wiry plumes on shoulders; yellow air sacs on side of throat; chest blackish before the breeding season, with black wiry feathers depending from the chest band; chest white after the breeding season, during which time the blackish tips are worn off by rubbing on the ground. *Adult female:* similar to male but smaller and without ruffs, air sacs, or nuptial plumes; throat white, chest band speckled grayish. *Young:* somewhat like adult female but brownish above, markings on under parts, including black of belly, less distinct." (Bailey) *Downy young:* "The sage-grouse chick is well colored to escape detection when crouching on the ground in the gray shadows of the desert. The crown, back, and rump are mottled and marbled with black, dull browns, pale buff, and dull white; the sides of the head and neck are boldly spotted and striped with black; there are two large spots of 'sayal brown' bordered with black, on the fore neck or chest; under parts grayish white, suffused with buff on the chest." (Bent) *Size:* "*Male*, length 26–30, wing 12–13, tail 11–13. *Female*, length 21.50–23.00, wing about 10.50–11.00, tail 8–9." (Bailey) *Nest:* A slight hollow near a sage bush, with little or no lining, eggs frequently being deposited on bare ground. *Eggs:* Usually 7 to 13, sometimes up to 17, olive or olive buff, quite evenly marked with small dark-brown spots.

Distribution.—*General:* Formerly from southern British Columbia, southern Saskatchewan, and northwestern North Dakota south to northeastern California, New Mexico, and northwestern Nebraska. Now exterminated or greatly reduced over much of its range. *In Oregon:* Formerly over all of eastern Oregon, with possible exception of Wallowa County, for which we have found no records, but now greatly restricted and confined to big sagebrush counties of southeastern part of State, overflowing in small numbers into some adjoining counties.

The lordly Sage Hen, largest and most magnificent of the North American grouse, has been greatly reduced in numbers in Oregon in the past few years. Up to 1920, a wonderful population of these great birds remained on the slopes of Hart Mountain in eastern Lake County, but at that time they were suddenly reduced in numbers, possibly by disease, almost to the point of extermination. Since about 1925, they have been slowly building back in the more isolated sections but nowhere have they reached their former abundance. Overgrazing, shooting, and the operations of natural enemies, combined, are apparently too much for these birds, and their future in this State does not look bright. They will probably have the best chance on Hart Mountain, which is now a Federal game preserve designed primarily to protect antelope and Sage Hens.

There have been for years a few small remnants of these magnificent birds in Union and Baker Counties that showed some tendency to build up in numbers. The hoggishness of a few local "sportsmen" in demanding and getting an open season, however, effectually blocked any hope that the Sage Hens might again become a common sight in these counties. There are still a few birds in Silvies Valley and also on Big Summit Prairie east of Prineville, but, aside from these scattered groups, the birds are in the vast sagebrush area of southeastern Oregon. We have found them in recent years most plentiful in Malheur, Harney, and Lake Counties, with small numbers in Crook, Deschutes, and Baker Counties. They may possibly be found in Klamath County also, as there have been, within the past few years, a few birds near the Oregon-California line on the east side of Lower Klamath Lake that might easily enter Oregon at times.

Townsend (1839) first reported the Sage Hen from Oregon, and Newberry (1857) and Suckley (1860) reported it as a common bird. Bendire (1892) took many sets of eggs during his stay at Camp Harney, the dates varying from April 4 to May 28. Since those times there has been much written about these great grouse, both in Oregon and elsewhere, as they attract the attention of everyone visiting their haunts.

Early in the morning with the first golden streamers of light in the eastern sky, the Sage Hens come to water, flying with alternate periods of flapping wings and sailing to alight one hundred or two hundred yards back from the stream or pond. In the dim light they become invisible as soon as they land, but an occasional head, bobbing against the sky line betrays them as they come waddling into the water for all the world like a flock of barnyard hens. In an hour or two they have all gone, departing as they came, walking some distance away from the watering place before taking wing.

The courtship of the Sage Hen is the most spectacular performance staged by any of the grouse. Finley at various times has watched and photographed this display and has given an account of it as follows (Bent 1932):

When the sage cock starts to strut, his tail spreads and the long pointed tail feathers radiate out in a half arc. The air sacs are filled and extend nearly to the ground, hiding the black breast feathers. This is the first movement. Then the bird takes one or two steps forward and throws up the pouch, apparently by drawing back the head and neck. The next movement is a repetition of throwing the air sacs up and down and getting under headway for the last toss of the pouch, which is brought down with a jerk, as one would crack a whip, making a "plop" that on a quiet morning we easily heard for a distance of 200 to 300 yards. The whole movement gives one the idea that the bird inflates the air sacs and then, by the rigid position of the body and throwing the head and neck back, gives these air sacs a very vigorous shaking. In the movement when the pouch spreads, the bare yellow skin on the lower part of the pouch or chest shows clearly. As the pouch is thrown up and down, the wings are held rigid, the tips of the wing feathers sometimes touching the ground. The white feathers that cover the chest are exceedingly stiff; these grate against the wing feathers, giving out a wheezy sound that at first I thought came from the inhaling and exhaling of air. I soon discovered that this rasping noise was made by the stiff feathers rubbing together.

The food of the Sage Hen consists largely of leaves of the sage, supplemented by a few leaves and seeds of other plants, and by miscellaneous insects, including beetles of several kinds, ants, and grasshoppers.

Partridges and Quails: *Family Perdicidae*

European Partridge:
Perdix perdix perdix (Linnaeus)

Description.—Smaller than a ruffed grouse but larger than our quail. "A very fine vermiculated intermixture of black, white, rusty and cream on back, neck, and breast, more rufous on lower back and nearly clear black and white with a general greyish effect on breast. Wing-coverts sharply shaft-streaked with cream. Flanks barred with white and chestnut. Face, throat, and superciliary line of tawny chestnut. A conspicuous double spot or horseshoe mark of rich chestnut occupies the upper abdomen. Sexes similar in coloration but female in duller tones." (Townsend, 1926.) *Downy young:* "Crown chestnut with a few small black spots sometimes extending to lines; back of neck with a wide black line down centre, at sides pale buff marked black; rest of upper-parts pale buff with some rufous and black blotches or ill-defined lines, at base of wings a spot, and on rump a patch, of chestnut; forehead and sides of head pale yellow-buff (sometimes tinged rufous) with spots, small blotches, and lines of black; chin and throat uniform pale yellow-buff; rest of under-parts slightly yellower, bases of down sooty." (Witherby, through Bent.) *Size:* Length 12.60, wing 6.50, tail 4.00. *Nest:* A slight depression in the ground, lined with dead leaves, grass, or straw. *Eggs:* 8 to 20, uniformly olive.

Distribution.—*General:* Breeds in western Europe. Introduced in many localities in North America. *In Oregon:* Introduced and now particularly common in Wallowa, Union, Umatilla, and Malheur Counties and in lesser numbers in practically all other eastern counties. Established on less successful scale in Multnomah and perhaps other Willamette Valley counties.

THE FIRST European or Hungarian Partridges, now almost universally known as "Huns," were brought into Oregon in 1900 and released in the Willamette Valley, in Multnomah County, and in Marion County, where they still persist, although they have not greatly increased. In 1913, 218 and in 1914, 1,522 were released in 23 counties of the State. They increased rapidly, particularly in Umatilla, Morrow, and Wallowa Counties and can now be considered as one of the most abundant upland game birds in those counties. Since that time the Oregon Game Commission has trapped and moved numbers of them to various parts of eastern Oregon, where many counties are becoming well stocked.

This plump-bodied little bird is a favorite with gunners and to date has caused far less complaint of crop damage than the China Pheasant. It is a fast, strong flier that gets away with blinding speed and seems able to hold its own in many parts of the State. It can be distinguished from any other of the gallinaceous birds in Oregon by the reddish-brown tail that is spread fanwise as the bird flies away.

Eastern Bobwhite:
Colinus virginianus virginianus (Linnaeus)

DESCRIPTION.—"*Adult male:* Line through eye white; throat white, bordered below by black; rest of under parts buffy or brownish—reddish brown on sides—narrowly barred with black; upper parts reddish brown and black; scapulars, tertials, and lower back strikingly blotched with black. *Adult female:* like male, but black of head replaced by brown, and white by buffy. *Young:* upper parts rusty, more or less spotted with black, and feathers with white shaft streaks widening at tip; breast grayish or brownish, streaked with white; throat and belly whitish." (Bailey) *Downy young:* "In a typical chick the forehead and sides of the head are from 'ochraceous-tawny' to 'ochraceous-buff,' with a stripe of brownish black from the eye to the nape; a broad band from the hind neck to the crown, terminating in a point above the forehead, is 'chestnut,' deepening to 'bay' on the edges; there is a similar broad band of the same colors from the upper back to the rump; the rest of the upper parts is mottled with 'chestnut,' dusky, and buff; the chin and lower parts are pale buff or buffy white. In some specimens from the South the back and rump are almost wholly 'chestnut,' mixed with some black." (Bent) *Size:* "Length 9.50–10.75, wing 4.55, tail 2.70, bill .59." (Bailey) *Nest:* A shallow depression, lined with dead grass or other dry vegetation, frequently arched over with woven grass, either dead or growing, and artfully concealed. *Eggs:* 12 to 20, usually 14 to 16, dull white to creamy white.

DISTRIBUTION.—*General:* Breeds naturally from South Dakota, southern Minnesota, southern Ontario, and Maine south to Texas, Gulf coast, and northern Florida. *In Oregon:* Introduced and successfully established in many parts of State, particularly in Willamette Valley, northern Morrow and Umatilla Counties, along Columbia and Umatilla Rivers, Wallowa County, and along Snake River Valley near Ontario. Less successful in Rogue River Valley, but there in small numbers.

The Eastern Bobwhite, the most widely hunted native American upland game bird, was introduced into Oregon many years ago and is now quite widely distributed in the State. So far as known, it was introduced by Solomon Wright of Tangent, Linn County, in 1882, who brought six birds from Indiana and released them on his own farm. He stated that they began to multiply at once. The birds that have been known from Malheur County for so long came from the increase of Bobwhite planted in the Boise Valley, Idaho, in 1875 by a group of local business men. The quail thrived and eventually spread into adjoining parts of Oregon. Since these early introductions Bobwhite have been released in various other parts of the State and have been established for many years.

This species has thrived best in Upper Sonoran localities in eastern Oregon and at present is probably most abundant in the vicinity of Hermiston, Umatilla County, where it has found conditions very much to its liking. The luxuriant growth of sweet clover along the irrigation ditches furnishes much ideal cover, as does the sagebrush, which has grown into great thickets in low places just outside the ditches but is subirrigated by them. The irrigated lands along the Snake and Malheur Rivers in Malheur County have also provided suitable conditions, and these quail are equally abundant there. In Wallowa County, the quail have not increased to great numbers, but they are there in small numbers and have maintained themselves for many years. They are also present in smaller numbers in the cultivated sections of the Transition Zone of western Oregon. In every county in the Willamette Valley from Multnomah to Lane, the diversified farming practiced there provides conditions suitable for these quail. Throughout this valley, the beautifully marked little cocks sit on the fence posts and whistle their love notes. In the morning and evening particularly, they can be found on full parade engaged in whistling their musical *bob-white*, *bob-bob-white* to a concealed lady love—a sight to bring a thrill to any observer.

The young are beautifully patterned little balls of down that grow and develop flight feathers with amazing speed, being able to fly in a very few days after hatching. The birds remain through the summer and fall in coveys that roost together in a compact circle and often feed together in close formation. When startled, they burst from the ground with the suddenness of a bomb, traveling in all directions and, after landing, call back and forth until the group is reunited.

Valley Quail:
Lophortyx californica vallicola (Ridgway)

Description.—*Adult male:* Crest chestnut and recurved, black; patches on back of head olive and dark brown, bordered front and sides by black and white lines; upper parts grayish brown with buffy or brown stripes along sides of back; throat black, bordered by white, breast bluish gray; belly scaled except for central deep-chestnut patch; flanks dark olivaceous or smoky brown, streaked with white. *Adult female:* Head without black or white markings, general color grayish brown, belly scaled, without chestnut patch; chestnut on sides; sides streaked with white. *Young:* chest gray, marked with triangular white spots, belly faintly barred with grayish; upper parts brownish, streaked and spotted with whitish. (Adapted from Bailey.) *Downy young:* "In the small chick of this species the front half of the crown and sides of the head are 'ochraceous-tawny'; a broad band of 'russet,' bordered with black, extends from the center of the crown to the hind neck, and there is an auricular stripe of the same color; the rest of the upper parts are from 'ochraceous-buff' to 'warm buff,' striped, banded, or blotched with black; the chin and throat are white, and the rest of the under parts are grayish white, suffused with buff on the breast." (Bent) *Size:* Length about 9.50, wing 4.35–4.70, tail 4.10–4.70. *Nest:* A slight hollow in the ground, lined with grass or leaves and well hidden. *Eggs:* 12 to 16, dull white to cream buff.

Distribution.—*General:* From Upper Klamath Lake and Rogue River Valley of southern Oregon south through California (except on coast) to Lower California. *In Oregon:* Native at least to Klamath, Lake, Jackson, and Josephine Counties. Now spread over entire State by transplanting.

Owing to the activities of sportsmens' organizations and the Oregon Game Commission, the Valley Quail is now widely distributed over the State. It is most abundant in the counties bordering on California, but can be found in goodly numbers in every other part of the State except the coast counties. We have had available a large series of skins taken from all over the State subsequent to the scrambling of local strains by transplanting operations that date back to about 1870. The largest single operation seems to have been in 1914 when some 1,200 birds were trapped in Jackson and Josephine Counties and liberated in many places throughout the State. We find all the specimens to be *L. c. vallicola*. Three birds in the group, from Brownsboro, Jackson County, tend toward the darker *L. c. californica*, but to date we have found no birds of this race in Oregon. We would expect to find them in Coos and Curry Counties, if they are present at all, and unfortunately we have no specimens from that territory. Newberry (1857) stated that the Valley Quail was common through the southern Oregon mountains and that he had taken specimens in the Willamette Valley. There is one *L. c. californica* in the National Museum taken by Newberry in that valley, which, in view of the lack of any other birds of this subspecies in Oregon, we feel may well have been collected farther south on his trip and mislabeled.

This little quail with its pert crest is a favorite all over the State. It is not so good a game bird as the Eastern Bobwhite, as it often runs to escape danger and does not work so well with dogs. It does, however, thrive better than its eastern cousin and has become a common and widely distributed bird in the past few decades. The rather harsh call note is a familiar sound to all bird lovers, and the sight of a covey running about in the gathering twilight is very common.

The eggs are laid in April and May. Patterson reported numerous dates from the Rogue River Valley between April 16 and June 8. On the Klamath side of the Cascades he took eggs from May 2 to 20.

Mountain Quail:
Oreortyx picta palmeri Oberholser

Description.—"*Adult male:* Crest black; *upper parts deep olive brown, usually to crest,* top of head bluish gray, stripes on sides of back buffy or yellowish brown, *throat and flanks deep chestnut,* flanks broadly banded with black and white; breast plain bluish slate. *Adult female:* crest usually shorter. *Young:* crest blackish, barred at end with pale brown, breast gray, marked with triangular spots, throat and belly whitish; upper parts grayish brown, specked with white." (Bailey) *Downy young:* Much like next species. *Size:* "Length 10.50–11.50, wing 5.25–5.40." (Bailey) *Nest:* A shallow depression, lined with grass, dead leaves, pine needles, and other vegetable matter; well concealed. *Eggs:* 8 to 12, pale cream to buff (Plate 35).

Distribution.—*General:* Humid coast strip from southwestern Washington to Monterey County, California. *In Oregon:* Permanent resident of coast counties and in Willamette Valley, including west slope of Cascades at least as far south as Eugene. (See Figure 6.)

The Mountain Quail of Oregon are divided into two subspecies—this one, which is the resident bird of the coastal slope of Curry and Coos Counties and of the balance of the coast area north to the Columbia, including the birds found in the Willamette Valley and on the west slope of the Cascades north of Eugene, and the next form, to which belong the birds of the Rogue River Valley east of the coastal range and all of the specimens we have examined from eastern Oregon. We have not seen any birds from the Umpqua Valley and therefore cannot say to which form they belong.

Douglas (1829) first recorded the Mountain Quail from the Oregon

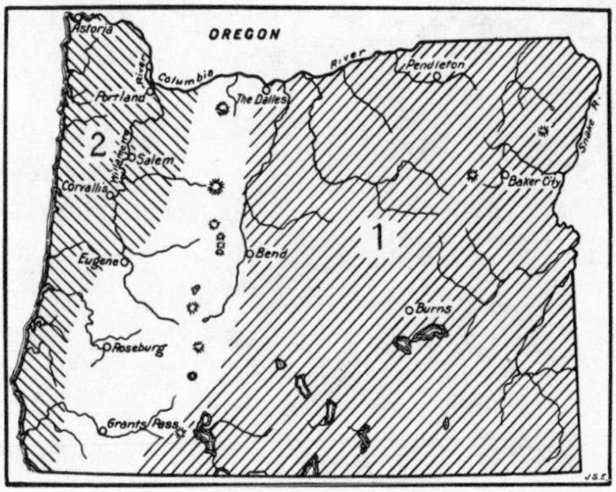

Figure 6.—Distribution of two forms of quail in Oregon: 1, Plumed Quail (*Oreortyx picta picta*); 2, Mountain Quail (*O. p. palmeri*).

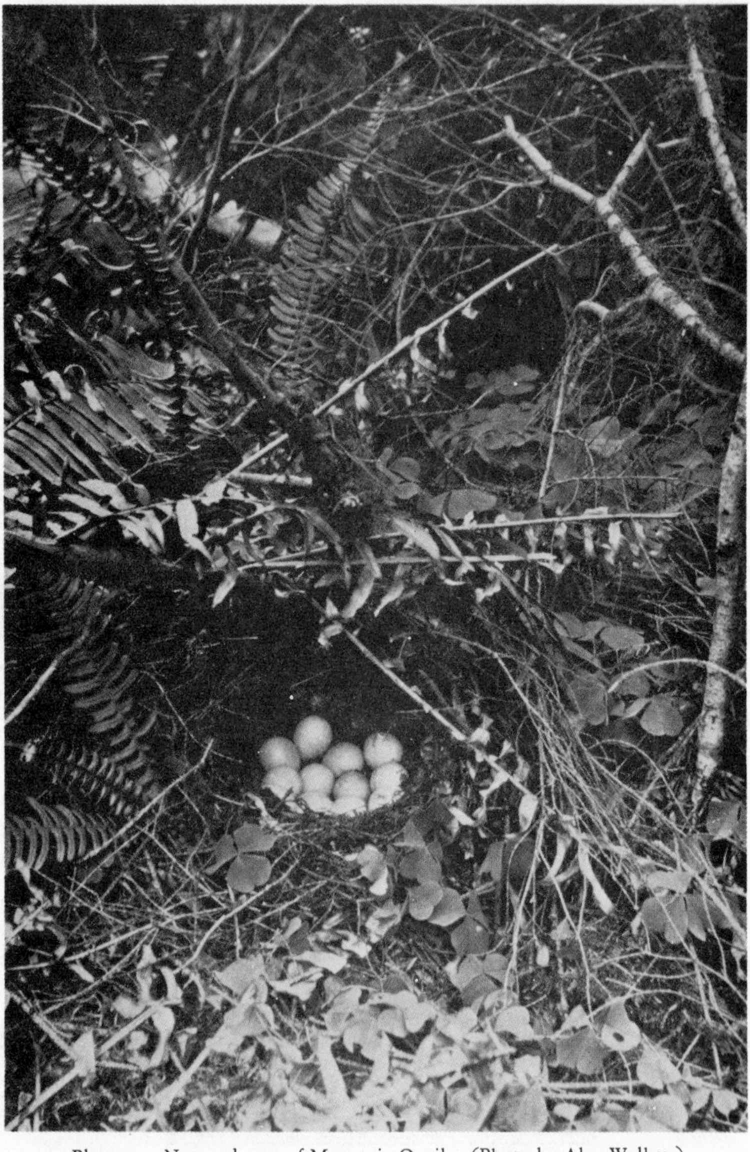

Plate 35. Nest and eggs of Mountain Quail. (Photo by Alex Walker.)

country, and it has been listed by nearly all subsequent writers. Bendire (1892) recorded a set of eggs taken near Coquille May 27, 1877, which was the first definite breeding record from the area now known to be inhabited by this subspecies. We have few actual nesting records available, either in literature or in our own notes, but those we have show that the eggs are laid in late May and early June. Alex Walker has furnished data on six nests found by him in Clackamas and Tillamook Counties between May 11 and June 13, the number of eggs varying from 8 to 15. Dr. Prill reported three nests at Scio, May 18, May 5, and May 18, with 9, 12, and 15 eggs, respectively.

The Mountain Quail is the largest member of the family found in Oregon and is essentially a brush and timberland bird. It is usually most common in cut-over lands or about the edges of clearings where it can find an abundance of wild berries and seeds to mix with the insects it consumes. As with other quail, the flight is strong and swift, the birds bursting cover like miniature bombs and diving again into the brush or weed patches after a short flight. It is also a very rapid runner on the ground, trusting to its heels to escape as frequently as it takes to the air.

Plumed Quail:
Oreortyx picta picta (Douglas)

Description.—"Like *O.* [*p. palmeri*] *pictus*, but upper parts olive, the hind neck usually partly or wholly bluish slate like the breast; forehead generally paler, often whitish, inner edge of tertials lighter buff or buffy whitish." (Bailey) *Downy young:* "In the downy young a broad band of deep 'chestnut,' mixed with and bordered by black, extends the whole length of the upper parts, terminating in a point in the middle of the crown; the rest of the upper parts, including the cheeks, are buffy or buffy white, with large blotches of 'chestnut' on the wings, thighs, and flanks and with a dusky line behind the eye; the under parts are grayish white or yellowish white, palest on the chin." (Bent) *Size:* Length 9.50, wing 4.35–4.70, tail 4.10–4.70. *Nest and eggs:* Like those of Valley Quail.

Distribution.—*General:* From northern Oregon east of Cascades south nearly to Mexican line. *In Oregon:* In almost every county of eastern Oregon and in Rogue River Valley (Jackson and Josephine Counties) west of Cascades. (See Figure 6.)

The Plumed Quail, the paler, grayer form, is the one originally described by Douglas, so that his name now applies to the eastern and southern Oregon birds, although his notes included the race *O. p. palmeri* as well. The 1931 A. O. U. Check-List gives the range of *O. p. picta* as west of the Cascades in northwestern Oregon, but we have carefully compared our specimens and find that birds from Portland, Newberg, and Willamette Valley points are much closer to the coast form than to the eastern Oregon form. In fact, one Portland bird is actually darker than birds from Yachats, which is only a few miles from the type locality of the humid coast form. At present, the Plumed Quail, which in habits and behavior is like the Mountain Quail, though it frequents more open country, is still common in Lake, Klamath, Crook, Jefferson, Wasco, and Wallowa Counties and less abundant in almost all other counties of that section. It is also fairly common in the foothills around the upper Rogue River Valley.

We have found no egg records in literature, and our only nesting record is of a set of eight eggs found by Gabrielson at Brownsboro, June 10, 1921. Patterson furnished records of five nests found in Jackson and Klamath Counties as follows: Ashland, May 8, 1924, and April 26, 1926; Pinehurst, May 6 and 10, 1924, and May 26, 1931.

Pheasants: *Family Phasianidae*

Ring-necked Pheasant: *Phasianus colchicus torquatus* Gmelin

Description.—"*Adult male:* Neck metallic greenish or bluish, back of head tufted; breast rich coppery chestnut, with metallic purple and coppery reflections; neck wholly or partly encircled by white collar. *Adult female:* tail brown, barred with black and white." (Bailey) *Downy young:* "Fore-head and sides of crown buff to yellow-buff with blackish line or spots down sides, centre of crown dark red-brown to blackish-brown; nape rufous; back of neck buff to yellow-buff with short blackish line in centre; rest of upper-parts rufous-buff with three wide black lines and wings with black blotches; sides of head pale yellow-buff to pale buff with a brownish streak from base of upper mandible and a black spot on ear-coverts; under-parts buff white to pale buffish-yellow, sometimes with a tawny tinge at base of throat." (Witherby, through Bent.) *Size:* "*Male*, length 30, wing 9.50–10.50, tail 17.50–20.00. *Female*, length 20–24, wing 8.50, tail 11–12." (Bailey) *Nest:* A slight hollow, often entirely without lining or at best scantily lined with dry vegetation. *Eggs:* 6 to 15, usually 10 to 12, brownish olive to buff.

Distribution.—*General:* Native to southeastern China, now widely introduced in North America. *In Oregon:* Introduced and now established in all parts except higher mountains.

The Ring-necked Pheasant, China Pheasant, Denny Pheasant, or Chink, was first shipped from China to Oregon in 1880, but the entire shipment of 70 birds died before reaching Portland. Undiscouraged, Judge O. N. Denny, then United States Consul General at Shanghai, sent 100 birds the following year, which were released in the Willamette Valley. They established themselves there and increased at an amazing rate for a number of years, only to decrease again later until at present, despite the continued release of new birds, they occur only in small numbers compared to former years. Meanwhile, they have been transplanted into all parts of the State and have evidently found the counties about the base of the Blue Mountains most to their liking. They are abundant in Wallowa and Union Counties and in northern Umatilla and Morrow

Counties, the little town of Hermiston being headquarters for many hunting parties during the open season. They are most abundant in the Snake and Malheur River Valleys of Malheur County, where they are exceedingly numerous. On December 6 to 7, 1933, after an open season when they had been hunted hard, the writers saw several hundred birds in a few hours in the fields along the edge of the irrigated area. They are present, though seemingly not doing so well, in the high plateau country of Harney, Lake, and Klamath Counties. In western Oregon, they do not increase as rapidly in the southern counties or on the coast as they do in the Willamette Valley. Eggs are laid in April and May, although later sets are sometimes found in the latter part of June—probably second sets following an earlier nesting disaster.

The introduction of the China Pheasant has been a success for the sportsman, but many damages to crops are charged to the bird. Many farmers bitterly resent its presence, complaining that much ripening grain is eaten and ridden down. The chief damage is in trucking sections, where the pheasants are accused of destroying ripening melons by picking them open, of pulling newly set plants of lettuce, spinach, and cabbage, of pulling sprouting corn, peas, and beans, and of digging up newly planted seeds of these and other vegetables. We have investigated some of these complaints and found many of them to be based on facts. On the other hand, pheasants are great consumers of insects and on many farms may easily earn their keep by their destruction of grasshoppers and other injurious insects. We believe that in general-farming districts these birds do little real harm but that in truck- and vegetable-producing sections they are often nuisances and many times become pests of considerable importance to individual farmers.

The Oregon Game Commission is now engaged in raising and liberating many thousands of these birds each year. In January 1924, a shipment of Mongolian Pheasants (*P. c. mongolicus*) was imported direct from China and added to the breeding stock. Possibly other shipments came at other times and may help account for the somewhat mongrel crop of pheasants now found in Oregon.

Order Gruiformes

Cranes: *Family Gruidae*

Little Brown Crane:
Grus canadensis canadensis (Linnaeus)

Description.—A smaller edition of the Sandhill Crane described next. *Size:* "Length 35, wing 17.50–20.00, bill 3.04–4.20, tarsus 6.70–8.44." (Bailey) *Nest and eggs:* Same as Sandhill Crane.

Distribution.—*General:* Breeds from northern and western Alaska, and Melville and Baffin Islands south to southern mainland of Alaska, southern Mackenzie, and Hudson Bay. Winters from California and Texas south into Mexico. *In Oregon:* Migrant in spring and probably fall.

Our knowledge of the status of the Little Brown Crane in Oregon is very unsatisfactory. Merrill (1888) recorded it from Fort Klamath and listed a specimen taken on June 10. Jewett saw a single bird that was killed in March 1905 in Harney County and mounted as part of the county exhibit in the Lewis and Clark Fair in Portland. The following item from Jewett's notebook summarizes the data:

November 6, 1912. Walter Donart has a mounted specimen without data that he claims was killed here (Klamath Falls) recently. I saw the Crane but took no measurements, although it was a small crane.

We have lost track of this specimen and know no more about it. Anthony listed the species as common in fall and rare in the spring at Portland in the list he furnished for Mrs. Bailey's *Handbook of Birds of the Western United States* (Bailey 1902). We do not know on what evidence this statement was based, but we have been unable to find any western Oregon specimen whatever. Willett (1919) listed it as common in Harney County in April. In response to an inquiry, he stated under date of June 3, 1934:

I do not know of any specimens [Little Brown Crane] having been taken in your State, but they were undoubtedly common in migration there in years gone by and probably come through in small numbers yet. I saw a good many of them in Harney Valley during the spring migration, as I noted in the *Condor*, but did not collect any. I was quite close to them and have no doubt as to their identity.

Willett is especially familiar with the water birds, and we therefore feel that his records are entirely acceptable and probably represent a close approximation to the former status of the species in the State. At present, cranes are scarce and wary, and it is difficult to obtain any evidence on their status in Oregon without killing a number of birds, a thing that any ornithologist, in view of the few birds remaining, is loath to do.

Sandhill Crane:
Grus canadensis tabida (Peters)

DESCRIPTION.—"Crown and lores naked except for scattered black bristles; cheeks and jaw well feathered. *Adults:* whole plumage slaty gray or light brownish, wings darker; cheeks and throat lighter and sometimes whitish. *Young:* head entirely feathered; plumage rusty brown." (Bailey) *Downy young:* "The small downy young crane is completely covered with thick, soft down and is very prettily colored. The color is deepest in the centers of the crown, hind neck and back and on the wings, where it is 'chestnut' or 'burnt sienna'; it shades off on the sides to 'ochraceous tawny' and on the throat and belly to dull grayish white." (Bent) (See Plate 36, *A*.) *Size:* "Length 40–48, wing 21.00–22.50, bill 5.15–6.00, tarsus 9.90–10.65." (Bailey) *Nest:* A bulky mass of marsh vegetation with a slight depression in the top. *Eggs:* 1 to 3, almost always 2, olive buff or drab, spotted with varying shades of brown (Plate 36, *B*).

DISTRIBUTION.—*General:* Breeds from British Columbia, Saskatchewan, and Manitoba south to California, Colorado, Nebraska, Illinois, and Ohio. Winters south into Mexico. *In Oregon:* Formerly common summer resident of eastern Oregon, particularly of Klamath, Lake, and Harney Counties, from late March to October. Elsewhere, migrant only, all of our own records from outside breeding territory being in April, September, and October. Now much diminished in numbers and only occasionally noted, except in breeding areas.

THE SANDHILL CRANE, most majestic of the wading birds, was first reported as a breeding bird by Bendire (1875) at Malheur Lake. Lewis and Clark (1814) recorded it as wintering near the mouth of the Columbia in 1805 and 1806, surely a mistake, as there are no other records of the species remaining so far north during the winter. Mearns (1879) stated that Wittich found it breeding at Fort Klamath, and Merrill (1888) also reported it as a breeding bird: Willett (1919) estimated that about 25 pairs bred in the vicinity of Malheur Lake in 1918, and Prill (1924) estimated 36 pairs bred in Warner Valley in 1923. These numbers have further diminished in recent years, but a few pairs still breed in those areas. Our earliest date is March 18; our latest, November 11 (both Harney County). Approximately 100 pairs still nest on the great cattle ranches of the Blitzen Valley and in the area east of the Steens Mountains, but this is a rapidly disappearing species so far as Oregon is concerned.

The Sandhill Crane formerly was reported by various observers as a common migrant in the Willamette Valley, but in recent years the sound of the raucous call of a flock of these huge waders passing far overhead in Indian file is sufficient to make the occasion a red-letter day for a western Oregon observer. The flight is steady and seemingly heavy, but it is really quick and swift for so ponderous a body. While in the air,

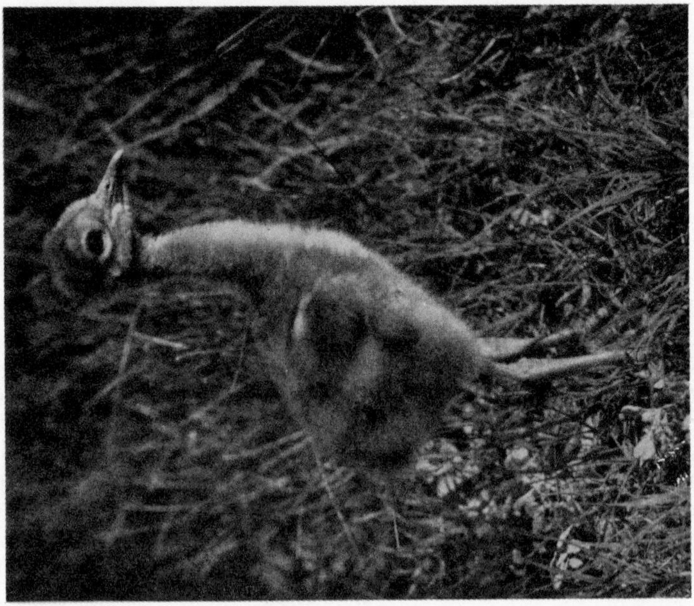

Plate 36, *A*. Downy young Sandhill Crane. (Photo by Alex Walker.)

Plate 36, *B*. Nest and eggs of Sandhill Crane. (Photo by Alex Walker.)

the legs are trailed straight behind and the long neck is thrust straight ahead to the fullest extent and not folded, as in the herons. In the hazy, lazy days of Indian summer the cranes often take wing and rise to great heights, spiraling upward on set pinions until finally lost to view, although the hoarse croaking may still be audible. In the wind the crane is also a master aerialist, taking every advantage of the air currents to sustain itself without effort.

The courting dance of these cranes is one of the most amazing sights of the bird world, the best account of which has been written by S. S. Visher (Bent 1926) as follows:

In the early spring, just after the break of dawn, the groups that were separated widely, for safety, during the night, begin flying toward the chosen dancing ground. These flocks of six or eight fly low and give constantly their famous, rolling call. The dancing ground that I knew best was situated on a large, low hill in the middle of a pasture of a section in extent. From this hill the surface of the ground for half a mile or more in every direction could be seen. As soon as two or three groups had reached this hill a curious dance commenced. Several raise their heads high in the air and walk around and around slowly. Suddenly the heads are lowered to the ground and the birds become great bouncing balls. Hopping high in the air, part of the time with raised wings, and part with dropping, they cross and recross each other's paths. Slowly the speed and wildness increases, and the hopping over each other, until it becomes a blurr. The croaking, which commenced only after the dancing became violent, has become a noise. The performance continues, increasing in speed, for a few minutes, and then rapidly dies completely out, only to start again upon the arrival of more recruits. By 7 o'clock all have arrived, and then for an hour or so a number are constantly dancing. Occasionally the whole flock of two hundred or so break into a short spell of crazy skipping and hopping. By 9 o'clock all are tired and the flock begins to break up into groups of from four to eight and these groups slowly feed to the windward, diverging slowly, or fly to some distance.

The huge nests (Plate 36, *B*) are usually located far out in the larger marshes, and the newly hatched young are quickly able to run about with the parents, with whom they remain until well grown, the brown-looking fledglings (Plate 36, *A*) appearing quite unlike the slate-gray adults. There are eggs in the United States National Museum taken by Bendire in Harney Valley, as follows: May 2 and 13, 1875, April 27, 1876, April 24, 1877, and April 14, 1888. Prill (1922b) has taken them in Warner Valley, May 30; and Patterson, in Klamath County, May 16, 1924.

The Sandhill Crane is somewhat omnivorous in its feeding habits--roots, bulbs, berries, grain, mice, frogs, snakes, and insects have all been reported as entering into its diet. The stomach of one taken by Gabrielson in Harney County (October 11, 1934) was entirely filled with barley. Complaints are sometimes received from farmers regarding destruction of potatoes and grain by these huge birds, but such losses to date have been very local. The species has already been so sadly reduced in numbers that it seems impossible that it should become of any economic importance, even though it should become much more destructive than at present.

Rails: *Family Rallidae*

Virginia Rail: *Rallus limicola limicola* Vieillot

Description.—"*Adults:* Upper parts olive brown, streaked with black; wing with a large chestnut patch; sides of head slaty gray, lores blackish, and chin white; throat and breast cinnamon brown; flanks black, barred with white. *Young:* plumage much mottled with black, but chestnut wing patch always present." (Bailey) *Downy young:* "The downy young Virginia rail is completely covered with long, thick, rather coarse, black down, glossed bluish on the head and greenish on the back. It can be distinguished from the young sora by the much longer bill, which is yellowish at the base and tip and crossed by a broad black band in the middle; there are also no orange bristles on the chin." (Bent) *Size:* "Length 8.12–10.50, wing 3.90–4.25, bill 1.45–1.60, tarsus 1.30–1.40." (Bailey) *Nest:* Of coarse grass and reeds, sometimes on the ground and sometimes woven into the tules, usually cleverly concealed. *Eggs:* 7 to 12, pale buff to white, irregularly spotted with varying shades of brown.

Distribution.—*General:* Breeds from southern Canada to Lower California, Utah, Colorado, Nebraska, Missouri, Ohio Valley, and New Jersey. Winters south to Central America. *In Oregon:* Rarely observed summer resident. Scattered records throughout State. Most frequently seen in Klamath and Harney Counties. Winters in western Oregon at least occasionally.

Newberry (1857) reported the Virginia Rail as common in Oregon, but Mearns (1879) recorded the first known specimen taken in the State, from Fort Klamath, July 2, 1875. Since that time it has been reported by various students in Washington, Lincoln, Yamhill, Marion, Benton, Lane, Clackamas, and Multnomah Counties in western Oregon, and from Baker, Malheur, and Klamath Counties east of the Cascades. Our own notes are quite fragmentary, but we have seen it in Tillamook (February 5 and November 26), Harney (August 29), Wallowa (June 14), Klamath (April 12 and September 16), and Multnomah (January 19 and August 10) Counties. The last date is the only record of special interest. On that day (August 10, 1914) Jewett saw an adult and a small downy young at Reed College Lake on the Eastmoreland Golf Course at Portland. Patterson reported nests found in Klamath County on May 8, 16, and 23, 1924, and Braly took two nests at Fort Klamath on May 14 and 16, 1930.

This medium-sized rail is undoubtedly much more common in Oregon than either the literature or our notes indicate. It is exceedingly difficult to observe unless an intensive search is made of its haunts. It is flushed only by accident and can run through the dense jungles of aquatic vegetation, in which it delights to live, at an astonishing rate. Its thin, flattened body is eminently suited to working through the thick grass, and its strong legs and big feet are able to carry it fast enough to outrun a dog. The startling cries and noises produced by this small bird are one of the surest guides to detecting its presence, if the observer is acquainted with them. An intensive search of the marshy areas of the State would undoubtedly add greatly to our knowledge of the status of the Virginia Rail.

Sora:

Porzana carolina (Linnaeus)

DESCRIPTION.—"*Adults:* Upper parts olive brown, spotted with black and finely lined with white; middle of crown, face, and throat black; breast and cheeks bluish gray, sides barred black and white; belly whitish; middle of lower tail coverts buff. *Immature:* similar to adult but without black face or bluish gray breast." (Bailey) *Downy young:* "The downy young sora is completely covered with thick, glossy, black down, except on the chin, which is ornamented by a small tuft of stiff, curly hairs of a 'deep chrome' color." (Bent) *Size:* "Length 7.85–9.75, wing 4.15–4.30, bill .75–.90, tarsus 1.25–1.35." (Bailey) *Nest:* Usually a fairly well-woven basket of flags or tules, anchored to the growing vegetation of the marshes. *Eggs:* 6 to 18, usually 10 or 12, buff ground color, irregularly spotted with browns of varying shades.

DISTRIBUTION.—*General:* Breeds from southern Canada to Lower California, Utah, Colorado, Kansas, Missouri, Ohio Valley, and Maryland. Winters south into South America. *In Oregon:* Summer resident in suitable marshes throughout State but most common in Klamath, Lake, and Harney Counties.

THE SORA, like the Virginia Rail, is without doubt much more abundant than the available records indicate, for unless one has time to devote to an intensive search of the marshes, it will seldom be seen. It is doubtless the commonest rail in the State. Its center of abundance is the great marsh country of south-central Oregon. Because of the lack of a suitable habitat, it is not a common bird in western Oregon at present, although Anthony (Bailey 1902) considered it as a tolerably common breeder in the vicinity of Portland. Our earliest date is April 17 (Sherman County); our latest, October 10 (Multnomah County); but records are too few to do more than indicate vaguely its present status.

Townsend (1839) made the first published reference to the Sora as an Oregon bird. Merrill (1888) found it breeding at Fort Klamath, and there is a set of eggs taken there June 2 and 3, 1883, in the United States National Museum. Jewett found a nest at Klamath Falls on May 30, 1916, containing 12 eggs and another the next day a few miles east of that town containing 3 eggs and 3 newly hatched young. Braly in 1930 took four sets of eggs in Klamath County between May 16 and June 5, 1930, and Patterson reported three sets in the same locality between May 20 and June 8. Preble in 1915 found it a fairly common species in southern Malheur County and reported seeing young between July 12 and 14 at Sheaville. The only recent records known to us from western Oregon are those of a badly decomposed bird picked up in Portland and brought to Gabrielson in 1928 (October 10) and of two brought to Jewett in 1931 (April 24 and September 23).

Yellow Rail:
Coturnicops noveboracensis (Gmelin)

Description.—"Upper parts dark buff, mottled with brown and black, feathers of back narrowly tipped with white in wavy cross-lines; wing dusky, with large white patch on secondaries; throat and breast plain buff or brownish; middle of belly whitish. Length: 6.00–7.75, wing 3.00–3.60, bill .50–.60, tarsus .80–1.00." (Bailey) *Nest:* A mass of dry grass, usually skillfully concealed. *Eggs:* 8 to 10, pale buff, finely speckled with brown and cinnamon.

Distribution.—*General:* Found during breeding season over States and Provinces bordering international line east of Rockies but actually found breeding only in North Dakota and California. Winters in southern United States. *In Oregon:* Known only from a single specimen from Scio, Linn County.

This rare and elusive bird, the Yellow Rail, is included in the Oregon list on the basis of only a single female taken by Prill near Scio, on February 1, 1900. This bird has been examined by Jewett and is correctly identified. It constitutes the sole record for the State.

Farallon Rail:
Creciscus jamaicensis coturniculus (Ridgway)

Description.—"*Adults:* Upper parts blackish, finely speckled and barred with white, patch on nape chestnut brown, color extending to top of head, forehead slaty; under parts rich plumbeous, lower belly, flanks, and under tail coverts barred with white. *Young:* white restricted. Wing 2.62, tarsus .79, culmen ,.54 depth of bill at base of nostril .18." (Bailey) *Nest:* A flimsy structure of fine, dry weed stems. *Eggs:* 4 to 8, with a creamy white to pure white ground color, "sparingly marked, chiefly at the larger end, with minute dots of browns and drabs." (Bent)

Distribution.—*General:* Coast marshes of California and Lower California. Casual in Washington. *In Oregon:* Casual, only records at Malheur Lake.

The admission of the Farallon Rail to the Oregon list rests solely on Bendire's records. He stated: "A single specimen of the black rail was noticed April 16th near Lake Malheur" (1875), and "Seen on two occasions in the swamps near Malheur Lake, where it unquestionably breeds" (1877). It has not been seen or taken in the State since.

American Coot:
Fulica americana americana Gmelin

Description.—"Toes lobed or scalloped along edges; bill stout, nearly as long as head; frontal shield narrow, ending in a point on crown. *Breeding plumage:* bill white, with brown spot near end, frontal shield brown; whole head and neck blackish; rest of body plumbeous except for white under tail coverts, edge of wing, and tips of middle wing feathers. *Winter plumage:* belly whitish; frontal shield smaller than in summer. *Young:* like winter adults, but with white of belly extending onto throat; bill dull flesh color, frontal shield rudimentary." (Bailey) *Downy young:* "The downy young coot is a grotesque but showy little chick; a black ball of down with a fiery head. The almost bald crown is but thinly covered with hairlike black down; the upper parts are thickly covered with glossy black, long, coarse down, mixed with long, hairlike filaments, which vary in color from 'orange chrome' on the neck and wings to 'light orange-yellow' on the back; the lores, chin, and throat are covered with short, stiff, curly hairs, varying in color from 'flame scarlet' to 'orange chrome'; the bill is 'flame scarlet,' with a black tip; the under parts are thickly covered with dense, furlike down, very dark gray to almost black, with whitish tips." (Bent) *Size:* "Length 13–16, wing 7.25–7.60, bill (to base of shield) 1.25–1.60." (Bailey) *Nest:* A well-woven floating basket, anchored to growing tules or other aquatic vegetation. *Eggs:* 6 to 22, usually 8 to 12, buff ground color, thickly and evenly colored with fine dots of black or brown.

DISTRIBUTION.—*General:* Breeds from central British Columbia, central Alberta, Manitoba, southern Quebec, and New Brunswick south into Mexico, Arkansas, and Tennessee. Winters south to West Indies and Costa Rica. *In Oregon:* Common year-around resident in every part of State where suitable nesting or resting grounds can be found.

THE AMERICAN COOT, or "Mud-hen," is undoubtedly the most common nesting water bird in the State and is equally common as a winter resident wherever open water occurs (Plate 37, *A*). It was first seen in Oregon by Lewis and Clark (1814), who found it common at the mouth of the Columbia on November 30, 1805, where it is still common as a wintering bird. It has been recorded in every county except Jefferson, Grant, Wheeler, Sherman, and Morrow in eastern Oregon and Clackamas and Josephine west of the Cascades, and undoubtedly it could be found in all of those with the possible exception of Jefferson.

There are definite nesting records for Washington, Yamhill, Benton, Lincoln, Multnomah, Coos, and Linn Counties in western Oregon, and for Umatilla, Baker, Malheur, Klamath, Lake, and Harney Counties east of the Cascades, most of them from the great marshes of the four last-mentioned, and the list could undoubtedly be greatly enlarged by intensive field work through the breeding season, as a pair or two is almost certain to be found on any permanent body of water large enough to furnish suitable feeding and nesting grounds. Their black bodies with their white bills riding high in the water are familiar sights to every school boy, and their harsh cackling voices are equally well known. The extreme dates of many nesting records are April 30 and June 11, but the eggs are usually laid between May 10 and June 1, and fleets of the funny little red-headed babies following their parents about are usually very much in evidence by mid-June.

Plate 37, *A*. American Coots. (Photo by Wm. L. Finley and Irene Finley.)

Plate 37, *B*. Black Oyster-catchers. (Photo by Wm. L. and Irene Finley.)

Order Charadriiformes

Oyster-catchers: *Family Haematopodidae*

Black Oyster-catcher:
Haematopus bachmani Audubon

Description.—"*Adults:* Head and neck dull bluish black; rest of plumage brownish black. *Young:* duller, more brownish." (Bailey) *Downy young:* "The downy young black oyster catcher is a swarthy little fellow, clothed in short, thick, dark, grizzly down, a color pattern well suited for concealment among the dark rocks where it lives. The down of the upper parts is basally sooty black and very dark gray, but the pale buffy tips give the bird its grizzly appearance. There is an indistinct loral and postocular stripe and two broad, more distinct, parallel stripes down the back of brownish black and two blackish areas on the thighs; between the back stripes and on the rump the buff tips produce a transverse barred effect. The under parts are dull grays, darkest on the throat and breast and lightest on the belly; the sides are faintly mottled or barred." (Bent) *Size:* "Length 17.00–17.50, wing 9.60–10.75, bill 2.50–2.95, tarsus 1.85–2.25." (Bailey) *Nest:* Usually a hollow in the bare rock, lined with bits of rock and shell. *Eggs:* 1 to 4, usually 2 or 3, cream buff to olive buff, covered with spots and scrawls of brown.

Distribution.—*General:* Breeds on Aleutian Islands and from Prince William Sound, Alaska, south to Lower California. Winters from southern Alaska to Lower California. *In Oregon:* Regular but not abundant permanent resident of coast rocks and islands.

The Black Oyster-catcher was described by Audubon (1838) from birds taken at the mouth of the Columbia River, probably by Townsend. Since that time little has been written about it. It is rapidly decreasing in numbers on the coast, as roads open up and beach resorts are developed, and each year we see fewer of them. Those that remain are wild and difficult to approach, showing a decided inclination to remain on the offshore rocks (Plate 37, *B*). The flight is strong and direct but rather slow, and the harsh voice will carry through the noisy roar of the surf, even when the latter is so deafening as completely to drown all other bird voices. Prill (1901) found eggs on Otter Rock, Lincoln County, on June 29, 1899, and Woodcock (1902) listed the species from Yaquina Bay. Finley (1902 and 1905d) found it breeding on Three Arch Rocks in both years, and Jewett found a nest on a bare rock there, July 3, 1914. Gabrielson saw a pair of adults and four partly grown young near Newport, July 4, 1926, and Braly collected a set of eggs at Otter Rock, June 3, 1932. We have numerous sight records and specimens from various points between Clatsop and Curry Counties for every month.

Plovers, Turnstones, and Surf-birds: *Family Charadriidae*

Western Snowy Plover: *Charadrius nivosus nivosus* (Cassin)

Description.—"Bill longer than middle toe without claw, slender, and entirely black. Chest band reduced to a spot at each side of breast. *Adults in summer:* crown and back pale buffy gray; face and under parts white; wide bar across front of crown, ear patch, and spot at side of chest black. *Adults in winter:* black replaced by dusky gray. *Young:* similar to winter adults, but with feathers of back tipped with white." (Bailey) *Downy young:* "The downy young snowy plover is quite unlike the young piping plover. The entire upper parts are pale buff, 'cream buff' to 'cartridge buff' mixed with grayish white. The crown, back, rump, wings and thighs are distinctly and quite evenly spotted with black. The under parts are pure white." (Bent) (See Plate 38, *A.*) *Size:* "Length 6.25–7.00, wing 4.20–4.30, bill about .60, tarsus .90–1.05." (Bailey) *Nest:* A hollow in the sand, lined with bits of shell and pebbles. *Eggs:* Sometimes 2, usually 3, olive buff, marked more or less evenly but not heavily with black and gray.

Distribution.—*General:* Breeds from Washington, northern California, and northern Utah south to Lower California. Winters from Oregon south along coast to Mexico. *In Oregon:* Permanent resident of the coast and rare summer resident of Harney Valley.

The only reference in Oregon literature (except for our own records) to the Western Snowy Plover, the pale little ghost of the sand dunes, is that by Woodcock (1902), who reported it from the coast on Anthony's statement. As a matter of fact, it is a permanent resident of such spits as those at Bayocean, Netarts, Siletz, and Pistol River, where its lacy tracks are in evidence everywhere among the thick evergreen patches of the sand verbena (*Abronia*) that grow above high-tide line in the dry sand dunes that it frequents. It is a silent little bird, running ahead of the observer on swift feet, only to blend almost indistinguishably into the sand the moment motion stops. Currier took sets of eggs in Tillamook County on July 13 and 14, 1921, and newly feathered young can occasionally be seen on sand areas there and elsewhere.

In winter the Snowy Plovers gather into small flocks of a dozen or less that frequent the dry dunes during stormy weather but often venture out on the wet beaches to feed to and fro with the movement of the surf. Though not as expert as Sanderlings in such maneuvers, they can be seen engaged in them at almost any tide. We have numerous winter specimens and records for the coast, particularly in Tillamook and Lincoln Counties, where this bird seems most common.

It is a rare species inland. Lewis saw three on Silver Lake, Harney County, on July 4, 1912, and Cantwell reported it from Malheur in 1916, from April 20 to May 1. Our only inland records are from Harney Lake, where on June 12, 1922, Jewett saw some birds on the lake bed and where on May 26, 1923, he watched a pair for some time. One bird was building a nest. Several sand hollows had been partially scooped out, and the process of scooping was still going on at the time he found the birds.

Semipalmated Plover:
Charadrius semipalmatus Bonaparte

Description.—"Size small; distinct basal webs between front toes; bill very small and short, less than middle toe without claw, the basal half yellow in adults. *Adults in summer:* throat encircled by a black collar, bordered above on back of neck with a white band; face black, with a white bar across forehead; upper parts brownish gray, under parts white. *Adults in winter:* black of summer plumage replaced by dark gray. *Young:* like winter adults, but with feathers of upper parts edged with buffy. *Length:* 6.50–7.50, wing 4.65–5.00, bill .48–.55, tarsus .95–1.05." (Bailey) *Nest:* A slight depression, sometimes lined with dry vegetation. *Eggs:* 3 or 4, buff with bold markings of dark brown or black.

Distribution.—*General:* Breeds from coast of Bering Sea to Baffin Island and Greenland, south to the Yukon, British Columbia, James Bay, New Brunswick, and Nova Scotia. Winters from central California, Louisiana, and South Carolina southward to southern Argentina. *In Oregon:* Regular migrant along coast in both spring and fall. Casual inland.

Little attention has been paid to shore birds in Oregon, and consequently little is on record regarding the Semipalmated Plover. Woodcock (1902) recorded it from Yaquina Bay, and Nichols (1909) saw it on the coast, July 26, 1908. We have found it to be a regular but by no means common migrant, most abundant in May and August, occurring usually as single birds frequenting the sand beach above the high-tide line. The earliest spring date is March 10, in Lincoln County (Bretherton, ms. reports, Biological Survey); and the latest, May 20, in Tillamook County. In the fall we have found it on the coast from July 21 to August 31 (both Lincoln County). We have no inland records, but Laing (ms. notes, Biological Survey) reported a few seen near Portland on August 24 and 29, 1919.

Killdeer:
Oxyechus vociferus vociferus (Linnaeus)

Description.—"*Adults:* Chest crossed by two black bands, the upper encircling the neck; forehead, collar, and under parts white; front of crown black; rump and sides of tail bright ochraceous yellow; rest of upper parts dull olive brown. *Young:* similar to adults but duller, with much rusty on back." (Bailey) *Downy young:* "The most distinctive feature of the downy young killdeer is the long, downy tail, black above and elsewhere barred with 'pinkish buff' and black with long, hair-like, buffy down below protruding beyond the rest of the tail; the forehead, chin, throat, a ring around the neck and the under parts are pure white, except for a tinge of pinkish buff in the center of the forehead; a broad, black stripe above the forehead extends around the crown to the occiput; a black stripe extends from the lores, below

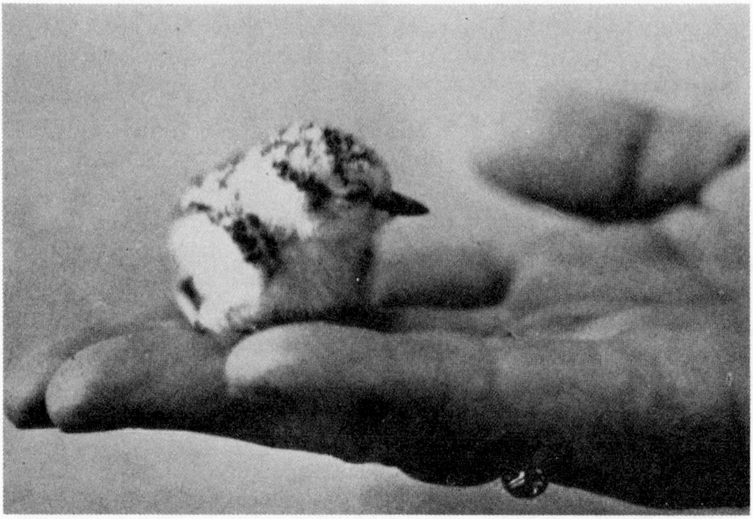

Plate 38, *A*. Downy young Western Snowy Plover. (Photo by Alex Walker.)

Plate 38, *B*. Nest and eggs of Killdeer. (Photo by Alex Walker.)

the eyes to the occiput; there is a broad black stripe entirely around the neck, below the white; the crown, auriculars, back and inner half of the wings are grizzled 'vinaceous buff' and dusky; there is a black space in the center of the back and a black band across the wing between the grizzled inner half and the white distal half." (Bent) *Size:* "Length 10.00–11.25, wing 6.20–6.75, bill .70–.90, tarsus 1.40–1.55." (Bailey) *Nest:* Usually a depression, with only the barest attempt at lining with bits of dry vegetable matter or small pebbles, although sometimes fairly well lined. *Eggs:* Usually 4, rarely 3 or 5, light buff or cream ground color, heavily marked with brown and black.

DISTRIBUTION.—*General:* Breeds from Mackenzie, Alberta, Saskatchewan, Manitoba, Ontario, Quebec, and Maine southward to Gulf States and Mexico. Winters from British Columbia, Utah, Colorado, Kansas, Iowa, Illinois, Indiana, and Massachusetts south into West Indies and Central America. *In Oregon:* Abundant permanent resident of every part of State, remaining through winter in small flocks wherever there is open water. Common summer resident of every county.

SINCE TOWNSEND (1839) first listed the Killdeer from Oregon, every ornithologist who has worked in the State has reported it. Bendire (1877) recorded it as a breeding species about Camp Harney, and we have since learned that it nests in every part of the State (Plate 38, *B*). In published records and in our own notes there are many egg dates between April 10 and June 12, but it is certain that the first date does not anywhere nearly approach the beginning of the nesting season, as we have on several occasions noted adults followed by newly hatched young between April 12 and 22. Most of the records refer to Jackson County, where it is evident incubation begins at least as early as mid-March. The beautifully marked downy young are able to travel soon after breaking the shell and move almost immediately to the nearest water. They are a familiar sight along the small ponds and streams from May to July as they feed about with the adults. Despite their conspicuous gray and white pattern, the youngsters blend beautifully with the landscape and are almost invisible so long as they remain motionless.

In summer, the Killdeers gather into flocks, sometimes of several thousand, and feed over the wetter meadows. At Malheur Lake, on August 19, 1932, Gabrielson watched for some time a flock that he estimated contained two to three thousand birds flying about the meadows and occasionally alighting for a time. The flight is direct, rapid, and somewhat ternlike in its gracefulness, the flocks being masters of the aerial evolution so commonly performed by members of the sandpiper family.

In winter the birds remain in small companies that feed about the ponds or along the shores of open streams. We have definite winter records for Crook, Grant, Baker, Umatilla, Wallowa, Malheur, and Klamath Counties in eastern Oregon, a list that could doubtless be extended by a little intensive field work. In western Oregon, the Killdeers winter commonly in every county and sometimes during heavy rains appear in numbers on large lawns, such as the campus of Oregon State College at Corvallis.

Like many other less common ground-nesting birds in the State, the Killdeers habitually feign injury to decoy an intruder away from the nest. Individuals vary greatly in their expertness at this ruse. We have watched them lie flat on the ground screaming lustily and beating their wings frantically, only to resume a normal posture and run a few steps to start the performance again. Some act so realistically as they flop along the ground barely beyond reach that the observer is certain every bone in their little bodies is broken. The performance is continued until the intruder is decoyed a safe distance from the nest, when the Killdeer takes wing screaming triumph. Occasionally both parents take part in the act, although it is usually carried out by the one that happens to be on the nest at the time of the intrusion.

American Golden Plover:
Pluvialis dominica dominica (Müller)

Description.—"Hind toe wanting, bill small and slender. *Adults in summer:* upper parts black or dusky, spotted with bright yellow and white; face, throat, and belly black, bordered with a line of white; tail dusky, barred with gray or yellow. *Adults in winter:* under parts mottled dusky gray; back less golden than in summer. *Young:* like winter adults, but with upper parts more golden, and yellow wash over neck and breast. *Length:* 9.50–10.80, wing 6.80–7.40, bill .80–1.00, tarsus 1.55–1.82." (Bailey) *Nest:* A hollow in the open tundra, lined with dead leaves. *Eggs:* Usually 4, sometimes 3 or 5, buff to cream color heavily marked with very dark browns or black.

Distribution.—*General:* Breeds from Point Barrow, Alaska, Baffin Island, and North Devon Island south to Keewatin and Mackenzie. Winters far south in South America. *In Oregon:* Rare fall migrant along coast with only three definite records, all in recent years.

The American Golden Plover, with its handsome spring plumage, is unknown as an Oregon bird up to this writing, and in the light of present knowledge it can be classed only as a casual migrant. Woodcock (1902) listed it as a migrant at Yaquina Bay, but the first Oregon specimen was one taken by Jewett (1914b) at Netarts on September 7, 1912. It was not again found in the State until September 12, 1926, when Jewett took two near the California line in Curry County. The third record is of a single bird taken by Overton Dowell, Jr., at Mercer, Lane County, in August 1929, and now in his collection.

Black-bellied Plover:
Squatarola squatarola (Linnaeus)

Description.—"Hind toe minute; bill rather short. *Adults in summer:* face, throat, and belly black, bordered with white; upper parts spotted with black and white; upper tail coverts white at base; outer half of tail barred with dusky. *Adults in winter:* under parts white, overlaid, streaked, and mottled with dusky and gray, becoming creamy or white on anal region; upper parts spotted with gray and dusky.

Young: like winter adults, but spotted above with light yellow, gray, and black. *Length:* 10.50–12.00, wing 7.50, bill 1.10, tarsus 1.95." (Bailey) *Nest:* A slight depression, lined with a few bits of grass and leaves. *Eggs:* 4, with a pink, green, or brown ground color, usually most heavily spotted with dark brown about the larger end.

Distribution.—*General:* Breeds on Arctic Coast from Alaska to Keewatin and on islands to north. Winters from western Washington on coast, Texas, Louisiana, and Virginia far south into South America. *In Oregon:* Uncommon migrant and winter resident along coast.

The Black-bellied Plover, with its checkered back and black breast and belly, is one of the handsomest and most striking of all shore birds, but unfortunately it seldom stops on the Oregon coast while in this showy attire. It seems far more abundant at Grays Harbor, Washington. In fact, the only spring record for Oregon known to us is of a small flock found by the authors together on the beach near Netarts, May 2, 1921. Fall records are more numerous. The first specimen taken in Oregon is one now in the United States National Museum labeled "Columbia River, October 21, 1836" and is listed by Cassin (Baird, Cassin, and Lawrence 1858) as an Oregon bird. Johnson (1880) reported the species as a Willamette Valley migrant, Nichols (1909) found it on the coast, July 26, 1908, and Walker (1924) saw two and took one at Netarts, October 1, 1921. Our earliest fall record is August 13 (Tillamook County). We have two winter records for the Lincoln County coast, taken by Gabrielson January 20 and November 24. In addition, we have noted it on August 13, 15, and 20, September 30, and October 19 and 20, all in Lincoln and Tillamook Counties. In fall and winter plumage, this grayish-looking bird with grayish-white under parts blends so well with the dry sand of the dune edges it loves to frequent that it often escapes notice so long as it remains motionless.

Surf-bird:
Aphriza virgata (Gmelin)

Description.—"Base of tail, upper coverts, and a broad bar on wing white. *Adults in summer:* upper parts, head, neck, and chest, slaty gray, specked and streaked with whitish, and spotted on scapulars with rufous; belly white, specked with dusky. *Adults in winter:* like summer adults, but with upper parts, head, and neck plain dusky or slaty gray. *Young:* back brownish gray, feathers edged with white; throat and breast white, streaked with dusky. *Length:* 10, wing 7, bill .95–1.00, tarsus 1.20–1.25." (Bailey) *Nest:* A slight natural depression, lined with bits of lichens and moss. *Eggs:* 4, buff, marked with splashes and spots of brown and fawn.

Distribution.—*General:* Breeds in mountains of south-central Alaska. Winters from Queen Charlotte Islands south to Straits of Magellan. *In Oregon:* Regular winter visitor to coast. Arrives in August and remains until April.

Townsend (1839) took the first Oregon specimen of the little-known Surf-bird on November 1, 1836, at the mouth of the Columbia River.

Woodcock (1902) recorded it from Yaquina Bay from Bretherton's reports. We have found it to be a regular but not common inhabitant of the coast, frequenting the rocky headlands, feeding on the mussels and barnacles exposed by low tide, and resting on the higher rocks when the tide is high. It is most abundant in April and October but is present in numbers all through the winter (earliest date, August 5, Lincoln County; latest, April 27, Clatsop County). In behavior and actions it resembles the Black Turnstone, and scattered individuals are often found feeding with their smaller cousins. Occasionally the early birds arriving from the north still have the beautifully marked breeding plumage, although most of them are in the duller winter dress.

Ruddy Turnstone:

Arenaria interpres morinella (Linnaeus)

Description.—"*Adults:* Throat and belly white, chest crossed by a broad black band; back coarsely mottled with rufous and black; head variously streaked. *Young:* similar to adult but duller, without rufous on back, and with the chest band mottled dusky gray. *Length:* 9.00–9.90, wing 6.00, bill .80–.90, tarsus 1." (Bailey) *Nest:* A slight depression, scantily lined with grass and leaves. *Eggs:* 4, olive to olive-buff, marked with warm browns.

Distribution.—*General:* Breeds from western Alaska to Southampton and western Baffin Island. Winters from central California, Texas, Louisiana, and North Carolina southward into South America. *In Oregon:* Irregular fall and rare spring migrant on coast.

The first known specimen of the Ruddy Turnstone from Oregon was taken by M. E. Peck at Seal Rocks, Lincoln County, on August 28, 1914. It was not again recorded until 1921, when between August 23 and 27 the writers took five at Netarts. Since that time it has been found more frequently, and in addition to the numerous skins in our collections, we have seen birds from Lane County in the Dowell collection and from Clatsop County in the Braly collection, all taken between Julv 24 and August 31, except three that Dowell took at Mercer on May 14, 1922. The latter furnish the only spring records for the State, although more extensive collecting would probably reveal the species as a more regular migrant. Most of the birds are in juvenile plumage and are found on the sand spits and long beaches rather than on the rocky headlands with their darker cousins.

Black Turnstone:

Arenaria melanocephala (Vigors)

Description.—"*Adults in summer:* Crown and upper back black, with greenish bronzy gloss; rest of head, neck, throat, and chest black, spotted on forehead and sides with white; a white spot in front of eye; belly and sides white. *Adults in winter:* similar, but with head, neck, and chest unspotted, sooty black. *Young:* head more grayish than in winter adults and feathers of back edged with buffy. *Length:* 9, wing, 5.80–6.10, bill .85–1.00, tarsus 1.00–1.10." (Bailey) *Nest:* A shallow depression in the dead grass, little or no lining. *Eggs:* 4, olive to buffy olive, marked with various shades of olive gray and yellowish olive, with scattered spots and streaks of brownish black.

Distribution.—*General:* Breeds from Bering Straits south to Sitka. Winters on coast south to Lower California. *In Oregon:* Common migrant and winter resident. Arrives in August and remains until late April. Casual straggler away from coast.

The Black Turnstone is another species to which little attention has been paid by previous workers. Woodcock (1902) reported it from Yaquina Bay on Bretherton's authority, but no one else has written anything regarding it. We have found it to be a common and at times abundant migrant and winter resident (earliest date, July 20, Lincoln County; latest, May 2, Tillamook County). It usually reaches its greatest numbers in September but is common through the winter on the rocky reefs and headlands. There the birds feed on the rocks exposed by ebb tide, being exceedingly expert at taking wing at the last possible moment before being sent tumbling by the breaking surf. When startled, they spring from the rocks, dive toward the water, and quickly gather into a compact flock, wheeling and circling low over the water before again alighting on the exposed rocks. We have specimens from scattered localities on the coast from Clatsop to Curry County, and they may be looked for in rocky places anywhere along the shore. We consider it the most common wintering shore bird in the State, with the single exception of the Killdeer.

The only inland record is of a bird killed at Wapato Lake, Washington County, November 12, 1913, by George Russell and now in Jewett's collection.

Snipe and Sandpipers: *Family Scolopacidae*

Wilson's Snipe; Jacksnipe: *Capella delicata* (Ord)

Description.—"Bill long and slender, mandibles grooved, roughened, and widened toward end; tip of upper overreaching the lower mandible; nostril small and at edge of feathers. Crown buff, with side stripes of black; back mainly black with stripes falling into two middle lines of buff and two outer lines of whitish; neck and breast spotted and streaked with buff, brown, and dusky; sides barred with black and white; belly white." (Bailey) *Downy young:* "The young snipe in its dark and richly-colored natal down is one of the handsomest of the young waders. The upper parts, including the crown, back, wings, and thighs, are variegated or marbled with velvety black, 'bay,' 'chestnut,' and 'amber brown'; the down is mainly black at the base and brown-tipped; the entire upper parts are spotted with small round white spots at the tips of some of the down filaments, producing a beautiful effect of color contrasts and a surprisingly protective coloration. The head is distinctly marked with a white spot on the forehead, a black crescent above it and a black triangle below it, partially concealed by brown tips; there is a distinct black loral stripe, extending faintly beyond the eye, and a less distinct black malar stripe; between these two is a conspicuous, large, white, cheek patch. The chin and upper throat are 'light ochraceous buff'; below this on the lower throat is a large sooty-black area, partially concealed by brown tips, these 'tawny' brown tips predominating on the breast and flanks, and shading off to 'pale pinkish cinnamon' on the belly." (Bent) *Size:* "Length 10.50–11.15, wing 4.90–5.60, bill 2.50–2.70, tarsus 1.20–1.30." (Bailey) *Nest:* A slight depression in the ground, lined with grass. *Eggs:* Usually 4, rarely 3 or 5, olive gray or buff, heavily spotted and blotched with dark brown.

Distribution.—*General:* Breeds from Yukon River, Mackenzie, northern Ontario, Ungava, and Newfoundland south to Pennsylvania, Ohio, Indiana, Illinois, Iowa, Colorado, Utah, and northern California. Winters regularly from Washington, British Columbia, Wyoming, Colorado, Oklahoma, Arkansas, Alabama, and Virginia southward into South America and occasionally farther north about Warm Springs. *In Oregon:* Permanent resident that breeds in suitable places throughout State and winters wherever open water prevails. More common in summer east of Cascades and more abundant in winter west of that range.

Wilson's Snipe, or Jacksnipe (Plate 39, *A*), was first seen in the territory now included in Oregon by Lewis and Clark (1814) in 1805–06 and was next recorded by Townsend (1839). Newberry (1857) found it common about the Klamath Lakes. Cassin (Baird, Cassin, and Lawrence 1858) listed a bird from Fort Dalles on November 16, and Suckley (1860) stated that several wintered there in 1854–55. Merrill (1888) first recorded it as a breeding bird from Fort Klamath, the territory where it still breeds most commonly in the State. Nearly every writer since then has mentioned the species as a breeding or wintering bird. There are definite breeding records for Klamath (Merrill; Jewett, 4 nests, May 15–31; Braly, 3 nests, May 10–17; Patterson, 2 nests, May 20 and 24; Furber; and numerous others); Douglas (Hardy); Multnomah (Finley); Marion (Johnson); Linn (Prill); Lake (Prill); Malheur (Becker and Preble); and Benton (Woodcock) Counties, and it doubtless breeds in many other counties where swampy ground is found.

It winters sparingly in eastern Oregon. Our own notes show winter records for Umatilla (December 10), Deschutes (several, January), Klamath (December 10, January 25), Wallowa (January 26, February 10), and Malheur (January 3) Counties, and the published literature contains winter records for Harney (February 15) and Wasco (all winter) Counties. Other winter records in the manuscript notes of Biological Survey members are for Klamath (January 9, Furber), Harney (Malheur Lake, December 18, 1913), and Jackson (January 15, Heckner) Counties. The last bird was in a small spring-fed meadow on the slopes of Mount McLoughlin at about 5,000 feet altitude. Winter records west of the Cascades are numerous and from every section of the territory.

This plump-bodied, long-billed, brown bird, exploding from the ground

Plate 39, *A*. Young Wilson's Snipe. (Photo by Wm. L. and Irene Finley.)

Plate 39, *B*. Long-billed Curlew chicks. (Photo by Wm. L. Finley and H. T. Bohlman.)

with a startling *scarp*, *scarp* from beneath the very feet of an observer, to corkscrew through the air for a short distance before dropping again into the grass, is a familiar sight to most Oregonians interested in the out-of-doors. The boring made in the soft mud in searching for earthworms and similar delicacies that are neatly seized by the flexible tips of the bill and extracted from their subterranean homes with skill and dispatch is likewise quite familiar. Less well-known but common in the spring evenings, though not always staged in the twilight, is the curious "winnowing" sound this snipe makes in connection with its courtship antics. Most observers believe the sound to be produced by the widely spread tail feathers, by the wing, or by a combination of both during the courtship flights.

On October 1, 1927, while hunting birds together on the Columbia bottoms east of Portland on a foggy rainy day, we saw a flock of about 25 heavy-bodied, long-billed snipe flash into view through the mist. They were in close formation, wheeling and turning abruptly in synchronized motion, exactly as is commonly done by the smaller shore birds. We first thought they were dowitchers, but the birds looked too big. Finally the flock swung close and we fired into it, bringing down one bird. To our astonishment, it proved to be this species. We have seen only one other published account of such a performance by the Jacksnipe, and neither of us has ever witnessed it except on that occasion.

Long-billed Curlew:
Numenius americanus americanus Bechstein

Description.—"Plumage light cinnamon, barred and mottled on upper parts with dusky and black; outer webs of outer quills wholly black; head, neck, throat, and chest streaked with dusky; crown mainly dusky; belly plain cinnamon; chin whitish." (Bailey) *Downy young:* "The young curlew, when first hatched, is completely covered with long, thick, soft down. The color varies from 'warm buff' on the breast and flanks, to 'cream buff' on the face, upper parts and belly and to 'cream color' on the throat; the crown is even paler. The markings, which are brownish black in color, consist of a broken and narrow median stripe on the forehead, irregular spotting on the posterior part of the head and large, bold, irregular spotting on the back, wings, and thighs." (Bent) *Size:* "Length 20–26, wing 10.00–11.00, bill 2.50 in young of year to 8.50 in old birds, tarsus 3.00–3.50." (Bailey) *Nest:* A slight depression in the ground, lined with grass. *Eggs:* 4, buff, with uniform spotting of browns and olives (Plate 40, *A*).

Distribution.—*General:* Breeds from British Columbia, Alberta, Saskatchewan, Manitoba, and Wisconsin south to Illinois, Iowa, Kansas, Oklahoma, Texas, Arizona, Nevada, and northern California. Winters from central California, Arizona, Texas, Louisiana, and South Carolina south to Mexico and Lower California. *In Oregon:* Rather uncommon summer resident and breeding bird of eastern Oregon. Arrives in April and remains until August. Casual west of Cascades.

Townsend (1839) first listed the Long-billed Curlew (Plate 39, *B*) for Oregon, and Suckley (1860) reported it as a breeding bird near The Dalles.

It formerly bred commonly in the grassy meadows of eastern Oregon, particularly in Klamath, Lake, Harney, Umatilla, Union, and Baker Counties, and still is to be found nesting in most if not all of these counties in limited numbers (earliest date, April 3, Umatilla County; latest, August 25, Harney County, Bailey ms.). In recent years we have found it in small numbers in Umatilla, Morrow, Lake, and Harney Counties in the breeding season. Egg dates in our own notes as well as in literature vary from May 4 to June 6. In western Oregon, the species may be regarded as a straggler only. Prill took one at Scio, Linn County, August 22, 1926, and Gabrielson took one on the Lincoln County coast near Yachats, July 24, 1922.

About the nesting ground the Long-billed Curlews are noisy birds, flying about in circles or diving frantically at an intruder, all the while uttering a constant succession of shrill cries. This is the largest of the shore birds found in Oregon; its brown color and long decurved bill, taken in connection with its size, render it a species easily identified. After the breeding season the birds are to be found in small flocks, often mingled with other shore birds and looking amusingly clumsy among their smaller companions. They are among the earliest of the shore birds to leave and after mid-August are seldom noted.

Hudsonian Curlew:
Phaeopus hudsonicus (Latham)

DESCRIPTION.—"Smaller than *longirostris* [*americanus*], with shorter bill and duller coloration; quills plain dusky. Upper parts specked, mottled, and barred with dusky and buff; crown black with middle and side lines of buff; a dusky stripe through eye; under parts buffy, barred and streaked on sides, chest, and neck with dusky. *Length:* 16.50–18.00, wing 9.00–10.25, bill 3–4, tarsus 2.25–2.30." (Bailey) *Nest:* A depression in the ground, lined with grass and leaves. *Eggs:* 4, olive green, marked with brown to lavender spots and blotches.

DISTRIBUTION.—*General:* Breeds on Arctic Coast of Alaska and northern Mackenzie. Winters from southern California, Louisiana, and South Carolina southward far into South America. *In Oregon:* Migrant only, somewhat more common in fall than spring, but not abundant in either season.

LITTLE has been published about the Hudsonian Curlew as an Oregon bird. Woodcock (1902) listed it as a migrant at Yaquina Bay on the authority of Bretherton, and there are a few migration notes by him in the Biological Survey files, ranging from March 30, earliest date, to June 6, latest date, and in the fall from August 10 to 24. In addition to this, we have only our own notes. We have found it only along the coast, in Clatsop, Lincoln, Tillamook, and Lane Counties, where it appears on the beaches in small flocks, sometimes along the edges of the surf and at other times on the mud flats of the bays. It is most abundant in early May and during August and with more field work will almost certainly

Plate 40, *A.* Nest and eggs of Long-billed Curlew. (Photo by S. G. Jewett.)

Plate 40, *B.* Nest and eggs of Upland Plover. (Photo by Ira N. Gabrielson.)

be found in all the coast counties. Our earliest spring date is April 29 (Clatsop County); our latest, May 17 (Tillamook County); and in the fall our records range from July 20 (Lincoln County), to September 11 (Tillamook County). There are no records for the interior of the State.

The Hudsonian Curlew is less brown than the Long-billed Curlew, has a much shorter bill, and in general is smaller. The occasional individual Long-billed Curlew associated with it on the coast can be easily picked from the flocks by the much longer bill. On the beaches the birds are rather quiet and shy, having been disturbed so much that they are usually difficult to approach except at the end of long migratory flights when they are sometimes so near exhaustion as to be utterly indifferent to human beings. Towering far above the usually abundant smaller shore birds, they seem like giants stalking about among crowds of pygmies, their leg movements appearing deliberate and clumsy in comparison to the twinkling feet of their small cousins.

Upland Plover:
Bartramia longicauda (Bechstein)

Description.—"Tail long and graduated, the end reaching well beyond tips of folded wings; base of toes webbed only between outer and middle. *Adults:* rump black, rest of upper parts dusky, or greenish black, scalloped and streaked with buff; crown blackish, with a median line of light buff; sides and lower surface of wing barred with black and white; throat streaked and chest marked with dusky; chin and belly white." (Bailey) *Downy young:* "In the downy young upland plover, the crown, back, and rump are prettily variegated, marbled, or mottled, with black 'wood brown,' 'pinkish buff,' and white, with no definite pattern. The sides of the head and the entire under parts are pale buff or buffy white, whitest on the belly and throat. A narrow, median frontal stripe and a few spots on the sides of the head are black." (Bent) *Size:* "Length 11.00–12.75, wing 6.50–7.00, bill 1.10–1.15, tarsus 1.90–2.05, tail 3.40–3.50." (Bailey) *Nest:* A slight depression, usually somewhat scantily lined with grass. *Eggs:* 4, cream or buffy, spotted with dark brown (Plate 40, *B*).

Distribution.—*General:* Breeds from Alaska, southern Mackenzie, Saskatchewan, Manitoba, Minnesota, Michigan, Ontario, Quebec, and Maine south to Connecticut, New Jersey, Virginia, Indiana, Illinois, Missouri, Texas, Utah, and southern Oregon. Winters in South America. *In Oregon:* Very rare summer resident in a few mountain valleys of eastern Oregon.

Merrill (1888) reported a pair of Upland Plover seen and the male taken at Fort Klamath on June 4 and a pair with three nearly grown young seen in the same locality July 18, 1887, and stated that Bendire also reported it from Harney Valley. After that time the bird long remained an unknown species to Oregon ornithologists, and Jewett in 1929 recommended that it be placed on the hypothetical list. Subsequent to his recommendation, however, we have obtained additional information. There is a specimen in the Overton Dowell, Jr., collection taken by Dowell on

August 9, 1919, at Summit Prairie, Crook County (Jewett, 1930e). In 1931 Jewett found it and collected specimens in Umatilla (May 16) and Grant (May 23 and 24) Counties, and we now know it to be a rare summer resident in the vicinity of Ukiah, Umatilla County, and Bear and Logan Valleys, Grant County.

This is one of the most interesting of the shore birds that breed within the United States. The haunting, melodious whistle given as the bird alights on a fence post with the wings extended far above the back is one of the sounds that once heard is never forgotten. It is to be hoped that the few birds remaining within the State may succeed in building up an increased population, though this sort of a biological miracle is not apt to occur.

Spotted Sandpiper:
Actitis macularia (Linnaeus)

Description.—"Small and slender, bill approximately the length of tarsus, or of middle toe and claw. *Adults in summer:* entire upper parts bronzy or greenish olive, faintly marked with dusky; under parts white, marked, except on middle of belly, with round spots dusky; quills dusky, secondaries tipped with white, with a conspicuous white line along the middle of open wing. *Adults in winter:* white of under parts unspotted. *Young:* like winter adults but finely barred on wings and back with dusky and buff." (Bailey) (See Plate 41, *A*.) *Downy young:* "The young spotted sandpiper in the natal down is quite uniformly grizzled or mottled on the upper parts, from crown to rump, with 'buffy brown,' 'wood brown,' grayish buff, and black. The forehead is grayish buff, and the entire under parts are white; a narrow black stripe extends from the bill through the eye to the nape; a black patch in the center of the crown extends as an indistinct median stripe down the nape and broadens to a black band along the back to the rump." (Bent) *Size:* "Length 7–8, wing 4.05–4.60, bill .90–1.05, tarsus .90–1.05." (Bailey) *Nest:* On the ground, lined with dry grass or weeds, usually in a tuft of grass or a small bush. *Eggs:* 4, rarely 3 or 5, buff ground color, spotted and blotched with dark brown.

Distribution.—*General:* Breeds from southern United States north to central Alaska, Yukon, Mackenzie, Manitoba, Ungava, and Labrador. Winters from British Columbia (on the coast), Arizona, Texas, Louisiana, and Virginia south into South America. *In Oregon:* Widely distributed summer resident and breeder from April to October. Uncommon winter resident of western Oregon.

The familiar little Spotted Sandpiper shares with the Killdeer the distinction of being the commonest breeding shore bird in Oregon. It becomes common by late April, and has been found in summer in practically every county. Breeding records are exceedingly numerous. Along every stream and about every lake and pond one can find it teetering unsteadily up and down on a rock or jerking about nervously as it hunts for food along the shores. Egg dates extend from May 2 to July 22, and by July the sight of the prettily marked glossy youngsters following the parents about is very common (Plate 41, *A*). The species remains numerous until September, after which it diminishes rapidly. It winters in

Plate 41, *A*. Spotted Sandpiper chick. (Photo by Wm. L. Finley and H. T. Bohlman.)

Plate 41, *B*. Western Willet. (Photo by Wm. L. Finley and H. T. Bohlman.)

the State sparingly at least. Jewett found it in Tillamook (February 22), Curry (February 21), and Jackson (November 29) Counties; and Gabrielson, in Benton County (January 1). Townsend (1839) first listed it for the State, and Bendire (1877) gave the first breeding record. Since then it has been noted by many observers and is one of the most frequently mentioned water birds in all the published literature on Oregon avifauna.

Western Solitary Sandpiper:
Tringa solitaria cinnamomea (Brewster)

Description.—*Adults in summer:* Upper parts, including upper tail coverts and two middle tail feathers, dark olive gray, finely specked with cinnamon brown; rest of tail barred with white; outer quills and edge of wing deep black; under parts white, streaked with dusky on chest and throat. *Adults in winter:* upper parts more dusky and less olive, chest less streaked. *Young:* specking of back buffy, and dusky of chest and sides tinged with buff. Wing 5.10–5.49, tail 2.18–2.30, bill 1.15–1.30. (Adapted from Bailey.) *Nest:* Unknown but presumably, like that of the Eastern Solitary Sandpiper, in old nests of robins, grackles, blackbirds, and jays. *Eggs:* Unknown.

Distribution.—*General:* Breeding range presumably in northern and western Alberta, northern British Columbia, and Alaska. Known to winter in the Argentine, Uruguay, Paraguay, and possibly other parts of South America. *In Oregon:* Uncommon migrant, both spring and fall, in eastern Oregon. Straggler only in western Oregon.

This is one of the rarer shore birds for Oregon, and the sight of a Western Solitary Sandpiper constitutes a red-letter day for any observer. Living up to its name the bird usually appears alone along the banks of small streams or ponds, where it frequents much the same kind of places as those chosen by the Spotted Sandpiper. Mearns (1879) first recorded this uncommon shore bird from Oregon from specimens taken at Fort Klamath in 1875, and Merrill (1888) reported specimens collected in the same place, May 12 and August 16, 1877. It was not again mentioned in Oregon literature, until Woodcock (1902) listed it as a winter resident on Yaquina Bay on the strength of reports by Bretherton. As this record is not substantiated by specimens and as the species is not known to winter on the Pacific Coast, we believe this to be a misidentification. Willett (1919) next recorded it for Oregon from Harney County, May 10 and August 24. All of our own records are for April and August (earliest spring date, April 15, Klamath County; latest, April 29, Deschutes County: earliest fall record, August 1, Baker County; latest, August 23, Umatilla County). It has been found in Umatilla, Lake, Deschutes, Grant, Baker, Harney, Klamath, and Malheur Counties in eastern Oregon. There are a number of skins in Jewett's and Gabrielson's collections, all from eastern Oregon, and two August birds in the United States National Museum. In the files of the Biological Survey are reports by

G. G. Cantwell of two birds at Malheur Lake in April 1915 and a note by F. M. and V. Bailey of one bird noted over that lake, August 30, 1920, the latest date for the State. The only authentic record for western Oregon is a specimen taken by Braly at Portland, May 5, 1930, and now in his collection.

The Western Solitary Sandpiper can be most easily confused with the Lesser Yellow-legs. It is darker, smaller, and has green legs that are somewhat shorter than those of the Yellow-legs and cause it to stand somewhat lower. In flight, the under surface of the wings appears blackish and the tail looks white with a dark center instead of pure white, as in the Yellow-legs. If a close approach is possible, the cinnamon-colored spots on the back can be distinguished as quite different from the black and white markings of the Yellow-legs.

Wandering Tattler:
Heteroscelus incanus (Gmelin)

DESCRIPTION.—"Web between middle and outer toes, but not between middle and inner; bill straight and slender, longer than tarsus; tarsus equal to length of middle toe and claw. *Adults in summer:* upper parts plain slaty or plumbeous gray; under parts thickly barred with white and dusky, becoming more spotted on throat and pure white on anal region. *Adults in winter:* middle of belly and chin white; chest, sides, and upper parts gray. *Young:* like winter adults but with fine specks and narrow scallops of white on wings and back. *Length:* 10.50–11.30, wing 6.50–7.30, bill 1.50–1.60, tarsus 1.25–1.35." (Bailey) *Nest:* A depression in the ground, lined with fine roots and twigs. *Eggs:* 4, greenish ground color, spotted and blotched with dark brown.

DISTRIBUTION.—*General:* Breeds in Alaska. Winters from Oregon southward along coast and also on Pacific islands and Asiatic coast. *In Oregon:* Regular and fairly common spring and fall migrant and probably a rare wintering bird. Away from coast, only a rare straggler.

THE STRIKING Wandering Tattler frequents the rocky headlands and off-shore rocks along the Oregon coast, where it obtains its food from among the abundant marine life associated with the mussels and barnacles that are exposed at low tide. At high tide it may occasionally be found perched on some convenient shelf high above the surging waters, but its colors blend so well with the rocky background that it is difficult to detect as long as it remains motionless. Birds taken in July and August occasionally retain the handsome heavily barred under parts of the spring plumage, though most of them even this early have donned the gray and white winter garb. In behavior they remind one of the Solitary or Spotted Sandpipers, nervously bobbing their bodies and twitching their tails as they feed over the rocks exposed by the ebb tide. These birds are usually solitary or appear at most in twos or threes. When startled, they fly away with sharp piercing calls that cut clearly through the thunder of the surf.

Curiously enough, the first recorded specimen of this species from Oregon (now in the United States National Museum) was taken at Crater Lake and is doubtless the "solitary female" that Bendire (1888a) saw there on July 27, 1882. This bird was of course only a straggler and is the only Oregon record of the bird away from the coast. Woodcock (1902) reported it from Yaquina Bay, and Nichols (1909) recorded it from Seaside. Our earliest fall records are July 21 (Lincoln County); our latest, November 22 (Tillamook County). In the spring our earliest record is April 27 (Clatsop County); our latest, May 20 (Tillamook County). There is one February 3 record for Cannon Beach (Gabrielson 1923b), which possibly indicates wintering birds. We have taken many specimens and noted it many times, between the dates mentioned, on suitable rocky places on the coast, from Clatsop, Tillamook, Lincoln, Lane, Coos, and Curry Counties. Only Douglas among the coast counties is missing, and this indicates lack of field work in that area rather than absence of the birds.

Western Willet:
Catoptrophorus semipalmatus inornatus (Brewster)

Description.—"Size large, bill slender, straight, about as long as tarsus; base of toes webbed; base of tail and large patch on wing always white. *Adults in summer:* upper parts mottled gray and dusky; end of tail gray; belly white; chest and sides buffy, barred with dusky, and throat streaked with dusky. *Adults in winter:* upper parts plain ashy gray; under parts white, grayish on sides of throat and breast. *Young:* like adults, but upper parts and sides more buffy or ochraceous." (Bailey) *Downy young:* The downy young is indistinguishable from that of the Eastern Willet, which Bent describes as follows: "There is a distinct loral stripe of brownish black, a post ocular stripe and a median frontal stripe of 'warm sepia.' The chin and throat are white and the rest of the head is pale buff, mixed with grayish white, heavily mottled on the crown with 'warm sepia.' The down of the hind neck and upper back is basally sepia with light buff tips. The rest of the upper parts are variegated with pale buff, grayish white and 'warm sepia'; but in the center of the back is a well marked pattern of four broad stripes of 'warm sepia' and three of light buff, converging on the rump and between the wings. The under parts are buffy white." (Bent) *Size:* "Wing 7.88–8.26, bill 2.28–2.70, tarsus 2.45–2.95." (Bailey) *Nest:* A hollow in the ground, lined with grasses and other dried vegetation. *Eggs:* 4, ground color buff, irregularly marked with dark browns.

Distribution.—*General:* Breeds from eastern Oregon, eastern Montana, Alberta, Saskatchewan, and Manitoba south to Illinois, Iowa, Nebraska, Wyoming, Utah, and northern California. Winters from Humboldt Bay, California, Texas, and Louisiana southward. *In Oregon:* Regular but not abundant summer resident and breeding bird of Malheur, Harney, Lake, and Klamath Counties. Casual transient anywhere else.

The neutral gray of the Western Willet (Plate 41, *B*) renders it a somewhat inconspicuous bird until it takes flight, when the black wing with the bold white band sets it off from any other species. It frequently alights on fence posts, throwing the wings high overhead and uttering its melodic whistle at the instant its feet touch the perch. It is not an abundant bird in the State. Townsend (1839) first listed it, but it was not actually found breeding until Bendire's (1877) time. He took eggs between May 8 and June 16, 1876, that are now in the United States National Museum. Merrill (1888) found it breeding at Fort Klamath, and Willett (1919) at Malheur. In June 1930, we found a few obviously breeding about the Cow Lakes in Malheur County, and we have found it on a number of occasions in the Warner Lake district of Lake County and regularly in Harney and Klamath Counties. There are only three records known from western Oregon, where it can be considered only a straggler. Anthony (Bailey 1902) called it a rare migrant about Portland, Vernon Bailey (ms. notes) noted one bird at Yaquina Bay, September 28 and 29 and October 1, 1909, and there is a record of a bird taken at Gresham by J. S. Stafford in October 1924. It arrives in April and remains until September (earliest date, April 15, Harney County, Fawcett; latest date, October 1, Lincoln County, Vernon Bailey) but is most noticeable in May, June, and July.

Greater Yellow-legs:
Totanus melanoleucus (Gmelin)

Description.—"*Adults in summer:* Upper parts heavily mottled with black, gray, and white; quills black; upper tail coverts white, tail white barred with gray; under parts white, spotted on chest and barred on sides with black; throat gray, streaked with dusky. *Adults in winter:* upper parts dark gray, finely spotted with white; under parts mainly white, with fine spotting of gray on chest and throat. *Young:* like adults in winter, but darker above and with buffy instead of white spotting. *Length:* 12.15–15.00, wing 7.50–7.75, bill 2.20–2.30, tarsus 2.50–2.75." (Bailey) *Nest:* A shallow depression, lined with bits of grass. *Eggs:* 4, buff ground color irregularly marked, chiefly about the larger end, with dark-brown shade.

Distribution.—*General:* Breeds from British Columbia, Quebec, and Newfoundland north to Alaska, Mackenzie, Alberta, Manitoba, and Labrador. Winters from Washington, eastern Oregon, Arizona, Texas, Louisiana, and Virginia south through the Argentine. *In Oregon:* Regular but not abundant migrant throughout State. Uncommon winter resident. Most abundant in April and from August to October.

Newberry (1857) reported the Greater Yellow-legs as not uncommon on the Columbia River, and since that time it has been reported by many observers from all parts of the State. It is a conspicuous wader, easily identified by its mottled back, white tail, and bright yellow legs. Single birds are likely to appear in the most isolated pools or meadows, either on the desert or on the high mountains. This is particularly true of the fall migration, which is a much more leisurely affair than the northward movement. It remains occasionally in small flocks far into the winter. Jewett took one on the Malheur River, December 13, 1927, and the authors together found a flock of six along this same stream, December 7, 1933. John Carter obtained a bird out of a flock of about twenty on Government Island (Multnomah County), November 24, 1933, and this flock was noted at intervals through December. Aside from these wintering records, it appears in Oregon in migration (Harney County, March 20), and migrates north in April (latest date, Wallowa County, May 10). The earliest fall migration date is July 9; the latest, November 20 (both Harney County).

The high-pitched cry is one of the most familiar sandpiper voices to Oregon bird lovers who are not privileged to live on the beaches or about the great swamps and lakes of eastern Oregon. The latter have an opportunity to know many shore birds that are seldom seen in most parts of the State, or at best so infrequently that one does not have an opportunity to become really acquainted with them.

Lesser Yellow-legs:
Totanus flavipes (Gmelin)

DESCRIPTION.—"Smaller than *melanoleucus*. Plumage similar in all its stages, but with finer markings. *Length:* 9.50–11.00, wing 6.10–6.65, bill 1.30–1.55, tarsus 2.00–2.15." (Bailey) *Nest:* A depression in the ground, lined with leaves and grass. *Eggs:* Usually 4, ground color buff, splotched and spotted with dark browns.

DISTRIBUTION.—*General:* Breeds from Alaska, Mackenzie, and Ungava south, formerly to New York, Indiana, Illinois, and Alberta. Winters from extreme southern United States southward. *In Oregon:* Uncommon migrant anywhere, but more abundant in eastern half of State and more frequent in fall than in spring migration.

WE REGARD the Lesser Yellow-legs as one of the less common migrating shore birds in this State. Townsend (1839) first listed it from this territory, and it has been reported since from eastern Oregon by Newberry (1857), Bendire (1877), Mearns (1879), and Willett (1919). Records from western Oregon are much scarcer. Woodcock (1902) reported a specimen from Corvallis, July 10, 1899; Hoffman (1926b) took one at Tillamook, September 10, 1925; and Currier (1929b) found two near Portland, November 21, 1928. Our only dates for spring are May 12 and 21, both in Lake County, but in the fall we have nine records extending from July 21 to September 28 from Klamath, Lake, Harney, Union, Crook, and Deschutes Counties.

The Lesser Yellow-legs is in every way a miniature of its larger relative and can easily be confused with it unless the difference in size is kept clearly in mind. The Greater Yellow-legs is one of the large shore birds, ranking next to the godwit and curlew in size, whereas the Lesser Yellow-legs, disregarding the length of its legs, is smaller in body than a Killdeer. Observers should be on the watch for this bird but should either collect the specimens or make most careful estimates of size before recording the identification, particularly in western Oregon.

American Knot:
Calidris canutus rufus (Wilson)

DESCRIPTION.—"The only species of *Tringa* in which the middle pair of tail feathers are not decidedly longer than the rest. *Adults in summer:* upper parts grayish and dusky, tinged with buff; rump and upper tail coverts white, barred and spotted with dusky; line over eye and most of under parts pale cinnamon; flanks and under tail coverts white. *Adults in winter:* upper parts plain gray; under parts, rump, and tail coverts white, barred or streaked with dusky except on belly and under tail coverts. *Young:* like adults in winter but gray feathers of back edged with whitish and dusky, and breast often suffused with buffy. *Length:* 10–11, wing 6.50, tail 2.50, bill 1.40." (Bailey) *Nest:* A hollow in the ground. *Eggs:* 4, olive buff, spotted and scrawled with brown.

DISTRIBUTION.—*General:* Breeding range is little known but is in far north on Arctic islands. Winters in southern hemisphere. *In Oregon:* Rare straggler on coast.

WOODCOCK (1902) first listed the American Knot as an Oregon bird on B. J. Bretherton's statement that it was a rare migrant on Yaquina Bay. It is of interest that the three specimens taken in Oregon since that time have all been taken at Seal Rocks, a few miles south of Newport. M. E. Peck collected two birds there on August 19, 1914, and Braly took the third 15 years later at almost the same spot on August 31, 1929. One of the curious anomalies that makes bird study such a fascinating subject is the behavior of this bird. It is common on the California coast and at times abundant at Willapa Harbor just to the north of the Columbia River, but the bird either has not scheduled any Oregon stops or passes along the coast at sea.

Aleutian Sandpiper:
Arquatella ptilocnemis couesi Ridgway

DESCRIPTION.—*Adult in spring:* Above, dark brown, variegated on the edges and tips of the feathers with a little whitish or grayish and much deep rusty; below, white, blotched or spotted with gray, rusty, or black in variable proportions without much pattern across breast and along flanks; throat paler; legs dull yellowish or yellowish green. *In winter:* Above, black with purple iridescence, feathers edged with grayish; below, white with broad breast band of ashy gray. *Size:* Length 7.50–9.00, wing 4.50–5.15, bill .98–1.25. *Nest:* A depression, scantily lined with dead leaves, grass, and feathers. *Eggs:* Usually 4, occasionally 5, olive to olive-buff, heavily and irregularly marked, chiefly about the larger end, with blotches and spots of dark brown.

DISTRIBUTION.—*General:* Breeds on northeastern coast of Siberia and west coast of Alaska and on adjacent islands south to Aleutians. Winters south to Oregon coast. *In Oregon:* Rare winter visitor.

THE ALEUTIAN SANDPIPER is a rare winter visitor on the Oregon coast from December 17 (Lincoln County) to April 15 (Tillamook County), where it frequents the rocky headlands most favored by the Black Turnstones, Surf-birds, and Wandering Tattlers. It looks superficially much like the Black Turnstone, with which it is frequently found, but is much smaller. Jewett (1914a) first recorded it from the State from a specimen taken at Netarts, December 31, 1912. Other records, all from Netarts and all supported by skins in his collection, are March 10, 1913, April 13, 1914, December 30, 1926, and December 29, 1928. The southernmost record for the State is at Roads End, in northern Lincoln County, where, December 17, 1930, the authors saw a small flock and took one bird.

Pectoral Sandpiper:
Pisobia melanotos (Vieillot)

Description.—"Bill longer than tarsus; middle pair of tail feathers pointed and longer than the rest; shaft of outer quill only, pure white; rump, upper coverts, and middle tail feathers, black. *Adults:* upper parts mottled dusky, black, and buffy; chest dark gray, finely streaked with dusky; chin and belly white. *Young:* similar to adults, but upper parts striped with ochraceous, brightest on edges of tertials and tail feathers; chest buffy, finely streaked with dusky. Length: 8.00–9.50, wing 5.00–5.50, bill 1.10–1.20, tarsus 1.00–1.10." (Bailey) *Nest:* A slight depression, lined with a little dry grass. *Eggs:* 4, dull white to olive buff, more or less evenly marked by blotches of brown.

Distribution.—*General:* Breeds mainly on Arctic Coast of Alaska and Mackenzie. Winters in South America. *In Oregon:* Occurs as uncommon migrant in both spring and fall. Most regular and abundant east of Cascades.

Woodcock (1902) first listed the Pectoral Sandpiper as an Oregon bird, stating that it was a rare spring migrant at Salem, as reported by Warner. This is the only published record for the State that we have been able to find, other than our own notes. We have found it much more abundant as a fall than as a spring migrant, a single record from Klamath County on April 19 and one from Harney County on May 24, both by Gabrielson, being the only spring records. Our earliest fall date is July 25 (Klamath County), but the first definite record of a specimen from the State is one taken by Jewett on October 16, 1905 (our latest fall date), on Government Island, Multnomah County. In the fall it is a fairly regular migrant east of the Cascades, where it can be expected in small numbers in Klamath and Harney Counties in the last half of September. In the notes of the Biological Survey, Preble reported it from Fort Klamath on September 15 to 18, 1896, and Cantwell, from Cold Springs Reservation, Umatilla County, in October 1914. In addition, Gabrielson obtained a specimen on September 23 from Crook County and at close range watched two birds running about over the permanent snow field just below the summit of Eagle Cap, Wallowa County, at about 9,600 feet altitude. These birds, hurriedly picking insects from the snow, were very tame and allowed slow approach to within 8 or 10 feet. The Multnomah County record above and one from the coast of Lincoln County, August 31, 1929, are our only records from western Oregon.

Baird's Sandpiper: *Pisobia bairdi* (Coues)

Description.—"Middle upper tail coverts plain dusky. *Adults in summer:* upper parts spotted and streaked with black, grayish, and buffy; chest buffy, streaked with dusky; line over eye, chin, and belly whitish. *Adults in winter:* plain grayish brown, obscurely streaked with dusky; under parts whitish, chest suffused with buffy. *Young:* feathers of back tipped with whitish, and chest less sharply streaked with dusky than in summer adult. *Length:* 7.00–7.60, wing 4.60–4.85, bill .90–1.00, tarsus 1.00." (Bailey) *Nest:* A slight depression in the ground, lined with leaves and grass. *Eggs:* Usually 4, pinkish buff, speckled and spotted with brown.

Distribution.—*General:* Breeds on Arctic Coast and islands of North America and adjacent parts of Siberia. Winters in South America. *In Oregon:* Known only as fall migrant on coast, with one record for eastern part of State.

Baird's Sandpiper was first reported from Oregon by Jewett (1914b), based on five specimens taken in August and September 1912. We find, however, that the first specimen was taken by Professor M. E. Peck near Woods, Tillamook County, on August 22, 1909, and is now in the Carnegie Museum. Since then the species has been taken regularly on the coast in Tillamook, Lincoln, and Curry Counties and at times is exceedingly abundant on the beaches. Our earliest date is July 30 (Lincoln County); our latest, September 13 (Curry County). The only record east of the Cascades is that of a small flock seen by Gabrielson and DuBois at Kinney Lake, Wallowa County, on August 20, 1930, from which one specimen was taken.

The ease with which this species might be confused with the Western or Pectoral Sandpiper undoubtedly has something to do with the previous scarcity of records. Comparative size is a poor criterion on which to separate similar species in the field unless they appear together, and birds are not always so considerate. Because of the strong general similarity of the two species we have confined our records to dates on which specimens were taken. In addition to our specimens, Braly has taken a number along the coast.

Least Sandpiper: *Pisobia minutilla* (Vieillot)

Description.—"Size very small, wing less than 4. *Adults in summer:* median parts of tail, upper coverts, and rump black; sides of coverts white, streaked with dusky; rest of upper parts mainly blackish, specked and spotted with brown and buff; chest buffy gray, specked with dusky; belly and flanks white. *Adults in winter:* upper parts dark gray, obscurely spotted and streaked with dusky; chest light gray, finely streaked. *Young:* crown and back heavily streaked with rusty, and back spotted with white; chest buffy gray, faintly streaked. *Length:* 5.00–6.75, wing 3.50–3.75, bill .75–.92, tarsus .75." (Bailey) *Nest:* A slight depression in the ground, lined with leaves and grass. *Eggs:* 3 or 4, cream buff to olive, blotched or speckled with brown.

DISTRIBUTION.—*General:* Breeds in Arctic north from Nova Scotia, Quebec, Keewatin, southern Mackenzie, southern Yukon, and southern Alaska and winters from Grays Harbor, Washington, Gulf coast, and North Carolina, southward. *In Oregon:* Spring and fall migrant, more abundant in fall than in spring migration movement. Regular winter resident in small numbers on coast.

THE LEAST SANDPIPER, the smallest of the Oregon shore birds, so closely resembles the Western Sandpiper that the two are easily confused. For that reason records of this species are not plentiful in Oregon literature. Townsend listed it in 1839, the only record until Woodcock (1902) reported it from Yaquina Bay and Corvallis. Anthony (Bailey 1902) stated that it was a common migrant near Portland. Willett (1919) found it in both spring and fall at Malheur Lake. In the Biological Survey field notes are records by Vernon Bailey, Preble, Becker, Streator, and Goldman from various localities in both eastern and western Oregon. Our date of latest spring departure is May 15 (Harney County). W. E. Sherwood took the earliest fall specimens we have seen, July 11, 1924, at Salem. The species is an abundant migrant on the coast during July, August, and September, after which most of the birds depart, leaving behind only a scant population that winters in the sand dunes, often in small flocks mixed with Snowy Plover. We have taken wintering birds on the coast on December 11 (Curry County, Jewett), December 27 (Tillamook County, Gabrielson), and November 24 (Lincoln County, both observers and John Carter). Like other small sandpipers, these little "peeps" are consummate masters of the art of synchronized motion, often wheeling and dipping in the most intricate aerial evolutions.

Red-backed Sandpiper:
Pelidna alpina sakhalina (Vieillot)

DESCRIPTION.—"Tarsus longer than middle toe and claw; bill longer than tarsus, slightly curved; middle of wing with a large white patch. *Adults in summer:* crown, back, and upper tail coverts bright rusty ochraceous, more or less spotted or streaked with black; middle of belly black; chest grayish white, thickly streaked with dusky; sides and back part of belly white. *Adults in winter:* upper parts plain ashy gray, obscurely streaked with dusky; chest light gray, more or less streaked with dusky; rest of under parts, sides of rump, and upper tail coverts white. *Young:* like adults in winter but upper parts spotted and streaked with black and ochraceous, and breast coarsely spotted with black. *Length:* 7.60–8.75, wing 4.60–4.95, bill 1.40–1.75, tarsus 1.00–1.15." (Bailey) *Nest:* A loose mass of dry grass in a shallow depression in the ground. *Eggs:* Usually 4, pale green to olive buff, spotted with dark browns.

DISTRIBUTION.—*General:* Breeds in Arctic America south to eastern Keewatin, northwestern Mackenzie, and Hooper Bay, Alaska. Winters from Washington and New Jersey south to Lower California, Florida, and Gulf coast. *In Oregon:* Common migrant on coast and less common but regular winter resident. Less common inland, although it occurs more or less regularly in migration. Arrives in October and remains until May.

The handsome Red-backed Sandpiper is a common migrant on the coast that in its spring plumage is not likely to be confused with any other species. In the fall, however, in its more demure dress, it is harder for the less observant to tell it from the hosts of other sandpipers present, but its heavy body and comparatively long bill serve to distinguish it from most of the others. This species was first reported for Oregon by Townsend (1839), and Newberry (1857) included it in his Oregon list. Johnson (1880) reported it as a migrant in the Willamette Valley, and Woodcock (1902) listed a specimen taken on the coast of Lincoln County, May 18, 1888, the date curiously coinciding with Jewett's record at Netarts, May 18, 1913, the latest date either of us has for the State. Walker (1917), however, reported it from Silver Lake, June 4, the latest date for the State and one of the few records for eastern Oregon. Willett (1919) saw several at Malheur Lake May 14. Neither of us has observed this bird east of the Cascades, no doubt because comparatively little field work has been carried on in the water areas during the proper season. In our experience, the species is most common in late April and early May and is sometimes present on the beaches and mud flats by the hundreds the first week in May. In the fall it becomes common in October (earliest date, October 4, Lane County), when other species of sandpipers are on the decrease and some of them have moved on southward. The birds remaining after November 1 are usually those that have elected to spend the winter on the coast, where they may be found feeding along the beaches at low tide or on the mud flats of the bays in small flocks, sometimes in company with a few Least Sandpipers.

Long-billed Dowitcher:
Limnodromus griseus scolopaceus (Say)

Description.—"*Adults in summer:* A light stripe over eye and dusky stripe from eye to bill; upper parts, except rump and lower back, specked and mottled with black, brown, and buff; rump white, spotted with black, tail feathers barred black and white; entire under parts bright cinnamon specked on throat and barred on sides and lower tail coverts with dusky. *Adults in winter:* belly and line over eye white; rest of plumage gray. *Young:* similar to adults but back and crown mottled with black and ochraceous; belly and chest suffused with light cinnamon. *Length:* 11.00–12.50, wing 5.40–6.00, bill 2.10–3.00, tarsus 1.35–1.75." (Bailey) *Nest:* A small depression in the ground, scantily lined with grass and leaves. *Eggs:* 4, olive in color, spotted and blotched with bright to dull brown.

Distribution.—*General:* Breeds from Point Barrow to mouth of Yukon, east to northwestern Mackenzie. Winters from Louisiana, Florida, central California, Cuba, Jamaica, and Mexico south to Panama and Ecuador; in migration on Pacific Coast and in western Mississippi Valley; occasional in summer (nonbreeding birds) south to western Ecuador. Casual on Atlantic Coast from Nova Scotia (Sable Island) southward and on northern coast of eastern Siberia south to Japan. *In Oregon:* Occurs as both a spring and fall migrant in eastern and western Oregon.

THE LONG-BILLED DOWITCHER is a regular but not abundant migrant in Oregon, though huge flocks will appear for a day or two in some localities during migrations. Its flight is swift and direct, and it is master of the intricate flock evolutions extensively practiced by many of its relatives. Townsend (1839) first recorded it from Oregon, and since his time Newberry (1857), Bendire (1877), Mearns (1879), Johnson (1880), and Willett (1919) have recorded it as either a spring or fall migrant, all of these referring to eastern Oregon except Johnson who found it in the Willamette Valley. For some unknown reason neither Woodcock (1902) nor any of his western Oregon correspondents seem to have noted this species; at least Woodcock failed to mention it.

In our own experience it is now regularly found on the coast and in the interior. The coastal birds are found usually in small compact flocks about the bays. In eastern Oregon the birds are often found in flocks of several hundred that stay about the marshes for several days or weeks, particularly on their movement southward. We have noted it in Clatsop, Tillamook, and Lincoln Counties on the coast and Harney, Klamath, and Crook Counties in the eastern part of the State. Our earliest spring date is April 29 (Clatsop County); our latest, May 15 (Harney County). In the fall our records range from July 20 (Lincoln County) to September 23 (Crook County).

Most of the specimens taken in Oregon are curiously speckled intermediates between the bright cinnamon of the summer and the gray and white of the winter dress. We have three taken by Gabrielson from a flock in Crook County, September 23, however, that are in complete winter plumage and two taken by him at Newport on May 3 that are in almost full nuptial dress.

Western Sandpiper:
Ereunetes mauri Cabanis

DESCRIPTION.—"*Adults in summer:* Ear coverts and upper parts bright chestnut, mottled with black and buffy gray; breast thickly spotted. *Adults in winter:* upper parts dull gray, obscurely streaked with dusky; under parts white, with a few scattered triangular spots of dusky on breast and sides. *Young:* back spotted with black and scalloped with dark chestnut and white; chest tinged with pinkish buff; rest of under parts white. *Male:* wing 3.60–3.75, bill .85–.95, tarsus .85–.90. *Female:* wing 3.70–3.90, bill 1.00–1.15, tarsus .90–.95." (Bailey) *Nest:* A depression in the ground, scantily lined with grass, leaves of berry-bearing vines and dwarf birch, and reindeer moss stems. *Eggs:* 4, rarely 5, creamy ground color, heavily marked with brown.

DISTRIBUTION.—*General:* Breeds only in Alaska from Hooper Bay north and east to Point Barrow and Camden Bay. Winters from Washington and Gulf coast southward into South America. *In Oregon:* Abundant spring and fall migrant.

THE WESTERN SANDPIPER is by far the most abundant shore bird in Oregon, often outnumbering all other species combined. It reaches its maximum numbers on the coast, but it is also common inland wherever suitable water conditions are to be found. It is most numerous in May, August, and September. Our earliest spring date is April 15 (Klamath County); the latest, May 22 (Tillamook County). In the fall movement, our earliest date is July 2 (Lincoln County); our latest, November 20 (Curry County). This last date suggests wintering birds, though we have not yet found this species anywhere on the Oregon coast between the months of December and March inclusive, but as it has been known to winter on the Washington coast, it may reasonably be expected to be found doing so in Oregon.

Townsend (1839) first reported the Western Sandpiper from Oregon. Bendire (1877) considered it a common spring migrant at Malheur Lake, and Willett (1919) also found it common in July and August at the same place. Woodcock (1902) recorded it from Yaquina, Scio, and Corvallis, and Anthony (Bailey 1902) considered it an abundant migrant about Portland. There is a specimen in the Carnegie Museum taken by Woodcock (1902) at Corvallis on April 21, 1899. The manuscript reports of Biological Survey workers contain many references to this bird during migrations. Those of particular interest are a specimen taken out of a flock of 10 by Preble, July 4, 1915, at Cow Creek, Lake Malheur, a specimen taken by him at Diamond Lake, August 12, 1896, and one taken at Lakeview October 1, 1914, by Goldman. From a huge flock on Yaquina Bay, July 2, 1934, Gabrielson and Braly took several birds showing incubation patches.

These little sandpipers, the most abundant of all the smaller species grouped under the name "Peep" or "Sand-peep" by the general populace, at times inhabit our beaches and lake shores in great swarms. Running back and forth with the surf along the beaches, or wheeling, dipping, and circling in perfect unison about the waterfront, they usually attract the attention of all eyes. Often when tired, apparently from a long migration trip, they settle on the beach in closely packed masses, all sitting tight to the ground and facing the same direction. On such occasions it is possible to approach almost within a step before the birds move, and a gun fired into the closely packed ranks will kill or wound dozens of the tiny creatures. It formerly was no unusual thing to find numerous crippled Western Sandpipers on the beaches, the luckless survivors of such a slaughter, but the practice seems to be dying out slowly.

Marbled Godwit:
Limosa fedoa (Linnaeus)

Description.—"*Adults:* Plumage mainly light cinnamon brown, heavily mottled with black on upper parts, and finely barred with blackish on chest, sides, and tail; throat streaked and chin whitish; edge of wing black. *Young:* similar to adults but more ochraceous brown, and breast and sides unmarked. *Length:* 16.50–20.50, wing 8.50–9.00, bill 3.50–5.06." (Bailey) *Nest:* A slight hollow in grassy places, sometimes lined with a little dry grass. *Eggs:* Usually 4, rarely 3 or 5, olive buff, sparingly marked with rounded spots of dull brown.

Distribution.—*General:* Breeds in interior, largely in Alberta, Saskatchewan, Manitoba, Wisconsin, Minnesota, Iowa, North and South Dakota—the principal remaining breeding area being in North Dakota and Saskatchewan. Winters from southern United States southward. *In Oregon:* Very rare transient. Only two recent records.

Although this large brown wader with the slightly upturned bill is a fairly common bird in October and November on the southern California coast, it has always been a rarity in Oregon. Townsend (1839) listed the Marbled Godwit for the State, and Woodcock (1902) said it was reported on the coast by Anthony. The only specimen we have seen is a bird taken at Netarts Bay from a flock of seven, September 12, 1922, by Gabrielson (1923). Kalmbach reported seeing two at close range in Klamath County, August 21 and 22, 1929, the only other recent report for the State.

Sanderling:
Crocethia alba (Pallas)

Description.—"Toes only 3, short and flattened; bill slender, about as long as tarsus; feet and legs black. *Breeding plumage:* upper parts, throat, and chest specked and spotted with rusty, black, and whitish; rest of under parts and stripe on middle of wing white. *Adults in summer:* upper parts and throat specked, spotted, and streaked with black, rusty and whitish; rest of under parts and stripe on wing white. *Adults in winter:* upper parts hoary gray, except blackish quills and bend of wing; under parts snowy white. *Young:* upper parts coarsely spotted with dusky and gray above; under parts white, sparsely marked with dusky and buffy on chest. Length: 7.00–8.75, wing 4.70–5.00, bill .95–1.00, tarsus .90–1.05." (Bailey) *Nest:* A slight depression in the ground, lined with withered leaves of Arctic willow and other plants of the extreme north. *Eggs:* 3 or 4, usually 4, greenish-olive ground color, marked with small, somewhat evenly distributed spots of dull brown.

Distribution.—*General:* Cosmopolitan in North America. Breeds from northern Alaska and Canada, on Arctic islands and Greenland. Winters from Washington and Massachusetts southward far into South America. *In Oregon:* Common migrant and winter resident of coast counties, where it is almost entirely a beach bird, that is nearly a permanent resident, being absent from coast for a short period in late spring and early summer.

Although the Sanderling is one of the most conspicuous and easily found sandpipers on the coast, for some unexplained reason it was overlooked by all of the early writers on Oregon birds. Woodcock (1902), who reported it as a common migrant at Yaquina Bay on reports of Bretherton, was the first to include it in any Oregon list. We have found it to be one of the most regular of all species. It is confined strictly to the coast counties. There are no inland records. It is most abundant on the beaches in August and September but is found also as the most common wintering sandpiper on the coast. When it arrives from the north it is already well advanced into the pale winter plumage that makes it the whitest appearing of all our small sandpipers. Before it departs in the spring it has completely donned the spotted and checked darker summer plumage. Our latest spring date is June 2 (Tillamook County); earliest fall date, July 20 (Lincoln County).

When the Sanderlings begin to arrive on the beaches in numbers in early August they appear in straggling flocks that follow the wash of the surf back and forth, always calculating to a nicety just how far they may follow the receding wave before turning to race shoreward on flying feet ahead of the surge of its successor. Seldom do they miscalculate enough to be forced to take wing ahead of the rushing waters. In September their numbers commence to diminish as many take off for points south. Enough of these hardy sandpipers remain, however, for a winter day's tramp of three or four miles to reveal a flock or two on almost any beach.

Avocets and Stilts: *Family Recurvirostridae*

Avocet:
Recurvirostra americana Gmelin

Description.—"Bill black, feet and legs bluish. *Adults in summer plumage:* head, neck, chest, and shoulders light cinnamon, shading into whitish around base of bill; under parts, rump, and large patches on wing white; primaries, base of wing, and half of scapulars black. *Adults in winter plumage:* cinnamon of head, neck, and chest replaced by grayish white. *Young:* like winter adults, but quills and scapulars tipped with whitish, and back of neck tinged with buffy." (Bailey) *Downy young:* "The downy young avocet is well colored for concealment on an open beach or alkaline flat. The colors of the upper parts are 'cinnamon buff,' 'cream buff,' and buffy grays, lightest on the crown and darkest on the rump; there is a distinct but narrow loral stripe of black; the crown is indistinctly spotted with dusky. Two parallel stripes of brownish black distinctly mark the scapulars and two more the sides of the rump; the wings, back, rump, and thighs are less distinctly spotted or peppered with gray and dusky. The under parts are buffy white, nearly pure white on the throat and belly." (Bent) *Size:* "Length 15.50–18.75, wing 8.50–9.00, bill 3.40–3.65, tarsus 3.70–3.80." (Bailey) *Nest:* Usually a depression, lined with a little dry grass. *Eggs:* Usually 4, occasionally 3 or 5, deep buff, more or less evenly covered with irregular spots and patches of dark brown (Plate 42, *A*).

Distribution.—*General:* Breeds from Washington, Idaho, Alberta, Saskatchewan, western Iowa, Kansas south to Texas, New Mexico, Utah, Nevada, and California. *In Oregon:* Breeds commonly about shallow alkaline ponds and lakes of Klamath, Lake, Harney, and Malheur Counties. Has bred in Baker County and probably in Umatilla County. Arrives in May and remains until October.

Townsend (1839) first reported the Avocet from Oregon, and Bendire (1877) first reported it breeding in the State (Plate 42, *B*). Since Bendire's time, every ornithologist who has visited the lake country of south-

Plate 42, *A*. Nest and eggs of Avocet. (Photo by Alex Walker.)

Plate 42, *B*. Avocet on nest. (Photo by Wm. L. Finley and H. T. Bohlman.)

central Oregon has had some comment to make about this striking bird. It is most abundant about the small alkaline ponds between Klamath Falls and the California line, at Abert, Summer, and the Warner Lakes in Lake County, about Malheur Lake and the smaller ponds in both the Silvies and Blitzen Valleys in Harney County, and about the Cow Creek Lakes in Malheur County. In addition, one or more pairs will be found about many of the smaller lakes and ponds in these counties. Its earliest date of arrival is April 5 (Klamath County); latest fall date, October 9 (Lake County). Aside from the counties in which it is found breeding, Oregon records of this bird are scarce. Woodcock (1902) reported two specimens from near Corvallis on July 29, 1900, the only record for the western part of the State. There are two records of its occurrence in Wallowa County: one was killed and mounted at the fish hatchery near Enterprise some time prior to 1927; and later a pair of wings taken by a game warden from a bird killed in the county was sent to us for identification.

In Oregon the nests are usually built in the edge of the short scant grass of the alkaline flats and are mere depressions, lined more or less with bits of dry vegetation (Plate 42, *A*). They are occasionally built so close to the water level that a heavy rain floods them, forcing the birds to move to higher ground for a second nesting. The eggs are laid in late May or early June (May 12 and June 25, extreme dates), and the long-legged youngsters are able to run about within a few hours after hatching, which occurs in mid-June.

The large size, the striking black, white, and chestnut color pattern, and the long, upturned bill serve to differentiate the Avocets from all other waders found within the State. In the fall the chestnut color of the head and neck is replaced by white, leaving the birds with a strictly black and white pattern. Nesting in the short grass and spending most of the time along the edges of the shallow pools, they are one of the most conspicuous marsh birds. When aroused by the presence of an intruder at the nests, they fly about in frantic circles, sweeping down with their long bills pointed straight ahead and continuously uttering low, piercing cries. At other times they are rather silent and spend their time feeding quietly near the shore line or resting in small companies on the mud flats. The upturned bill, a clumsy-looking affair, is an appropriate tool for use in feeding in the shallow water. The bird walks or runs forward, with the bill plowing the water and scooping up the aquatic larvae and other food.

Black-necked Stilt:
Himantopus mexicanus (Müller)

Description.—"Bill black, feet and legs pinkish. *Adult male:* back of head and neck, shoulders, and wings greenish black; tail gray; rest of plumage white, breast tinged with dull pinkish in breeding plumage. *Adult female:* like male, but black duller, or slaty. *Young:* similar to adult female, but feathers of back bordered with buffy, and blackish of head and neck mottled with buffy." (Bailey) *Downy young:* "Upper parts light buffy grayish mottled with dusky, the back and rump with several large blotches of black; head, neck, and under parts buffy whitish or brownish white, the crown, occiput, and hindneck grayish, the crown with a mesial streak of black, the occiput with several irregular spots of the same." (Ridgway 1919.) *Size:* "Length 13.50–15.50, wing 8.50–9.00, bill 2.50, tarsus 4." (Bailey) *Nest:* A hollow, lined with bits of vegetation. *Eggs:* Usually 4, occasionally 3 to 7, dull yellow to buff, irregularly spotted with small blotches of dark brown or black (Plate 43, *A*).

Distribution.—*General:* Nests north to Oregon, Utah, Colorado, Louisiana, and Florida and southward into South America. Winters in Central and South America. *In Oregon:* Summer resident of alkali ponds of Klamath, Harney, and Lake Counties. Arrives in May and leaves for south in August.

The Black-necked Stilt, an odd black and white bird with elongated pink legs (Plate 43, *B*), is a summer resident and one of the striking species of the alkaline lake country. It reaches its northernmost breeding grounds in Oregon, where nesting colonies are known at present from Klamath (several ponds near Midland), Lake (Warner Lakes and Chewaucan Marsh), and Harney (Malheur Lake) Counties. Newberry (1857) first recorded the species from the State, and Bendire (1877) found it breeding at Malheur Lake. Mearns (1879) listed it at Fort Klamath, and subsequent observers have found it in these two counties and in Lake County also. The earliest date of arrival is April 19 (Klamath County); latest fall date, August 31 (Lake County), the birds leaving for the south while the weather is still warm in the great interior plateau. The species is not common in Oregon, the numbers being limited to a few pairs at each of the above-mentioned localities. It has not been found even as a straggler outside the breeding area.

The flimsy nests (Plate 43, *A*), built in much the same situations as those selected by the Avocets, are occasionally flooded by rising waters. At such times, the birds have been known to build them up by thrusting bits of sticks and debris under the eggs until they are occasionally raised as much as 8 inches above the ground level. The eggs are usually laid during the last half of May (May 21 to June 21).

In walking, the Black-necked Stilts raise the feet with a very exaggerated knee action, which sometimes makes them appear clumsy and awkward in handling their pipestem legs, but in reality they are very competent waders in the slime and muddy waters of their chosen home. Their flight is well sustained but not particularly swift, the long legs projecting behind giving the birds an exceedingly slender appearance. During their brief stay in Oregon, the stilts are exceedingly noisy and aggressive, scolding with harsh, shrill clatter at any one who invades their haunts.

Plate 43, *A*. Nest and eggs of Black-necked Stilt. (Photo by Wm. L. and Irene Finley.)

Plate 43, *B*. Black-necked Stilt on nest. (Photo by Wm. L. and Irene Finley.)

Phalaropes: *Family Phalaropodidae*

Red Phalarope:
Phalaropus fulicarius (Linnaeus)

Description.—"Bill about as long as head, flat, widest toward end. *Adult male in summer:* back streaked with black and buff; wing bluish and dusky, crossed by a white band; side of head whitish; under parts dark cinnamon brown. *Adult female in summer:* crown and face plumbeous or blackish, sides of head pure white. *Adults in winter:* head, neck, and under parts pure white, except for plumbeous on back of head and around eyes; upper parts plain blue gray. *Young:* upper parts blackish, the feathers edged with yellowish; under parts whitish, with dusky brown across breast. *Length:* 7.50–8.75, wing 5.25–5.50, bill .80–.95." (Bailey) *Nest:* A depression in the ground, lined with bits of grass and leaves or moss of the tundra. *Eggs:* Almost invariably 4, buff, more or less irregularly spotted and blotched with bright to dark brown.

Distribution.—*General:* Breeds in Arctic regions of both Old and New World. Winters on oceans to below equator. *In Oregon:* Regular and at times abundant migrant along coast, spending much time at sea and appearing on shore in numbers only during severe storms. Casual straggler inland.

The beautiful little Red Phalarope (Plate 44, *A*) is a common and at times abundant migrant shore bird off the Oregon coast, but it usually stays well offshore so that the scattered individuals found on the beaches furnish a most unsatisfactory clue to its movements and abundance in our State. During the periods of abundance the birds are found flying low over the water in small flocks or riding the ocean swells like puffs of down. They ride high on the water, and a more incongruous picture can hardly be imagined than these dainty mites riding the waves during rough weather, apparently entirely indifferent to the tumult of the waters. Our earliest spring date is March 27 (Lane County); latest, May 11 (Lincoln County). In the fall migration, July 20 (Lincoln County) is our earliest and November 22 (Tillamook County) our latest date of their appearance. Inland, the species is known only as a casual straggler. A female taken at Fort Klamath, October 31, 1882, by Bendire and now in the United States National Museum was the only specimen prior to the storm of October 1934, when birds were found as far inland as Carleton.

Several times in our experience in Oregon, fall storms have been too much for these little navigators and they have been driven onto the beach by the hundreds and sometimes thousands. When this occurs the birds, weak and usually extremely emaciated, sit on the sand above the breaking waves or crouch among the logs in the drift above the storm tide line. They are frequently so weak that it is almost possible to capture them in the hand, and numbers are killed along the coast highways by passing cars. Jewett first encountered one of these great groups of storm-driven phalaropes at Netarts Bay between September 17 and 29, 1920. The next

Plate 44, *A*. Red Phalarope. (Photo by Alex Walker.)

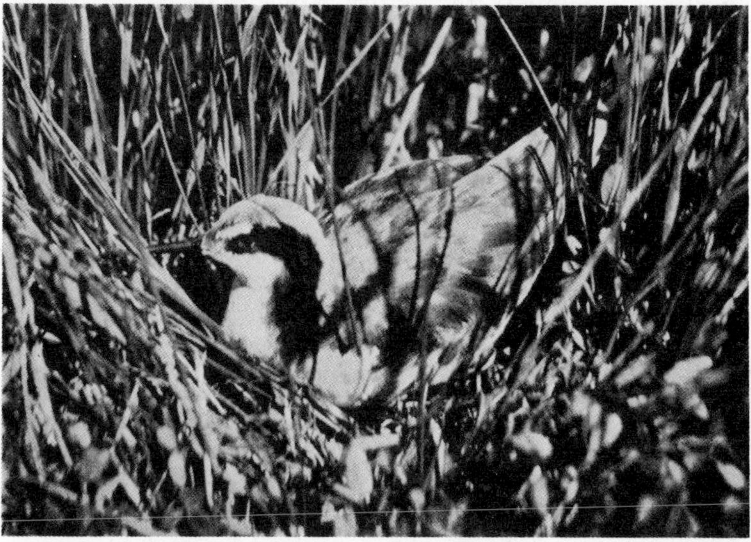

Plate 44, *B*. Male Wilson's Phalarope. (Photo by Wm. L. Finley and H. T. Bohlman.)

year Gabrielson observed a similar occurrence on the Tillamook beaches on October 18 and 19. Most of the birds soon disappeared, but a few remained on the beaches on a second visit on November 22. During the last week of October 1934, a heavy storm killed hundreds of these birds along the beaches and drove thousands more inland, some into the Willamette Valley, to be killed by cars or various other agencies. It was one of the most spectacular cases of bird destruction ever to come to our attention.

On offshore trips taken during the late summer and fall by one or both of the writers at irregular intervals during the past few years, these phalaropes were the most abundant small bird encountered; and every offshore trip at that season revealed their presence in numbers. On July 20, 1933, Gabrielson found them common off Depoe Bay. Their breasts were still curiously speckled and blotched with the remaining red of the summer plumage. On August 30 and 31, 1929, the two writers and Braly saw great numbers scattered over the ocean out 12 to 15 miles, and a few of those collected showed an occasional red feather. At that time the phalaropes were scattered in small flocks feeding on the surface and frequently indulging in the familiar whirling, treading performance. They seemed particularly partial to the "tide rips" (so called by local fisherman) that are produced by a combination of wind, surface current, and tidal movements. These rips are usually an irregular broken line roughly paralleling the shore and marked by masses of floating kelp, logs, and drift thrown overboard from passing steamers. They may be close to shore or many miles at sea, depending on the variations of wind and water movements. The phalaropes, gulls, and shearwaters, in particular, seem to find them a prolific source of food supply, and when a rip forms it is usually followed by a noticeable concentration of such birds. We have not had an opportunity to get offshore so regularly in the spring, and therefore our spring records are much more scanty, depending on the shore stragglers that have appeared between March 27 and May 11.

Few writers have had much to say regarding this little bird as an Oregon species. Townsend (1839) credited it to Oregon, and Woodcock (1902) said it was found at Yaquina Bay. Aside from these two references we have had to rely entirely on our own notes for the discussion of its status.

Wilson's Phalarope:
Steganopus tricolor Vieillot

Description.—"Bill slender, longer than head; toes with straight-edged marginal membranes; wing without white bar; female larger and handsomer than male. *Male in breeding plumage:* crown and upper parts dusky, touched with brown; sides of neck with a chestnut stripe; throat and chest buffy; stripe over eye, chin, and belly white. *Female in breeding plumage:* crown and back bluish gray; black stripe along sides of head and neck shading into rich chestnut along lower neck and shoulders; chest and lower part of throat delicate cinnamon buff; upper part of throat, belly, and line over eye white. *Adults in winter plumage:* upper parts plain gray, chest and sides of breast grayish; rest of under parts white. *Young:* upper parts dusky, streaked with light cinnamon; under parts white, with tinge of cinnamon across breast." (Bailey) *Downy young:* "In its natal down the young Wilson phalarope is entirely unlike the other phalaropes and quite different from any other young wader. The slender bill and long slender legs and feet are characteristic. It is prettily and distinctively colored also. The prevailing color of the upper parts and of a band across the chest is 'ochraceous buff,' deepening on the crown, wings, and mantle almost to 'ochraceous orange,' and paling to buffy or grayish white on the belly and to pure white on the chin and throat. There is a narrow, median, black line on the crown extending nearly or quite to the bill; this is continued in a broad, more or less broken, black stripe down the center of the back to a large black patch on the rump; a black spot on each side of the crown, one on the occiput and several more on wings, thighs, and sides of the back, sometimes run together to form stripes." (Bent) *Size:* "*Female*, length 9.40–10.00, wing 5.20–5.30, bill 1.30–1.35, tarsus 1.30–1.35. *Male*, length 8.25–9.00, wing 4.75–4.80, bill 1.25, tarsus 1.20–1.25." (Bailey) *Nest:* A depression in the ground, more or less lined with grass. *Eggs:* Usually 4, rarely 3, buff, sometimes evenly and sometimes irregularly spotted or blotched with dark brown.

DISTRIBUTION.—*General:* Breeds from Washington, Alberta, Saskatchewan, Manitoba, Minnesota, Michigan, and southern Ontario south to Indiana, Missouri, Kansas, Colorado, Wyoming, Utah, Nevada, and central California. Winters from southern United States southward far into South America. *In Oregon:* Abundant summer resident and breeding bird in Klamath, Lake, Harney, and Malheur Counties. Breeds less commonly in Crook, Union, and perhaps other eastern Oregon counties where suitable marshes are found. Rare straggler west of Cascades.

TOWNSEND (1839) first discovered Wilson's Phalarope (Plate 44, *B*), as he did so many other species, as an Oregon bird. Although it is an abundant summer resident and breeding bird in eastern Oregon, it appears west of the Cascades only as a rare straggler, the only record being that of Overton Dowell, Jr., from Mercer, May 15, 1917. It appears on the nesting ground in May (earliest date, April 21, Malheur County) and remains until August (latest date, September 22, Harney County). The eggs are laid in late May or early June (we have no definite dates), and the beautifully marked youngsters can run about as soon as hatched.

This phalarope is one of Oregon's most interesting nesting birds. That the lady of the house wears the breeches is abundantly demonstrated by the fact that the male does all of the incubating and cares for the young. The more brilliantly colored female lays the eggs and retains an interest in the family as shown by her anxiety whenever any one approaches the nest, but so far as known, her interest does not extend to the point of relieving her hen-pecked spouse of any of the housekeeping drudgery.

Throughout the breeding season, flocks—sometimes of considerable size—of nonbreeding birds are found on the marshes, and as soon as the young are feathered out and able to fly they join them. The flocks remain until August, when the southward movement begins. The birds are strong, swift fliers, and on occasion the flocks go through the intricate aerial evolutions so commonly seen among the sandpipers.

Northern Phalarope:
Lobipes lobatus (Linnaeus)

Description.—"Bill about as long as head, very slender and sharp; margins of toes scalloped; wing with white bar in all plumages. *Male in breeding plumage:* upper parts dark plumbeous, striped on back with buff and black; sides of neck rufous; chest gray; upper throat and belly white. *Female in breeding plumage:* brighter colored rufous extending across throat as well as on sides of neck. *Fall and winter plumage:* face, line over eye, and under parts white; line under eye, and back of head, dusky; upper parts mainly gray. *Young:* like winter adults, but upper parts darker, striped with buff and black. *Length:* 7–8, wing 4.00–4.45, bill .80–.90." (Bailey) *Nest:* A slight depression, lined with leaves and grass. *Eggs:* 4, buff to olive, with irregular spots and blotches of dark brown.

Distribution.—*General:* Arctic regions of both hemispheres. Breeds farther south than Red Phalarope, being found south to western Quebec, northern Manitoba, and Nushagak Island in Alaska. Winters largely at sea, its range at this season (imperfectly known) extending far south into southern hemisphere. *In Oregon:* Common migrant along coast. Less common but regular migrant inland.

The tiny Northern Phalarope, smallest and daintiest of its kind, is also the most widely distributed of the three species and, all things considered, the one the average bird student is most likely to encounter, unless it be Wilson's Phalarope in its eastern Oregon breeding grounds. It may be expected anywhere in the State during the migration periods, often appearing at pools seemingly too small or too remote from any other water to have any possible attraction for a water or shore bird. It is most abundant as a migrant in May and again in July, August, and September. Townsend (1839), who made the first general list of birds from this region, first credited it to Oregon, and Newberry (1857) stated that it was supposed to have nested on the Deschutes River in 1885, on report of Williamson. This record is undoubtedly a confusion with Wilson's Phalarope and cannot be considered authentic, as there is no existing evidence that the species ever bred so far south. It is interesting, though, that our latest spring record, an adult female, was collected from a roadside pool between Redmond and the Deschutes River by Gabrielson on June 12, 1924. The sex organs, however, showed no signs of breeding.

Bendire (1877) saw a flock on April 26, 1876, at Malheur Lake, and Mearns (1879) reported it from Klamath. Since that time numerous observers have reported it in migration. Peck (1911a) reported seeing it in northern Malheur County on July 21, and our own notes and collections contain records and specimens from the following eastern Oregon counties: Klamath, Harney, Umatilla, Grant, Deschutes, and Morrow. Two of these specimens warrant special mention, as they furnish the two earliest fall records of this little phalarope. One, in the Jewett collection, was taken by E. Rett at the Narrows, Harney County, July 2, 1925; and the second, now in the United States National Museum, was collected by Jewett at Strawberry Lake, high in the Blue Mountains of Grant County, on July 15, 1915. This leaves little gap between the last spring bird (June 12) and those first going southward in the fall. We consider, however, that the June 12 bird was a very belated straggler—perhaps weakened enough from some cause to prevent the northward flight at the normal season. Except for this one bird, our latest spring record is May 19, which may be regarded as much nearer the normal period of departure. These few early southward-moving individuals, moreover, might easily be nonbreeding birds or individuals whose nests had been destroyed too late in the season to allow a second clutch. Aside from the two birds mentioned above and a July 6 sight record for Tillamook County, about July 20 seems to be the normal date for the arrival of the southbound birds. Our latest fall record is October 6 (Klamath County). In western Oregon we have noted the species in Jackson, Josephine, and Multnomah Counties as straggling individuals or in small flocks, and along the coast, from Curry to Clatsop Counties, as a common bird.

Although this dainty little phalarope is most abundant offshore, sometimes exceeding the Red Phalarope in numbers, it is not such a confirmed lover of the briny deep as the latter and is found much more commonly along the beaches and tide flats. When on the ocean, it acts much as does its larger and heavier cousin; when in the tide pools and shallows of the bay, numbers of them can frequently be seen sitting quietly on the water or converting themselves into tiny "Whirling Dervishes" as they tread up the water, pausing now and then to pick up some small representative of the abundant aquatic life disturbed by the small feet.

Jaegers: *Family Stercorariidae*

Pomarine Jaeger:
Stercorarius pomarinus (Temminck)

Description.—"*Adults: Light phase:* face, crown, and upper parts, except collar, sooty black; throat white, becoming silky yellow on cheeks and around back of neck; breast white, chest and sides mottled with sooty. *Dark phase:* wholly dark sooty or plumbeous. All grades are found between the dark and light phases. *Young:* back dusky, feathers tipped with buff; rest of plumage dull buff, barred with dusky." (Bailey) *Downy young:* "Immaculate grayish brown (between benzo brown and deep brownish drab) passing into paler (between benzo brown and drab) on chin and under parts of body; bill brownish, the legs and feet much paler brownish." (Ridgway 1919.) *Size:* "Length 20–23, wing 13.50–14.00, tail 8–9, bill 1.45–1.75." (Bailey) *Nest:* A slight depression in the soil, just large enough to accommodate the eggs. *Eggs:* 2 to 3, ground color "brownish olive" to "dark olive buff," sparingly spotted with brown, drab, or gray.

DISTRIBUTION.—*General:* Breeds on shores of Arctic Ocean and migrates south along coast to winter in southern hemisphere. *In Oregon:* Along coast in spring and fall migrations, known from three specimens only.

THE POMARINE JAEGER, the largest of the jaegers, may undoubtedly be looked for along the Oregon coast in both spring and fall migrations. It is most likely to occur in April, May, August, and September, although stragglers may possibly be found at any time. It seems to keep well offshore, as do so many of the species that travel this coast. In our numerous bird-collecting trips offshore we have met with it only twice and have taken only three specimens—an immature female (Gabrielson Coll. No. 1822), September 23, 1932, just south of the end of the south jetty at the mouth of the Columbia, and an adult female (Gabrielson Coll. No. 2567) and an immature bird (Jewett Coll.), both September 8, 1933, off Depoe Bay. We saw perhaps a dozen birds on those days, some of them adults with the characteristic twisted tail feathers and odd plumage very well marked. Five of them flew across our stem just out of gunshot. Their flight, in contrast with that of the gulls, consisted of rather steady, deliberate, and powerful wing beats. As the birds were not feeding and were not molesting the swarming gulls and shearwaters, as is their custom, we were not fortunate enough to see the wonderful aerial acrobatics in which they indulge at such times.

The jaegers are the hawks of the sea. On their breeding grounds they feed on the eggs and young of other birds and harry the gulls and terns until they drop any food they may have obtained and then dive after the morsel themselves, usually seizing it before it strikes the water.

Parasitic Jaeger:
Stercorarius parasiticus (Linnaeus)

DESCRIPTION.—"*Adults. Light phase:* upper parts slaty, becoming blackish on crown, wings, and tail; throat and under parts white; sides of head and neck white or grayish, tinged with yellow. *Dark phase:* entire plumage slaty or sooty, darkest on crown, wings, and tail. *Young:* head and neck streaked, and under parts spotted and barred with buff and dusky." (Bailey) *Downy young:* "Sooty brown above, paler below; but the downy young of dark parents are deepest in hue." (Saunders, 1896.) *Size:* "Length 15.50–21.00, wing 12.67, tail 7–9, bill 1.27." (Bailey) *Nest:* An unlined depression in the ground. *Eggs:* 2, dull olive, varying to green, gray, or brown ground color, with spots, blotches, and lines of a sepia, drab, dark chocolate, or umber vinaceous.

DISTRIBUTION.—*General:* Breeds in Arctic and Subarctic regions of both hemispheres. Winters from southern coast of United States southward, also along southern shores in Old World. Passes in migration along United States coasts in spring and fall. *In Oregon:* Spring and fall migrant along coast. One definite record only.

THE PARASITIC JAEGER undoubtedly is a regular migrant along the Oregon coast, both spring and fall, although a skin (Jewett Coll. No. 3470) taken by Dr. Flynn near Scappoose, just below Portland on the Columbia

River, in September 1909, is the only definite specimen recorded for the State. This bird was badly decomposed when found and it was impossible to tell the sex. We saw one or two birds off Newport, August 30, 1930. In comparison with the larger Pomarine Jaeger, the Parasitic Jaeger is a rapid and graceful flier and more falconlike in appearance. We have not met with it frequently in our offshore trips, but it should be looked for, particularly during April, May, August, and September.

This jaeger is included by Woodcock (1902), on A. W. Anthony's statement concerning Parasitic and Long-tailed Jaegers: "I have seen both species off the Oregon coast in winter." As there are no recent records of the Long-tailed Jaeger and we are unable to find any actual specimens from Oregon, we are placing that species in the hypothetical list until such time as we are able to gather more definite information regarding its status.

Gulls and Terns: *Family Laridae*

Glaucous Gull: *Larus hyperboreus* Gunnerus

DESCRIPTION.—Primaries white or light gray, shading into white at ends. *Adults in summer:* Mantle, *i.e.* back and top of wings, light pearl gray; rest of plumage white. *Adults in winter:* head and neck streaked with grayish. *Young:* whitish, tinged below and mottled above with brownish gray." (Bailey) *Downy young:* "The young chick is covered with long, soft, thick down, grayish white above and almost pure white below, tinged with buff on the throat and breast. The back is clouded or blotched with 'smoke gray,' and the head and throat are distinctly marked with numerous large and small spots of 'fuscous black,' the number and extent of the markings varying in different individuals." (Bent) *Size:* "Length 26–32, wing 16.75–18.75, bill 2.30–2.70." (Bailey) *Nest:* Usually a depression, lined with soft grass and moss. *Eggs:* 2 or 3, ground color brown or buff, irregularly spotted and blotched with darker brown or drab.

DISTRIBUTION.—*General:* Breeds on Arctic Coasts of both hemispheres south in this continent to Kuskokwim River and Newfoundland. Winters south to Monterey Bay, California, and Long Island. *In Oregon:* Rare winter visitor to coast and Columbia River.

ON THE BASIS of present records, the Glaucous Gull, or burgomaster, must be listed as an unusual visitor to Oregon. There are three known specimens—one (University of Oregon Coll. No. 1277) taken April 28, 1915, by Shelton, a second (Jewett Coll. No. 3515) taken on Sauvies Island, December 12, 1914 (Jewett and Gabrielson 1929), and the third taken by Gabrielson at Tillamook Bay, January 28, 1933. In addition, the authors have occasionally seen large pale gulls on the Willamette River in Portland harbor that were probablv this species. One individual noted several times in January 1922 was almost certainly a Glaucous Gull. We have seen several similar birds on Tillamook Bay in addition to Gabrielson's specimen.

This, the largest gull that visits Oregon, is distinguishable from all others by its pale pearl-gray mantle and wings, the latter fading to pure white at the tips. The remainder of the body is pure white, with some dusky mottling and clouding in immature birds. There are no traces of the dusky coloring and white mirrors that are found on the wing tips of the other gulls. It can be confused only with the Glaucous-winged Gull, its smaller and more abundant relative but can be distinguished from it by the differences of the wing pattern.

Glaucous-winged Gull:
Larus glaucescens Naumann

Description.—"*Adults in summer:* Mantle light pearl gray; primaries gray, with distinct white tips; rest of plumage white. *Adults in winter:* head and neck clouded with sooty gray. *Young:* deep ashy gray; head and neck streaked, and rest of upper parts mottled with grayish white or dull buff." (Bailey) *Downy young:* "The downy young is 'drab gray' above, variegated with 'avellaneous,' and a paler shade of the same color below, fading to 'tilleul buff' on the center of the breast. It is heavily spotted on the back with 'fuscous black' and on the head and throat with pure black." (Bent) *Size:* "Length 23.70–27.75, wing 16.25–17.30, bill 2.20–2.60, depth of bill at angle .80–.90." (Bailey) *Nest:* Well made of grass, seaweed, or kelp, placed either on ledges on a steep cliff or on grassy or sandy flats of small islands. *Eggs:* 2 or 3, much like those of similar gulls, ground color buff to pale olive, more or less spotted or blotched with darker browns.

Distribution.—*General:* Breeds on coast and adjacent islands of north Pacific as far south as Destruction Island, Washington. Winters on Pacific Coast as far south as Lower California. *In Oregon:* Abundant winter resident of coast, probably most common wintering gull. Recorded from Clatsop, Tillamook, Lincoln, Douglas, Lane, Coos, and Curry Counties on coast and regularly from Columbia, Multnomah, and Clackamas Counties inland. Straggles inland at least as far as Morrow County.

The Glaucous-winged Gull, the largest of the common gulls on the Oregon coast, first listed by Newberry (1857), may be distinguished from all others by the silvery-gray lining of its wings and the distinct white tips of the primary feathers. In other words, it entirely lacks the black wing tips that are found in all other gulls common in Oregon. It has been observed in every month except July, although it is not known to breed south of Destruction Island, Washington. It is common from mid-August to late May, being found throughout the latter part of May and June in diminishing numbers. Those that spend most of the summer with us are probably nonbreeding individuals. As soon as the young are able to fly, however, immature birds commence to appear on our coast. This usually happens in early August, and by September 1 this species is common. The great wintering flocks of gulls that frequent every harbor and the mouth of every fresh-water stream in winter are composed of several species, but the Glaucous-winged Gull is probably the most abundant of them all. It has been found in every coast county of the State, not only along the shore but following the streams inland to feed on dead salmon that spawn in the fall and winter months. It follows the Columbia and is the most common wintering gull at Portland and up the Columbia, at least as far as Vancouver, and to the Falls of the Willamette on that stream. It occasionally goes farther inland. It has been observed in midwinter as far up the Columbia as Heppner Junction in Morrow County and can be looked for up the Willamette occasionally and probably up the Rogue farther than we have observed it.

One of the interesting things on the Oregon coast during the winter is the great congregation of gulls that takes place in rough weather. Apparently during fair weather the gulls scatter widely along the coast and out to sea, taking refuge in the more sheltered bays and inlets at the beginning of a severe storm. In December 1930 the writers were together at Gold Beach, Oregon, just as a rather severe southwester broke. Before the storm there had not been an unusual number of gulls in the river mouth. As the storm broke, gulls commenced to arrive in straggling groups from all directions, alighting on a sand spit at the river mouth, until there were acres of birds congregated. In this great conglomeration, Glaucous-winged Gulls were the most abundant species and remained so during two days that we stayed in the territory. December 7, 1931, there was a similar congregation of gulls on the Columbia River bottoms at Portland, and again the Glaucous-winged Gulls were the most abundant species. This great congregation persisted for three days and then broke up until only the usual number of birds were present.

Like all gulls, these are masters of the air, and the sight of them on the wing is one of the real attractions on the Oregon coast. Even in the heaviest storms, when nearly all other birds are glad to find sheltered places, the gulls may be seen over the breakers fighting their way into the teeth of the gale with powerful wing beats and cleverly taking advantage of the breakers themselves to make progress against the wind. We have often seen them indulging in this pastime apparently for the pure joy of fighting the storm. They will fight their way against the wind for some distance, whirl upward, and drift with the storm for long distances before again taking up their flight. We have also watched them apparently feeding on small schools of surface-feeding fish off the breakwaters during the stormiest periods that come on the Oregon coast.

Few of the larger salt-water gulls are of any particular economic significance, although as they come into the fields for rest during the stormy periods they may do some good by catching mice. They certainly do no damage, as the fish they obtain are small surface-feeding anchovies and other small species that abound on the Oregon coast. Primarily gulls are scavengers. They clean up quickly any dead birds and fish brought in along the beaches and follow the migrating salmon into the streams, sometimes in countless thousands, quickly consuming the fish that perish after spawning. They also follow the great smelt runs into the Columbia River, and the progress of the runs can be marked by the horde of gulls circling and screaming over the myriads of fish. One of two stomachs taken at Netarts, December 13, 1920, contained 47 *Lepas anatifera;* the other, 18. One taken at Portland, December 12, 1914, contained scales and bones from a large fish that was evidently refuse matter. The Glaucous-winged Gull is conspicuous in the great numbers of birds that congregate around salmon canneries, where they quickly clean up the refuse. In all, these gulls do no harm while in the State and add much of interest to the winter bird life of the beaches.

Western Gull:
Larus occidentalis occidentalis Audubon

Description.—"*Adults in summer:* Mantle dark slaty gray; primaries, including inner webs of first, second, and usually third, black, tipped with white; rest of plumage white. *Adults in winter:* top of head and back of neck streaked with dusky. *Young:* upper parts brownish slaty, varied with buff and whitish; quills and tail dull black, usually tipped with white; under parts brownish gray, specked or spotted with whitish." (Bailey) (See Plate 45, *A.*) *Downy young:* "The downy young is 'drab gray' above varied with 'avellaneous' or other shades of buff. Some individuals are grayer and others are brighter buff in color. The lower parts are lighter colored, paling to 'tilleul buff' on the center of the breast; sometimes the breast is bright clear 'avellaneous' buff in newly hatched young, the colors fading as the youngster grows. The back is heavily spotted with 'fuscous black' and the head and throat with pure black." (Bent) *Size:* "Length 24–27, wing 15.75–17.00, bill 2.00–2.35, depth of bill at angle .85–.95." (Bailey) *Nest:* Of seaweed, grass, and similar material, usually placed in a slight depression on rocky ledges or on more level ground on small offshore islands. *Eggs:* 2 or 3, much like those of other gulls, buff to olive ground color, heavily splotched and marked with various shades of brown (Plate 45, *B*).

Distribution.—*General:* Breeds on Pacific Coast from Washington south to Lower California. Winters over same territory, spreading north to British Columbia and south to Mexican coast. *In Oregon:* Remains year round. Breeds along entire coast wherever it can find suitable conditions. In winter, wanders inland to at least Portland, The Dalles, and Corvallis.

The Western Gull (Plate 46), the largest and darkest-backed of any of the black-primaried gulls, is the only one that breeds on the Oregon coast. It remains the year around and travels from the coast up the rivers to at least as far as Portland, Oregon City, occasionally Corvallis (Woodcock 1902), and The Dalles, but it is not as abundant inland as some of the other species. In fact we consider it one of the less common gulls on the Columbia and Willamette Rivers near Portland, where it is usually outnumbered in the Portland Harbor by the Glaucous-winged,

Plate 45, *A*. Young Western Gull. (Photo by Reed Ferris.)

Plate 45, *B*. Nest and eggs of Western Gull. (Photo by Alex Walker.)

Short-billed, and California Gulls. It seems to be confined more to the seacoast than the Glaucous-winged and is one of the abundant species in the great wintering flocks there. It can be distinguished from other gulls in adult plumage by its large size, dark slaty-blue back, and black-tipped wings, the ends of which are decorated with small white oval mirrors.

So far as we know, there are no valid records for this species east of the Cascade Mountains. Bendire's notes (Brewer 1875 and Bendire 1877), made at Old Fort Harney, contain references to the Western Gull; but he collected no specimens, and he himself questioned whether or not the birds were of this species. Since there are no specimen records for the Western Gull in that territory and the California Gull is exceedingly abundant there, we believe that Bendire's records cannot be accepted. The status of the Western Gull then, as we know it at present, is that of an abundant coastal resident that straggles inland up the streams to a less extent than do some of the other coast-loving species.

During the summer it is the all-abundant resident gull on the coast, where its beautiful white plumage and dark slaty-gray mantle form an attractive feature of the beaches and rocky points. It nests on nearly every suitable rock from Curry to Clatsop County. The largest and best-known colony is the one on Three Arch Rocks Reservation. Other colonies known to us are on Otter Rock, the rocks at the mouth of Pistol River, and the rocks off Bandon. In addition, there are many smaller colonies in suitable spots. The nests are rather bulky affairs of seaweeds, grasses, and other material, usually built in a somewhat slight depression in the rocks (Plate 45, *B*). There these gulls lay their two or three eggs and raise their fuzzy, buffy youngsters. The nests are usually fairly well constructed for gulls' nests, but become filthy before the nesting season is over. When the young are able to fly, they too forage up and down the beach and in their first plumage are the darkest-colored gulls in Oregon (Plate 45, *A*).

A great deal of propaganda is directed against gulls by certain sportsmen who feel that these birds destroy immense numbers of game birds and fish. So far as the Western Gull is concerned, there is no ground for such an indictment, as it does not enter any territory where game birds live and such fish as it gets are small surface-feeding ones of little use to man. It is essentially a scavenger of the beaches, quickly pouncing upon and eating any dead fish or other marine life that may be washed ashore and working up the streams to feast on the spawned-out salmon. One of the most interesting and intelligent performances of this bird is its habit of taking small clams high in the air and dropping them onto a rocky beach or other hard surface to break them open. It drops a clam, then quickly follows it down, reaching the ground almost as soon as the missile. We have watched this performance many times while waiting for the ferry on the South Ferry Slip at Newport, where from one or two to a dozen Western Gulls may be observed carrying on this type of aerial bombardment, which is one of the most amusing spectacles on the Oregon coast. Many of the clams miss the slip entirely and land in the mud below. The birds seldom try to reclaim these wild shots. Some of the gulls become quite skillful in gauging their speed and height and hit the narrow roadway with a high degree of regularity and accuracy. We have observed this species at various times dropping clams on rocky or stony beaches also, particularly Netarts Bay in Tillamook County.

About summer resorts and salmon canneries, where they become accustomed to feeding from garbage dumps and cannery refuse, the Western Gulls become exceedingly tame during the summer as they forage about. They may then be observed at very close range and their plumage studied in detail. During salmon-canning season, every cannery is decorated with a line of gulls along the roof ridge and usually every available piling, as well as every perch, is taken by these white-robed scavengers. When material is dumped, it immediately becomes the center of a screaming, fighting horde of gulls, each struggling to obtain more than its share of the food, completely destroying any opinion of daintiness or refinement that might have been derived from its angelic livery.

Few actual stomach examinations of Western Gulls taken in Oregon have been made. One taken on December 6, 1913, was full of remains of clam shells and fish bones, another taken on December 27 of the same year was full of unidentified fish roe, and a third, taken on December 28, 1920, contained one earthworm and pieces of mollusk shell. The earthworm item might indicate that the gulls have a habit of picking up earthworms when, during heavy storms at sea, they are driven for shelter to pasture lands, congregating in great white fleets to rest between buffetings by the storms.

Herring Gull:

Larus argentatus smithsonianus Coues

Description.—"*Adults in summer:* Mantle delicate pearl gray; five outer primaries black toward ends, and tipped with white; a distinct gray wedge on inner web of second quill; rest of plumage white; bill, yellow, with red spot near end of lower mandible; feet pale flesh color. *Adults in winter:* head and neck streaked with grayish. *Young:* brownish gray; head and neck streaked with white; back mottled with buffy and gray; quills and tail blackish; bill dusky, feet purplish." (Bailey) *Downy young:* "The downy young are of a buffy yellow color, nearly white below and dusky on the back. They are thickly marked with black spots above. The bill is horn color, with a pink tip, after the white pipping knob has disappeared; the feet, dusky pink." (Bent) *Size:* "Length 22.50–26.00, wing 17.24, bill 2.24, depth of bill through angle of lower mandible .68–.85." (Bailey) *Nest:* Usual gull nest of grass, weeds, and seaweeds, built on the ground or rocks, though sometimes in trees. *Eggs:* 1 to 4, usually 2 or 3, ground color varying from light blues and grays to dark browns, more or less irregularly marked or blotched with darker browns or chocolate.

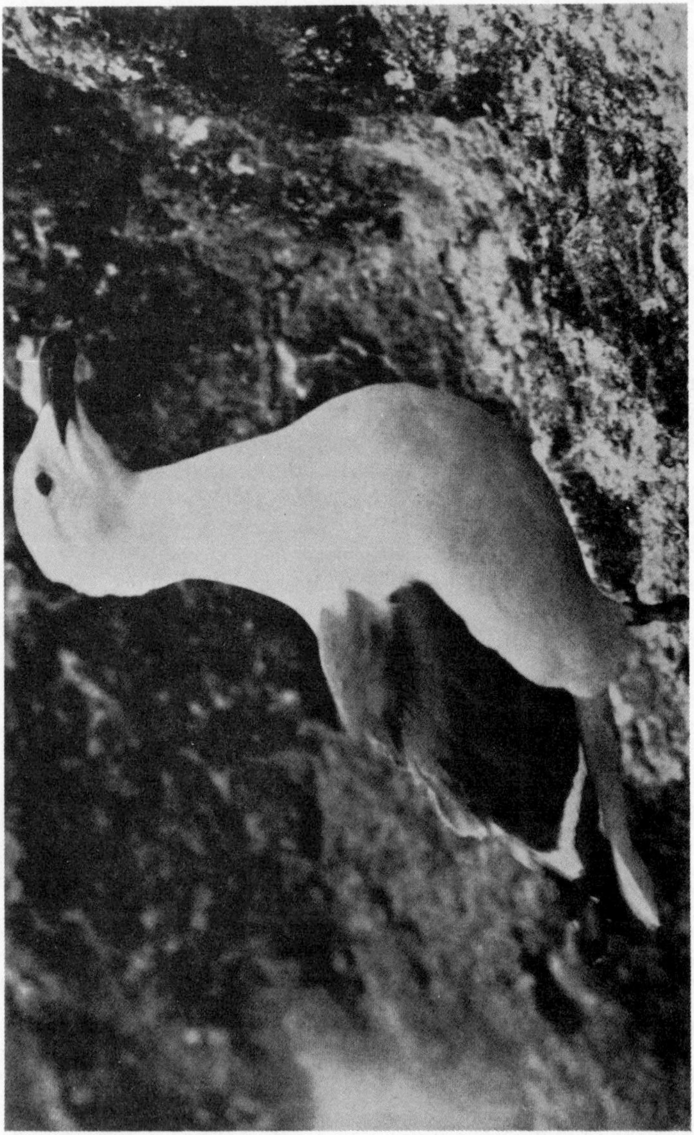

Plate 46. Western Gull. (Photo by Wm. L. Finley and H. T. Bohlman.)

Distribution.—*General:* Almost world-wide in northern hemisphere. In North America, breeds south to Maine, Great Lakes, and central British Columbia and winters irregularly south to West Indies and to Mexico on west coast. *In Oregon:* Uncertain status. In light of our present knowledge, can only be considered an uncommon winter visitor represented by five specimens and a number of unsatisfactory sight records.

Many observers have reported the Herring Gull on the Oregon coast, some of them as a common species. Townsend (1839) was the first to record it, but so far as we can learn left no specimens to confirm the statement. A. W. Anthony, according to Woodcock (1902), reported it as equally abundant with the Glaucous-winged Gull on the Oregon coast, a statement that certainly is not applicable to present-day conditions. Jewett reported it in 1921 as found on Netarts Bay but had only one specimen. Whatever its status in the past, we are not able to find it as a common visitor to the Oregon coast today, although it is reported commonly from Washington and as a regular winter resident of the California coast.

We have collected a great many gulls in an endeavor to determine the correct status of the Herring Gull, and so far as we know the following are the only specimens of this species: T. R. Peale collected one, labeled Oregon, that is now in the United States National Museum (No. 12587); Jewett has an adult male that was picked up dead on the beach near Seal Rocks, Lincoln County, on December 15, 1930, while we were on a trip up the Oregon coast; Gabrielson collected two adult males on the Columbia River (Coll. Nos. 2194 and 2195) on January 25, 1933, and saw a number of others; and John Carter has a female (No. 61) collected on the same trip. These specimens confirm the sight records of Rufus Comstock, of Vancouver, who reports a few individuals regularly about the Vancouver water front. At other times we have seen large pale gulls that we took to be this species but have not been able to collect them, and even these have not been at all common on the Oregon coast. The species may be more common than our records indicate, however, as it could easily be overlooked in the great hordes of gulls found during the winter months at the mouth of every fresh-water stream that enters the ocean.

Thayer's Gull:
Larus argentatus thayeri Brooks

Description.—Like the Herring Gull but paler and with less black in the wing tips. The bill shows a tendency to be more slender than the average of *smithsonianus*. *Size: Male*, wing 16.18–16.93, tail 6.42–6.89, tarsus 2.44–2.68, toe without claw 2.01–2.20, culmen 1.93–2.44, depth at base of bill 0.65–0.79; *female*, wing 14.96–15.95, tail 5.71–6.50, tarsus 2.28–2.56, toe without claw 1.85–2.13, culmen 1.69–2.20, depth at base of bill 0.55–0.75 (Dwight, 1925). *Nest and eggs:* Same as for Herring Gull.

DISTRIBUTION.—*General:* Arctic Coast and islands west of Greenland, to Point Barrow in migration, south in winter to coast of British Columbia and California. *In Oregon:* Uncommon winter visitor known with certainty from a few specimens.

ON DECEMBER 22, 1932, Gabrielson collected an adult female (Gabrielson Coll. No. 2098) on the Columbia River near Portland that proved to be a Thayer's Gull. An immature bird (Gabrielson Coll. No. 2196), taken January 25, 1933, near the same spot, was very puzzling. It matched closely a single bird in Jewett's collection, taken at Netarts, August 20, 1925, but we could not find similar birds in any of the collections available to us—including those of the Biological Survey and the United States National Museum. By process of elimination the birds were finally placed as *L. a. thayeri.* Later they were sent to George Willett for comparison with the fine series of northern gulls in the Bishop collection. He confirmed the identification, and today these are the only definite records for this form from the State. Thayer's Gull cannot be distinguished in life from the Herring Gull, and careful comparison with the skins in hand is required to establish its identity. In habits and behavior it is like the other species that make up the swarming hordes of gulls found on the Oregon coast and the Columbia River during winter.

California Gull:
Larus californicus Lawrence

DESCRIPTION.—"*Adults:* Mantle clear bluish gray; outer primaries black, tipped with white, the first two with subterminal white spots; a distinct gray wedge on inner web of second; bill yellow, with red and black spot near end of lower mandible; feet greenish. *Young:* upper parts coarsely spotted and mottled with dusky, buffy, grayish, and whitish; under parts mottled and streaked; quills and tail blackish; bill dusky, with black tip." (Bailey) *Downy young:* "The young bird when first hatched, is covered with thick, soft down of plain, light colors to match its surroundings, 'light buff' to 'cartridge buff,' brightest on the head and breast; the upper parts and throat are clouded or variegated with light grayish, and the head is sparingly spotted with dull black." (Bent) *Size:* "Length 20–23, wing 15.00–16.75, bill 1.65–2.15, depth of bill at angle .60–.75." (Bailey) *Nest:* Of usual gull type, usually on ground, composed of weeds, grass, bits of sticks, feathers, and other similar available material. *Eggs:* 2 or 3, similar to other gulls' eggs, ground color varying shades of brown or buff, irregularly spotted and blotched with browns and grays.

DISTRIBUTION.—*General:* Breeds from Great Slave Lake, Canada, and Stump and Devils Lake, North Dakota, south to northern Utah and west to central British Columbia and northeastern California. Winters on Pacific Coast from British Columbia to Lower California. *In Oregon:* Breeds in Klamath (Spring and Upper Klamath Lakes), Lake (Summer and, formerly, Silver Lakes), and Harney (Malheur Lake) Counties. Winters largely on coast and sparingly on open water anywhere in State. A few summer birds remain on coast but do not breed.

THE BEAUTIFUL medium-sized California Gull (Plate 47, *A*) was first noted by Newberry (1857), who found it at the mouth of the Columbia in October 1855. It is now one of the most widely distributed and

Plate 47, *A*. California Gulls. (Photo by Ira N. Gabrielson.)

Plate 47, *B*. California Gull colony. (Photo by Ira N. Gabrielson.)

abundant gulls found in Oregon and has been recorded for every month and from every county. Somewhat smaller than the Western and Herring Gulls and larger than the Ring-billed, it is one of the species that make for confusion in the identification of gulls. It can be distinguished from the Western Gull by its much paler back and by its paler under parts in comparable plumages, but it is more or less easily confused with the smaller Ring-billed Gulls, particularly by those who are just beginning the study of birds.

In general, the California Gull, the most abundant breeding gull in Oregon, will be found during the breeding season in the great alkaline lakes and swamps in the eastern part of the State, where it forms huge nesting colonies (Plate 47, *B*). In these great interior nesting colonies, nest construction and egg laying usually start in late April or early May, and young birds commence to hatch in increasing numbers around June 1. There is great variation in the nests built. Some of them are fairly compact structures of dry grass and other vegetation, and in some cases the eggs are laid on almost bare ground. The gulls stay as long as there is open water, and stray individuals remain along the Columbia, Snake, and Klamath Rivers well into the winter, if not through the entire season. There are colonies at Malheur Lake in the Harney Valley, at Summer Lake in the Warner Valley, and usually one or more on Upper Klamath Lake in the Klamath Basin; and recently a colony has been established in Spring Lake, a small pond a few miles out of Klamath Falls. There is a colony just across the line on the Clear Lake Reservation in California.

The colony in Harney Valley has been written about by every observer who has traveled this country since Bendire's time. In some years, it is on Malheur Lake, in others in some of the other swamps in the valley, and frequently during the past few years has been on the Island Ranch north of Malheur Lake. There, in 1926, the season when we made the last careful inspection of the colony, we estimated that on a little sage- and greasewood-grown island there were between 1,500 and 2,000 pairs of California Gulls nesting and a smaller number of Ring-billed Gulls and Caspian Terns. At the time of our visit on June 4, numerous nests contained two or three fresh-looking eggs and there were many young just hatched and quite a number grown to the size of pigeons or larger that were able to walk and swim off in little groups as we approached the island.

The visit to this colony, as to all other great bird rookeries, was an exciting event. From a distance the colony looked like gigantic swarms of bees, circling and darting as the parent gulls traveled to and from their feeding grounds to the colony. As the intruders approached, a constantly growing swarm of gulls hovered overhead until the screaming became almost deafening. The colony, as usual, was filthy and odoriferous. The birds had been feeding the young on grasshoppers, and the surface of the ground was strewn with remains of these insects. After half an hour or so had been spent in the colony, we were glad to get away from the din and smell, although it was an interesting and fascinating place.

After the breeding season, as soon as the young are able to fly, the gulls commence to scatter. In late July or early August, individual California Gulls, Ring-billed Gulls, and sometimes other species appear in the high mountain lakes of Oregon, where they cause great consternation among the hatchery men engaged in releasing trout in these lakes. Such observations and stomach examinations as we have been able to make, however, indicate that the gulls gather there to feed on the abundance of wind-blown insects found on the surface of the lakes at that season and to perform their usual office of scavengers along the shore line. By the first of October, the numbers of California Gulls in eastern Oregon are very greatly depleted, although scattered individuals and small groups may be found through the entire winter where open water is available. In late July these gulls commence to appear in increasing numbers in western Oregon, on the Willamette and Columbia Rivers near Portland, and on the coast, until by October they are one of the abundant gulls found there. Gulls banded in the Klamath colonies have been taken frequently on the Lincoln County coast, showing a definite north and west movement from the breeding grounds.

Like all other gulls, the California Gulls are scavengers, particularly during the winter. We have made no stomach examinations of this species, and the only stomach available, taken June 21 at Portland, contained bones of one catfish. Undoubtedly the species is of economic benefit in the vicinity of its great colonies, where remains of ground squirrels, mice, crayfish, carp, small minnows, grasshoppers, crickets, and other insects indicate its omniverous food habits. A monument to this species was erected in Salt Lake City many years ago in commemoration of its destruction of crickets.

Ring-billed Gull:
Larus delawarensis Ord

Description.—"*Adults:* Mantle light pearl gray; bill greenish yellow, crossed near end by a distinct black band, tip yellow or orange; eyelids vermilion, iris pale yellow; feet pale yellow, sometimes tinged with greenish. *Young:* upper parts dusky, feathers bordered and marked with grayish buff or whitish; under parts white, spotted along sides with grayish brown; quills blackish, the shorter ones gray at base and tipped with white." (Bailey) *Downy young:* "The downy young have at least two distinct color phases, both of which are often found in the same nest. In the gray phase the upper parts are 'smoke gray' or 'pale smoke gray,' in the buffy phase the upper parts are 'pinkish buff' or 'vinaceous buff.' They are lighter below and almost white on the breast; they are distinctly spotted with 'hair brown' or 'sepia' on the head and neck, and more faintly mottled with the same color on the back." (Bent) *Size:* "Length 18–20, wing 13.60–15.75, bill 1.55–

1.75, depth at angle of lower mandible .50–.65." (Bailey) *Nest:* Usually on the ground on small islands, occasionally in the tules, constructed of the usual dried grasses, weeds, and small sticks (Plate 48, *A*). *Eggs:* 2 to 3, ground color various shades of brown or buff, spotted and blotched with browns, grays, and drabs.

Distribution.—*General:* Breeds from southern Canada through North Dakota to Great Salt Lake and west to southern Oregon and southern Alaska. Winters along both coasts of United States and northern Mexico and north to Idaho, Montana, and Great Lakes in winter. *In Oregon:* Breeds in Klamath (Spring Lake), Lake (Warner Lake), and Harney (Malheur Lake) Counties. Winters regularly on coast, Columbia River, at least as far inland as Portland, and occasionally, at least, inland on any open water.

The Ring-billed Gull, a beautiful little bird, in some of its immature phases is one of the most daintily marked of any of the gulls in Oregon. In many respects it is a miniature California Gull, except for the dark band about the bill during the breeding season, which easily distinguishes the adults from their larger relatives. In some of the immature plumages, a subterminal tail band of black is also a distinct mark and enables one with little or no difficulty to pick out particular individuals as Ring-billed Gulls. In other seasons, it might well be confused with both California and Short-billed Gulls on the wing. Gulls seen in eastern Oregon at any season of the year are almost certainly this species or the California Gull.

Since Townsend (1839) first reported it from Oregon, and Bendire (1877) published the first breeding record, the Ring-billed Gull has been mentioned frequently in the papers of field workers in the State. As these birds are great wanderers, they are likely to be found anywhere in the State, particularly on inland waters (Plate 48, *B*). They remain in the interior until the lakes and ponds begin to freeze, and straggling individuals remain about open water, occasionally at least, throughout the winter. The few individuals that once in a while remain on the coast during the breeding season are undoubtedly nonbreeders, as there is nothing in our records to indicate that this species ever breeds anywhere in the State except in the great alkaline marshes in the southeastern part.

Each of the great colonies of California Gulls in Warner Valley, Malheur Lake, and the Klamath Basin contains its quota of Ring-billed Gulls nesting in a separate and distinct area that is usually almost entirely surrounded by nests of the more abundant California Gulls. The Ring-bills are in such decided minority, however, that they are a negligible factor in the noise and bustle of the gull colony. They lay their eggs in late April or early May, and by the first of June hatching is well under way. Following the breeding season they spread from their inland homes to the high Cascade lakes and the coast. In late July or early August, they are usually found in the Cascades and by mid-August, on the coast, where they form a rather minor element in the great wintering gull flocks.

Their food, as reported in various sources, consists of a great variety

Plate 48, *A*. Nest and eggs of Ring-billed Gull. (Photo by Alex Walker.)

Plate 48, *B*. Ring-billed Gulls. (Photo by Alex Walker.)

of insects, small fish, and crayfish, and the species is undoubtedly of value in the destruction of grasshoppers, crickets, and various species of beetles, particularly on its breeding grounds. One stomach from Klamath Falls, taken September 23, 1916, contained fragments of a dragonfly and pieces of a small fish. Another, from Warner Valley, taken May 18, 1920, contained three minnows, a weevil, and a water beetle. A third, from Warner Valley, taken May 20, 1923, contained 27 carabid beetles, a water beetle, a cricket, and a spider. In the winter, in common with the other gulls, the Ring-bill becomes a scavenger on the Oregon coast and inlets and helps to keep the beaches clear of dead fish, birds, and other animal matter.

Short-billed Gull:
Larus canus brachyrhynchus Richardson

Description.—"*Adults in summer:* Mantle light pearl gray; rest of plumage, except quills, white; outer primary mainly black, with a large white spot near end; second primary with a smaller white spot, white tip, and wedge of gray on inner web; third with white tip and a large white space on inner web between gray and black; bill greenish, with yellow tip; feet and legs greenish. *Adults in winter:* head, neck, and chest mottled with dusky. *Young:* upper parts grayish brown, feathers bordered with pale grayish buff; head, neck, and lower parts brownish gray; tail gray at base, brownish gray toward end, and narrowly tipped with white." (Bailey) *Downy young:* The young, when first hatched, is well covered with a warm coat of soft, thick down, 'pale drab-gray' to 'pale smoke-gray' on the upper parts, sides, and throat; 'pale pinkish buff' on the breast and belly; and tinged with the latter color on the sides of the head and neck. The frontal and loral region is clear black. The sides of the head and neck are boldly and clearly spotted with black in a very distinct pattern, the spots coalescing into an indistinct Y on the crown; an irregular W on the occiput; a large distinct crescent on the cervix; and a small crescent on the throat. The remainder of the upper parts are heavily but less distinctly mottled with duller black, becoming grayer posteriorly. The under parts are unspotted." (Bent) *Size:* "Length 16.50–18.00, wing 13.95, bill 1.45, depth of bill at angle .40–.50." (Bailey) *Nest:* Poorly constructed of twigs and grass in small trees or on the ground. *Eggs:* 2 or 3, ground color brown to buff, spotted and blotched with various shades of brown and drab.

Distribution.—*General:* Breeds in northwestern America east to Mackenzie River and south to Alberta and British Columbia. Winters on Pacific Coast from Vancouver Island south. *In Oregon:* Winter resident from August to April, chiefly in coast counties and along Columbia River.

The Short-billed Gull is a regular and sometimes abundant winter visitor to the Oregon coast, where it can easily be confused with the somewhat larger Ring-billed Gull. It has a noticeably smaller and weaker bill than the latter, however, and is appreciably smaller. It appears on the coast in August usually, although we have one record from Newport Bay on July 22. It becomes more common by October and at times during the winter is one of the abundant species present on the seashore, which it frequents from the mouth of the Columbia River to the California line. At times it is exceedingly abundant also on the Columbia as far inland as Portland, where it rests in little fleets on the golf courses and public parks near the Willamette River. The grounds of the Benson Polytechnic School are a favorite resort when the birds are in the harbor, and hundreds of them are present there at times. Occasionally, the species wanders inland in other parts of the State, but so far as we know there are no authentic records of it east of the Cascades. Prill reported taking three specimens near Scio, September 21, 1900, and Gabrielson shot two out of a mixed flock of gulls, on Diamond Lake, September 16, 1927. Except for these, our own records are confined to the coast counties and the Columbia River. The birds remain in abundance well into March and then diminish in numbers rapidly. Our latest date is April 10 (Clatsop County).

These small gulls are beach scavengers in Oregon, as are most of the other wintering gulls, although they feed on insects and small crustaceans to a greater extent than do some of the larger species. The two Diamond Lake birds collected by Gabrielson were crammed with insects picked from the surface of the water. The great bulk of the food of one of them had been ants, more than 500 of which were counted in one full stomach. A strong offshore breeze had blown the insects onto the lake to perish, and in one bay their bodies were so thick as to form almost a solid film on the surface. The gulls, numerous little Eared Grebes, and other waterfowl were gobbling them up eagerly in competition with the little trout that had just been released by State Game Commission employees. As these little trout broke water, it appeared from the shore that they were being eaten by the gulls, and the two gulls were collected to satisfy the game warden and Gabrielson as to what was actually happening. A specimen collected January 24, 1921, at Netarts by Alex Walker contained quite a collection of insects, largely beetles, some of which indicated the presence of carrion in the stomach. As none of the feeding habits of this little gull are inimical to man and as it acts as a scavenger, its protection while in the territory is fully justified.

Bonaparte's Gull:
Larus philadelphia (Ord)

Description.—"*Adults in summer:* Bill and head black; mantle delicate pearl gray; three outer quills chiefly white, outer web of the first, and terminal portion of all, black; tail and under parts white; feet orange red. *Adults in winter:* head white, tinged with gray behind and with a dusky spot on ear coverts; feet pale flesh color. *Young:* top of head, back, and spot on ear coverts dusky; sides of head, neck, and under parts white, including tail coverts and base of tail; band across end of tail blackish, feathers tipped with white." (Bailey) *Downy young:* Little known, but described by Dr. Jonathan Dwight (1901) as "much like that of *Sterna hirundo*, yellowish with dusky mottling above." (Bent) *Size:* "Length 12–14, wing 10.25, bill 1.20." (Bailey) *Nest:* In trees, 4 to 20 feet from ground, built of twigs, lined more or less with grass and mosses. *Eggs:* 2 to 4, ground color brown or dark buff, spotted and blotched with various shades of brown and drab.

Distribution.—*General:* Breeds in timbered regions of northern Canada and Alaska. Winters on both coasts, on Pacific Coast from Gray's Harbor, Washington, southward to Peru. *In Oregon:* Common but erratic migrant on coast and in great alkaline marshes in Lake (Goose, Crump, and Guano Lakes) and Klamath (numerous records) Counties.

Beautiful little Bonaparte's Gull, the smallest and daintiest of the gulls known in Oregon, is one of the most graceful of birds, and nothing more attractive is to be seen along the coast than a huge flight of these little gulls. The slow, leisurely, effortless beat of the bird's wings carries it along at a surprising speed as it travels up and down the coast or through the interior of the State in its migratory flights. In the spring its black head and beautifully tinted rosy breast set it apart from all other species of gulls found in the State. It is likely to be seen in any part of Oregon but is more frequently found on the alkaline lakes of the interior or on the more open bays and estuaries, where it flies aimlessly and leisurely about in a ternlike flight, picking up insects or small marine forms of life from the surface of the water.

Newberry (1857) first recorded this tiny gull from Oregon, and Bendire (Brewer 1875) found it abundant at Harney Lake. Since then it has been reported frequently. It is more regular as a fall migrant on the coast from August to December (August 20 to December 28, both Tillamook County) but appears also from April to May (April 5 to May 2, both Tillamook County). In the interior of the State it migrates north in the spring from April to May (March 31 to May 15, both Klamath County), with occasional stragglers remaining into June (June 13, Klamath County, Jewett and Gabrielson). In the fall, it appears in July (July 24, Deschutes County) and is present until November (November 22, Klamath County, latest date).

The few gulls whose stomachs have been examined fed almost entirely on crustaceans and isopods while in the State. In fact, four stomachs collected by R. C. Steele on Tillamook Bay, May 1, contained practically nothing but the small isopod *Exosphaeroma oregonensis* that resembles the common sowbug. One stomach contained 42, one 248, one 141, and one 18 of these creatures. A stomach collected in November 1920 at Netarts Bay contained bits of fish and an aquatic beetle. Certainly the feeding habits of Bonaparte's Gulls in this territory cannot cause any possible harm from an economic standpoint, and there is no excuse whatever for any persecution of these little gulls like that sometimes carried out by sportsmen and fishermen against the larger species.

Heermann's Gull:
Larus heermanni Cassin

Description.—"*Adults:* Bill bright red with black tip; feet and ring around eye red; head and upper neck white; back sooty gray, secondaries tipped with white; primaries and tail black, tail tipped with white; under parts dark gray. *Young:* bill brownish; body sooty gray, feathers of upper parts bordered with whitish or pale buff; or, entire plumage sooty gray except blackish tail and quills." (Bailey) *Downy young:* "The downy young is covered with short, thick down, which on the head, throat, breast and flanks is 'pinkish buff' or 'pale pinkish buff,' becoming paler toward the belly, which is pure white. The back is grayish white, mottled with dusky, and there are a few dusky spots on the top of the head." (Bent) *Size:* "Length 17.50–21.00, wing 13.50, bill 1.50." (Bailey) *Nest:* In some colonies, a depression in the ground, with little or no lining; in others, well-built structures of weeds, sticks, and grass. *Eggs:* Pearl gray to blue gray, spotted and blotched with lavender and brown.

Distribution.—*General:* Breeds along Mexican Pacific Coast and wanders north as far as British Columbia after breeding season. *In Oregon:* On coast from about July to late December in small numbers. Very rare in recent years.

Heermann's Gull, a beautiful slate-colored bird with a white head, has become rather rare on the Oregon coast in the past 10 years. Prior to that time there is evidence that it was much more common. Bretherton indicated to Woodcock (1902) that it was a very abundant summer bird on Yaquina Bay, outnumbering other species in the late summer and early fall. He suspected that it nested there but did not find any positive evidence of its breeding. We know it to be a breeding bird of the Mexican and Lower California coasts that wanders north after the breeding season, and there is no evidence that it has ever bred in Oregon. It usually appears on the coast in July (June 22, Curry County, earliest date) and remains through the summer and fall. The latest fall record is December 28, when Alex Walker took a specimen at Netarts Bay.

In recent years we have the following specimens, all adult birds: One in the Jewett collection (No. 3707) taken by Gabrielson on Netarts Bay, August 24, 1921, and two in the Gabrielson collection (Nos. 606 and 658) taken August 21 and November 20, 1921. Alex Walker reported two specimens taken December 28, 1913, and one taken November 8, 1921, all in Tillamook County, and one taken December 28, 1930, while collecting for the Cleveland Museum that is now in the collection of that museum. Neither of us has taken any specimens in Oregon since that date. Our last record of this species on the Oregon coast was a sight record, June 22, 1929. Our observations bear out reports from its nesting grounds and from California observers that this beautiful gull is rapidly decreasing in numbers on the coast. It is so distinctly marked that it is readily picked out from other species present, and we do not believe we could have overlooked the presence of many individuals during our visits to the coast.

The only stomach examined was one taken December 28, 1930, by Alex

Walker that contained a variety of small beetles and a few other insects. Undoubtedly many of the insects eaten by these and other gulls in the winter are picked up along the streams and bay shores, although some of them may well be taken from the cultivated fields, as the gulls habitually forage over such areas during heavy storms.

Pacific Kittiwake:
Rissa tridactyla pollicaris Ridgway

Description.—"Appearance gull-like; hind toe minute, with or without a nail; feet and legs black; tarsus shorter than middle toe with claw; bill yellow, with greatest depth at base; tail slightly emarginate, or forked. *Adults:* back and wings light bluish gray, five outer primaries tipped with black; rest of plumage pure white. *Young:* like adults, but with black or slaty on back of neck and across ear coverts." (Bailey) *Downy young:* "The newly hatched young is covered with long, soft, glossy down, which is white and spotless, but tinged basally with yellowish gray and buffy on the back and thighs, and tipped with dusky, giving it a grizzly appearance, quite unlike other young gulls." (Bent) *Size:* "Length 16.00–17.70, wing 12.25, bill 1.40–1.50." (Bailey) *Nest:* Usually placed on tiny shelves or projections on vertical cliffs, composed of grass and mud cemented with mud. *Eggs:* Usually 2, gray or buff, spotted with drab or gray.

Distribution.—*General:* Breeds on coast and islands of North Pacific, Bering Sea, and adjacent Arctic Ocean. Winters south along Pacific Coast casually at least to northern Lower California. *In Oregon:* Irregular winter visitor along coast.

The Pacific Kittiwake is an irregular winter visitor to the Oregon coast. When in the hand, it can be identified readily by the rudimentary or missing hind toe. In the air, its long, pointed wings would be most likely to attract attention. In the adult plumage, the solid-black tips of the primaries, unbroken by white spots or "mirrors," distinguish it from other wintering gulls, and immature birds display a black cape on the back of the neck that, among other species present on the Oregon coast, is found only in the much smaller Bonaparte's Gull. Observers fortunate enough to be on the coast during the winter should keep a sharp watch for this beautiful little gull.

Prill (1891b) recorded a Pacific Kittiwake from Sweet Home, Linn County, on December 16, 1890. This bird, now in the University of Oregon, proved on examination to be a Ring-billed Gull. Woodcock (1902) recorded this same bird and also stated that the species was found at Yaquina. Jewett (1914b) recorded the first actual specimen—a bird picked up dead on the beach at Netarts Bay on March 13, 1913, by Murie. Alex Walker took the second specimen, also at Netarts, on December 25, 1920. Since that time, Braly, Jewett, and Gabrielson have found numerous dead specimens on the beaches of Lincoln, Tillamook, and Clatsop Counties, and Jewett caught a live bird in his hand at Bayocean. These specimens were taken between December 27 and March 13, in 1932–33 and 1934–35, when the birds were more frequent than usual.

Red-legged Kittiwake:
Rissa brevirostris (Bruch)

Description.—"Legs and feet bright red (becoming yellowish in dried skins). *Summer adult:* Pure white, the mantle dark bluish gray, or plumbeous; fine innermost quills plumbeous, the inner webs broadly edged with white, the outer tipped with the same; five outermost quills black toward ends, the third, fourth, and fifth tipped with plumbeous. *Winter adult:* Similar but hind-neck and auriculars washed with plumbeous. *Young:* Similar to winter adult, but hind-neck crossed by blackish band, ear-coverts crossed by a smaller black band, and a suffusion of same in front of eye." (Ridgway, 1887.) *Size:* Length 14.00–15.80, wing 13.00, culmen 1.20, tarsus 1.25. *Eggs:* 2 to 5, olive white, grayish white, or buffy, blotched and spotted with brown and lavender gray.

Distribution.—*General:* Coast and islands of Bering Sea. *In Oregon:* Rare straggler, known from one record only.

The only Oregon record of the Red-legged Kittiwake is of a fresh adult female specimen picked up on the beach at Delake, Lincoln County (January 28, 1933), by C. A. Leichhardt and Gabrielson. The bird had been torn open by gulls but was in otherwise perfect condition and is now in Gabrielson's collection. This is a species that remains far to the northward but that—like the other northerners that made up the phenomenal flight of the winter of 1932–33—is capable of moving far to the south on occasion.

Sabine's Gull:
Xema sabini (Sabine)

Description.—"Bill gull-like, tail conspicuously forked, the feathers rounded, not narrow and pointed at ends. *Adults in summer:* head and upper neck dark plumbeous, bordered below by a black collar; mantle slaty gray; tail and middle of wing white; outer quills black, with inner webs and tips white; under parts white; bill black, tipped with yellow. *Adults in winter:* head and neck white, with dusky on ear coverts and back of head. *Young:* like winter adults, but mantle brownish, feathers with buffy or grayish edges; tail with a subterminal black band, white tip and base; bill black." (Bailey) *Downy young:* "The downy young is dark colored, from 'ochraceous tawny' to 'tawny olive' on the upper parts and throat, paler on the chin, fading off to 'pale pinkish buff' or paler on the belly. The crown and sides of the head are distinctly spotted or streaked with black and the rest of the upper parts are thickly but indistinctly mottled with 'fuscous black,' the under parts are immaculate." (Bent) *Size:* "Length 13–14, wing 10.10–11.15, bill 1.00, tail 4.50–5.00, fork .60–1.00 deep." (Bailey) *Nest:* A few blades of grass and stems, arranged about the eggs or in a slight hollow in the ground. *Eggs:* 2 or 3, brown or olive buff, faintly and irregularly spotted blotches with shades of brown.

Distribution.—*General:* Breeds on Arctic Coasts of both hemispheres. Winters, so far as known, on coast of Peru. *In Oregon:* Migrates north along coast in May (one record) and south in fall from August to September.

The beautiful black-headed, fork-tailed Sabine's Gulls (Plate 49, *A*) are undoubtedly more common on the Oregon coast than our records indicate. They migrate north along the coast in May and south in the fall from August (August 30, Lincoln County) to September (September 27, Tillamook County). As do many migratory water birds, they seem to travel well offshore, and unless one goes out to them, only casual stragglers are seen from the shore. In 1920, from September 19 to 27, there was a considerable flight of these birds on the Tillamook County coast, centered largely at Netarts Bay, during which period both Alex Walker and Jewett collected numbers of specimens. Shaw (1924) recorded one taken at Yaquina Bay, September 4, 1904; and Jewett (1921b), one taken at Netarts, May 1, 1916. These are the only shore records we have.

On August 30, 1929, the authors and Braly made a trip offshore from Newport, Lincoln County, and were on the ocean from 8 a.m. until 5 p.m., most of the time from 6 to 9 miles out. All day long there was a constant flight of Sabine's Gulls headed southward, either single individuals or small companies. Many hundreds passed us during the day, but no particular effort was made to count individuals. Anyone who has ever seen this exceedingly graceful little gull with the distinctive white marks on the edges of its wings will not confuse it with any other species, and we enjoyed to the utmost our experience in watching them by the hundreds. It is evident that we struck the major southward flight of this beautiful bird, as we have been offshore a number of times since and have never been fortunate enough to repeat the experience.

The food of two birds collected by Alex Walker in Tillamook County in 1920, one at Sand Lake and the other at Netarts, consisted entirely of insects—weevils, carabid beetles, ants, and a few miscellaneous ones. These gulls are so rare in Oregon that their choice of food while in the State cannot possibly be of any economic consideration.

Forster's Tern:
Sterna forsteri Nuttall

Description.—Outer web of outer tail feathers white, inner web dusky; tail very narrow and long. "*Adults in summer:* under parts white; upper parts light pearl gray, top of head black; outer web of outer tail feather white; feet orange red, bill dull orange, dusky at tip. *Adults in winter:* top of head white, back of head tinged with gray, a dusky stripe around eye and across ear coverts; bill and feet duller colored. *Young:* upper parts, crown, and sides of head washed with brownish; tail feathers dusky toward ends." (Adapted from Bailey.) *Downy young:* "The downy young is quite different from that of the common tern. The upper parts vary from light 'clay color,' through 'cinnamon buff' to 'pinkish buff,' shading off to paler shades of the same color below, paling on the breast and belly almost to white, and darkest on the throat, which is 'wood brown' or 'drab' in some specimens, but never so dark as in the common tern. The upper parts are heavily spotted or streaked with black or 'blackish brown,' less heavily on the head and more heavily

Plate 49, *A*. Sabine's Gull. (Photo by Wm. L. and Irene Finley.)

Plate 49, *B*. Forster's Tern on nest. (Photo by Wm. L. Finley and H. T. Bohlman.)

on the back, where these markings are confluent into great blotches or longitudinal bands." (Bent) *Size:* "Length 14–15, wing 9.50–10.30, bill 1.50–1.65, tail 5.00–7.70, forked for 2.30–5.00." (Bailey) *Nest:* In Oregon and other western States, a floating mass of decaying cattails or tules, the eggs being deposited in a neat depression above the water (Plate 49, *B*). *Eggs:* 2 to 6, usually 3 or 4. Ground color olive to buff, marked and spotted with dark browns.

DISTRIBUTION.—*General:* Breeds throughout temperate North America, from Alberta and Manitoba south to Gulf coast and west to central Oregon and California. Winters from southern California and Gulf coast southward. *In Oregon:* Breeds in Klamath (Klamath Lake), Lake (Warner and Summer Lakes), and Harney (Malheur Lake) Counties in great shallow alkaline lakes and marshes. Arrives in April and remains until October.

FORSTER'S TERN is the most common Oregon representative of the medium-sized terns of swallowlike flight, black cap, and forked tail. It unquestionably ranks with the most beautiful and graceful of all birds in flight, during which it displays not only beauty of action but beauty of form and color as well. The soft pearl gray of its back and the jet black of its head in the breeding plumage contrast beautifully with the snowy whiteness of the remainder of its body (Plate 49, *B*). To observe these beautiful birds at their best, one must again go to the great alkaline marshes of interior Oregon, where they may be seen winging their way over the marshes or waterways, wheeling, turning, darting, or hovering a moment before diving headlong into the water after some luckless minnow. They are fairly common summer resident and breeding birds of Harney, Lake, and Klamath Counties from the middle of April (April 14, Klamath County) until some time in October (latest date, October 14, Harney County), but are seen in other parts of the State only as stragglers or in migration. When their nesting colonies are invaded, they will dart and dive at the intruder, uttering raucous cries as they fly, displaying great bravery and determination in their attempts to drive the intruder away. Eggs are laid in May or early June. Our earliest date is May 6; our latest, June 11.

The food of this tern consists almost entirely of small fish, principally of the top-minnow type, and water insects. Two stomachs taken in May 1923 from Warner Lakes were examined. One contained two *Leuciscus*, a small minnow; and the other, one *Mylocheilus caurinus*. A September stomach from Klamath Falls contained only fragments of fish bones. As do most fish-eating birds, this tern almost invariably swallows a fish head first to facilitate its passage down the throat. Digestion is extremely rapid, as it is in many other water birds, and the fish's head may be entirely dissolved in the tern's stomach while the tail is still intact in the throat. The birds certainly do no harm to any economic interests in the State by their food habits, and they add a most attractive feature to central Oregon landscape.

Common Tern:
Sterna hirundo hirundo Linnaeus

Description.—"Outer web of outer tail feather dusky, inner web white. *Adults in summer:* bill and feet bright orange red, the bill tipped with black; top of head black; mantle light pearl gray; tail and its coverts mainly white; throat white, breast light gray. *Adults in winter:* crown mainly white; under parts pure white; bill and feet duller. *Young:* marked with blackish around eyes and on back of head; forehead and under parts white; back light gray with buffy edgings to feathers and dusky spots on wings; bill and feet brownish or pale reddish." (Bailey) *Downy young:* "The commonest type is 'cream buff,' 'ochraceous buff,' or 'clay colored' above, irregularly mottled with 'sepia' or 'seal brown'; the throat is sometimes 'smoke gray' but more often 'drab' or 'sepia'; and the under parts are pure white." (Bent) *Size:* "Length 13–16, wing 9.75–11.75, bill 1.25–1.50, tail 5–7, forked for about 3.50." (Bailey) *Nest:* Often merely a slight hollow in the sand, though sometimes lined with bits of vegetation. *Eggs:* 3 or 4, ground color buff or brown, quite heavily spotted or blotched with darker browns.

Distribution.—*General:* Breeds on Gulf coast and in Old World and from Nova Scotia south to North Carolina on the east coast and northwest to Great Slave Lake south to Minnesota, North Dakota, and Alberta. Winters in South America in our hemisphere. *In Oregon:* Rare straggler. Listed on basis of two specimens.

The Common Tern can be distinguished from the much more abundant Forster's Tern only by careful examination of the bird in hand, when the difference in the color of the tail feathers, as indicated in the description, will classify the birds. It is one of the most widely distributed North American water birds but gains a place in the Oregon list on the basis of two specimens only, both collected by Kalmbach at Ontario, Malheur County, in 1920. On October 3, 1920, several of these birds were flying over the Snake River, and Kalmbach collected one, a female (Gabrielson Coll. No. 399). Because of its puzzling appearance, he went back the next day and took another specimen (Biol. Surv. Coll. No. 272,362). Although these two are the only definite Oregon records, this species should be looked for in eastern Oregon in the spring and fall, where there is no reason why it should not be a more or less regular migrant, particularly along the Snake and Columbia Rivers. It has been reported as nesting on some of the sand islands in the Columbia River in Washington and should occur in Oregon also in similar situations. On several June days we have noted small terns that may well have been this species flying over the Columbia near Umatilla but have had no opportunity to take specimens.

Arctic Tern:
Sterna paradisaea Brünnich

Description.—"Outer web of outer tail feather dusky, rest of tail white. *Adults in summer:* bill carmine, feet vermilion, bill without black tip; top of head black, bordered by white superciliary; body clear deep gray. *Adults in winter:* under parts white, or tinged with grayish; forehead white, rest of crown streaked with black. *Young:* similar to young of *hirundo*, but with breast and throat washed with dull brownish." (Bailey) *Downy young:* "The downy young of the Arctic Tern may be distinguished from that of any other American tern by the black or dusky frontal space, which includes the lores and extends across the base of the bill. This dark area matches in color the dark-colored throat, which varies from 'dusky drab' to nearly black. The breast is pure white, becoming more grayish posteriorly. The upper parts show at least two distinct color phases, both of which are sometimes found in one brood. In the brown phase the head, back, and wings, vary from 'cinnamon' to 'pinkish buff.' In the gray phase these parts are 'pale drab gray' or 'pale smoke gray,' shading off gradually into the white or paler color of the under parts. In both phases the head is distinctly spotted and the back is heavily mottled or variegated with 'fuscous' or black; the markings are usually blacker in the brown phase than in the gray." (Bent) *Size:* "Length 14–17, wing 10.00–10.75, bill 1.08–1.40, tail 6.50–8.50, forked for 4–5." (Bailey) *Nest:* Generally a depression in sand, gravel, or moss, sometimes lined with a few bits of grass. *Eggs*: 2 or 3, ground color from olive to dark brown, more or less spotted and blotched with black and brown.

Distribution.—*General:* Circumpolar, south on Atlantic Coast to Massachusetts and to southern Quebec, Great Slave Lake, and on Pacific side to Commander and Aleutian Islands and north far into Arctic. Winters in Antarctic Ocean. *In Oregon:* Casual visitor to coast, probably passing offshore in its southward migration.

The Arctic Tern, another of the beautiful fork-tailed, medium-sized terns, migrates more or less regularly up and down the Oregon coast, as it is reported regularly from north and south of this territory. It must pass by offshore as a usual thing, and such records as we have from the coast are of casual birds that come in closer. There is a specimen in the University of Oregon collection from Lane County, and Jewett has one in his collection (No. 4349) that was found dead on the beach in Tillamook County, August 20, 1926. These are the only two Oregon specimens that we know of. There is one record for Multnomah County made by Jewett in August 1902 of a flock of about 40 seen flying over a small island on Government Lake and reported in the *Birds of the Portland Area* (Jewett and Gabrielson 1929). Gabrielson, Jewett, and Braly saw a number of birds that were undoubtedly this species off Newport on August 30, 1929, and Gabrielson saw five or six birds in the mouth of the Columbia River on September 29, 1930. These few and scattered records undoubtedly are only indications of the presence of these birds that must sometimes occur on the coast in greater numbers and would be seen more frequently if there were more observers present on the coastal bays.

Caspian Tern:
Hydroprogne caspia imperator (Coues)

Description.—"Tail not very deeply forked, the outer feathers pointed, but not much narrowed; bill red, feet black. *Breeding plumage:* crown and back of head black; mantle light gray; wings darker gray, the outer quills tipped with black," remainder of plumage pure white. "*Winter plumage:* black of head streaked with white. *Young:* crown grayish, mixed with black posteriorly; back and tail feathers with dusky spots." (Adapted from Bailey.) *Downy young:* "The downy young varies on the upper parts from dark grayish buff or 'vinaceous buff' to 'cartridge buff' or pale grayish white. The throat is very pale dusky and the remainder of the under parts are white. There are sometimes no dark markings, but usually the upper parts are more or less heavily spotted or mottled with dusky." (Bent) *Size:* "Length 19.00–22.50, wing 15.00–17.40, bill 2.48–3.10, tail 5.30–6.75, forked for .75–1.60." (Bailey) *Nest:* Usually a small depression lined with a few bits of broken vegetation. *Eggs:* 2 to 4, much like gull eggs, buff ground color, sparingly marked and blotched with various shades of brown.

Distribution.—*General:* Breeds in widely scattered locations over most of North America. Winters from South Carolina and San Francisco Bay southward. *In Oregon:* Summer resident and breeder in Klamath, Lake, and Harney Counties, where it is present from April to October.

The Caspian Tern is not only the largest but also the most spectacular of the terns that have come into Oregon. It is swift and beautiful in flight and exceedingly graceful, but it is more gull-like than the smaller terns. To see this beautiful big bird in life in the State, one must go to the great shallow lakes and marshes of south-central Oregon where it is resident from April (April 17, Klamath County) until about October 1 (October 9, Harney County). There are breeding colonies (Plate 50) in Klamath County, usually at Spring Lake, in Lake County, at Summer and Warner Lakes, and in Harney County, in the vicinity of Malheur Lake.

The terns usually nest in companies with the California and Ring-billed Gulls and keep their eggs together in one spot. Egg dates vary from May 12 to June 16 in the various colonies in different seasons. Single sets can be found earlier, but the dates given represent numerous sets in each colony. An intruder in one of these mixed colonies becomes the center of a screaming mass of birds, and in their anxiety for their eggs and young, the Caspians are much fiercer in their attacks than the gulls. Frequently they come at the intruder from high in the air, dive upon him, screaming at the top of their voices, and turn aside only at the last possible moment, when a collision with the object of their wrath seems unavoidable.

The Caspian Tern is not as abundant in Oregon as it was a few years ago. Undoubtedly the decrease in numbers has been due to drought and drainage rather than to persecution by man. The great summer colonies first reported by Finley (1907a) in 1905 in Lower Klamath Lake have disappeared with the draining of that lake, and in late years the only colony remaining in Klamath County has usually been at Spring Lake and has contained from 20 to 50 pairs. The colonies on Malheur Lake have also diminished in numbers. It is hoped that this royal bird will be present in Oregon always and that with the development of bird sanctuaries and more breeding areas for water birds in the State it will again increase in numbers to its former abundance.

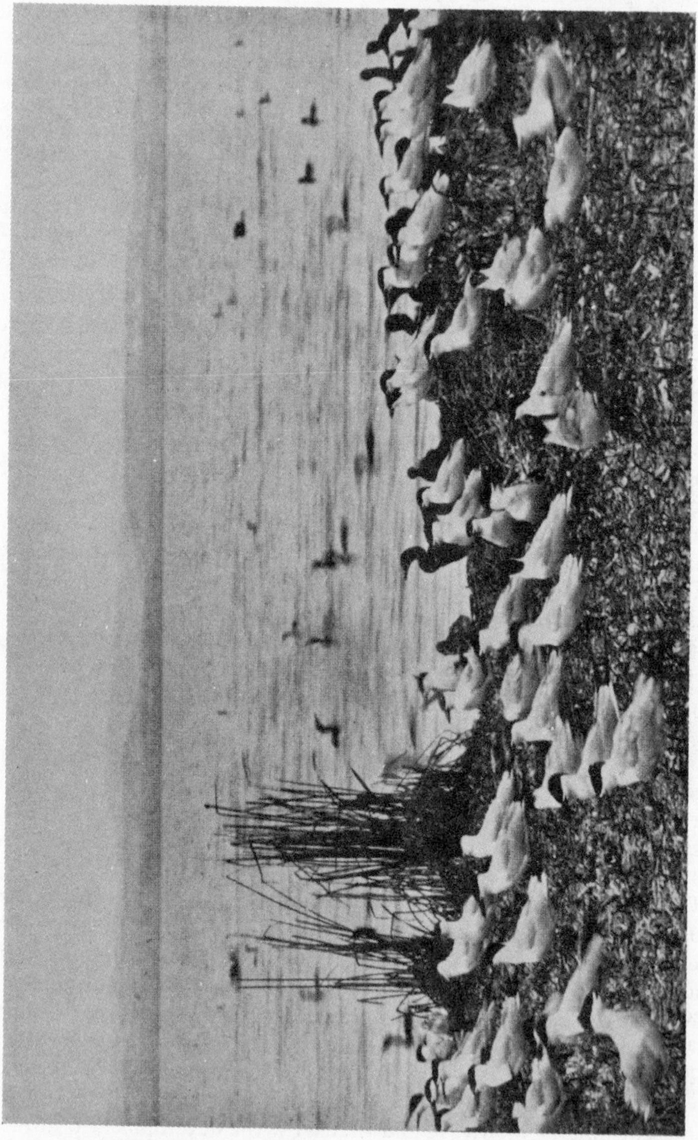

Plate 50. Caspian Terns and Farallon Cormorants. (Photo by Wm. L. Finley and H. T. Bohlman.)

Its food consists almost entirely of small fish that it catches by graceful dives into the water, and as it is largely a surface feeder, most of the fish obtained are top minnows and slow-moving trash fish that are easily caught. It does not destroy any appreciable number of valuable food fish and cannot, by the widest stretch of the imagination, be considered any detriment to the game fisherman. Along with many other birds, however, it is subject to more or less senseless persecution on the part of sportsmen and fishermen who believe that they have the sole and divine right to every game fish in the waters and to every game bird in the air in our western country.

Black Tern:

Chlidonias nigra surinamensis (Gmelin)

Description.—"Web of feet reaching only to middle of toes. *Adults in breeding plumage:* head, neck, and breast black; wings and tail slaty gray; under tail coverts white; bill and feet black. *Winter plumage:* head, neck, and under parts white, orbital ring and ear coverts dusky; upper parts blue gray. In late summer the white and black feathers are mixed on the breast. *Young:* similar to winter adults, but with edges of scapulars brown, and crown and back of head dusky." (Bailey) (See Plate 51.) *Downy young:* "The young of the black tern, when first hatched, is a swarthy individual, entirely different from the young of other terns. It is thickly covered with long, soft, silky down, 'cinnamon drab' on the throat, neck, and sides, shading off to 'pale drab gray' on the belly and cheeks; the upper parts are rich 'cinnamon,' heavily blotched with 'fuscous black.' When very young the sides of the head, including the orbital region, the cheeks, the lores, and sometimes a narrow frontal strip are pure white." (Bent) *Size:* "Length 9.00–10.25, wing 8.25, bill 1.10, tail 3.75, forked for .90." (Bailey) *Nest:* Usually a floating platform of dead and rotting reeds containing a slight depression; sometimes a fairly well-built nest of tules and reeds. *Eggs:* 2 or 3, brown or buff ground color, heavily spotted and blotched with dark browns.

Distribution.—*General:* Breeds in interior of North America from central Alaska, Great Slave Lake, and central Manitoba south to northern Ohio, northern Nebraska, northern Utah, and southern California. Winters from Gulf of Mexico and Pacific coast of Mexico southward. *In Oregon:* Breeds in eastern Oregon abundantly in the great swamps of Klamath, Lake, and Harney Counties and in many scattered small swamps in these and probably other counties. Likely to be seen in any part of eastern Oregon in spring migration and after breeding season.

The dainty little Black Tern, dressed in jet black with shimmering satiny gray wings during the breeding season, is the smallest tern and one of the most beautiful and graceful birds in Oregon. Townsend (1839) first listed it from the State, and since his time most ornithological workers in eastern Oregon have had something to say about it. Black Terns are strictly summer residents, arriving in late April (earliest date, April 10, Klamath County) and remaining until early October (October 11, Harney County). They are abundant in the great alkaline marshes of Klamath, Lake, and Harney Counties, where they breed not only in such large swamps as Klamath, Warner, and Malheur Lakes, but also in many of

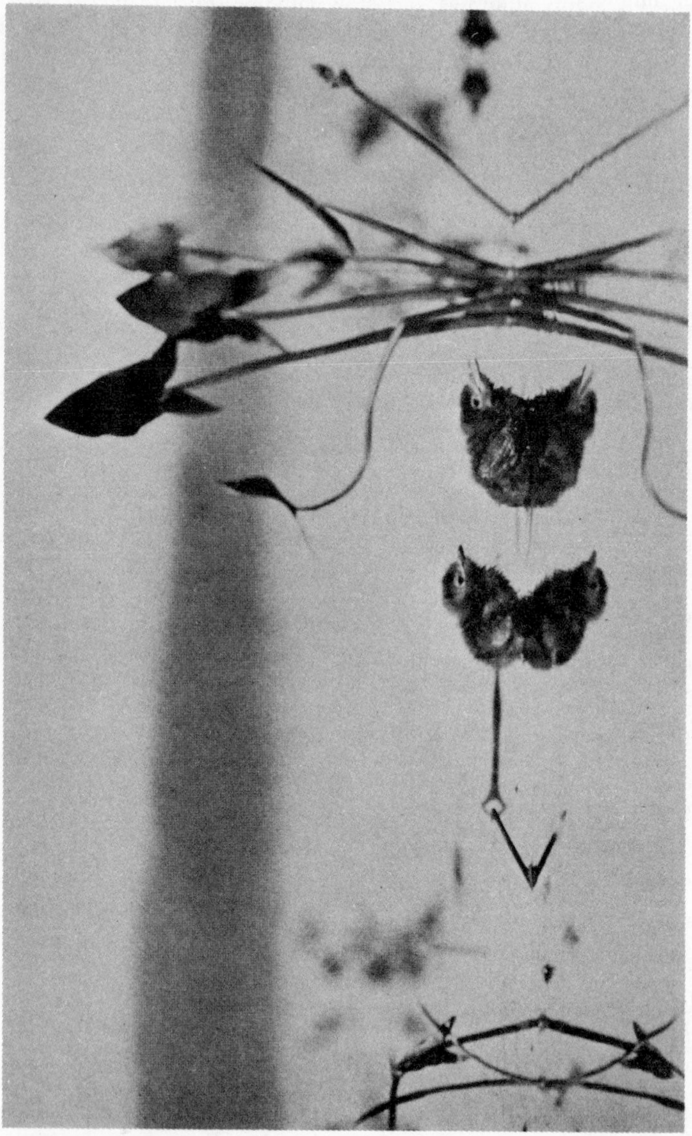

Plate 51. Young Black Terns. (Photo by Wm. L. Finley and H. T. Bohlman.)

the smaller swampy lakes scattered throughout those counties and others. They are likely to be seen anywhere in eastern Oregon not only in the spring migration in April or early May, at which time they are in the black breeding plumage, but also after the breeding season in August and September when they wander away from their nesting grounds. At that time they still retain the pearl-gray wings, but the body is white with more or less of the black about the head and eyes still in evidence. In any plumage, this is a dainty, lovable inhabitant of the marshes. It has something of the swallow about it, darting, twisting, and turning about the tops of the tules, from which it expertly picks the insects that form a large part of its food. Few people can watch it without getting a thrill as it winnows the marshes on graceful wings. It is such an expert on the wing and performs so easily that it is most impressive.

The Black Terns do not congregate in nesting colonies as do other terns in the State, although there may be many pairs in the same swamp. They are exceedingly brave in defense of their nests, diving squarely in the face of an intruder, screaming all the while at the tops of their voices. The eggs are usually laid on a mass of floating vegetable matter, with little or no attempt at nest building, or even on floating boards, although sometimes there is more effort at nest construction. Dates on which we have found fresh eggs vary from May 20 to June 20.

The food of these small terns consists generally of water insects or their larvae, sometimes small crayfish, and perhaps fish. The stomach contents of three birds collected in Warner Valley, May 21, 1923, by Prill and examined by the Biological Survey all contained insects and either nymphs or larvae of aquatic insects. Many of the insects and nymphs are picked from the tule and reed stems as the terns flash by on the wing, a practice in which they are so expert that only the performance of the swallows in drinking while on the wing, can compare with it. These beautiful little birds certainly do no harm in their feeding habits; in fact such economic value as they may have is certainly on the favorable side, although the insects on which they habitually feed usually have no economic significance.

Auks, Murres, and Puffins: *Family Alcidae*

California Murre:
Uria aalge californica (Bryant)

Description.—"Bill narrow and slender, nostril concealed in feathers; a deep groove in feathers back of eye. *Breeding plumage:* upper parts slaty or blackish, secondaries tipped with white; sides of head, neck, and throat velvety sooty brown; under parts pure white. *Winter plumage:* sides of head, neck, throat, and under parts pure white; a dusky stripe back of eye. *Young:* like winter adults, but with white

Plate 52. California Murre colony. (Photo by Wm. L. Finley and H. T. Bohlman.)

more restricted on sides of head and lower throat faintly mottled with dusky." (Bailey) (See Plate 53, *B.*) *Downy young:* "When first hatched the young murre is covered with short down which varies from 'bone brown' to 'hair brown' above, almost black on the head and neck, except that the throat is mottled with white; the under parts are white; the head and neck are sparsely covered with long, hair-like filaments, grayish white or buffy white in color, giving the bird a coarse hairy appearance." (Bent's description of the young of murre, *U. troille troille*, which is, in this plumage, indistinguishable from the California Murre.) *Size:* Length 17, wing 8.30, bill 1.86. *Nest:* None, single egg laid on bare, rocky ledge. *Egg:* 1, almost endlessly variable in color and markings, ground color pure white to light blues and greens, sometimes without spots, but usually beautifully speckled, scrawled, or blotched with various shades of brown or black.

Distribution.—*General:* Breeds from Santa Barbara, California, north to Pribilofs and westward through Aleutians to Asiatic coast. Winters from Aleutians southward. *In Oregon:* Abundant year-around resident of coast, breeding on every suitable island and rocky headland.

The California Murre is undoubtedly the most abundant seafowl of the Oregon coast and next to the American Coot the most abundant breeding water bird in the State. It remains on the coast throughout the year but is less common in winter than in summer. It frequents the rocky headlands, more particularly the high offshore rocks, where it lays its single egg on a bare, rocky ledge, usually in early June, and where the incubating birds stand in soldierly rows in almost unbelievable numbers (Plate 52). By August, the young are able to leave their rocky ledges and take to the water. During the latter part of July and August, the ocean near shore is covered with California Murres, each young bird in the company of an adult that it follows about begging for food (Plate 53).

Despite its abundance we can find no earlier published reference to it as an Oregon bird than that of Finley (1902). His writings and those of Bohlman many years ago made nationally famous the immense bird colonies on Three Arch Rocks off the Tillamook coast. Probably no one knows how many hundreds of thousands of birds nest on this reservation, but the murres make up the largest single element in the bird population, flying about the rocks like a giant swarm of bees. Although Three Arch Rocks is the most famous Oregon colony, it is by no means the only one, as other offshore rocks with suitable ledges and nesting places have their quota of these birds.

Their food in general consists of a great variety of marine life—small fish, worms, and other invertebrates—but we have no definite data on their food habits in Oregon.

Pigeon Guillemot:
Cepphus columba Pallas

Description.—"Bill black, straight, and slender, upper edge of nostril feathered; feet bright red in summer, pink in winter. *Breeding plumage:* black, except for large

Plate 53, *A*. California Murre. (Photo by Wm. L. Finley.)

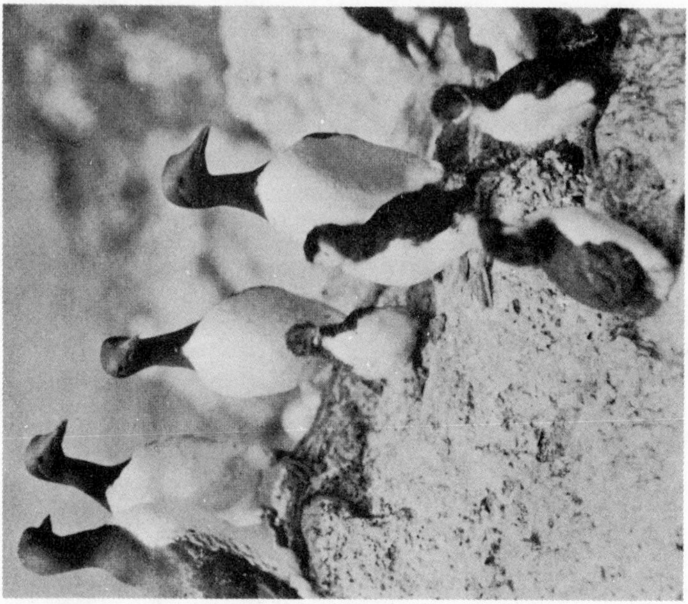

Plate 53, *B*. California Murres and young. (Photo by Alex Walker.)

white patch on base of wing which half incloses a black triangle. *Winter plumage:* wings and tail as in summer, rest of plumage mainly white, varied above and sometimes below with black. *Young:* similar to winter adults, but white of wings obscured by dusky, tips of quills marked with white." (Bailey) *Downy young:* "The young guillemot is hatched with a complete covering of soft, thick down, 'fuscous black' above, shading into 'clove brown' below." (Bent) *Size:* "Length 13–14, wing 6.90–7.30, bill 1.20–1.40." (Bailey) *Nest:* A crevice or cranny of the rocks, where the eggs are laid on the bare rock. *Eggs:* 2, pale greenish white, bluish white, or pure white, usually heavily spotted and blotched with dark brown or black.

DISTRIBUTION.—*General:* Breeds from Pacific Coast from southern California through Aleutians to Bering Strait. Winters from Aleutians southward. *In Oregon:* Breeds on nearly every suitable rocky headland along coast, being particularly abundant in Lincoln, Tillamook, Coos, and Curry Counties, where there are many available sites. Becomes common in April and remains until October in numbers. Winters casually.

THE BRIGHT-RED FEET, jet-black plumage, and conspicuous white wing patches of the Pigeon Guillemot make it one of the most striking and easily recognized summer birds of the Oregon coast, where it is one of the prominent features of the bird life and may be seen flying in and out of crevices in precipitous headlands or feeding offshore among the myriads of sea birds that gather during the anchovy runs. Its flight is very rapid and strong, and its swimming and diving—like that of its relatives—expert. It was first mentioned as an Oregon bird by Townsend (1839). Prill (1901) found it breeding at Otter Rock, Woodcock (1902) listed it from Yaquina Bay, and Finley (1902) found it on Three Arch Rocks. Since then little has been written about it.

It breeds on practically every rocky Oregon headland suitable for the purpose from the mouth of Pistol River north to the Columbia, but is particularly abundant in Lincoln, Tillamook, Coos, and Curry Counties, where it becomes common in April (April 12, Tillamook County). The species nests abundantly on the headlands adjacent to the Three Arch Rocks, Tillamook County, where it lays its eggs rather late in the season. Our only egg records are from July 2 to 6. The guillemots in this colony are usually busily engaged in feeding young in August after all the other sea birds have left their rocky homes and are to be found scattered over the surface of the ocean. There is also a particularly fine colony in the seal caves on Heceta Head, Lincoln County, where in the dark crevices and crannies of this huge water-worn cavern at least 100 pairs of birds breed. A visit to this cave on August 4, 1932, showed guillemots feeding just offshore on a huge run of small fish and making frequent direct flights between this school of fish and their noisy young in the cave. The birds remain in numbers until October (October 10, Coos County). Winter records so far are few, but the species undoubtedly occurs in small numbers off the Oregon coast throughout the year. Gabrielson saw 10 scattered birds on Yaquina Bay during a heavy storm on February 7, 1919.

We have no definite records regarding food of this species in Oregon except that it is found commonly feeding on the great schools of small fish that abound on the coast.

Marbled Murrelet:
Brachyramphus marmoratus (Gmelin)

Description.—*Breeding plumage:* "Upper parts dusky, back and sides barred with deep rusty brown; under parts white, mottled with sooty brown. *Winter plumage:* upper parts slaty, with white band on back of neck; scapulars mixed with white; feathers of back tipped with plumbeous; flanks with dark gray stripes. *Young:* upper parts dusky, collar and scapular spots indistinct; under parts white, mottled, or speckled with sooty. *Length:* 9.50–10.00, wing 5, bill .60–.70." (Bailey) *Downy young and nest:* Unknown. *Eggs:* One egg taken by Cantwell from body of a bird is pale yellow, thickly spotted with dark brown to black.

Distribution.—*General:* Summer range, coast of central Oregon northward to Aleutian Islands. Winters from British Columbia southward to central California (Monterey Bay and Santa Barbara). *In Oregon:* Regular summer resident of coast of Lincoln, Lane, and Tillamook Counties. Found throughout year in coastal waters.

The home life of the Marbled Murrelet is still one of the unsolved mysteries of ornithology. When and where this small bird nests and rears its young is still its secret, but it is assumed that it nests either in the timber or on the bald hills facing the Coast Ranges from Oregon northward. A number of years ago, in May, in the Prince of Wales Archipelago, George Cantwell took a nearly perfect egg from a bird he had shot. There is also a single egg in the J. H. Bowles collection, probably this species, that was taken in Alaska by Stanton Warburton. Woodcock (1902) first listed the species for Oregon from Yaquina Bay, which is still one of its centers of abundance. It is a regular summer resident of the coast, particularly in Lincoln, Tillamook, and Lane Counties, and is found in winter in the same general territory, but no one has yet found its nest or eggs in Oregon, although Jewett (1934d) recorded one newly hatched downy young bird caught by Stanley Jewett, Jr., on September 4, 1933, in the dense woods back of Devils Lake, Lincoln County. It is much the youngest bird of the species the authors have seen. It was not able to fly and presumably was at or near the nest site. The authors have also seen a specimen just out of the down that A. B. Johnson picked up near Minerva, Lane County, on September 8, 1918, and gave to Overton Dowell, Jr., that is undoubtedly a young Marbled Murrelet. Alex Walker collected several young birds at Pacific City in the summer of 1931, and the authors have numerous immature specimens taken off Depoe Bay during the summers of 1933 and 1934.

Marbled Murrelets are rather shy and difficult to approach, and when they are on the water considerable maneuvering on the part of the collector is usually required before specimens can be taken. Ordinarily this little diver is found in the mouths of bays and in the ocean just offshore, where its expertness in the water is a marvelous sight. Gabrielson has had numerous opportunities to watch these birds working about the docks on Puget Sound. As they dive beneath the surface, the wings are spread out and used exactly as a pair of oars to drive the birds through the water. The feet are also used, at least part of the time. The birds actually fly under the surface, sometimes emerging from the water in full flight. The flight is strong and direct.

Very little is known about the food of this species in Oregon waters, but it undoubtedly consists of small marine life of the same general type as that eaten by its near relatives.

Ancient Murrelet:
Synthliboramphus antiquus (Gmelin)

Description.—"Bill small and short, nostrils exposed; front of tarsus covered with transverse scutellae. *Breeding plumage:* head and neck black, with large white patch on side of the neck, a wide stripe of white filaments along back edge of crown, and scattered white filaments over back of neck; back slaty; sides black; under parts white. *Winter plumage:* throat white; head and back without white filaments; sides gray." (Bailey) *Downy young:* In the downy young the upper parts are of jet black, including the back, wings, crown, and sides of the head to a point below the eye; there is a whitish auricular patch in the black area back of the ear; the occiput and the whole dorsal region seems to be clouded with bluish gray, due to a subterminal portion of each filament being so colored; the under parts are pure white, slightly tinged with yellowish." (Bent) *Size:* "Length 9.50–10.80, wing 5.25–5.50, bill .60." (Bailey) *Nest:* An abandoned burrow of Cassin's Auklet, a crevice in the rocks, or a burrow under a tussock of grass. *Eggs:* 2, deep buff, spotted and marked with light brown and lavender of various shades.

Distribution.—*General:* Breeds on coast and islands of north Pacific, from northern Japan and Queen Charlotte Islands northward to Aleutians. Winters southward to southern California and Japan. *In Oregon:* Winter visitor to coast.

The Ancient Murrelet is another of the northern nesting Alcidae that is fairly rare on the Oregon coast. Our only records are of birds found dead or dying on the beaches of Clatsop, Tillamook, and Lincoln Counties, mostly in the winter months. Jewett has four winter skins from Netarts Bay in his collection (December 28 and 31, 1912; December 30, 1928; and December 14, 1933) and one from Delake (January 14, 1933). He has one skin from Neskowin as early as August 12, 1928, and a spring specimen from Netarts Bay as late as April 28, 1915. In the winter of 1932–33 Ancient Murrelets died by the dozens along the Oregon coast, and every collector who visited the coast obtained a number of these somewhat erratic visitors. Gabrielson caught several alive that were exhausted and emaciated on December 27 to 28, 1932, and more birds were picked up at intervals well into February. Prior to this visitation its appearance had been that of a straggler, of which a specimen was occasionally taken.

Cassin's Auklet:
Ptychoramphus aleuticus (Pallas)

Description.—"Bill broader than deep at base; upper outline nearly straight. Upper parts slaty black; sides of head, neck, and throat plumbeous; spot on lower eyelid, and under parts white." (Bailey) *Downy young:* "The downy young is 'blackish brown' or 'fuscous black' when first hatched, fading to 'fuscous' or 'hair brown' when older, on the upper parts; the throat, breast, and flanks are paler; and the belly is 'ecru drab,' 'drab gray,' or 'drab.' " (Bent) *Size:* "Length 8.00–9.50, wing 4.75–5.25, bill .75." (Bailey) *Nest:* A burrow from one to several feet in length or a natural cavity or crevice on rocky islands off the coast. *Egg:* 1, white, unmarked, though often with a greenish-bluish tinge.

Distribution.—*General:* Breeds on Pacific Coast from Lower California to Aleutian Islands. Winters from Puget Sound southward. *In Oregon:* Found off coast throughout year.

Cassin's Auklet is found throughout the year on the Oregon coast, although most of our records are in July and August. Visitors to the Oregon coastal waters will have no difficulty in identifying it, as it is the smallest of the offshore species regularly found there. It is usually found commonly off the mouths of harbors and bays, where it feeds on the surface or under water, using both wings and feet during its underwater activities. Frequently the birds are seen apparently flying directly out of the surface of the water. Despite their plain dresses of gray and white, it is rather interesting to watch their absurd, chunky bodies bobbing about on the surface. Dead birds are at times washed up on the beach during December, January, and February, following heavy offshore storms in which these auklets suffer in common with many of the other offshore species. Little attention has been paid to the species as an Oregon bird, our first record being that of Loomis (1901), who in 1898 found it abundant off the mouth of the Rogue. It is not otherwise mentioned except in our own notes and publications. There is only one inland record. It was taken in Portland and brought to Jewett on October 4, 1921 (Jewett Coll. No. 3452).

The bird breeds on little rocky islands offshore along the Pacific Coast. It apparently is absent on Three Arch Rocks. At least Jewett and Finley have been unable to find it there on any of the trips they have made. The only definite breeding record we have for the Oregon coast is reported by Braly (1930a), who obtained adults and young on June 15, 1930, on Island Rock just off Port Orford. A careful search of the other rocky islands along the Oregon coast would certainly reveal the presence of this bird as a breeding species.

A number of Oregon stomachs collected by Alex Walker at Netarts during December and January showed forms of mollusks, bones of small fish, pieces of sand dollar, seeds of *Ceanothus* and *Lathyrus*, forms of lichens, and remains of one *Nereis*.

Paroquet Auklet:
Cyclorrhynchus psittacula (Pallas)

Description.—"Bill dark red, high, and thin, with sickle-shaped lower mandible curved upward. *Breeding plumage:* throat and upper parts sooty black; under parts white; a white line from lower eyelid back over ear ending in a thin white crest. *Winter plumage and young:* throat as well as rest of under parts white." (Bailey) *Downy young:* " 'Fuscous black' on the crown, 'fuscous,' 'benzo brown,' or 'hair brown' on the back, sides, throat and breast, and 'pale drab gray' on the belly." (Bent) *Size:* "Length 9.00–10.40, wing 5.40–6.00, bill .60." (Bailey) *Nest:* Crevice or cranny in the rocks, egg being laid on bare rock. *Egg:* 1, pure white or bluish white.

Distribution.—*General:* Breeds on coasts and islands of Bering Sea. Winters on north Pacific south casually to central California. *In Oregon:* Rare offshore winter visitor.

The curious little Paroquet Auklet, with its upturned bright-red bill and tiny white crest, is only an irregular winter visitor to Oregon waters. It is seldom seen alive, and all our records are of birds found dead on the beaches and preserved. The first specimen taken in the State was found dead on the beach at Netarts, January 1, 1913, by M. E. Peck and was recorded in the *Condor* by Jewett (1914b); the second was obtained at Newport, January 27, 1914, by Jewett; and the third was found at Netarts, January 1, 1921, by Alex Walker. In 1932 and 1933 several more specimens were found by Jewett and Braly. Jewett has skins in his collection taken at Taft (February 21, 1932), Delake (February 5, 1933), Sunset Beach, Clatsop County (3 skins, February 23, 1933), and Gleneden (February 26, 1933). Our last record consisted of several specimens that were too far gone to save, found on Clatsop County beaches January 12, 1935, while we were on our last field trip together gathering material for this book.

The stomach of the bird found by Walker contained four seeds of *Rhus* (sumac) and one of *Lathyrus* (a wild perennial pea), but the usual food of the species undoubtedly consists of the varied forms of marine life eaten by other similar sea birds.

Rhinoceros Auklet:
Cerorhinca monocerata (Pallas)

Description.—"Bill much compressed, longer than deep; in breeding season base of bill surmounted by upright horn. *Breeding plumage:* upper parts dusky; sides of head, throat, and rest of under parts plumbeous, except for whitish belly; side of head with two series of white pointed feathers. *Winter plumage:* breast more uniformly gray; belly purer white; horn absent." (Bailey) *Downy young:* "Uniform sooty grayish brown, very similar to corresponding stages of *Lunda cirrhata* [Tufted Puffin], but rather lighter in color and with more slender bill." (Ridgway, 1887.) *Size:* "Length 14–15.50, wing 7.25, bill from front edge of horn 1." (Bailey) *Nest:*

A burrow, several feet in length, ending in a dome-shaped chamber. *Egg:* 1, dull white, often spotless, but usually with faint spots of pale lavender, gray, or light brown.

Distribution.—*General:* Breeds from Destruction Island, Washington, northward to southern Alaska, Aleutian Islands, and northern Japan. Winters on open sea from Washington coast southward to Lower California. *In Oregon:* Winter visitor all along coast.

The first Oregon record for the Rhinoceros Auklet was that of Woodcock (1902) for Yaquina Bay. The only other references to it as an Oregon bird are by Finley (ms.) and Jewett (1914b). Although it is the largest auklet found on the Oregon coast, it is one of the least-known Oregon sea birds. In life, its short, heavy body and intermediate size distinguish it from any other auklet likely to occur. It is noticeably larger than the other auklets and murrelets and decidedly smaller than the puffins and murres with which it is associated. The chances for a person to see it are very limited, however, unless he goes to sea, which, in winter, is a rather robust sport off the Oregon coast and one seldom indulged in by nature lovers and ornithologists. Although the species is present off the coast from August until March we did not meet with it in life in any of our offshore trips until Gabrielson and John Carter collected several off Depoe Bay, September 10, 1934. Its presence is usually made known by the finding of dead birds washed up on the beach. The earliest record of this type that we have is of one found at Cape Meares on August 6; the latest, March 1. Records during August, January, and February are quite numerous so that the bird is certainly present in numbers off the shore at times.

Two Oregon stomachs, one taken in August and one in December, both nearly empty, contained fragments of small fish bones. This auklet is known to feed generally on small crustaceans and fish and cannot be regarded as having any effect, detrimental or otherwise, on man's economic interests.

Horned Puffin:
Fratercula corniculata (Naumann)

Description.—*Adults in breeding season* (sexes alike): Top of head uniform grayish brown; sides of head white; neck and back, black; throat sooty, changing to brownish-gray on the chin; under parts white; bill brilliantly colored with salmon-red, yellow, and orange; legs and feet bright red. *Winter plumage:* Sides of head gray, legs and feet pale red, and bill much duller colored in dusky and pale yellow. *Downy young:* Uniform dark sooty grayish brown, the breast and upper abdomen rather abruptly white. *Nest:* A shallow burrow, sometimes lined with a little grass or other vegetable matter. *Egg:* 1, ground color dull white or creamy white, with some markings of lavender, gray, or olive.

Distribution.—*General:* Breeds on coasts and islands of north Pacific from southern

Alaska northward. Winters south along coast to Queen Charlotte Islands. *In Oregon:* Found as an irregular winter resident, common only from December 1932 to February 1933.

The Horned Puffin, a northern cousin of the common Tufted Puffin, is found in Oregon only as a winter straggler. The first specimen was one found dead on the beach at Netarts Bay, March 7, 1916, and recorded by Jewett (1923b). It was so badly decomposed that it was possible to save only the head, which is now in Jewett's collection. There are also two skins in the Overton Dowell, Jr., collection, a male and a female, found dead on the beach, 3 miles northwest of Mercer, Lane County, on March 15, 1919.

On December 27, 1932, Gabrielson found dozens of dead and dying birds on the beach north of Netarts. Many, badly oil-soaked and thus rendered helpless, drifted in on each high tide. In two days 35 specimens were saved. Many dozens more were so badly torn and injured by the gulls that no attempt was made to save them. Among this lot were many Horned Puffins, Ancient Murrelets, and other species that do not normally winter in numbers on our coast. Two days later Jewett was on the beaches a few miles north and had the same experience. From that time until mid-February every bird observer who visited the beaches reported the same condition.

Curiously enough, Tufted Puffins remained through the winter in far greater numbers than usual. We can find nothing in weather conditions on the Oregon coast or in Alaskan waters to account for the visitation of puffins, murrelets, auklets, and kittiwakes in numbers far exceeding anything we had previously known. The only logical explanation that comes readily to mind is a change in food conditions. A marked decrease in the normal supplies in northern waters and a comparative abundance on the Oregon coast would logically explain both the southward movement of northern birds and the unusual abundance of Tufted Puffins and other resident birds. We have no evidence, however, to substantiate this surmise.

Tufted Puffin:
Lunda cirrhata (Pallas)

Description.—"Bill compressed, nearly as high as long. *Adults:* upper parts sooty black; under parts dark grayish. *Breeding plumage:* sides of face white, a long crest of fine silky yellow feathers over each eye; terminal half of bill, and feet, bright red. *Winter plumage:* sides of head dusky, and without crests; horny covering of base of bill replaced by soft dusky brown skin; feet flesh color. *Young in first winter:* similar to winter adult, but with rudiments of light brown crests, and sides of upper mandible without grooves." (Bailey) *Downy young:* "Completely covered with long, soft, silky down, sooty black above and sooty grayish below." (Bent) (See

Plate 54, *A*. Downy young Tufted Puffin. (Photo by Reed Ferris.)

Plate 54, *B*. Close-up of a Tufted Puffin. (Photo by Wm. L. Finley and H. T. Bohlman.)

Plate 54, *A.*) *Size:* "Length 14.40–15.60, wing 7.75, bill 1.30–1.45." (Bailey) *Nest:* A shallow burrow, usually lined with feathers and grass. *Egg:* 1, pale bluish white or dull, dirty white, with a few to many spots or scrawls or various shades of gray or pale brown.

DISTRIBUTION.—*General:* Coastal islands from California northward to northwestern Alaska, and from Japan to northeastern Siberia. *In Oregon:* Nests on suitable offshore rocks and headlands along entire coast.

COMPARATIVELY LITTLE has appeared in Oregon literature about the Tufted Puffin (Plate 54, *B*). Prill (1901) recorded it as breeding at Otter Rock in 1889, and Loomis (1901) found it off the mouth of the Rogue River, but Finley's (1905d) account of it on Three Arch Rocks gave the first adequate published material on this species that is now one of the most abundant of the sea birds breeding on the Oregon coast. There, above the thunder of the surf, on the steep slopes of offshore rocks or precipitous headlands it digs its shallow nesting burrow, lays its single egg, and rears its young. It nests, or has recently nested, to our knowledge, on the rocks at the mouth of Pistol River, Island Rock near Port Orford, the rocks near Bandon, Heceta Head, Seal Rocks, Yaquina Head, the rocks off the mouth of Salmon River, those off the mouth of the Nestucca River, Cape Lookout, Cape Meares, and Three Arch Rocks and adjacent points on the mainland. Normally, few remain through the winter, but from December 1932 to February 1933 many hundreds were present off the Tillamook and Lincoln County coasts, where they were associated with a great flight of more northern species.

Tufted Puffins are most curious dumpy little birds. When sitting up in front of the nest or on a rocky ledge above the water, their black bodies, white plumes, and enormous bright-colored bills give them an air of comical gravity found in no other bird. They are quite social, usually nesting in colonies of considerable size and frequently fishing together in similar groups. During the summer months, they are a conspicuous element in the enormous mixed groups of seafowl that follow the movements of the hordes of anchovies and other small fish along the coast. Their flight is quite characteristic, the short, heavy bodies being driven at high speed by their comparatively small, blunt wings. It is difficult for them to rise off the water in calm weather or to launch themselves into the air from the land. This may be one reason for their usual choice of nesting sites on steep slopes (Plate 55) from whence they can dive downward until sufficient momentum is gained to carry them along. When once launched their flight is swift and direct. The birds find it difficult, however, to alter the line of travel, either to rise or to turn aside, and any such changes in their course are usually made in long gradual curves.

This bird was evidently a staple article of diet of the Oregon coast Indians, as it is today with the Aleuts, because puffin bones have been

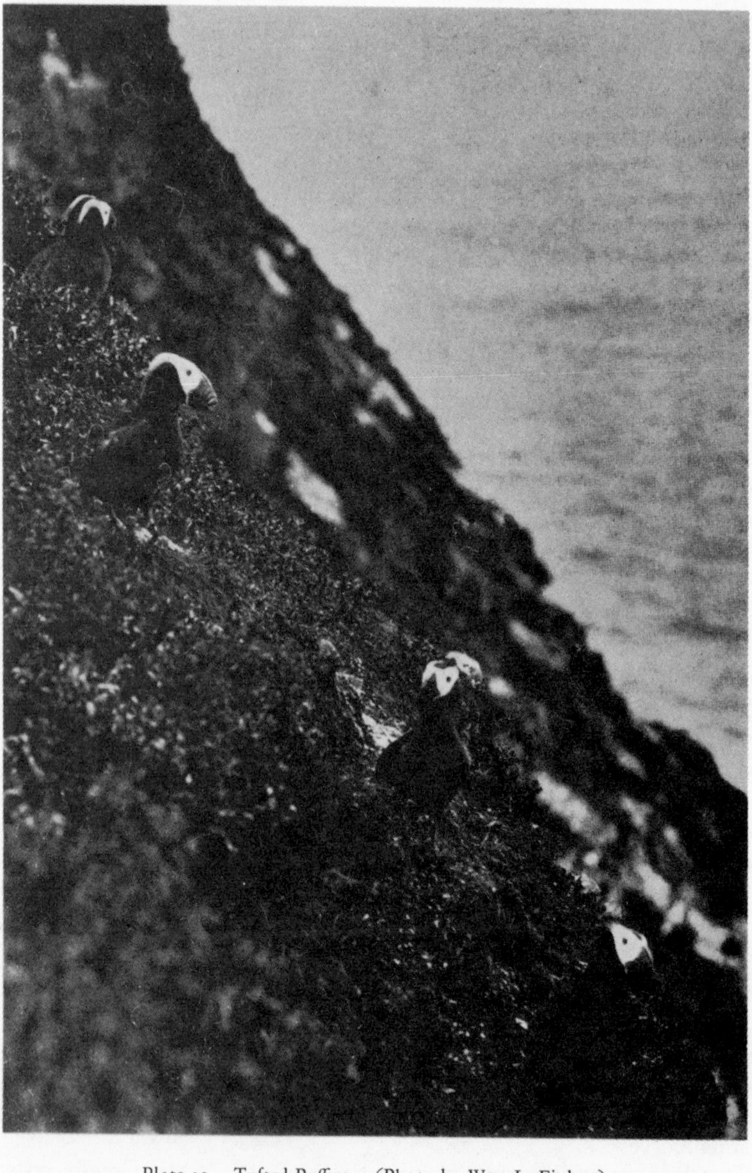

Plate 55. Tufted Puffins. (Photo by Wm. L. Finley.)

found abundantly by Jewett in the shell mounds on the Tillamook County coast.

The Tufted Puffin feeds on small fish and marine life. Few Oregon stomachs were available, but several stomachs from other places along the coast were full of small fish (*Clupea pallasii*). So far as known these odd-appearing little Sea Parrots do no harm to anything of economic consequence to man and therefore can well be allowed to remain as an attractive feature of the Oregon shore line.

Plate 56, *A*. Band-tailed Pigeon squab on nest. (Photo by Alex Walker.)

Plate 56, *B*. Western Mourning Dove on nest. (Photo by Ira N. Gabrielson.)

Order Columbiformes

Pigeons and Doves: *Family Columbidae*

Band-tailed Pigeon: *Columba fasciata fasciata* Say

DESCRIPTION.—"*Adult male:* End of tail with *broad—two inch—band*, pale gray, bordered above by black; *back of neck with white collar* adjoined by iridescent bronzy patch spreading back as a greenish wash; head and under parts purplish pink, fading to whitish on belly; fore part of back tinged with brownish, hinder part bluish gray; wing quills blackish, coverts bluish gray, faintly edged with white. *Adult female:* like male but duller and much grayer; white nuchal band often obsolete, iridescent patch restricted, head grayish instead of pink, under parts largely grayish. *Young* without white on nape, under parts dull grayish, tinged with brown on breast; upper parts with feathers more or less lightly bordered with paler; head and neck dull bluish gray in male, light grayish brown in female. *Length:* 15–16, wing 8.00–8.80, tail 6.00–6.50." (Bailey) *Nest:* A flimsy structure of twigs on the flat limb of a tree (Plate 56, *A*). *Eggs:* Usually 1, rarely 2, pure white.

DISTRIBUTION.—*General:* Breeds from British Columbia and north central Colorado south into Mexico. Winters from southwestern United States southward. *In Oregon:* Common summer resident and breeding species west of Cascades. Most abundant in Coast Ranges. Casual in winter in western Oregon. Straggler only to eastern Oregon.

DOUGLAS (1914) collected the first Band-tailed Pigeon (Plate 56, *A*) for the State at the mouth of the Santiam River, August 19, 1825, and since that time it has been reported regularly by ornithologists visiting western Oregon. It is greatly prized as a game bird and at one time was reduced in numbers, but a long Federal closed season has restored the species to something of its former abundance. It is now common in the western part of the State, where it is found in the greatest abundance on the coast (earliest date of arrival, March 5, Lane County; latest date of fall departure, October 28, Lincoln County). There it builds a nest, usually high in a coniferous tree, and lays its one or two eggs on a flimsy platform of twigs. Egg laying is at its height in late May and June, the extreme dates being May 3 and July 12. There is one winter record from Curry County: Jewett reported 150 birds feeding on madrone berries at Agness, January 18, 1928. Our only definite record for eastern Oregon is one by Jewett for Harney County of a bird found October 19, 1928, at the Home Creek Ranch at the western base of the Steens Mountains, a most unlikely place for a Band-tailed Pigeon.

When the Passenger Pigeons disappeared in the eastern States, a theory advanced to account for their disappearance was that they had moved to a new territory, presumably farther west, and the Band-tailed Pigeons are still occasionally reported as being that long-lost species. Nothing could be farther from the truth. Except in size, the two do not resemble each other in any way, the differences between them being about the same as those between the Band-tailed Pigeon and the Mourning Dove. In fact, the Passenger Pigeon might be described as a much enlarged and more highly decorated Mourning Dove.

The food of the Band-tailed Pigeons consists largely of acorns, mountain-ash berries, the numerous species of *Rubus* (blackberry, raspberry, salmonberry, and thimbleberry), elderberries, currants, kinnikinnick, dogwood, and many others, and seeds of grain, peas, legumes of various kinds, and doubtless many others. After the breeding season the birds gather in large flocks, feeding on the berries of salal, salmonberry, blackberries, and the numerous abundant fruits of the fall months. The flocks wander somewhat, occasionally appearing above timber line to feed about the heather patches, apparently to obtain seeds of *Lupinus lyalli*, which grows in abundance in such places. Gabrielson first noted this on August 25, 1926, when a single bird was flushed from a heather patch on Mount Hood, and has seen the same behavior several times since.

There is, at times, considerable complaint regarding the depredations of Band-tailed Pigeons on agricultural crops. Green prunes are eaten to some extent, though usually not so heavily as to materially reduce the crop, and every year it is alleged that these birds do great damage to grain and peas. Where grain is broadcast, they do pick up kernels that are left on the surface, but in no instance have we found them scratching out the covered grain. Where peas are grown for canning they also eat the peas remaining on the surface, which causes considerable concern among the farmers. Gabrielson at one time spent two weeks checking on this behavior and collected a number of stomachs. The birds had been eating peas, but a careful check on the fields in question revealed no damage to the crop. The flock showed a tendency to feed in the same part of the field for several days in succession. Comparisons between those areas and areas where the pigeons did not feed showed the stand on the supposedly damaged area to be as good as that on other areas. As the peas are drilled to a depth of 4 to 6 inches, this is logical. The birds were at no time observed to scratch out seed, being content to wander about picking up the spilled seed from the surface.

Rock Dove:
Columba livia livia Gmelin

Description.—Sexes alike. In original form, pale gray all over, except the rump, which is white. Two distinct black bars across the wing, greenish metallic area on either side of neck. In domestication, these have developed wide variations into white-reddish browns and other colors, possibly from crosses with other species. The wild birds in Oregon are a motley lot, though there are many birds approaching the original species in color and markings. *Size:* Length 14, wing 8.80. *Nest:* A few straws, bits of grass, or other material about buildings or on the rocks. *Eggs:* 2, white.

DISTRIBUTION.—*General:* Southern Europe, northern Africa, and Asia Minor. Introduced and widely reared as the Domestic Pigeon. Escaped and breeding about many towns in United States. *In Oregon:* Has gone wild and become established as a breeding bird about docks and waterfront of Portland, grain elevators and railroad yards of numerous other towns, and rocky cliffs along Umatilla River.

THE ROCK DOVE, or common domestic pigeon, has become naturalized and established about numerous towns in both eastern and western Oregon. It is particularly abundant along the Portland waterfront, where it breeds on the buildings and feeds about the grain docks. It has been established and breeds about Pilot Rock and in the cliffs along the Umatilla River below Pendleton, and these are the only Oregon colonies we have noted that have reverted to ancestral habits. Incidentally, the Umatilla River colony is greatly appreciated by a pair of Prairie Falcons that have lived for years on a nearby cliff. Many of the doves have reverted to the ancient slate-blue and white plumage of their ancestors, but there are still many mixed colored individuals among these naturalized birds.

Western Mourning Dove:
Zenaidura macroura marginella (Woodhouse)

DESCRIPTION.—"Tail of fourteen feathers, graduated, more than two thirds as long as wing; feathers more or less narrowed at tips; wings pointed; tarsus naked, side toes of unequal length, the outer shortest; space around eye bare. *Adult male:* tail bordered with white and with subterminal black spots; back and wings with a few roundish black spots; rest of upper parts brown; top of head washed with bluish gray, sides of head with blue-black spot and pink iridescence; under parts brownish, tinged with pink on breast. *Adult female:* similar but paler throughout, with little if any bluish gray on head, black ear spot smaller, and metallic gloss less distinct. *Young:* duller than female, without metallic gloss or distinct ear spot; feathers of upper parts and breast with grayish tips. *Length:* 11–13, wing 5.70–6.10, tail 5.70–6.50, bill .50–.55." (Bailey) *Nest:* A flimsy platform of twigs, usually on a low horizontal limb but sometimes on the ground (Plate 56, *B*). *Eggs:* 2, pure white.

DISTRIBUTION.—*General:* Breeds from Minnesota and Oklahoma west to Pacific Coast and north to Manitoba, Saskatchewan, and British Columbia. South through Mexico. *In Oregon:* Common summer resident and breeder, most abundant in eastern Oregon but widely distributed in western Oregon, even to coast, where it is uncommon. Casual winter resident in scattered localities east of Coast Ranges.

THE WESTERN MOURNING DOVE (Plate 56, *B*) is not mentioned either in the reports of the Lewis and Clark Expedition or in Douglas' Journals for this territory, but beginning with Townsend (1839) it has been included in every local list published in the State and in numerous manuscript notes in the files of the Biological Survey. In eastern Oregon, it is an abundant bird in all counties, coming north in late March and early April and remaining in numbers until late September and early October. It is most abundant in the Upper Sonoran and Transition Zones of that part of the State, although it is common in the mountains up to 7,000 feet. It is an uncommon winter resident along the Columbia and Snake Rivers. We have winter records for Umatilla (January 12, February 17 and 22), Wasco (January 25), and Malheur (December 6) Counties. In western Oregon, it remains in small numbers through the winter. There are winter records for Multnomah, Polk, Yamhill, eastern Lane, Jackson, and Josephine Counties. It is much less common on the coast, but it has been noted in Tillamook, Lincoln, western Lane, Coos, and Curry Counties, and is doubtless found from May 20 to September 3, though most of the records are for June. Egg laying is spread over a long period, dates for fresh eggs extending from April 20 to September 3, with the height of the laying season coming in June.

These doves are not hunted for food or sport in Oregon, and consequently they are tame and unsuspicious in most localities, nesting and living commonly about farms and in smaller towns, where they may be found feeding about the farmyards or seen in a strong and rapid flight, the wings giving off a whistling sound as they flash by. Outside the breeding season they congregate in loose flocks that may be found feeding in scattered formation along the roadsides or in cultivated fields or sitting in solemn and dignified rows on the fence wires. When alarmed they take wing, the flock scattering as single birds or in pairs or trios. It is evident that they are not as gregarious as the Band-tailed Pigeons, for the flocks are not usually as large nor as persistent as in that species. In the arid section the doves frequent the vicinity of streams and water holes, feeding out sometimes for long distances into the sage lands.

The food consists of all sorts of weed seed and grain, the latter largely waste grain. Even when feeding in the ripening grain, the Mourning Doves are so few in numbers in any one field as to cause little apparent damage. They consume enormous quantities of weed seed, the numbers sometimes found in a single stomach reaching almost unbelievable proportions.

Order Cuculiformes

Cuckoos: *Family Cuculidae*

California Cuckoo:
Coccyzus americanus occidentalis Ridgway

Description.—"*Adults:* Upper parts grayish brown, with faint green gloss; under parts white, grayish across chest; *lower half of bill mainly yellow;* side of head with blackish streak; tail graduated, middle feathers like back, tipped with black, the rest blue black, *with broad white thumb marks* on tips; wing quills mainly rugous on inner webs. *Young:* like adults, but tail duller, without blue, and white not strikingly contrasted with brown. *Length:* 12.30–13.50, wing 5.50–6.00, tail 6.10–6.90, bill 1.02–1.08, depth of bill through base .37–.40." (Bailey) *Nest:* A flimsy platform of twigs, sometimes scantily lined with bits of finer vegetation. *Eggs:* 3 to 4, light greenish blue.

Distribution.—*General:* Breeds from British Columbia south to Lower California and inland to Colorado and Texas. Winters in an unknown territory southward. *In Oregon:* Rare summer resident, most abundant west of Cascades but recorded sparingly from eastern Oregon.

The California Cuckoo, the western representative of the familiar Yellow-billed Cuckoo, is not a common bird anywhere in Oregon. In our own experience, as well as in that of others, it is most abundant in the willow bottoms of the Columbia and Willamette Rivers but is rather erratic, appearing to be more common some seasons than others. Our earliest date is May 19, and our latest September 5, both Multnomah County; but the notes and specimens are too few to use as a basis for any definite statement regarding arrival and departure dates. Townsend (1839) listed it from the territory of Oregon, and Prill (1891g) recorded eggs on November 7, 1891, from Sweet Home. Johnson (1880) considered it rare in the Willamette Valley, as did Anthony (Bailey 1902), Woodcock (1902), and Shelton (1917). During 1923, 1924, and 1925, we found it to be a fairly common bird along the Columbia. We observed at least a dozen birds on June 8, 1923, and obtained many other records and specimens during each of the three seasons. Since then our records have been rather sporadic.

It is a rare bird in eastern Oregon, only three records being available to us up to the present time. Bendire (1877) wrote as follows:

August 2, 1876, camping under a clump of willow bushes near Keeney's Ferry, on the Oregon side of the Snake River, I found a nest of this species containing half grown young birds.

The parents, at first rather uneasy, soon lost their fears and attended to the wants of their young. They were constantly going back and forth bringing crickets, and judging from the number disposed of in the three hours I noticed them, the amount required in a day must be enormous.

Streator (Biological Survey field notes) stated that he noted them every day between June 25 and July 3, 1896, at Plush, and Peck (1911a) noted it on Willow Creek, Malheur County, on July 6, 1910.

The eggs are laid on flimsy platforms of twigs, usually within a few feet of the ground. Occupied nests have been recorded from June 1 to August 2. The November nesting recorded by Prill is abnormal. The young, decorated with an abundance of blackish-purple quills, are repulsive looking until the sheaths burst. Then, within a few hours, the slim babies are transformed into elegant creatures clad in waistcoats of white satin and coats of brown satin.

The weird call notes of the California Cuckoo, or "rain crow," are most often heard in June and early July in the thickly wooded stream bottoms. There the bird conceals his slim, satiny elegance of plumage while giving voice to the peculiar chant directed to the rain gods. Although the effort is commendable in that the cuckoo is reputedly doing his earnest best to bring showers during the dry months, more and better results would be obtained by scheduling the performance either earlier or later in the season.

Order Strigiformes

Barn Owls: *Family Tytonidae*

Barn Owl:
Tyto alba pratincola (Bonaparte)

Description.—"Wings long, pointed, folding beyond tail; tail short, about half as long as wing; tarsus nearly twice as long as middle toe without claw, closely feathered above, slightly feathered and bristly below, as on toes; feathers of back of tarsus pointing upward; inner toe as long as middle toe; inner edge of middle claw pectinated. Facial disk pure white to tawny; under parts pure white to yellowish brown, dotted with triangular brown or blackish spots; upper parts yellowish brown, more or less overlaid with mottled gray, finely streaked with black and white; wings and tail with a few dusky bands. *Length:* 14.75–18.00, wing 12.50–14.00, tail 5.50–7.50, bill .90–1.00." (Bailey) *Nest:* In hollow trees and old buildings or on cliffs where eggs are usually laid on accumulated debris. *Eggs:* 3 to 6, white.

Distribution.—*General:* Breeds from Oregon, Colorado, Nebraska, Illinois, Great Lakes, and southern New England south to Central America. *In Oregon:* Uncommon permanent resident, likely to be found in any part of State but probably most common in western Oregon.

Cassin (1856) first credited the Barn Owl (Plates 57 and 58) to Oregon. Newberry (1857) found it an uncommon species in the Klamath Basin. Woodcock (1902) reported it from Scio, Haines (Baker County), and Corvallis. Finley (1906c) found it at Portland. Shelton (1917) listed specimens from Eugene, the mouth of the Siuslaw River, and Diamond Peak, the latter a surprising place to find this owl. We have seen specimens from Benton (4), Multnomah (2), and Umatilla (1) Counties and have seen it in Tillamook, Klamath, and Wallowa Counties. These records are scattered throughout the year. The Barn Owl undoubtedly breeds sparingly in this State. The only definite nesting records are Patterson's two dates of April 20 and 24, 1924, in southern Oregon. The birds seem to be most numerous in the southern Willamette Valley, where Gabrielson has repeatedly seen them in barns on farms south of Corvallis. The farmers there protect them as they value highly their services as rat and gopher catchers.

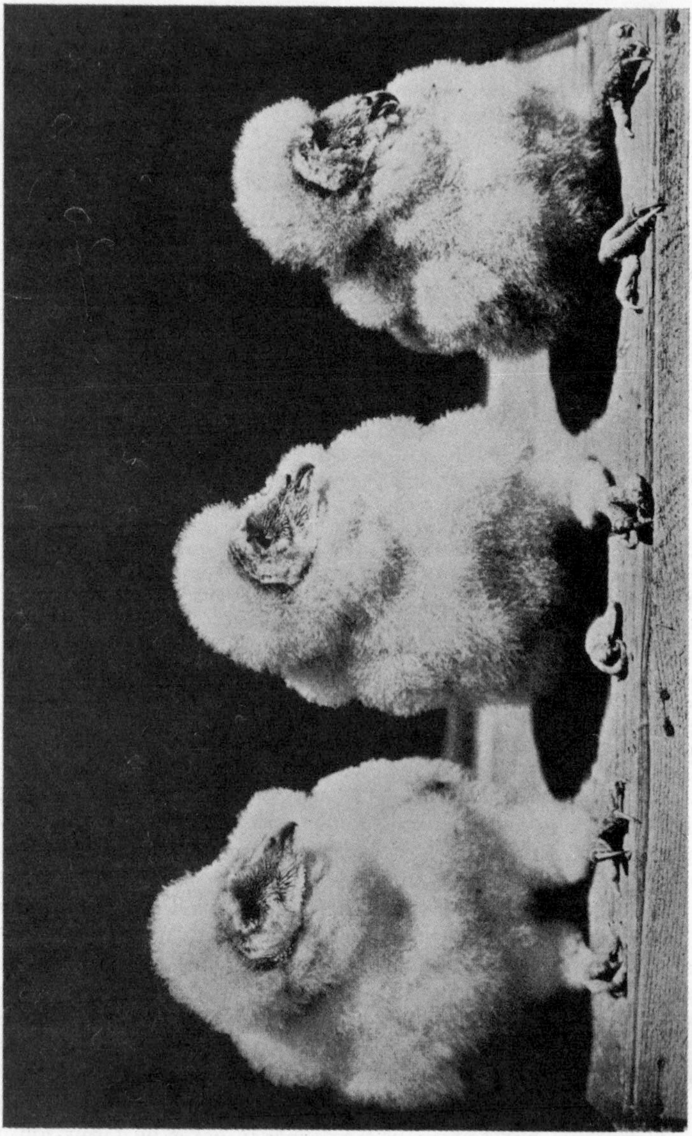

Plate 57. Downy young Barn Owls. (Photo by Wm. L. Finley and H. T. Bohlman.)

Plate 58. Barn Owl. (Photo by Wm. L. Finley and H. T. Bohlman.)

Typical Owls: *Family Strigidae*

MacFarlane's Screech Owl:
Otus asio macfarlanei (Brewster)

Description.—"Upper parts brownish or sooty gray with black shaft streaks and creamy stripes on scapulars and edge of wing; lower parts with heavy shaft streaks and numerous fine cross-lines of black; legs and feet buffy, slightly mottled with dusky. *Male:* wing 6.96, tail 3.80, bill from nostril .53. *Female:* wing 7.23, tail 3.85, bill from nostril .57." (Bailey) *Nest:* A hollow in a tree or an old woodpecker hole. *Eggs:* 4 to 5, white.

Distribution.—*General:* Permanent resident of southern British Columbia south to eastern Oregon, northeastern California, and southern Idaho. *In Oregon:* Regular permanent resident everywhere east of Cascades except in extreme southern Klamath County. (See Figure 7.)

The large MacFarlane's Screech Owl, with the pale colors of the smaller California Screech Owl (*O. a. bendirei*), is found throughout eastern Oregon where it behaves much as do Screech Owls elsewhere. It is almost strictly nocturnal, usually retiring to some hollow tree or dense thicket to spend the day, and is therefore difficult to see. Bendire (1892) mentioned a nest and eggs taken near Malheur Lake on April 16, 1877, the first record for this subspecies within the State. Miller (1904) reported it from Wheeler County, Peck (1911a) from northern Malheur County, and Walker (1917b) from near Maupin and from Moody's Ranch, both on the Deschutes River. Patterson took eggs May 1 and 14, 1928, in Klamath County. There are three specimens in the Biological Survey collection identified as this species, one taken at Wapinitia, Wasco County, June 17, 1897, one at McKenzie Bridge, Lane County, July 8, 1914,

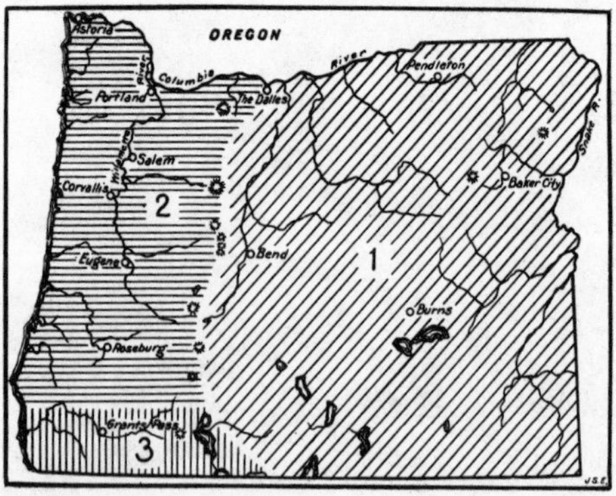

Figure 7.—Distribution of three forms of Screech Owls in Oregon: 1, MacFarlane's Screech Owl (*Otus asio macfarlanei*); 2, Brewster's Screech Owl (*O. a. brewsteri*); 3, California Screech Owl (*O. a. bendirei*).

and one at Ontario, Malheur County, September 24, 1920. We have 15 specimens in our collections, well scattered both geographically and seasonally through eastern Oregon, that are clearly this subspecies, which is therefore the Screech Owl found as a permanent resident in that part of the State.

Brewster's Screech Owl:
Otus asio brewsteri Ridgway

DESCRIPTION.—Slightly larger than the California Screech Owl with brownish or buffy markings on the upper parts and sometimes a buffy suffusion beneath. *Size:* Length, male 8.98, wing 6.65, tail 3.35, culmen .58. *Nest:* In hollow tree or old woodpecker hole. *Eggs:* 2 to 5, white.

DISTRIBUTION.—*General:* Western Oregon and extreme southern part of eastern Washington. *In Oregon:* Resident Screech Owl of western Oregon, the subspecies having been described from Salem by Ridgway in 1914. (See Figure 7.)

BREWSTER'S SCREECH OWL (Plate 59) is the most common small owl found in western Oregon, and all Screech Owl records in literature from western Oregon north of the Rogue River Valley now properly belong under this name. This owl is not seen by the average observer as frequently as the Great Horned Owl; but it is equally common, and its quavering call is one of the regular night sounds of spring and early summer. It is strictly nocturnal, seldom moving voluntarily from its hiding place in a hollow tree or in a dense foliage mass until well after sundown. There are exceptions to all rules, however, and occasionally we have found it hunting on rainy winter days. Once on the Columbia River bottoms a Screech Owl flew into a weed patch, remained a moment, and left again with a small bird in its claws. It vanished behind a clump of low, deformed willows where a little search revealed a likely looking hollow tree. Sure enough, the owl was there and was unceremoniously hauled out for inspection still clutching firmly a freshly killed song sparrow. The first record of the bird from this territory seems to have been by Ridgway (1879). Johnson (1880) listed it as a common breeding species of the Willamette Valley, and Bendire (1892) stated that eggs were taken in Marion County, July 13, 1883, and May 8, 1891. Since that time there have been numerous records published and many specimens taken.

California Screech Owl:
Otus asio bendirei (Brewster)

DESCRIPTION.—Smaller than *O. a. brewsteri* or *O. a. macfarlanei* and paler than the former, it is like other gray Screech Owls with heavy shaft streaks of black on both the back and breast feathers and has somewhat inconspicuous cross-lining below. (Adapted from Mrs. Bailey.) *Size:* Length 8.58, wing 6.35, tail 3.17, culmen .55. *Nest and eggs:* As for other forms.

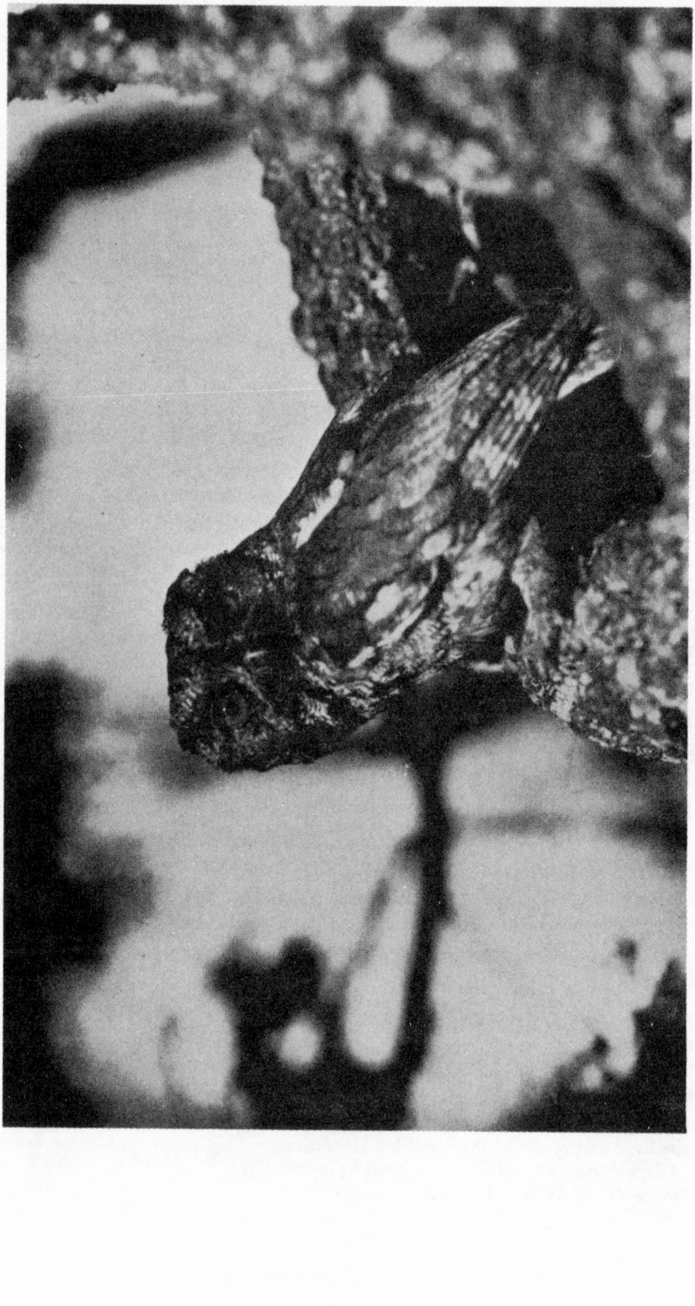

Plate 59. Brewster's Screech Owl. (Photo by Wm. L. Finley and H. T. Bohlman.)

DISTRIBUTION.—*General:* Over most of California and extreme southern Oregon. *In Oregon:* Found only in southern Klamath, Jackson, Josephine, and Curry Counties. (See Figure 7.)

THE REFERENCES by Prill (1895a) and Woodcock (1902) to the California Screech Owl refer to Brewster's Screech Owl (*O. a. brewsteri*), which has since been described from the Willamette Valley with Salem as the type locality. With these records assigned to the proper form, there are now no published records of the California Screech Owl for Oregon. We find, however, that the birds from the extreme southern edge of the State may properly be referred here. There are four specimens in Jewett's collections as follows: from Klamath County (no definite date); Eagle Point, Jackson County (March 21, 1925); Sixes, Curry County (July 23, 1920); and Agness, Curry County (September 18, 1919). Gabrielson has one bird taken near Grants Pass (September 12, 1934). These birds are undoubtedly closer to the California form than to the one described from the Willamette Valley.

Flammulated Screech Owl: *Otus flammeolus* (Kaup)

DESCRIPTION.—"*Adults: Toes entirely naked to extreme base;* ear tufts small; upper parts grayish, finely mottled and marked with blackish; stripes on sides of back yellowish brown or orange, white beneath the surface; under parts whitish, marked with broad mesial streaks and narrow cross-bars; face, throat, and upper parts sometimes washed with orange brown. *Young:* upper parts mottled transversely with gray and white, but without black streaking; under parts similarly but coarsely and regularly barred. *Wing:* 5.10–5.60, tail 2.60–3.00." (Bailey) *Nest:* In old woodpecker holes. *Eggs:* 3 to 4, white.

DISTRIBUTION.—*General:* From southern British Columbia, eastern Washington, and Idaho south to Central America. *In Oregon:* Extremely rare resident of eastern Oregon.

THE FLAMMULATED SCREECH OWL, a tiny bird no bigger than the Pygmy Owl, but with prominent ear tufts that are exact duplicates of those adorning its larger namesakes, is one of the least known of Oregon owls and is listed from the State on the basis of two specimens only. Jewett (1928c) recorded as the first Oregon specimen one taken at Old Fort Warner on Hart Mountain, eastern Lake County, May 25, 1927. We find an earlier skin, however, in the Biological Survey collection (No. 259602), taken June 9, 1916, at Homestead, Baker County, by H. H. Sheldon, a record of which has never been published. These are our only definite records.

Montana Horned Owl: *Bubo virginianus occidentalis* Stone

DESCRIPTION.—"*Adults:* Ear tufts blackish; iris bright yellow; ring around face black; throat white; rest of under parts white or buffy, mottled and barred with brownish; flanks buffy; upper parts mottled dark brown, light grayish, and buffy, *lighter colors prevailing;* wing quills and tail banded with dull brown; whole plumage irregularly varied with buffy, tawny, whitish, and dusky. *Young:* wing quills and tail feathers as in adult, rest of plumage dull buffy or ochraceous, everywhere barred with dusky." (Bailey) (See Plate 60, *A.*) *Size: Male*, wing 13.71, tail 8.34, culmen 1.06; *female*, wing 14.78, tail 9.04, culmen 1.18. *Nest:* A cave or hollow in the rocks, a hollow tree, or an old crow's or hawk's nest. *Eggs:* 2 to 3, white.

Distribution.—*General:* Breeds from Minnesota, South Dakota, Nebraska, and Kansas west to Nevada, southeastern Oregon, northeastern California, Wyoming, and Montana, north to central Alberta. *In Oregon:* Known as a winter bird.

This subspecies, the Montana Horned Owl, differs from the Pacific Horned Owl in having darker feet and legs, more or less heavily barred with black, and in lacking—or at least being less conspicuously marked with—the buffy wash, both above and below, that is found in the more common form. Horned Owls are of common occurrence in Oregon, where their fierce hunting calls are well known and where, particularly in eastern Oregon, they are a familiar sight, usually perched in the heavier branches of the cottonwoods and willows of the wooded stream bottoms. The historical records of the Horned Owl in eastern Oregon are so much involved in the shifting about from one subspecies to another that has characterized the treatment of this group that it is impossible to trace the various forms without having the actual specimens at hand. Out of some thirty Oregon specimens available for our study we have three skins from east of the Cascades, all winter birds, that are undoubtedly this form. They were taken at Hermiston (December 10, 1916), Burns (December 17, 1919), and Silver Lake (November 26, 1920). The first two are in Jewett's collection; the third, in Gabrielson's.

Northwestern Horned Owl:
Bubo virginianus lagophonus (Oberholser)

Description.—Similar to *B. v. occidentalis* but larger and with somewhat more contrast between the buffy and black-and-white markings of the under parts. *Size: Male*, wing 13.95, tail 8.76, culmen 1.07; *female*, wing 14.74, tail 9.31, culmen 1.14. *Nest and eggs:* Same as for other forms of Horned Owls.

Distribution.—*General:* Breeds in Idaho, northeastern Oregon, and eastern Washington north through British Columbia and interior Alaska. *In Oregon:* Breeds in Blue Mountain section and probably scatters out over eastern Oregon somewhat in winter.

We have three specimens of this big black-and-white looking subspecies, the Northwestern Horned Owl, all in the Jewett collection. They are from Pilot Rock (January 29), Wallowa (September 29), and Enterprise (October 28). In addition, we have at various times had other skins from this area that were of this form.

Plate 60, *A*. Young Montana Horned Owls. (Photo by Wm. L. and Irene Finley.)

Plate 60, *B*. Dusky Horned Owl. (Photo by Wm. L. and Irene Finley.)

Dusky Horned Owl:
Bubo virginianus saturatus Ridgway

Description.—"Like *B. v. pallescens*, but plumage extremely dark, face generally sooty brownish mixed with grayish white; plumage usually without excess of yellowish brown, sometimes with none." (Bailey) *Size:* Length (skins) 19–24, wing 13.58–15.08, tail 8.07–9.53, exposed culmen 1.50–1.65. *Nest:* Same as for other Horned Owls. *Eggs:* 2 to 4, white.

Distribution.—*General:* Resident of Pacific Coast region from southern Alaska to northern California. *In Oregon:* Permanent resident west of Cascades.

The first reference in Oregon ornithological literature that seems to refer to this subspecies, the Dusky Horned Owl (Plate 60, *B*), is Anthony's (1886) statement that it probably occurs in winter in Washington County. Prill (1891b) listed it as a breeding bird in Linn County, and there is a specimen in the Carnegie Museum that was taken at Beaverton, May 22, 1890. It is mentioned many times in the field notes of the Biological Survey and in our own notes. We have available for examination numerous specimens in our own collections and several belonging to others, and all skins seen from western Oregon clearly belong to this subspecies. In habit, voice, and behavior this dusky representative of the race does not differ appreciably from its paler-colored relative to the east. It is the same fierce and aggressive hunter, able and willing to kill chickens, turkeys, grouse, rabbits, squirrels, and even skunks, although it does not carry olfactory evidence of so frequent an association with the latter, as does the eastern bird.

Like others of its group, the Dusky Horned Owl nests early in the season, usually selecting an old hawk's or crow's nest for the home site. Egg-laying commences in late February or early March, and full sets have been taken in the early part of March. Braly has given us notes on one nest found near Salem on March 18 that contained a single young bird, which would indicate an exceptionally early laying period in that case. He also took a set of three well-incubated eggs on March 19, 1932, on Sauvies Island.

Pacific Horned Owl:
Bubo virginianus pacificus Cassin

Description.—Smallest of the forms found in eastern Oregon, much washed with buffy and brown on both the back and under parts; feet and legs white, or at most faintly buffy and slightly barred with blackish. *Size: Male*, wing 13.19, tail 8.02, culmen 1.02; *female*, wing 14.11, tail 8.60, culmen 1.07. *Nest and eggs:* Similar to those of other subspecies.

Distribution.—*General:* Most of California and eastern Oregon. *In Oregon:* Breeds in south-central Oregon.

Most of the eastern Oregon breeding birds, as well as many of the winter skins taken outside the Blue Mountains, are certainly closer to skins from

California than they are to *lagophonus* or *occidentalis*. We have numerous specimens from Burns, Malheur, Maupin, Gateway, and Cayuse that are almost identical with birds from Los Angeles. In addition to these there is a peculiar looking bird in Jewett's collection, taken at Hart Mountain on June 21, 1933, that seems referable only to this species, perhaps as a slightly albinistic individual. In color it is most like *subarcticus* of the north and *pallescens* of the southern border, falling somewhat between these two. It lacks entirely the dark black and white barring of *occidentalis* and has only a slight touch of the buffy wash associated with *pacificus*, although in size it corresponds to the latter.

Snowy Owl:
Nyctea nyctea (Linnaeus)

Description.—"Ear tufts rudimentary; ear openings small, without anterior flap, the two ears not distinctly different; tail not reaching beyond tips of longest under coverts; four outer quills emarginate; toes covered with long hair-like feathers, partly or wholly concealing the claws; bill nearly concealed by loral feathers. *Adult male:* body pure white, sometimes almost unspotted, but usually marked more or less with transverse spots or bars of slaty brown. *Adult female:* much darker, pure white only on face, throat, middle of breast and feet, the head spotted, and the rest of the body barred with dark brown. *Male:* length 20–23; wing 15.50–17.30, tail 9.00–9.70, bill 1. *Female:* length 23–27, wing 17.30–18.70, tail 9.70–10.30, bill 1.10." (Bailey) *Nest:* A slight depression in the ground, lined to some extent with feathers, moss, or lichen. *Eggs:* 5 to 7, white.

Distribution.—*General:* Circumpolar. Breeds on Arctic islands and on mainland of this continent, Yukon delta, central Mackenzie, central Keewatin, and northern Ungava, and migrates south sporadically to California, Texas, and Gulf States. *In Oregon:* Irregular winter visitor most frequently seen in eastern Oregon but occasionally appearing in western Oregon in November and December.

The Snowy Owl (Plate 61, *A*) was first reported for Oregon by Townsend (1839), who simply listed it as one of the species of that territory with no date. Bendire (Brewer 1875) reported one at Camp Harney, January 25, 1875, and a little later (Bendire 1877) listed it as "a rare winter visitor, observed on several occasions, but no specimens procured." Johnson (1880) stated it was a winter bird of the Willamette Valley, and Merrill (1897) reported: "In December, 1896, there was a general migration of Snowy Owls into northern Idaho, Oregon and Washington and dozens were killed." Woodcock (1902), in addition to references to some of the above records, reported that it was occasionally taken at Corvallis, Scio, Dayton, and Yaquina Bay. The Yaquina Bay record was from Bretherton, who considered it "a rare winter visitor, quite numerous in 1897." Walker (1924) stated it was common during the winter of 1916–17 at Netarts and Tillamook Bays, and from all the records available to us, it is evident that that winter and the following one witnessed the last flights that brought this great predator into Oregon in numbers. In almost every village and town in the northern part of eastern Oregon are

Plate 61, *A*. Snowy Owl. (Photo by Wm. L. and Irene Finley.)

Plate 61, *B*. Young Northern Spotted Owl. (Photo by Wm. L. and Irene Finley.)

mounted specimens taken in those winters. There are two birds in the Jewett collection and two in Gabrielson's collection, all taken in Umatilla County in 1916–17 and 1918. Since that time there have been sporadic newspaper references and reports of individual birds taken in various parts of the State. The last actual skin to come into the hands of either author was taken at Seaside, November 29, 1929, and is now in Jewett's collection.

This white terror of the north is not only the most beautiful but also the most conspicuous of all owls found in the State. Its habit of daylight hunting and its preference for open country cause it to be the victim of the first hunter to get within range, and few Snowy Owls that reach the settled sections of the State live to return to their northern homes. While in Oregon, they prey chiefly upon jack rabbits but are powerful enough to successfully attack China Pheasants, grouse, ducks, or even barnyard fowl when driven by hunger to hunt in the dooryards for something edible.

Rocky Mountain Pigmy Owl:
Glaucidium gnoma pinicola Nelson

Description.—Like the California Pygmy Owl, but the browns entirely replaced by gray. "Upper parts *grayish* brown; head *specked* and tail *barred* with white; under parts white, streaked with brown. Eyes lemon yellow; bill and feet dull greenish yellow." (Bailey 1928.) *Size:* About same as *G. g. californicum*. *Nest:* Old woodpecker holes. *Eggs:* Usually 4, white.

Distribution.—*General:* Rocky Mountain region from Montana, Idaho, and Washington south to Mexican line. *In Oregon:* Permanent resident of Blue Mountains, including Wallowa, Union, Baker, Grant, and Umatilla Counties, and of northern Malheur and Harney, eastern Crook, and southern Gilliam and Morrow Counties. (See Figure 8.)

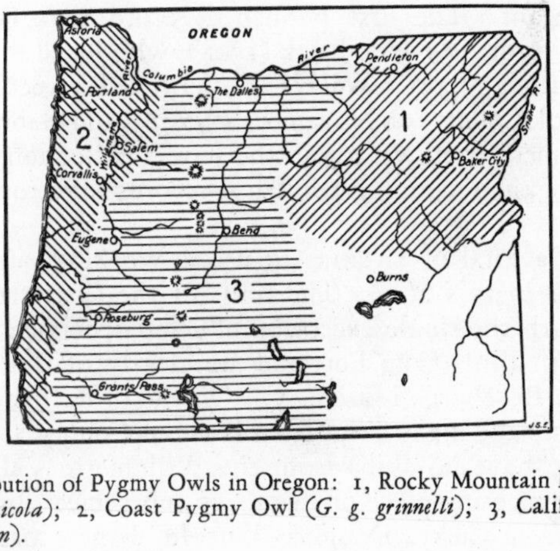

Figure 8.—Distribution of Pygmy Owls in Oregon: 1, Rocky Mountain Pygmy Owl (*Glaucidium gnoma pinicola*); 2, Coast Pygmy Owl (*G. g. grinnelli*); 3, California Pygmy Owl (*G. g. californicum*).

THE LITTLE GRAY Rocky Mountain Pygmy Owl is easily distinguished from the browner forms found to the west, as it is entirely lacking in any brown wash on the plumage. We regard it as rather rare in this State, although there are seven Oregon specimens available for examination. Like the other races, owls of this species are usually seen sitting motionless on a limb at the top of a small tree. Though more or less diurnal in habit, they are most frequently seen on cloudy days or late in the afternoon. In habits and general behavior, they do not differ materially from the better-known subspecies.

The only published reference to this little owl as an Oregon bird was Gabrielson's (1924a) recording of Jewett's Wallowa County specimen, taken in the town of Wallowa, February 28, 1919, on the first field trip the writers made together. Bendire (1877), however, recorded under the name *G. g. californicum* a bird taken at Camp Harney in 1875 that should be referred to this subspecies as it is now understood.

Coast Pigmy Owl:
Glaucidium gnoma grinnelli Ridgway

DESCRIPTION.—Like the California Pygmy Owl but much browner, particularly on the back. *Size:* About size of *G. g. californicum*. *Nest:* Old woodpecker holes or other excavations in stumps and trees. *Eggs:* About 4, white.

DISTRIBUTION.—*General:* Pacific Coast district from southeastern Alaska to Monterey, California, and east to interior valleys. *In Oregon:* Found in all coast counties and coast mountains. (See Figure 8.)

THE RECORDS of the various subspecies of these little owls in Oregon are much confused. Townsend (1839) listed it as "found in the territory of Oregon," but the lack of locality records makes it impossible to say which subspecies is meant. The first published record that is undoubtedly referable to this form is by Woodcock (1902), who listed it from Yaquina Bay on Bretherton's report. Walker (1924) listed a specimen taken at Blaine, Tillamook County, on November 12, 1919, and Gabrielson (1924a) listed two specimens from Netarts in the Jewett collection. So far as we are able to learn, the remaining published records refer to the California Pygmy Owl.

We have had a total of 41 skins to use in working out the range of these little owls in this State. The birds of the Coast Mountains and coastal strip, with the single exception of a fall specimen from Netarts, are of this form. Birds from Portland are clearly of this form, as is a single bird from Roseburg (March 25). On the other hand, late March birds from Eugene and many skins from Douglas County are clearly *G. g. californicum*. We have no skins from the Willamette Valley, which is undoubtedly the meeting place of these two subspecies. In our own collections, skins from Curry, Douglas, Lincoln, Lane (coast slope), and

Tillamook Counties are of this subspecies, and birds seen by Jewett at various times from Portland are also of this form. From the skins available, we conclude that the Coast Pygmy Owl is the breeding form inland to the inner base of the Coast Ranges and merges with *californicum* in the Willamette and Umpqua Valleys.

California Pigmy Owl:
Glaucidium gnoma californicum Sclater

Description.—"*Adults:* Very small, under parts white, thickly streaked with dark brown; sides brownish, indistinctly spotted with lighter; *upper parts dark, slaty gray, olive brown,* or *dark rusty brown;* head specked with white; tail blackish or brownish, *barred with white. Young:* like adult, but top of head plain gray. *Length:* 6.50–7.50, wing 3.40–4.00, tail 2.40–2.80." (Bailey) *Nest:* In old woodpecker holes. *Eggs:* 4 to 6, white.

Distribution.—*General:* California, except humid coast, through central Oregon and Washington to British Columbia. *In Oregon:* Permanent resident of Cascades, wooded parts of Klamath and Lake Counties, and Rogue River Valley extending into Umpqua and Willamette Valleys where it passes into the coast form. (See Figure 8.)

Most of the early Oregon records apply to the California Pygmy Owl. Newberry (1857) reported it as rare in the Cascades, and Bendire (1892) reported nesting birds from Corvallis that probably refer to this form. Since that time there have been numerous references to Pygmy Owls, mostly from territory occupied by this form. We have numerous specimens, including a pair of birds and six eggs taken from an old woodpecker hole in an aspen tree at Fort Klamath on May 21, 1930. The eggs are now in Braly's collection and the skins in Jewett's. In addition, we have skins that are strictly comparable to these breeding birds from Gold Hill (March 24), the Umpqua Valley, Oakland (December 6, January 8, February 24), Dillard (December 13), Ten-mile (Douglas County, November 2), and Eugene (March 17). There is also an adult fall bird (September 16) from Netarts in the Jewett collection that is undoubtedly of this form and can only be considered a straggler that has wandered from the normal range of the race. Skins from Warner Valley (February 10) and Redmond (January 13) seem to be intermediate between this and *G. g. pinicola* but closer to *californicum.*

These little owls generally hide in the foliage of evergreen trees so that they are difficult to detect. As a matter of fact they are much more common than the casual observer would expect, and their peculiar call notes are a familiar sound in the twilight hours. They are usually observed when by accident they select a conspicuous perch, such as a telephone pole, the topmost branch of a thick shrub, or the spire-pointed tip of some small conifer where the tiny owls appear as conspicuous spots in the gathering twilight.

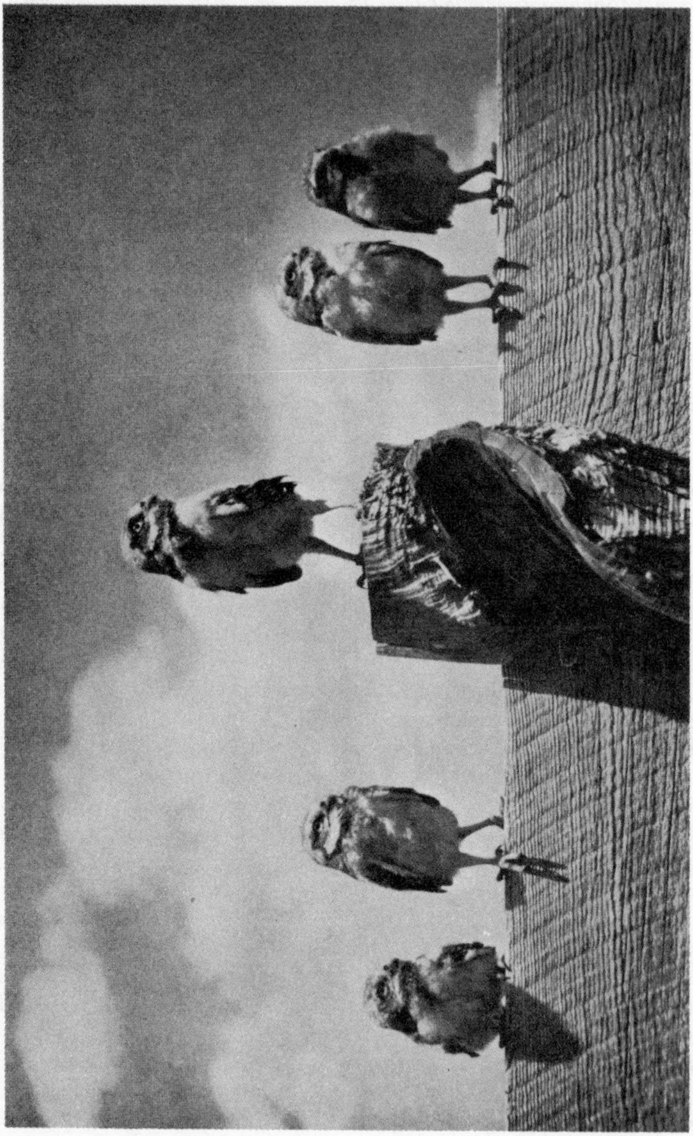

Plate 62. Young Western Burrowing Owls. (Photo by Wm. L. Finley and H. T. Bohlman.)

Western Burrowing Owl:
Speotyto cunicularia hypugaea (Bonaparte)

Description.—"Tail only about half as long as wing; tarsus more than twice as long as middle toe, scantily feathered in front, bare behind; toes bristly. *Adults:* Upper parts dull earth brown, spotted and barred with white and buffy; under parts mainly buffy barred with brown. *Young:* under parts mainly buffy, unmarked; upper parts plain brown except wings and tail, which are as in adults [Plate 62]. *Length:* 9-11, wing 5.80-7.20, tail 3.15-3.50, bill .55-.60." (Bailey) *Nest:* Usually an old rodent burrow or similar excavation. *Eggs:* 6 to 11, white.

Distribution.—*General:* Breeds from Pacific Coast east to Minnesota and Iowa and from British Columbia and Manitoba south to Central America. *In Oregon:* Breeds throughout eastern Oregon, except in higher mountains, and in Rogue River Valley. Straggler only elsewhere in western Oregon. Largely migratory in eastern Oregon, although a few individuals may remain through winter.

The Western Burrowing Owl, a curiously long-legged little bird, is a familiar sight in the lower sections of eastern Oregon as well as in the pasture lands of the Rogue River Valley. Often it may be seen perched on the fence posts or sitting by the open mouth of an old rodent burrow. It was first reported for Oregon by Townsend (1839). Newberry (1857), Cassin (1856), Suckley (1860), and Bendire (1875) all found it in eastern Oregon, and many subsequent writers have listed it from various places there. There are many references to it in the field notes of Biological Survey members who have worked eastern Oregon, and these, combined with our own material, show it to be present in every county east of the Cascades but most abundant in Wasco, Morrow, Umatilla, Malheur, Harney, and Lake Counties. Although a few individuals may remain during the winter, it is largely migratory in eastern Oregon, where it is present from April (earliest date, March 20, Baker County) to October (latest date, October 31, Wasco County).

Woodcock (1902) reported four specimens from Corvallis and stated on the authority of Prill that the species bred in Linn County, and Shelton (1917) recorded it as found sparingly in Lane County and considered it a probable resident. It is a regular inhabitant of the prairie district north and east of Medford, Jackson County, and a more or less irregular straggler to the Willamette Valley, where three birds in Jewett's collection from the Corvallis Game Farm were taken on October 19, November 1, and January 10.

The eggs are laid in April and early May in the old burrows of ground squirrels and other digging rodents. We find the following egg dates in our own notes and those of Braly: April 16 (4 eggs), May 11 (5 young and 2 addled eggs), May 11 (8 eggs), and June 20 (large young). One nest excavated by Jewett on April 11, 1932, near Boardman, contained no eggs as yet but four kangaroo rats, two pocket mice, two lizards, and one horned toad, all freshly killed. Patterson reported nests in Jackson County, April 16, and May 4, 12, and 18, 1925.

Northern Spotted Owl:
Strix occidentalis caurina (Merriam)

Description.—Upper parts dark brown, head and neck spotted with round white spots, wing quills spotted with pale brown and white and slightly tipped with whitish; tail banded, under parts whitish, barred and spotted with brown. (Adapted from Mrs. Bailey.) *Size:* Length 16–19, wing 12–13, tail 8–9. *Nest:* In a hollow tree or crevice in a cliff. *Eggs:* 2 to 3, white.

Distribution.—*General:* Permanent resident from British Columbia to San Francisco Bay, California. *In Oregon:* Permanent resident west of Cascades.

The Northern Spotted Owl (Frontispiece and Plate 61, *B*), a strictly nocturnal resident of the thick fir and spruce forests, is rarely seen except by accident, and little is known regarding its abundance or habits in Oregon. Jewett (1916b) published the first record for the State, an adult male taken at Netarts April 12, 1914. Shelton (1917) listed a specimen in the University of Oregon collection. Prill (1928) recorded one taken at Scio November 1, 1924. In 1929, we published the record of one taken near Oswego, November 15, 1914, by E. F. Gonty and referred to two specimens without data in the Portland City Museum, presumably taken near Portland (Jewett and Gabrielson 1929). A specimen taken November 9, 1914, by W. H. Riddle at Ocean View is now in Jewett's collection. W. E. Sherwood located a nest containing young near Trail, Jackson County, in June 1925. He kept several of these young birds as pets, taking numerous photographs of them, and collected at least one of the birds, which went into the Dr. L. C. Sanford collection. In addition to these known specimens, there are a few sight records by competent observers. In the migration reports to the Biological Survey, Overton Dowell, Jr., reported seeing one at Mercer, April 25, 1920, and Vernon Bailey (field notes) saw one at Eugene between June 15 and 20, 1914. Gabrielson saw a single bird near Corvallis on December 27, 1918. It swooped at him while he was "squeaking" to attract the attention of some small birds. These notes are given in detail to show how little we know about this bird that is probably much more common than these records indicate.

Great Gray Owl:
Scotiaptex nebulosa nebulosa (Forster)

Description.—"Ear tufts wanting; ear openings large, with conspicuous anterior flap, the two ears strikingly different; bill and feet small, bill inconspicuous among facial feathers; toes entirely covered with feathers; eyes yellow, eye ring black; face with concentric rings of gray and dark brown; upper parts sooty, mottled with gray and blackish; wing quills and tail banded; under parts mixed sooty and whitish, with irregular sooty streaking; flanks and legs barred. *Length:* 25–30, extent 54–60, wing about 16–18, tail 11.00–12.50." (Bailey) *Nest:* A bulky nest of sticks, lined with feathers and moss. *Eggs:* 2 to 4, white.

Distribution.—*General:* Breeds in Hudsonian and Canadian Zone from tree limit in Alaska and Mackenzie south to central California, Montana, Idaho, and Ontario, south in winter to northern United States. *In Oregon:* Rare permanent resident.

Townsend (1839) listed the Great Gray Owl for Oregon. Newberry (1857) found it in the Cascade Mountains, Deschutes Basin, and along the Columbia River. Shelton (1917) reported finding the remains of one at a hunter's cabin near Diamond Peak, Johnson (1880) included it in his list of birds from various points in the Willamette Valley, and there is a record of one killed near Milwaukie by Guy Stryker (Jewett and Gabrielson 1929). There are a number of mounted specimens in Oregon, all without adequate data but reported killed close to the area where the birds are now located. Such specimens have been seen at Medford, Bear Valley (Grant County), Pendleton, and Eugene. In addition to these, there are five specimens in the Jewett collection, from Sherwood (December 11, 1914), Baker (November 10, 1915), Bear Valley (Grant County, October 18, 1922), Marr Flat (Wallowa County, September 13, 1930), and Hardman (Morrow County, August 14, 1932). Other than these records little is known about the Great Gray Owl as an Oregon bird. It is shot by every hunter who comes within range, a circumstance that is true of all other large owls and that undoubtedly contributes materially to their scarcity.

Long-eared Owl:
Asio wilsonianus (Lesson)

Description.—"Ear tufts dark brown, conspicuous; face mainly yellowish brown; under parts whitish and yellowish, with dark brown shaft streaks and horizontal bars on belly; flanks yellowish brown, unspotted; upper parts mottled gray, tawny, and blackish; wings and tail barred. *Length:* 13–16, wing 11.50–12.00, tail 6.00–6.20, bill .65." (Bailey) *Nest:* Usually an old crow's or magpie's or hawk's nest, lined with grass, leaves, etc. *Eggs:* 3 to 6, white.

Distribution.—*General:* Breeds from British Columbia, Mackenzie, Ontario, Quebec, and Newfoundland south to southern California, Texas, Arkansas, and Virginia. Winters from southern Canada to central Mexico. *In Oregon:* Common summer resident of eastern Oregon, less common in winter. Winters sparingly in western Oregon and possibly breeds occasionally.

To know the Long-eared Owl and its wonderful variety of hisses, catcalls, and clatterings, one must go to the willow-bordered streams of eastern Oregon. Since Townsend (1839) listed it as an Oregon bird, many observers have reported it from that part of the State, including Bendire (1877), who took a number of sets of eggs in the Harney Valley. It makes its home in the abandoned nests of crows, magpies, or hawks, which it repairs, sometimes rather sketchily, before depositing its set of pure white eggs. The breeding season falls in late April and early May. April 4 and May 15 are the extreme dates published by others or noted by us. The young (Plate 63), like those of all other owls, remain in the nest for a comparatively long period and are fed a variety of small animals and occasionally birds by the industrious parents. When an intruder approaches the nest the adults usually show great concern and produce an astonishing variety of noises. The bills are snapped rapidly, and a medley of catcalls, hisses, and throaty *wuk-wuk* notes pours forth. The anxious parents may dive at the intruder or sit on a nearby branch, with feathers erect, scolding the disturber and threatening dire things.

This owl is found sparingly in winter in western Oregon. Woodcock (1902) listed a number of specimens and localities, and Shelton (1917) recorded it for Lane County. Pope reported taking eggs in 1894, presumably near Sheridan, to Woodcock (1902), the only indication we have that the species might breed in western Oregon.

In the fall and winter, numbers of these Long-eared Owls, together with a few Short-eared Owls, often roost in willow thickets where the mouse population furnishes an adequate diet. On November 17, 1930, on the Malheur River, we flushed more than a dozen from a single willow clump, the largest congregation of this species yet seen. All sorts of mice with which the willow bottoms and sage-coated slopes abound are grist to the digestive mill of this medium-sized owl that is in fact one of the most valuable mousers we have in the State and should be rigidly protected. Contrary to popular belief, it does little or no harm to birds and poultry.

Short-eared Owl:
Asio flammeus flammeus (Pontoppidan)

DESCRIPTION.—"*Adults:* Ear tufts inconspicuous; eyes with black ring and white eyebrows; body varying from yellowish brown to buffy white, conspicuously streaked with dark brown; wings and tail irregularly banded with dark brown and buffy or yellowish brown. *Young:* face brownish black, under parts plain dull buffy, tinged with gray in front; upper parts dark brown, the feathers tipped with yellowish brown. *Length:* 13.80–16.75, wing 11.80–13.00, tail 5.80–6.10, bill .60–.65." (Bailey) *Nest:* A loose mass of sticks and grass on the ground. *Eggs:* 4 to 7, white.

DISTRIBUTION.—*General:* Breeds from Alaska, Mackenzie, northern Quebec, and Greenland south to California, Colorado, Missouri, Great Lakes, and New Jersey. Winters from British Columbia and northern United States south to West Indies and Central America. *In Oregon:* Regular permanent resident, whose numbers increase during winter, when the birds sometimes congregate in considerable numbers in small areas.

THE SHORT-EARED OWL was first reported from Oregon by Townsend (1839), and Newberry (1857) found it common about the Klamath Lakes and in the Deschutes Basin. It prefers the great grassy flats and meadows of eastern Oregon, where an abundant supply of mice can usually be found. One or the other of us has noted winter concentrations in Malheur River

Plate 63, *A*. Downy young Long-eared Owls. (Photo by Ira N. Gabrielson.)

Plate 63, *B*. Young Long-eared Owl. (Photo by Wm. L. Finley and H. T. Bohlman.)

Valley, the Grande Ronde Valley, and in the Klamath Basin. Except during these gatherings, this owl is only occasionally seen by the average observer, even though it is widely distributed in the State. It has been reported breeding in Harney Valley (Bendire 1877), Malheur and Klamath Lakes (Cantwell, Biological Survey files), Umatilla County (Lewis, Biological Survey files), and Morrow County (Jewett) in eastern Oregon. For a nest it gathers together a nondescript mass of material on the ground and there lays its eggs.

In western Oregon it is much less common and is most often noted in the southern Willamette Valley, between Corvallis and Eugene, and along the Columbia in the vicinity of Portland. Scattered individuals have been recorded for many localities in that part of the State, where an observer may expect to see an occasional wintering bird almost anywhere. In the winter of 1934–35, a considerable flight of these owls arrived on Sauvies Island and remained throughout the winter. At various times we saw from 6 to 10 birds in a single morning.

This owl is a day-flying bird to some extent. On cloudy days it is frequently seen flying slowly about over the marshlands with steady vigorous sweeps of the long wings, and it often starts its hunting activities before sundown. Even when flushed in bright sunlight, it is able to see its way about without a great deal of difficulty. One stomach taken at Enterprise, May 31, 1928, contained three young *Microtus*, just about what one would expect, considering the foraging habits of the bird.

Richardson's Owl:
Cryptoglaux funerea richardsoni (Bonaparte)

Description.—"*Adults:* Eye ring black, face whitish; under parts gray, heavily blotched with dark brown across breast and streaked with dark brown on belly; upper parts dark brown, spotted with white; flanks and feet usually ***buffy, more or less spotted*** with brown; under tail coverts ***striped with brown***. *Young:* face blackish, eyebrows and malar streak white in sharp contrast; wings and tail like adult; body plain seal brown except for yellowish brown on belly and flanks; flanks more or less spotted with brown. *Length:* 9–12, wing 6.60–7.40, tail 4.10–4.70." (Bailey) *Nest:* In holes in trees. *Eggs:* 3 to 6, white.

Distribution.—*General:* Breeds from tree limit south to northern parts of British Columbia, Alberta, Manitoba, and Nova Scotia. Winters south to United States boundary and casually farther south. *In Oregon:* Rare winter straggler from the north.

Audubon (1838), Townsend (1839), Cassin (Cassin 1856; Baird, Cassin, and Lawrence 1858), and Bendire (1892) all listed Richardson's Owl. The first three references were based on Townsend's statement that it was "found in the territory of Oregon," and Bendire said it was not rare at Camp Harney. The only definite record since Bendire's work is a specimen now in the Biological Survey collection (No. 184845) that was taken at Fort Klamath, March 21, 1902, by B. S. Cunningham.

Saw-whet Owl:
Cryptoglaux acadica acadica (Gmelin)

Description.—"*Adults:* Eye ring whitish, face streaked with dark brown; ***under parts white, streaked vertically with reddish brown,*** most thickly on breast; upper parts olive brown, marked with white, finely streaked on head, and coarsely streaked or spotted on back, wings, and tail; ***feet plain white or buffy.*** *Young:* face blackish, in sharp contrast to white eyebrows and white malar streak; upper parts and breast plain dark seal brown; wings and tail as in adult; belly yellowish brown. *Length:* 7.25–8.50, wing 5.25–5.90, tail 2.80–3.25." (Bailey) *Nest:* A deserted woodpecker hole, old squirrel nest, or hollow tree. *Eggs:* 3 to 7, white.

Distribution.—*General:* Breeds from southern Alaska, British Columbia, Alberta, Manitoba, Quebec, and Nova Scotia south to California, Mexico, Nebraska, the Great Lake States, and Maryland. Winters through most of breeding range and south to Gulf of Georgia. *In Oregon:* Uncommon but widely distributed resident.

Although the little Saw-whet Owl is not common anywhere in Oregon, it has been recorded throughout the State since Townsend's time. Most of the reports have been of actual specimens taken, including one at The Dalles (Cooper and Suckley 1860), several specimens at Camp Harney (Bendire 1877), one in the Willamette Valley (Johnson 1880), one at Fort Klamath (Merrill 1888), specimens at Corvallis (Woodcock 1902), and a nest reported from Camp Harney, May 2, 1881 (Bendire 1892). There is one skin in the Biological Survey collection from Malheur County (October 1916), and there are three in the Overton Dowell, Jr., collection taken in Lane County (June 1, November 3, and December 12). In addition to the above, we have or have seen skins from Douglas, Umatilla, Malheur, Benton, Tillamook, Multnomah, and Jackson Counties. This little owl is so small and usually so inconspicuous when perched in the heart of a dense tree that it can easily be passed by, something that no doubt frequently occurs.

Order Caprimulgiformes

Goatsuckers: *Family Caprimulgidae*

Nuttall's Poor-will: *Phalaenoptilus nuttalli nuttalli* (Audubon)

DESCRIPTION.—"*Adult male:* Plumage of upper parts moth-like, soft, and velvety, finely mottled ***grayish brown*** with sharply contrasting velvety black bars and sagittate markings; tail with all but middle feathers tipped with white; ***sides of head and chin black***, white throat patch bordered by black below; rest of under parts barred except for plain buffy under tail coverts. *Adult female:* similar, but with white tips to tail feathers narrower. *Young:* upper parts more silvery gray mixed with rusty; black markings smaller and less distinct; white of throat and tail restricted and tinged with buffy. *Wing:* 5.78, tail 3.67." (Bailey) *Nest:* Eggs laid on bare ground. *Eggs:* 2, pure white or slightly marked (Plate 64, *A*).

DISTRIBUTION.—*General:* Breeds from southeastern British Columbia, western North Dakota, and western Iowa south to central Texas, Arizona, and Mexico. *In Oregon:* Summer resident and breeding species in sage lands of eastern Oregon. One straggler reported from western Oregon.

SUCKLEY (Cooper and Suckley 1860) found Nuttall's Poor-will at Fort Dalles. Bendire (1877) reported it rare at Camp Harney. Woodcock (1902) listed it from Baker County on Anthony's report; Miller (1904) recorded it from Wheeler County; Peck (1911a) included it from northern Malheur County; and Walker (1917b) recorded it from Wasco and Sherman Counties. Walker (1934a) also reported a specimen from Tillamook County taken October 27, 1933, the only record we know of for western Oregon. Although these are all of the published records for this little-known bird, the files of the Biological Survey contain many manuscript notes on its occurrence in practically every county in eastern Oregon. It is present from May (earliest date, May 12, Lake County) to September (latest date, October 6, Wasco County).

Our own notes show it to be a widely distributed species that is generally overlooked because of its nocturnal habits. Abundant as it is in places, we have seldom flushed it in the daytime but have had to wait until sundown stirred the birds into activity before we could find them. On one such rare occasion Dr. W. B. Bell and the writers, while tramping across the slopes of Hart Mountain on June 14, 1926, flushed a bird from two eggs laid on the bare ground under a sage bush. So far as we can learn, this is the only nest of the species actually discovered in Oregon.

Few Oregonians are acquainted with this bird by sight, and those who are, know it as a pair of shining eyes that gleam from the roadway in the lights of a car or as a ghostly shape that flits for an instant across the beam from those same headlights. More people know it by its rapid, oft-repeated call, *poor-will, poor-will*, whistled endlessly from the vantage point of some hillside on a June evening. Although the unseen musician is easily heard, an attempt to locate the singer quickly reveals the ventriloquial character of the note. This, combined with a color that matches the surroundings so exactly, makes the attempt to find it a more or less hopeless one that succeeds only by accident.

Dusky Poor-will:
Phalaenoptilus nuttalli californicus Ridgway

Description.—"Similar to *nuttallii* but much darker; middle of crown largely blackish; hind neck extensively marked with black, back dull blackish gray or wood brown instead of light brown." (Bailey) *Size:* About same as Nuttall's Poorwill. *Nest and eggs:* Identical with previous subspecies.

Distribution.—*General:* From southern Oregon south to Lower California. *In Oregon:* Rare summer resident of chaparral lands bordering Rogue River Valley in Jackson County.

The status of the Dusky Poor-will as an Oregon bird rests on a single specimen (Gabrielson Coll. No. 1884) taken at Brownsboro, Jackson County, on June 21, 1929, that is strictly comparable to birds from Sonoma County, California, although slightly darker than several other California specimens. On numerous dates between May 21 and September 17, Gabrielson has heard poor-wills calling in this locality and several times has flushed birds when driving a car through the district at night. The bird is undoubtedly a regular summer resident of this area in eastern Jackson County and probably of other parts of the Rogue River Valley. It is difficult to collect in the dense brush of the territory it frequents and consequently escapes detection except under favorable circumstances.

Pacific Nighthawk:
Chordeiles minor hesperis Grinnell

Description.—"Entire upper parts black, mottled with gray and marked with buffy brown; outer tail feathers crossed near the tip by a white band; a broad band of white across throat; breast black, speckled with gray; *wings long and narrow crossed by a broad white bar;* tail forked. Bill very small, black; feet flesh-color. *Female:* Throat-band buff, no white bar on tail." (Hoffman 1927.) *Size:* 9–10, wing 7.30–8.20, tail 4.10–4.60. *Nest:* None, eggs laid on bare ground or on roofs of buildings. *Eggs:* 2, creamy, olive, or buff, heavily spotted or blotched with black, gray, and lavender.

Distribution.—*General:* Breeds from southeastern British Columbia south to northern California and in Sierra Nevada Mountains south to southern California. Winters southward. *In Oregon:* Abundant summer resident.

THE EARLY RECORDS of the Pacific Nighthawk (Plate 64, *B*) are all under the name Western Nighthawk, as the present subspecies was not recognized and named until 1905. The bird was first recorded from Oregon by Newberry (1857) and later by Suckley (Cooper and Suckley 1860). All the earlier naturalists mentioned it, and Rockwell (1878) recorded eggs from St. Helens. It has since been listed by many others and is known as an abundant summer resident of all parts of the State. It is perhaps the latest migrant to arrive in Oregon. For several years, a pair that nested on Gabrielson's place in East Portland appeared for the first time on June 3, and our earliest records for the State are about June 1 each year (earliest date, May 24, Harney County; latest, September 23, Klamath County). The eggs are laid in late June, numerous Oregon sets having been taken between June 20 and July 10. No nest is built; the eggs are placed on the bare ground or occasionally on tarred and gravelly roofs.

The aerial evolutions of the "bull bat" are a familiar sight of the long summer evenings. They include not only the twisting and turning carried on in search of food but also the nose dives indulged in at irregular intervals. One watching them circling and wheeling over the treetops, opening their capacious mouths and scooping in luckless insects as they dart through the swarms of gnats, midges, flying ants, and similar insects, will see a bird suddenly turn straight downward toward the earth, ending the dive in a quick upturn that sends it shooting skyward to the accompaniment of a sharp "whizzing boom" caused by the sudden change of angle of the wing feathers.

Plate 64, *A*. Nest and eggs of Nuttall's Poor-will. (Photo by Alex Walker.)

Plate 64, *B*. Pacific Nighthawk. (Photo by Wm. L. and Irene Finley.)

Order Micropodiformes

Swifts: *Family Micropodidae*

Black Swift:
Nephoecetes niger borealis (Kennerly)

Description.—"Tail slightly forked; tarsus and toes naked, the hind toe pointing backward. *Adults:* dusky or blackish, lighter on head and neck, the forehead hoary, a velvety black area in front of eye. *Young:* similar, but feathers tipped with whitish. *Length:* 7.00–7.50, wing 6.50–7.50, tail 2.30–3.00." (Bailey) *Nest:* On cliffs, built of straw, etc. *Eggs:* 5, white.

Distribution.—*General:* Breeds from southeastern Alaska and southern Colorado south to southern Mexico. Winters southward. *In Oregon:* Known only as rare straggler.

One of the mysteries of Oregon ornithology is the absence of the Black Swift from the State. It is known to breed in both California and Washington but so far has escaped detection in Oregon except for a single specimen picked up dead in a field near Albany, September 22, 1924, and sent to Oregon State College. It is now in the collection of that institution and was recorded by Miss Florence Hague (1925) as the first Oregon specimen. These swifts undoubtedly pass over Oregon regularly during migration flights, but apparently they make long journeys, as the above specimen is the only one ever seen within the State, unless the swifts noted by Bretherton in September 1898 at Cape Foulweather were of this species, as he suspected. It is peculiar that they pass over the intricate system of canyons and mountains of western Oregon entirely, only to nest in apparently exactly similar places farther north.

Vaux's Swift:
Chaetura vauxi (Townsend)

Description.—"Upper parts sooty brown, lighter on rump and tail; tail tipped with spines; under parts gray, lighter on throat. *Length:* 4.15–4.50, wing 4.30–4.75, tail (including spines) 1.50–1.90." (Bailey) *Nest:* Of small twigs, glued together and fastened to the inside of a hollow tree or chimney. *Eggs:* 3 to 5, white.

Distribution.—*General:* Breeds from southeastern Alaska, central British Columbia, and Montana south to central California and Nevada. Winters in Central America. *In Oregon:* Regular but not common summer resident and breeding bird of western Oregon, including Cascade Range, and of the Blue Mountain area.

Vaux's Swift was first described by Townsend (1839) from specimens taken along the Columbia near Fort Vancouver, Washington, where it is still fairly common, and since then numerous ornithologists have mentioned it. It is much more common in Oregon in the Cascades and the valleys westward than in the eastern half of the State, although it occurs regularly in smaller numbers in the Blue Mountains, particularly in the Wallowa Range. It arrives in early May (earliest date, April 27, Tillamook County) and remains until September (latest date, September 22, Benton County). It usually nests in hollow trees, but is repeatedly found nesting in chimneys after the fashion of its eastern relative, the Chimney Swift. Nests have been found in many localities in western Oregon. In migration it sometimes gathers in huge flocks, one of which roosted for several years in a greenhouse chimney in East Portland. The sight of this company of rapidly moving birds circling about the chimney like a huge whirlpool, with the birds in the vortex dropping like plummets into the chimney, excited much interest among local bird lovers who made many trips to watch the performance.

Vaux's Swift is a swift, strong flier, its oarlike wings sending the slender body through the air at astonishing speed. Often the bird appears to work the wings alternately, and again, in orthodox fashion. Its speed far surpasses that of the swallows with which it often associates in migration, enabling the swift to dart past the swallows with no apparent effort.

White-throated Swift:
Aeronautes saxatalis saxatalis (Woodhouse)

Description.—"Tail about one half as long as wing, forked, with stiffish and narrowed but not spiny feathers; tarsus and part of toes feathered; hind toe directed either forward or to the side, but not backward. Upper parts blackish; *throat and breast and patches on wing and sides of rump white;* sides blackish; tail without bristles. *Length:* 6.50–7.00, wing 5.30–5.90, tail 2.50–2.70." (Bailey) *Nest:* Of feathers and straws or other vegetable matter, glued to the rocks. *Eggs:* 4 or 5, white.

Distribution.—*General:* Breeds from southern British Columbia and southern Alberta south to Lower California and southern Mexico. Winters from California southward. *In Oregon:* Known only from Malheur County.

As does the Black Swift, the White-throated Swift apparently passes over most of Oregon to nest on the cliffs along the Columbia in eastern Washington, though why the exactly similar rims that abound in eastern Oregon are not chosen is one of the intriguing mysteries of the bird world. In addition to our own lone bird, the only records we find for the State are manuscript notes in the Biological Survey files made by E. A. Preble on a trip through Malheur County in July 1915. He saw one near Disaster Peak on July 14, reported a breeding colony of about six pairs on Mahogany Mountain, and saw four at Watson, July 24, one of which he collected.

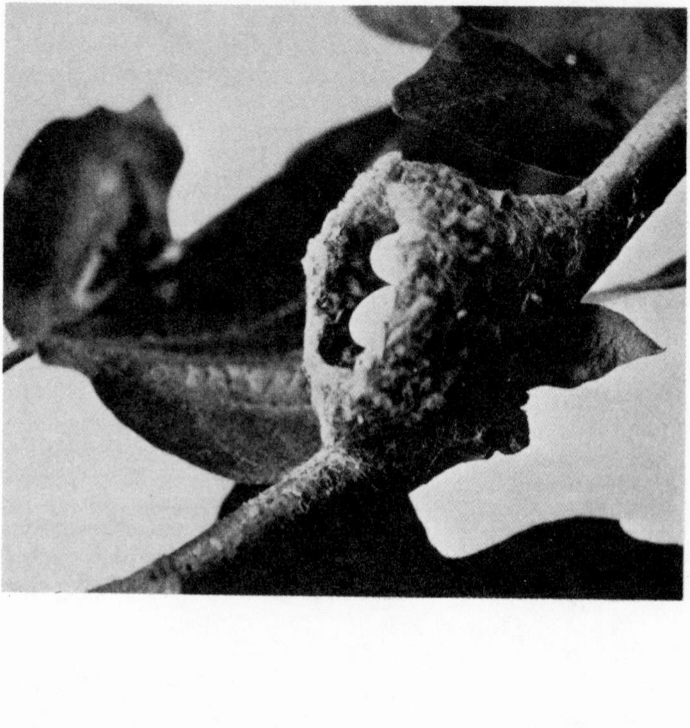

Plate 65, *A*. Nest and eggs of Black-chinned Hummingbird. (Photo by Wm. L. Finley and H. T. Bohlman.)

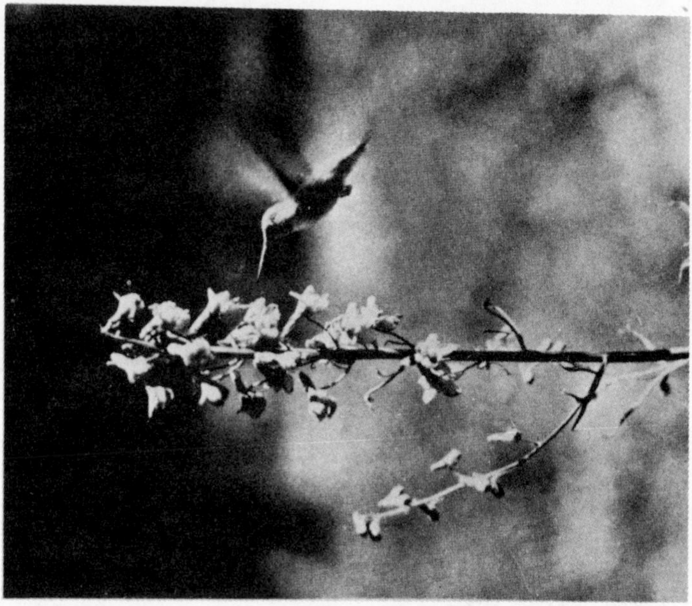

Plate 65, *B*. Broad-tailed Hummingbird. (Photo by Alex Walker.)

It is now in the Biological Survey collection. We were unaware of these unpublished records when we published our note (Gabrielson and Jewett 1930) listing a specimen taken at the Battle Creek Ranch, Malheur County, June 18, 1930 (Gabrielson Coll. No. 1717), as the first Oregon record.

This big, boldly marked swift, with the conspicuous white throat, cannot possibly be confused with any other Oregon bird once it becomes familiar to an observer. It can quickly and easily be picked out of any group of swallows or swifts with which it may be associated by its larger size, black and white coloration, and almost incredible speed of flight. As it darts by, it seems to pass with almost the speed of light, and he is indeed a good wing shot who can bring down even an occasional bird.

Hummingbirds: *Family Trochilidae*

Black-chinned Hummingbird: *Archilochus alexandri* (Bourcier and Mulsant)

Description.—"*Adult male: Gorget above opaque velvety black, below metallic violet* glittering with purple, blue, and peacock green lights; upper parts greenish; under parts soiled whitish, green on sides. *Adult female:* upper parts bronzy green; under parts grayish; *tail much rounded*, middle pair of feathers about the longest and wholly green, next two feathers green tipped with black, outer three tipped with white. *Young:* similar to adult female but feathers of upper parts tipped with buffy or rusty and throat of male streaked with dusky. *Male:* length 3.30–3.75, wing 1.70–1.75, tail 1.25, bill .70–.75. *Female:* length 3.90–4.10, wing 1.90–2.00." (Bailey) *Nest:* A beautiful cup, made of plant down, usually within a few feet of the ground. *Eggs:* 2 or 3, white (Plate 65, *A*).

Distribution.—*General:* Breeds from southern British Columbia to northern California and east to Montana and Texas. Winters in Mexico. *In Oregon:* Rare. Included on basis of two specimens.

Although the Black-chinned Hummingbird doubtless migrates more or less regularly through eastern Oregon and probably nests in small numbers, its place in the Oregon bird list rests entirely on two female specimens. One, now in the Biological Survey collection, was taken by Jewett near Mount Vernon (Grant County) on June 30, 1915. Walker (1934b) took the second at Adel (Lake County) on June 7, 1925. Cantwell reported seeing a bright male near Paradise (Wallowa County) on June 10, 1919. A male was shot in the same locality on June 11 but was lost in the brush. The absence of any permanent observers in eastern Oregon probably accounts for the fact that this bird is not detected more frequently, as it certainly should be present.

Plate 66. Rufous Hummingbird at nest. (Photo by Wm. L. Finley and H. T. Bohlman.)

Broad-tailed Hummingbird: *Selasphorus platycercus platycercus* (Swainson)

DESCRIPTION.—"*Adult male: Gorget without elongated sides, deep rose pink; top of head bronzy green* like back and middle tail feathers; other tail feathers purplish black, some of them *edged with rufous;* under parts whitish, sides glossed with green. *Adult female and young:* upper parts bronzy green; under parts whitish, the throat with dark specks, sometimes with a few central feathers like gorget of male; sides brownish; three outer tail feathers rufous at base, with a black subterminal band and white tip; a touch of green on the second and third feather between the rufous and black, the fourth feather green but marked with a terminal or subterminal spot of black, and edged with rufous, tip often white. *Male:* length 4.00–4.25, wing 1.92–2.05, tail 1.40–1.60, bill .62–.70. *Female:* length 4.10–4.70, wing 2.00–2.10, tail 1.45–1.50, bill .70–.72." (Bailey) *Nest:* Usually within 15 feet of the ground, made of vegetable down, covered with lichens, bark, leaves, and plant fiber. *Eggs:* 2, white.

DISTRIBUTION.—*General:* Breeds from southern Idaho, Montana, and Wyoming to Mexico. Winters in Mexico. *In Oregon:* Rare summer visitor found only in extreme eastern part of State.

ALTHOUGH Bendire (1895a) and Woodcock (1902) mentioned probable Oregon records, our information concerning the status of the Broad-tailed Hummingbird (Plate 65, *B*) is meager and quite unsatisfactory. Preble (ms.) noted it several times in various localities in southern Malheur County between June 9 and July 25, 1915, and Sheldon (ms.) saw it in the Steens Mountains in July and August 1916. The authors together saw an adult male in Wallowa County, July 27, 1921, and Jewett has seen the species at Adel, Lake County. Like the Black-chinned Hummingbird, this species would doubtless be detected more frequently if more observers were available in the eastern part of the State.

Rufous Hummingbird: *Selasphorus rufus* (Gmelin)

DESCRIPTION.—"*Adult male:* Gorget fire red, orange, and brassy green; *general body color bright reddish brown*, glossed with bronzy green on crown and sometimes back, and fading to white next to gorget and on belly; tail feathers rufous, with dark mesial streaks; middle tail feather broad, pointed at tip, *second from middle deeply notched on inner web*, *sinuated on outer web*. *Adult female:* upper parts bronzy and rufous, rufous on rump and tail coverts; under parts whitish, throat sometimes with a few central brilliant feathers; sides shaded with rufous; tail feathers rufous at base, the middle ones green nearly to base; outer ones with broad blackish subterminal band and white tips; outside feather more than .10 wide. *Young males* similar to adult female, but feathers of upper parts edged with rusty, rump rufous, and throat showing specks of metallic red. *Young females:* similar to young males, but rump green and throat specked only with green. *Male:* length 3.25–3.70, wing 1.50–1.60, tail 1.30–1.35, bill .60. *Female:* length 3.50–3.90, wing 1.75–1.80, tail 1.25–1.30, bill .65–.70." (Bailey) *Nest:* Of plant fiber and down, decorated with moss or lichens, usually close to the ground, often in bushes overhanging banks (Plate 66). *Eggs:* Usually 2, white.

DISTRIBUTION.—*General:* Breeds from Alaskan coast, southern Yukon, and southern Alberta south to Oregon and southwestern Montana. Winters in Mexico. *In Oregon:* Most common hummingbird in State. A common summer resident and breeding species.

THE RUFOUS HUMMINGBIRD (Plate 66) is the brown-looking hummingbird of the dooryards, familiar to almost every Oregonian. It is the most abundant one in the State and is found in migration and as a breeding species in every county. The females and young, lacking the reddish-brown back and brilliant gorget of the adult male, are frequently taken for some other species. It is, however, the only hummer one is likely to see in western Oregon, as it is the only one found regularly west of the Cascades. East of that range, many more than half the hummingbirds seen are of this species, and in the mountains of eastern Oregon it is abundant. It usually arrives in early March (earliest date, February 16, Coos County) and remains until September (latest date, September 24, Washington County). It was first recorded as arriving at the mouth of the Columbia River near the encampment of the Lewis and Clark expedition on March 26, 1806 (Lewis and Clark 1814). Nuttall (1840) reported a set of eggs taken at the mouth of the Willamette on May 29, 1835. Since then a great number of records of this species have been published, including many nesting records. The latter are largely in May, which is the great breeding month, although Braly took eggs on Sauvies Island as early as April 12 and Jewett found a fresh set on June 9 at Portland.

Allen's Hummingbird:
Selasphorus alleni Henshaw

DESCRIPTION.—"*Adult male:* Similar to *rufus*, but whole *back as well as crown bright bronzy green*, two outer tail feathers very narrow, and second from middle without notch or *sinuation;* outer feather much less than .10 wide. *Adult female:* similar to female *rufus*, but with *outer tail feathers not more than* .10 *wide*. *Male:* length 3.25–3.30, wing 1.50–1.55, tail 1.10–1.20, exposed culmen .60–.65. *Female:* length 3.40, wing 1.65–1.70, tail 1.05–1.15, exposed culmen .68–.70." (Bailey) *Nest:* A beautiful cup of plant down, covered with moss and usually placed on a plant or bush overhanging the water. *Eggs:* 2, white.

DISTRIBUTION.—*General:* Breeds along coast from southern Oregon to southern California. Winters on Santa Barbara Islands and probably in northwestern Mexico. *In Oregon:* Known definitely from only two specimens.

ALTHOUGH MANY of the earlier books gave general ranges that listed Allen's Hummingbird as a summer resident of the Oregon coast, definite evidence of its presence was not obtained until Jewett collected two specimens, an adult male and an immature male, on Pistol River, Curry County, June 23, 1929. In July, 1933, the authors while together in that same locality shot two more hummers that were unquestionably of this species, but both were lost in the dense jungle of vines through which the tall stalks of *Scrophularia* about which they were feeding grow.

Calliope Hummingbird:
Stellula calliope (Gould)

Description.—"Six middle tail feathers contracted in the middle and widened at end; adult male with feathers of chin and throat narrow, those on the outside of the ruff elongated; base of ruff white. *Adult male:* Gorget rose purplish, white bases giving effect of streaking; upper parts metallic green; tail feathers dusky, bases edged with rufous, tip wider than base; under parts white; sides tinged with brown and green. *Adult female:* upper parts bronzy green; tail rounded and tail feathers greenish gray basally with touch of rufous, black-banded, and tipped with white, except middle pair, which are green ending in dusky. *Young:* similar, but under parts washed with rufous, throat specked with dusky. *Male:* length 2.75–3.00, wing 1.50–1.60, tail .90–1.10, exposed culmen .55–.58. *Female:* length 3.50, wing 1.75–1.80, tail 1.10–1.15, bill .58–.60." (Bailey) *Nest:* Willow down, decorated with bits of bark and shreds of cone, and often saddled on a pine cone. *Eggs:* 2, white.

Distribution.—*General:* Breeds from northern British Columbia and southwestern Alberta south in high mountains to Lower California and New Mexico. Winters in Mexico. *In Oregon:* Regular summer resident of Blue Mountains and isolated high ranges of eastern Oregon.

Next to the Rufous Hummingbird, the Calliope Hummingbird is the most abundant hummer in the State, although it is found only in eastern Oregon. There are, however, a few scattered records from the Siskiyou Mountains, Jackson County, and one from Glendale, Douglas County, on July 3, 1916 (specimen in Carnegie Museum).

This is the smallest bird in the State—probably the smallest in the United States—but despite its minute size it is quite hardy. It frequents the open mountain meadows, where it finds an abundance of flowers during the short summer. It arrives in early May (earliest date, April 24, Klamath County) and remains until September (latest date, September 24). Merrill (1888) published the first record for Oregon when he listed it as a common bird at Fort Klamath. Bendire (1895a) listed the first set of eggs, taken June 11, 1883, near the same spot. He found several other nests and collected three sets of eggs in a few days in June of that year. Anthony took a set of fresh eggs in Baker County, July 2, 1902. Since that time the species has been listed by various observers as a summer resident of all mountain ranges in the State east of the Cascades. There are numerous skins in the Biological Survey collection as well as in our own collections.

Plate 67. Western Belted Kingfisher row. (Photo by Wm. L. Finley and H. T. Bohlman.)

Order Coraciiformes

Kingfishers: *Family Alcedinidae*

Western Belted Kingfisher: *Megaceryle alcyon caurina* (Grinnell)

Description.—"*Adult male:* Under parts white, with blue gray belt across breast; crest and upper parts bluish gray; nuchal collar white; wing quills black, marked with white; tail with middle feathers bluish gray, the rest black, spotted with white. *Adult female:* similar, but belly partly banded and sides heavily washed with rufous. *Young:* like adults, but male with breast band and sides tinged with rusty. *Length:* 11.00–14.50, wing 6.00–6.50, tail 3.80–4.30, bill 2 or more." (Bailey) *Nest:* A burrow in a perpendicular bank. *Eggs:* 5 to 8, white.

Distribution.—*General:* Breeds from northern Alaska and Yukon territory south to southern California and from Rockies to Pacific. *In Oregon:* Permanent resident throughout State. Less common in winter.

The rattling cry and flashing blue wings of the Western Belted Kingfisher (Plate 67) have been familiar to frequenters of Oregon's water courses and lakes since the Lewis and Clark expedition first noted this bird at the mouth of the Columbia on March 24, 1806 (Lewis and Clark 1814). Every ornithologist since then has listed this industrious fisherman among the birds observed in the State, and the field records of the Biological Survey contain dozens of records. Our own records cover every month and all parts of the State. Eggs are laid in May and June (May 12 to July 1), usually in a long tunnel excavated in a perpendicular bank near the water. There the young remain and are fed by the parents until able to launch out from the mouth of the burrow to start fishing for themselves.

Until recent years, every small stream and lake in Oregon big enough to support a population of fish and other aquatic life had its pair of kingfishers, but the relentless and senseless persecution of this striking bird by sportsmen has sadly reduced its numbers. As in many other instances, the persecution is the result of ignorance and misunderstanding. Fishermen, whipping their favorite stream, see the flash of blue and white as this expert diver plunges into the stream to emerge almost instantly with a tiny fish in its beak and jump to the conclusion that trout and other game fish are being terribly depleted by these birds. Nothing could be further from the truth. Although this kingfisher would undoubtedly take trout and bass, food is furnished in such abundance by other fish, crayfish, aquatic larvae, and batrachians, that few game fish are taken. Frequently one hears the statement that the fish-eating birds *must* be eating trout "as we have only trout in our river." Possibly there may be such a favored spot, but we know of no Oregon streams that do not swarm with many other species of fish, mostly of the nonfood group. The statement is true of some of the high mountain lakes that were without fish until planted with game fish, but there is an abundance of aquatic insect larvae and other forms of life, even in those areas. If it were not so, the fish themselves would find it hard to live save by cannibalism.

Order Piciformes

Woodpeckers: *Family Picidae*

Northern Flicker:
Colaptes auratus luteus Bangs

Description.—"*Adult male:* Upper parts brown, barred with black, except for red nuchal band, white rump, and black tail; wings and tail with *shafts and under side of feathers bright yellow;* throat and sides of head pinkish brown, with black malar stripe or 'mustache' and black crescent on chest; rest of under parts brownish white, washed with yellow and spotted with black. *Adult female:* similar, but without black mustache, though sometimes with faint indications of one. *Young male:* similar to adult male, but crown marked with dull red, nuchal band dull scarlet. *Young female:* with dark mustache. *Male:* Length 12–14, wing 6.18, tail 4.09, exposed culmen 1.33. *Female:* wing 6.06, tail 4, exposed culmen 1.25." (Bailey) *Nest:* In old stumps or trees, usually not far from ground. *Eggs:* 5 to 9, white.

Distribution.—*General:* Breeds from Canada and Alaska east of Rocky Mountains from tree limit south to edge of Lower Austral Zone and in winter south to Gulf. *In Oregon:* Rare straggler that has occurred twice.

There are two records of the Northern Flicker in Oregon, both stragglers. The first is of a bird taken by Walker (1924) at Blaine, Tillamook County, on November 3, 1921; the second is of a bird taken in Portland, February 23, 1932 (Jewett Coll. No. 7175).

Although typical *C. a. luteus* seems to be a rarity in Oregon, hybrids between it and *C. cafer collaris* are common, particularly on the coast. Overton Dowell, Jr., at Mercer, and Walker, in Tillamook County, took numerous specimens; we have three from Portland (Jewett Coll. No. 3380; Gabrielson Coll. Nos. 1897 and 1898); and there is a single bird from Adel, Lake County (Gabrielson Coll. No. 332). These birds exhibit curious combinations of the mustaches and crown markings of the two forms, often complicated further by association of dominant head markings of one species with the color of wing linings and tail feathers of the other. Such a series is an interesting study in possible character combinations but would be out of place in this book. It is evident, however, that the wintering flickers of northwestern Oregon originate somewhere in Canada along the line where these two forms meet. In addition to the specimens of these hybrid birds that we have examined, Bendire (1877) reported one from Camp Harney in 1875, and Woodcock (1902) listed two from Corvallis.

Northwestern Flicker:
Colaptes cafer cafer (Gmelin)

Description.—Similar to *C. c. collaris* but darker. *Size:* Length 12.75–14.00, wing 6.35–7.00, tail 4.70–5.20, exposed culmen 1.35–1.60. *Nest:* Similar to *C. auratus luteus*. *Eggs:* 5 to 10, white.

Distribution.—*General:* Northwest coast district from Sitka, Alaska, to Humboldt County, California. *In Oregon:* Permanent resident that breeds throughout Willamette Valley, Umpqua Valley, and along entire Coast Ranges through coast counties.

The Northwestern Flicker is the breeding form of all of Oregon west of the Cascades, except Jackson and Josephine Counties. It winters throughout its range and occasionally in the Rogue River Valley. In the country it inhabits, it is by far the most common woodpecker and ranks as one of the characteristic and most common birds of the district. Townsend (1839) first listed it as an Oregon bird, and since his time much has been published about this very widely distributed species, although most of the literature is applicable to the Red-shafted Flicker.

It is impossible to assign this bird to any definite habitat, as it is found so universally through western Oregon that it vies with the robin as the most commonly observed bird. It is frequently most unwoodpeckerlike in its behavior. Although it feeds in the orthodox manner, it also essays the fly-catching stunt of Lewis's Woodpecker and is inordinately fond of ants. It can be regularly seen on lawns and in meadows digging away in the ground, tearing up ant hills, and catching the excited inhabitants of the disrupted fortress on its sticky tongue.

Normally these flickers nest, as do other woodpeckers, in holes that they have excavated in trees for the purpose, either close to the ground or high up in the branches of a giant tree. Frequently, however, a flicker will cause some trouble and complaint by persistent attempts to drill a nesting hole in a building; and in the St. Johns district of Portland, despite an abundance of trees for normal nesting sites, several pairs have for years excavated burrows in a steep bank along a railroad cut and raised their families in these kingfisherlike apartments. Eggs are laid in early May. Jewett located five nests on Government Island from April 29 to May 10 that contained five to seven eggs each.

Red-shafted Flicker:
Colaptes cafer collaris Vigors

Description.—"*Adult male:* Ground color of head and body brownish, back barred and under parts spotted with black; rump white and tail black; no nuchal band; *mustache red;* chest marked with black crescent; *under side of wings and tail red. Female:* Similar, but usually with a buffy or brown malar stripe. *Young:* Similar, but without mustache. *Length:* 12.75–14.00, wing 6.45–7.15, tail 4.40–5.20, exposed culmen 1.34–1.53." (Bailey) *Nest:* Same as *C. auratus luteus*. *Eggs:* 5 to 10, white.

DISTRIBUTION.—*General:* From southeastern British Columbia and southern Alberta east to Great Plains and south to southern California and Mexico. *In Oregon:* Permanent resident of all of eastern Oregon, including eastern slope of Cascades, and of Jackson and Josephine Counties of Rogue River Valley.

NEWBERRY (1857) first listed the Red-shafted Flicker (Plate 68) from the territory now assigned to it, and Bendire (1877) collected the first set of eggs at Camp Harney in 1875. Since then many writers have mentioned the bird. It is common even in the treeless areas of eastern Oregon, where it nests in posts or in holes in banks and forages in the sagebrush in competition with the Horned Larks and Meadowlarks. The eggs have been collected from April 20 to June 10, according to published records and to our own and other manuscript notes, and the habits and behavior of the bird are in every way similar to those of the two preceding species.

In addition to eastern Oregon birds, we have a fair series of breeding and wintering birds from the Rogue River Valley and find upon comparison that these birds are much nearer to *C. c. collaris* than they are to the darker *C. c. cafer* of the Northwest coast. Breeding birds are quite definitely of this form, as are a majority of the wintering individuals, although some of the latter approach the darker race.

Western Pileated Woodpecker: *Ceophloeus pileatus picinus* (Bangs)

DESCRIPTION.—"Head conspicuously crested; bill longer than head, straight with wedge-like tip, beveled sides, and strong ridges, broader than high at base; nostrils concealed by large nasal tufts; feet peculiar, outer hind toe shorter than outer front toe, tarsus shorter than inner front toe and claw. *Adult male:* Brownish or grayish black; entire top of head, occipital crest, and malar stripe bright red; chin and wide stripe on side of head white, or sulphur yellow; patches on wings and under wing coverts white; feathers of belly tipped with whitish. *Adult female:* similar, but forepart of head and malar stripe brown instead of red. *Young:* similar to female, but crest salmon." (Bailey) *Size:* Length 17–18, wing 9.00, tail 6.30, bill 2.05. *Nest:* Usually excavated, well up in either deciduous or coniferous trees. *Eggs:* 3 to 5, white.

DISTRIBUTION.—*General:* From British Columbia and Montana south to central California. *In Oregon:* Permanent resident of forests of entire State.

BENDIRE (Brewer 1875) first included the Pileated Woodpecker in Oregon's fauna when he listed it as resident in the pine woods about Camp Harney, and he (Bendire 1895a) first reported finding an Oregon nest of the species, which contained young birds, at Fort Klamath, in June 1882. He commented on the rarity of this woodpecker everywhere in the West, and several of the other earlier writers listed it as a rare bird in Oregon. Bowles (1901a) reported taking eggs near Waldo, Josephine County.

Plate 68. Red-shafted Flicker. (Photo by Wm. L. Finley and H. T. Bohlman.)

Woodcock (1902) listed 12 localities in the State where the bird has been noted and quoted Bretherton as follows:

A rather rare resident, breeding, and frequenting the large timber. The Indians believed that the red scalp of this bird was a talisman against all evil, and, in consequence, the birds were constantly hunted and their numbers greatly reduced, but as the Indians are being rapidly civilized out of existence the birds are now on the increase.

Perhaps in this statement there is a hint as to the apparent increase of this great woodpecker that we now find to be fairly common and widely distributed for so large and conspicuous a bird. Our notes contain records for every month and for all of the wooded sections of the State. It is most common in the open forests of the Wallowa Mountains and in the ranges bordering the Rogue River Valley, though it is also found in lesser numbers throughout both the Cascades and Coast Ranges and in the wooded portions of the Willamette Valley. Braly found a nest containing one egg near Fort Klamath, May 11, 1931.

The borings of this great bird are more frequently seen than the bird itself. Old stumps are literally torn to pieces in its search for wood-boring insects, and deep pits are to be found in many other trees. These drillings are carried out with amazing speed, one pair of the birds soon effectively riddling all of the stumps and snags in the immediate neighborhood of their chosen home.

Usually shy, these largest of the woodpeckers in Oregon can dodge behind a tree trunk with amazing speed for creatures so big and clumsy looking. At times they lose their shyness and flit about from one tree to another in supreme indifference, as Gabrielson has twice observed, once in Wallowa County, where a family of six furnished a wonderful entertainment as the parents taught their newly fledged offspring the intricate art of dashing through the thick growth at top speed, and once in Lincoln County, where two males and a female darted about through the trees as do the Downy Woodpeckers in mating season. The flight in such performances is swift—the birds zigzagging among the trees, flashing the white wing patches and linings that contrast strongly with the dark body plumage. At other times the flight resembles that of a crow, with much less of the undulating movement of the woodpecker family generally.

Of all bird notes to be heard, the ringing bugle calls of the Pileated Woodpecker, the clear peal of the Loon, and the wild free notes of the Olive-sided Flycatcher seem most fittingly to express the very spirit of the great western forests. Heard in the early morning, when the perpetual twilight of the heavy forests is still only a shade lighter than the blackness of night, the ringing notes of the "Black Woodcock" bring a thrill to the listener that few other wild voices can produce. Not only are the calls thrilling, but the sight of this great black woodpecker, flame-crested and white-winged, intrigues every lover of the out-of-doors.

California Woodpecker: *Balanosphyra formicivora bairdi* (Ridgway)

Description.—"*Adult male:* Feathers around base of bill and chin black, bordered by band of white or yellow; crown red; sides of head, upper parts, and chest band glossy *greenish;* rump, wing patch and belly white. *Adult female:* similar but with a black band separating white or yellow forehead from red crown. *Young:* similar to adults and with same sexual differences in crown, but colors duller." (Bailey) *Size:* Length 8.50–9.50, wing 5.30–5.90, tail 3.10–3.60, bill .87–1.12. *Nest:* Usually drilled in living trees. *Eggs:* 4 or 5, white.

Distribution.—*General:* Breeds from southwestern Oregon south to southern California. *In Oregon:* Permanent resident of southwestern Oregon from Umpqua River south.

The handsome, sleek-looking California Woodpecker was first found in Oregon by Newberry, who collected it in the Umpqua Valley in 1855 (Baird, Cassin, and Lawrence, 1858). Bendire (1895a) reported that he saw three birds near Pelican Bay, Upper Klamath Lake. He also listed the first Oregon breeding record, June 15, 1883, between Fort Klamath and Jacksonville on the west slope of the Cascades and reported that J. K. Lord saw this woodpecker, May 25, 1860, on the headwaters of the Deschutes River and on the eastern slopes of the Cascades among a mixed growth of pines and oaks. We have numerous records for Jackson and Josephine Counties and fewer for Douglas, Coos, and Curry Counties. There is one record for Lane County and an early record or two from east of the Cascades.

After Bendire's time, Jones (1900) and Woodcock (1902) were the only writers who mentioned this species as an Oregon bird until Gabrielson (1931) listed it in *The Birds of the Rogue River Valley*. Bendire remarked on its great abundance in that valley, and we wish to emphasize the fact that nowhere else in Oregon is any species of woodpecker so abundant. There it is one of the most conspicuous birds of the oak belt; its shining plumage flashes ever in the sun as it dodges about a limb or flies in undulating lines from tree to tree; and its noisy calls break the midday silence of the hottest summer day.

This is the species that so delights in wedging acorns into telephone poles and trees until at times there seems to be no room for another nut. Wherever the oaks are found from Eugene south, one is likely to find this striking bird or evidence of its presence, though it does not become common until south of the Umpqua. The nests are usually drilled in the oak trees about which this woodpecker spends most of its life and are generally well up from the ground. Patterson has reported egg dates between May 2 and 19 in the Rogue River Valley.

Lewis's Woodpecker:
Asyndesmus lewis Gray

Description.—"*Adults:* Under parts iridescent greenish black except for gray collar; face dull crimson; throat and chest gray changing to soft rose on belly; plumage of lower parts harsh and hairlike. *Young:* head without red, neck without collar, under parts with less red [Plate 69, *A*]. *Length:* 10.50–11.50, wing 6.50–6.80, tail 4.40–4.70." (Bailey) *Nest:* In trees of many kinds, at almost any height. *Eggs:* 6 to 7, white.

Distribution.—*General:* From British Columbia and southern Alberta to Arizona and New Mexico and from Black Hills west to Pacific. *In Oregon:* Summer resident in every part of State. Winters more or less regularly in Columbia, Snake, John Day, and Willamette Valleys and more commonly in Umpqua and Rogue River Valleys.

The striking red and dark bronzy green Lewis's Woodpecker is an exceedingly familiar sight in Oregon from timber line on the highest peaks to the straggling growth of willows and cottonwoods along the stream beds of the eastern part of the State. There is much in its behavior and actions reminiscent of the Red-headed Woodpecker of the Eastern States. It has the same trick of sitting on fence posts and telephone poles and the identical habit of catching insects, both by short sallies from the high perch and by more intricate aerial evolutions amid the insect swarms. It is also fond of the oak groves, athough it is by no means so closely associated with them as the California Woodpecker. It nests in May and June. The dates at which eggs have been taken vary from May 12 to June 29. Nests are usually high above the ground and difficult of access.

Townsend collected the first Oregon specimen, September 22, 1834, along the Columbia River (Baird, Cassin, and Lawrence 1858), and Dr. Suckley (Cooper and Suckley 1860) obtained two others at The Dalles, January 9, 1855. Since that time nearly every writer on Oregon birds has had something to say about this abundant species. Newberry (1857) noted its habit of congregating at and near timber line in the fall months to compete with the robins and bluebirds in harvesting the ripening crop of mountain-ash berries.

Red-naped Sapsucker:
Sphyrapicus varius nuchalis Baird

Description.—"*Adult male:* Upper parts black, thickly marked with white; wing coverts plain black, with wide white outer stripe; head with *red crown and red nuchal patch separated by a plain black area;* sides of head with white stripes; *chest black between red throat and pale yellow belly. Adult female:* similar, but duller, and black chest patch mostly mottled gray. *Young:* duller, red of head and throat wholly wanting or only suggested by pale claret-colored tinge. *Length:* 8.00–8.75, wing (male) 4.92–5.10, tail 3.10–3.40, bill .95–1.02." (Bailey) *Nest:* Usually in an aspen tree, in this State, 5 to 20 feet from the ground. *Eggs:* 4 or 5, white.

Plate 69, *A*. Young Lewis's Woodpeckers. (Photo by Wm. L. Finley and H. T. Bohlman.)

Plate 69, *B*. Gairdner's Woodpecker. (Photo by Wm. L. Finley and H. T. Bohlman.)

Distribution.—*General:* Breeds from British Columbia and Alberta south to northeastern California, Arizona, New Mexico, and Texas. Winters south to central Mexico and Lower California. *In Oregon:* Regular but not common resident and breeding bird of eastern slope of Cascades, Blue Mountains, and timbered parts of isolated ranges in eastern Oregon.

The Red-naped Sapsucker, the handsome representative of the familiar Yellow-bellied Sapsucker, was first listed for Oregon by Bendire (1877), who found a nest containing good-sized young, June 12, 1875, in the Blue Mountains. He stated:

Their nests are in aspens, and generally inaccessible. I noticed three in the season of 1876 in such situations, too late for their eggs.

The authors and Dr. W. B. Bell discovered a nest containing large young in an aspen thicket on Hart Mountain, June 15, 1926, and in the Braly collection there is a set of five eggs taken at Beattie, Klamath County, May 25, 1930. The birds arrive in April (earliest date, April 8, Klamath County) and remain until October (latest date, October 19, Harney County). We have no winter records, but Bendire (1895a) occasionally observed the birds in Harney Valley in winter, and Woodcock (1902) reported two January records for Baker County in 1896 on the authority of Robert W. Haines. There are no recent winter records. Eastern Oregon observers should keep on the lookout for winter specimens.

In common with other sapsuckers, this one drills rows of neat square holes in the bark of various species of trees to collect the exuding sap or the small insects that gather about it, or both. If it were more abundant, the species might do some economic damage, but it is too scarce to cause any concern.

Northern Red-breasted Sapsucker: *Sphyrapicus varius ruber* (Gmelin)

Description.—Similar to southern Red-breasted Sapsucker but red of a darker shade and belly olive yellow. *Size:* About as southern Red-breasted Sapsucker. *Nest:* In holes in living trees. *Eggs:* 5 or 6, white.

Distribution.—*General:* Breeds from Alaska south to western Oregon. Winters south to central California. *In Oregon:* Permanent resident of Willamette Valley and Coast Mountains.

The Red-breasted Sapsucker is such a striking bird that it is well known to most residents of western Oregon. Most highly colored of resident woodpeckers, it excites admiration and interest whenever seen. Like the other sapsuckers, it is a comparatively quiet bird except during the mating season when it becomes quite noisy. Johnson (1880) listed it as a breeding bird of the Willamette Valley, the first printed record of the present subspecies that we have found. Anthony (1886) and Bendire (1889b) also reported it as a breeding bird of that territory, and Bendire

(1895a) listed a number of sets of eggs taken in the eighties, some near Salem by Clinton T. Cooke, and some in Washington County by Anthony. He also referred to many nests and specimens that he took himself about Fort Klamath at about the same time, but those records properly belong to the next form. Woodcock (1902) presented records from Lincoln, Yamhill, Multnomah, Marion, and Benton Counties.

In checking the ranges for the two subspecies now listed for this State, we find a lack of breeding birds from the southern Willamette and the Umpqua Valleys, so that we are not able to define the area of intergradation as closely as is desirable. All of our specimens from the Willamette Valley and the coast district as far south as Coos County, both winter and summer, undoubtedly belong to this subspecies. There is in addition a single bird (Gabrielson Coll. No. 3559) from Grants Pass, taken December 9, 1918, that is unquestionably a northern bird. Breeding material from the northern Cascades is lacking, but these birds should also belong to this form.

As this is the only sapsucker found in the Willamette Valley and adjacent Coast Mountains, to it alone must be credited the damage to orchard and shade trees that at times calls forth bitter complaint. Prune trees and English walnut trees seem most subject to its attacks, although few fruit trees are entirely immune. Individual trees are often attacked year after year until damage results from direct physical injury. In addition, many orchardists fear the entry of disease organisms in the open wounds left by the birds.

Southern Red-breasted Sapsucker:
Sphyrapicus varius daggetti Grinnell

DESCRIPTION.—"*Adults: Whole head, neck, and chest plain red*, or black and white markings of *nuchalis* only suggested; back, wings, and tail black, heavily marked with white; belly dusky or yellowish. *Young:* duller, and color pattern less distinct, the red replaced by claret brown. *Length:* 8.50–9.25, wing (male) 4.70–5.05, tail 3.10–3.50, bill 1.00–1.08." (Bailey) *Nest:* Usually in aspens, not far from the ground. *Eggs:* 5 or 6, pure white.

DISTRIBUTION.—*General:* Breeds from southern Oregon south through California mountains. Winters in adjacent lowlands. *In Oregon:* Permanent resident of Klamath, Jackson, Josephine, and possibly extreme southern Lake Counties, where it breeds in highlands and winters sparingly in valleys, most of the birds going south into California from October to April.

THE RECORDS of Mearns (1879), Merrill (1888), and Bendire (1895a), all from Fort Klamath, apply to this subspecies, the Southern Red-breasted Sapsucker, which is more abundant about Fort Klamath and the adjoining section of the Cascades than any sapsucker elsewhere in Oregon. Bendire found numerous nests and remarked at length on the abundance of the species, a condition that remains unchanged to this time. We have found it commonly about the Klamath Lakes as well as about the base of Mount McLoughlin. In the Rogue River Valley it is much less common. Our breeding birds from that area are much nearer breeding birds from southern California than those from northwestern Oregon.

Its breeding habits and behavior are much like those of other sapsuckers. About Fort Klamath it shows a marked preference for aspen trees as nest sites. Eggs are laid in May, and there are six sets in the Braly collection taken from this locality, May 21 and 22, 1930, containing from three to five eggs each.

Williamson's Sapsucker: *Sphyrapicus thyroideus thyroideus* (Cassin)

DESCRIPTION.—"*Adult male:* Upper parts glossy black except *white rump*, large *white patch on wing* coverts, and fine white spots on quills; sides of head with two white stripes; throat and breast black, with a median stripe of bright red; belly bright yellow. *Adult female:* entire body barred with brown or black and white, except for brown head and white rump and, rarely, a red median stripe on throat; chest usually with a black patch; middle of belly yellow. *Young male:* similar to adult male, but black duller, belly paler, throat stripe white. *Young female:* similar to adult female, but markings and colors duller, belly whitish, and chest without black patch. *Length:* 9.00–9.75, wing 5.25–5.50, tail 3.80–3.90, bill 1.00–1.20." (Bailey) *Nest:* In both coniferous and deciduous trees. *Eggs:* 3 to 7, white.

DISTRIBUTION.—*General:* Breeds from southern British Columbia through Washington, Oregon, and Sierra Nevada Mountains of California. Winters south to Lower California. *In Oregon:* Summer resident of summit and eastern slope of Cascades, Blue Mountains, and isolated ranges of eastern Oregon on which are found yellow pine forests.

THE FIRST SPECIMEN of Williamson's Sapsucker known from Oregon was taken by Newberry near Upper Klamath Lake, August 23, 1855. Baird (Baird, Cassin, and Lawrence 1858) wrote about this specimen, and Merrill (1888) also reported the species from Fort Klamath. Walker (1917b) reported it from Jefferson County, and Shelton (1917) from Crescent Lake and Three Sisters. All of the published records, except these last two and our own, refer to the Fort Klamath district, where the species is indeed common. We have found it to be equally common in the Blue Mountains, however; particularly in the yellow pine belt. There are many specimens and field notes in the Biological collection and files. These specimens and our own have been taken in extreme northeastern Oregon, on the summit of the Siskiyou Mountains south of Ashland, in and along the entire eastern slope of the Cascades, in the Warner Mountains, in the wooded ranges between Klamath Falls and Lakeview, and in the Maury Mountains east of Bend. We have no records for the isolated ranges of southeastern Oregon from the Warner Mountains eastward to the Idaho line.

The birds arrive in April (earliest date, March 3, Klamath County) and remain until October (latest date, December 1, Lake County). The eggs are laid in May and June. Bendire (1895a) recorded the first set from Oregon as taken June 3, 1883, from an excavation 50 feet up in a yellow pine tree on the road between Fort Klamath and Crater Lake, and he took other sets during June of that year. Patterson took several sets in Klamath between May 2 and 12.

This handsome sapsucker, the males among the most contrastingly marked of Oregon summer birds, is by choice a resident of the open yellow pine forests, where it frequently builds its nest in the pines in preference to the aspens and other deciduous trees chosen by its relatives. It is a quiet bird and somewhat solitary. On April 28, 1926, in the vicinity of Sled Springs Ranger Station on the Wallowa National Forest, Gabrielson observed a dozen or more in a loose flock chasing each other through the forest and uttering shrill cries in a manner entirely unlike their usual decorous behavior.

Harris's Woodpecker:
Dryobates villosus harrisi (Audubon)

Description.—"*Adult male:* Upper parts black, with scarlet nape, white stripe down back, ***wing coverts and tertials plain black or lightly spotted*** with white; outer primaries with white spots; outer tail feather plain white; ***under parts smoky gray or light smoky brown.*** *Adult female:* similar, but without scarlet nape. *Young:* similar, but forehead spotted with white and scarlet of nape extending partly or wholly over crown. *Length:* 9–10, wing 4.70–5.30, tail 3.20–3.75, bill 1.12–1.40." (Bailey) *Nest:* Usually a freshly constructed hole. *Eggs:* 3 to 6, white.

Distribution.—*General:* Permanent resident of humid coast belt from British Columbia to northern California. *In Oregon:* Western part of State from summit of Cascades to Pacific Ocean and south to northern Jackson and Josephine Counties. In these counties, there is an intermingling with next species, though this is the form on coastal slope of Coos and Curry Counties. (See Figure 9.)

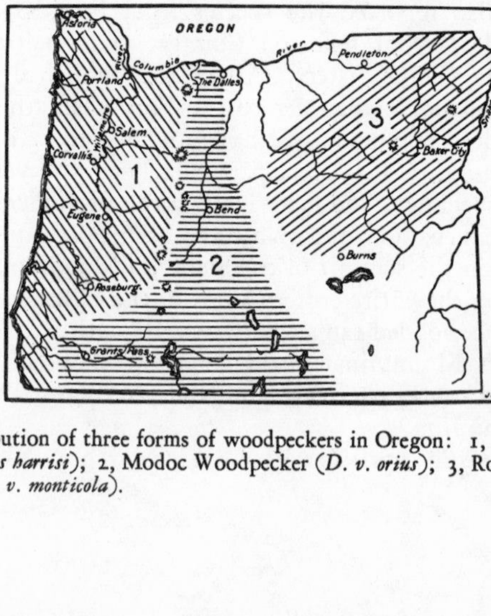

Figure 9.—Distribution of three forms of woodpeckers in Oregon: 1, Harris's Woodpecker (*Dryobates villosus harrisi*); 2, Modoc Woodpecker (*D. v. orius*); 3, Rocky Mountain Hairy Woodpecker (*D. v. monticola*).

Early records in this group of woodpeckers, as in many other variable species, have been greatly confused, and it is impossible to assign many of them to the correct subspecies. All records in the above outlined territory, however, belong to Harris's Woodpecker unless otherwise specified. We have had 98 Oregon skins available for working out the distribution of the three subspecies that occur here. Audubon (1839) described the present form from specimens taken at Vancouver, Washington, and there have been many records since of this common woodpecker, although the records of Suckley (Cooper and Suckley 1860) at The Dalles and those of various early collectors for eastern Oregon must now be referred to other races. One of the curious anomalies of bird distribution is presented by the comparative abundance of the woodpeckers of the *villosus* and *pubescens* groups. Within the range of *D. v. harrisi*, the *villosus* group is comparatively much less abundant than its smaller relative, whereas the reverse is true in southern and eastern Oregon. Within the territory assigned to it, Harris's Woodpecker is a permanent resident, and, in addition, we have a summer bird from Butte Falls, Jackson County, July 22, 1926, (Gabrielson Coll.) and one bird taken at Grants Pass, December 11, 1918, (Jewett Coll.) that are *harrisi*. Curiously enough, a Modoc Woodpecker was taken at the same time. Our own notes contain records for every month for the Willamette Valley and along the coast.

The eggs are laid in April and May in holes excavated by the powerful chisel-like beak, usually in living trees, and the young are usually hatched by May 15. Woodcock (1902) recorded a set of four fresh eggs taken May 30, near Salem.

These handsome big woodpeckers are essentially birds of the coniferous forests, where their rolling *tattoo* and high-pitched alarm note are familiar sounds. They are usually shy and not too easily seen within the heavy forests. Even in the open cut-over lands they are adept at keeping a branch or tree trunk between themselves and an intruder. If an observer remains quiet, the birds, which freeze into instant silent watchfulness at his approach, soon forget him and proceed about their business of drilling for insects and larvae in the trees. If he scrambles noisily through the woods, however, the first intimation of the woodpecker's presence will be a high-pitched alarm note given as it hastily leaves its perch in undulating flight and seeks a safer vantage point.

Modoc Woodpecker:
Dryobates villosus orius Oberholser

Description.—Very similar to *harrisi*, except paler beneath and somewhat smaller. *Size:* Length (skins) 7.25–9.25, wing 4.92–5.20, tail 2.74–3.29, bill 1.06–1.36. *Nest and eggs:* Identical with those of *D. v. harrisi*.

DISTRIBUTION.—*General:* Sierra Nevada Mountains of California, northern Oregon, and south central Washington and east into Nevada. *In Oregon:* Permanent resident along east slope of Cascades from Columbia River south to vicinity of Diamond Lake, at which point it crosses over summit to intergrade with *harrisi*, although most breeding birds of Rogue River Valley are of this form. Eastward, the birds from Redmond and Bend east and south through Silver Lake, Adel, and Hart Mountain, belong here. (See Figure 9.)

THE BREEDING RANGE of the Modoc Woodpecker in Oregon is roughly a great triangle with the apex at The Dalles and the base extending from southern Josephine County eastward to southeastern Lake County. It includes western Wasco and Jefferson Counties and the timbered parts of Deschutes, Lake, Klamath, Jackson, and Josephine Counties. The bird wanders about somewhat in the winter. Walker (1924) took one at Tillamook, January 13, 1916, and Jewett has a specimen in his collection taken August 11, 1925, at Netarts. Working out the range of this bird is a puzzling proposition at best, but the general line of intergradation can best be illustrated by noting that birds of intermediate character have been taken by us at Crane Prairie (April 29), Bend (February 15), Keno (March 22), Rustler Peak (November 25), and Brownsboro (April 17, June 19, and December 8). The correct allocation of the birds from the Rogue River is particularly difficult, but after careful consideration of the specimens we feel that they properly belong here. An adult male (Gabrielson Coll. No. 1511) taken east of Butte Falls on July 22, 1926, is clearly *harrisi*, whereas birds taken at Hayden Mountain (2), Four-mile Lake, Mosquito Ranger Station, Williams, and Grants Pass are identical with birds from Lake County and northeastern California. In addition, the bird from Rustler Peak and the three from Brownsboro above are also from this Rogue River territory. There is also an intermediate bird from Portland (December 27, 1924), probably a winter straggler that came through the Columbia Gorge from the eastern slope of the Cascades. The records of Newberry (1857) in the Cascades, Suckley (Cooper and Suckley 1860) at Fort Dalles, Bendire (1888) at Fort Klamath, Baird (Baird, Cassin, and Lawrence 1858) at Fort Dalles, and Mearns (1879) and Merrill (1888), both at Fort Klamath, apply to this particular subspecies.

The nest and eggs of the Modoc Woodpecker are not different from those of Harris's Woodpecker, but the latter is a bird of the spruce and fir forests, whereas the former is associated to a great extent with the yellow pine forests and aspen thickets of the more open timber of the eastern slope of the Cascades and the great timber belt of south-central Oregon. There are three sets of four eggs and one of three in the Braly collection that were taken in the vicinity of Fort Klamath between May 13 and 30, 1930, and one set of four eggs taken in the same territory, May 10, 1931.

Rocky Mountain Hairy Woodpecker:
Dryobates villosus monticola Anthony

Description.—Like *D. v. orius*, but larger with heavier and longer bill and much clearer white below. *Size: Male*, wing 5.23, tail 4.00, bill from nostril 1.12; *female*, wing 5.04, tail 3.80, bill from nostril .95. *Nest and eggs:* Indistinguishable from *D. v. harrisi*.

Distribution.—*General:* From British Columbia, Washington, and Montana southward through the Rocky Mountains to eastern Utah and northern New Mexico. *In Oregon:* Breeds in Blue Mountain area, which includes all of Wallowa, Union, Baker, and Grant Counties, all of Umatilla except lower sage lands along Columbia, southern Morrow, timbered parts of Wheeler and Crook, a small area in extreme southeastern Jefferson, and northern Harney and Malheur Counties. In winter, may straggle outside this area, but is common permanent resident of its breeding range in Canadian and Transition Zones of these counties. (See Figure 9.)

Bendire's (1877) records from Camp Harney are the first ones published for the Rocky Mountain Hairy Woodpecker in Oregon. His set of eggs taken May 29, 1876, "in the Blue Mountains" from a dead pine 20 feet from the ground is the first definite breeding record and the only published one available, but we can add the following notes: Jewett took large young from a nest on East Eagle Creek, Baker County, on June 21, 1925; and while traveling together we found a nest containing five fresh eggs on Lookout Mountain, Baker County, May 27, 1933. This nest was drilled in a living aspen tree 12 feet from the ground. Walker (1917b) recorded the bird from eastern Jefferson County, and there are specimens in the Biological Survey collection from that same locality. Our own published records and notes list it for every month in the area outlined above. In addition we have a single bird (Jewett Coll. No. 4411) taken at Adel, Lake County, October 23, 1926, that is undoubtedly a migrant from farther north.

This large and white-looking race, living in open timber, is a conspicuous member of the avifauna of the Blue Mountains, probably seen more frequently than any other woodpecker except the Red-shafted Flicker. The habits and behavior are no different than those of the other Hairy Woodpeckers found in the State.

Batchelder's Woodpecker:
Dryobates pubescens leucurus (Hartlaub)

Description.—Like *D. p. gairdneri* but large with under parts pure white; under tail coverts pure white instead of spotted and barred with black; outer tail feathers with much less black and tertials more spotted with white. *Size:* Length 6–7, wing 4.00, tail 2.62, bill .63. *Nest and eggs:* As in *D. p. gairdneri*.

Distribution.—*General:* From southern Alaska and British Columbia east of Cascade Range south to northeastern California, New Mexico, and Arizona and east to

Montana, western Nebraska, and Colorado. *In Oregon:* Blue Mountain area and desert ranges of Malheur, Harney, and Lake Counties, including Warner Mountains. (See Figure 10.)

Baird (Baird, Cassin, and Lawrence 1858) first reported the small Batchelder's Woodpecker from the range now occupied by this race, and Bendire (1877) considered it rare in the John Day Valley. We believe the various Fort Klamath records of Bendire and Merrill probably should now be referred to one or the other of the two other races of this species. Peck (1911a) recorded it from Malheur County, and there are numerous specimens and field records in the Biological Survey from the territory outlined above. We have records and specimens covering every month from the territory outlined but know of no definite breeding records for eastern Oregon, though the bird is a permanent resident. We have found the species to be scarce in this State and consider it a noteworthy day when more than one individual is seen. Like its relatives, it frequents the cottonwood and willow growth along the streams, being seen very infrequently in the coniferous timber. It is rather quiet except at mating time and may consequently escape detection even when present.

Gairdner's Woodpecker:
Dryobates pubescens gairdneri (Audubon)

Description.—"*Adult male:* Upper parts black, with dingy whitish forehead, scarlet nape, and white stripe down back; middle and greater *wing coverts plain black*, or only lightly spotted with white; *outer tail feathers white*, barred with black; *under parts smoky gray* or light smoke brown. *Adult female:* similar but without scarlet on nape. *Young:* similar, but with red of nape extending partly or wholly over crown. *Length:* 6.25–7.00, wing 3.55–4.15, tail 2.30–2.70, bill .70–.80." (Bailey) *Nest:* A freshly excavated hole, usually in deciduous tree. *Eggs:* 4 or 5, white.

Distribution.—*General:* Coast zone from southern British Columbia to Mendocino

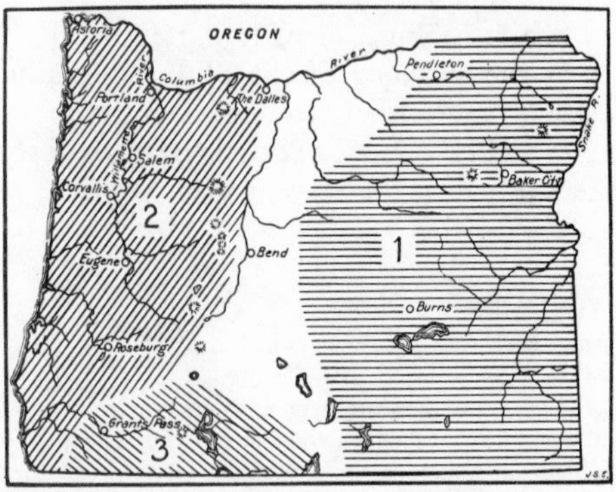

Figure 10.—Distribution of three forms of woodpeckers in Oregon: 1, Batchelder's Woodpecker (*Dryobates pubescens leucurus*); 2, Gairdner's Woodpecker (*D. p. gairdneri*); 3, Willow Woodpecker (*D. p. turatii*).

County, California. *In Oregon:* Permanent resident of western Oregon from Columbia River south to Rogue River and thence southwestward to Coos and Curry Counties, including western slope of Cascades south to northern edge of Rogue River Valley. (See Figure 10.)

AUDUBON (1839) described Gairdner's Woodpecker (Plate 69, *B*) from specimens collected at Fort Vancouver, Oregon; Cooper and Suckley (1860) reported it from western Oregon; and Johnson (1880), Anthony (1886), and Woodcock (1902) listed it as a common resident of western Oregon. Our own numerous specimens, published records, and field notes reveal it to be an exceedingly common bird in the Willamette Valley and a less common but regular resident of the coast country. We have one winter bird of this race from Grants Pass, taken December 16, 1918 (Jewett Coll. No. 4739), and numerous intergrades that will be discussed under *D. p. turatii*.

The species is most abundant along the Columbia and Willamette Rivers, where it builds its nest in the old willow stubs and branches, usually within 10 to 12 feet of the ground. Woodcock (1902) stated that Mr. Warner's collection contained four sets of eggs from Salem, taken between May 4 and 15, with four or five eggs in each set. Braly furnished us with the unpublished record of a nest containing young that he found on Sauvies Island, May 19, 1932.

This tiny black and white woodpecker, smallest representative of the family in Oregon, is a familiar sight in the wooded bottoms along the streams, where, because of the thick, almost junglelike growth, the *tap-tap-tap* of the chisel-like bill is frequently heard long before the industrious carpenter is sighted. Tame and unsuspicious, it is one of the birds most easily observed by the person just beginning the study of birds; and, because of its relative abundance, it is one of the most constant elements of the winter bird population. It is equally abundant in summer, but the thick foliage makes it much more difficult to see it at that season.

Willow Woodpecker:
Dryobates pubescens turatii (Malherbe)

DESCRIPTION.—Like *D. p. gairdneri*, but smaller, with lighter under parts and the tertials spotted with white. *Size:* Length 5.55–6.42, wing 3.46–3.82, tail 2.00–2.38, exposed culmen .57–.67. *Nest and eggs:* Identical with those of *D. p. gairdneri*.

DISTRIBUTION.—*General:* Upper Austral and Transition Zones of California, except desert ranges, and extreme northwest coast extending into southern Oregon. *In Oregon:* Permanent resident of Klamath, Jackson, and Josephine Counties. (See Figure 10.)

THE BREEDING WOODPECKERS of this group from southern Klamath County and the Rogue River Valley are exceedingly puzzling. One from Medford, May 21, 1919 (Gabrielson's Coll. No. 340), has been identified by Oberholser as *D. p. turatii* and so recorded (Gabrielson 1923c). We now have available for comparison a series of 96 skins of the small woodpeckers, including 10 from this southern Oregon territory. Most of these birds seem to be intermediate between *D. p. gairdneri* and *D. p. turatii*, with summer birds matching well in color of the under parts a good series of comparable birds in California. The bills seem slightly heavier, though the measurable difference is negligible, and the spotting of the tertials is not quite so pronounced, although more so than in summer birds from Portland. We are convinced that the breeding population here is in the aggregate a group of intergrades appearing somewhat closer to *turatii*, though individuals tending toward either subspecies are available.

Northern White-headed Woodpecker:
Dryobates albolarvatus albolarvatus (Cassin)

Description.—"Outer hind toe longer than outer front toe; bill with nasal groove extending nearly to tip; terminal half of bill not distinctly compressed; tongue very slightly extensile. *Adult male: head and neck white*, whole body black except for *white patch on wings* and red patch on back of head. *Adult female:* similar, but without red on head. *Young male:* similar, but back and red on crown duller. *Length:* 8.90–9.40, wing 5.00–5.10, tail 4.00–4.05." (Bailey) *Nest:* A hole in a tree, from 4 to 15 feet or more from ground. *Eggs:* 4 to 7, white.

Distribution.—*General:* From Cascades and Sierra Nevadas east to Idaho and Nevada and from Washington to central California. *In Oregon:* Permanent resident of entire timbered section from summit of Cascades eastward and of western slope in Jackson County and westward along Siskiyous at least to Redwood Highway.

The curiously colored Northern White-headed Woodpecker, unexpectedly inconspicuous in its contrasting white and black garb, is a regular permanent Oregon resident wherever the yellow pine is found in good stands. It is one of the more silent woodpeckers that is surprisingly difficult to see so long as it remains motionless against the yellow pine bark. In flight it is exceedingly conspicuous, however, the white wing patches and head showing in startling contrast to the velvety black body plumage. It is a regular inhabitant of the yellow pine area of the Blue Mountains and scattered ranges to the southward and equally common along the eastern slope of the Cascades from the Columbia River southward. Somewhere in the vicinity of Crater Lake it crosses the summit and is found somewhat sparingly in the mixed yellow pine and oak forests of Jackson County and across into Josephine County along the timbered flanks of the Siskiyous. There is an area on the head of the Umpqua as yet too little worked by ornithologists where it may occur, although to date we have no definite record of its appearance there.

Newberry (1857) listed it as not common in the Cascades, and Baird (Baird, Cassin, and Lawrence 1858) recorded it from Oregon, giving the locality as "Cascade Mountains 50 miles south of the Columbia," referring to specimens collected by Newberry. Cooper (1869) listed it as a breeding species near Fort Dalles, but Bendire (1877) reported the first actual nest as taken at Camp Harney, May 27, 1875. He (1895a) also recorded a nest taken at Crater Lake, May 29, 1883. Many writers since that time have listed it, and our own notes show it to be a widely distributed permanent resident. It is not common west of the Cascades, but Gabrielson saw it on Rustler Peak near Mosquito Ranger Station on the Rogue River National Forest and collected a female on Little Gray-back Mountain, just south of the Oregon-California line, on July 16, 1933. On the next day the authors watched a pair feeding a nest full of young in an old pine snag in the same vicinity. Patterson found eggs from May 8 to 16 in the southern Cascades.

Arctic Three-toed Woodpecker:
Picoïdes arcticus (Swainson)

Description.—"*Adult male:* Upper parts *glossy* blue black except for squarish yellow crown patch, fine white spotting on wings, and plain white outer tail feathers; sides of head black and white; under parts white, heavily barred with black on sides. *Adult female:* similar, but without yellow on head. *Young male:* like adult, but yellow crown patch more restricted, black of upper parts duller, under parts tinged with brown. *Young female:* crown black, sometimes with traces of yellow. *Length:* 9.50–10.00, wing 4.85–5.25, tail 3.60, bill 1.40–1.60." (Bailey) *Nest:* In dead trees or stumps, usually close to the ground. *Eggs:* 1 to 4, usually 4, white.

Distribution.—*General:* From Alaska, Yukon, and northern Mackenzie, northern Minnesota, Michigan, and New York. *In Oregon:* Permanent resident in lodgepole pine forests of Canadian Zone in Blue Mountains, Cascades, and Siskiyous.

Newberry (1857) first reported the Arctic Three-toed Woodpecker for Oregon, from the Cascades. Bendire (1877, 1895a) found it at Camp Harney and recorded eggs taken at Linkville (Klamath Falls), May 25, 1883, and Merrill (1888) listed it as breeding at Fort Klamath. Since that time there have been numerous records for the State. We have collected 34 specimens, the most easterly from Whitney, Baker County, and the most westerly from Bolan Lake, Josephine County.

As the yellow pine is preferred by the Northern White-headed Woodpecker, so the lodgepole pine is the chosen haunt of the Arctic Three-toed Woodpecker, and our notes show that the great lodgepole pine forest lying between Bend and Klamath Falls in a more or less unbroken body from the summit of the Cascades to the eastern spurs of the Paulina Mountains (East and Paulina Lakes) is the center of abundance of this beautiful woodpecker. Outside of this area it is much less common but is found in small numbers throughout the lodgepole patches of both the Blue and Siskiyou Ranges.

The nests are usually found within a few feet of the ground in old snags or stumps. Four sets of eggs in the Braly collection, taken in 1930 between May 15 and June 7 in the lodgepole pine area north of Klamath Falls, contained one, two, or four eggs, and a nest found by Jewett in Lake County on June 18 contained three nearly fledged young. Patterson reported nests with eggs from May 6 to 30.

The shiny black back and handsome yellow crown patch lend a distinction to this species missing in most of its relatives. The bird is usually silent, calling neither as frequently nor as noisily as the Hairy Woodpecker, and is almost always located by its industrious tapping as it works over the bark of the pines.

Alaska Three-toed Woodpecker:
Picoïdes tridactylus fasciatus Baird

Description.—*Adult male:* Upper parts mainly black with a whitish nuchal band and a white back, strongly barred with black, wing quills barred with white and secondaries noticeably spotted with the same color, outer tail feathers mainly white, somewhat sparingly barred with black, a conspicuous yellow crown patch and back of head dark glossy blue, under parts white, sides and flanks barred with black. *Adult female:* Similar but without yellow crown. *Size:* Length 9.50, wing 4.50–4.70, tail 3.10–3.75, bill 1.10–1.25. (Adapted from Bailey.) *Nest:* In holes in coniferous trees. *Eggs:* Usually 4, white.

Distribution.—*General:* Hudsonian and Canadian Zones from Alaska, Yukon, and western Mackenzie south to Oregon, northern Idaho, and northern Montana. *In Oregon:* Rare permanent resident of higher parts of Wallowa Mountains and Cascades south at least to east base of Mount McLoughlin in Jackson County.

We have found the Alaska Three-toed Woodpecker to be one of the rarer species. The only published record of it as an Oregon bird is that of Shelton (1917), who listed it as breeding on the Three Sisters. He based his statement on specimens in the Oregon Game Commission collection, a pair and two young collected by Jewett on the Three Sisters, July 19, 1914, which are the first known specimens from the State. On July 24, 1926, Gabrielson collected a young male out of three birds found on the shores of Four-mile Lake at the east base of Mount McLoughlin, the most southerly record for the State. The other two were evidently a newly fledged young and an adult. There are five other specimens, all taken in the higher part of the Wallowa Range on various dates between May 19 and October 26.

In general behavior, this woodpecker is much like the more abundant Arctic Three-toed Woodpecker, frequenting dense lodgepole forests and remaining comparatively silent in most seasons. The call is a peculiar nasal note, quite unlike that of any other woodpecker save those of its other three-toed cousins.

Order Passeriformes

Tyrant Flycatchers: *Family Tyrannidae*

Eastern Kingbird:
Tyrannus tyrannus (Linnaeus)

Description.—"*Adults:* Under parts and ***band on end of tail pure white;*** head and tail black; rest of upper parts slate gray; middle of crown with a concealed patch of orange red. *Young:* crown patch wanting and colors duller, wing and tail coverts edged with brownish, tail band and chest tinged with brownish. *Length:* 8–9, wing 4.45–4.75, tail 3.40–3.75, bill from nostril .50–.57." (Bailey) *Nest:* A rather bulky structure of weed stems, grass, wool, string, feathers, or other similar available material, placed in the crotch of bushes or trees, on telephone poles, or about buildings. *Eggs:* 3 or 4, white or pink, spotted and blotched with browns and lavender.

Distribution.—*General:* Breeds from southern Canada to Nevada, Texas, and Florida. Winters in Central and South America. *In Oregon:* Common summer resident east of Cascades and Klamath Lake country.

Bendire (1877) reported the Eastern Kingbird as a common summer resident of the John Day Valley, and Miller (1904) found it in the same valley in 1899. Woodcock (1902) reported it from the Grand Ronde Valley and eastward on Anthony's authority; Peck (1911a), in Malheur County; Walker (1917b), at the mouth of the Deschutes River in 1914; Willett (1919), common in Harney County; and Prill (1922a), as a breeding species from the Warner Valley. In the manuscript notes of various members of the Biological Survey and in our own notes, it has been recorded for every county in eastern Oregon except Klamath and Deschutes, and undoubtedly it will be found to be a more or less regular inhabitant of the eastern part of the latter. It arrives in May and remains until September (earliest date, May 5; latest, September 15, both Harney County). The eggs are laid in June. The few actual nesting dates we have occur between June 13 and 26, although the nesting period undoubtedly extends over a much longer season.

The Eastern Kingbird, or Bee Martin, is a familiar sight in the irrigated valleys and about the big stock ranches of the eastern part of Oregon, where it is often closely associated with the Western Kingbird. Particularly is this true in August when the young of the year have joined their parents in the sport of capturing a winged meal by a short dash from some vantage point. At this season they sit on the telephone wires or the barbed wire fences in straggling formation, the two species intermixed, as individual birds watch every few yards from their chosen perches. The Western Kingbird is much the more common of the two throughout this section of the State, although the Eastern Kingbird is plentiful enough in the John Day River, Burnt River, and Malheur River Valleys, to mention only a few typical habitats chosen by this bird in Oregon.

Arkansas Kingbird:
Tyrannus verticalis Say

Description.—"*Adult male:* Upper parts and breast light ash gray; throat paler; belly lemon yellow; tail black, outer web of outer feather abruptly white; wings brown, *end of long quills with gradually narrowed points;* concealed crown patch red. *Adult female:* similar, but tips of outer quills less narrowed and crown patch restricted. *Young:* like adults, but crown patch wanting and colors duller, wing coverts bordered with buffy. *Length:* 8.00–9.50, wing 4.75–5.25, tail 3.65–4.00, bill from nostril .50–.55." (Bailey) *Nest:* Rather untidy, of weed stems, feathers, string, paper, straw, or any other available material, usually in small trees, low bushes, or on fence posts and telephone poles or sometimes on ledges on the face of cliffs. *Eggs:* Usually 4, white or flushed with pink, heavily spotted or blotched with brown (Plate 70, *A*).

Distribution.—*General:* Breeds from southern British Columbia, Alberta, and Manitoba south to Lower California and northern Mexico. Winters south to Nicaragua. *In Oregon:* Regular summer resident. Abundant in eastern Oregon and Rogue River Valley, where it is a conspicuous breeding species. Less common elsewhere west of Cascades, although there are many records.

The Arkansas Kingbird, or Western Kingbird, as it is called by most western ornithologists, is a conspicuous summer resident of the open country east of the Cascades from mid-April (earliest date, April 6, Wasco County) to late August (latest date, August 30, Jackson County). There it may be found perching on fences or telephone lines, capturing its insect prey by short twisting sallies in approved flycatcher fashion. Frequently during the late summer mixed groups of this species and the Eastern Kingbird will be found strung out along the telephone lines, bright yellow bellies of these birds showing in striking contrast to the pure white of the eastern species. Except in the higher mountains, it is one of the most conspicuous birds and is particularly abundant in irrigated districts where the swarming hordes of insects make fat living for many summering birds.

West of the Cascades it is almost equally common in the Rogue River Valley but becomes more of a rarity to the northward. We have found it in Lane, Douglas, Clackamas, Josephine, Jackson, Multnomah, Coos, Curry, Marion, Polk, and Benton Counties, including nests in Douglas and Benton Counties. Shelton (1917) recorded it from Lane County, and Woodcock (1902) listed it from Benton and Marion Counties. Walker (1924) recorded a pair taken in Tillamook County, May 8, 1918, and

Overton Dowell, Jr., took several specimens at Mercer Lake, on the coast of Lane County, these latter two being the only coast records except for a single bird noted in Curry County by Gabrielson on May 16. We consider it a bird of rare but regular occurrence in the northern Willamette Valley, where one or more individuals is seen or taken along the Columbia River near Portland nearly every season.

Historically, it is interesting to know that Audubon's (1838) reference to it as a bird of the "Wahlamet" (Willamette) River is the first published record for the State, although it has since been recorded by a long list of writers. No ornithologist could well overlook this conspicuous member of the Oregon avifauna. Manuscript notes of the Biological Survey are filled with references to its abundance in the sagebrush sections of eastern Oregon.

The usual nest sites are in bushes or small trees where the somewhat untidy nests are built in a convenient fork (Plate 70, *A*). Frequently, where trees are not handy, the nests are saddled on the cross arms of telephone poles or built in the broken and weathered tops of fence posts. Preble (ms.) found a nest on Rock Creek, Gilliam County, built on the face of rocky cliffs—a practice that does not seem to be common, although rock rims are plentiful. The eggs are laid in early June. Our dates for eggs range from May 14 to July 21, and most of the records are between June 1 and 15.

The Arkansas Kingbird, like its near relatives, is exceedingly pugnacious and promptly makes life miserable for any bird, large or small, that intrudes on its chosen domain. Hawks, crows, ravens, or magpies all look like fair game to this agile bird, who promptly worries them by a darting, twisting attack from above until they pass the forbidden line on the way out. Many farmers rejoice in the presence of this kingbird because they feel that hawks are less likely to steal their poultry in the face of such a noisy and pugnacious watchman.

Ash-throated Flycatcher:
Myiarchus cinerascens cinerascens (Lawrence)

Description.—"Throat and chest *pale* ashy, sometimes almost white on throat; belly *pale* sulphur yellow; upper parts grayish brown; wings with two white bars, quills edged with reddish brown, tertials edged with white; tail with middle feathers dusky brown, the rest chiefly brown on inner webs; outer tail feathers with *inner web dusky at tip, outer web distinctly whitish*. *Young:* tail feathers rufous, with dark median stripe. *Length:* 8.00–8.50, wing 3.80–4.25, tail 3.65–4.20, bill from nostril .52–.60, tarsus .88–.95." (Bailey) *Nest:* Usually in old woodpecker holes, behind strips of bark, or in cavities in stumps, built of a great variety of vegetable and animal debris that is most convenient. *Eggs:* 3 to 6, creamy to buff, streaked with purple.

Distribution.—*General:* Breeds from Washington, northern Utah, Colorado, and

Plate 70, *A*. Nest and eggs of Arkansas Kingbird. (Photo by Wm. L. Finley and H. T. Bohlman.)

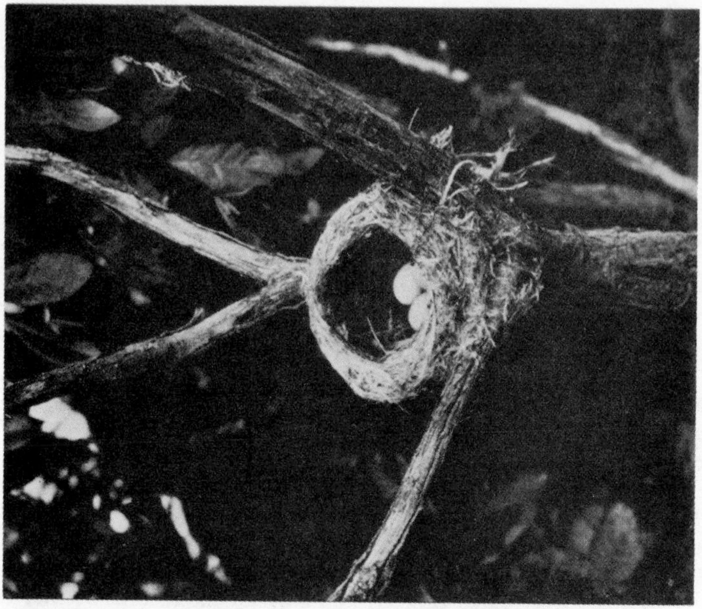

Plate 70, *B*. Nest and eggs of Wright's Flycatcher. (Photo by Alex Walker.)

Texas south into Mexico. Winters to Central America. *In Oregon:* Not common summer resident of lower timber and slopes of eastern Oregon and Umpqua and Rogue River Valleys west of Cascades.

The shy and comparatively silent Ash-throated Flycatcher is the direct antithesis of the noisy and quarrelsome kingbirds. It is a bird of the mixed juniper or yellow pine and deciduous growth in the hot canyons or dry hillsides where the forest and desert meet. Although found over quite a wide territory it is locally most abundant in the timbered foothills of the eastern Rogue River Valley and in the hot dry canyons along the eastern slope of the Cascades in Wasco and Deschutes Counties. There it may be found perched silently on the dead lower limbs of some gnarled tree, remaining motionless except for short dashes after insects.

Little has been written about this retiring flycatcher, although it is a constant summer resident of the State. Bendire (Brewer 1875) first recorded it from Oregon on the basis of a sight record near Camp Harney, and he found the first nest on June 20, 1876, in the same locality (Bendire 1877). Miller (1904) listed it from the John Day Valley, Woodcock (1902) quoted Bryant as recording its presence at Jacksonville in 1883, and Walker (1917b) found it at Redmond, Sisters, and The Dalles. The manuscript files of the Biological Survey contain a number of notes that were of use in drawing up the ranges given above, but all other published records have been our own. We have found it in Douglas, Jackson, and Josephine Counties west of the Cascades and in Wasco, Grant, Sherman, Umatilla, Wheeler, Crook, Deschutes, Lake, Harney, and Malheur Counties east of the Cascades. It arrives in May (earliest date, May 11, Jackson County) and remains until late August, decreasing rapidly in numbers in mid-August. The latest fall date in our own records is September 3, but there is a specimen in the Bishop collection (Willett 1933) taken by W. E. Sherwood at Ashland, on October 25, 1923, which is not only the latest fall date for Oregon but for the Pacific Coast States.

We have few nesting records, although this indicates a lack of observers rather than a scarcity of birds. Patterson took a set of eggs, May 10, 1930, in Jackson County; and Braly, a set of five eggs near Sisters, June 15, 1931, which so far as known to us are the only actual sets of Oregon eggs taken recently.

Say's Phoebe:
Sayornis saya saya (Bonaparte)

Description.—"Upper parts olive gray, darker on head; under parts whitish, tinged below with pale yellowish, sides of breast with olive gray. *Length:* 6.25–7.00, wing 3.25–3.55, tail 3.00–3.40." (Bailey) *Nest:* On beams in barns, bridges, and houses, or on ledges in caves, banks, or cliffs, built of mud mixed with weak stems, grass, moss, hair, feathers, paper, or similar material. *Eggs:* 3 to 6, white, sometimes dotted with brown about the large end.

Distribution.—*General:* Breeds from Alaska, northwestern Mackenzie, Alberta, Saskatchewan, and Manitoba to southern California and northern Mexico. Winters from central California south into Mexico. *In Oregon:* Summer visitor throughout State, except along coast. May winter rarely.

Audubon (1838), who reported Say's Phoebe from the Blue Mountains, first put this bird on the Oregon list, and most of the later writers have recorded it. It is a hardy species that starts its northward movement almost as soon as do the robins and bluebirds. We have seen it as early as February 22 in Wasco and Jackson Counties, February 26 in Klamath County, and February 28 in Wallowa County, and by March 15, though the ground may still be frozen, it can be found regularly throughout its range in the State. It is never an abundant bird, except for a few days in the migration period, but it is widely distributed, single pairs being found about nearly every deserted cabin. It is more common east of the mountains but is a regular resident of the Rogue, Umpqua, and Willamette Valleys. To date it has not been taken on the coast, although stragglers might be taken there if more observers were at work. It often remains until late September (latest normal date, October 29, Wasco County). Jewett noted one in Malheur County, November 26, 1928, and Gabrielson saw a single individual in Coos County, December 6, 1927, and one in Benton County, December 29, 1918. These might have been belated stragglers, but their occurrence more probably indicates occasional wintering individuals, as these dates make records for every month except January.

Say's Phoebes probably begin nesting operations immediately upon their arrival in the State, as Jewett found a nest in Morrow County on April 3 that was ready for eggs and another on April 10 that contained young. The nesting season covers an extended period, as we have found nests containing eggs and newly hatched young as late as June 16 in Harney County.

In Oregon, these birds take the place of the phoebe, or "Bridge Phoebe," dear to the heart of boyish egg collectors of the Middle West. They build in similar places on the beams of small wooden bridges and sit on the fences or telephone wires, emitting occasional mournful protests, accompanied by vigorous jerks of the tail, when an intruder interferes with domestic affairs. They find the tumbling ruins of homesteaders' buildings much to their liking also, and nearly every such ruin harbors at least one pair of phoebes, even though great cliffs containing an abundance of nesting sites may be close by.

Little Flycatcher:
Empidonax trailli brewsteri Oberholser

Description.—"Width of bill at nostrils decidedly greater than half the length of exposed culmen. *Adults: eye ring whitish;* upper parts olive, darker on head from dusky centers of coronal feathers; wing bars varying from brownish to whitish; ***under parts white***, shaded with gray across breast, tinged with yellow beneath; under wing coverts yellowish white. *Young:* browner above, yellower beneath; wing bands buff or yellowish brown. *Male:* length 5.80–6.25, wing 2.70–2.85, tail 2.35–2.60, bill .64–.73, bill from nostril .35–.40, width at base .27–.31, tarsus .65–.72. *Female:* length 5.55–6.00, wing 2.55–2.65, tail 2.20–2.50." (Bailey) *Nest:* Usually close to ground in low shrubs and bushes, woven of dry grasses, pine needles, shreds of bark, plant fibers, and other similar materials and lined with finer material. *Eggs:* 2 to 4, white, dotted and blotched with brown, mostly about the large end.

DISTRIBUTION.—*General:* Breeds from British Columbia, Idaho, and Wyoming south to Mexico. Winters in Central and South America. *In Oregon:* Common summer resident and breeding species. Found in suitable situations throughout State.

THE LITTLE FLYCATCHER is the most abundant and widely distributed small flycatcher in the State and is the common small flycatcher of western Oregon, especially the Willamette Valley, where the Western Flycatcher is the only other *Empidonax* regularly found. It arrives in May (earliest date, April 21, Multnomah County) and remains until early September (latest date, September 17, Lake County). Audubon (1840) listed it from Sauvies Island, and there have been many subsequent records. The name "Little Flycatcher" was revived in the last A. O. U. Check-List, because of the confusion over the name "Traill's Flycatcher," formerly applied to this subspecies.

It frequents the wooded stream bottoms where it builds its nests in small trees and bushes, usually within a few feet of the ground; but like many others of its family, it waits until insect life has reached its summer abundance before undertaking the task of raising a family entirely on such food. Therefore it is well into June before egg laying is finished. We have 12 nests with eggs from June 15 to July 29, but it is probable that these extremes can be extended considerably by more observations.

Its habits are like those of other small members of the family. When at rest, it perches silently and motionless on some dead twig, often low down in the bushes or willow thickets, though occasionally on the topmost branch of a tree. From such a vantage point it captures its insect prey by short quick dashes, returning to the same perch or alighting on a similar one nearby.

Hammond's Flycatcher:
Empidonax hammondi (Xantus)

DESCRIPTION.—"*Adults:* Upper parts ***grayish olive***, grayer anteriorly; wing bars whitish or yellowish; outer tail feather more or less edged with whitish; throat grayish; ***breast olivaceous, almost as dark as back;*** belly and under tail coverts yellowish; width of bill at nostrils less than half the exposed culmen. *Young:* tinged with brown, wing bars yellowish brown. *Male:* length 5.50–5.75, wing 2.60–2.80, tail 2.30–2.50, bill .53–.59, bill from nostril .26–.29, width at base, .22–.24, tarsus .60–.68. *Female:* length 5.25, wing 2.45–2.75, tail 2.15–2.40." (Bailey) *Nest:* Neatly woven structure of plant fiber, shreds of bark, and down, lined with finer material, moss and feathers, sometimes built on horizontal limbs of conifers and sometimes in aspens and cottonwoods. *Eggs:* 3 or 4, creamy white, immaculate or sparingly spotted with brown about the larger end.

DISTRIBUTION.—*General:* Breeds from southern Alaska, Yukon, and southern Alberta to Sierra Nevadas of central California and Colorado. Winters in Mexico. *In Oregon:* Common summer resident of mountainous areas except Coast Ranges, where it is of only casual occurrence.

THE SMALL Hammond's Flycatcher is difficult to distinguish from the several similar species found in the State. It has a narrow bill and a more or less conspicuous dark chest band, characters that at times enable one to identify it with reasonable certainty in the field, but there is much chance of confusion, and for this reason we are ignoring our sight records and are basing our statements regarding it on specimens actually collected. It is commonly found in the Blue Mountains, including the Wallowa Range, on both slopes of the Cascades, and in such isolated ranges as the Steens, Hart, and Warner Mountains, where it frequents the edges of coniferous forests, of mountain glades, and the shores of lakes and tumbling streams. It arrives in May (earliest date, May 8, Baker County) and remains until September (latest date, September 23, Wallowa County). The eggs are laid in June and July. Our three nesting records from the Blue Mountains are June 19, June 24, and July 17.

This little flycatcher has appeared infrequently in the literature of Oregon ornithology. Bendire (1877) listed it from Camp Harney, although there is a possibility that he had it confused with the Gray Flycatcher, a common bird in that territory that had not yet been described. Merrill (1888) took specimens at Fort Klamath, and Shelton (1917) listed it from several localities in eastern Lane County. All other records, except our own published ones, are repetitions of these two. There are specimens in either our own collections or those of the Biological Survey from Wasco, Grant, Wallowa, Baker, Harney, Umatilla, Jackson, Deschutes, Lake, Crook, and Lane Counties.

Wright's Flycatcher:
Empidonax wrighti Baird

DESCRIPTION.—"Similar to *hammondi*, but bill wider, plumage grayer above, whiter below, throat often whitish; *outer web of outer tail feather abruptly paler than inner web*, usually whitish. *Length:* 5.75–6.40. *Male:* wing 2.70–2.95, tail 2.55–2.80, bill .62–.69, bill from nostril .32–.38, width at base .24–.27, tarsus .71–.77. *Female:* wing 2.55–2.75, tail 2.50–2.65." (Bailey) *Nest:* Of plant fibers and shreds of bark, lined with feathers, hair, or moss, and usually placed in a fork of a bush or small tree or fastened to the twigs. *Eggs:* 3 to 5, dull white (Plate 70, *B*).

DISTRIBUTION.—*General:* Breeds from central British Columbia, Yukon, and Saskatchewan south to California, Arizona, New Mexico, and Texas. Winters in Mexico. *In Oregon:* Common summer resident from eastern slopes of Cascades eastward. Casual west of Cascades.

WRIGHT'S FLYCATCHER is as much at home in eastern Oregon on the dry sage slopes as it is among the aspen groves of the mountain meadows and is a common species in its chosen haunt, where it flits about from a perch in the top of a sage bush to one on the lower limb of a gnarled aspen. It arrives in May (earliest date, May 15, Baker County) and remains until September (latest date, September 21, Wallowa County). It so closely resembles Hammond's Flycatcher that it is almost impossible to distinguish it in life, although occasionally its whitish outer tail feathers can be seen and, taken in conjunction with its paler breast, make a fairly good field mark. With the specimens in hand, the difference in the length of the primaries serves best to separate these two very similar forms.

This species was first listed from Oregon by Merrill (1888), who found it at Fort Klamath. Bendire (1895) recorded three Oregon nests, two from Fort Klamath, June 24 and July 14, 1882, and one from the Deschutes River, June 12, 1882. Woodcock (1902) repeated Bendire's records. Peck (1911a) reported it from Malheur County. Shelton (1917) listed it from Crescent and Diamond Lakes, and Prill (1922a) from Warner Valley. Keller (1891b) recorded a set of eggs taken at Salem in 1890, but we are inclined to believe that this may have been confused with some other small flycatcher, as there are few records of this bird in western Oregon. Walker took one at Mulino, Clackamas County, May 5, 1913, and Jewett (Coll. No. 989) has one taken at Tillamook, May 24, 1913. It is possible, of course, for such an obscure bird to be overlooked, but we have collected many small flycatchers in western Oregon since then and not one of them has been *E. wrighti*.

Aside from the egg records of Bendire, we have two, one June 5 (Baker County) and the other June 13 (Klamath County), which would indicate about the same breeding season for this as for the other small flycatchers. Patterson listed two nests in the vicinity of Pinehurst, one May 5 and the other May 20.

Gray Flycatcher:
Empidonax griseus Brewster

DESCRIPTION.—"Nearest to *wrighti*, but larger and much grayer, washed with darker on chest; bill longer, basal half of lower mandible flesh colored in strong contrast to blackish tip." (Bailey) *Nest:* In sagebrush or small trees, built of plant fibers and shredded bark. *Eggs:* 3 or 4, cream buff.

DISTRIBUTION.—*General:* Breeds in intermountain country from eastern Oregon and eastern California to northeastern Colorado. Winters from southern California and Arizona southward into Mexico. *In Oregon:* Regular summer resident and breeding bird of sagebrush areas east of Cascades.

THE GRAY FLYCATCHER closely resembles Wright's but is larger and grayer. While in Oregon, it is most at home in the luxuriant growth of sage along the dry washes, where a combination of good soil and better moisture conditions produce plants with the stature of small trees. It seems somewhat out of place there, although the gray of its coat fits perfectly into the gray landscape. Jewett (1913b) published as a first record for the State two specimens taken in Harney County, June 25, 1908, by Wm. L. Finley, but we find that there are a number of prior specimens in the Biological Survey collections. The earliest one we have located was taken May 25, 1896, at Elgin, Union County, by Vernon Bailey, who also took one at Burns, Harney County, July 6, 1896 (Oberholser 1920b). Preble, who was with Bailey at Elgin, took an adult and a nest with two eggs at the Narrows, Harney County, July 25, 1896 (Oberholser 1920b). Since Jewett's publication, Walker (1914b and 1917b) has reported nesting records from the Paulina Mountains and the vicinity of Bend, Deschutes County, and Willett (1919) has reported the bird common in central Oregon. Numerous specimens have been collected, by the writers and others, from Jefferson, Deschutes, Lake, Harney, Malheur, and Union Counties, and we know that the species is a regular summer resident of the great eastern Oregon sagebrush plateaus. The Union County records are the only ones today from outside this area.

The birds arrive in May and remain until late August (earliest date, April 28; latest, August 29, both Harney County). Jewett found them building nests in the sagebrush in southern Harney County on May 23, and Braly took a set of eggs in Deschutes County, June 15, 1930. Preble's nest taken at the Narrows on July 25 is the latest egg date.

Western Flycatcher:
Empidonax difficilis difficilis Baird

Description.—"*Adults:* Upper parts olivaceous (brownish in winter), wing bars dull buffy (brighter in winter); *under parts dull yellow*, shaded with brown across breast, brightening to sulphur yellow on belly and under tail coverts; under wing coverts buffy, deepening to ochraceous on edge of wing; width of bill at nostrils decidedly greater than half the length of exposed culmen. *Young:* similar, but browner above, with wing bands yellowish brown or rusty buff, sulphur yellow of belly replaced by dull white. *Length:* 5.50–6.00. *Male:* wing 2.50–2.90, tail 2.35–2.60, bill .57–.63, bill from nostril .29–.33, width at base .25–.28, tarsus .64–.69. *Female:* wing 2.30–2.60, tail 2.20–2.45." (Bailey) *Nest:* Usually near water, in trees, bushes, or on rock ledges or beams of buildings or any similar location; built of plant fiber, rootlets, leaves, moss, feathers, and other available material. *Eggs:* 3 or 4, white, blotched and spotted with brown and buff.

Distribution.—*General:* Breeds from Glacier Bay, Alaska, British Columbia, and Montana south to California and Texas. Winters in Mexico. *In Oregon:* Fairly common summer resident west of Cascades. Much less common in eastern Oregon.

Like the other small flycatchers of its group, the Western Flycatcher is not conspicuous or easily identified and is usually overlooked among the more abundant Little Flycatchers. Because of the difficulty of field identification of this dull-colored species, we have based our discussions of the group on specimens only. The Western Flycatcher is the yellowest flycatcher found in the State and can usually be distinguished in the field from the larger and grayer Little Flycatcher with which it is associated in western Oregon. West of the Cascades it is a fairly common bird, more abundant along the coast where it frequents stream bottoms grown up with willow and alder thickets. It arrives in May (earliest date, May 5, Benton County) and remains until August (latest date, September 9, Tillamook County).

Although we have collected flycatchers carefully throughout eastern Oregon for many years, neither of us has taken a specimen of this species in that part of the State. Bendire (1877, 1895a) recorded seeing a number at Camp Harney, May 8, 1876, and finding a nest with four young on Anna Creek near Fort Klamath, July 6, 1882, and Vernon Bailey took a specimen, together with a set of four eggs, at Drews Creek (Lake County), June 17, 1897. These are the only eastern Oregon records available at present. Bendire (1895a) reported also that Dr. C. T. Cooke found several nests and eggs near Salem. These and Bendire's Fort Klamath nest and young constitute the earliest certain records of the species for the State.

Although the nest is usually placed in a crotch of a small tree or bush, the Western Flycatcher is not set in its ways and often builds in an upturned root, on a rock ledge, or on the beams of some building. We have records of a completed nest as early as May 12 and of nests with fresh eggs as late as June 20.

Western Wood Pewee:
Myiochanes richardsoni richardsoni (Swainson)

Description.—"*Adults:* Upper parts dark grayish brown; under parts heavily washed with dark gray; belly and under tail coverts whitish or pale yellowish; wing at least six times as long as tarsus; tarsus longer than middle toe with claw; exposed culmen much less than twice the width of bill at nostril. *Young:* with buffy or brownish wing bars. *Length:* 6.20–6.75, wing 3.15–3.55, tail 2.50–2.95, exposed culmen .44–.51, width of bill at base .27–.32, tarsus .49–.56." (Bailey) *Nest:* A neat structure of plant fiber, grasses, etc., saddled on a horizontal limb usually not more than 30 or 40 feet above the ground. *Eggs:* 2 to 4, white, specked and blotched in an irregular wreath of brown about the larger end.

Distribution.—*General:* Breeds from central Alaska, southern Mackenzie, Saskatchewan, and Manitoba south to Mexico. Winters in South America. *In Oregon:* Common summer resident throughout timbered sections.

The mournful *pee-ar* of the Western Wood Pewee is a familiar sound in the forested sections of the State, where the small dull-colored vocalist may be found sitting quietly on a dead branch of some giant tree. In fact, its mournful call is better known to most Oregonians than its dull colors and rather retiring habits. The call note is given persistently through the long summer days, long after the spring bird chorus has broken up into a few scattered individual singers that are comprised largely of the wood pewees and some of the vireos.

Despite its ability to adapt itself to variable conditions, this pewee shows a definite preference for the glades and parks of the more open coniferous forests and is most abundant in such areas. It frequents also the smaller timbered patches along the watercourses and the artificial groves about farmsteads. It has been noted by us or given in the manuscript records of other members of the Biological Survey in every county in the State. It arrives in May (earliest date, April 27) and remains until the last of August (latest date, September 14). Baird (Baird, Cassin, and Lawrence 1858) listed it from the Columbia River, the first record definitely assignable to the State.

The nests are usually saddled on a horizontal limb of a tree anywhere from 6 to 7 feet up to 50 feet from the ground, and nest building is somewhat late, occupied nests being found mostly in late June or July. Available records range between May 16 and July 27 for nests containing eggs or partially grown young. Bendire (1895a), who first recorded the species as an Oregon breeding bird, reported nests with eggs at Fort Klamath on July 7, 1882, and July 18, 1883.

Olive-sided Flycatcher:
Nuttallornis mesoleucus (Lichtenstein)

DESCRIPTION.—"*Adults:* Under parts with *whitish median tract between dark, somewhat streaked lateral parts*, white sometimes faintly tinged with yellow; upper parts sooty, *conspicuous tuft of white cottony feathers on sides of rump* (usually concealed by wings). *Young:* similar, but wing coverts tipped with buffy, or brownish instead of white. *Length:* 7.10–7.90, wing 3.90–4.50, tail 2.80–3.50, exposed culmen .58–.70, tarsus .55–.60." (Bailey) *Nest:* Saddled on coniferous branches, usually high above the ground, skillfully woven of vegetable fibers. *Eggs:* Usually 3, creamy white, generally with a wreath of brown and lavender spots about the larger end.

DISTRIBUTION.—*General:* Breeds from central Alaska, Mackenzie, Manitoba, Quebec, south in coniferous forests of western United States to Mexican borders and in eastern mountains to North Carolina. Winters in South America. *In Oregon:* Common summer resident of forested sections.

THE RINGING CALL of the Olive-sided Flycatcher, thrown out as he sits on the topmost twig of a giant conifer, typifies all that is wild and free and untamed in the great spire-pointed forests of spruce and fir that clothe the mountain slopes of the State. No other bird note, save the clear peal of the Loon coming through the fog of early morn across a mountain lake or the ringing bugle call of the Pileated Woodpecker flung out in the gray dawn of the heavy forests, can stir such unnamed primitive emotions and arouse in the sensitive listener so strong a desire to go back to the days when the world was young. It is perhaps the surroundings, but there is something in that call that makes it the vocal expression of all that is wild and intractable in the wilderness. No matter how many times it has been heard, it is a red-letter day when *Nuttallornis* completes his spring journey northward and announces to all concerned that he is back again to take up the love-making and fly-catching left unfinished at the fall departure.

The Olive-sided Flycatcher prefers the spruce and fir forests and consequently is a common resident of the higher parts of the Cascades, the Blue Mountains, and the Canadian Zone strip along the coast. It is also found, though less commonly, along the foothills of the Willamette Valley, in the Warner Mountains and on Hart Mountain in eastern Lake County. It arrives in May (earliest date, May 1, Tillamook County) and remains until September (latest date, September 15).

As in so many other cases, the honor of being the first to list this bird as an Oregon species goes to Bendire (1877), who found it rare in the hills above Camp Harney. Not far behind, Mearns (1879) found it at Fort Klamath, and since that time it has been listed by many others. Loomis (1901) stated that on September 9, 1898, one came aboard ship off the mouth of Rogue River. Bendire (1895a) listed it as a breeding species, as have several others in manuscript notes, but the only actual nest we have found was one located by Jewett at Strawberry Lake (Grant County), July 13, 1915. This nest was on the lower limb of a spruce about 8 feet from the ground and contained five downy young. Patterson discovered two nests in the Klamath country on June 20 and 26, 1923.

Larks: *Family Alaudidae*

Pallid Horned Lark:
Otocoris alpestris arcticola Oberholser

Description.—*Adult male:* Front of crown hornlike tufts; lores, cheeks, and shield on breast black; back of head and neck, upper tail coverts, and bend of wing pinkish cinnamon; forehead, superciliary stripe, ear coverts, and throat white; rest of under parts white, sides and flanks shaded with cinnamon; back pale grayish streaked with brown. *Female:* Like male, but black of head replaced by brownish and buffy; back of neck, bend of wing, and upper tail coverts cinnamon without pinkish tinge; back of neck narrowly streaked, superciliary and ear coverts buffy; sides and flanks streaked with dusky. (Adapted from Bailey.) *Size:* Length (skins) 6.30–7.50, wing 4.00–4.50, tail 2.44–2.91, bill .37–.47. *Nest:* A slight depression in the ground, lined with fine grasses and roots. *Eggs:* 3 or 4, grayish or greenish marked with brown.

Distribution.—*General:* Breeds from Alaska (except in Pacific Coast strip) south in mountains to northern Washington. Winters to Oregon and Utah. *In Oregon:* Known only as winter migrant from December to February.

The Pallid Horned Lark is present in Oregon as a winter migrant from December to February (earliest date, December 16, Baker County; latest, February 28, Wallowa County). Little is known about its abundance and distribution in the State, as most observers have not troubled to distinguish it in the great wintering flocks of Horned Larks that frequent eastern Oregon. Contrary to the usual experience in field identification of subspecies, we do not find it difficult to select individuals of this form out of the flocks of the Dusky Horned Lark with which it is usually associated. Both of us have done so and then confirmed our identification by collecting the birds. They are conspicuously larger and paler than the Dusky Horned Larks, and their white throats stand out noticeably when they are among their yellow-throated companions. The only prior published record of the Pallid Horned Lark is by Gabrielson (1924a), who included it in a list of Wallowa County birds from specimens collected in that county by the authors in February 1919 and 1920.

In working over the collections we found that Jewett had a bird belonging to this race taken at Hermiston, January 14, 1917, that is, so far as we can learn, the first specimen taken in the State. Since that time we have taken the species in Wallowa, Umatilla, Morrow, Gilliam, Baker, and Lake Counties. More intensive collecting will undoubtedly show it to be a regular winter visitor to most of the open country east of the Cascades and the length of its stay to extend over a longer period than our records to date indicate.

Streaked Horned Lark:
Otocoris alpestris strigata Henshaw

Description.—"Back heavily streaked with black in sharp contrast to deeply ruddy nape; under parts partly or wholly yellow. *Male:* length 6.75–7.25, wing 3.70–4.10, tail 2.70–3.05. *Female:* 6.25–6.50, wing 3.60–3.85, tail 2.50–2.80." (Bailey) *Nest and eggs:* Same as those of Pallid Horned Lark.

Distribution.—*General:* Breeds on west side of Cascades in Washington and Oregon south to Siskiyou County, California. Winters throughout its range and into eastern Washington and Oregon and northern California. *In Oregon:* Common permanent resident that breeds in Willamette, Umpqua, and Rogue River Valleys as well as in many other smaller valleys of western Oregon. Winters throughout this area and eastward regularly along Columbia to Morrow County, less commonly to other parts of eastern Oregon.

The Streaked Horned Lark is darker on the back and conspicuously more yellow beneath than any other subspecies in Oregon. The extremely yellow under parts distinguish it easily from the paler Dusky Horned Lark. It was first described by Henshaw (1884) from specimens among which was an adult female collected at Albany, January 22, 1881. Henshaw's reference is the first in Oregon literature that can be assigned definitely to this subspecies, but many subsequent records have been published. It is a common breeding bird of the open fields in suitable localities throughout western Oregon, and we have found it to be particularly abundant in the rolling open hills of Polk and Yamhill Counties and in the great, flat, pasture-land area of Linn, Lane, and Benton Counties. It is equally abundant in the rocky grasslands east of Medford, Jackson County. We have taken many winter specimens along the Columbia River, particularly in the area between Boardman, Irrigon, and Cecil, on dates ranging from September 25 to January 31; and Jewett has a bird taken on February 11, 1932, at Abert Lake, Lake County.

The species is scarce on the coast, though we have found it in Curry (November 22), Coos (February 16–17), Tillamook (February 7), and Clatsop (September 22) Counties, and it is probable that more time spent in the open valleys of the coast would result in more records. The area of open pasture land is slowly increasing as land is cleared and put into cultivation, and such changes are frequently followed by an influx of birds that find the new conditions to their liking.

Mating begins in January or early February, and by March 1 the wintering flocks are broken up into mated pairs or trios in which two males are still contesting for the favor of a female. During the mating and incubation period, the males habitually perch on fence posts, where, with the tufts of black feathers erected like two tiny horns, they sing a tinkling little song that may be likened to a whispered song of the meadowlark. At times the song is given on the wing. Two and possibly three broods are raised each season, and eggs can be found from March 15 to June 4, or possibly later. The only two recent nests known to us were discovered by Elmer Griepentrog (ms.) near Salem on May 21 and 27, 1929. Each contained four eggs. The funny spotted youngsters begin to be a conspicuous element of the roadside fauna in May and June, and from that time on flocks of the birds may be found. They are perhaps family flocks at first, though they gradually increase in size as the season advances until by fall dozens or even hundreds of individuals are associated together.

Dusky Horned Lark:
Otocoris alpestris merrilli Dwight

Description.—"Similar to *strigata*, but larger, grayer above, streaking of back blacker and back of neck paler, pinkish instead of ruddy brown; less yellowish below; eyebrow usually yellowish. *Male:* wing 4.07, tail 2.80, bill from nostril .35. *Female:* wing 3.72, tail 2.50, bill from nostril .34." (Bailey) *Nest and eggs:* Same as those of Pallid Horned Lark.

Distribution.—*General:* Breeds from British Columbia and Idaho south through Washington and Oregon to northern California and Nevada. Winters south to California. *In Oregon:* Common permanent resident found in every county east of Cascades.

THE DUSKY HORNED LARK is one of the most abundant birds of the sagebrush sections of the State. In spring and summer scattered individuals and pairs are to be found everywhere, and in fall and winter huge wintering flocks comprised largely of this form are often the only living things to be seen in miles of travel. Its habits and behavior are the same as other races previously discussed. Like all of its relatives, it nests early. Our dates for nests and eggs extend from April 3 to June 20. Two and possibly three broods are regularly raised in the lower altitudes, and two are frequently hatched in the higher plateaus.

Bendire's (1877) records of Horned Larks in the vicinity of Camp Harney undoubtedly are referable to this form, although this subspecies was not recognized until 1890 when Dwight described it, giving Fort Klamath as the type locality.

Swallows: *Family Hirundinidae*

Violet-green Swallow: *Tachycineta thalassina lepida* Mearns

DESCRIPTION.—"*Adult male:* Top of head parrot green; nape with a narrow purple collar; back bottle green, glossed with violet in some lights; rump and upper tail coverts violet, shaded with purple; wing and tail quills black, glossed with indigo; wing coverts violet, edged with green; rump with white patches on sides almost confluent in life; under parts white. *Adult female:* similar, but smaller and duller. *Young:* like those of *bicolor*, but feathers of under parts grayish beneath the surface, and bill smaller [Plate 71, *A*]. *Length:* 5.30, wing 4.65, tail 1.97, bill .26." (Bailey) *Nest:* In cliffs, hollow trees, or bird houses, lined with straw and feathers. *Eggs:* 4 or 5, white.

DISTRIBUTION.—*General:* Breeds from central Alaska, Yukon, and central Alberta south to Lower California and Mexico. Winters in Mexico and Central America. *In Oregon:* Abundant breeding species throughout State.

AUDUBON (1838) said that the Violet-green Swallow bred along the "Wahlamet" (Willamette) River, and Nuttall (1840) made the same statement. Bendire (1877), Johnson (1880), and Merrill (1888) found it to be common in the territories worked by them. At present it is found throughout the State—records for every county being available to us—and can be considered common not only in the settled sections but in many mountainous districts. It is one of our most abundant dooryard birds and builds its untidy nest of feathers and straw in bird houses (Plate 71, *B*) and in crannies about outbuildings, as well as in holes in trees and fence posts and crevices in rocky cliffs. Together with the bluebirds, it usually occupies bird boxes about city homes and parks, taking the place the Purple Martin occupies in many of the Eastern States.

Plate 71, *A*. Young Violet-green Swallows. (Photo by Wm. L. Finley and H. T. Bohlman.)

Plate 71, *B*. Violet-Green Swallow at nest box. (Photo by Wm. L. Finley, Jr.)

Its intimate, confiding ways, constant cheerful twittering, and brilliantly contrasting violet and green back combine to make it a favorite with all bird lovers.

It is the earliest swallow to arrive. It reaches southern Oregon by late February and can be counted on to appear in the Columbia River bottoms near Portland by March 6 or 7. We have a number of records for the Rogue River Valley between February 20 and March 1 in different years and could perhaps find it there still earlier by more continuous observation (earliest date, February 20, Lane County). Eggs have been found from May 7 to July 1, and the height of the nesting season is reached about June 1.

By early July, flocks of swallows, composed in many instances mostly of this species, begin to form. They grow steadily in size until by September hordes of graceful, darting forms swirl over the meadows and lakes, feeding on the abundant insect life of late summer. These swarms are conspicuous—either in flight or lining the telephone wires for rods—for many days until suddenly, as the nights grow chill, one awakes to the fact that they are no longer present (latest date, October 6, Multnomah County). They depart in a body, and the emptiness of the air is emphasized by the occasional straggler that flits about—perhaps looking for the departed clans.

Tree Swallow:
Iridoprocne bicolor (Vieillot)

Description.—"*Adult male: Under parts pure white;* upper parts burnished *steel blue;* lores deep black; wings and tail blackish, slightly tinged with green. *Adult female:* upper parts usually duller than in male, but sexes often indistinguishable. *Young:* above entirely dull brownish slate. *Length:* 5.00–6.25, wing about 4.50–4.80, tail 2.30–2.50." (Bailey) *Nest:* In holes in trees or bird boxes, lined with grass and feathers. *Eggs:* 4 or 5, white.

Distribution.—*General:* Breeds from northwestern Alaska, southern Mackenzie, northern Manitoba, and northern Quebec south to southern California, Colorado, Kansas, northern Arkansas, and Virginia. Winters from central California, coast and south Atlantic States to Central America. *In Oregon:* Common summer resident and breeding species for western Oregon. Less common in eastern Oregon, except in Klamath, Lake, Deschutes, and Wasco Counties, and not noted in higher parts of Blue Mountains.

The Tree Swallow, unlike the Cliff Swallow, is most common in western Oregon and about the high lakes in the Cascades. For several years there was a thriving colony at the southeast base of Mount McLoughlin in the dead trees that had been killed by the raising of Fish Lake for irrigation purposes; and nearly every one of the high Cascade lakes, as well as such coastal bodies of water as Tahkenitch, Siltcoos, and Devils Lakes, has its quota of these swallows with steel-blue backs and pure white under parts, which are among the most beautiful of our summer birds. They are somewhat larger than the other swallows, comparatively slower of wing, and a little more sedate in behavior. They are usually tame and unsuspicious and will hunt for insects low over the water or weeds and fly all about a human being as if entirely unconscious of his presence. They arrive in March (earliest date, February 22, Tillamook County) and remain until September (latest date, September 24, Benton County).

The nests are almost invariably built in old woodpecker holes or other cavities in dead stumps and snags. The eggs are laid in May (May 10–30), and we have records of young being fed in the nest as late as June 28 but have no definite June egg dates. There has been a small colony about an alder stump near Gabrielson's place at Devils Lake, Lincoln County, for many years that invariably have young on the wing by July 4, which means the eggs must have been laid in early June.

Suckley (Cooper and Suckley 1860), who found Tree Swallows common at The Dalles, was the first to report them for the State. Mearns (1879) listed them as abundant at Fort Klamath on April 28, 1875, and Merrill (1888) considered them common at the same point. Since that time they have been frequently recorded, particularly in lists from western Oregon. Curiously enough there is no mention in literature of this bird from northeastern Oregon. Neither is there any record in the Biological Survey files or in our own voluminous notes to indicate its presence in that section. It probably occurs, at least occasionally, but has escaped detection during the brief visits we and others have made to that territory.

Bank Swallow:
Riparia riparia riparia (Linnaeus)

Description.—"Tarsus with a small tuft of feathers on back near toes; bill small, nostrils opening laterally; tail much shorter than wings, emarginate. Upper parts sooty, darkest on head and wings; under parts white, with *sooty band across chest and sides*, and sometimes sooty spot on breast. *Young:* similar, but feathers of wings and rump with buffy or whitish edgings. *Length:* 4.75–5.50, wing 3.70–4.25, tail 2.10–2.25." (Bailey) *Nest:* A burrow excavated in a perpendicular bank, the back end lined with bits of grass. *Eggs:* 3 to 6, white.

Distribution.—*General:* Breeds from northern Alaska and northern Quebec south to southern California, Arizona, Texas, central Alabama, and Virginia. Winters in South America. *In Oregon:* Breeding species. Least abundant swallow in State.

The Bank Swallow is the least common of all the members of the family over the State as a whole, although it is abundant in the colonies found. It appears in April (earliest date, April 3, Yamhill County) and remains until September (latest date, September 12, Harney County). It was first reported from the State by Bendire (1877), who found a colony near Malheur Lake on May 27, 1875. Jones (1900) reported it from Portland, and Woodcock (1902) listed it from Dayton (Hadley), Sheridan (Pope),

Elkton (Andrus), Corvallis, and Malheur Lake (Bendire's record mentioned above)—all localities in the Willamette Valley except Elkton and Malheur. Shelton (1917) found it in Lane County but stated that many of the reported occurrences probably referred to the Rough-winged Swallow. Willett (1919) stated that it bred at Malheur Lake, and Prill (1922a) also reported it as breeding in the Warner Valley.

In the manuscript notes of the Biological Survey it has been reported as breeding at Klamath Lake (J. J. Furber and L. A. Lewis), Portland (Finley), Malheur Lake (V. Bailey), and Juntura (Shelton). In our own experience, we have found it in recent years mostly in eastern Oregon, where for many years there have been colonies at Adel (Lake County), Arlington (Gilliam County), Irrigon (Morrow County), and near Ontario (Malheur County). Undoubtedly there are other large colonies in eastern Oregon, because often, in that part of the State particularly, competent observers who publish their notes are rare, rather than the birds, which may well be the case in this instance.

The colony near Ontario has been the largest. Several hundred pairs nest there in a cut above the Old Oregon Trail. On May 27, 1933, as we were driving toward Ontario, we witnessed a curious incident in this colony. A car, traveling at a high rate of speed, passed us and as it roared through the swarm of birds passing to and fro over the highway killed a swallow. We slowed down to pick up the bird, when a crow that had been sitting in the shelter of a sage bush at the top of the bank swooped down, seized the dead swallow in its beak, and flew off across Snake River. We have passed the place several times since and each time have noted a crow hanging about the colony, evidently retrieving the birds knocked down by speeding cars.

The colony at Adel contained full sets of eggs on May 26, 1925, when Jewett dug into several nests, and the Arlington group had half-grown young on June 6, 1926. We have not disturbed the nests on other occasions, although one or the other of us has seen the birds in these various colonies nearly every year since. In July 1922, Gabrielson found a few pairs nesting near Yachats, in Lincoln County, the only colony either of us has noted in recent years west of the Cascades.

Rough-winged Swallow:
Stelgidopteryx ruficollis serripennis (Audubon)

Description.—"Bill small; tail short and slightly emarginate; tarsus slightly feathered above; lateral claws curved and not reaching beyond the base of the middle claw; *outer web of outer primaries saw-toothed* in male, roughened in female. *Adults:* upper parts dull grayish brown, darker on wings and tail, tertials usually margined with grayish; under parts soiled gray, belly and under tail coverts white. *Young:* like adults, but plumage more or less washed with brown; wings with broad cinnamon tips and margins. *Length:* 5.00–5.75, wing 4.00–4.70, tail 2.05–2.35." (Bailey)

Nest: A burrow excavated in a perpendicular bank (Plate 72). *Eggs:* 3 to 6, white.

Distribution.—*General:* Breeds from southern British Columbia, Montana, North Dakota, Minnesota, central Wisconsin, Ontario, New York, and western Massachusetts south to southern United States and Mexico. Winters in Mexico and Central America. *In Oregon:* Fairly common summer resident and breeding species.

It is our own observation that Rough-winged Swallows are more widely distributed than Bank Swallows and are scattered in colonies of a few pairs or as single pairs nesting in earthen banks rather than being assembled in great aggregations. They are present from April (earliest date, April 7, Lane County) to August (latest date, August 28, Harney County). The little dull-colored birds are easily distinguishable from all other swallows except the Bank Swallows. As many observers do not distinguish between these two species, some of the records of each may apply to the other. In the hand or at rest, however, these two are also easily recognizable, but on the wing it often takes keen eyes to determine surely whether the distinct dark breast band of the Bank Swallow is present or only the indistinct shading of the Rough-wing. In habits and manner of flight, the two are very similar. Both birds spend much time wheeling about near the low banks in which the nests are located. and in the summer both mingle with the great swallow swarms, of which they are usually an inconspicuous part.

Merrill (1888) first reported the Rough-winged Swallow for the State, from Fort Klamath. Keller (1892b) found it at Salem, and Woodcock (1902) listed it from Yaquina Bay, Portland, Salem, and Corvallis. Miller (1904) recorded it from Wheeler County, and Shelton (1917) considered it common in west-central Oregon. Peck (1911a) included it in his list from northern Malheur County, as did Walker (1924) from Tillamook. Gabrielson (1924a) found it to be common in Wallowa County, and in our *Birds of the Portland Area* (Jewett and Gabrielson 1929) we included it as a regular summer resident and reported two nests dug out by Jewett on June 23 and 28, one of which contained a large young bird and the other an addled egg. We have not excavated other nests but know the young birds are generally on the wing in early July, which would bring the height of the egg-laying period around the first of June.

Barn Swallow:
Hirúndo erythrogaster Boddaert

Description.—"Tail forked for about half its length, outside feather tapered to point; tarsus shorter than middle toe and claw; upper part feathered. *Adults: under parts tawny brown;* darkest on throat; forehead dark brown, rest of upper parts glossy steel blue; wings and tail tinged with purple and green; tail feathers—except middle pair—marked with large whitish spots. *Young:* fork of tail shorter; upper parts paler, under parts duller, brown of forehead indistinct or wanting; throat and chest light rusty. *Length:* 5.75–7.75, wing 4.60–4.90, tail 3.70–4.10, forked in adult male

Plate 72. Young Rough-winged Swallows at nest. (Photo by Wm. L. Finley and H. T. Bohlman.)

for about 1.85–2.10." (Bailey) *Nest:* A bowl-shaped structure of mud mixed with straw, lined with feathers, and cemented to timbers in barns and bridges and other buildings or in a cave or crevice. *Eggs:* 3 to 5, white, speckled with brown and lavender (Plate 73, *A*).

Distribution.—*General:* Breeds from northwestern Alaska, Mackenzie, southern Manitoba, and central Quebec south to southern California, Mexico, southern Texas, northern Arkansas, Tennessee, and North Carolina. Winters in Central and South America. *In Oregon:* Fairly common summer resident and breeding bird.

The Barn Swallow (Plate 73, *A*) is found throughout the State, as records are available from every county, though nowhere is it as abundant as the Cliff Swallow in the large colonies. This bird shows little tendency to colonize. One or two pairs about the ranch yards are about the usual quota. It has been known as an Oregon bird since it was found at Fort Klamath, June 15, 1875, by Lieutenant Wittich (Mearns 1879). Bendire (1877) reported it as a breeding species near Camp Harney, and subsequent writers have reported it from many localities in the State. In our own notes and those of other Biological Survey members we find references to its presence in small numbers in every section of the State. It appears in April (earliest date, April 6, Marion County) and remains until September (latest date, September 26, Jackson County). With its long, forked tail and long wings, it is the most graceful of all land birds and reminds one of the smaller terns not only in shape but in behavior. It darts about over the grasslands in quick, intricate evolutions that outdo those of any of its relatives—a speeding insect trap—snaring victims that are not alert enough to escape.

The cup-shaped mud nests (Plate 73, *A*) are almost invariably placed on a rafter inside some building or beneath a bridge, and in some communities the birds are known as bridge swallows. The eggs are usually laid in May and June, although nests occupied by unfledged young have been reported as late as August 20. The earliest egg date we have actually recorded is May 6, the latest, June 5, though we are certain this latter date does not represent the end of the egg-laying period. After the breeding season the Barn Swallows join the great mixed flocks of swallows that swarm over the lowlands or decorate the telephone wires for rods, like strings of jewels. These swarms are usually most abundant in early September. By the middle of that month they are gone except for a few stragglers.

Northern Cliff Swallow:
Petrochelidon albifrons albifrons (Rafinesque)

Description.—"*Adults: Forehead white, buffy, or brown;* crown, back, and patch on chest glossy blue black; throat and sides of head chestnut; *rump conspicuous pale rufous;*

Plate 73, *A*. Barn Swallow at nest containing eggs. (Photo by Wm. L. Finley and H. T. Bohlman.)

Plate 73, *B*. Northern Cliff Swallows. (Photo by Reed Ferris.)

belly white. *Young:* similar, but colors duller and pattern less sharply defined; throat usually, and other parts of head sometimes, spotted with white; tertials and tail coverts edged with brown, chestnut of head partly or wholly wanting; upper parts dull blackish. *Length:* 5–6, wing 4.05–4.55, tail 2.00–2.20." (Bailey) *Nest:* A gourd-shaped structure built of bits of mud mixed with straw, lined with feathers, and cemented to cliffs or buildings. *Eggs:* 3 to 5, white, spotted with brown and lilac.

Distribution.—*General:* Breeds from central Alaska, Mackenzie, northern Ontario, southern Quebec, and Cape Breton Island south over entire United States except Florida and Rio Grande Valley. Winters in South America. *In Oregon:* Common summer resident and breeding species throughout State, least abundant on coast.

In suitable localities the Northern Cliff Swallow (Plate 73, *B*) is an abundant summer bird that breeds in great colonies on the faces of overhanging cliffs or under the eaves of barns and other buildings. Its gourd-shaped nests of mud are conspicuous and easily located. The bird is most abundant in eastern Oregon where the great basaltic lava rims furnish innumerable nesting sites. For several years there was a great colony beneath a highway bridge near Arlington, and the birds swarmed both above and below the bridge all day long. We have located other large colonies at various times. In 1926 we found hundreds of their curious nests plastered on the rocks along the Blitzen River in southern Harney County, and along the Malheur River at times there has been a great colony in the basaltic rims that abound in that section. In western Oregon, particularly in the Willamette Valley, the colonies are much smaller and are frequently located beneath the eaves of barns and other outbuildings. They normally contain a dozen or more pairs, though sometimes as many as 50 nests will be found on one building.

The earliest published reference to the Cliff Swallow in Oregon was in 1857 when Newberry reported it as common in the Willamette Valley and not common east of the Cascades. Baird (Baird, Cassin, and Lawrence 1858) recorded it from The Dalles in May 1855, and Cooper (Cooper and Suckley 1860) listed it as a common breeding species at Portland. Since that time there have been many references to it, as workers have had something to say about this common bird nearly every summer. It arrives in April (earliest date, April 8, Sherman County) and remains until September (latest date, September 18, Klamath County).

In flight it is not as graceful as the Barn Swallow, with which it is frequently associated about farmyards. Neither is it as swift nor as erratic as its forked-tailed relative. Both species may be found in late April or early May gathering mud from the damp spots, each pellet so collected making a single brick in the nest structure being built for family occupancy at a later date. By June 1, nests containing unfinished sets of eggs or fledglings several days old may be found in the larger colonies. Patterson reported egg dates for Klamath County from May 12 to 30.

Purple Martin:
Progne subis subis (Linnaeus)

DESCRIPTION.—"*Adult male:* Whole body glossy blue black; wings and tail black; feathers of ventral region entirely sooty grayish beneath the surface. *Adult female and immature males* with forehead grayish and upper parts sooty glossed with blue black, interrupted by grayish collar; lower parts grayish in front, whole under parts streaked, the feathers, especially on chest, with distinctly sooty grayish centers. *Length:* 7.25–8.50, wing 5.65–6.20, tail 3.00–3.40 (forked for .70–.90)." (Bailey) *Nest:* In holes in trees, about buildings, or in bird boxes. *Eggs:* 3 to 5, white.

DISTRIBUTION.—*General:* Breeds from Alaska, Alberta, Saskatchewan, Manitoba, Ontario, New Brunswick, and Nova Scotia south to Mexico, the Gulf Coast, and Florida. Winters in South America. *In Oregon:* Rather uncommon summer resident and breeding species of western Oregon; most common in coastal counties; decidedly rare east of Cascades.

WE CONSIDER the beautiful and companionable Purple Martin a decidedly uncommon bird in Oregon and much regret that it is not more abundant. Its gentle social nature has endeared it to mankind throughout the Eastern States, and the sight of a flock of Purple Martins circling about an elaborate martin house set upon a long pole brings a thrill to any bird lover. For several years colonies nested near Bridge, Coos County; near the mouth of Sixes River, Curry County; at St. Helens, Columbia County; and at Klamath Falls. In addition to these, Braly collected birds out of a colony near Sand Lake, Tillamook County, June 3, 1928, and in the same year the writers obtained specimens from a small colony at Drews Creek Reservoir, Lake County. This colony, which persisted for several subsequent seasons, nested in old woodpecker holes in the tops of a clump of giant old yellow pines that had been killed by the impounded waters of the reservoir. At the time of our first visit there was perhaps 10 feet of water about the base of the trees, the lower limbs of which held a colony of Farallon Cormorants. This was a rather bizarre combination—martins and cormorants going about their daily business in the same clump of trees. The coastal county colonies were all found breeding in old spruce snags, and those at St. Helens and Klamath Falls in the business buildings, as the birds do in eastern cities.

The first published Oregon record of this species was Anthony's (1886) from Washington County. Woodcock (1902) listed it from Portland, Beaverton, and Corvallis, the records including a set of 5 eggs taken in Fulton, south of Portland, by W. L. Finley on July 3, 1895. Shelton (1917) found it in the Mackenzie Valley and the coast of Lane County. Willett (1919) reported one bird from Malheur Lake on May 10. Finley (Finley and Finley 1924) listed it as breeding in trees in the Willamette Valley. This completes the published references to the species except our own notes. The files of the Biological Survey contain the following manuscript records in addition to our own given above. Dr. A. K. Fisher reported the species from Astoria, Clatsop County, in July 1897; Peck, from Roseburg, Douglas County, and vicinity in June and July 1916; and Overton Dowell, Jr., breeding birds at Mercer, Lane County, in 1917, 1920, and 1922. Patterson (ms.) took eggs between May 15 and 26 in Klamath County, the spot in Oregon where the birds are most abundant.

Jays and Magpies: *Family Corvidae*

Rocky Mountain Jay: *Perisoreus canadensis capitalis* Ridgway

DESCRIPTION.—"*Adults: Top of head white* shading to dark gray on back of neck; rest of upper parts light slate gray; tail tipped with white; throat whitish; rest of *under parts brownish gray. Young:* top of head dull white, tinged with grayish brown. *Length:* 11.25–13.00, wing 5.90–6.30, tail 5.80–6.35, bill .97–1.08." (Bailey) *Nest:* Built of twigs inclosing an inner nest of stems, plant fibers, and down, and placed on horizontal branch. *Eggs:* 3, grayish white, blotched with purplish brown.

DISTRIBUTION.—*General:* Breeds from southern British Columbia, southern Alberta, and Black Hills south to Arizona and New Mexico. *In Oregon:* Common permanent resident of higher parts of Blue Mountain area. (See Figure 11.)

BENDIRE (1877, 1895a) found the Rocky Mountain Jay, commonly known as "Camp Robber" or "Whiskey Jack," on Canyon Mountain to the north of Camp Harney. The first two he saw, on October 31, 1875, were on the headwaters of Bear Creek near Silvies Valley. We have taken numerous specimens throughout the timbered sections of the Blue Mountains and find the species to be fairly common. It is somewhat erratic in appearance; sometimes a dozen will be seen in one day and then several days' travel will pass before another is sighted. So far as we can find,

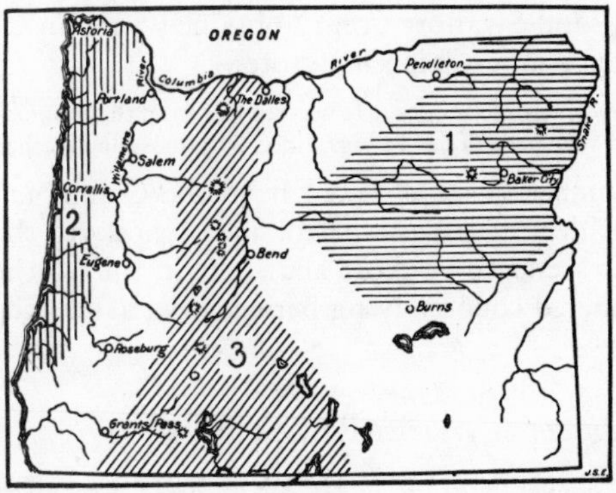

FIGURE 11.—Distribution of three forms of jays in Oregon: 1, Rocky Mountain Jay (*Perisoreus canadensis capitalis*); 2, Oregon Jay (*P. obscurus obscurus*); 3, Gray Jay (*P. o. griseus*).

no actual nests have been taken in Oregon, but there is no question as to its breeding in the State, as we frequently meet small flocks containing newly fledged young in June and July.

These jays often follow a person through the woods, swooping from their perches in a downward swing that ends in a sharp upturn to suitable perches in the next tree, where they will then sit motionless or hop upward through the tree in deliberate movements, eventually to sail out of the tree in another similar movement. When disturbed, they fly rapidly away through the woods, often uttering their half-whistled call as they go.

Oregon Jay:
Perisoreus obscurus obscurus Ridgway

DESCRIPTION.—"*Adult:* Like *P. c. capitalis*, but *white only* on forehead; *top of head and back of neck blackish*, and rest of upper parts brownish gray; feathers of back with white shaft streaks; tail only slightly if at all tipped with white; under parts white. *Young:* dull sooty brown, darkest on head, browner below. *Length:* 9.50–11.00, wing 5.15–5.75, tail 5.20–5.90, bill .84–.99." (Bailey) *Nest:* Of twigs and moss, grass lined, usually placed high in a bushy conifer. *Eggs:* 4 or 5, gray or greenish, spotted with lavender and gray.

DISTRIBUTION.—*General:* Pacific slope from western Washington to northern California. *In Oregon:* Permanent resident of Coast Ranges throughout length of State, except in Curry County. (See Figure 11.)

THE FIRST OREGON record of the Oregon Jay, the habits and behavior of which are quite similar to those of other members of the genus, was made near the mouth of the Columbia, January 2, 1806, by members of the Lewis and Clark Expedition (Lewis and Clark 1814), and since that time the species has been recorded many times. Despite the common local belief that "camp robber eggs have never been taken," two nests have been recorded from Oregon: Anthony (1886) took eggs at Beaverton, March 31, 1884, and Swallow (1891) obtained a set in Clatsop County, May 8, 1891, concerning which he wrote:

> I found a nest May 8, with four eggs. It was ten feet from the ground in a small hemlock in thick woods, and was made of dead twigs, lined with moss and feathers.

We have a number of skins taken from the Columbia River to Coos County and consider this race to be confined strictly to the Coast Ranges in this State. It seems to be most abundant in the northern part of the State in the timbered country lying between Portland and Tillamook.

Gray Jay:
Perisoreus obscurus griseus Ridgway

DESCRIPTION.—"Similar to the Oregon Jay, but decidedly larger except for feet, and much grayer; back dark gray instead of brown, and under parts grayish white instead of brownish white." (Bailey) *Size:* Length (skins) 9.10–10.60, wing 5.30–

5.95, tail 5.14–5.65, bill .69–.81. *Nest:* Of long slender twigs and straw, woven into a basketlike platform, thickly lined with moss and feathers of the Coast and Gray Jays. *Eggs:* 3 or 4, similar to those of the Oregon Jay.

Distribution.—*General:* Breeds from southern British Columbia through Cascades of Washington and Oregon to northern California. *In Oregon:* Permanent resident of both slopes of Cascades from Mount Hood south to California line, westward in Siskiyous at least to vicinity of Oregon Caves, and eastward to vicinity of Lakeview. (See Figure 11.)

This paler form, the Gray Jay, inhabits an area in Oregon roughly triangular in shape, with the apex at Mount Hood and the base extending along the California line from near Lakeview to a point south of Grants Pass. There it is a common permanent resident, being particularly partial to the lodgepole pine and spruce belts on the higher parts of the range. Mearns (1879) listed it from Fort Klamath on February 2, 1875, and Merrill (1888) reported it common from the same territory. Bendire (1895a) reported seeing young west of Linkville (Klamath Falls) on June 9, 1883, and others on the Deschutes River, June 12, 1882.

Braly took two sets of eggs from one pair of birds near Sandy in the spring of 1932. The first set, containing three eggs, was taken April 3; the second, containing four eggs, April 20. Both nests were obtained, and the description given above was written from them. Braly had first seen these birds on March 16 breaking twigs and carrying them to the nest site, which was some 75 feet from the ground in a fir tree. There is a set of three eggs in the Jack Bowles collection taken May 16 (?) that passed through several hands before it reached him. Jewett received the nest through Jack Horton, of the Forest Service, and gave it to Bowles. The set originally contained four eggs, but one was broken in handling. These are the only Oregon nests of which we have been able to get any record.

Coast Jay:
Cyanocitta stelleri carbonacea Grinnell

Description.—*Adults:* "Conspicuously crested; *fore parts of body dull blackish*, changing to pale blue on lower back and belly; wings and tail purplish blue, barred with black. *Young:* similar, but duller; wing bars faint or wanting." (Bailey) *Size:* Length (skins) 10.00–12.50, wing 5.35–6.22, tail 4.92–5.75, bill .98–1.25. *Nest:* Usually in conifers, made of twigs or grass, cemented with mud, and lined with fine vegetation. *Eggs:* 3 to 5, pale blue-green, spotted and blotched with brown.

Distribution.—*General:* Humid coast strip from northern Oregon to central California. *In Oregon:* Permanent resident of western Oregon, including west slope of Cascades, excepting Siskiyous and foothills around Rogue River Valley. Birds of northern half of eastern slope of Cascades also are closer to this form, though individuals are found that superficially resemble *frontalis*. (See Figure 12.)

The beautiful dark-blue crested jay in some of its various forms is a well-known inhabitant of the Oregon forest lands. This particular subspecies, the Coast Jay, is the one found in the Willamette Valley and the

Coast Ranges. The ranges and intergradations of this bird are exceedingly puzzling. Along the northern coast at the mouth of the Columbia, the birds closely approach *Cyanocitta stelleri stelleri*, whereas in the southern Cascades and Siskiyous, they intergrade with *Cyanocitta stelleri frontalis*. Similarly, along the eastern slope of the Cascades the resident birds are more like *frontalis*, approaching more nearly *carbonacea* to the northward, until at Mount Hood the birds of the eastern slope are either intermediate between the two forms or much closer to *carbonacea*. Along the western slope of the Cascades, the Willamette Valley, and southern coast, the birds are quite typical of *carbonacea*.

Like all jays, the Coast Jay is a noisy, boisterous bird, its screams and calls echoing through the woodlands whenever an intruder appears. About the nest, however, it is a silent blue ghost that slips through the fir branches in an astonishing vanishing act for one so highly colored. The nests are usually well concealed in the thick branches of some spruce or fir and are seldom discovered, so that comparatively few data are available on the nesting season. Bendire (1895a) listed sets of eggs taken at Beaverton April 14, 1891, and Salem April 26, 1891, and Swallow (1891) recorded a nest with eggs nearly ready to hatch in Clatsop County on May 13, 1891, and these records still represent the extreme dates of which we have any knowledge. Braly, however, found a nest near Portland on April 22, 1931, that contained young, which is evidence that this particular bird must have commenced laying soon after April 1. It is interesting to note that members of the Lewis and Clark Expedition (Lewis and Clark 1814), who first recorded this bird in Oregon on November 30, 1805, at the mouth of the Columbia, noticed the birds building on January 31, 1806. Currier, of Portland, who has probably taken more Crested Jay nests than any recent collector in the State, kindly furnished us with

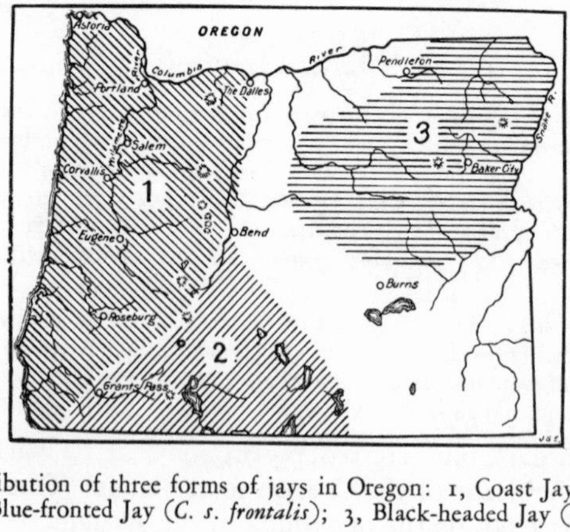

FIGURE 12.—Distribution of three forms of jays in Oregon: 1, Coast Jay (*Cyanocitta stelleri carbonacea*); 2, Blue-fronted Jay (*C. s. frontalis*); 3, Black-headed Jay (*C. s. annectens*).

his manuscript notes. He listed four nesting records for the Coast Jay: April 15, 1906, nest and four eggs; May 17, 1908, nest and three eggs; and May 8, 1927, nest and four eggs, all from Portland; and a nest and four eggs from the headwaters of Hood River, May 5, 1919. All eggs were fresh. Prill took a nest containing three eggs from a "small fir bush within reach of hand" near Scio, Linn County, June 4, 1920. Griepentrog, in a letter, reported one "carrying sticks for nesting material" at Salem, Marion County, April 8, 1934. In 1934 Jewett took a set of five incubated eggs from a nest 12 feet from the ground in a lone fir tree at Jennings Lodge, Clackamas County, on April 15, and Braly a set of four eggs from a nest "low in a fir sapling" at Depoe Bay, Lincoln County, on April 17.

The "Blue Jay," as these vividly colored woodlanders are wrongly called by many local residents, is a well-known but scarcely well-loved bird. Sportsmen and nature lovers cry out against it because of its undoubted fondness for the eggs and young of other birds. No one can deny that the handsome rascal is guilty, though the extent of his depredations can be easily exaggerated by a good imagination. Farmers, particularly those engaged in the comparatively new Oregon industry of growing filberts, complain bitterly at the loss of nuts. To many of these people who operate small tracts the loss of the entire crop from a tree or two is a serious matter. Such losses usually are most severe when filberts are planted adjacent to timber growth. Shooting the culprits, about the only feasible method of getting relief, is not always an easy matter. The Coast Jays, like their relatives, are intelligent and cunning and soon become adept at slipping in and out of an orchard where shooting is undertaken, without undue danger to themselves. Their depredations commence as the nuts begin to fill and continue up to harvest time. Complaints are received also of the destruction of fruits, particularly cherries, and once in a while is heard a story of the killing of young chickens.

Much could be written about these jays, which, despite their bad habits, are among the most interesting as well as the most beautiful of our feathered neighbors. Somehow the woodlands would lose a great deal of their charm if there were no chance of seeing the handsome dark-blue coat or of hearing the raucous voice of this typical bird of the fir forests.

Blue-fronted Jay:
Cyanocitta stelleri frontalis (Ridgway)

Description.—"*Adults:* Fore parts of body brownish slate, with *blue tinge to crest and blue streaks on forehead;* wings and tail dark blue, barred; rump and under parts dull turquoise. *Length:* 11.75–13.00, wing 5.50–6.10, tail 5.10–5.75, exposed culmen 1.00–1.20." (Bailey) *Nest and eggs:* As for *C. s. carbonacea.*

DISTRIBUTION.—*General:* South-central Oregon, western Nevada, and California, except humid coast strip south to San Diego County. *In Oregon:* Permanent resident of Warner Mountains and timbered area westward to Klamath Falls, intergrading with *C. s. carbonacea* in Siskiyous and southern Cascades and along eastern slope of Cascades. (See Figure 12.)

MEARNS (1879) first listed the Blue-fronted Jay as a common breeding species at Fort Klamath, and Willett (1919) found it at Old Fort Warner on Hart Mountain. It is a common and conspicuous permanent resident in the yellow-pine forests of south-central Oregon. Its nesting habits and behavior are identical with those of the Coast Jay. Patterson (ms.) has egg dates from the southern Cascades from April 20 to May 10, and Gabrielson flushed a bird from a nest containing four eggs on April 18, 1923. The nest was built about 8 feet from the ground in a small yellow-pine sapling. It was made of sticks and was lined with fine vegetation.

Black-headed Jay:
Cyanocitta stelleri annectens (Baird)

DESCRIPTION.—"Head black, back slaty, blue of under parts dark as in *stelleri; streaks on forehead bluish white*, sometimes indistinct; *small white spot over eye*. *Remarks:* The black-headed [jay] has the general body colors of the Steller jay, with the eye spot and streaks approaching those of the long-crested [form]. *Length:* 12.50–13.75, wing 5.90–6.60, tail 5.80–6.65, exposed culmen .97–1.08." (Bailey) *Nest and eggs:* As for *C. s. carbonacea.*

DISTRIBUTION.—*General:* Boreal and Transition Zones of the Rocky Mountains, from British Columbia south to eastern Oregon, Idaho, and Wyoming. *In Oregon:* Permanent resident of Blue Mountain area, including all forested parts of Wallowa, Union, and Baker Counties, of northern Malheur, northern Harney, Grant, Wheeler, Crook, extreme eastern Jefferson, southern Gilliam, and southern Morrow Counties, and of Umatilla County, except sagebrush area along Columbia. (See Figure 12.)

THE BLACK-HEADED JAY remains in Oregon as a permanent resident of the breeding range, though there is a noticeable altitudinal movement that concentrates a large part of the jay population in the lower elevations during cold weather. Nuttall's (1840) mention of the Steller Jay of the Blue Mountains is the first record for the State that can be assigned definitely to this form. Bendire (Brewer 1875) found it near Camp Harney, and he gave a little more information on its habits in his 1877 paper on the same region. Miller (1904) recorded it from Wheeler County and Walker (1917) from extreme eastern Jefferson County. We have found it to be a common resident of the Blue Mountains, from the yellow pine zone well up toward timber line, and have at hand many specimens well distributed over the territory assigned to it. We have one typical bird (Jewett Coll. No. 6969), taken on Hart Mountain, October 13, 1931; the only specimen that we have taken outside of its normal range in the State. Its nesting habits and behavior are identical with those of the other subspecies. Unfortunately, we have few nesting data, the only nest found by either of us being one containing four young, discovered by Jewett near Anthony, Baker County, July 8, 1906.

Long-tailed Jay:
Aphelocoma californica immanis Grinnell

DESCRIPTION.—"*Adults:* Upper parts blue except for ***brownish back*** and scapulars; under parts white except for bluish streaking on throat and ***partial blue and brownish necklace;*** white superciliary clearly defined; sides of head blackish. *Young:* head only tinged with blue, nearly uniform with brownish back; throat white, unstreaked; chest washed with brownish gray; belly whitish." (Bailey) *Size:* Length (skins) 10.00–11.50, wing 4.80–5.28, tail 5.12–6.00, bill .94–1.06. *Nest:* A structure of sticks, sometimes containing moss, grass, and other material, and lined with fine rootlets. *Eggs:* 3 to 6, buff to green, spotted and splotched with brown (Plate 74, *A*).

DISTRIBUTION.—*General:* Breeds from Columbia River south to central southern California (except in Coast Ranges). *In Oregon:* Permanent resident from Columbia River south through Willamette, Umpqua, and Rogue River Valleys and in Klamath and Lake Counties. (See Figure 13.)

THE FIRST published Oregon record of the Long-tailed Jay was by Henshaw (1880), who recorded a specimen from The Dalles, October 4, 1879, and stated that the species was tolerably common near Portland. Bendire (1895a) noted it in the Fort Klamath and Klamath Falls districts in 1883, and numerous writers have included it in their lists since. Walker (1926) recorded a bird seen at Tillamook, November 19, 1924, the only record for the northern coast counties. This jay has one of the most peculiar distributions of any Oregon bird. It reaches the northernmost limits of its range along the Columbia bottoms near Portland. There is a thriving colony on Sauvies Island from which occasional individuals straggle across to the Washington shore. In the vicinity of Portland and in the northern

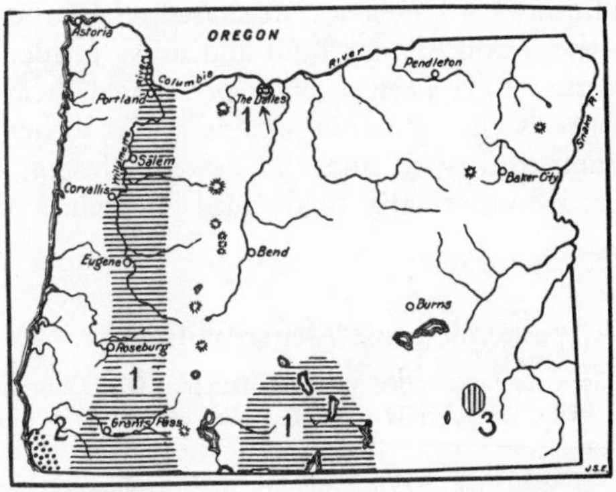

FIGURE 13.—Distribution of three forms of jays in Oregon: 1, Long-tailed Jay (*Aphelocoma californica immanis*); 2, Nicasio Jay (*A. c. oocleptica*); 3, Woodhouse's Jay (*A. c. woodhousei*).

Willamette Valley the species is represented by scattered pairs. At Salem and Dallas it is much more common, becoming less so again toward the south until the Umpqua Valley is reached. There, and in the Rogue River Valley and surrounding foothills, it becomes really abundant. It is found in small numbers about the town of Klamath Falls and also in the brushy hillsides across the southern part of the county. There is a thriving colony along the slopes above the western shore line of Summer Lake, and the species is found along both slopes of the Warner Mountains southward from Abert Lake. The farthest east we have taken it is on Hart Mountain, where Jewett obtained a specimen on September 16, 1928.

Currier took two nests on Columbia Slough near Portland, May 13, 1906, and May 10, 1907, each containing five eggs. Jewett found a nest containing five small young near Gold Hill, Jackson County, May 17, 1916. Prill collected a set of four eggs at Scio, Linn County, June 4, 1922, and found four nests in the Warner Valley, three at Adel, June 12, 1924, June 3, 1925, and June 4, 1932, containing three, four, and five eggs, respectively, and one at Twenty-Mile Creek, May 27, 1927, containing five eggs. The nests were all made of dry sticks and fine roots and were lined with hair. Walker collected a nest (Plate 74, *A*), four eggs, and both parent birds in the Warner Valley on a hillside near Blue Creek, 14 miles west of Adel, June 4, 1925, and took eggs in the Rogue River Valley, April 16 and 20, 1928. There is a set of six eggs in the Braly collection that were taken on Sauvies Island, April 19, 1932.

This is a bird of the manzanita and wild plum thickets, preferring such cover as that of oaks or other deciduous trees to the coniferous forests chosen by the crested jays. There the blue color and continual squawking of the birds as they sail from one tree to another draw the attention of every observer to their presence. The birds are a curious mixture of timidity and boldness, a trait shared with others of the family. If undisturbed, they soon become bold and noisy residents about buildings, but where they have been severely persecuted, it is a real sporting proposition to get within gunshot of one. Like other jays, they are notorious for their ability to find and destroy the eggs and young of smaller birds and are universally condemned for such practices.

Nicasio Jay:
Aphelocoma californica oocleptica Swarth

Description.—Same as Long-tailed Jay, but darker. *Size:* Length (skins) 10–11, wing 4.80–5.04, tail 5.08–5.59, bill .91–1.06. *Nest and eggs:* Same as for Long-tailed Jay.

Distribution.—*General:* Coastal slope from San Francisco Bay north to southern Oregon. *In Oregon:* Uncommon permanent resident of Curry County coast from Pistol River south to California line. (See Figure 13.)

The Nicasio Jay, in habits, behavior, and appearance identical with the Long-tailed Jay, extends its range into Oregon only along the coast of Curry County, where there are small permanent colonies at Brookings and Pistol River. Neither of us has seen it farther north than the latter point, although we have maintained a careful watch for it. The only Oregon specimens known to us are four from these colonies that definitely match Nicasio Jays collected in the type locality in Marin County, California—an adult male and an adult female (Jewett Coll. Nos. 4451 and 8284) collected at Brookings on November 4, 1926, and March 16, 1934, respectively, and two male birds from Pistol River, taken November 22, 1932 (Gabrielson Coll. No. 1912), and March 17, 1934 (Jewett Coll. No. 8285).

Woodhouse's Jay:
Aphelocoma californica woodhousei (Baird)

Description.—"Upper parts dull blue except for *slate gray back and scapulars;* under parts gray except for blue tail and under tail coverts, and throat, which is *whitish streaked with dark gray*. *Young:* back darker than in young of *californica;* under parts dark gray instead of white. *Length:* 11.50–12.75, wing 4.70–5.35, tail 5.20–6.20, bill .93–1.06." (Bailey) *Nest:* A platform of sticks lined with fine roots. *Eggs:* 3 to 6, pale green, sparingly marked with irregular brown and lavender markings.

Distribution.—*General:* Possibly breeds from southeastern Oregon, southern Idaho, and southern Wyoming south to southeastern California, southern Arizona, New Mexico, and Texas. *In Oregon:* Rare. Known only from extreme southeastern part of State. (See Figure 13.)

Bendire (1895a) stated: "I observed this species on the southern slopes of the Steens Mountains, in southeastern Oregon in August 1877, which locality marks about the northwestern limit of its range." No other record of the presence of Woodhouse's Jay in the State was made until August 8, 1921, when two birds were collected from a small flock present in the brush along the banks of Wild Horse Creek near Andrews on the southeastern slope of the Steens Mountains where the authors were camped. One of these birds recorded by Jewett (1926a) is now in the Biological Survey collection and the other is in Gabrielson's collection (No. 531). We have made a number of trips into this general territory without again meeting with the species and believe it may be an irregular visitor that wanders into this area after the breeding season, although it may possibly breed there or on the headwaters of the Owyhee River in southern Malheur County.

American Magpie:
Pica pica hudsonia (Sabine)

Description.—"*Adults:* Black, varied with bronzy iridescence, except for white belly and wing patches; tail long and graduated; bill and naked skin of orbital

Plate 74, *A.* Nest and eggs of Long-tailed Jay. (Photo by Alex Walker.)

Plate 74, *B.* Nest of American Raven on windmill. (Photo by S. G. Jewett.)

region *black.* *Young:* head without bronzy gloss. *Length:* 17.40–21.75, wing 7.30–8.40, tail 9.30–11.95, exposed culmen 1.15–1.42, tarsus 1.70–1.92." (Bailey) (See Plate 75, *A.*) *Nest:* A mud cup, lined with rootlets and fine grasses, located in the center of a bulky mass of sticks, and reached through an entrance in the side; in bushes and small trees. *Eggs:* 5 to 9, grayish, uniformly heavily marked with brown.

Distribution.—*General:* Breeds from Alaska Peninsula, Yukon, Alberta, Saskatchewan, and Manitoba south to Arizona and New Mexico. Winters over most of its range. *In Oregon:* Common permanent resident found in every county east of Cascades. Straggles irregularly west of Cascades.

The American Magpie is without doubt the most conspicuous bird throughout the sagebrush and grain country of eastern Oregon. Its noisy cries and conspicuous black and white color pattern bring it into the limelight as it flies in straggling formation over the tops of the willows, with its long tail feathers streaming out behind. By choice, the magpies frequent the thick willow and cottonwood patches of the stream bottoms from which they forage out into the open country in search of anything edible. An old carcass, a bird's nest, a concentration of meadow mice, or a horde of insects is each equally acceptable to this jovial freebooter. Every man's hand is against him, but, wise in the ways of the world and as able to fend for himself as the crow, the magpie continues to thrive.

Newberry (1857) first made mention of the magpie in the State, and since that time many others have written about its abundance and distribution. No one can visit the eastern section of the State without seeing it, and there are many records of its appearance in western Oregon. Johnson (1880) listed it from Forest Grove; Anthony (Bailey 1902) stated that a few were to be found along the Columbia; Woodcock (1902) recorded it for Dayton, Scio, The Dalles, and Beaverton; and we have numerous records of its appearance along the Columbia near Portland. Walker's (1924) record of a small flock seen at Blaine, Tillamook County, on October 8, 1919, is the only one from a coastal county.

With the first break in winter, the magpies commence collecting sticks to build their bulky nests, and by early March these structures are well under way. The nesting season is long drawn out, though the later nests may be those of pairs that for some reason failed to successfully raise their first brood. Our earliest date of a nest with a full set of eggs is March 21. Most of the eggs are laid in April and early May, although we have records of eggs as late as June 21. By early May the short-tailed youngsters can be found in the willow bottoms, and June 1 finds them everywhere, the youngest clambering about in the branches while their elder brethren are trying their wings overhead. From this time on through the summer small bands of magpies wander over the country, forming the most conspicuous living element in the landscape.

Farmers dislike these birds because of their propensity for stealing eggs and killing young chicks; livestock men despise them because of their habit of pecking the sores on cattle and horses that have been caused by branding or accident, sometimes almost literally eating the victims alive; sheepmen accuse them of pecking out the eyes of new-born lambs; and sportsmen persecute them unmercifully because of their belief that quail, grouse, China pheasants, and other game birds have disappeared from their favorite coverts because of the nest-destroying ability of the magpies. There is a measure of truth in all of these accusations, though one may seriously question the sportsman's belief that the magpies are solely responsible for the decreasing supply of game birds. It seems reasonable that too much shooting, destruction of food supplies and shelters by agricultural development, climatic conditions, and perhaps many other factors have a greater influence on the supply of game than the nest destruction practiced by the magpies a few weeks in the year. There are local areas where a concentration of magpies is undoubtedly an important factor in the decrease of game birds, but we are not optimistic enough to believe that removal of this or any other predatory species will solve even a few of the many problems involved in the proper management of the game-bird population.

American Raven:
Corvus corax sinuatus Wagler

Description.—"Black, entire plumage glossed with lustrous purplish, tinged with dull greenish on belly; feathers of throat lanceolate, distinct from one another; *feathers of neck dull gray at base;* nasal tufts covering more than basal half of upper mandible. *Length:* 21.50–26.00, wing 15.10–18.00, tail 9–11, exposed culmen 2.40–3.05." (Bailey) *Nest:* On cliffs, buildings, in trees, or in old windmill towers, built of sticks and lined with shredded bark, moss, hair, or wool. *Eggs:* 5 to 7, green, olive, or drab, spotted and blotched with brown and lavender.

Distribution.—*General:* Breeds from Oregon, southeastern British Columbia, Montana, and North Dakota south to Nicaragua. *In Oregon:* Permanent resident throughout State. Most abundant in eastern Oregon, but still quite common on coast. Rare in area between Cascades and Coast Ranges, though seen occasionally.

To see the American Raven at its best one must go to the great lava rims of eastern Oregon. There its black coat and harsh *croak*, as it sails over the gray landscape, seem to harmonize with the surroundings. From the vantage point of those rims, which furnish an abundance of suitable nesting sites, it can see everything that occurs in its chosen hunting ground and can instantly take advantage of the death of a rabbit, killed by a speeding car, or spy the carcasses of dead livestock. Along the coast it is not nearly as abundant as in the interior. Old records indicate that it was formerly more abundant in the Willamette and other western Oregon valleys. Now, an occasional glimpse of one sailing high overhead or the sound of its guttural voice is all that can be expected there. Some of the coastal birds, particularly in winter, may closely approach

C. c. principalis, but we do not have any specimens that are definitely assignable to this northern race. In Allen's edition of the Lewis and Clark expedition, it is stated that the raven was abundant at the mouth of the Columbia on November 30, 1805 (Lewis and Clark 1814).

This raven, like many of the desert birds, nests early. Most of the egg sets are completed and incubation is under way in early April. Our earliest date for a completed set is March 24 and our latest May 16, although Bendire (Brewer 1875) who listed the first eggs taken in Oregon —two sets from Camp Harney—took fresh eggs as late as May 29. Many of the nests are built in the scattered juniper trees so common in the eastern section of the State, although occasional ones are found in other trees. We know of several that were built on the remains of old windmill towers and on abandoned sheds (Plate 74, *B*). In the rimrock country the usual site is a ledge on the face of the sheer cliffs, and along the coast the nests are usually built on the rocky headlands.

Although ravens have largely disappeared from the settled sections of western Oregon, they are still so abundant in eastern Oregon that they are one of the real factors in reducing the numbers of waterfowl produced on the great marshes of Harney and Lake Counties. During the breeding season they work not only on the nesting colonies of herons, egrets, cormorants, and other similar birds but search out and destroy many dozen ducks' nests. The drought conditions in these counties in recent years, by causing the nesting birds to concentrate in a much restricted area, have greatly increased the toll of waterfowl taken by ravens, until at the present low ebb of bird life there the ravens are an important factor in preventing any increase, even under improved conditions.

Western Crow:
Corvus brachyrhynchos hesperis Ridgway

Description.—"Black, whole plumage glossed with violet, more strongly on upper parts; feathers of throat short, blended." (Bailey) *Size:* Length 18.50–19.25, wing 11.10–12.75, tail 6.45–7.80, bill 2.00–2.20. *Nest:* A bulky mass of sticks, plant stalks, and similar material, lined with rootlets, grass, hair, and other fine material. *Eggs:* 4 to 8, pale green or olive buff, blotched and spotted with browns and grays.

Distribution.—*General:* From central British Columbia, southern Saskatchewan and Montana south to Lower California and central New Mexico. *In Oregon:* Common permanent resident of entire State, except higher mountain peaks.

Lewis and Clark (1814) found crows abundant on November 30, 1805, at the mouth of the Columbia and listed them as Northwestern Crows, but unless the distribution of the two species has radically changed since that time, the Western Crow (Plate 75, *B*) was the more abundant species. Suckley (Cooper and Suckley 1860) reported the crow as an abundant breeder at The Dalles, still under the name *caurinus*. Bendire (1895a)

Plate 75, *A*. Young American Magpie. (Photo by Wm. L. Finley and H. T. Bohlman.)

Plate 75, *B*. Western Crow. (Photo by Wm. L. Finley and H. T. Bohlman.)

recorded it from Camp Harney as *americanus* and reported eggs taken May 4, 1877. Since that time, many records of the Western Crow have been published, and our own notes refer to every county in the State.

Although this western counterpart of the common crow is widely distributed, it is most at home along the timbered banks of the larger streams, where it nests in the cottonwoods and willows, usually building well above the ground. Eggs are laid in early May. Extreme dates are April 20 and June 9. The young are out of the nest in late June and early July.

After the nesting season, the birds wander about the country feeding along the stream banks and irrigation ditches and exploring the forests or sage-clad hills for food. In August the clans gather in flocks that increase in size until late fall, when winter roosts number thousands of individuals that remain during the winter and begin to break up in February or March as mating begins. From these great roosts the birds range out over the countryside in somewhat definite flight lines. They leave just before sunrise—spreading out in flights like spokes in a wheel. In the afternoon the return flight commences, and for an hour or more before sunset they pour back in a number of waving noisy black lines, not to the roost, but to a point some distance from it. The assembly is a noisy and conspicuous performance, seemingly designed to call everyone's attention to the birds, but as darkness falls the entire group flies quietly away to the chosen roost.

The largest roost is on an island in the Snake River near Ontario, where a large portion of the crow population of that and tributary valleys gathers to spend the winter months. From this roost the flyways extend up and down the Snake River, up the Malheur to the westward, and up the Payette and Weiser to the eastward. The population varies seasonally and is usually at its peak about December 1. In some winters it has reached an estimated total of 50,000 birds, and in others only a small fraction of that number. There is a similar but smaller roost on an island in the Columbia near Portland, and still smaller local roosts occur near Astoria, at various points in the Willamette Valley, and at Roseburg.

Northwestern Crow:
Corvus brachyrhynchos caurinus Baird

Description.—"Black, upper parts glossed with dull violet. *Length:* 16–17, wing 10.10–11.50, tail 5.90–7.00, exposed culmen 1.60–1.90." (Bailey) *Nest:* Made of sticks, sometimes mud, lined with cedar bark. *Eggs:* 4 or 5, like those of Western Crow but smaller.

Distribution.—*General:* Breeds from Kodiak Island south to Puget Sound, Washington, along coast. Winters in about same area. *In Oregon:* Straggler to Columbia River in winter.

When we wrote our *Birds of the Portland Area* (Jewett and Gabrielson 1929), we based our statement that the Northwestern Crow was a common bird along the Columbia on two specimens (one taken by Gabrielson, November 11, 1920, and one by Jewett, November 4, 1923) that happened to be the only Portland skins in our possession at that time. Since then, numerous specimens have been taken along the Columbia, and only two (both taken February 16, 1929) are of this race. All of the breeding birds and most of the wintering population are Western Crows. Because of the confusion of the two races in literature, we cannot segregate any individuals other than those listed above from among the records of more abundant forms, but the Northwestern Crow undoubtedly occurs down the Columbia as a winter visitor, and persistent collecting at Astoria would doubtless reveal it to occur there and along the Clatsop beaches at least as frequently as it does at Portland.

Pinon Jay:
Cyanocephalus cyanocephalus (Wied)

Description.—"Head not crested; bill cylindrical; nostrils exposed; tail nearly square, much shorter than wings; feet stout, claws large, strong, and much curved. *Adults:* almost uniform grayish blue, brightest on head; throat with white streaks. *Young:* dull grayish blue, lighter beneath. *Length:* 10.00–11.75, wing 5.70–6.00, tail 4.80–4.85." (Bailey) *Nest:* A bulky mass of twigs and bleached grasses, well lined with wool, moss, hair, and feathers. *Eggs:* 3 to 5, bluish white, covered with small specks or wreathed around the larger end with coarser spots.

Distribution.—*General:* Breeds from central Washington, Idaho, and Montana south to Lower California, Arizona, and New Mexico, in juniper and pinon-pine belt that lies east of Cascades and Sierra Nevadas. *In Oregon:* Common permanent resident of juniper belt that begins near Redmond and Prineville and extends south and southeast to Klamath Falls and Lakeview. Abundant in four counties, Klamath, Lake, Deschutes, and Crook, and noted in Harney, Malheur, Wheeler, Wasco, and Marion. Casual west of Cascades.

The Pinon Jay is the characteristic bird of the great juniper forests of central Oregon, where it roams the country in straggling flocks that feed and behave exactly the same as those of Clark's Nutcracker. Like the latter, it is a sociable bird and may be found in flocks throughout the year, even breeding in scattered colonies. This soft-blue, short-tailed jay was first reported by Newberry (1857) from Deschutes County. Bendire (1877) listed it from Camp Harney; Merrill (1888) stated it was a visitor at Fort Klamath; Miller (1904) saw it in Wheeler County in 1899; Walker (1917b) listed it from Deschutes and Wasco Counties; and Peck (1911b) recorded two specimens from Salem on December 21, 1910, the only known appearance of the species west of the Cascades.

No definite nesting records for the State were known until Braly (1931), who has done a great deal in the last few years to increase our knowledge of the breeding habits of this species, published his notes, showing it to be a common breeding bird of the juniper forests. Once the colonies are located, it is not difficult to find nests. Braly and his companions found as many as 14 in a single day, and between April 9 and 21, 1931, Braly found 76 nests in the mixed yellow pine and juniper forests in the vicinity of Redmond and Grandview. The nests contained from three to five eggs each, mostly four, and were located from 4 to 85 feet above the ground, most of them at 20 feet or less. The lower nests were usually built in juniper trees; the higher ones, in yellow pine, ordinarily 10 to 15 feet out from the trunk on a large limb. According to Braly, the males regularly fed in a loose flock one-quarter to three-quarters of a mile from the nests and carried food to the incubating females, usually perching on top of a tree 40 or 50 feet from the nest and calling the females from the nest. After feeding their mates the males flew directly back to the feeding ground.

Clark's Nutcracker:
Nucifraga columbiana (Wilson)

Description.—"Bill cylindrical, nostrils concealed by a tuft of feathers; wings long and pointed, folding to the end of tail; tail little over half as long as wing; tarsus shorter than middle toe and claw; claws large, sharp, and much curved. *Adults:* Body ash gray, whiter on forehead and chin; wings black, with white patch on secondaries; tail with middle feathers black, outer ones white. *Young:* similar, but colors duller and upper parts brownish gray; under parts brownish ash indistinctly barred. *Length:* 12–13, wing 7.10–8.00, tail 5.10–5.40." (Bailey) *Nest:* In conifers, usually 8 to 40 feet from the ground, built of twigs and lined with shredded bark, dry grass, etc. *Eggs:* 3 to 5, pale green, slightly spotted with tiny dots of brown and gray.

Distribution.—*General:* Breeds from southern Alaska, Alberta, and western South Dakota to Lower California, Arizona, and New Mexico. *In Oregon:* Regular permanent resident of Blue Mountains, Cascades, Siskiyous, and Warner Mountains, straggling to other isolated ranges. Known in coast mountains as a straggler only.

This striking black and white crow, Clark's Nutcracker, is associated in the minds of most of us with the timber-line forests of spruce and pine. There it sits on the treetops observing and scolding the intruder, eventually to take swift wing across a canyon or to a distant tree. It is a high-mountain bird but also can be found lower down in the yellow pine forests and the scattered groves of juniper over the higher plateaus. It is an abundant bird in our major ranges, such as the Cascades and Blue Mountains. Audubon (1839) listed it as a common bird in the Blue Mountains, and Newberry (1857) considered it common in the Cascades between 4,000 and 10,000 feet, a statement that still describes its status in that region. Several fall specimens have been taken on Hart Mountain, but it has not yet been recorded from the Steens Mountains. It has been found a number of times on the coast of western Lane County. Harry Telford collected a specimen there on November 11, 1913 (Jewett

Coll. No. 2488), and we saw two birds on Heceta Head on September 30, 1930, one of which was taken. Walker (1924) recorded one taken at Blaine on October 12, 1919, which is the only record for Tillamook County.

This bird breeds early, as Bendire (1882b) reported taking a full set of eggs on April 4, 1878, near Camp Harney and finding a nest containing newly hatched young on April 22, 1876 (Bendire 1876, 1877, 1882b). On April 1, 1932, Braly took a newly hatched bird from a nest near Sisters. The egg from which this bird was hatched must have been laid early in March. Young birds are on the wing by May 1 and are common about their timber-line haunts by June 1.

After the nesting season the birds gather into loose flocks, from a dozen to several hundred in number. They travel over the country, feeding either in the trees or on the ground. In the latter case, the birds in the rear are continually rising and flying to the front ranks, the movement appearing as that of a flattened wheel rolling slowly forward. The birds are noisy, keeping up a continual scolding and calling, so that one is instantly aware of the presence of a flock. The largest flock of this kind we have seen was feeding steadily along the yellow-pine forests of Wallowa County on September 24, 1933. Four birds collected from the several hundred present were all crammed with seeds of yellow pine.

Titmice and Bush-tits: *Family Paridae*

Long-tailed Chickadee: *Penthestes atricapillus septentrionalis* (Harris)

Description.—"Like *atricapillus* [the Black-capped Chickadee], but paler; throat, top of head and nape black; back pale ash, tinged with brownish; wings with white patch and edgings; tail feathers edged with white; sides of head and under parts white; sides and flanks washed with pale buffy. *Size:* Length 4.75–6.00, wing 2.55–2.80, tail 2.55–3.00." (Bailey) *Nest:* In holes in trees, made of fur, feathers, hair, and vegetable fibers. *Eggs:* 4 to 8, white, spotted with reddish brown and lilac, particularly around the larger end.

Distribution.—*General:* Breeds from Kenai Peninsula, central Michigan, and northern Manitoba south to eastern Oregon, northern Mexico, Kansas, and western Iowa. *In Oregon:* Permanent resident and breeding species from various localities in eastern part of State.

The Long-tailed Chickadee is a species of the cottonwoods and river bottoms, though it extends also into the mountains along the stream bottoms. It is quite a common bird, particularly in the valleys that lie around the base of the Blue Mountains in Wallowa, Union, Baker, Grant, and Umatilla Counties. Our records extend through the year, and the birds seem to be as abundant in winter as in summer. Bendire (Brewer 1875) reported it at Camp Harney in November and December 1874, and in 1877 (Bendire 1877) stated that it was a common winter bird. Peck (1911a) found it in northern Malheur County, and Walker (1917b) listed it from the mouth of the Deschutes as well as at Maupin and Warm Springs. These notes were partly based on a collecting trip into the district with Jewett, who took specimens at Maupin and Warm Springs that are now in the Biological Survey collection. In addition to numerous skins from the eastern part of the State in this collection, there is one from The Dalles, taken by W. K. Fisher, July 2, 1897, that is the farthest west specimen we have seen.

The birds along the eastern base of the Cascades, along the Deschutes River, and from north-central Oregon generally are very puzzling. Oberholser in a letter regarding them said:

> These birds are certainly not *Penthestes a. septentrionalis* as can be seen at a glance when a series of typical birds of the latter is compared with them. They are nearer as a whole to the coast bird, *P. a. occidentalis*, than they are to *septentrionalis* but they are of course, almost exactly intermediate between the two. They are in fact so nearly identical with *P. a. atricapillus* from eastern North America that Mr. Ridgway has referred them to this form. . . . If this is not done they must of course be referred either to *P. a. septentrionalis* or *P. a. occidentalis*. If this disposition of them however is followed, they are certainly much nearer, both in size and color to the coast bird than they are to the bird of the interior, and I should call them *P. a. occidentalis* with this explanation.

It is quite evident that we have again an area of intergradation which makes for confusion. Birds from the Blue Mountains and southeastern Oregon are much more like the Long-tailed Chickadee, whereas the intervening territory presents a series of intermediates that cannot be satisfactorily identified under the present recognized dividing lines.

Oregon Chickadee:
Penthestes atricapillus occidentalis (Baird)

DESCRIPTION.—Top of head and back of neck glossy jet black, ***back dark gray***, tinged with olive brown; sides of head clear white, in sharp contrast to black of head and throat; median under parts white, contrasting with tawny-brown sides. *Size:* Length 4.50–5.25, wing 2.35–2.60, tail 2.30–2.55. (Bailey) *Eggs:* 4 to 9, white, spotted with brown and lilac, mostly about the larger end.

DISTRIBUTION.—*General:* Breeds from southwestern British Columbia to northern California west of Cascades. *In Oregon:* Permanent resident and breeding species from western foothills of Cascades to Pacific, most abundant in interior valleys such as Willamette, Umpqua, and Rogue.

SUCKLEY (Cooper and Suckley 1860) found the small, dark-colored Oregon Chickadee (Plate 76) to be a common bird in the Willamette Valley, and every subsequent writer has accorded it the same status in that territory. Jewett (1916b) first recorded it from the coast as a resident of Tillamook County, and Gabrielson (1931) reported it as a common species in the Rogue River Valley. Although it is less common on the coast than in the interior valleys west of the Cascades, we have records from Tillamook and Lincoln Counties, and there are records in the files of the Biological Survey from Scottsburg (specimen, October 8, 1908, V. Bailey), Douglas County; Wedderburn (specimen, October 26, 1909, V. Bailey), Curry County; Mercer, Lane County on coast (various dates, O. Dowell, Jr.); Tillamook County (specimen, December 10, 1915, Alex Walker); and Empire (October 20–29, 1909), Coquille (November 3–12, 1909), and Bandon (November 13–27, 1909), Coos County, (D. D. Streeter, Jr.) Our own specimens are scattered from Portland to Grants Pass, Williams, and Ashland in the Rogue River Valley, which, together with the above Survey records, blanket the entire western part of the State.

The species nests commonly. Egg dates range from April 28 to June 19, and the number of eggs varies from three to nine. There were nine in each of two sets collected by Jewett on Government Island on May 10 and June 19, 1902.

This is one of the characteristic ever-present species of the lowlands along the Columbia and Willamette. During the winter, flocks of these friendly little birds, sometimes mixed with kinglets, nuthatches, and creepers, work over the buds and bark of the deciduous trees. Occasionally they will be found in the conifers in company with the Chestnut-backed Chickadees, but usually each sticks to its own territory. This chickadee's cheerful, whistled note and confiding ways endear it to the nature lovers who make a specialty of feeding birds during the winter, and it is usually one of the first and most persistent visitors to the feeding stations.

Grinnell's Chickadee:
Penthestes gambeli grinnelli van Rossem

Description.—"Throat and top of head jet black; black of head broken by *white superciliary* line; sides of head white; back gray; median under parts grayish white; sides dark gray, tinged with brown." (Bailey) *Length:* 5–6, wing 2.60, tail 2.29. *Nest:* In holes in trees, usually lined with fur. *Eggs:* 5 to 9, plain white or spotted with reddish brown, mostly about the large end.

Distribution.—*General:* Breeds from northern British Columbia south to east-central Oregon and northern Idaho. *In Oregon:* Permanent resident and breeding species of northeastern Oregon in Blue Mountain area.

Grinnell's Chickadee, the somewhat poorly differentiated form described from northern Idaho, extends into northeastern Oregon. We have specimens from Wallowa, Baker, Grant, and Crook Counties that are fairly typical of the race, and there are birds in the Biological Survey collection from Steens Mountains and Rome. Our sight records from Umatilla, Union, and northern Harney and Malheur Counties belong here. Captain Bendire (Brewer 1875) collected specimens near Camp Harney "about December 5, 1874, and prior" and found a nest containing one egg on Canyon Mountain on June 8, 1876 (Bendire 1877). Miller's (1904) records from Wheeler County in 1899 doubtless belong here. Jewett's (1909c) specimens from Baker County and Gabrielson's (1924a) birds from Wallowa County are also of this race. This and the next race are the present names of the subspecies of the familiar Mountain Chickadee.

Short-tailed Chickadee:
Penthestes gambeli abbreviatus Grinnell

DESCRIPTION.—Similar to Grinnell's Chickadee but with slight differences in color shading and with a relatively shorter tail. *Size:* Length 5–6, wing 2.70, tail 2.27. *Nest and eggs:* Similar to those of Grinnell's Chickadee.

DISTRIBUTION.—*General:* Cascades and southern range of Oregon, northwestern Nevada, northern and eastern California south to Mount Whitney. *In Oregon:* Permanent resident of Cascades, Siskiyous, and ranges of Klamath and Lake Counties east to and including Hart Mountain in east-central Lake County. Has strayed to Portland and Netarts in winter.

THE SHORT-TAILED CHICKADEE is the breeding form in the Cascades, the Siskiyous, and the isolated ranges from west of Bend east and southward to and including Hart Mountain in eastern Lake County. Six October specimens in our collection from the head of Marks Creek, Little Summit Prairie, seem to be closer to this form than to Grinnell's Chickadee. Birds from Redmond, Pine Mountain east of Bend, Silver Lake, Lakeview, and Hart Mountain record about the eastern limit of the range, and similarly a summer skin from Bolan Mountain, Josephine County, in Jewett's collection, marks its western limit so far as known at present.

Jewett (1909d) recorded a winter straggler "along the Columbia," December 10, 1908, and Walker (1926) published a record of a specimen taken at Netarts, December 17, 1924, which are the only two records west of the Cascades north of the Siskiyous. Baird (Baird, Cassin, and Lawrence 1858) recorded a specimen of Mountain Chickadee taken by Suckley at Fort Dalles in February 1855, but in Cooper's report (Cooper and Suckley 1860) Dr. Suckley said: "I obtained one of these birds at Fort Dalles, in February 1854. It must be very rare in that vicinity, as I never succeeded in getting another." Norris (1890) reported eggs taken at Fort Klamath, June 8, 1890, and both Mearns (1879) and Merrill (1888) found this chickadee abundant at the same spot. Since this time it has been listed by numerous observers and writers.

Aside from the Norris record, we have only the following nesting data: Three nests were located by Jewett, June 14, 1923, southeast of Lapine on the Deschutes National Forest. The first contained eight small young just out of the eggs; the second, six eggs advanced in incubation; and the third, seven eggs—one broken, three addled, and three in an advanced stage of incubation. Two of these nests were built in lodgepole pine

Plate 76. Oregon Chickadee and young. (Photo by Wm. L. Finley and H. T. Bohlman.)

and the third in an old stump. Currier (ms.) reported a nest containing six eggs, "with incubation well underway" from Wasco County, May 18, 1931. His notes are as follows:

In very rotten pine stump and entrance only 18 inches above the ground. Entrance very freshly picked through the bark and irregular in shape. The tunnel was fully 20 inches long following around the stump just behind the bark. Nest a felted quilt of rabbit fur. The bird remained on the nest until I touched her with my finger, drawing back with bill open in a threatening manner.

Braly took two nests containing seven and six eggs, May 28 and 30, 1930, near Fort Klamath.

Chestnut-backed Chickadee:
Penthestes rufescens rufescens (Townsend)

DESCRIPTION.—*Adults:* "Throat blackish brown; top of head and back of neck hair brown; superciliary black; back, sides, and flanks dark reddish brown; rest of under parts and sides of head white. *Young:* top of head, back of neck, and throat dark sooty brown; back dull chestnut, tinged with olive; sides ashy, partly washed with brown. *Size:* Length 4.50–5.00, wing 2.35–2.60, tail 2.00–2.30." (Bailey) *Nest and eggs:* Similar to those of other chickadees.

DISTRIBUTION.—*General:* From Prince William Sound, Alaska, south to central California, east to western Montana and eastern Oregon. *In Oregon:* Common permanent resident from Cascades west to coast. Less common but present in Blue Mountain area.

THE CHESTNUT-BACKED CHICKADEE is the common representative of the family in the coast mountains and in the heavy spruce forests of the coast. It is common but not quite so abundant in the Cascades. In the Willamette Valley, it is often to be found on the fir knolls, but the Oregon Chickadee replaces it in the cottonwood bottoms. Sometimes the two species will be found traveling together, but more often each remains in the type of timber it seems to prefer. The Chestnut-backed Chickadee is common from the Columbia to the California line along the Cascades, preferring the spruce, fir, and lodgepole of the higher areas. Jewett took young birds in Baker County in July 1906 (1909c) and an adult, May 14, 1907, in the same canyon of the Blue Mountains. The only other eastern Oregon record known to us is a single straggler taken by Jewett in the Warner Valley, November 12, 1933.

Historically, the species was described by Townsend (1837) from the forests of the Columbia, which has been worked out to mean in this case Fort Vancouver, Washington, although Townsend or some of the other men working out of that post at about that time undoubtedly also found it on the Oregon side, which they frequently visited. Ridgway (1879), more than forty years later, listed the species from the Columbia River; Gadow (1883) recorded it from Upper Klamath Lake; Swallow

(1890) reported it from Clatsop County; and Keller (1891c) reported eggs taken at Salem, May 27, 1889, and May 3, 1891. In August 1914, Goldman found the species at Bend and Fremont, the latter place in the extreme eastern edge of the forest belt northwest of Silver Lake. These are the farthest east records except Jewett's specimens from Baker County, mentioned above.

Dr. A. K. Fisher found these chickadees feeding young at Tillamook between June 30 and July 4, 1897, and on June 28 of the same year took a nearly developed egg from a bird collected on Wilson River and now in the Biological Survey collection. Jewett found a nest near Portland, May 3, 1908, containing one egg and in the same district saw a pair building a nest, May 21, 1909. Braly took eggs, May 13, 1932, in Washington County, and May 22, 1930, in Klamath County.

Oregon Titmouse:
Baeolophus inornatus sequestratus Grinnell and Swarth

Description.—*Adults:* Plain, unmarked; upper parts, including crest, brownish or olive gray, becoming whitish on the belly. *Young:* upper parts washed with brown; under parts ashy white. *Length:* 5.00–5.60, wing 2.68–2.90, tail 2.20–2.60, bill .38–.40. (Adapted from Bailey.) *Nest:* In holes in trees, made of plant fibers, feathers, wool, and other soft materials. *Eggs:* 6 to 8, white.

Distribution.—*General:* Jackson and Josephine Counties, Oregon, and Siskiyou County, California. *In Oregon:* Permanent resident of chaparral and oak areas of Jackson and Josephine Counties.

The Oregon Titmouse, a plain gray little bird, is a common denizen of the chaparral thickets of southern Oregon, where its chickadeelike calls and notes, as well as its deliberately whistled song, are characteristic sounds. Its movements are somewhat slow but otherwise much like those of the chickadees, with which it is frequently found associated.

The first published reference we have found that ascribed this bird to Oregon is Mrs. Bailey's (1902) statement that *Parus inornatus* is a resident in the Pacific Coast region of California and Oregon. She gives no further information. Henninger (1920) recorded a specimen taken by W. M. Clayton at Ashland, April 17, 1900, as the first record for the State. It is the first definite publication for the State that is based on a specimen, but it is not the first actual specimen, as Henshaw took one at Ashland, February 10, 1881. Jewett (1921a) recorded a number of specimens from various points in the Rogue River Valley, and Gabrielson (1931) listed it as one of the common permanent birds of the valley. These are the only published Oregon records, a fact that again emphasizes the lack of field work on birds in the State. Patterson (ms.) reported one nest, May 12, 1926.

Gray Titmouse:
Baeolophus inornatus griseus (Ridgway)

Description.—"Similar to *inornatus* [Oregon Titmouse], but lighter; upper parts light gray; under parts whitish gray. *Length:* 5.75–6.10, wing 2.80–3.00, tail 2.40–2.70, bill .40–.48." (Bailey) *Nest:* In holes in trees, made of feathers and other soft material. *Eggs:* 6 to 8, white.

Distribution.—*General:* Breeds from northern California, extreme southern Oregon, Nevada, southern Idaho, Utah, and southwestern Wyoming and Colorado to southeastern California, Arizona, New Mexico, and west-central Texas. Winters throughout most of its range. *In Oregon:* Known definitely only from Warner Valley in extreme southern Lake County.

The Gray Titmouse is known as an Oregon species from five specimens, four of which were collected in the extreme southern part of Warner Valley. Two, taken by Walker at the Murial Jacobs Ranch, May 3, 1930, are now in the Cleveland Museum and form the basis for Oberholser's (1932) recently described subspecies *zaleptus*, which is the only published reference to the Gray Titmouse in any form as an Oregon bird. Because of the lack of comparative material and the fact that this form was described subsequent to the last A. O. U. Check-List and so has not yet been passed by the A. O. U. committee, we prefer to let it stand as the above-recognized form. The third and fourth specimens were collected by Jewett at South Warner, May 19, 1932. He also saw two titmice at Barley Camp a few miles west of the Jacobs Ranch, October 17 and 19, 1932, but did not obtain them. The fifth was taken by Jewett, February 9, 1936, in the Blitzen Canyon, Steens Mountains, in Harney County. The Gray Titmouse is not uncommon in the juniper belt of northern California in the vicinity of Clear Lake, and the species will undoubtedly be found in the similar country in southern Klamath County.

Coast Bush-tit:
Psaltriparus minimus minimus (Townsend)

Description.—"Top of head *sooty brown;* back *dark grayish* brown or brownish gray; under parts smoky brownish on sides. *Length:* 4.00–4.50, wing 1.95, tail 2.20." (Bailey) *Nest:* Skillfully woven pendent structure (huge for size of bird) made of plant fibers, moss, feathers, and other material, usually hung on small trees and bushes. The entrance is a small opening to one side (Plate 77, *A*). *Eggs:* 5 to 9, white.

Distribution.—*General:* Along coast from British Columbia south to southern California. *In Oregon:* Regular permanent resident and breeding bird of Willamette Valley and at least as far south inland as Glendale, Douglas County, and along coast into California. (See Figure 14.)

The tiny Coast Bush-tit (Plate 77, *A*) is a fairly common resident of the Willamette Valley and of the coast along the entire length of the State.

Its actions remind one of a miniature chickadee, but its absurdly long tail is out of all proportion to the size of the tiny ball of fluff hanging upside down on a swaying tree. These birds are usually found in small companies working through the willows and low bushes, keeping up a friendly exchange of faint notes all the while. Nuttall (1840) reported the species from the banks of the Willamette River in May 1835, and Audubon (1841) repeated his statement. Johnson (1880) considered it common at East Portland, Forest Grove, and Salem, and Anthony (1886) listed it as a resident of Washington County. Woodcock (1902) listed it from eight stations, all, except Elkton, in the Willamette Valley, and numerous records have been published since. The Biological Survey collection contains specimens from Oregon City (October 24, 1893, C. P. Streator), Glendale June 13, 1894, C. P. Streator; (June 18, 1897, A. K. Fisher), Scottsburg (October 8, 1909, V. Bailey), and Reston (July 4, 1916, M. E. Peck). There are also specimens in the Carnegie Museum collected by A. W. Anthony at Beaverton. Our own collections contain specimens from Portland and one from Bridge, Coos County, June 19, 1920 (Gabrielson Coll.).

The nest is a wondrous structure composed of a dangling mass of skillfully woven material in which the tiny side entrance is easily overlooked (Plate 77, *A*). Included in Woodcock's (1902) list were four nesting records from Portland (credited to H. T. Bohlman), May 23, 1893, May 10 and 11, 1895, and April 29, 1897. A nest taken at Cedar Mills, Washington County, May 5, 1894, by W. B. Malles, contained five fresh eggs; and Jewett has two records for Portland, June 5, 1908, four eggs, and June 15, 1908, seven eggs.

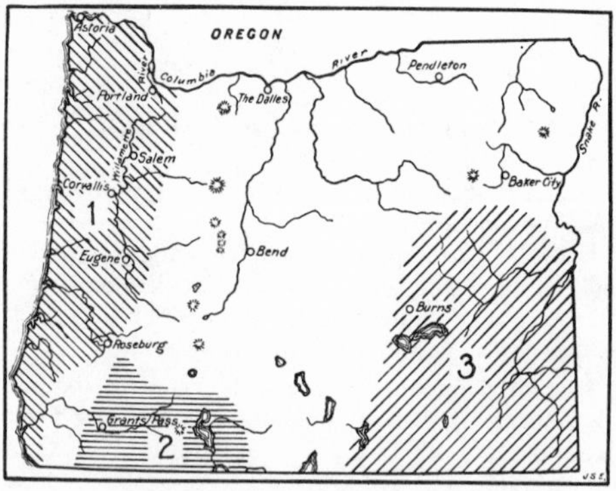

FIGURE 14.—Distribution of Bush-tits in Oregon: 1, Coast Bush-tit (*Psaltriparus minimus minimus*); 2, California Bush-tit (*P. m. californicus*); 3, Lead-colored Bush-tit (*P. m. plumbeus*).

Plate 77, *A.* Coast Bush-tit at nest. (Photo by Wm. L. Finley and Irene Finley.)

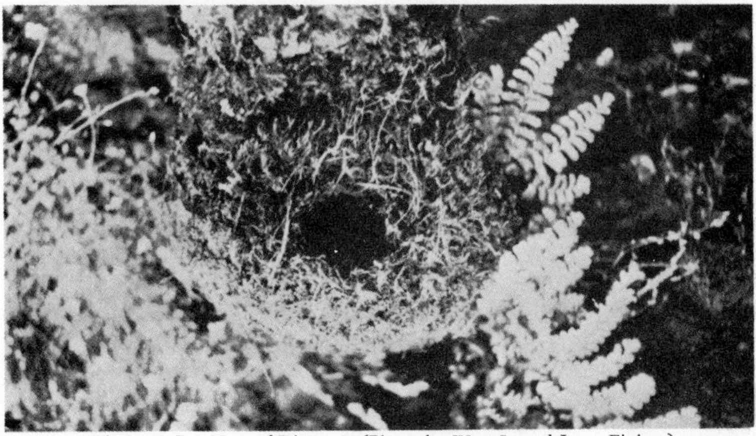
Plate 77, *B.* Nest of Dipper. (Photo by Wm. L. and Irene Finley.)

California Bush-tit:
Psaltriparus minimus californicus Ridgway

DESCRIPTION.—"Similar to *minimus*, but lighter, top of head *light brown*, contrasting more sharply with *light gray* of back; under parts light brownish. *Length:* 4.00–4.50, wing 1.85–2.10, tail 2.00–2.30." (Bailey) *Nest and eggs:* Same as for Coast Bush-tit.

DISTRIBUTION.—*General:* From Rogue River Valley and southern Klamath County south through interior of California to Kern County. *In Oregon:* Permanent resident of Rogue River Valley, Umpqua Valley, and Klamath County. (See Figure 14.)

MERRILL (1888) reported bush-tits from Fort Klamath but took no specimens. Although Fort Klamath is a few miles farther north than any of our records, the birds were undoubtedly California Bush-tits. Ridgway (1904) listed a bird from Wilbur, Douglas County, as one of this race, and Gabrielson (1931) listed the species as a common resident of the Rogue River Valley. We have many skins from the Rogue River and from the vicinity of Klamath Falls and Olene in Klamath County. It is about equally common in Jackson and Klamath Counties and somewhat less abundant in Josephine County, though present in all three throughout the year.

Lead-colored Bush-tit:
Psaltriparus minimus plumbeus (Baird)

DESCRIPTION.—"*Upper parts plain bluish gray;* sides of head brown; under parts grayish white, faintly tinged with pale brownish on belly. *Length:* 4.12–4.60, wing 2.00–2.15, tail 2.35–2.50." (Bailey) *Nest and eggs:* Same as those of other bush-tits in Oregon.

DISTRIBUTION.—*General:* Breeds from eastern Oregon and western Wyoming south to Mexico and western Texas. *In Oregon:* Permanent resident and breeding species from Canyon Mountain, Grant County, and Sumpter, Baker County, south to Nevada-California line and west as far as Lakeview. (See Figure 14.)

THE LEAD-COLORED BUSH-TIT, which acts exactly like its relatives, is probably most common in Oregon in the Steens and other desert ranges but is a regular resident on Hart Mountain and in the Warner Mountains east of Lakeview. Bendire (Brewer 1875) took a specimen at Camp Harney, November 14, 1874, and he (Bendire 1877) saw others near the summit of Canyon Mountain in June 1876. This record still remains the farthest north and west for the species. H. Dobyns took one near Sumpter, Baker County, October 28, 1928, which was recorded by Jewett (1930c). A specimen collected by Gabrielson at Lakeview, October 28, 1919, is the westernmost record to date. Jewett has taken several in Malheur County, and there are others in the Biological Survey collection taken by Preble. We have numerous specimens from southern Harney County, which seems to be the center of abundance.

We found one nest, containing six eggs, hung 3 feet up in a rosebush on Trout Creek in southern Harney County, June 21, 1930. It was discovered by Gabrielson when the adult flushed almost in his face as he was following a stock trail through the brush. Jewett has twice watched birds carrying nesting material. On Hart Mountain, May 15, 1924, he saw a pair using fiber from a piece of burlap for their raw material, and again on Hart Mountain, June 14, 1926, he observed a pair nest building. In neither instance was he able to return to see the completed nests.

Nuthatches: *Family Sittidae*

Rocky Mountain Nuthatch: *Sitta carolinensis nelsoni* Mearns

DESCRIPTION.—Same as *S. c. aculeata* but averaging larger with stouter, heavier bill. *Size:* Length 5.95, wing 3.70, tail 2.17, bill .80. *Nest and eggs:* Same as for Slender-billed Nuthatch.

DISTRIBUTION.—*General:* Breeds from southern Alberta south to Mexico, from Cascades and Sierra Nevadas eastward through Rockies. *In Oregon:* Permanent resident and breeding species in timbered sections east of eastern base of Cascades.

BENDIRE (Brewer 1875) first reported the Rocky Mountain Nuthatch for Oregon, from Camp Harney in November and December 1874, and on June 6, 1876, collected the first set of eggs near the same station (Bendire 1877). From that date until Jewett (1909c) included it in his Baker County list, it did not appear in Oregon bird literature, although the files of the Biological Survey contain notes from the Blue Mountains (Preble 1896; Cantwell 1919), Wallowa Lake (Young and Bailey 1897), and Grande Ronde Valley (McLellan 1894). Walker (1917b) listed the bird for Jefferson County, and Gabrielson (1924a) for Wallowa County. We have specimens available from Ochoco Ranger Station and Fossil (Wheeler County), Wallowa Mountains (both in Wallowa and Baker Counties), and northern Harney County, taken during the breeding season; October and November birds from Hart Mountain and Lakeview (Lake County), and Lapine (Deschutes County); and a February bird from Bend (Deschutes County). We found a nest in a pine snag near Lava Butte south of Bend. It was lined with wadding from an old mattress lying beside the trail and contained eight eggs.

Slender-billed Nuthatch: *Sitta carolinensis aculeata* Cassin

DESCRIPTION.—"Top of head and back of neck glossy blue black in sharp contrast to clear white of sides of head and under parts; back bluish gray; wings and tail marked with black and white, tertials dark or *dull bluish* gray, with black patch along shaft of longest feather *pointed at tip*. *Adult female:* top of head grayish. *Length:* 5.00–

6.10, wing 3.35–3.75, tail 1.90–2.20, bill .80–.95, greatest depth of bill .13." (Bailey) *Nest:* In natural cavities or old woodpecker holes, lined with moss, grass, fur, and feathers. *Eggs:* 5 to 7, creamy, lightly dotted with brown and lilac.

Distribution.—*General:* Breeds from southern British Columbia to northern Lower California west of Cascades and Sierras. *In Oregon:* Permanent resident and breeding species from Coast Ranges to and including Cascades and from Columbia River to California line.

The Slender-billed Nuthatch is found during the breeding season from the Coast Ranges to the eastern edge of the timber on the Cascades—Bear Springs (east of Mount Hood), Wamic, Hay Creek, Jefferson County, Summit Stage Station, Fremont, and Klamath Canyon just below Keno. In western Oregon, it is a regular resident in the Willamette, Umpqua, and Rogue River Valleys but is not yet recorded from any of the coast counties. It is not a common bird throughout most of its territory and is generally most abundant in the yellow-pine forests on the eastern slope of the Cascades and in similar stands in eastern Jackson County on the western side of the range. In the Willamette Valley, it frequents both the coniferous and deciduous timber, though seeming to show some preference for the oaks and cottonwood. There these nuthatches may be seen in mixed flocks with chickadees, kinglets, and other nuthatches, the members of this acrobatic family hanging indifferently upside down or traveling head first down the trunks of some forest monarchs, busily searching for insects or their eggs or larvae.

Mearns' (1879) records from Fort Klamath for June 1875 are the first for the State. These were soon followed by Merrill's (1888) notes from the same locality and Anthony's (1886) records from Washington County. Woodcock (1902) listed seven stations, all in the Willamette Valley. Jewett observed a pair carrying food to a nest full of young at Gold Hill, Jackson County, May 16, 1916, and Braly discovered a nest containing young at Portland, May 23, 1931. Patterson (ms.) took eggs, May 10 to 16, 1922.

Red-breasted Nuthatch:
Sitta canadensis Linnaeus

Description.—"Top of head glossy black, side of head with *white superciliary and black eye stripe; under parts reddish brown;* back bluish gray; wings plain; tail with white patches on outer feathers. *Adult female:* black of head replaced by bluish gray; under parts lighter reddish brown. *Young:* similar, but duller. *Length:* 4.12–4.75, wing 2.60–2.85, bill about .60." (Bailey) *Nest:* In small cavities in trees, lined with shredded bark. *Eggs:* 4 to 8, white, sparingly spotted with red at larger end.

Distribution.—*General:* Breeds over most of timbered country of Canada south in western ranges into Arizona and New Mexico, across northern tier of States and south to North Carolina in eastern mountains. Winters over most of United States and in Oregon. One of most common and widely distributed of smaller timber birds. *In Oregon:* Permanent resident and breeding species in all timbered sections. In winter apt to be found anywhere.

The Red-breasted Nuthatch is common in all types of timber found in the State, though perhaps it is most abundant during the summer in the fir, spruce, and lodgepole-pine forests. It has been found breeding at Portland, however, where Jewett found a slightly incubated set of six eggs on May 17, 1908. At the other extreme of the State, Cantwell found a nest containing young near Sled Springs Ranger Station on the Wallowa National Forest, May 1, 1919. Braly found four nests near Fort Klamath between May 15 and 30, 1930. Three sets contained six eggs each; the fourth, five. Outside of the breeding season the birds are found over the entire State. It is no uncommon thing to hear their nasal *yank yank* and watch their acrobatic performances on the sage branches far from the nearest timber, and on several occasions we have found small bands of them working up and down the tule stalks on the edges of Malheur Lake.

This nuthatch was first listed for the State by Mearns (1879), who had three specimens taken by Lieutenant Willis Wittich at Fort Klamath in 1878, two of them on May 9. Since that time it has been mentioned by most of the contributors to Oregon ornithological literature.

Black-eared Nuthatch:
Sitta pygmaea melanotis van Rossem

Description.—"*Adults:* Top of head grayish brown or olive gray, nape usually white; rest of upper parts bluish gray; tail with basal half of middle feathers white; eye stripe black; chin white; rest of under parts dull buffy. *Young:* wing coverts usually more or less distinctly edged with pale buffy. *Length:* 3.80–4.55, wing about 2.60, bill .60–.65." (Bailey) *Nest:* In crevices of bark and holes in trees, lined with feathers, down, and wool. *Eggs:* 6 to 9, white, covered with red spots.

Distribution.—*General:* Breeds from southern British Columbia and northern Idaho south to Mexican boundary. *In Oregon:* Permanent resident and breeding species of Blue Mountains, yellow-pine belt in Cascades, and timbered sections of Klamath and Lake Counties.

The tiny little Black-eared Nuthatch is to us indelibly associated with the yellow pine—so much so that we instinctively begin to look for it whenever we get into one of the beautiful parklike forests on the eastern slope of the Cascades or in the Blue Mountains. We have found it commonly in the yellow-pine forests of Wallowa, Union, Baker, Umatilla, Wheeler, Grant, Malheur, Crook, Jefferson, Wasco, Deschutes, Lake, Klamath, and eastern Jackson Counties. It probably occurs also in the southern part of Morrow County and in the yellow-pine areas of southern Douglas County, although we have no records from either place.

In its chosen haunts, it travels through most of the year in little flocks. Its shrill calls are much unlike the nasal ones of its relatives, but its acrobatic abilities are on a par with those of the larger forms. It is the most abundant of the three found in its territory, and one often finds mixed companies comprised largely of this species and chickadees, with a few of either Slender-billed, or Rocky Mountain, and Red-breasted Nuthatches intermingled. They forage through the pines, the shrill high voices of the pygmies often leading the observer to the group.

Bendire (Brewer 1875) first reported this nuthatch, as he did so many other eastern Oregon birds, and later (Bendire 1877) stated that it nested in the Blue Mountains. Norris (1889e) listed eggs from Fort Klamath between May 3 and 18, 1888. Prill (1895a) stated that the species wintered near Sweet Home, Linn County, although in the absence of other western Oregon records we cannot help wondering about the correctness of this identification. Walker (1917b) found a nest containing young on the Warm Springs Indian Reservation on June 18, 1913. In addition to published nesting records, Jewett found a nest 8 feet up in a yellow-pine stump near Zumwalt, Wallowa County. It was lined with fur, feathers, and wool, and contained eight eggs. When he tapped on the stump, three adult birds emerged from the nest opening. Braly's egg data show four nests taken at Sisters and Fort Klamath May 17 and June 10, and Patterson (ms.) took nests in the same territory between May 2 and 16.

Creepers: *Family Certhiidae*

Rocky Mountain Creeper: *Certhia familiaris montana* Ridgway

Description.—Bill slender, sharp, and decurved, tail rounded, of rigid, sharp-pointed feathers; claws greatly curved and sharp. Upper parts *grayish*, head and back streaked conspicuously with white; rump tawny, under parts white, becoming darker on the flanks. *Size:* Length 4.50–5.50, wing 2.56, tail 2.71, bill .75. (Adapted from Bailey.) *Nest:* A mass of fiber and feathers, behind loosened bark on stumps or dead trees. *Eggs:* 5 to 9, white, spotted with brown.

Distribution.—*General:* Breeds in mountains from central Alaska and Alberta south through Rockies to Arizona and New Mexico. Winters south to Mexican line. *In Oregon:* Permanent resident and breeding species of Blue Mountain area. (See Figure 15.)

The Rocky Mountain Creeper is a permanent resident of the Blue Mountain area, being found in Wallowa, Union, Baker, and Grant Counties, and it probably occurs in the adjoining mountain districts of Umatilla, Wheeler, Crook, Harney, and Malheur Counties. Curiously enough, the first published record for the State was Jewett's (1909c) from Baker County and the second, Gabrielson's (1924a) from Wallowa County, where it is more abundant than elsewhere in the State. In winter many individuals leave, but a part of the population remains throughout the year. We have only one winter skin from outside of the regular range. This was taken at Ontario, January 4, 1927, by Jewett. The bird is neither common nor conspicuous—consequently, it is overlooked by many observers. We have found it sparingly throughout the year in the above localities, but its insignificant notes and brown-streaked dress render it difficult to find, even when present.

We have only one nesting record. Jewett located a nest near Lick Creek, July 17, 1926, having been attracted to it by noticing the female come from behind a slab of loose lodgepole bark. The nest was about 8 feet from the ground and contained five newly hatched young.

Sierra Creeper:
Certhia familiaris zelotes Osgood

DESCRIPTION.—"Upper parts *dusky* anteriorly, becoming bright rusty on rump; superciliary, streaks on scapulars, and spots on primaries white; throat and breast pure white, sides and flanks tinged with brownish." (Bailey) *Size:* Length (skins) 4.53–5.16, wing 2.30–2.65, tail 2.07–2.55, bill .55–.67. *Nest and eggs:* Same as for *C. f. montana*.

DISTRIBUTION.—*General:* Breeds in Cascade Mountains of Washington and Oregon and Sierra Nevadas of California, spreading to adjacent valleys in winter. *In Oregon:* Breeds along summit and eastern slope of Cascades and through timbered parts of Klamath and Lake Counties. Winters throughout much of its range. (See Figure 15.)

OUR KNOWLEDGE of the range of the various forms of creepers both in summer and winter is still far from complete. They seem to be somewhat more abundant in the territory normally occupied by this race, the Sierra Creeper, or at any rate we have more specimens of this form with which to work. All our specimens from the summit of the Cascades east to Tumalo, Bend, Cougar Peak, and Lakeview and west to the head of

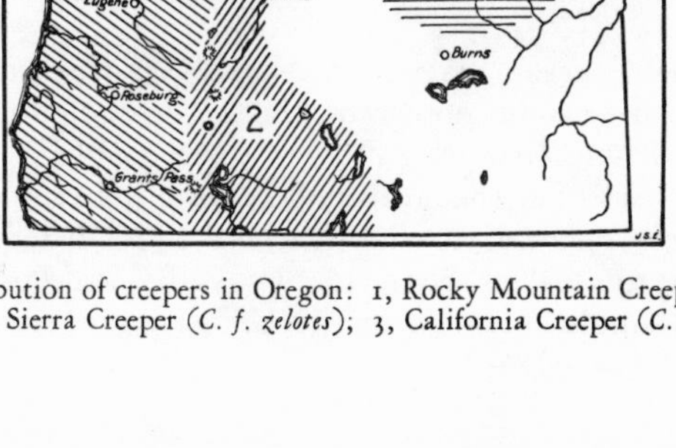

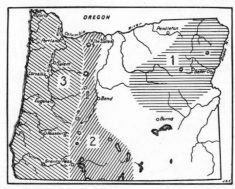

FIGURE 15.—Distribution of creepers in Oregon: 1, Rocky Mountain Creeper (*Certhia familiaris montana*); 2, Sierra Creeper (*C. f. zelotes*); 3, California Creeper (*C. f. occidentalis*).

Little Butte Creek in Jackson County are of this race. Undoubtedly individuals winter in the Willamette and other valleys of western Oregon, although the winter bird specimens we have taken happen to be *occidentalis*.

The different races are identical in behavior. All have the unique habit of flying to the base of the tree and spiraling upward about the trunks searching the crevices of the bark for edible tidbits in the ascent. When the top is reached the birds drop down to the base of another tree and repeat the process. All of this is done silently or with an occasional faint call that is inaudible to some human ears.

Merrill's (1888) Fort Klamath records are the first that can be definitely ascribed to this form in Oregon. He found it abundant in winter and not rare as a breeding bird, saying that he found a pair feeding fledgling young on June 6, 1887. He also stated that he found several of their characteristic nests but did not give any details. Shelton's (1917) records from the Cascades of Lane County certainly apply to this form, and the bird Walker (1917b) listed from Warm Springs Agency as *C. f. occidentalis*, taken May 2, 1915, is apparently the same as one now listed in the Biological Survey collection as this race. The later records published from the State have been our own, based on specimens from the localities listed above. Patterson (ms.) reported two nests, May 10 and 14, 1924, from the southern end of the Cascades. Currier (ms.) furnished the following notes:

Have never seen an occupied nest of this subspecies but in 1931, I tore out an old used nest from behind a piece of bark on a tree trunk near Fort Klamath that was undoubtedly made by this bird. Again in 1933 I found an old Creeper's nest on the trunk of a large pine in Wasco County.

California Creeper:
Certhia familiaris occidentalis Ridgway

Description.—"Upper parts *rusty brown*, brightest on rump; superciliary and streaks on head and back often tawny." (Bailey) *Size:* Length 4.53–5.16, wing 2.47, tail 2.45, bill .72. *Nest and eggs:* Same as for *C. f. montana*.

Distribution.—*General:* Breeds on Pacific Coast from Sitka, Alaska, south to Monterey County, California. Winters throughout its range. *In Oregon:* Permanent resident and breeding species from Columbia River to California line and from western slope of Cascades to Pacific. (See Figure 15.)

The California Creeper, like other creepers, is frequently overlooked except by the most careful observers. In the dense fir forests frequented by this inconspicuous little tree climber there could be many times the present numbers without the creepers becoming noticeable. The earliest records definitely referable to this race are those listed by Woodcock (1902) from Dayton, Salem, Beaverton, Corvallis, and Portland. Shelton (1917) listed a single specimen in the University of Oregon collection taken at Forest Grove, November 13, 1912, as of this race but considered the bulk of the birds at Eugene to be *C. f. zelotes*. This is somewhat at variance with our present-day concept of the two forms. From our specimens taken at Portland, Sauvies Island, Newberg, Netarts, Crater National Forest, Jackson County, and Bolan Mountain, Josephine County, this is the bird of the Coast Ranges and the lowlands between those ranges and the Cascades. On the western slope of this latter range, the two merge and some specimens are intermediates that cannot be satisfactorily placed in either race.

Braly took a nest at North Plains, Washington County, May 6, 1932, containing five eggs, and one at McMinnville, May 7, 1933, containing six eggs. Currier (ms.) furnished the following notes:

June 24, 1917, nest and four eggs, St. Johns. Twenty feet up on side of fir tree 18 inches in diameter at nest. Birds seen building June 18th and on. Left the nest today as I started up. Nest looped in behind a loose strip of bark with much material hanging out at both sides. Outside nest of coarse outer bark of cedar with several balls of spider web worked in—inner nest a beautiful felted mass of inner cedar bark. Eggs fresh and clear.

He also found a nest containing six eggs, May 1, 1932, and one with five young, May 25, 1933, both in Washington County.

Wren-tits: *Family Chamaeidae*

Coast Wren-tit:
Chamaea fasciata phaea Osgood

Description.—Upper parts dark brown becoming sooty on head; under parts ***dark ruddy brown***, indistinctly streaked with dusky. *Size:* Length (skins) 5.59–6.10, wing 2.24–2.32, tail 2.95–3.15, bill .41–.47. *Nest:* Usually in low bushes, made of twigs, straw, and grass, mixed with feathers. *Eggs:* 3 to 5, pale greenish blue.

Distribution.—*General:* Humid coast slope of Oregon from Astoria to California line. *In Oregon:* Permanent resident along entire coast.

The Coast Wren-tit, with its long tail and loud clear song, is distinctly a bird of the seashore, never wandering far from the salt water, and is much more often heard than seen. The dark brown of its coat blends admirably with the shadows of the lowlands that it frequents, and its mouselike habits add to the difficulty of sighting the author of those bell-like notes that Mrs. Bailey has phrased as ***keep-keep-keep-keep-keep-it keep-it keep-it***. This song, combined with the elusiveness of the bird, makes this Wren-tit one of the distinctive avian personalities of our coast.

At Astoria, at the extreme northern point of its range, the Coast Wren-tit is a common bird. Gabrielson has on several occasions heard as many as six singing males in the residential section of town. The bird is equally abundant along the coast to the California line. Perhaps it has increased in abundance in recent years; otherwise, it is hard to account for the fact that Lewis and Clark missed this brilliant songster, as did all the succeeding ornithologists who visited the coast. There is a manuscript note in the Survey files from B. J. Bretherton stating that he saw a few on February 13, 1897. A skin taken by Dr. A. K. Fisher at Astoria, July 17, 1897, and one taken by Bretherton at Newport, March 14, 1899, are the earliest ones in the Biological Survey collection, the latter being the type specimen selected by Osgood (1899) when he described this race in 1899. Woodcock (1902) included a note of Bretherton's on its abundance in the vicinity of Newport and stated further: "Warner and Cooke's collection contained a specimen taken at Newport on Yaquina Bay, May 28, 1888." Jewett (1916b) reported it as common at Netarts Bay, Bailey (1917) listed it from Tillamook Bay, and Shelton (1917) considered it an abundant resident of western Lane County.

In addition to these few published records, there are numerous specimens and notes in the Biological Survey by Bailey, Streator, Dearborn, Fisher, Peck, and Shaw from various points along the coast, most of them being from Newport and Yaquina Bay, although Coos Bay, Astoria, Empire, Norway, and Anchor are included as locality records. Our own collections contain numerous specimens and notes well distributed along the entire coast line of the State. The only actual nesting record we know of is a set of four eggs taken by Braly at Depoe Bay, June 11, 1932.

Pallid Wren-tit:
Chamaea fasciata henshawi Ridgway

Description.—"Upper parts gray, tinged with olive or brown on posterior part; tail long, graduated; under parts fawn, buffy brown, or pinkish brown, more or less obscurely streaked with dusky. *Wing:* 2.37, tail 3.41, bill .42." (Bailey) *Nest and eggs:* Same as for Coast Wren-tit.

Distribution.—*General:* Upper Austral Zone from Rogue River Valley south through interior valleys of California and along coast from Santa Barbara County to Mexican Boundary. *In Oregon:* Regular but not common resident of Rogue River Valley in Josephine and Jackson Counties that has straggled once to Klamath County.

On November 7, 1912, Jewett collected a pair of Wren-tits at Klamath Falls that belong to this race. No other individuals have ever been detected in this county although they are found regularly in the Rogue River Valley. Murie collected a specimen on Louse Creek near Grants Pass on June 10, 1916, which we understand is now in the Carnegie Museum, and Jewett took one at Grants Pass, December 10, 1918. Since that time we have noted the birds in the chaparral thickets near Grants Pass on numerous occasions, and Jewett noted them in Jackson County, March 22 to April 6, 1916, during a stay at Gold Hill, and November 13, 1917, at Medford. This is a considerable extension of the range northward over that given in the 1931 A. O. U. Check-List, but these birds are apparently established permanently in the Rogue River Valley. The only published reference to this species in Oregon is that of our notes by Gabrielson (1931) in *The Birds of the Rogue River Valley, Oregon*. We have no breeding records.

Dippers: *Family Cinclidae*

Dipper:
Cinclus mexicanus unicolor Bonaparte

Description.—"Bill shorter than head, slender, and compressed; wing short, stiff, rounded, with ten primaries, the first spurious; *tail shorter than wing*, soft, of twelve broad rounded feathers almost hidden by coverts; tarsus without scales; claws strongly curved. *Adults in summer:* whole body nearly uniform slate gray, a trifle lighter below; head and neck faintly tinged with brown. *Adults in winter:* similar, but feathers of wings and under parts lightly tipped with white. *Young:* similar to winter plumage, but under parts more or less mixed with white and tinged with rusty. *Length:* 7.00–8.50, wing 3.40–3.81, tail 1.90–2.12, bill .60–.70." (Bailey) *Nest:* An oven-shaped structure of green moss, opening on the side, and placed among rocks or behind waterfalls (Plate 77, *B*). *Eggs:* 3 to 5, white.

Distribution.—*General:* Breeds from northwestern Alaska, British Columbia, and western Alberta south to southern California, Arizona, and New Mexico. Winters throughout its breeding range. *In Oregon:* Common permanent resident of Blue and Warner Mountains and territory from Cascades west to Pacific.

The Dipper, or Water Ouzel, a cheerful mountain songster, is a common sight bobbing up and down on a rock or slipping into the water to forage for insects and small aquatic life beneath the waters of our rushing mountain streams (Plate 5, *B*). Since Newberry (1857) first listed it for the State from the Cascade Mountains many writers have commented on the curious combination of songster and fisherman in one small dull-colored bird. It is a permanent resident of the Blue and Warner Mountains and of the territory from the Cascades west to the Pacific. It winters on streams with tumbling waters that never freeze, seemingly not minding at all the chilly temperature.

The nest is often built over the water on a moss-covered bank or behind a waterfall in a convenient niche. Nesting records are numerous, and dates extend from March 30, 1925, Prill's record (ms.) of a set of four eggs at Scio, to May 31, Jewett's note of a nest on the western base of Mount Hood. Jewett found a nest on April 22 at Traill, Jackson County, at which the parents were feeding young; and Gabrielson discovered one, May 8, 1929, on the moss-covered bank of Eagle Creek, Clackamas County, that contained two eggs, now in the Braly collection.

Trout fishermen persist in repeating their belief that these small underwater acrobats are terrifically destructive to young trout. Undoubtedly when a Dipper discovers a hatchery pond crowded to overflow by trout fingerlings he helps himself. Who wouldn't if they liked such fare! Stomach examinations have shown, however, that its bobbing and probing among the pebbles is to obtain aquatic insects and their larvae and not baby trout.

Wrens: *Family Troglodytidae*

Western House Wren: *Troglodytes aëdon parkmani* Audubon

Description.—"Upper parts dull brown, all but head barred with blackish; tail coverts barred with black and whitish; under parts dingy, lightly barred. *Length:* 4.25–5.25, wing 2.02, tail 1.85, exposed culmen .49." (Bailey) *Nest:* A cavity in a tree or about buildings, filled with sticks and lined with feathers. *Eggs:* 5 to 7, pinkish, thickly spotted with brown.

Distribution.—*General:* Breeds from British Columbia, Alberta, Saskatchewan, Manitoba, and northern Wisconsin south to Lower California, Arizona, Texas, and Missouri. Winters south into Mexico. *In Oregon:* Regular summer resident and breeding species throughout State.

The Western House Wren (Plate 78, *A*) has been known from the Pacific Northwest since Audubon (1839) described it from the Columbia River, territory that was later identified as Vancouver, Washington. It did not definitely appear in literature from the present territory of Oregon, however, until Bendire (1877) listed it as a common breeding bird at Camp Harney, describing several odd nesting sites. Since that time it has been found widely and may appear anywhere in the State as the same sort of cheerful, inquisitive songster that is known farther east. Records are available for every county except Columbia, Curry, Hood River, and Morrow, and the absence of records there is unquestionably due merely to lack of field work. The bird arrives in April (earliest date, April 8, Sherman County) and remains until September (latest date, October 1, Multnomah County). It cannot be considered an abundant species, though it does reach that status in some localities. It is common in some parts of Lake and Harney Counties and becomes one of the really conspicuous songsters in Benton, Polk, and Yamhill Counties in the little valleys between the oak-covered foothills of the Coast Ranges. We have comparatively few egg dates. They extend from June 5 to July 5, a range that could possibly be extended considerably by more field work.

The eastern cousin of this species has been bitterly accused of destroying other small birds' nests and for that reason is under fire from bird lovers. The Western House Wren is so comparatively scarce in Oregon, however, that there would be no great cause for alarm over the safety of the other small nesting species, even should it have a fondness for breaking eggs.

Western Winter Wren:
Nannus hiemalis pacificus (Baird)

Description.—"Tail less than three-fourths as long as wing; outstretched feet reaching far beyond its end. Upper parts dark brown, brighter on rump and upper tail coverts; wings, tail, and often back and rump narrowly barred with blackish; superciliary stripe, throat, and breast, tawny; belly and under tail coverts barred; flanks darker. *Length:* 3.60–4.25, wing 1.80–1.90, tail 1.20–1.35, exposed culmen .40–.45." (Bailey) *Nest:* In heavy timber, in crevices of logs or stumps, made of moss, lined with feathers. *Eggs:* 5 to 7, white or cream, sparingly spotted with small brown dots.

Distribution.—*General:* Breeds from Prince Williams Sound, Alaska, and western Alberta south to southern California and Colorado. Winters throughout western United States. *In Oregon:* Common permanent resident of timbered sections.

This pert little bit of brown fluff, the Western Winter Wren (Plate 78, *B*), is one of the comparatively few birds that like the dense shade of the heaviest fir and spruce forests in Oregon. In their gloomy depths, whether it be at seashore or timber line, this mouselike mite will be found darting about in the thick brush or hopping about the fallen logs. One can often hear it scolding, but it is impossible to catch a glimpse of the bird itself in the dense jungles. During the nesting season, however, the male mounts to the top of a convenient stump and bursts forth in the most amazing loud, clear song that ever came from a brown protuberance. Lewis and Clark (1814), who seldom mentioned small birds, listed this one as present at the mouth of the Columbia on January 2, 1806. Merrill (1888) published the first record from eastern Oregon, from Fort Klamath, but since then the species has appeared frequently in Oregon literature. It is present throughout the year and has been found in every county of western Oregon, and in Wallowa, Baker, Union, Grant, Umatilla, Deschutes, Lake, Klamath, Wasco, and Hood River Counties in eastern Oregon. It is particularly common in the higher areas where spruce and fir thickets abound. Jewett has two nesting records, a set of three fresh eggs found at Anthony (Eagle Creek), Baker County, May 8, 1907, and a set of five fresh eggs found at Milwaukie, Clackamas County, April 5, 1908.

Seattle Wren:
Thryomanes bewicki calophonus Oberholser

Description.—"Superciliary white; upper parts *rich dark brown*, slightly deeper on head; *tail black*, middle feathers sepia brown barred with black, the rest tipped with gray and barred with brown, outer pair barred toward end with whitish; under parts grayish white, lightest on throat, tinged with brown on sides and flanks; under tail coverts barred with black. *Wing:* 2.07, tail 2.03, exposed culmen .56." (Bailey) *Nest:* A bulky mass of sticks, lined with feathers and placed about buildings, holes in stumps, and similar places. *Eggs:* 5 to 7, white or pinkish, finely speckled with brown—sometimes evenly over the entire eggs and at others only about the larger end.

Plate 78, *A*. Western House Wren. (Photo by Wm. L. Finley, Jr.)

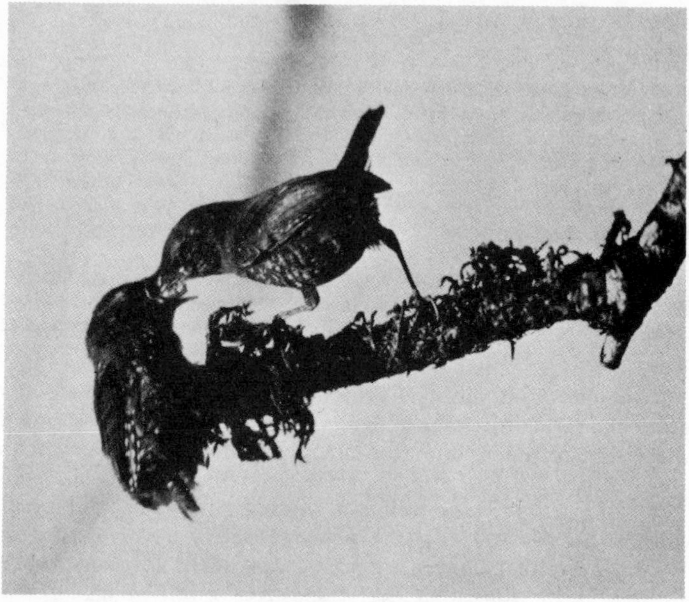

Plate 78, *B*. Western Winter Wren feeding young. (Photo by Wm. L. Finley.)

Distribution.—*General:* Pacific slope from Vancouver Island and southern British Columbia to Oregon. *In Oregon:* Common permanent resident west of Cascades from Columbia River to but not including Curry, Josephine, and Jackson Counties, though it occasionally winters in those counties. (See Figure 16.)

The Seattle Wren (Plate 79), one of the characteristic birds of the brush patches and woodlands in both the stream bottoms and on the foothill slopes, is the commonest wren in the territory it inhabits and ranks almost with the Song Sparrow in all-year-round abundance and wide dispersion over the occupied territory. It is a comparatively large wren, with energetic mannerisms and a loud, pleasing song, and is the one most frequently found occupying nest boxes about homes. It is a permanent resident in all but the southern counties west of the Cascades but is found there in winter. We have winter birds from Ashland, Medford, Gold Hill, Powers, and Gold Beach. The nesting season is largely in May, fresh egg dates extending from April 4 to May 31, the number of eggs varying from three to six.

This wren was first listed as an Oregon breeding bird from Fort William (Portland) by Nuttall in 1840. Its next appearance in literature is in Anthony's (1886) paper on the birds of Washington County. Since Woodcock's (1902) list, a number of publications have referred to it, though for so common a species it has made scant appearance in the ornithological literature of the territory.

San Joaquin Wren:
Thryomanes bewicki drymoecus Oberholser

Description.—Similar to the Seattle Wren but grayer and paler. *Size:* Length (skins) 4.25–5.00, wing 1.93–2.17, tail 1.85–2.17, bill .53–.63. *Nest and eggs:* Same as for Seattle Wren.

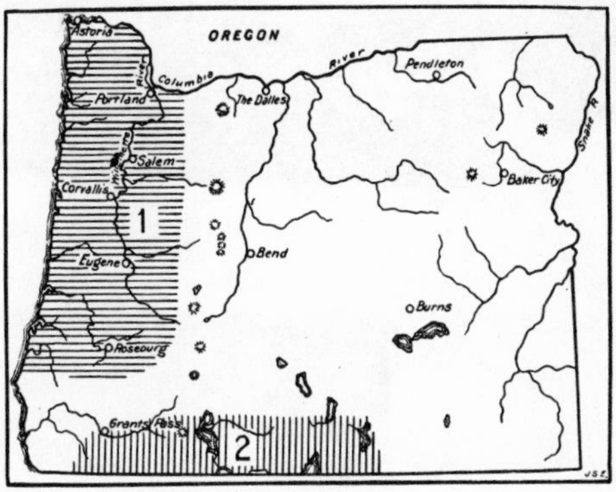

Figure 16.—Distribution of two wrens in Oregon: 1, Seattle Wren (*Thryomanes bewicki calophonus*); 2, San Joaquin Wren (*T. b. drymoecus*).

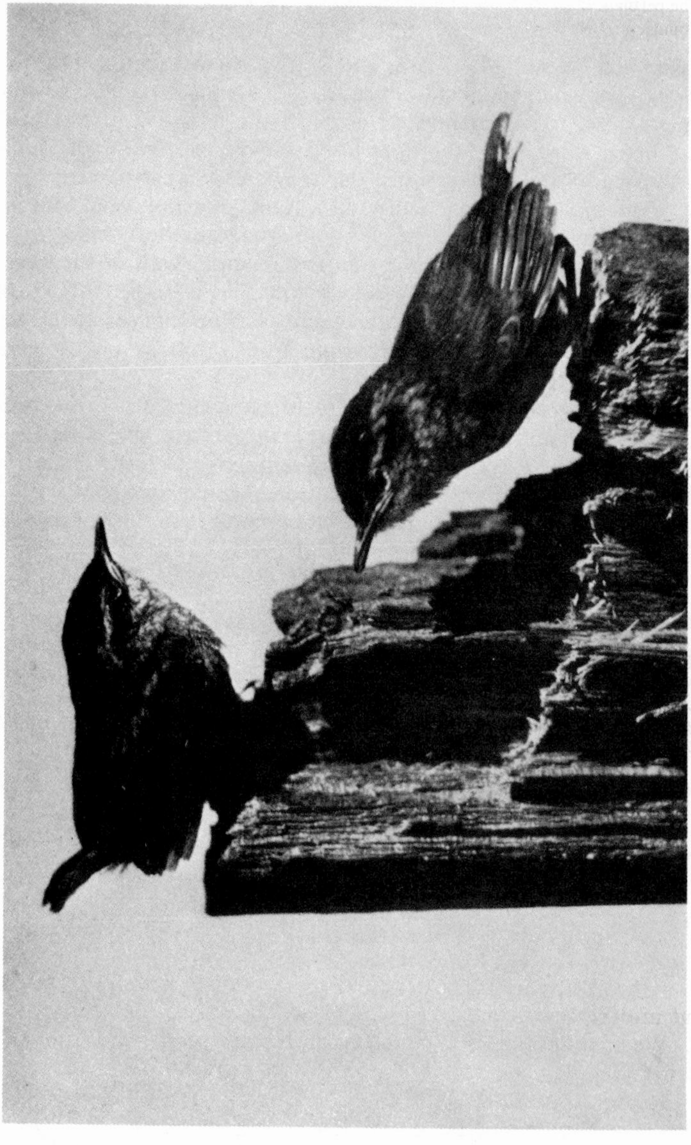

Plate 79. Young Seattle Wrens. (Photo by Wm. L. Finley and H. T. Bohlman.)

DISTRIBUTION.—*General:* Southern Oregon east of Coast Ranges to Warner Mountains south through Sacramento Valley to central San Joaquin Valley. *In Oregon:* The permanent resident and breeding bird of Lake, Klamath, Jackson, and Josephine Counties. (See Figure 16.)

THE SAN JOAQUIN WREN is a common bird in the Rogue River Valley and almost equally abundant in the vicinity of Klamath Falls. Over most of Klamath and Lake Counties it is comparatively scarce, although it is locally common in the Warner Valley. It is a permanent resident of Lake, Klamath, Jackson, and Josephine Counties. Oberholser (1932) set the birds of this territory apart as *T. b. atrestus*, but as this new race has not yet been passed on by the A. O. U. committee and we lack adequate comparative material from California we are leaving the bird under the present race.

Bendire (1877) included a wren of this genus in his Camp Harney list with the statement that it was "rather rare in this vicinity." So far as we can learn no specimen was taken, so that the easternmost birds we have seen are from the Warner Valley. Birds of this group appearing in Burns as stragglers would probably belong in this subspecies. Wrens of the genus *Thryomanes* were not again mentioned from this territory until Oberholser (1920a), in his synopsis of the genus, included southern Oregon in the range of the present form. Gabrielson (1931) listed the breeding birds of Jackson and Josephine Counties as *T. b. drymoecus*, the only subsequent reference to the race.

Western Marsh Wren:
Telmatodytes palustris plesius (Oberholser)

DESCRIPTION.—Like *T. p. paludicola* but upper parts paler, under parts grayer, middle tail feathers heavily barred, and upper and lower tail coverts barred; paler and more sharply barred than *paludicola*. *Size:* Wing 2.06, tail 1.82, bill .50. *Nest:* A globule of tule stems and grass on the tules above the water. *Eggs:* 5 to 9, lavender brown.

DISTRIBUTION.—*General:* Breeds from central British Columbia east of Cascades south to northern California, Nevada, and Colorado. Winters south into Mexico. *In Oregon:* Common summer resident and breeding species east of Cascades. Occasionally winters where there are open water and tules.

THE RATTLING NOTES of the Western Marsh Wren are one of the characteristic sounds in the great marshes of interior Oregon. This wren is most abundant in Klamath, Harney, and Lake Counties but can also be found in other parts of eastern Oregon wherever suitable conditions prevail. We have specimens from Klamath, Harney, Lake, and Crook Counties that are all typical of this race. In addition, we have seen birds in Malheur, Union, and Umatilla Counties that without doubt belong here, though none were collected.

Curiously enough the first winter record of the species is also the first record for the State. Bendire (Brewer 1875) collected one, January 18,

1875, along a willow-fringed stream, and later (Bendire 1877) found the species to be an abundant summer resident. A few individuals winter regularly in Klamath, Lake, and Harney Counties, usually about the warm springs in which the country abounds or along some of the little streams that have open areas throughout the winter. A few can likewise be found along the Snake River in Malheur County. These few wintering individuals are increased to an abundant number about mid-April, and from that date to late September the Western Marsh Wrens are much in evidence, audibly if not visually. One can seldom stop near a tule patch without facing a vigorous scolding from this small denizen of the marshes, though a long period may pass before a good look at it is obtained.

The curious globular nests are a common sight, though each nest by no means indicates a breeding pair. On the contrary, each pair builds several dummies in the vicinity of the real nest. No one has ever certainly accounted for all of this extra labor. Perhaps they are actually dummies to attract attention away from the real nest. The explanation has been advanced that at least one provides sleeping quarters for father wren. At any rate they are there, and an intruder must pry into several before finding the handsome brown eggs. These are present from May 6 to June 20 and perhaps later.

Tule Wren:
Telmatodytes palustris paludicola (Baird)

Description.—"Top of head and triangular patch on middle of back black; middle of crown washed with brown; back patch streaked with white; rest of back light brown; *middle tail feathers and tail coverts generally distinctly and continuously barred with black;* under parts soiled whitish, flanks brownish. *Length:* 4.50–5.75, wing 1.95–2.22, tail 1.80–2.05, bill .48–.55." (Bailey) *Nest and eggs:* Same as for *T. p. plesius*.

Distribution.—*General:* Breeds from southern British Columbia south along coast to southern California. Winters south into Mexico. *In Oregon:* Permanent resident and breeding species in suitable localities west of Cascades.

The Tule Wren is not an abundant bird in Oregon due to lack of suitable breeding sites. A few scattered pairs can be found along the Columbia River from Portland to the Pacific and likewise along the Willamette. It is even less common in the Rogue River Valley, although we have records of it in a few places in Jackson County. Along the coast it is found in scattered colonies in all counties from Clatsop to Curry, Tillamook and Lincoln having the greatest population, in our experience. There the birds are found along the tide flats wherever vegetation is rank enough to furnish cover, although at Devils Lake they frequent the thick clumps of wild rose bushes at the south end of the lake. The only eggs known to us from the State are a set of five collected by Stanley G. Jewett, Jr., at Devils Lake, April 29, 1933.

Anthony (1886) listed the Tule Wren from Washington County, the first Oregon record applicable to this form. Woodcock (1902) added Corvallis as a locality record. Swarth (1917b) recorded two from Netarts Bay. Shelton (1917) stated it was common in west-central Oregon. Walker (1924) published records of specimens taken along the Tillamook River (December 25, 1917) and Netarts Bay (October 27, 1922). The writers (Jewett and Gabrielson, 1929) added Multnomah County to the list and have since collected specimens at Siletz Bay and Devils Lake in Lincoln County.

Swarth (1917b) listed three birds from Oregon—one from Netarts, one from Elmira, and one from Eugene—as *T. p. aestuarinus*, the Suisun Marsh Wren, but in his discussion he stated:

> Of these three specimens just one is fairly typical of *aestuarinus* in appearance, the others tending towards *paludicola*. Possibly all three are merely variants of the latter race, showing individual variation toward *aestuarinus*.

This appears to be the only published basis for the statement in the 1931 A. O. U. Check-List that this strictly local race, the Suisun Marsh Wren, spreads to Oregon in the winter. We doubt the advisability of including the form in the list of Oregon birds on the above statement.

Dotted Wren:
Catherpes mexicanus punctulatus Ridgway

DESCRIPTION.—"*Adults:* Brown except for white throat and breast; upper parts light brown, grayish on head, speckled with white and blackish; tail rusty brown, crossed by narrow black bars; belly dark rusty brown. *Young:* essentially like adults, but usually without white specks on upper parts or posterior under parts, which are, instead, mottled, more or less, with dusky." (Bailey) *Size:* Length (skins) 4.69–5.39, wing 2.19–2.46, tail 1.83–2.15, bill .75–.85. *Nest:* A bulky mass in crevices of rocks or caves. *Eggs:* 3 to 5, white, spotted on larger end with brown.

DISTRIBUTION.—*General:* Breeds from southern Washington through Oregon and California into Lower California. *In Oregon:* Uncommon permanent resident of eastern part of State. Crosses Cascades only into Jackson County.

THIS BRILLIANT SONGSTER, the Dotted Wren, is a very little-known inhabitant of the rocky sides and basaltic rims of the eastern part of the State. It is most abundant in southern Malheur and Harney Counties, where it is a not infrequent inhabitant of the Steens and the lesser ranges to the eastward. In addition, there are records of the bird in Baker, Grant, Jefferson, Jackson, Sherman, Wasco, and Wallowa Counties. We have numerous specimens from Harney, and there are specimens in the Jewett collection from Moody (July 30, 1914) and Maupin (March 24, 1928), both Wasco County; Imnaha Canyon, Wallowa County (April 15, 1928); and Grass Valley, Sherman County (February 7, 1930). Gabrielson took the species in Hay Creek, Jefferson County (July 18, 1919); Newbridge, Baker County (February 20, 1932); and Brownsboro, Jackson County (December 8, 1926). The Biological Survey collection contains specimens from Crane, Harney County (July 28, 1916); Malheur Caves, Malheur County (October 6, 1916); Homestead, Baker County (June 17, 1916); and Mount Vernon, Grant County (July 1, 1915). Patterson (ms.) reported two nests in the Klamath country, May 16 and 30, 1930.

The first authentic record for the State was Miller's (1904), who found it at Shearers Bridge, Wasco County (May 27, 1899); at Bridge Creek, Wheeler County (June 5, 1899); and at Cove in the same county (June 22, 1899). Woodcock (1902) listed it as a "tolerably common resident" at Yaquina Bay on the authority of B. J. Bretherton, but in the absence of any subsequent supporting specimens or authentic records from the coast we are convinced that this was a case of mistaken identification. Jewett (1916a) recorded a bird taken at Mount Vernon, Grant County, and Sherwood (1924) published the first record for Jackson County, a male taken near Ashland, February 21, 1924.

The song of this tiny brown wren is exceptionally loud and powerful for one so small. It echoes up and down the cool canyons until one is at a loss to locate the singer. We have become best acquainted with the bird in the rugged gorges of the Steens where it is fairly common. It frequents the tumbled talus piles of huge blocks of rock found in these deep gorges and is as elusive as a mouse when one actually tries to get a view of it. Elsewhere in the State it is found only as widely scattered individuals or pairs and one may follow a rim or canyon for many miles without seeing or hearing one.

Common Rock Wren:
Salpinctes obsoletus obsoletus (Say)

Description.—"Bill about as long as head, slender, compressed, decurved at tip; wing longer than tail; tail rounded, feathers broad; feet small and weak; tarsus longer than middle toe, scaled behind. *Adults:* upper parts *dull grayish brown*, finely flecked with black and white dots; rump light brown; tail graduated, tipped with buffy brown and with *subterminal band of black;* middle tail feathers narrowly barred with blackish; under parts dull whitish, brownish on flanks; chest usually finely speckled. *Young:* upper parts rusty gray; under parts whitish anteriorly, brownish on flanks and under tail coverts. *Length:* 5.12–6.35, wing 2.68–2.80, tail 2.12–2.40, bill from nostril .44–.54." (Bailey) *Nest:* In crevices in rocks, or sometimes about buildings. *Eggs:* 7 or 8, white, spotted on larger end with brown.

Distribution.—*General:* Breeds from southern British Columbia, Alberta, and Saskatchewan south to Mexico. Winters through much of its range and into Mexico. *In Oregon:* Common permanent resident east of Cascades, rather rare west of Cascades. Most abundant from April to October but present in smaller numbers throughout winter.

The Common Rock Wren makes its cheerful presence known musically from every rock slide in eastern Oregon, where it is one of the characteristic inhabitants. The notes are startlingly loud and clear for so small a bird and have little competition in the gray landscape, unless perchance a meadowlark or sage thrasher happens to be musically inclined at the same time. West of the mountains, the species is much less common, although it appears often enough to afford an occasional thrill to the enthusiastic hunter of new records.

Newberry (1857) first reported it for the State from the Klamath Lakes and the head of the Deschutes River. Bendire (Brewer 1875), who found the first Oregon nest at Camp Harney, May 9, 1875, wrote:

> The nest and eggs of the rock wren were found accidentally by two of my men, who were getting building-stone yesterday. In moving a flat rock lying on the side of a hill close to my quarters, they found a nest and four fresh eggs under it. Unfortunately a small bit of stone fell into the nest and broke two of the eggs. The nest is not such a bulky affair as wrens' nests usually are, no doubt on account of want of room under the rock. It was about a foot and a half from the opening under the rock, on a steep hillside covered with boulders. The nest was composed externally of sticks and bark, and lined with fine rootlets and a little hair.

In a later paper (Bendire 1877) he mentioned several nests from the same locality. Walker (1917b) listed a nest of six fresh eggs from Twickenham, in the John Day Canyon. There have been many published references since, and our notes and those of other Biological Survey men show the species to be found in every county east of the Cascades.

Anthony (Woodcock 1902) recorded a specimen taken near Beaverton, May 21, 1885, the first record for that part of the State. Jewett (1913a) reported one collected by O. J. Murie at Netarts, December 27, 1912, and Shelton (1917) stated that it bred at Spencer Butte, near Eugene, as well as along the eastern edge of Lane County in the Cascades. Gabrielson (1931) included it in the *Birds of the Rogue River Valley* on a sight record by Jewett. In addition to these western Oregon records, there is a specimen in the Jewett collection taken by Overton Dowell, Jr., at Mercer, western Lane County, May 21, 1915. It is curious that when this bird does go to western Oregon it should go to the coast twice out of five records.

Mockingbirds and Thrashers: *Family Mimidae*

Western Mockingbird:
Mimus polyglottos leucopterus (Vigors)

Description.—*Adults:* upper parts grayish drab; wings and tail blackish, wings with large white patch at base of primaries, wing bars, white-tipped wing quills, and tertick with whitish edgings; under parts white, washed with clay color. *Young:* more brownish above; back indistinctly spotted or streaked; breast spotted. (Adapted from Mrs. Bailey.) *Size:* Length 10.00, wing 4.25–4.72, tail 4.43–5.32.

Distribution.—*General:* From northwestern Mexico and southwestern United States north to southeastern Oregon. *In Oregon:* Known only from Steens Mountains, Harney County.

The Western Mockingbird is one of the most characteristic birds of farms and gardens in our southwestern States where its mimic song is heard throughout the day and often all night long during periods of moonlight. It imitates every other bird call from that of the jay to the varied notes of the gnatcatchers and the kingbirds and often gives even a good imitation of the shrill call of the rock squirrel. The mockingbird was not recorded as occurring in Oregon until Jewett (1937) published the report of one seen in the Blitzen Valley by Mrs. Stanley G. Jewett in August 1935 and one seen there by him on November 21, 1935; an adult male collected in the Steens Mountains on February 9, 1936, one seen there on March 26, 1936, and an immature male in the spotted plumage collected there at an elevation of 7,500 feet on August 30, 1936. From this meager evidence it would appear that rare as the "mocker" is in Oregon, it must be a permanent resident in small numbers in the Steens Mountains.

Catbird:

Dumetella carolinensis (Linnaeus)

Description.—"Rictal bristles well developed; tail longer than wing, much rounded; scales of tarsus indistinct. *Adults:* dark slaty gray; crown and tail black; under tail coverts dark rufous. *Young:* similar, but washed with brownish. *Length:* 8.00–9.35, wing 3.45–3.75, tail 3.70–4.25, bill .65–.75." (Bailey) *Nest:* Largely of roots and rootlets, placed in bushes or low trees. *Eggs:* 3 to 5, deep blue green.

Distribution.—*General:* Breeds from central British Columbia, southern Alberta, central Saskatchewan, Manitoba, Ontario, Quebec, and Nova Scotia south to northern Oregon, northern Utah, New Mexico, and the Gulf States. Winters south to Panama. *In Oregon:* Regular summer resident of northeastern corner. Undoubtedly breeds, although there are no actual breeding records.

The Catbird has evidently become increasingly common in the past few years, although it is still confined to the extreme northeastern section of the State. It arrives in May and remains until August (our earliest date, May 21; latest, August 4, both Union County). Peck (1911a) published the first Oregon record. He found it along Willow Creek in extreme northern Malheur County in the summer of 1910. Jewett (1916a) collected a specimen at Mount Vernon, Grant County, June 30, 1915, that is now in the Biological Survey collection, and Gabrielson (1924a) published three records for Wallowa County. We have specimens also from Union and Umatilla Counties. Preble (Biological Survey ms.) reported it at Pendleton in 1896. M. E. Peck (1915 ms.) reported it as having been observed at La Grande "several years ago," and H. H. Sheldon (ms.) from Baker County in 1916.

In Oregon, the extreme of its western range, the Catbird is somewhat more shy than farther east. Occasionally one is observed perched on a conspicuous twig—particularly in the courting season—but more frequently the song or meowing alarm note is given from the shelter of some thick bush, and it is often necessary to search the thickets carefully in order to catch a glimpse of the slate-colored songster.

Sage Thrasher:
Oreoscoptes montanus (Townsend)

DESCRIPTION.—"Bill much shorter than head; rictal bristles well developed; wings and tail of equal length; tail graduated. *Adults:* upper parts dull grayish brown, indistinctly streaked; wings with two narrow white bars; tail with inner web of 2 to 4 outer feathers *tipped with white;* under parts whitish, buffy on flanks and under tail coverts; breast and sides marked with brown to sooty spots. *Young:* like adults, but upper parts indistinctly streaked with darker, and streaks on under parts less sharply defined. *Length:* 8-9, wing 3.95-4.19, tail 3.20-3.35, bill .60-.65." (Bailey) *Nest:* Of sage twigs, plant stems, and grasses, lined with rootlets; in sagebrush or other bush near the ground. *Eggs:* 3 to 5, rich greenish blue, spotted with brown (Plate 80).

DISTRIBUTION.—*General:* Breeds from southern British Columbia, central Montana, and western Nebraska south to southern California and northern New Mexico. Winters south into Mexico. *In Oregon:* Common summer resident and breeding species of sagebrush areas of eastern Oregon. Casual straggler in western Oregon.

THE SAGE THRASHER is one of the characteristic sagebrush birds. Its dull color matches the gray landscape that its rollicking song does so much to enliven. It is the supreme songster of the sage and has been noted in every county in eastern Oregon, but is most abundant in the great sage slopes and valleys of Malheur, Harney, and Lake Counties. It appears in April (earliest date, April 8, Morrow County) and remains until September (latest date, October 19, Harney County).

There are two records for western Oregon where it may be regarded as a casual straggler only. Shelton (1917) reported a specimen from Oakridge, July 6, 1916, and in our *Birds of the Portland Area* (Jewett and Gabrielson 1929) we recorded an individual that appeared at a bird bath in Gabrielson's yard in Portland, August 12, 1924.

Bendire (Brewer 1875) is credited with the first record and also with the first nesting record when he took eggs at Camp Harney, May 29, 1875. He stated (Bendire 1877) that the species commenced to nest about the end of April and left the valley in September. The nests are usually located in the sage and are not difficult to find. Our records of egg dates extend from May 6 to June 20.

Plate 80. Nest and eggs of Sage Thrasher. (Photo by Alex Walker.)

Thrushes, Bluebirds, Stonechats, and Solitaires: *Family Turdidae*

Northwestern Robin:
Turdus migratorius caurinus (Grinnell)

Description.—"Head all around black, interrupted by slaty tippings to the feathers posteriorly, so that there is dorsally and laterally a mergence into the color of the back. Eyelids white, except on loral side. Whole dorsal surface uniform dark mouse-gray with a tinge of sepia. Wings and tail blackish, edged with color of back. Outer pair of tail feathers with a terminal bar of white, mostly on inner web, at most 3 mm. wide. Proximal to this is an indistinct grayish interval merging into the blackish of the basal portion of the feathers in question. Extreme chin pure white. Throat streaked black on a white ground. Some hazel in malar region. Whole lower surface from behind throat to anal region, including sides and under wing-coverts, clear deep brown of a shade between hazel and chestnut. Anal region abruptly white and crissum mainly white, the fuscous bases showing through, giving a clouded effect." Similar to *Turdus migratorius migratorius* "but lacks the extended white patch on inner web of outer tail feathers; resembles *Turdus migratorius propinquus* in the extremely narrow white tippings of the outer tail feathers, but coloration much darker and size smaller." (Grinnell 1909b.) *Size:* Length (skins) 8.25–10.00, wing 4.92–5.35, tail 3.58–4.21, exposed culmen .71–.79. *Nest:* A cup of mud and grass, lined more or less with fine grass and rootlets and placed usually in a fork of a tree or on a projecting shelf in a building or on a cliff. *Eggs:* 3 to 5, greenish blue.

Distribution.—*General:* Breeds from Glacier Bay, Alaska, south through the Pacific Coast district to Willamette Valley and northern coast district of Oregon. *In Oregon:* Permanent resident that breeds in northwestern Oregon and Willamette Valley and at least Clatsop, Tillamook, and Lincoln Counties. Winters throughout State.

The breeding birds from the Willamette Valley, from Portland to Eugene, although not quite as dark as birds from the Olympic Mountains, Washington, are much closer to *caurinus* than to *propinquus*. This is likewise true of the birds of the coast, at least as far south as Lincoln County. When we came to check up on skins we found we had no breeding birds from farther south than Eugene in the western half of the State, so that we are unable to state the exact line that divides the form from *propinquus*, which breeds in the Rogue River Valley.

In winter the Northwestern Robin spreads over the State, and every winter specimen we have is *caurinus*, but we cannot help but believe that more intensive collecting will reveal a fair proportion of *propinquus* in the winter population. We have numerous winter specimens from western Oregon and winter birds from Mitchell, Klamath Falls, and Wallowa also that are identical with them. Apparently the breeding birds in the eastern part of the State move out and those from farther north and west take their places, though more intensive collecting may reveal that our obtaining only representatives of the race by sporadic winter collecting is only a coincidence.

The bird is too well known to warrant any extended comment. This, or the Western Robin, is a familiar dooryard bird in every part of the State, and there are few ornithologists whose early interest was not stimulated by watching this bird pulling worms from the lawn grass. As would be expected, the notes on this species are more extended than for any other, and an historical resume of the literature would involve a recitation of all the major papers on Oregon birds. It is sufficient to say that since Lewis and Clark (1814) noted it at the mouth of the Columbia on February 15, 1806, it has been included in every list of birds of this territory or any of its subdivisions.

Chapman (Multnomah 1879) reported an albino robin from Portland, an interesting fact in view of our now well-established annual outbreaks of newspaper reports of albino robins in that vicinity. There seems to be a marked albinistic strain in the birds of that locality, as we see one or more albinos each season and have collected several.

The robin's mud-cupped nest, greenish-blue eggs, and spotted-breasted young are familiar to every bird student. Beginning in early May, the parents are seen leading little squads of squalling youngsters over the lawns and through the bushes, a daily sight until well into July, as two and sometimes three broods are raised by this abundant bird, which has a long breeding season. Nests with full sets of eggs have been noted from April 11 to July 8. Jewett (1928a) observed an odd and interesting incident near Portland. He saw a Russet-backed Thrush repeatedly feed young fledgling robins, voluntary assistance probably greatly appreciated by the hard-working parents.

When the strawberries and cherries are ripe the robins take their toll. Later they switch to wild fruits, leaving the less edible fruits, such as snowberries and rose hips, for emergency winter rations. In the fall months, they are found in the mountains feasting on the ripening mountain-ash berries and the squads that remain about the town see that any such trees planted as ornamentals do not lack for attention. A sudden snowstorm often concentrates the birds, and on such occasions the snowberries in the bottoms or the red berries of the ornamental cotoneasters soon vanish under the onslaught of the hungry hordes. Sometimes the robins come alone, but on other occasions they are accompanied by Varied Thrushes, Evening Grosbeaks, or sleek Bohemian Waxwings.

In good berry years in the extensive juniper forests near Redmond, the robins gather in great winter roosts that in the evening look like huge swarms of bees as the birds swirl over the treetops in the twilight before settling down for the night. It is one of the real winter bird sights of eastern Oregon, and it is worth a trip to that section to watch the great numbers of birds entering and leaving the roost. In February or early March, these roosts begin to break up as the arrival of birds from farther south swell the robin population.

Western Robin:
Turdus migratorius propinquus Ridgway

Description.—"*Adults:* Head, wings, and tail blackish; rest of upper parts slaty gray, *black of hind neck sharply contrasting with gray of anterior part of back;* outer tail feather without distinct white tip, often with no white; throat black, streaked with white; rest of under parts, except tail coverts, rufous; in female paler and duller. *In winter:* upper parts tinged with brown; under parts with feathers edged with white. *Young:* under parts spotted; upper parts streaked with white. *Young in first winter:* head and neck brownish gray, like upper parts; rufous of breast paler, more olivaceous. *Length:* 10–11, wing 5.20–5.70, tail 3.80–4.70, bill .85–.95." (Bailey) *Nest and eggs:* As for Northwestern Robin.

Distribution.—*General:* Breeds from southeastern British Columbia and Montana south to California. Winters over much of its range and southward. *In Oregon:* Abundant breeding species from summit of Cascades eastward throughout State and in Rogue River Valley and southern counties along coast.

All of the breeding birds from and including the summit of the Cascades eastward are of this race. We have breeding individuals in the Biological Survey collection from Fort Klamath, Davis Lake, Hart Mountain, Ione, Mount Vernon, and Wallowa Lake. There are also summer birds from Elgin, Heppner, Millers Head of Crooked Creek, Crook County, head of Drews Creek, Lake County, and Lapine. There are egg dates from published data, from our notes, or from notes in the Biological Survey files from April 12 to July 26.

To date we have not seen a winter bird of this race from Oregon, but we are unable to believe that it withdraws entirely from the State and feel sure that more winter collecting, particularly east of the Cascades, will reveal it.

Pacific Varied Thrush:
Ixoreus naevius naevius (Gmelin)

Description.—"*Adult male: Under parts bright rusty brown, throat crossed by blackish necklace;* belly mixed white and gray; upper parts dark bluish slate, feathers edged with lighter; wings banded and edged with brown; side of head black, bordered above by brown streak. *Adult female:* similar, but much duller; upper parts washed with brown—deeper in winter—and collar obscured by brown feathers. *Young:* like female, but duller; collar less distinct, and more or less spotted with yellowish brown; feathers of breast with dusky and those of upper parts with distinct paler shaft streaks. *Length:* 9–10, wing 4.90–5.20, tail about 3.60–3.80, bill about 1." (Bailey) *Nest:* Much like that of a robin and in much the same position. *Eggs:* 4, pale greenish blue, sparingly speckled with brown.

Distribution.—*General:* Breeds from Yakutat Bay, Alaska, south to Humboldt County, California. Winters south to southern California. *In Oregon:* Permanent resident west of eastern edge of timber on Cascades running through Wasco, Jefferson, Deschutes, and Klamath Counties. We have specimens and notes from every county west of this line.

The Pacific Varied Thrush, or Alaska Robin, as it is sometimes called, attracted the attention of early visitors. Lewis and Clark (1814) found it wintering at the mouth of the Columbia. Newberry (1857) reported it from the Cascades and Willamette Valley in October 1855, and Suckley (Cooper and Suckley 1860) said it was common at Astoria in winter. Swallow (1891) was the first to find it breeding in the State when he located a nest, 4 feet up in a small hemlock, at Astoria on April 27. Woodcock (1902) published a record sent him by Prill of a nest and four eggs taken at Scio, Linn County, June 1901, and Jewett's notes list one taken by Prill at Scio, June 12, 1900. These are surely the same nest, with an error of a year made somewhere in transcribing the dates. Jewett found a nest near Linnton on April 19, 1906, that contained three eggs. It was in a crotch of a small cedar tree about 20 feet from the ground. He found a second nest on the Collowash Burn, Mount Hood National Forest, on May 12, 1919, containing four small young.

The Pacific Varied Thrush is most in evidence in the lowlands during the winter months, where it is often seen with the robins or in little flocks of its own species. It usually disappears from the lowlands in early May, though a few may remain to breed in favored spots, and returns again in late September. It is an abundant bird despite the comparatively few nesting records available. The endless miles of fir forests in the State make finding a nest either a lucky accident or the happy ending of a painstaking search that takes time few of us have to give.

The song is a single, long-drawn-out, high-pitched note that manages to bring with it some of the mystery of the virgin forests in much the same manner as does that of the Hermit Thrush. One who has heard this vibrant note will ever after associate it with the dark spruce and fir forests that are the chosen home of the Varied Thrush.

Northern Varied Thrush:
Ixoreus naevius meruloides (Swainson)

Description.—*Male:* Like *I. n. naevius*. *Female:* "Similar to female *naevius*, but grayer and paler, white markings more extended, wing longer, more pointed." (Bailey) *Size:* Length (skins) 7.87–9.49, wing 4.75–5.22, tail 3.23–3.68, bill .73–.87. *Nest and eggs:* As for Pacific Varied Thrush.

Distribution.—*General:* Breeds from Yukon and Mackenzie Deltas south through mountains to eastern Oregon and northwestern Montana. Winters south into California. *In Oregon:* Regular summer resident and breeding species of northeastern Oregon in Wallowa, Union, Baker, and Umatilla Counties. In migration southward through Harney and Lake Counties.

We have four Oregon specimens of the Northern Varied Thrush—two taken at Union (April 16, 1922, Gabrielson), one at Lick Creek Ranger Station (June 20, 1927, Jewett), and one on Hart Mountain (October 12, 1931, Gabrielson). There are also two in the Biological Survey collection, one taken at Bourne, Baker County (August 4, 1915, Jewett), and one at Wallowa Lake (April 9, 1919, George Cantwell). In addition, we have numerous manuscript notes, both of our own and other Survey members, for the counties listed above under "Distribution." Our earliest spring date is March 2; and latest fall record, October 24. We consider it a regular but not common bird over the district in which it is found and feel certain that more intensive work would considerably extend its range in Oregon.

Bendire (1877) reported collecting a female at Camp Harney on March 7, 1876. Jewett (1909c) recorded the species from Baker County and included a nest and young found on Eagle Creek, Baker County, on May 14, 1907. Henderson (1920) found it in eastern Oregon, and Gabrielson (1924a) encountered it commonly at some points in the Wallowas. These are the only published references to its occurrence in Oregon. Since the Baker and Wallowa accounts were published, we have collected a few specimens, and Jewett found a second nest at Lick Creek, Wallowa County, June 20, 1927. It was located 12 feet up in a small spruce and contained four fresh eggs.

Alaska Hermit Thrush:
Hylocichla guttata guttata (Pallas)

Description.—"Upper parts *dark grayish brown*, more olive in winter, tail *deep rufous;* chest thickly marked with broad, wedge-shaped spots. *Length:* 6–7, wing 3.25–3.80, tail 2.60–3.00, bill .45–.52." (Bailey) *Nest:* On ground in damp woods, made of leaves and dried grass. *Eggs:* 4 or 5, plain greenish blue.

Distribution.—*General:* Breeds from south-central Alaska south to Kodiak Island, Cross Sound, and northern British Columbia. Winters south to southern California. *In Oregon:* Rather uncommon winter visitor that arrives in October and remains until April. Most abundant in western Oregon valleys and along Cascades but appears also east of mountains.

An anonymous note (Anonymous 1897) reporting the Alaska Hermit Thrush seen in Oregon, April 2, 1896, and a specimen taken, January 8, 1897, was the first published reference to the bird for the State. Osgood (1901) recorded winter specimens for Fort Klamath. Walker (1915, 1917b) reported an albino from Hemlock, Tillamook County, December 18, and recorded specimens from Warm Springs, Wasco County, April 30, 1915. All of the birds of this group are shy, elusive inhabitants of the denser timber and brushlands and are somewhat difficult to locate unless they are in song.

There are specimens in the Biological Survey collection from Detroit (September 28, 1897) and Gold Beach (October 24, 1909). According to Biological Survey records there are five skins in the Carnegie Museum, one collected April 17, 1901, at Corvallis by A. R. Woodcock, and four collected April 10, 1909, at Salem, by M. E. Peck. Walker took one at Tillamook, December 11, 1915, and sent it to the Biological Survey for identification.

In our own collections, we have three skins from Portland, two from Grants Pass, and two that deserve special mention, one from Mosquito Ranger Station on the Rogue River National Forest, Jackson County, taken September 26, 1926 (Gabrielson) that is the earliest fall record as well as the one farthest south in the Cascades, and the second from the Steens Mountains, Harney County, taken May 14, 1934 (Jewett) that is the farthest inland station and the latest spring record. Because of the impossibility of distinguishing these subspecies of Hermit Thrush in the field, we have limited our discussion of ranges and dates to specimens actually secured and identified by some competent ornithologist.

Dwarf Hermit Thrush:
Hylocichla guttata nanus (Audubon)

Description.—"Like *guttata*, but color darker and richer; upper parts brownish olivaceous, tending toward raw umber; top of head and rump browner than back; upper tail coverts and tail burnt umber; under parts more buffy than in *guttata*. *Wing:* 3.25, tail 2.75, bill .50, tarsus 1.12." (Bailey) *Nest and eggs:* Similar to those of the Alaska Hermit Thrush.

Distribution.—*General:* Breeds from Cross Sound, Alaska, to southern British Columbia. Winters south into Mexico. *In Oregon:* The common wintering Hermit Thrush on coast that occasionally goes inland as far as Portland, Corvallis, Grants Pass, and Brownsboro.

We have 21 specimens of the Dwarf Hermit Thrush from Oregon, 17 of which are from the coastal slope in Tillamook, Lincoln, and Curry Counties. Our earliest fall specimen was taken September 22 and our latest spring bird March 26, both from Multnomah County. Of the four inland birds, two are from Portland (September 22, 1907, and March 26, 1908, Jewett), one from Corvallis (March 25, 1919, Gabrielson), and one from Brownsboro, Jackson County (November 8, 1926, Gabrielson). There are two in the Biological Survey collection, one from Yaquina (December 11, 1893, C. P. Streator) and the other from Empire (October 13, 1909, D. D. Streeter, Jr.).

On December 17 and 18, 1924, while they were together in Tillamook County, the authors witnessed a curious phenomenon. Usually the wintering Hermit Thrushes and Fox Sparrows stay close within the brush that, on this well-watered district, reaches the proportion of a jungle. In such a place, the dull brown of the birds makes them difficult to see if they happen to be at all shy. During the night of December 16–17 a heavy wet snow fell down to the very edge of the Pacific, matting the brush down into a soggy mass. Evidently the birds did not like it, for on the morning of the 17th and through the 18th the open glades, beaches, and pasture lands were alive with Hermit Thrushes and Fox Sparrows hopping about in the drift on the beach and among the cattle in the fields. As soon as the snow melted the birds returned to their usual haunts and again became shy, elusive shadows.

Because of the intermingling of *guttata* and *nanus* in the Willamette Valley, it is impossible to separate the early records according to present-day conception of the races of Hermit Thrush. Anthony (1886) reported Dwarf Hermit Thrushes common in Washington County. He also reported to Belding (1890), whose statement was copied by Woodcock (1902), that it was a common summer resident whose first nest was seen June 7, 1884. As the only thrush now breeding commonly in this district is the Russet-backed Thrush, this record undoubtedly applies to it. Woodcock's (1902) own records from Corvallis of a "rare migrant, late in both March and October," might well apply to this form in part. The same may be said of Shelton's (1917) records of Lane County, though we have found no evidence to support his statement that it breeds there. The only other published records are our own (Jewett and Gabrielson 1929) from the Portland area, consisting of the two Portland skins mentioned above.

It will be noticed that several writers stated that Hermit Thrushes bred in western Oregon, a statement that we have not yet been able to substantiate. Hermit Thrushes do breed up to the Sikiyous and along the higher parts of the Cascades, but no one has found them breeding in the coast mountains of Oregon nor have we been able to obtain any summer skins, although a large part of the area would seem to be ideal thrush territory.

Monterey Hermit Thrush:
Hylocichla guttata slevini Grinnell

Description.—"Above hair brown slightly browner on top of the head; upper tail-coverts and tail isabella color. Ground color of under parts and sides of head white, except a scarcely discernible tinge of cream buff across the breast; sides and flanks faintly washed with drab gray. Spots on breast sepia, small in size and few in number; a series extends on each side up to the ramus of the lower mandible forming two malar stripes which enclose an immaculate throat patch. Outer surface of closed wing isabella color." (Grinnell 1901.) "Similar to *H. g. guttata*, but paler and grayer, and decidedly smaller." (Ridgway 1907.) *Size:* Length (skins) 5.00–6.00, wing 3.07–3.43, tail 2.30–2.80, exposed culmen .47–.53. *Nest and eggs:* As in preceding forms.

Distribution.—*General:* Breeds from Siskiyous of southern Oregon south through coast mountains of California to southern Monterey County. *In Oregon:* Breeds in that part of summit main ranges of Siskiyous that lies in Josephine and probably Jackson County.

On July 17, 1933, the authors were encamped in the Siskiyous on the California-Oregon line, where Gabrielson collected a thrush that proved to be this form. We were certain that it was also in Oregon and resolved to be on the lookout for it on future visits to that territory. Later in the summer (August 18) Jewett collected two birds at Bolan Lake, a few miles north of the State line, that Grinnell identified as this subspecies. We heard other Monterey Hermit Thrushes singing during the July visit and believe the birds to be fairly common summer residents of that district.

Sierra Hermit Thrush:
Hylocichla guttata sequoiensis (Belding)

Description.—"Similar in coloration[1] to *H. g. sleveni* but decidedly larger and slightly darker or browner; similar to *H. g. guttata*, but larger, paler, and grayer; similar to *H. g. auduboni*, but decidedly smaller." (Ridgway 1907.) *Size:* Length (skins) 5.63–6.65, wing 3.39–3.82, tail 2.52–3.05, exposed culmen .47–.57. *Nest and eggs:* As in preceding subspecies.

Distribution.—*General:* Breeds from southern British Columbia south through Cascades and other ranges to southern California. Winters south into Mexico. *In Oregon:* Summer resident and breeding species along summit of Cascades, in Blue Mountains, except highest points of Wallowas, and in Warner Mountains.

All of our summer skins from the Cascades and Blue Mountains in Oregon, with the exception of the three mentioned under *H. g. auduboni*, are of the Sierra Hermit Thrush. These include late May birds from the Warner Mountains and from Bly Mountain in Klamath County that should be breeding birds. Our earliest specimen was taken April 12 and our latest in eastern Oregon on October 7. We have 14 summer skins, and there are six in the Biological Survey collection from this breeding area. The localities represented are Aneroid Lake, Canyon City, summit of the Blue Mountains above Mitchell, Huntington, Mill Creek, 20 miles west of Warm Springs, Lakeview, Barley Camp, Warner Mountains (migrant), Hay Creek, Jefferson County (migrant), Paulina Lake, Three Sisters, Reston, and Robinson Butte, eastern Jackson County. In addition to these summer records, there are notes in the Biological Survey records indicating that specimens sent to the Survey for determination from the following places had been identified as *sequoiensis* by Oberholser: Corvallis (April 27, 1901, and February 3, 1903), Portland (April 26, 1901, and March 28, 1908), Forest Grove (April 24, 1911), and Salem (February 24, 1912). These records would indicate occasional wintering individuals as well as a migration movement through western Oregon before the birds head into the mountains.

Bendire (1877) is undoubtedly entitled to the honor of finding the first nest at Camp Harney, June 28, 1875, which is the first record as well that

[1] "Both *H. g. sequoiensis* and *H. g. sleveni*, in addition to being paler and grayer on upper parts have the spots on chest, etc., lighter and duller in color." (Ridgway, 1907.)

can be definitely ascribed to the race. The nest was on the ground and contained three nearly fledged young and one addled egg, which was collected. Merrill (1888) collected birds at Fort Klamath that belong in this race. Shelton (1917) reported it common in the Cascades in the vicinity of the Three Sisters, and Gabrielson (1931) found it to be a fairly common summer resident of the higher part of the Cascades in Jackson County. Patterson (ms.) found a nest in Crater Lake Park, May 16, 1926.

Audubon's Hermit Thrush:
Hylocichla guttata auduboni (Baird)

Description.—"Similar to *guttata*, but larger, and upper parts lighter, grayer, with rufous of tail much lighter (fulvous). *Length:* 7.50–8.25, wing 3.65–4.35, tail 2.95–3.45, bill .53–.60." (Bailey) *Nest and eggs:* As in other subspecies.

Distribution.—*General:* Breeds from southeastern British Columbia and Montana south to Nevada, Arizona, and New Mexico. Winters southward. *In Oregon:* Summer resident and breeding bird in higher peaks in Wallowa Mountains and found in migration south through Blue Mountains.

Jewett (1916a) published an account of finding the nest of Audubon's Hermit Thrush at Bourne, Baker County, on August 3, 1915. It was 8 feet up in a fir sapling in a deep thicket and contained three incubated eggs. Gabrielson (1924a) recorded one found at Lick Creek Ranger Station, July 27, 1920. These two comprise the only published records for the species. In addition to these, we have specimens from Silvies Valley (September 9, 1919, Gabrielson), Ice Lake (June 27, 1934, Jewett), Lick Creek (June 30, 1934, Jewett), and Hart Mountain (September 17, 1934, Jewett). There are skins in the Biological Survey collection from Bourne (August 3, 1915, Jewett), Beech Creek (July 2 and 3, 1915, Jewett), Strawberry Mountains (July 13, 1915, Jewett), and Meacham (June 10, 1915, M. E. Peck). In addition to the published breeding record above, Jewett has notes as follows: A nest with four fresh eggs, June 19, 1927, on Aneroid Lake Trail, 6 feet up in a spruce tree, collected by Braly; one at Lick Creek, June 20, 1927, 5 feet up in a spruce tree and containing two eggs; and one on Little Eagle Creek, July 20, 1929, 6 feet up in a fir sapling and containing two eggs.

This race and the Sierra Hermit Thrush rank together as among our finest song birds. Not only are their songs of superior quality, but the setting of beautiful parks, clear lakes, and sparkling streams combine with the music to give it an emotional quality that could not prevail under more prosaic surroundings. We know of no more enchanting experience than to watch the sun set behind a jagged sky line of snow-clad peaks to the accompaniment of their ethereal songs. Surely then, if ever, one listens to the music of the stars.

Russet-backed Thrush: *Hylocichla ustulata ustulata* (Nuttall)

Description.—"Upper parts *olive brown, wings and tail often browner;* buffy eye ring distinct; sides of head tinged with tawny; chest pale buff, whitish in summer, marked with narrow triangular spots; under parts white, sides tinged with olive brown. *Length:* 6.90–7.60, wing 3.60–4.00, tail 2.80–3.30, bill .50–.60." (Bailey) *Nest:* In bushes or low in tree, compact mass of mosses and shreds of bark (Plate 81, *A*). *Eggs:* 4 or 5, pale greenish blue, spotted with rusty.

Distribution.—*General:* Breeds from Juneau, Alaska, to southern California. Winters from Mexico south. *In Oregon:* Common summer resident of western Oregon to and including summit forests of Cascades and Klamath Lake district.

One of the characteristic summer birds of the fir forests of the Willamette Valley foothills as well as those along the summit of the Cascades and the coast districts is the Russet-backed Thrush (Plate 81, *A*). Heard in those somber forests, its beautiful eerie song brings the spirit of the wilderness as few other sounds can. Heard either as the early morning light first begins to penetrate the gloomy shadows or in the gathering twilight of a golden orange sunset, it carries a spiritual quality found only among these soft-colored songsters. The bird itself is only a brown shadow among a hundred other shadows, though if one enters a salmonberry thicket and remains quiet long enough to be forgotten, some of the shadows will begin to move independently and reveal the soft-brown bird with breast beautifully marked with irregular spots of brown.

The type specimen came from the "forests of the Columbia River," now considered by the American Ornithologists' Union to mean Fort Vancouver, Washington, although Nuttall (1840) stated the type was taken June 10, 1835, at Fort William. Cooper (Cooper and Suckley 1860) wrote that the bird arrived on the Columbia River May 1, 1854, and that eggs were found June 15 to July 13, 1854. Johnson (1880) reported it for the Willamette Valley. Merrill (1888) found a few at Fort Klamath, including a nest with four eggs, June 8, 1887. Woodcock (1902) included eight Willamette Valley and coast stations, including nesting dates at Portland, June 29, 1894, and June 20 and 21, 1895, furnished by H. T. Bohlman. Since these publications, there have been numerous references to the species in western Oregon, where it arrives in April (earliest date, April 24, Multnomah County) and remains until September (latest date, September 22, Clatsop County). Our own records cover practically every county in that part of the State, the farthest-east specimen being one from Fish Lake on the southeast base of Mount McLoughlin, Jackson County, June 12, 1921 (Gabrielson Collection). This lake is only a few miles from Upper Klamath Lake and Fort Klamath where Merrill made his breeding record.

Numerous nesting records in our notes and the files of the Biological Survey show nests with fresh eggs to be most frequent about mid-June, the extreme dates being May 30 and July 15.

Plate 81, *A*. Russet-backed Thrush at nest with young. (Photo by Wm. L. Finley, Jr.)

Plate 81, *B*. Nest and eggs of American Pipit. (Photo by S. G. Jewett.)

Olive-backed Thrush:
Hylocichla ustulata swainsoni (Tschudi)

Description.—"*Upper parts uniform olive* or grayish olive; buffy eye ring conspicuous; *sides of head buffy*, marked with darker; chest bright buff, marked with wide blackish streaks; under parts white, sides olive brown. *Length:* 6.35–7.55, wing 3.80–4.10, tail 2.80–3.10, bill .50–.55." (Bailey) *Nest and eggs:* Similar to those of Russet-backed Thrush.

Distribution.—*General:* Breeds from northern Alaska, Mackenzie, Manitoba, Quebec, and Newfoundland south to Kenai Peninsula, eastern Oregon, northern California, Nevada, Utah, Colorado, Michigan, West Virginia, and Pennsylvania. Winters in Central and South America. *In Oregon:* Fairly common summer resident of eastern Oregon, including Blue Mountains, Steens, and higher peaks in Malheur County.

Jewett (1909c) published the first record of the Olive-backed Thrush from notes and specimens taken on Eagle Creek, Baker County, in 1906. He found eight nests between June 23 and July 7 in that locality. Of these, one contained three eggs; six, four eggs; and one, five eggs. Peck (1911a) published the only other record for the State, from Willow Creek in northern Malheur County. Our records extend from May 13 to September 11 (both Baker County).

There are several Oregon specimens in the Biological Survey collection. Preble, on his trip in 1915, took specimens at Disaster Peak on June 15, and in Jordan Valley on June 29 and July 1. There is a skin from Cornucopia, collected by Jewett, September 2, 1915. Becker took the species in Kiger Gorge in the Steens Mountains during his stay from August 10 to September 4, 1916. There are skins in the Jewett collection from Billy Meadows (June 13, 1925), West Fork of the Wallowa River (July 21, 1925), Lick Creek Ranger Station (July 17, 1926), and Lostine River (July 18, 1926), all in Wallowa County. Gabrielson has one skin taken June 8, 1934, from just across the State line between Wallowa County and Washington. These specimens establish a definite breeding range that at present includes Wallowa, Baker, Malheur, and Harney Counties. We would expect the species to be found eventually in Grant, Union, Umatilla, and probably Lake Counties. In connection with the latter county, a note in the Biological Survey files tells of a bird sent to the Biological Survey and identified by A. K. Fisher as this species. It came from the Warner Mountains, August 4, 1896, but we have not been able to trace it farther.

Willow Thrush:
Hylocichla fuscescens salicicola Ridgway

Description.—"Upper parts *uniform olive brown, chest pale buffy*, marked with triangular brown spots; median under parts white, sides gray. *Length:* 6.90–7.90, wing 3.80–4.25, tail 2.95–3.40, bill .55–.60." (Bailey) *Nest:* On or near the ground, made largely or entirely of leaves. *Eggs:* Usually greenish blue, occasionally with a few faint brown spots.

DISTRIBUTION.—*General:* Breeds from southern British Columbia, central Alberta, central Saskatchewan, southern Manitoba and northern Wisconsin south to central Oregon, Nevada, Utah, northern New Mexico, and central Iowa. Winters in South America. *In Oregon:* Rather uncommon summer resident of Blue Mountain area, of which we have too few records to accurately determine range or season.

THE ONLY published reference to the Willow Thrush as an Oregon species is Jewett's (1913b) note of a specimen taken June 24, 1908, by Wm. L. Finley near Burns. There is a skin in the Biological Survey collection taken by Jewett at Howard, June 10, 1915, and two in his own collection, one obtained by Ralph Hoffman at Enterprise, July 12, 1925, and one that he himself took on Hart Mountain, May 26, 1927. Preble noted the species at Elgin while he was there from May 21 to 30, 1896, and at Fossil, Wheeler County, in June 1896; and he and Bailey found it at Prineville, June 23 to 26, the same year. Preble also found the bird at Disaster Peak, Malheur County, on June 10, 1915. These are all the available notes from Oregon to date, and this scarcity of records emphasizes the need for more systematic collecting in the State.

Western Bluebird:
Sialia mexicana occidentalis Townsend

DESCRIPTION.—"*Adult male:* Upper parts dark purplish blue and chestnut; *throat purplish blue;* breast dark rufous; rest of under parts mixed brown, dull purplish and gray. *Adult female:* head, neck and upper parts gray, washed with brown on back; rump and tail bright blue; outside tail feathers edged with white. *Young:* Like young of *sialis*, but slenderer. [Plate 82, *A*.] *Male:* length 6.50–7.12, wing 3.95–4.45, tail 2.62–3.05, bill .45–.50. *Female:* wing about 4, tail 2.50." (Bailey) *Nest:* In woodpecker holes or natural cavities, or in bird houses. *Eggs:* 3 to 6, pale blue.

DISTRIBUTION.—*General:* Breeds from southern British Columbia, northern Idaho, and western Montana south to southern California. Winters through much of its range. *In Oregon:* Permanent resident and breeder west of Cascades. Summer resident east of that range.

THE WESTERN BLUEBIRD (Plate 82) is a permanent resident and breeder in western Oregon, where it vies with the robin for first rank as a dooryard bird. Although not so abundant in the State east of the Cascades, it is a summer resident and common species there, arriving in March and remaining until October (earliest date, February 12; latest, November 17, both Klamath County). A nest box will be more certain to attract this species than any other, and once established, the birds are likely to remain and produce at least two broods. Their gentle nature, clear, musical calls, and bright colors make them favorites with all, and any other bird that presumes to intrude upon a pair of bluebirds using a nest box erected for their benefit will doubtless draw down the wrath of the person who

Plate 82, *A*. Western Bluebird and young at feeding station. (Photo by Mrs. L. J. Merrill.)

Plate 82, *B*. Western Bluebird at nest box. (Photo by Wm. L. Finley, Jr.)

placed the box. Two or more broods are raised each season, and fresh-egg dates extend from May 6 to June 27, both extremes from Portland.

The species was described by Townsend (1839) from specimens collected near Fort Vancouver, some of which may well have come from Oregon; but the first definite State record was made from east of the Cascades nearly 20 years later when Newberry (1857) reported the species from the Deschutes Basin. Suckley (Cooper and Suckley 1860) listed it from The Dalles. Since then the Oregon literature on this species has been voluminous, and the numerous published records, together with our own notes, cover every county.

Mountain Bluebird:
Sialia currucoides (Bechstein)

Description.—"*Adult male:* Upper parts light purplish blue or greenish blue; under parts pale greenish blue. In winter, color dulled by dull brownish tips to feathers above and below. *Adult female:* upper parts brownish gray, wings and tail bright blue; under parts fawn color, with blue showing through. *Young:* brownish or grayish, streaked with white; wings and tail blue. *Male:* Length 6.50–7.90, wing 4.60–4.80, tail 3.00–3.15. *Female:* Length 7.00–7.20, wing about 4.25, tail 2.75–2.90." (Bailey) *Nest:* In old woodpecker holes or natural cavities. *Eggs:* 5 to 7, pale greenish blue.

Distribution.—*General:* Breeds from Yukon, British Columbia, central Alberta, Saskatchewan, and Manitoba south into Mexico and from Cascades and Sierra Nevadas to western Dakotas and Nebraska. Winters south into Mexico. *In Oregon:* Permanent resident and breeding species from summit of Cascades through eastern Oregon.

The Mountain Bluebird, most brilliant blue of any native species, winters in small numbers throughout the sagebrush country of eastern Oregon but becomes much more abundant in early March when the southern birds arrive. Its numbers decrease again in November to the comparatively few wintering individuals. We have recorded it in every county east of the Cascades as well as in those that reach the summit from the west. These birds furnish a brilliant and irreplaceable color note in the gray sage landscape; particularly when in migration their brilliant blues flash in the desert sun in startling contrast to the prevailing dull colors of most of the other birds. They have learned to use the fences and telephone wires to good purpose, both as a resting place and as a vantage point from which to watch for a luckless insect that may crawl into view.

Bendire (Brewer 1875, Bendire 1877), who found the species nesting in Oregon, first in 1875 and again in 1876, stated that it commenced to nest about May 20 and probably raised two broods. Most ornithologists who have worked eastern Oregon since his time have had something to say about this brilliant songster. Nesting dates vary from April 20 to June 21, and the habits and behavior of this bluebird are much the same as those of the Western Blackbird except that it is not so fond of artificial nest boxes. Jewett's notes mention an old flicker hole, a box on a house, a tin mail box, and a pine stump as nesting sites, the number of eggs or young varying from two to five, and Gabrielson, in addition to two nests in old woodpecker holes, mentioned a nest containing three young in a natural cavity in a fence post.

Townsend's Solitaire:
Myadestes townsendi (Audubon)

Description.—"Bill short, flattened, widened at base, deeply cleft; legs weak; tail feathers tapering. *Adults:* brownish gray, paler beneath; wings with two whitish wing bars, bases of primaries and secondaries buffy or yellowish brown; tail feathers with outer web and tip of inner web grayish white. *Young:* wings and tail as in adult; rest of plumage, including wing coverts, conspicuously spotted with buff. *Length:* 7.80–9.50, wing 4.35–4.85, tail 4.15–4.70." (Bailey) *Nest:* On the ground, a bulky mass of sticks and pine needles, usually placed near or on logs or stumps, or among rocks. *Eggs:* 3 to 6, white, spotted with reddish brown.

Distribution.—*General:* Breeds from central Alaska, southwestern Mackenzie, and western Alberta south in mountains to California, Arizona, and New Mexico. Winters through much of its breeding ground. *In Oregon:* Permanent resident that breeds in Cascades and Blue Mountains and probably in Warner Mountains and spreads in winter to lower valleys in eastern Oregon. Straggles more or less regularly to western Oregon after breeding season.

By one of those curious happenings that occasionally occur in the bird world, the type locality of Townsend's Solitaire, this bird of the high mountains and juniper-clad slopes of eastern Oregon, is at Fort George, or Astoria. The type specimen collected by Townsend and described by him in 1839 was one of those stragglers to western Oregon that occasionally reach the coast. Newberry (1857) found it to be an abundant species in the Deschutes River Basin. Bendire was greatly intrigued by this first-rank songster, which he found there in numbers, and on December 5, 1874, wrote to Brewer (1875) as follows:

In their habits they remind me very much of *Phainopepla nitens*. Like that species, they prefer to perch on dry limbs, and as high as they can get on the juniper trees, which they seem to frequent exclusively. At this season of the year they seem to feed on juniper berries entirely. I can bear witness to the excellence of their song. I find it very varied, soft and flutelike at times, strong and powerful at others, and it reminds me, in many respects, of that of the European sky-lark. I most certainly consider it fully equal, if not superior, to the song of our mocking-bird. Its usual call note is peculiar, and hard to describe. I took it down at the time of hearing it, and do not give it from memory. It comes as near as possible to the occasional sound produced by an axle of a wagon just about commencing to need greasing—like *hit-it* and sometimes like *wa-ip*, with quite an interval between each syllable. Generally the bird is seen singly, rarely in flocks. It prefers isolated patches of juniper to the dense timber, and so I have only noticed it in junipers, or on rocks on the edges of the bluffs.

Since that time, numerous writers have referred to these birds, but none has written a better account of their behavior in winter, when these summer residents of the higher mountains descend to the lowlands. They are particularly fond of the juniper forests of central Oregon, where they will be found competing with the great companies of robins for the juniper berries. The Wallowa Valley and Powder River are two other favorite winter haunts of this soft-colored songster.

The species has appeared frequently in western Oregon, for which we find other published records in addition to the type specimen from Astoria. Woodcock (1902) listed the following: Yaquina Bay, September 1900, Bretherton; Portland, January 1901, Anthony; and Corvallis, "rare spring visitor." Jewett (1922c) gave a record for the coast of Tillamook County, February 28, 1922, and in our *Birds of the Portland Area, Oregon* (Jewett and Gabrielson 1929) listed specimens in Multnomah County, September 22, 1907, April 27, 1908, and April 25, 1916. The Biological Survey files contain the following manuscript notes: Wilson River, Tillamook County (June 27, 28, 1897, A. K. Fisher), Scottsburg (October 8, 1909, D. D. Streeter), Corvallis (March 4, 1911, V. Bailey), Mercer (February 9, 1922, Overton Dowell, Jr.), and Portland (October 24, 1928, Mrs. Twining). The species is much more abundant in Jackson County. It is found regularly in the eastern part of that county, and we have numerous records for the valley and foothills.

A. W. Anthony (1903b) reported it as nesting on Eagle Creek in Baker County, and in 1906 Jewett found four nests on the same creek. One, on May 29, contained four eggs, and of three found on May 31 two contained four fresh eggs each and one, four newly hatched young. In 1907, in the same locality, Jewett again found a nest with four eggs, May 26, and on May 29 a deserted nest with one egg. Shelton (1917) reported finding a nest containing young on the headwaters of the McKenzie, June 11, 1914, and Vernon Bailey (ms.) reported a nest with four fresh eggs near Bourne, Baker County, July 29, 1915. On July 27, 1926, Gabrielson collected spotted young barely able to fly at Mosquito Ranger Station at the west base of Mount McLoughlin. Patterson (ms.) reported several nests between May 12 and 28 at Pinehurst and on the Klamath Indian Reservation.

Kinglets: *Family Sylviidae*

Western Golden-crowned Kinglet: *Regulus satrapa olivaceus* Baird

Description.—"*Adult male: Crown encircled anteriorly with black, bordered inside by yellow, with a central orange patch;* rest of upper parts grayish olive, more olive toward rump; wings with two whitish bands; under parts dingy whitish. *Adult female:*

similar, but crown patch wholly yellow. *Young:* crown patch wanting, but white line over eye; breast washed with fawn color. *Length:* 3.15–4.55, wing 2.10–2.25, tail 1.60–2.00, exposed culmen .25–.30." (Bailey) *Nest:* A mass of moss, lined with hair and feathers. *Eggs:* 5 to 10, white or buffy, faintly speckled with deeper buff, largely around large end.

DISTRIBUTION.—*General:* Breeds from Kenai Peninsula, Alaska, south to southern California and New Mexico. Winters from British Columbia south. *In Oregon:* Common permanent resident in coniferous covered mountains. Winters everywhere in lowlands.

THE WESTERN GOLDEN-CROWNED KINGLET is one of the most widely distributed timber-loving birds in the State. The first Oregon record is for birds seen at Camp Harney, November 7, 1875, by Bendire (1877). Johnson (1880) listed it as a common winter resident of the Willamette Valley, and since that time there have been numerous references to the species in the literature. We have found it in all parts of the State. It may be looked for almost anywhere in western Oregon throughout the year, but it is to be expected only in the mountains in eastern Oregon in summer. During that season, the spruce and fir thickets of all the ranges have their quota of these tiny mites. In winter the species is apt to appear in willow- and cottonwood-filled stream bottoms anywhere in the State.

There are comparatively few breeding records. Dr. A. K. Fisher (ms.) took a young bird at Tillamook Bay, June 30, 1897, and reported seeing a family of eight to ten in the same locality, July 4. V. Bailey (ms.) caught one of a family of young kinglets in his hands at Garibaldi, June 10, 1914, and H. M. Laing watched a pair building a nest at Portland, April 2, 1919. Jewett found a nest containing one fresh egg at Netarts, May 17, 1913, and saw a pair feeding young in Sellwood, June 4, 1909. Braly took a set of seven eggs at Fort Klamath, May 23, 1930. Shelton (1917) reported a breeding record near Eugene, but gave no details, and wrote of a pair noted feeding young at the mouth of the Siuslaw River.

Western Ruby-crowned Kinglet:
Corthylio calendula cineraceus (Grinnell)

DESCRIPTION.—"*Adult male: crown patch bright red;* upper parts grayish, brightening to greenish on rump, and with greenish yellow edges to feathers; wings with two narrow whitish bands; under parts dingy whitish. *Adult female and young:* similar, but without crown patch." (Bailey) *Size:* Length (skins) 3.66–4.33, wing 2.24–2.40, tail 1.63–1.96, bill .30–.37. *Nest:* A partially hanging mass of barks, feathers, and moss, lined with hair and feathers and usually attached to the end of a coniferous branch. *Eggs:* 5 to 9, white or buff, faintly spotted around the large end with light brown.

DISTRIBUTION.—*General:* Breeds from Cascades and Blue Mountains of Oregon south to southern California. Winters in California. *In Oregon:* Breeds in Cascades and Blue Mountains. Winters south of borders.

THE FIRST SPECIMENS of Western Ruby-crowned Kinglets ever reported for the State were taken at Fort Dalles, May 4 to 6, 1856, and of course

Bendire, Merrill, and Johnson, among the other early workers in this field, reported the species from the districts in which they worked. As it is impossible to distinguish the two races of kinglets in the field, we find it difficult to properly segregate our winter sight records and are therefore being guided entirely by specimens in discussing ranges. Our summer birds are all of this race, *C. c. cineraceus*, but the winter specimens from eastern as well as western Oregon prove to be *C. c. grinnelli*. We have birds from Corvallis (April 22, 1919, Gabrielson) and Portland (April 30, 1929, Jewett) that are of this race, as well as birds from Klamath, Deschutes, Wallowa, and Umatilla Counties (May, June, and July). On June 12, 1915, on Lookout Mountain, eastern Crook County, Jewett watched a pair of Western Ruby-crowned Kinglets building a nest of moss. On June 12, 1925, at Billy Meadows, Wallowa County, he saw a Rocky Mountain Jay take the eggs from a Western Ruby-crowned Kinglet nest 40 feet up in a Douglas fir, one of the few times, if not the only occasion, on which anyone has witnessed this particular act of vandalism. Braly has a nest and two eggs taken from a small fir along the Aneroid Trail, Wallowa County, June 19, 1927.

Sitka Kinglet:
Corthylio calendula grinnelli (Palmer)

Description.—"*Adult male:* similar to *calendula* [*cineraceus*], but smaller and darker; upper parts sooty olive, darkening to blackish along sides of vermilion crown patch; wing with dark parts nearly black; throat and breast dusky gray; belly whitish, tinged with yellowish. *Young male:* rich brownish olive, much darker than corresponding *calendula* [*cineraceus*], and under parts brighter. *Wing:* 2.17, tail 1.70, bill .16." (Bailey) *Nest and eggs:* Probably similar to *C. c. cineraceus*.

Distribution.—*General:* Breeds along southern Alaska coast and in British Columbia. Winters south into California. *In Oregon:* Regular and common winter visitor that arrives in October and remains until April. Appears rarely in winter in eastern Oregon.

It is a curious fact that every wintering Ruby-crowned Kinglet that either of us has taken is of this race, the Sitka Kinglet. In the vicinity of Portland it is a very common bird in October and November (earliest date, September 18, Lake County) and again in March and April (latest date, May 2, Tillamook County). It remains common all winter along the coast and in the foothills of the Rogue River Valley. We have numerous specimens from various points in western Oregon.

East of the mountain, wintering birds are rare, and because the three actual specimens we have are all *grinnelli* we are making no effort to allocate our few winter notes to either race. More winter collecting of these birds in eastern Oregon will be necessary to determine definitely the status of the two races. These specimens are all in Jewett's collection and were taken at Ontario (January 4, 1927), Vale (November 17, 1930), and Hart Mountain (September 18, 1934).

Pipits: *Family Motacillidae*

American Pipit:
Anthus spinoletta rubescens (Tunstall)

Description.—"Hind claw about equal to toe. *Adults in summer:* upper parts grayish brown, indistinctly streaked; wing blackish brown, with two buffy wing bars and light edgings; tail blackish, inner web of *outside feather largely white*, second feather tipped with white; superciliary stripe and under parts light buffy, chin lighter, chest streaked with dusky. *Adults in winter:* browner above, lighter below, streaks on breast usually broader. *Young:* similar, but washed with brown, and more distinctly streaked. *Length:* 6-7, wing 3.20-3.50, tail 2.65-2.85." (Bailey) *Nest:* On ground, bulky, compact, made of moss and grass, lined with hair and feathers. *Eggs:* 4 to 6, nearly uniform brown from heavy spotting (Plate 81, *B*).

Distribution.—*General:* Breeds in Arctic Zone, south in mountains to Oregon, Colorado, and New Mexico. Winters from Oregon and Ohio Valley south to Central America. *In Oregon:* Common migrant throughout State. Regular winter resident of western Oregon and lower valleys of eastern Oregon. Breeds regularly on higher peaks of Wallowa Mountains and perhaps rarely in Cascades and Steens Mountains.

Bendire (1877) found the American Pipit to be an abundant migrant at Malheur Lake, and since his time many others have noted it from different parts of Oregon. During migration it is widely distributed and can be looked for in every part of the State. At times during such movements it is one of the most abundant birds along the beaches and tidelands of the coast, in the pasture lands of the Willamette Valley, and in the great valleys of eastern Oregon. In the Klamath Basin and the Harney Valley, particularly, it sometimes appears in almost incredible numbers, and the same thing is true to a lesser extent in other localities. It arrives from the north in September (earliest date, September 10, Klamath County), and in late October the numbers commence to diminish, but the species winters regularly along the Columbia River between Portland and Astoria and in the Rogue, Umpqua, and Willamette Valleys. It is a common winter resident of the tidelands along the coast, also, from Clatsop County to Curry County and winters more or less commonly along the Malheur and Snake Rivers in eastern Oregon. It remains until April (latest date, April 30, Deschutes County).

V. Bailey and Young (ms. notes, Biological Survey) reported it common between August 24 and September 17, 1897, in the Wallowa Mountains and collected specimens during that time. Bailey found it, July 31, 1916, on the top of Steens Mountains and suggested that it probably bred. We have no other records for the Steens Mountains but have found it regularly during summer in the Wallowas. On July 23, 1923, Jewett collected an adult female at Aneroid Lake, and between July 20 and 22, 1924, he took numerous skins of adults and fledgling young and one nest in the same locality. The nest, containing four eggs, was found near the margin of a small lake at an altitude of about 8,000 feet. It was built of dry grass in a slight depression protected by rocks on two sides and sheltered by one above (Plate 81, *B*). The female was very tame and greatly excited at the intrusion. Gabrielson, who was in another part of the range at the same time, collected an adult and newly fledged young on July 25 and 26, 1924, near Swamp Lake and on the head of Last Chance Creek, both points toward the western extremity of the higher ridges. Since that time we have found this pipit to be a regular summer resident throughout the range.

We have no breeding records for the Cascades, although Jewett saw these birds on Mount Jefferson on September 6 and 7, 1925, and on Broken Top on August 11, 1933. We have at times spent considerable time on Mount Hood and in the Three Sisters country without detecting this species as a summer resident.

Waxwings: *Family Bombycillidae*

Bohemian Waxwing: *Bombycilla garrula pallidiceps* Reichenow

Description.—"*Adults:* Whole body, including high crest, soft fawn color, fading to grayish on rump and flanks, and washed with yellowish on middle of belly; forehead, cheeks, and under tail coverts deep brown; chin, lores, and eye streak extending back under crest, velvety black; wings and tail blackish, wing coverts extensively tipped with whitish or yellow, the tertials sometimes with red wax-like appendages; tail with a terminal band of yellow. *Young:* duller; under parts streaked. *Length:* 7.40–8.75, wing 4.40–4.60, tail 2.75–2.90." (Bailey) *Nest:* A bulky mass of twigs, rootlets, leaves, grass, and mosses, lined with finer materials and feathers and placed in a tree 5 to 20 feet up. *Eggs:* 3 to 5, bluish gray, spotted with brown and black.

Distribution.—*General:* Breeds from western Alaska, northern Mackenzie, and northeastern Manitoba south to southern British Columbia and Alberta. Winters south irregularly over northern United States and occasionally south, even to California and Arizona. *In Oregon:* Irregular but at times abundant winter visitor.

The Bohemian Waxwing is an irregular winter visitor over most of the State but appears most regularly in the mountain valleys about the base of the Blue Mountains. We have found it in at least small numbers in the Wallowa Valley in many different years, and nearly every winter we see a few scattered small flocks, usually in the Blue Mountain districts. In the winter of 1919–20 there occurred a big invasion of these birds, and they were present in numbers in Portland, Corvallis, and other points in western Oregon as well as over most of eastern Oregon, reaching at least as far south as Adel, Lake County, where Gabrielson collected a bird out of a flock of approximately three hundred on April 3, 1920. Again in the winter of 1931–32 the birds appeared in numbers, going far south into California, according to published reports. We find we have specimens and notes from the following counties: Baker, Benton, Deschutes, Grant, Klamath, Lake, Malheur, Multnomah, Union, Wallowa, and Wasco. Our own records have been published from Baker (Jewett 1909c), Wallowa (Gabrielson 1924a), and Multnomah (Jewett and Gabrielson 1929) Counties. The species arrives in November (earliest date, November 11, Klamath County) and remains until March (latest date, April 19, Multnomah County).

Bendire (1877), who first recorded the species from Oregon, found it as a winter visitor to Camp Harney; Johnson (1880) recorded a pair from Hillsboro in January 1876; Woodcock (1902), on various authorities, listed it from Camp Harney between November 1875 and March 1876, from Haines, January 10, 1897, from Salem as "a rare winter migrant," and from Forest Grove in January 1876; and Raker (1918) saw waxwings in Portland in February 1917.

The Bohemian Waxwings are among the most beautiful of all Oregon birds. Their plumage has a silky texture that is lacking in many birds, and the soft pastel shades of gray and brown merging imperceptibly into one another are beautifully contrasted with the brilliant yellow tips to the tail feathers and the waxen ruby drops on the secondary wing feathers. The birds fly in compact flocks, usually in silence or with faint notes that do not attract attention. When in Portland they showed a decided preference for the berries of such cultivated shrubs as *Pyracantha* and *Cotoneaster*. As they sit on these dooryard shrubs, their conspicuous crests and sveldt appearance cause wonderment among the householders as to the native home of these strange outlanders. No bird is more stylish and distinctive in appearance, and it is indeed a red-letter day when a flock comes within the observation of a bird student.

Cedar Waxwing:
Bombycilla cedrorum Vieillot

DESCRIPTION.—"*Adults:* Streak through eye velvety black; crest, head, and under parts fawn color, fading to olive yellow on flanks; upper parts olive gray becoming blackish on wing quills and tail; tail tipped with yellow and both wing and tail sometimes tipped with red wax-like appendages. *Young:* similar, but duller, and under parts strongly, upper parts lightly, streaked. *Length:* 6.50–7.50, wing 3.60–3.90, tail 2.30–2.60." (Bailey) *Nest:* A bulky structure, built of twigs, weed stems, grasses, and vegetable fibers, lined with leaves and rootlets, and placed in bushes or small trees. *Eggs:* 3 to 5, bluish gray, spotted with brown or black.

DISTRIBUTION.—*General:* Breeds from central British Columbia, central Alberta, central Manitoba, Ontario, Quebec, and Cape Breton Island south to northern California, New Mexico, Kansas, northern Arkansas, and North Carolina. Winters south to Central America. *In Oregon:* Permanent resident and breeding species throughout State. Frequents stream bottoms and open woodlands.

Unlike its aristocratic northern cousin that appears in Oregon as a winter visitor, this smaller and paler species, the Cedar Waxwing, is a permanent resident. True, it is more common in summer, but a number remain throughout the year, so that the sight of them against a snowy background is no novelty. Although it remains permanently with us, it is one of the last birds to nest. Our breeding records show nests with fresh eggs from June 1 to 20, most of them between the 15th and 20th, and nests containing unfledged young have been noted as late as July 21 in Wallowa County by Gabrielson. Jewett examined six nests in Multnomah County on June 6, 10, 16, 17 (2 nests), and 20, and all contained fresh eggs. These dates cover the extreme range of eggs noted by us. Jewett found one other nest, in Lake County, June 20, with comparatively fresh eggs. Braly has taken several sets between June 1 and 20.

There have been numerous references to the Cedar Waxwing in Oregon literature, Merrill (1888) first finding it at Fort Klamath. Since that time, published literature, field notes of the Biological Survey, and our own notes have listed it from practically every section of the State except the highest parts of the mountains.

This is the "cherry bird" that occasionally causes loss of ripening cherries. Such loss is always local and usually insignificant, although one would not suspect this to be the case after listening to some of the heart-rending complaints put forth by indignant owners of cherry trees. Sometimes a considerable flock will appear and strip a large percentage of the fruit from a tree, but this does not happen often enough to justify any persecution of these soft-plumaged dandies.

Shrikes: *Family Laniidae*

Northwestern Shrike: *Lanius borealis invictus* Grinnell

Description.—"*Adults in summer:* Wide streak on side of head, and wings and tail black, wings and tail extensively marked with white; ***under parts white, barred or undulated with grayish;*** upper parts pale ash gray becoming whitish on forehead, superciliary, and rump; ***lores black and grayish,*** a whitish spot on lower eyelid. *Adults in winter:* similar, but basal half of lower mandible light brownish horn color, grayish in life, and lores chiefly light grayish or whitish. *Young:* largely washed with brownish." (Bailey) *Size:* Length (skins) 8.00–10.25, wing 4.30–4.70, tail 4.23–4.90, bill .71–.79. *Nest:* In bushes or thorny trees, bulky, made of twigs, stems, and grass, lined with feathers, moss, etc. *Eggs:* 4 to 6, pale bluish green, spotted with brown and purple.

Distribution.—*General:* Breeds from northwestern Alaska and Mackenzie south to northern British Columbia, Alberta, and Saskatchewan. Winters south to northern

California, Arizona, New Mexico, and Texas. *In Oregon:* Regular winter visitor to every county east of east base of Cascades. Irregular and rare west of that range.

The Northwestern Shrike is most at home along the willow-bordered streams of eastern Oregon, where it sits on the topmost twig of some low tree or perches motionless on a convenient telephone wire, its keen eyes scanning the landscape for a luckless mouse or a venturesome small bird that may stray too far from a safe shelter. Once in Antelope Canyon, in southern Wasco County, we watched one of these shrikes pursue a Ruby-crowned Kinglet for some time. The smaller bird was winging its way from one juniper tree to a smaller, thicker one, when the shrike, appearing from nowhere, swung into sight behind the intended victim. The kinglet, putting on a frantic burst of speed, literally dove into the thick juniper with the shrike so close behind that it all but crashed into the tree. The terror-stricken kinglet hopped quickly to the other side of the bush. Like a flash the shrike was around the tree to again strike viciously. Several times the butcher bird swung around the tree to meet the frantic moves of the smaller bird, which was wise enough to stay in the thickest part of the top of the tree, until finally it gave up in disgust and flew away to seek a less fortunate victim.

Bendire (1877) published the first record for the State, from Camp Harney, January 5, 1876, and Merrill (1888) found it at Fort Klamath in the fall and winter. Prill (1895a) found it at Sweet Home, Linn County, in winter. Woodcock (1902), in addition to his own statement that it was a rare winter visitant to Corvallis, listed a specimen taken at Ross Island, January 3, 1898, by Herman T. Bohlman and gave Warner's comment that it was a "winter resident found only in very stormy weather" at Salem. Shelton (1917) considered it an irregular winter resident of western Oregon, and Walker (1924) recorded a specimen from Blaine, October 31, 1919. Gabrielson (1924a) recorded it from Wallowa County, and we listed one skin and several sight records from Portland in our *Birds of the Portland Area* (Jewett and Gabrielson 1929). We have skins also from the following points in western Oregon: Corvallis (December 23, 1913, Jewett Coll. No. 1289), Salem (November 25, 1928, Jewett Coll. No. 5596), and Forest Grove (December 20, 1932, Gabrielson Coll. No. 1953). We have many specimens and sight records from widely scattered points throughout eastern Oregon, where in some seasons it is one of the common winter birds. It arrives in October (earliest date, September 9, Crook County) and remains until March (latest date, April 9, Wallowa County).

California Shrike:
Lanius ludovicianus gambeli Ridgway

Description.—*Adults: Bill, lores and nasal tufts wholly black*, upper parts slate gray tinged with brownish, upper tail coverts sometimes abruptly whitish as in *excubi-*

torides; under parts dull white or grayish, darker on sides, breast usually distinctly vermiculated and sometimes tinged with pale brown. *Young:* like adults but base of lower mandible light colored, general colors less strongly contrasted, washed with brown and narrowly barred, the wing coverts tipped with buffy. (Adapted from Bailey.) *Size:* Length 8–10, wing 3.70–4.00, tail 3.75–4.50, bill from nostril .43–.48, depth of base .30–.35. *Nest:* In trees, hedges, or cactus, a bulky structure of sticks, leaves, wool, and feathers. *Eggs:* 4 to 6, grayish to yellowish white, spotted with brown and lilac.

Distribution.—*General:* Breeds from interior valleys of British Columbia south to Lower California and east to Montana and Utah. Winters in California and Mexico. *In Oregon:* Common summer resident and breeding species east of Cascades. Rare or accidental west of that range.

The California Shrike (Plate 83, *A*) arrives in Oregon from the south in numbers about the time its larger northern cousin begins to leave its winter quarters, so that there is a gradual replacement of one species by another, a process that is reversed in the fall. Bendire (Brewer 1875) listed it from Camp Harney and published breeding data for the same locality (Bendire 1877). Merrill (1888) recorded it from Fort Klamath. Woodcock (1902), on the basis of A. W. Anthony's observations, stated that it was found at Sparta. He regarded it as an uncommon winter visitor to Corvallis. Peck (1911a), Walker (1917b), Willett (1919), and Prill (1924) recorded it from various localities in eastern Oregon.

Our own voluminous notes and those of other members of the Biological Survey who have worked in Oregon present a better picture of its status than these rather fragmentary published records. We find it to be a regularly distributed and conspicuous member of the avifauna throughout the summer months over all of the eastern section of the State, arriving in February or early March (earliest date, February 9, Lake County) and remaining until late October (latest date, November 14, Harney County). There are shrikes on the telephone and fence wires throughout the year, but there is little danger of confusion of records save for a short time in spring and again in the fall. This is the summer bird that keeps vigil along the highway with the western kingbirds through the long, hot summer days. We have only one record for western Oregon, a bird collected by Jewett at Medford, March 19, 1934.

The nests are bulky affairs of sticks, usually placed in junipers or small deciduous trees, that are often easily located by the grasshoppers, beetles, or small mammals or birds found impaled on thorns or on the barbs in wire fences in the vicinity of the nest. The birds commence to lay in early April along the Columbia and persist till well toward the first of June at some of the higher elevations. Available egg dates extend from April 8 to May 20. Fresh eggs are undoubtedly present at a later date, as Jewett found a freshly built nest as late as May 21, 1917, near Plush.

Plate 83, *A*. California Shrike. (Photo by Wm. L. and Irene Finley.)

Plate 83, *B*. Lutescent Warbler feeding young. (Photo by Wm. L. Finley and H. T. Bohlman.)

Starlings: *Family Sturnidae*

Starling:
Sturnus vulgaris vulgaris Linnaeus

Description.—"Primaries ten, but first quill minute; bill straight, nasal feathers erect or inclined backward; nostrils with conspicuous nasal scale. *Adults in summer:* glossy, greenish or purplish black, speckled with buffy brown and whitish; wing and tail feathers largely edged with brownish buff; bill yellow. *Adults in winter:* upper parts light brown; under parts whitish, spotting often so conspicuous as to obscure the underlying green and purple. *Length:* 7.50–8.50, wing 5.00–5.10, tail 2.60–2.90, bill .95–1.00." (Bailey) *Nest:* A mass of straw, feathers, and other debris, built in a box, hollow tree, or about crevices of buildings. *Eggs:* 4 to 7, pale greenish or bluish white.

Distribution.—*General:* Introduced from Europe and now widely distributed over eastern half of United States and Canada. *In Oregon:* Introduced in Portland but now, fortunately, extinct.

In 1889 and 1892, the Portland Song Bird Club released 35 pairs of Starlings in Portland. These birds established themselves and remained for a number of years, but some time about 1901 or 1902 disappeared, which, in the light of the troubles with this species in the Eastern States, was a fortunate thing for the Pacific Coast, for if the Starling ever becomes abundant there the small-fruit industry will suffer severely.

Crested Mynah:
Aethiopsar cristatellus cristatellus (Linnaeus)

Description.—Entire plumage black except for white wing patches. Head crested with tuft of feathers that project forward. Iris, back, and feet yellow in adult. About size of a robin. *Nest:* In holes about buildings or in trees, a messy structure of almost any available material such as grass, weeds, straw, feathers, papers, etc. *Eggs:* 4 to 6, light blue to greenish blue.

Distribution.—*General:* Introduced and established about Vancouver, British Columbia, and Fraser River Valley. *In Oregon:* Straggler from colony in Vancouver, of which there is one record.

A single Crested Mynah came to a bird-feeding station near Mount Tabor Park in Portland and remained for several days. Gabrielson saw it, February 4 and 6, 1922, and from its appearance and behavior did not think it to be an escaped cage bird. It was probably a straggler from the British Columbia colony. It will be a sorry day for Oregon if the Crested Mynah should ever become numerous, and every effort should be made to prevent that happening.

Vireos: *Family Vireonidae*

Hutton's Vireo:
Vireo huttoni huttoni Cassin

DESCRIPTION.—"*Adults:* Lores and orbital ring dull whitish; ***upper parts dull olive brown***, greener on rump, wings, and tail; wing bars narrow, white; under parts dingy, tinged on sides with olive yellow; spurious primary well developed. *Young:* similar, but upper parts lighter brown, sides of head buffy brown, under parts paler. *Length:* 4.25–4.75, wing 2.40–2.45, tail 2.00–2.10, bill from nostril .26–.29, tarsus .72–.76." (Bailey) *Nest:* Hung from twigs, woven of moss, and lined with dry grass. *Eggs:* 2 to 4, white, marked about the large end with brown.

DISTRIBUTION.—*General:* Pacific Coast from southern British Columbia south to Lower California. Resident throughout range. *In Oregon:* Rather uncommon permanent resident west of Cascades.

HUTTON'S VIREO is a dull-colored little bird, somewhat more silent than its more common relatives, although it has a characteristic scolding note one soon learns to recognize. It was first recorded from Oregon by Anthony (1890b), who described the now discarded subspecies (*V. h. obscurus*) from Beaverton as a new form. Oregon records are listed as Hutton's or Anthony's Vireos, though both are now considered as one race (Grinnell 1922). Andrus (1894) found a nest with eggs at Elkton, May 31, 1892, which he recorded as this species, but Woodcock (1902) published the following statement from Mr. Andrus: "Have recorded this species and collected a set of eggs but am now rather doubtful as to identity being correct." Woodcock (1902) listed it as a winter resident at Salem on the authority of Wm. Warner, who stated it was "always found with Ruby-crowned Kinglets and Oregon Chickadees." Bowles (1907) found it to be a winter resident along the Columbia River, and Shelton (1917) considered it a common resident of Lane County, being the only observer to place it in that category.

We consider Hutton's Vireo to be a regular but not common resident of the western part of Oregon, but more field work—particularly in the Willamette, Rogue, and Umpqua Valleys—is needed to determine accurately its status in the State. We have records of it in our notes in Multnomah, Yamhill, Benton, Lane, Douglas, Jackson, Josephine, Tillamook, Coos, and Curry Counties for every month except August and published records for Washington and Marion Counties. Jewett found a nest, 7 feet up in an oak tree, at Oak Grove, July 4. It contained four newly hatched young.

Cassin's Vireo:
Vireo solitarius cassini Xantus

DESCRIPTION.—"*Adults: Top and sides of head gray in sharp contrast to white of loral streak, orbital ring, and throat;* back *dull* olive green; wings with two clear white bands;

under parts clear white, washed with yellow and olive on sides and flanks. *Young in first winter:* dull grayish brown above, dull buffy below. *Length:* 5.00–5.60, wing 2.85–3.00, tail 2.10–2.30, bill from nostril .28–.31, tarsus .70–.78." (Bailey) *Nest:* Like that of the Red-eyed Vireo, but often decorated with bits of white cocoon or fragments of a hornet's nest and hung low in bushes or trees (Plate 84, *A*). *Eggs:* 4 or 5, white, spotted with reddish on big end.

Distribution.—*General:* Breeds from central British Columbia, southwestern Alberta, Idaho, and Montana south through California and western Nevada to Lower California. Winters in Mexico and Central America. *In Oregon:* Regular summer resident and breeder.

Cassin's Vireo is second in abundance among Oregon members of the family. It is found in the smaller second growth and in brushy areas either on the hillsides or along the stream bottoms. It is more deliberate in both song and motion than its more abundant cousin, the Western Warbling Vireo, and is often seen hopping about the inner branches of a tree, its movements timed to somewhat the same cadence as its full-throated song. Like so many of our more common birds, it was first listed from the State from Fort Klamath, in Lieutenant Wittich's records published by Mearns (1879). Many subsequent observers have listed it from various localities, until now with our notes and the unpublished records of other Biological Survey workers it is known from every section of the State. It arrives in April (earliest date, April 13, Jackson County) and remains until September (latest date, September 21, Lake County). It breeds commonly and builds its dainty nest low in bushes or trees. Eggs have been found from May 10 to June 28.

Red-eyed Vireo:
Vireo olivaceus (Linnaeus)

Description.—"*Adults: Top of head gray, conspicuously bordered by white superciliary* and narrow black line; blackish line through eye; rest of upper parts olive green; wings without bands or spurious primary; under parts clear white. *Young:* similar, but back brownish ash; sides washed with brown. *Length:* 5.50–6.50, wing about 3.10–3.30, tail 2.15–2.30, exposed culmen, .50–.55." (Bailey) *Nest:* A beautiful cup, woven of strips of bark, vegetable fibers, and wool, and hung in a forked twig, usually close to the ground. *Eggs:* 3 to 5, sparingly dotted with brown, chiefly around larger end.

Distribution.—*General:* Breeds from central British Columbia, western Mackenzie, Manitoba, Ontario, and Cape Breton Island south to northern Oregon, Idaho, Montana, Wyoming, Texas, Alabama, and central Florida. Winters in South America. *In Oregon:* Summer resident and breeding species of northern edge of State in Wallowa, Baker, and Umatilla Counties and westward along the Columbia at least to Sauvies Island.

The history of the Red-eyed Vireo in Oregon is most interesting. The first knowledge that it was to be found within the State limits goes back to 1897 when Vernon Bailey, who was entirely familiar with the species, saw one in Klamath County but failed to collect the bird. So far as we

Plate 84, *A*. Young Cassin's Vireos at nest. (Photo by Wm. L. Finley and H. T. Bohlman.)

Plate 84, *B*. Western Warbling Vireo at nest. (Photo by Wm. L. Finley and H. T. Bohlman.)

can determine, H. H. Sheldon, of the Biological Survey, collected the first actual Oregon specimen at Homestead, Baker County, on May 31, 1916. He stated that no others were seen, and neither of the two above records has been previously used. The credit for the first publication of the species from the State goes to A. C. Shelton (1917), who took an adult male near Oakridge, Lane County, June 22, 1916, less than a month after the Baker County bird was taken. The next evidence is that of Cantwell, who saw one bird June 7 and another June 10, 1919, near Paradise, Wallowa County. This may have been the same individual or possibly two different birds. On June 14, 1923, W. E. Sherwood collected an adult male at Imnaha, Wallowa County, that is now in Jewett's collection (No. 2940).

Evidently in recent years this bird has become increasingly common, for since 1924, when we first found it in Portland, we have encountered it with increasing frequency. On July 6 of that year, while on a field trip together on the Hall Ranch east of Portland on the Columbia River bottoms we found a nest containing three eggs and collected two adult birds. The nest was located in a wild crab-apple tree about 8 feet from the ground. We saw additional birds in that vicinity on numerous occasions that summer, and each season since we have found the species along the Columbia as far down the river as Sauvies Island. We have seen it repeatedly on that island, which to date is the farthest-west station for the species. In some years we have heard as many as a dozen singing males in a June or early July tramp of a few miles along the dikes that edge the Columbia near Portland. The species has undoubtedly spread westward and become more common in recent years and has also doubtless grown more abundant in northeastern Oregon, as we have found it present there with greater frequency. It arrives in May and remains until September (earliest date, April 27; latest, September 8, both Multnomah County).

Western Warbling Vireo:
Vireo gilvus swainsoni Baird

Description.—"*Adults: Upper parts olive gray*, grayest on head and most olive on rump and upper tail coverts; *white streak through eye;* wings and tail dusky brown, unmarked, wing with a well-developed spurious primary; sides of head pale brownish or buffy; under parts white, shaded with olive yellow on sides. *Young:* top of head and hind neck pale grayish buff; rest of upper parts buffy, wings with buffy bars; under parts pure white, except for yellowish tail coverts." (Bailey) *Size:* Length (skins) 4.29–5.08, wing 2.44–2.87, tail 1.77–2.13, bill .35–.43. *Nest:* Similar to that of Red-eyed Vireo, but usually higher above the ground (Plate 84, *B*). *Eggs:* 4 or 5, white, spotted around larger end with brown and lilac.

Distribution.—*General:* Breeds from southern British Columbia, southwestern

Mackenzie, and central Alberta south to Lower California and Mexico and central western Texas. Winters south to Central America. *In Oregon:* Common summer resident and breeding species of wooded areas.

THE WESTERN WARBLING VIREO (Plate 84, *B*) is the most common and widely distributed vireo in the State. It is much more often heard than seen, as its soft colors blend into the foliage until it is indeed difficult to distinguish. Since Bendire (1877) first discovered it in Oregon at Camp Harney it has been listed by many writers from all sections. It is equally abundant on the stream bottoms in eastern and western Oregon, except on the coast, where it is a decidedly less conspicuous element of the fauna. It has been recorded, however, from practically every county. It arrives in May and remains until September (earliest date, April 21; latest, October 1, both Multnomah County). Its somewhat monotonous song, repeated endlessly through the long summer days as the birds work through the leafy treetops, is heard everywhere throughout June and July, even at midday, when the balance of the bird chorus is stilled. After the nesting season, however, the singing ceases and the birds become silent shadows that slip about in the treetops so quietly that they are seldom seen.

The eggs are most commonly laid in May and June, and the young are on the wing by July 1. Our nesting data are rather scanty, but Jewett has a Portland record for May 16, 1917, of a nest and four fresh eggs, 12 feet up in an alder tree. Together we found a nest near Fort Klamath, May 30, 1934, in an aspen thicket. It contained three fresh eggs. Patterson (ms.) has egg dates on May 20 and 25 at Pinehurst and June 20 and 27 on Williamson River in Klamath County.

Wood Warblers: *Family Compsothlypidae*

Orange-crowned Warbler: *Vermivora celata celata* (Say)

DESCRIPTION.—"*Adult male:* Upper parts *dull* olive green, brighter on rump; sometimes tinged with gray, especially on head; *crown with dull orange patch* concealed except in worn midsummer plumage by grayish olive tips to feathers; orbital ring and superciliary yellow; under parts *dull* yellowish, indistinctly streaked with darker on throat and chest. *Adult female:* crown patch usually duller and restricted, sometimes obsolete. *Young:* generally without crown patch. *Young in first plumage:* crown patch wanting; upper parts dull olive; wings with two light bands; belly white; rest of under parts brownish gray, tinged with buffy. *Male:* length (skins) 4.25–4.80, wing 2.39–2.49, tail 1.92–2.07, bill .37–.41. *Female:* length (skins) 4.35–4.65, wing 2.26–2.33, tail 1.78–1.94, bill .37–.42." (Bailey) *Nest:* On the ground, made of strips of bark, stems, and grasses, and lined with grass, hair, or fur. *Eggs:* 4 to 6, white, finely speckled with brown, mostly on larger end.

DISTRIBUTION.—*General:* Breeds from Kobuk River, Alaska, south to northern

Manitoba. Winters in Gulf Coast States, Mexico, and southern California. *In Oregon:* Uncommon breeding species, of which we have only a few records east of eastern base of Cascades.

The Orange-crowned Warbler is one of Oregon's more uncommon breeding birds, and very little is known about it. Bendire (1877) listed one from Camp Harney as a breeding bird, and his record undoubtedly belongs here. Gabrielson (1924a) erroneously published a sight record from Wallowa County as Lutescent Warbler that should have been recorded as this form, and the correction is herewith made. Since 1927 Jewett has collected a number of birds in June and September on Hart Mountain, and on May 27, 1933, while the authors were together, Gabrielson collected one of several birds on Lookout Mountain, Baker County. Our few sight records and nine skins from eastern Oregon are placed here for want of better classification. The elimination of the form *V. c. orestera* from the 1931 Check-List has left us somewhat in doubt as to the proper identity, but they are certainly closer to this than to any other form now recognized. Our earliest date of arrival for the species is April 27, Wallowa County; our latest, September 21, Harney County. We have only one nesting record. Jewett (1934b), with the aid of a small, keen-eyed boy, collected a female and nest containing four incubated eggs on Hart Mountain, June 18, 1934.

Lutescent Warbler:
Vermivora celata lutescens (Ridgway)

Description.—"Similar to *celata*, but brighter colored; upper parts bright olive green; under parts bright greenish yellow, streaks on under parts dull olive greenish. *Young in first plumage:* upper parts olive green, wing bars paler or buffy; under parts buffy or straw color shaded with olive on chest, sides, and flanks. *Male:* length (skins) 4.20–4.45, wing 2.29–2.41, tail 1.76–1.93, bill .37–.38. *Female:* length (skins) 4.00–4.40, wing 2.24–2.40, tail 1.80–1.85, bill .39–.40." (Bailey) *Nest and eggs:* Similar to those of Orange-crowned Warbler.

Distribution.—*General:* Breeds along Pacific Coast from Cook Inlet in Alaska south to southern California. Winters to Central America. *In Oregon:* Common summer resident of northwestern Oregon and common migrant and less common summer resident of southwestern section.

The Lutescent Warbler (Plate 83, *B*), while in Oregon, is a bird of the brushlands, where the males utter their wheezy little song as they work restlessly about in the low shrubs. Its dull, yellowish-green coloration makes it difficult to detect it unless it is in motion or song, and consequently it is often overlooked. It is, however, one of the common summer birds in the Willamette Valley and on the coast in Clatsop, Tillamook, and Lincoln Counties. It is less common as a breeding species in the Rogue River district but is found there throughout the summer. It crosses the Cascades to Klamath, Deschutes, and Wasco Counties and continues along the eastern edge of the timber, but records from farther east are doubtful, probably being referable to *V. c. celata*. It appears in March (earliest date, March 12, Lane County) and remains until September (latest date, October 1, Multnomah County).

Baird (Baird, Cassin, and Lawrence 1858) published the first known record for the State, when he listed two birds collected on the Columbia River by J. K. Townsend, May 15 and 16, 1835. Although these might have been taken on either shore of the river, the bird listed as taken at Fort Dalles, May 4, 1855, by Dr. Suckley, and the one without date, but certainly not much later, taken at Fort Umpqua by Dr. Vollmer, were undoubtedly within the present limits of Oregon. Suckley (Cooper and Suckley 1860) reprinted the record of the Fort Dalles bird. Anthony (1886) considered the species common in Washington County; Merrill (1888) listed it as a common migrant and stated that a few remained to breed; and Finley (1904b) published photos of nests from Portland.

The eggs are laid in May. Our few dates and those published extend from May 6 to June 3. V. Bailey found the birds feeding young near Eugene between June 15 and 20, 1914. Woodcock (1902) reported that the Finley collection contained two sets of eggs taken May 11 and one set taken June 3, 1895, at Portland. A number of later writers have listed these warblers as breeding birds but give no definite data.

Calaveras Warbler:
Vermivora ruficapilla ridgwayi van Rossem

Description.—"*Adult male: Under parts bright yellow;* upper part of head gray, with conspicuous white orbital ring and *chestnut crown patch*, but feathers tipped with gray; back olive green, brightening to yellowish green on rump and upper tail coverts; wings and tail unmarked. *Adult female:* similar, but duller, and crown with little if any chestnut. *Young:* throat, chest, and under tail coverts dull yellowish; belly buffy brown; upper parts brownish gray, becoming olive gray on rump. *Male:* length (skins) 4.05–4.75, wing 2.32–2.46, tail 1.70–1.88, bill .37–.40. *Female:* length (skins) 3.85–4.10, wing 2.12–2.19, tail 1.53–1.62, bill .34–.38." (Bailey) *Nest:* On or near the ground, of stems, grass, and bark, lined with root fibers. *Eggs:* 4 or 5, creamy white, with wreath of brown and lavender spots about the large end.

Distribution.—*General:* Breeds from southern British Columbia south to central Sierra Nevadas of California, eastern Oregon, and Idaho. Winters in Mexico. *In Oregon:* Widely distributed summer resident, most abundant in Jackson, Josephine, and Klamath Counties but found throughout Blue Mountain area and along western slopes of Cascades and in valleys below.

The tiny Calaveras Warbler is one of the common birds of the cutover lands of southern Oregon, being particularly abundant in the brushy areas and in the oak-covered hillsides of Jackson, Josephine, and Klamath Counties. It is less common but is found northward along the Cascades to Portland. In addition, we have found it in Lake, Baker, Wallowa, Sherman, Wasco, and Hood River Counties east of the Cascades and are sure that more field work would add greatly to our knowledge of the extent of territory occupied by this little midget. It appears in April (earliest date, April 9, Sherman County) and remains until August (latest date, August 21, Baker County).

Little has appeared in literature regarding this rather inconspicuous bird of the oak- and brush-covered slopes. Sharpe (1885) listed a specimen from Upper Klamath Lake on May 18. Merrill (1888) considered it common at Fort Klamath, but it was not again mentioned in Oregon ornithological literature until Jewett (1909c) published his records from Baker County. Jewett (1916a) later listed it from Baker and Sherman Counties. Walker (1917) referred to the Sherman County bird mentioned above, and the authors (Jewett and Gabrielson 1929) included several records from the Portland area. Gabrielson (1931) considered it common in the Rogue River Valley and recorded the only nesting record so far published for the State, a nest found at Gold Hill, Jackson County, May 16, 1916, by Jewett. It was located on the upper bank of an old roadway in the timber, well sunk into the ground and concealed from above by a small plant of poison oak. Both parents were present, and the female and a set of five well-incubated eggs were collected. Patterson (ms.) reported two nests at Pinehurst, May 20, 1920, and May 23, 1928.

Eastern Yellow Warbler:
Dendroica aestiva aestiva (Gmelin)

Description.—"*Adult male:* Under parts yellow; breast and belly *streaked with rufous;* forehead bright yellow, front of crown often tinged with orange; hind neck and rest of upper parts yellowish green, brightest on rump; *wing* edgings yellow; inner webs of tail feathers, except middle pair, *light yellow. Adult female and male in first autumn:* upper parts plain yellowish green, usually darker than in male, lighter on forehead and rump; under parts paler and duller, usually unstreaked. *Young female in first autumn:* like adult female, but duller olive green above, olive whitish slightly tinged with yellow below; under tail coverts pale yellow. *Male:* length (skins) 3.94–4.92, wing 2.36–2.80, tail 1.65–2.09, bill .39–.43. *Female:* length (skins) 4.02–4.57, wing 2.24–2.68, tail 1.54–1.77, bill .39–.43." (Bailey) *Nest:* A compact cup of gray plant fibers, lined with down and feathers and placed in a fork in a bush or tree. *Eggs:* 2 to 6, greenish white, wreathed with brown, black, and lilac spots about large end.

Distribution.—*General:* Breeds throughout North America from tree limit south to Nevada, New Mexico, southern Missouri, northern Alabama, Georgia, and South Carolina. Winters in South America. *In Oregon:* Abundant summer resident throughout State.

There has been much confusion of the races of Yellow Warbler in Oregon. We have a fair series of breeding birds from the different sections of the State, and after a careful comparison we are unable to find any constant character or combination of characters either of size or coloration by which we are able to differentiate the two forms. The 1931 A. O. U. Check-List includes the birds west of the Cascades in the race *D. a.*

brewsteri Grinnell and those east of the mountains in the present race. The two seem to be poorly differentiated in this State, and we can see little value in continued recognition of a race based on such slight and variable characters. Therefore we are including all of our breeding Yellow Warblers here.

The Eastern Yellow Warbler was first reported from Oregon by Bendire (1877), who found it breeding in abundance at Camp Harney, a status that persists to this day. Many subsequent writers have mentioned it, and we now know it to be a common summer resident in every county. It usually arrives in early May (earliest date, April 24, Multnomah County) and remains until September (latest date, September 21, Lake County). It is the most conspicuous of all breeding warblers, the bright-yellow coloring and simple song being familiar to everyone interested in birds. It is very common in the willow thickets and brush patches of the State, and along stream bottoms the eggs are laid in June. Our extreme dates for numerous nests with complete sets, largely in Multnomah County, are May 24 and June 27, although doubtless these could be considerably extended by more observations. Patterson (ms.) reported numerous sets from southern Oregon between May 2 and June 6.

Alaska Yellow Warbler:
Dendroica aestiva rubiginosa (Pallas)

Description.—Similar to *Dendroica a. aestiva*, but slightly smaller and much duller in color. *Adult male:* darker and duller olive green above, the pileum concolor with the back, or else becoming slightly more yellowish on the forehead and fore part of crown-wing edgings less conspicuous. *Adult female:* darker and duller olive-green above, duller yellow below. *Nest and eggs:* Similar to those of *D. a. aestiva*.

Distribution.—*General:* Breeds in Alaska and south to Vancouver Island. Winters from Mexico southward. *In Oregon:* Detected only as spring migrant to date.

The differences between the recognized races of Yellow Warbler are so vague that it is difficult to distinguish with certainty the Alaska Yellow Warbler. Birds that appear identical with breeding birds from the British Columbia coast are considered to be this form. We have specimens from Bend (May 11), Brownsboro (May 13), Newberg (May 15), Baker (May 27), Portland (June 5 and 7), and Prineville (June 21) that seem to belong here. These birds are somewhat smaller and slightly darker than breeding birds and have more yellow on the forehead, but the line between these specimens and local birds is not clearly defined.

Myrtle Warbler:
Dendroica coronata (Linnaeus)

Description.—"*Adult male in spring and summer: Crown patch and rump bright yellow;* rest of upper parts bluish gray, streaked with black; wings with two white bars; tail black with gray edgings; outer pair of tail feathers with large spots of white; *throat white;* rest of under parts black, yellow, and white. *Adult female in spring and summer:* similar, but smaller and duller; upper parts tinged with brown; color patches restricted. *Adult male in fall and winter:* upper parts grayish brown, streaked with black on back and scapulars; yellow crown patch concealed by brown tips to feathers; throat and chest brownish white or buffy brown, chest streaked with black; yellow patches obscured, black patches with white edges to feathers. *Adult female in fall and winter:* like winter male, but smaller, upper parts browner, yellow crown patch restricted or obsolete; under parts pale buffy brown in front and on sides; median parts of breast and belly yellowish white; yellow breast patches indistinct or obsolete. *Young, first plumage:* streaked above and below; wings and tail much as in adults. *Male:* length (skins) 4.72–5.51, wing 2.76–3.07, tail 1.97–2.36, bill .35–.43. *Female:* length (skins) 4.65–5.51, wing 2.64–2.95, tail 2.02–2.32, bill .32–.41." (Bailey) *Nest:* Usually in coniferous trees, well woven of grass, twigs, and rootlets and lined with fine grass, feathers, and hair. *Eggs:* 3 to 6, white, wreathed on the larger end with brown and lavender spots.

Distribution.—*General:* Breeds from tree limit in Alaska, Mackenzie, Manitoba, and Quebec south to northern British Columbia, southern Alberta, Minnesota, Michigan, Ontario, New York, and Massachusetts. Winters from Oregon, Kansas, Ohio Valley, and New Jersey southward to Panama. In *Oregon:* Regular but not common spring and fall migrant and winter resident of western Oregon. Found only once east of Cascades.

The Myrtle Warbler has long been known as a migrant through Oregon. Johnson (1880) first recorded it for the State in his list of birds from East Portland, Forest Grove, and Salem. Keller (1891f) listed it from Salem, November 26, 1891, and Prill (1892b) stated that it bred at Sweet Home, a statement for which there has been no subsequent confirmation. Woodcock (1902) published records from Yaquina Bay, Salem, Portland, and Corvallis. Shelton (1917) took a specimen near Eugene, March 18, 1915. Walker (1924) recorded a specimen taken near Tillamook, April 28, 1919. We published a number of records for the Portland district in our *Birds of the Portland Area* (Jewett and Gabrielson 1929) and since that date have continued to find it a regular migrant and at least an occasional winter resident. In addition to these published records, which include Multnomah, Washington, Marion, Linn, Benton, and Tillamook Counties, there are manuscript notes in the Biological Survey files that add Polk, Yamhill, and Clackamas Counties to the list, and we have specimens from Jackson, Lane, and Multnomah Counties. The only record east of the Cascades is of a male seen by Jewett on the Springer Ranch near Malheur Lake, May 14, 1932. The species arrives in October (earliest date, October 11, Multnomah County) and remains until May (latest date, May 14, Harney County).

While in Oregon, it is usually found intermingled with the much more abundant Audubon's Warbler along the fence rows or in the deciduous thickets along the streams. It is not conspicuously different from its more familiar cousin, unless one can look directly at the throat, which is white instead of bright yellow. As an opportunity for such a close view is not always available, it requires careful search for the observer to pick this bird out of the regular migrating warblers.

Audubon's Warbler: *Dendroica auduboni auduboni* (Townsend)

Description.—"*Adult male in spring and summer: Throat, crown patch, and rump yellow;* under parts white, yellow, and solid black; upper parts bluish gray, streaked with black; wing coverts with large white patches; tail black, inner webs of four or five outer feathers with large submarginal patch of white. *Adult female in spring and summer:* like summer male, but duller, and with less black on under parts; upper parts usually more or less tinged with brown; yellow crown patch restricted, and partly tipped with brownish gray; wings with narrower bands; chest and sides grayish, marked with black; color patches restricted. *Adult male in fall and winter:* duller and browner than summer male, upper parts washed with brown, wing markings tinged with brown; black of chest and sides mostly concealed by brownish white edges to feathers. *Adult female in fall and winter:* like winter male, but smaller and duller, back without sharply defined streaks; yellow patches paler and more restricted; black chest spots more sharply defined. *Young, first plumage:* upper parts thickly streaked with dusky on brownish gray ground; lower rump grayish white, narrowly streaked with dusky; under parts grayish white, streaked. *Male:* length (skins) 4.80–5.39, wing 2.95–3.19, tail 2.09–2.42, bill .39–.43. *Female:* length (skins) 4.80–5.08, wing 2.87–3.07, tail 2.13–2.32, bill .39–.43." (Bailey) *Nest:* In trees and bushes, usually within a few feet of the ground, a compact cup of strips of bark and pine needles, lined with rootlets, hair, and feathers. *Eggs:* 3 or 4, olive white, sparingly spotted with black and brown (Plate 85, *A*).

Distribution.—*General:* Breeds from central British Columbia, Alberta, and Saskatchewan south to mountains of southern California, Arizona, New Mexico, and Black Hills. Winters from Oregon and Rio Grande to Central America. *In Oregon:* Permanent resident that has been noted in every county during summer and throughout western Oregon in winter.

Audubon's Warbler is one of the abundant birds of Oregon. Bendire (1877) published the first State record when he stated it was common and breeding at Camp Harney. Many subsequent writers have referred to it from places well distributed over the State until the species has now been recorded, either in literature or in our own notes, for every county. It is a regular summer resident in the mountains as well as in the western valleys. Its little song is heard on every side during May and June, and its peculiarly distinct call or alarm note is a familiar sound throughout the balance of the year. This is true not only of the wooded slopes and bottoms but equally so of the weedy fence rows of the Willamette Valley, where during the short days of fall and winter these warblers may be found associating with the Golden-crowned Sparrow and Willow Goldfinches or sitting on the telephone wires with the Western Bluebirds. In mid-March the arrival of the individuals that wintered farther south greatly swells the population, and the species becomes one of the really abundant birds, remaining so through April and into early May, when the migrant population disappears to the north, leaving only resident birds until late August. At that time the birds travel southward, and during September and October they again swarm over the landscape, until by the last of October they are reduced in numbers to the wintering

Plate 85, *A*. Nest and eggs of Audubon's Warbler. (Photo by Alex Walker.)

Plate 85, *B*. Black-throated Gray Warbler feeding young near nest. (Photo by Wm. L. Finley and H. T. Bohlman.)

population. In eastern Oregon our latest fall date is October 24 (Lake County) and our earliest spring record is March 22 (Klamath County), except for a single straggling record of two birds seen by Jewett in Wasco County, January 2, 1917. West of the Cascades the species remains in numbers every winter.

We have only one definite nesting record, that of a nest in an aspen tree on Hart Mountain containing three small young and one addled egg, found June 15, 1926, while the authors and Dr. W. B. Bell were traveling together toward the summit of the mountain. We have, however, numerous records and some specimens of newly fledged young from the Blue Mountains, the Cascades, and the Willamette Valley. Braly took eggs, May 24 and 27, 1930, in Klamath County, and Patterson (ms.) reported sets, May 6, 1922, May 10, 1920, and May 20, 1924, for the same territory. There is a set of eggs in the National Museum taken by Bendire near Fort Klamath in 1882.

Black-throated Gray Warbler: *Dendroica nigrescens* (Townsend)

DESCRIPTION.—"*Adult male in spring and summer: Whole head, throat, and chest black,* except for white streaks on side of head and along throat, and *bright yellow spot over lores;* breast and belly pure white; sides streaked with black; back gray, more or less streaked with black; wings with two white bars; tail with inner webs of two outer feathers mainly white. *Adult female in spring and summer:* similar, but colors duller; crown usually gray, streaked with black; black of throat largely mixed with white. *Adult male in fall and winter:* like summer male, but gray of upper parts tinged with brown, and black markings restricted, sometimes nearly obsolete. *Adult female in fall and winter:* like summer male, but plumage softer and streaks on back and upper tail coverts obsolete or wanting. *Young male in first fall and winter:* like adult winter male, but gray of upper parts browner; crown brownish gray except on front and sides; streaks on back and upper tail coverts obsolete or concealed; black of throat with white tips to feathers; white of under parts tinged with yellowish. *Young female in first fall and winter:* entire upper parts brownish gray, crown bordered with dusky; white of under parts strongly tinged with brown. *Male:* length (skins) 4.13–4.65, wing 2.35–2.62, tail 1.92–2.17, bill .32–.38. *Female:* length (skins) 4.21–4.80, wing 2.13–2.47, tail 1.85–2.01, bill .33–.38." (Bailey) *Nest:* A compact cup of plant fibers, lined with feathers, sometimes placed low in bushes or small trees and at other times high in big conifers (Plate 85, *B*). *Eggs:* 3 or 4, white, spotted on the larger end with brown and lilac.

DISTRIBUTION.—*General:* Breeds from southern British Columbia, Nevada, and northern Utah south to Lower California, Arizona, and New Mexico. Winters in Mexico. *In Oregon:* Common summer resident of western Oregon and also of eastern Oregon in juniper trees in Wasco, Jefferson, Deschutes, Crook, Klamath, Lake, and Harney Counties. Not common elsewhere in eastern Oregon.

THE BLACK-THROATED Gray Warbler (Plate 85, *B*) has a peculiar distribution for the State. It is a common summer resident and breeding species of the valleys and lower slopes throughout western Oregon, where there are records for every county, and in eastern Oregon it occupies a broad triangle with its apex on the Columbia River near The Dalles and its base extending from the eastern base of the Cascades near Klamath Falls to the Steens Mountains in Harney County. Outside of the counties listed above, where it is a common summer bird frequenting the junipers, we have one record for Wheeler County, where Jewett saw one bird in a juniper tree near Twickenham, June 25, 1915. It arrives in April (earliest date, March 31, Jackson County) and remains until September (latest date, October 1, Multnomah County).

Undoubtedly the first published record for Oregon was by Audubon (1839), who listed birds seen along the Columbia River in 1835, presumably by Townsend, one on May 23 and others on June 14 and 16. Nuttall (1840) based his original description on a bird seen but not taken at Fort William (Portland), Oregon, May 29, 1835. Bendire (1877) published a record for Canyon City Mountain, which was probably within the present boundaries of Grant County, and Miller (1904) found it in Wheeler County, June 2, 1899.

There have been numerous published breeding records for the species. Johnson (1880) recorded a nest taken June 17, 1879, and Charles Warren Bowles (1901a, 1901b, 1902) contributed a number of notes to the *Condor* regarding nesting dates from 1901 to 1902. A number of our own nesting records, together with these previously published ones, indicate that fresh eggs are to be found from May 14 to June 24, which happen to be the outside dates mentioned by Bowles (1902) for southern Oregon.

Townsend's Warbler:
Dendroica townsendi (Townsend)

Description.—"*Adult male in spring and summer:* Head and throat black, except for bright yellow superciliary and malar streak bordering throat; *breast bright yellow* fading to white on middle of belly; sides streaked with black; back bright olive green; with black arrow-point streaks; wings and tail blackish, wing with two white bars, tail with inner webs of three lateral feathers white at ends. *Adult female in spring and summer:* like winter male, but black streaking of upper parts and sides restricted or obsolete; crown sometimes blackish; throat often blotched with black. *Adult male in fall and winter:* like summer male, but black obscured; crown and hind neck with olive green edges to feathers; cheek patch with olive green tips to feathers; throat lemon yellow; chest and sides spotted with black. *Adult female in fall and winter:* like summer female, but upper parts slightly brownish, streaks indistinct; sides and flanks brownish. *Young male in first fall and winter:* like adult winter male, but streaks on crown and back obsolete, and yellow of throat paler. *Young female in first fall and winter:* like adult fall female, but yellow paler, and markings less distinct. *Male:* length (skins) 4.21–4.80, wing 2.56–2.72, tail 1.89–2.01, bill .32–.35. *Female:* length (skins) 4.25–4.92, wing 2.48–2.60, tail 1.93–1.97, bill .32–.39." (Bailey) *Nest:* In small conifers, made of grasses, plants, skins, or cedar bark, lined with horsehair, moss, etc. *Eggs:* 3 or 4, white, sprinkled and wreathed with browns and purples.

DISTRIBUTION.—*General:* Breeds from Prince William Sound and Upper Yukon south to Washington and east to southern Alberta and Montana. Winters from Oregon south to Nicaragua. *In Oregon:* Regular spring and fall migrant. At least occasional summer resident that possibly breeds in State. Casual winter resident.

TOWNSEND'S WARBLER first appeared in the ornithological literature of Oregon when Bendire (1877) recorded a specimen taken May 11, 1875, and described a supposed nest and eggs taken near Camp Harney on June 7 of the same year. Merrill (1888) recorded one taken at Fort Klamath, May 14, 1887. Anthony (1886) considered it rare in Washington County, and Peck (1896) listed it from Salem under date of April 22, 1896. Woodcock (1902) listed it from several Willamette Valley points, and Jewett (1916b) published records from Tillamook County. Abbott (1915) recorded a set of eggs from Yamhill County, May 25, 1895, a statement that we have not been able to confirm. Walker (1917b) listed it from Gateway, Hay Creek, and Cascade Mountains. It was not again mentioned in Oregon literature until we published two of Gabrielson's records for Multnomah County (Jewett and Gabrielson 1929). One of these was of a bird picked up dead on a Portland street by a school girl and brought to Gabrielson through the courtesy of Miss Ruth Russell on January 13, 1928. Since then two more winter birds (January 12, 1931, and January 13, 1932) have reached Jewett in the same way. They are our only winter records for the State and indicate that careful search might reveal the birds southward through the valleys of the Willamette, Umpqua, and Rogue Rivers. Most of our specimens have been taken in May, June, and September, although we have some taken in both July and August. Jewett has one taken July 20, 1916, at Meacham, and one taken August 28, 1923, at Bonanza, and Vernon Bailey's notes contain a record of one collected at 6,000 feet altitude in the Steens Mountains on July 30.

We find the species most abundant on the coast and in the Blue Mountains and desert ranges of eastern Oregon. It is difficult to detect, as it persistently remains in the tops of tall conifers, preferring spruce, fir, or lodgepole pine. Along the coast at times it becomes exceedingly abundant in migration but on account of the heavy timber is not so easily observed as in the more open growth of the Blue Mountains. We have specimens from the Blue Mountains, Hart Mountain, and the ranges about Bly, as well as those from the coast and the Willamette Valley. It arrives in May (earliest date, May 5, Tillamook County) and remains until September (latest date, September 15, Lake County).

Possibly this warbler nests within the State, though to date we have no evidence to confirm the two supposed records mentioned above. At least occasional birds remain through the summer and also through the winter, but it is only during the migration movements that it can be searched for with any real hope of success. At all other times it can be considered a rare bird.

Hermit Warbler:
Dendroica occidentalis (Townsend)

Description.—"*Adult male in spring and summer: Top and sides of head bright yellow*, crown spotted with black, occiput usually mainly or wholly black; throat black; rest of under parts white, sometimes streaked on sides; hind neck streaked black and olive green; rest of *upper parts gray*, tinged with olive green and streaked with black; wings and tail black, wings crossed by two white bands; tail with two outer pairs of feathers largely white. *Adult female in spring and summer:* like winter male, but forehead and crown largely yellow; streaks on back restricted; body less brownish; throat and chest often with dusky patch. *Adult male in fall and winter:* like summer male, but yellow of crown and occiput obscured by olive tips to feathers, black streaks of back obscured by grayish edges to feathers, and black throat patch with whitish tips. *Adult female in fall and winter:* upper parts plain grayish olive, crown with traces of yellow; under parts brownish white, throat and chest with feathers dusky below the surface. *Young male in first fall and winter:* like adult fall male, but crown olive green, back more olive, streaking concealed or obsolete; sides of head paler yellow washed with olive; throat and chest whitish or yellowish, feathers black under the surface; rest of under parts soiled white; sides and flanks tinged with olive brown. *Male:* length (skins) 4.41–4.80, wing 2.48–2.72, tail 1.93–2.05, bill .37–.43. *Female:* length (skins) 4.37–4.72, wing 2.44–2.48, tail 1.83–2.01, bill .35–.39." (Bailey) *Nest:* Usually in conifers, made of plant stems, pine needles, wood-plant fibers, and cobwebs, lined with strips of bark. *Eggs:* 4 or 5, white or grayish, spotted and blotched around the larger end with lilac and brown.

Distribution.—*General:* Breeds chiefly west of Cascades from Washington to southern California. Winters in Mexico and Central America. *In Oregon:* Regular but not abundant summer resident of Cascades and west to coast.

Although Townsend described the Hermit Warbler in 1837 from a pair taken at Fort William (now Portland), Columbia River, May 28, 1835, little has since appeared in print regarding the species as an Oregon bird. It frequents the heavy timber, particularly dense stands of second growth, and for that reason is difficult to detect except when in song during May and June. Merrill (1888) took a specimen, May 12, 1877, at Fort Klamath. Peck (1896) recorded the species from Salem. Woodcock (1902) reported it as a rare summer resident at Dayton on the authority of Hadley and gave the following note from A. W. Anthony: "Both (*D. townsendi* and *D. occidentalis*) are equally common, and in heavy second-growth fir are not at all rare; they no doubt nest high as no nests were found." Bowles (1912) considered it a common breeder at Kerby. Jewett (1916b) recorded specimens from Tillamook and Nehalem. Shelton (1917) stated it was found breeding above Oakridge and near Triangle Lake.

In our *Birds of the Portland Area* (Jewett and Gabrielson 1929) we published two records for Multnomah County and stated we considered it a rare summer resident, a statement that still seems to apply. It arrives in May (earliest date, April 29, Washington County) and remains until August (latest date, August 16, Tillamook County). Gabrielson (1931) found it to be a fairly common summer bird about the base of Mount McLoughlin, and we have found it to be most abundant in southern

Oregon, where it is regularly found in some numbers. We have a number of specimens and eight records from Coos and Jackson Counties in addition to those published previously. The Biological Survey files contain manuscript records by Fisher, from Forest Grove and Glendale, and by Peck, from Reston. There are also several specimens in the Carnegie Museum from Beaverton.

Western Palm Warbler:
Dendroica palmarum palmarum (Gmelin)

Description.—"*Adults in summer:* Crown chestnut, bordered by yellow superciliary; back olive or brown, narrowly streaked with darker and becoming olive green on rump and upper tail coverts; two outer tail feathers with large terminal spots of white; throat, breast, and under tail coverts light yellow; chest, and sometimes sides of throat, more or less streaked; *belly whitish*, more or less mixed with yellowish. *Adults in winter:* chestnut of crown obscured or concealed; throat and chest whitish instead of yellowish. *Young in first fall and winter:* similar, but upper parts browner, superciliary less distinct, and markings of under parts more suffused. *Length:* 4.50–5.50, wing 2.52, tail 2.24." (Bailey) *Nest:* On ground, made of grass, shreds of bark, and moss, lined with plant down and feathers. *Eggs:* Creamy white, spotted, around larger end mostly, with brown and purple.

Distribution.—*General:* Breeds from southern Mackenzie and northern Manitoba south to northern Minnesota. Winters from southern Florida to West Indies and Mexico. *In Oregon:* Rare straggler for which there is only a single record.

The Western Palm Warbler is a species normally found east of the Rockies and can be considered only as an accidental visitor to Oregon. Jewett took a single specimen, a male, in Catlow Valley, Harney County (Jewett Coll. No. 1949) on September 26, 1913. It was in a little clump of willows and is the only record to date.

Grinnell's Water Thrush:
Seiurus noveboracensis notabilis Ridgway

Description.—"*Adults:* Upper parts sooty olive brown; superciliary dingy white; stripe through eye dark brown; under parts usually white with little if any yellow tinge; throat finely, and breast and sides broadly streaked with blackish. *Young:* like adults, but streaks on under parts less distinct, and feathers of upper parts tipped with light fulvous, producing a spotted appearance. *Male:* length (skins) 5.14–5.84, wing 2.90–3.20, tail 2.00–2.25, bill .49–.63. *Female:* length (skins) 5.01–5.99, wing 2.88–3.11, tail 1.92–2.28, bill .48–.56." (Bailey) *Nest:* On or near the ground, in wet woods, made of moss and dried grass. *Eggs:* 3 to 6, white, spotted with reddish brown or lilac.

Distribution.—*General:* Breeds from northwestern Alaska, northern Yukon, and central Mackenzie south to southern British Columbia, central Montana, northwestern Nebraska, and northern Minnesota. Winters in West Indies and Mexico south into South America. *In Oregon:* Rare straggler that has occurred only once.

Reed Ferris took a male Grinnell's Water Thrush at Beaver, on August 26, 1931, which is the only record for the State. This skin was included by McCabe and Miller (1933) in their newly described *S. n. linnaeus* from British Columbia. We can see no appreciable difference between it and skins from the Middle West and are therefore continuing to use the above name for it.

Macgillivray's Warbler:
Oporornis tolmiei (Townsend)

Description.—"*Adult male in spring and summer: Head, throat, and breast slate gray;* throat feathers edged with ash; rest of under parts yellow; lores deep black; eyelids with distinct white spots; back olive green, sometimes tinged with gray. *Adult female in spring and summer:* like adult male, but crown, hind neck, and sides of head and neck mouse gray fading to pale grayish or grayish white on throat and breast. *Adult male in fall and winter:* like summer male, but feathers of crown and hind neck tipped with brown and light edges of feathers on throat and chest broader, sometimes almost concealing black centers. *Adult female in fall and winter:* like summer female, but plumage softer, and sides of throat and chest more grayish. *Young female in first autumn:* like fall adult female, but crown and hind neck like back instead of gray, throat and chest yellowish instead of grayish; marks on eyelids yellowish, and streak over lores pale yellow. *Male:* length (skins) 4.67–5.44, wing 2.34–2.56, tail 2.08–2.48, bill .43–.46. *Female:* length (skins) 4.63–5.04, wing 2.15–2.36, tail 1.91–2.28, bill .42–.48." (Bailey) *Nest:* Low in bushes or weeds, made of dried grass and lined with same. *Eggs:* 3 to 5, white or creamy white, speckled on larger end with brown and lilac and sometimes marked with irregular lines (Plate 86).

Distribution.—*General:* Breeds from Alaska, central British Columbia, central Alberta, and southern Saskatchewan south to central California, northern Arizona, and New Mexico. Winters to South America. *In Oregon:* Common summer resident of timber and brush areas.

This dark-headed little inhabitant of the brush patches, Macgillivray's Warbler, is a common bird in the Cascades and west to the coast as well as in the Blue Mountains and desert ranges to the south. It arrives in late April and remains until late September (earliest date, April 20; latest, October 12, both Multnomah County). In western Oregon, it frequents the blackberry patches and dense thickets of *Spiraea* or *Salal*, and in the eastern part of the State, it is equally at home in the dense growth of willow about the springs and along the stream bottoms. The birds are much in evidence in their chosen haunts in late April and early May while the courtship is in progress, but when household cares occupy the daylight hours they become as elusive as field mice, slipping about through the thickets like shadows, only the sharp alarm note betraying their presence to an intruder.

Historically, this warbler has been known as an Oregon bird since Townsend collected specimens in May 1835. Audubon (1839) reported this date and also the first nesting record, a nest containing young found on June 12, 1835. Both these records are from the Columbia River near the present site of Portland (Fort William). Since then many writers

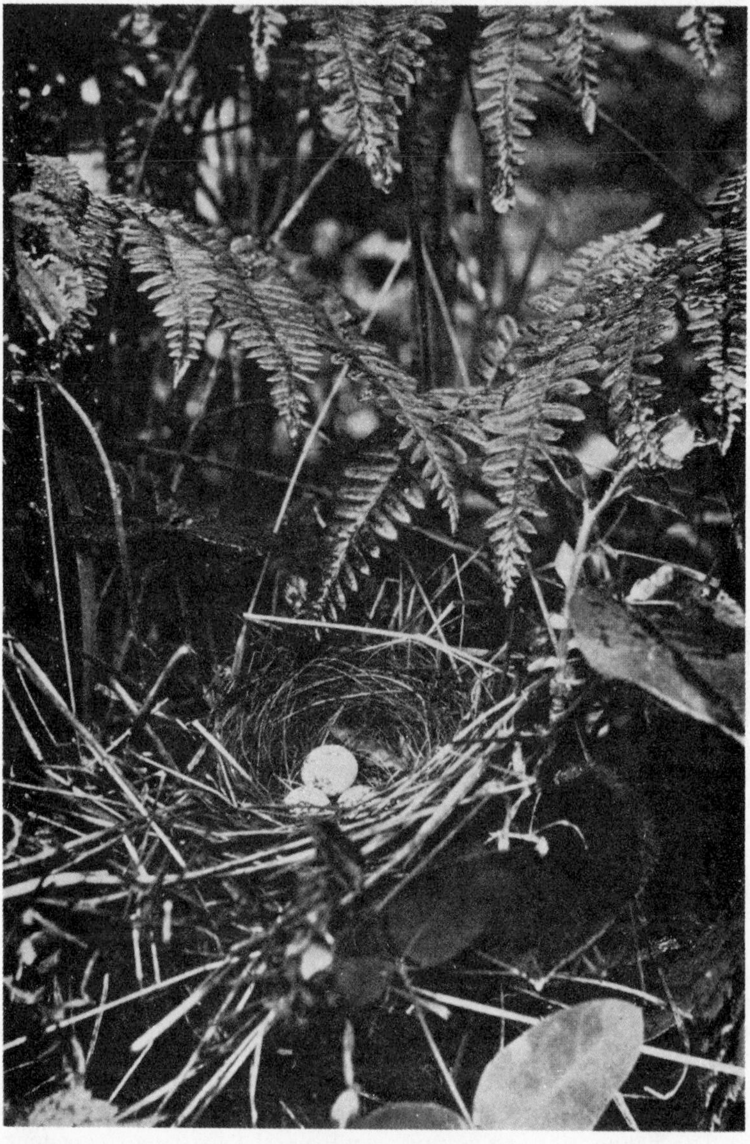

Plate 86. Nest and eggs of Macgillivray's Warbler. (Photo by Alex Walker.)

have listed the species until, including our own notes, it has been recorded in every county, either in migration or as a breeding species.

The courtship commences immediately upon the arrival of the birds in the State, and complete sets of eggs are found by early June (our earliest date, May 30). The breeding season is somewhat extended, as Jewett found one set of four slightly incubated eggs as late as July 18 in Baker County. Published breeding records, in addition to that from Multnomah County referred to above, include Harney County (Bendire 1877), Clackamas County (Dietrich 1914, Abbott 1915), Marion County (Cooke 1891b, who gave May 15 as the earliest and June 19 as the latest date, and Peck 1896). Our own records include nests found in Clackamas, Lake, Crook, Baker, and Multnomah Counties in addition to summer skins from many other localities.

Western Yellow-throat:
Geothlypis trichas occidentalis Brewster

Description.—"*Adult male: Forehead and sides of head black*, bordered above with white, sometimes tinged with yellow; rest of upper parts plain olive green; under parts deep yellow. In winter, washed with brown. *Adult female:* without black, ashy, or white; upper parts olive brown, often tinged with reddish brown on crown, greenish on tail; under parts pale yellowish or yellowish white. *Young male in first winter:* like adult, but black mask less distinct. *Male:* length (skins) 4.53–5.00, wing 2.17–2.36, tail 2.01–2.22, bill .43–.47. *Female:* length (skins) 4.33–4.76, wing 2.05–2.15, tail 1.93–2.09, bill .41–.43." (Bailey) *Nest:* On or near ground, a deep cup woven of grass and lined with same material and hair. *Eggs:* 3 or 4, white, dotted on larger end with brown and black.

Distribution.—*General:* Breeds from southern Alaska, central British Columbia, and central Alberta south to central California, southern Nevada, and Texas. *In Oregon:* Summer resident and breeding bird east of Cascades.

We have been greatly puzzled by our series of breeding birds from Oregon and Washington. When all young and fall birds are eliminated, the series shows much greater differences than do the forms of Yellow Warbler ascribed to Oregon. Our eastern Oregon birds are larger, the females are much paler, particularly on the under parts, and some have only a faint trace of yellow, and the males are much paler, with a conspicuously greater amount of white on the forehead. We feel that the two forms are subspecifically distinguishable and are therefore proposing the revival of Oberholser's *G. t. arizela* for the race in Oregon and Washington west of the Cascades. We hesitate to take such a step when a race has once been eliminated, but we believe that this form is a much more easily recognized variation than many still included in the list.

With this restoration in mind, the present race, the Western Yellow-throat, is limited to eastern Oregon, where it is a common bird under suitable ecological conditions. It is most abundant in the great tule marshes of Klamath, Lake, and Harney Counties and is found there in company with the energetic and noisy Western Marsh Wren. It arrives in April (earliest date, April 9, Lake County) and remains until September (latest date, September 15, Klamath County). It is most conspicuous in May and June when its loud, clear song, which has been interpreted *wreech-ity*, *wreech-ity*, *wreech-ity*, *wreech-ity*, is one of the most familiar bird notes. It was first recorded by Merrill (1888) from Fort Klamath as a common summer resident and since that time has been frequently listed from various sections of the State.

Nothing has been written about its nesting habits in this State, its secretive ways making intensive search necessary to learn anything about its domestic affairs, and we have record of only one nest, containing three fresh eggs, which Jewett found at Harriman Lodge, Klamath County, May 28, 1916.

Pacific Yellow-throat:
Geothlypis trichas arizela Oberholser

Description.—"Similar to *occidentalis*, but smaller, and with smaller bill, shorter wing and tail, duller coloration, and white band on head narrower; yellow of under parts less orange. *Male:* length (skins) 4.49–4.92, wing 2.07–2.28, tail 1.94–2.24, bill .39–.43. *Female:* length (skins) 4.25–4.72, wing 2.00–2.08, tail 1.89–1.97, bill .39." (Bailey) *Nest and eggs:* Similar to *occidentalis* (Plate 87, *A*).

Distribution.—*General:* Pacific coast, Washington, and Oregon west of Cascades. *In Oregon:* Breeding form west of Cascades.

As indicated in our discussion of the Western Yellow-throat, we feel that there is a much greater and more constant difference between our eastern and western Oregon yellow-throats than there is between many recognized subspecies. We see little point in the endless multiplication of named forms based on slight average differences of size or color, but if such distinctions are to be recognized at all, the breeding race of yellow-throats west of the Cascades in Oregon and Washington is deserving of a name, and we are therefore using the name, "Pacific Yellow-throat," (Plate 87, *B*) to designate it. The form probably extends to British Columbia, but material from that source is not available to us at this time.

Johnson (1880) first recorded the yellow-throat from the territory assigned to this race. Anthony (1886) listed it from Washington County, and Woodcock (1902) gave numerous stations in western Oregon. It is a regular summer resident and breeding species, not only in the Willamette Valley but along the coastal marshes as well. It arrives in April (earliest date, March 22, Jackson County) and remains until September (latest date, October 6, Multnomah County). Currier (ms.) took eggs near

Plate 87, *A*. Nest and eggs of Pacific Yellow-throat. (Photo by Ira N. Gabrielson.)

Plate 87, *B*. Male Pacific Yellow-throat feeding young. (Photo by Wm. L. Finley and H. T. Bohlman.)

St. Johns, a suburb of Portland, on May 9, 1914; June 23, 1927; and June 19, 1927. Each nest contained four eggs. Braly took sets on May 6 and 26, 1931, near Portland.

Long-tailed Chat:
Icteria virens longicauda Lawrence

Description.—"Bill curved, stout, higher than broad at nostrils, without notch or bristles; wings much rounded; tail long, feet stout; outside of tarsus almost without scales; tarsus decidedly longer than middle toe with claw, its scutella indistinct or obsolete on outer side. *Adults:* throat and breast vivid yellow; belly white; upper parts olive gray; superciliary, orbital ring, and malar stripe, white; lores, and line under eye black. *Young:* upper parts olive; lores gray instead of black; throat whitish, chest, sides, and flanks grayish; rest of under parts white. *Male:* length (skins) 6.26–7.28, wing 2.95–3.31, tail 3.01–3.39, bill .53–.59. *Female:* length (skins) 6.38–6.97, wing 2.87–3.15, tail 2.83–3.23, bill .53–.59." (Bailey) *Nest:* In bushes, made of grass, leaves, and shredded bark and lined with grass. *Eggs:* 3 to 5, white, spotted with gray and brown.

Distribution.—*General:* Breeds in low valleys from southern British Columbia, Montana, and North Dakota south to Lower California and Mexico. Winters in Mexico. *In Oregon:* Common summer resident and breeding species in tangled thickets of stream bottoms throughout State, except coastal counties.

The weird notes of this clown of the thickets are a familiar sound on May mornings throughout Oregon. If you would become acquainted with this maker of cat calls, whistles, and screeches, take an early May morning pilgrimage to the thickest blackberry or willow tangle in the vicinity and after finding a comfortable seat wait for the birds to forget that an intruder is there. If a Long-tailed Chat is present, he will soon make himself known, vocally at least. The scolding and calling will come at irregular intervals from the thicket where the bird is hopping about in the tangle. Eventually he will work upward to a visible perch and perchance take wing in the queer courting flight for which he is famous. Upward he will go in narrow circles, flying with an odd, jerky wing motion until at a height of perhaps a hundred feet he will pitch back toward the sheltering thicket in an amazing series of aerial gyrations. All through his eerie show the performer sings his own liquid song or gives vent to some of the wide assortment of other calls at his command.

Although this chat is conspicuous, Oregon nesting records are rather scarce. Bendire (1877) not only is to be credited with the first published record for the State, but he also found the first nest near Camp Harney, June 5, 1876. Jewett found two nests, one at Portland, June 17, 1908, that contained three eggs and was recorded in our *Birds of the Portland Area* (Jewett and Gabrielson 1929), and one at Gold Hill, May 22, 1916 (Gabrielson 1931). In the manuscript records of the Biological Survey we found mention of a nest found at Homestead, Baker County, June 14,

1916, with a grass snake in possession, its jaws filled with eggs (Becker). Another note recorded a nest containing four eggs at Paradise, Wallowa County, June 10, 1919 (Cantwell). Braly (ms.) took nests at Portland, May 26, 1931, and Tygh Valley, Wasco County, May 30, 1931. Patterson (ms.) in the years he has worked in the Klamath country reports six nests between May 6 and 28. Records of fledgling young being fed by the parents are quite common in our own notes and also occur in the manuscript notes of other Biological Survey workers.

In addition to these breeding records, various writers since Bendire's time have published notes on the occurrence of the bird for all sections of the State with the exception of the coastal counties. It has yet to be detected on the seaward slope of the Coast Ranges or in the valleys beyond, although it is a common species in Jackson and Josephine Counties in the upper valley of the Rogue, along the Umpqua in the vicinity of Roseburg, and throughout the Willamette Valley. It arrives in May and remains until late August (earliest date, May 2; latest, September 9, both Multnomah County).

Wilson's Warbler:
Wilsonia pusilla pusilla (Wilson)

Description.—"Similar to *pileolata*, but not so bright; wings and tail shorter, bill broader and darker colored. *Male:* length (skins) 4.05–4.45, wing 2.09–2.64, tail 1.83–1.97, bill .28–.35. *Female:* length (skins) 4.10–4.45, wing 2.05–2.17, tail 1.81–1.95, bill .31–.35." (Bailey) *Nest:* On ground, in damp woods, made of grass and lined with finer vegetation and hair. *Eggs:* 4 or 5, usually 4, white or creamy white, speckled with reddish or purple.

Distribution.—*General:* Breeds from limit of trees in northern Canada south to northern United States. Winters in Central America. *In Oregon:* Rare straggler known from only one record.

A single specimen (Jewett Coll. No. 685) collected December 11, 1908, on Government Island, is the only record of Wilson's Warbler for the State. This bird was one that evidently lost its way on the southward migration that normally should have taken it east of the Rockies.

Northern Pileolated Warbler:
Wilsonia pusilla pileolata (Pallas)

Description.—"*Adult male:* Crown glossy blue black; back bright yellowish olive green; under parts vivid yellow; forehead often orange yellow. *Adult female:* similar, but crown patch often wanting. *Young:* like adult male, but black of crown nearly obscured by olive wash. *Male:* length (skins) 4.13–4.49, wing 2.17–2.36, tail 1.85–2.05, bill .28–.35. *Female:* length (skins) 4.13–4.57, wing 2.15–2.24, tail 1.87–1.97, bill .30–.35." (Bailey) *Nest:* Of leaves, weed stems, and grasses, on or near the ground. *Eggs:* 2 to 4, creamy white, spotted with brown and lilac, either over the entire egg or about the large end.

Distribution.—*General:* Breeds from northern Alaska south through eastern Oregon and California to mountainous New Mexico and Texas. Winters in Mexico and Central America. *In Oregon:* Fairly common summer resident and breeding species in mountains east of Cascades.

The Northern Pileolated Warbler as now classified was first detected at Fort Klamath (Mearns 1879). Merrill (1888) also listed the bird as common at Fort Klamath, Miller (1904) recorded it from Wheeler County, and Walker (1917b) from Haycreek, now in Jefferson County. The records of Nuttall (1840), Cooke (1891b), Peck (1896), and Finley (1902) from western Oregon are referable to the form now known as the Golden Pileolated Warbler. In addition to these published records, we have noted or taken the species in Klamath, Lake, Harney, Malheur, Baker, Wallowa, Umatilla, Jefferson, Deschutes, and Wasco Counties. It arrives in May (earliest date, April 29, Wallowa County) and remains until September (latest date, September 21, Lake County). It undoubtedly occurs in Union and Grant Counties, although we have no records for either, and it most certainly will be detected at least as a migrant in the remaining counties of eastern Oregon.

We have no actual nesting records, although we have collected the species throughout the breeding season, and our specimens include juveniles that certainly had not traveled far from their homes. So far as our own notes or published records go, however, the first actual Oregon nest remains to be discovered.

Golden Pileolated Warbler:
Wilsonia pusilla chryseola Ridgway

Description.—Like the previous subspecies but smaller and much brighter colored. *Size:* Length (skins) 4.12–4.55, wing 2.12–2.34, tail 1.83–2.05, bill .28–.35. *Nest and eggs:* Same as for the previous subspecies.

Distribution.—*General:* Breeds along Pacific slope from British Columbia to southern California. Winters in Mexico and Central America. *In Oregon:* Common summer resident and breeding species west of Cascades.

The Golden Pileolated Warbler is the western Oregon counterpart of the Northern Pileolated Warbler—differentiated by the deeper and more golden yellow color. It is a bird of the brushlands, being most abundant along the coast, where it is one of the common summer birds. It arrives in May (earliest date, May 5, Coos County) and remains until late August (latest date, September 10, Tillamook County). Nuttall (1840) recorded fledged young, May 12, 1835, on the Columbia River, surely a mistake, as it is one of the latest warblers to arrive. He also listed eggs taken along the Willamette River on May 16. As stated previously,

Cooke's (1891b) and Peck's (1896) records of the Pileolated Warbler from Salem and Finley's (1902) note as to its breeding in the coastal mountains of Oregon all properly belong in this subspecies. In addition to these records, numerous other published notes from western Oregon refer to this form.

We have no breeding records, but Currier (ms.) has kindly supplied us with the following notes on a nest taken by him at Linnton, Multnomah County, June 17, 1917:

Hillside nest one foot above the ground in a crotch of fallen dead bush well hidden by sword ferns. Eggs four, well advanced in incubation. Female on nest when found.

American Redstart:
Setophaga ruticilla (Linnaeus)

Description.—"*Adult male:* Black with bluish gloss, except for white belly and under tail coverts, and salmon or orange patches on sides of breast, wings, and tail. *Adult female:* black of male replaced by grayish olive, and orange by yellow. *Immature male:* similar to female, but smaller, browner, and color patches deeper; after first winter plumage interspersed with black feathers. *Immature female:* like adult female, but gray more brownish, throat and chest tinged with brownish buff; yellow of breast less distinct, and that on wings partly or wholly concealed. *Young, first plumage:* upper parts grayish brown; under parts grayish white, pale gray on chest; breast without yellow; wings and tail like older birds, but with two whitish or yellowish bands. *Male:* length (skins) 4.61–5.00, wing 2.40–2.64, tail 2.05–2.28, bill .28–.35. *Female:* length (skins) 4.41–4.76, wing 2.28–2.60, tail 1.93–2.28, bill .31–.35." (Bailey) *Nest:* In trees, sometimes high up, a compact cup of plant fibers, bark, and down. *Eggs:* 3 to 5, white, greenish, or grayish, spotted around the larger end with brown and lilac.

Distribution.—*General:* Breeds from British Columbia, Mackenzie, Quebec, and Newfoundland south to Washington, Utah, Colorado, Oklahoma, Arkansas, and North Carolina. Winters in West Indies and in Central and South America. *In Oregon:* Casual migrant and perhaps rare summer resident of Blue Mountain district.

So far as we know, the American Redstart is of only casual occurrence in Oregon. Emerson (1901) recorded a specimen in the University of California Collection taken July 1, 1899, at John Day, which was the first published record for the State. Miller (1904) listed the same specimen. Peck (1911a) reported the species from Willow Creek in northern Malheur County, June 30 and July 14, 1910, and Jewett (1916a) took two specimens at McEwen, Baker County, August 19 and 20, 1915. The last specimen that we have seen from the State is one taken by Jewett at Minam, Wallowa County, July 12, 1916. It will be noted that these locality records are well distributed throughout the Blue Mountain area. Furthermore, the fact that all of them are July and August dates would indicate that the bird breeds at least occasionally in that part of the State, although we have no definite information regarding it.

Weaver Finches: *Family Ploceidae*

English Sparrow:
Passer domesticus domesticus (Linnaeus)

Description.—"Form stout and stocky; bill very stout, curved, side outlines bulging to near the end; wing pointed; tail shorter than wings, nearly even; feet small. *Adult male:* lores, throat, and chest patch black; rest of under parts grayish; top of head and ear coverts grayish, with bright chestnut patches between eye and nape; wing with chestnut patch and two white bands; rest of upper parts brown, back streaked with black; upper parts dull brown; under parts dull gray. *Adult female:* crown and hind neck grayish brown or olive; entire under parts brownish white or gray; back browner, less rufescent than in male. *Length:* 5.50–6.25, wing about 2.85–3.00, tail 2.35–2.50." (Bailey) *Nest:* An untidy mass of stray feathers, grass, wool, or any other available material, either about buildings or in trees. *Eggs:* 4 to 7, white, thickly spotted with brown and purple.

Distribution.—*General:* Introduced into America in 1850 at Brooklyn and later, at many other places. Now established throughout country and southern Canada. *In Oregon:* Permanent resident in every part.

This ubiquitous little foreigner, the English Sparrow, introduced by extended and painful efforts into Oregon and other sections of the United States, is now well established and thoroughly at home throughout Oregon. No hamlet or ranch is too remote for the English Sparrows to discover, and they make themselves at home with all the assurance of the domestic stock. In the grain-raising sections of the State they are sometimes seen in great swarms flying into the grain to feed and returning to the weedy fence rows for shelter when alarmed. Their adaptability, which accounts for their success in an alien and hostile land, is best illustrated by their newly acquired habit of picking insects from the radiators of autos parked just after having been driven at high speeds. We have frequently found sparrows busily at work on the radiators of our cars by the time we reached the curb.

Meadowlarks, Blackbirds, and Troupials: *Family Icteridae*

Bobolink:
Dolichonyx oryzivorus (Linnaeus)

Description.—"Bill conic-acute, cutting edges bent in; tail shorter than wing, with stiffened acute feathers; wings long and pointed; feet stout, tarsus shorter than middle toe and claw; claws all very large. *Adult male in spring:* under parts wholly black, upper parts black, with cream or buffy brown patch on hind neck, light streaking on wing and fore parts of back, grayish scapulars, and white hind back, rump, and upper tail coverts. *Adult female:* ground color yellowish brown, paler and plain on under parts except for blackish streaks on flanks; heavily streaked on upper parts; crown with buffy brown median stripe. *Adult male in fall and winter:* similar to adult female, but streaking of upper parts blacker. *Young, first plumage:* like adult female but more buffy, with necklace of faint dusky spots, flank streaks obsolete. *Male:* length (skins) 6.30–7.40, wing 3.69–4.00, tail 2.47–2.70, bill .58–.69. *Female:* length (skins) 6.00–6.55, wing 3.35–3.53, tail 2.31–2.54, bill .57–.61." (Bailey) *Nest:* A slight depression in the ground, lined with dry grass. *Eggs:* 5 to 7, gray to reddish brown, irregularly spotted and blotched with browns and purples.

Distribution.—*General:* Breeds from southeastern British Columbia, central Alberta, Saskatchewan, Manitoba, Ontario, and Quebec, south to northeastern California, northern Nevada, Utah, Colorado, Missouri, and Ohio Valley. Winters in South America. *In Oregon:* Summer resident and breeder in valleys about base of Blue Mountains. Records from Wallowa, Union, Baker, Malheur, Harney, Lake, Crook, and Grant Counties.

The Bobolink seems to be a comparatively new arrival in this State, as so good an observer as Bendire failed to find it in the Harney Valley during his stay, though it is now a regular resident of that area. The first definite published record for Oregon was from Ironside, in northern Malheur County (Peck 1911a), although Woodcock (1902) listed a questionable record from Scio by Prill. As no specimen was taken, the record has never been accepted as a definite first record for the State. Finley and Bohlman collected specimens in Harney Valley in 1908 but failed to record them. Anthony (1912) listed the species from Malheur, and Willett (1919) included it in his list of breeding birds for the vicinity of Malheur Lake. Prill (1922a) found it in Warner Valley, and Shaw (1923) listed it from several localities.

The Bobolink arrives in May (earliest date, May 21, Lake County) and remains until September (latest date, September 18, Harney County). Our notes show that in the past few years the colonies in Wallowa and Harney Valleys are the largest in the State and that the bird is present in smaller numbers in Baker, northern Malheur, Grant, Lake, Union, and Crook Counties. In the latter case, the birds noted east of Prineville in July 1919 (Gabrielson) might have been wandering individuals from either the John Day or Harney Valleys. So far as we can tell, the species has made little advance in recent years. Although the farm lands of the Willamette Valley would seem ideal for it, there has been no indication that it has spread in that direction. Its conspicuous black and white markings and rollicking song make it easy to detect, and it does not seem probable that it would long be present in a territory without some bird lover noticing it. Watch should be kept for it in western Oregon, to which it may possibly spread at some future date.

Western Meadowlark:
Sturnella neglecta Audubon

Description.—"*Adult male in breeding plumage:* Crown with median buffy stripe; lores yellow; superciliary buffy; rest of upper parts grayish brown, with buffy white streaks and black streaks and bars; middle of back heavily marked with black, and tertials, rump, and tail heavily barred; outer tail feathers mainly white; under parts bright yellow, *yellow of throat spreading over cheeks;* crescent on breast and spotting on sides black. *Adult female in breeding plumage:* similar, but paler, and yellow restricted. *Adults in winter plumage:* upper parts lighter, from unworn light tips and edgings of feathers; black and yellow of under parts veiled by light edgings. *Male:* length (skins) 8.31–10.14, wing 4.66–5.08, tail 2.69–3.25, bill 1.17–1.44. *Female:* length (skins) 7.74–9.00, wing 4.12–4.59, tail 2.39–2.84, bill 1.09–1.28." (Bailey) *Nest:* In a tuft of grass, usually more or less arched over with dried grasses (Plate 88, *A*). *Eggs:* 3 to 7, white, spotted with brown and purple.

Distribution.—*General:* Breeds from British Columbia, Alberta, and Manitoba south to Lower California, Mexico, and Texas. Winters throughout its breeding range and southward into Mexico. *In Oregon:* Permanent resident throughout State except on highest mountains.

The Western Meadowlark was chosen by vote of the school children as Oregon's State bird, and the choice was ratified by the Legislature. Suckley (Cooper and Suckley 1860) reported it as abundant about The Dalles, and nearly every person who has written on Oregon birds since has had something to say about this species that is probably the most widely distributed and among the most abundant of the permanent resident birds. It is equally at home in the arid sage plateaus of southeastern Oregon and the tide flats of the humid coast district. It appears in our field notes from every county in the State, and its cheery song is known to our school children everywhere, facts that probably account for its choice as State bird.

During the winter the birds withdraw somewhat from the State and those remaining gather into small wintering bands that seek the sheltered valleys during the worst weather. In late February or early March, they increase in numbers as the migrants move north. By early April, mating is completed and eggs may be found. We have notes on egg dates varying from April 3 to June 16, although the height of the nesting season is reached in early May.

Adult ♂ 4/25/74 Lewiston

Yellow-headed Blackbird:
Xanthocephalus xanthocephalus (Bonaparte)

Description.—"Bill decidedly shorter than head, its depth through base less than half the length of the exposed culmen; culmen straight, flattened; sexes different in size; wing long and pointed; tarsus nearly one fourth as long as wing; claws large, lateral ones reaching beyond base of middle one. *Adult male in summer:* black except for yellow or orange of head, throat, and chest, and white patch on wings. *Adult male in winter:* similar, but yellow of top of head obscured by brownish tips to feathers. *Adult female:* brownish, throat and chest dull yellowish, breast mixed with white. *Young male in first winter:* similar to female, but larger and deeper colored. *Male:* length (skins) 8.60–10.10, wing 5.32–5.73, tail 3.66–4.27, bill .83–.99. *Female:* length (skins) 7.50–8.30, wing 4.33–4.64, tail 3.10–3.45, bill .77–.83."

(Bailey) *Nest:* Neatly woven basket of marsh grass, tules, and similar vegetation, fastened to tule stems over the water. *Eggs:* 3 to 5, grayish to greenish white, heavily and evenly spotted and blotched with brown.

DISTRIBUTION.—*General:* Breeds from British Columbia, southern Mackenzie, central Manitoba, and northern Minnesota south to Mexico and east to Wisconsin and Indiana. Winters south into Mexico. *In Oregon:* Common breeding species of Lake district of south-central Oregon (Klamath, Lake, and Harney Counties), less abundant in Blue Mountain area, and only irregular visitor west of Cascades.

THE EARLIEST MENTION of the Yellow-headed Blackbird (Plate 88, *B*) in Oregon was Newberry's (1857) report of it as an abundant breeding species about Klamath Lake; and all of the other earlier ornithologists who worked that territory, including Bendire (1877), Mearns (1879), and Merrill (1888), had something to say about it. It is most at home in the tule beds of the alkaline lakes of Klamath, Lake, and Harney Counties, where it is an abundant breeding species, conspicuous both because of its color and its queer love song. It arrives there in April and remains normally until late September (earliest date, April 1; latest, November 20, both Harney County). It has been found less commonly in Malheur (2 specimens in Biological Survey Collection from Ontario by Kalmbach), Union, Baker, Crook, Umatilla, and Deschutes Counties in eastern Oregon. In all of these counties our records are April, May, and June dates, many of which are probably for migrating birds, although Braly took four sets of eggs at Davis Lake in Deschutes County, June 7, 1931.

Prill (1895a) reported this blackbird as a rare winter bird at Sweet Home. In this or any other western Oregon locality, it cannot be regarded as a winter resident but only as a straggler. We have noted several individuals near Portland and took specimens while together on May 18, 1928. In addition to these, there are several sight records by others from the Columbia bottoms in the same general territory, and Overton Dowell, Jr., took an adult male in Curry County on June 24.

The nests are invariably built over the water, usually a foot or two above the surface. They are neatly woven baskets of available heavy grass, tules, or rushes and contain three to five eggs each. Egg dates for numerous nests vary in our notes from May 16 to June 17, although earlier dates could probably be noted by someone who lived on the ground.

Before the young birds are able to fly, many of them leave the nests to clamber about in the tules until their wings become strong enough to carry them. During this period they are fair game for hawks, turtles, and the larger fish that get them from perches close to the water. Numbers of them are also drowned when they fall into the water in places from which they are unable to clamber back onto the tules.

After the breeding season the Yellow-heads join the rapidly growing mixed flocks of blackbirds that roam the country in the vicinity of the nesting marshes and sometimes cause heavy losses to the ripening grain.

Plate 88, A. Young Western Meadowlarks in nest. (Photo by Wm. L. Finley and H. T. Bohlman.)

Plate 88, *B*. Yellow-headed Blackbird. (Photo by Wm. L. Finley and H. T. Bohlman.)

These flocks are made of Yellow-heads, Red-wings, Brewer's Blackbirds, and some Nevada Cowbirds, but the first two are generally the most abundant. Wherever grasshoppers appear, the blackbird swarms descend upon them and devour great numbers, often without making any noticeable inroad into the insect hordes.

Nevada Red-wing:
Agelaius phoeniceus nevadensis Grinnell

DESCRIPTION.—"*Adult male in breeding plumage:* Black except for red and buffy brown or whitish shoulder patches. *Adult male in winter:* like summer male, but buff of wing coverts deeper and scapulars and interscapulars edged with rusty. *Adult female in breeding plumage:* plumage of harsh texture compared with the silky plumage of the male: streaked, top of head dark brown, with buffy median crown stripe and superciliary; nape and fore part of back dark brown, lightly marked with buffy; shoulders faintly tinged with red; under parts whitish, heavily streaked with dark brown; throat variably tinged with creamy, buff, or pinkish. *Adult female in winter:* lighter markings of upper parts more conspicuous, under parts tinged with buffy. *Immature male:* epaulettes flecked with black and varying from orange to red; black of plumage obscured by heavy rusty and buffy edgings above, and light ashy or brownish tips below. *Young:* like adult female, but throat, superciliary, and malar stripes yellowish; ground color of under parts pale buffy or yellowish with narrow dusky streaks." (Bailey) *Size:* Length (skins) 5.75–8.30, wing 3.90–5.04, tail 2.70–3.86, bill .75–.96. *Nest:* In small trees, bushes, attached to stems of rushes and tules, or sometimes on the ground. Well-woven basket of dried grasses and similar vegetation. *Eggs:* 3 to 5, pale bluish, scrawled and blotched with black, brown, and purple.

DISTRIBUTION.—*General:* Breeds from British Columbia and northern Idaho south through California (east of the Sierras) and Nevada to northern Arizona, New Mexico, and Texas. Winters south to Mexico. *In Oregon:* Abundant summer resident east of Cascades. Less common winter resident. (See Figure 17.)

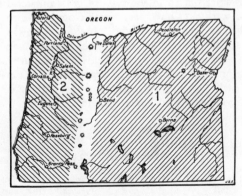

FIGURE 17.—Distribution of two forms of red-wings in Oregon: 1, Nevada Red-wing (*Agelaius phoeniceus nevadensis*); 2, Northwestern Red-wing. (*A p. caurinus*).

NEVADA RED-WINGS winter along the rivers and smaller streams of eastern Oregon in small flocks but become much more abundant in late February as the migrants return. They migrate in sex flocks. The old males arrive first, their glistening black uniforms and scarlet epaulettes standing out in startling contrast to the drab landscape. Later the females and younger birds return, and the flocks gradually break up as each male selects a territory and commences to sing his love song and to indulge in aerial evolutions and strutting display of his brilliant wing patches. One or more females may eventually fall for his charms and consent to build a nest and raise a family in the particular patch of swamp that he claims. Some especially favored gallant may have several wives, for polygamy is practiced to some extent by these interesting birds.

Three counties, Klamath, Lake, and Harney, contain most of the breeding population of Red-wings in eastern Oregon, where the birds are present in the large swamps in uncounted thousands, and where in the fall the gathering swarms look like black clouds on the horizon. In the remainder of eastern Oregon, the Red-wings are more common than the Yellow-heads. Every little swamp provides a nesting place for one or more pairs, and many are found along the willow-grown stream beds. Bendire (Brewer 1875) first recorded this species from Camp Harney. Mearns (1879) and Merrill (1888) listed it from Fort Klamath. Since that time little has been written about the bird in that particular area, although every observer who has made a general list has included it.

The nests are built in a variety of places, but the swamps seem to be the first love of the Red-wing. There the nests, shallower and more heavily walled than those of the Yellow-head, are woven about the upright stems of the tules. Along streams the birds frequently build in the willows or bushes that overhang or are close to the water, and occasionally the nests are placed in the tufts of grass on small hummocks in the bogs. Nests with eggs have been found from May 2 to June 20, with the height of the egg-laying season about June 1. Following the breeding season the birds gather into huge mixed flocks that through July, August, and September swarm over the grain fields and pasture lands adjacent to the breeding grounds. These flocks gradually decrease in size in late September and early October, as the birds drift southward, until usually only small wintering groups of males remain.

Northwestern Red-wing:
Agelaius phoeniceus caurinus Ridgway

DESCRIPTION.—Very similar to *A. p. nevadensis*. "*Male:* length (skins) 8.60–9.10, wing 4.57–5.10, tail 3.39–3.83, bill .90–1.01. *Female:* length (skins) 6.80–7.80, wing 3.85–4.22, tail 2.80–3.27, bill .77–.86." (Bailey) *Nest and eggs:* Same as for Nevada Red-wing.

DISTRIBUTION.—*General:* Breeds on northwest coast from British Columbia to Mendocino County, California. *In Oregon:* Common permanent resident of counties west of Cascades. (See Figure 17.)

THERE ARE no great breeding colonies of the Northwestern Red-wing comparable to those great aggregations of Nevada Red-wings in the south-central Oregon swamps. It lives in small colonies along the willow-bordered streams or in the much less extensive swamp areas of the stream bottoms and tide flats. In habits and behavior, it is quite similar to other Red-wings, except that the migrating flocks and summer congregations are much smaller than those east of the mountains. Johnson (1880), who listed it from the Willamette Valley (Salem and Forest Grove) as "very abundant in summer, breeding with the usual habits of the species," seems to have been the first to record it from western Oregon, though it is odd that the earlier explorers missed so conspicuous a bird. He was closely followed by Anthony (1886), who reported it as a common breeder at Wapato Lake, and later by many others who found it a widely distributed bird in that part of the State, where it is found in every county. We have egg dates between May 3 and June 6, mostly around Portland, although a few are from Devils Lake in Lincoln County.

Tricolored Red-wing:
Agelaius tricolor (Audubon)

DESCRIPTION.—"*Adult male:* Glossy blue black, plumage with silky luster; *epaulettes dark red, bordered with white*, more or less tinged with buff; *in winter*, plumage softer, more glossy, and white on epaulettes more or less tinged with buff. *Adult female:* texture of plumage like that of male; upper parts dusky with greenish or bronzy luster; crown narrowly streaked; scapulars and interscapulars with grayish edgings; wings with grayish and whitish bands; head with superciliary and malar streaks; throat and chest streaked; rest of under parts dusky with paler edgings to feathers. *Immature female, first winter:* like adult female, but browner. *Young:* like female, but browner, and under parts narrowly streaked; wings with two bands. *Male:* length (skins) 8.00–9.05, wing 4.63–4.87, tail 3.32–3.75, bill .87–.95. *Female:* length (skins) 7.10–7.85, wing 4.11–4.32, tail 2.92–3.16, bill .78–.83." (Bailey) *Nest and eggs:* Similar to those of Nevada Red-wing.

DISTRIBUTION.—*General:* Breeds from Klamath Lake south through California to Lower California. *In Oregon:* Found only at Klamath Lake.

THE TRICOLORED RED-WING has been reported from Oregon many times, beginning with Newberry (1857). Bendire failed to find it and said it must be rare in this territory, which he felt must be the northernmost point reached by the species. Anthony (1886) called it an abundant breeding species in Washington County. Merrill (1888) reported seeing a few among the commoner Red-wings. Woodcock (1902) listed it from Klamath and Portland. Peck (1911a) recorded it from northern Malheur County. These records were all unsupported by specimens. Neff (1933), however, actually took specimens near Klamath Falls between June 14 and 19, 1933, when he found two small colonies about Agency Lake and Upper Klamath Lake. There has been no confirmation of the presence of this bird elsewhere in Oregon, and we feel that the records from Portland and vicinity should not be accepted. The species is naturally an inhabitant of the great tule swamps, and conditions in western Oregon are not particularly to its liking.

Bullock's Oriole:
Icterus bullocki (Swainson)

Description.—"*Adult male in summer:* Under parts, sides of head and neck, and superciliary orange; narrow throat patch, crown, back of neck, back, and stripe through eye, black; wings with conspicuous white patch and edgings; tail with middle feathers black, changing to almost pure yellow on outer feathers. *Adult male in winter:* like summer male, but scapulars and interscapulars edged with gray, feathers of rump and upper tail coverts tipped with gray, of under parts edged with whitish. *Adult female:* under parts lemon yellow, fading to gray on belly; throat usually with more or less of black; upper parts olivaceous, fading to brownish and sometimes streaked with black on back, but brightening to olive yellow or deeper on rump and tail; wings with white bands. *Immature male in second year:* similar to adult female, but lores and median line of throat black. *Young in first plumage:* similar to female, but colors duller, washed more or less with buffy, with no trace of black on the throat, and yellow sometimes almost wanting. *Male:* length (skins) 6.75–7.60, wing 3.82–4.03, tail 2.98–3.22, bill .65–.81. *Female:* length (skins) 6.60–7.50, wing 3.52–3.87, tail 2.73–3.12, bill .67–.78." (Bailey) *Nest:* A skillfully woven pendent basket, usually well out toward the end of a branch, made of dry grasses, horse hair, or shredded bark. *Eggs:* 3 to 6, dull white or buffy, more or less marked with scrawled lines of black, usually more heavily around the large end.

Distribution.—*General:* Breeds from southern British Columbia, Alberta, and Saskatchewan, to Lower California, Mexico, and Texas. Winters in Mexico. *In Oregon:* Regular summer resident and breeder throughout valleys of entire State, except on coast.

Bullock's Oriole is to the Western States what the Baltimore Oriole is to the Eastern States. Throughout the West it is a bird of those valleys and irrigated sections that lie in the Transition Zone. Baird (Baird, Cassin, and Lawrence 1858), who listed it from The Dalles, May 7, 1855, seems to have made the first published record for Oregon, and Bendire (1895) seems to have been the first to collect the eggs when he took a set, June 10, 1877.

We have found it to be common throughout eastern Oregon except in the higher mountains. It is primarily a bird of the river bottoms and farming districts, where its brilliant colors and liquid musical notes combine to make it a well-known and well-loved species, and there are few farmsteads with a scraggly growth of cottonwoods or willows about the house that do not have at least a pair of these brilliantly garbed songsters as summer residents. It is less abundant, but still common, in the Rogue and Umpqua Valleys but becomes scarcer in the Willamette and tributary valleys, where it is confined largely to the brushy growths along the watercourses, with only an occasional pair frequenting the farmyards. The only record we have for the coast is one from Coos County, June 19, 1920, when Gabrielson saw a bird at Bridge. It arrives in April (earliest date, April 13, Josephine County) and remains until August (latest date, September 10, Klamath County).

The hanging nests, skillfully attached to small twigs by their rims, are airy baskets made of dry grasses, horse hair, and other similar material and are among the most beautifully woven of birds' nests. The same pair will often return year after year to nest in the same grove or even the same tree, three to five or more nests in various stages of destruction being visible when the leaves have fallen. Eggs are laid from May 16 to June 15.

Brewer's Blackbird:
Euphagus cyanocephalus (Wagler)

Description.—"*Adult male in summer:* Glossy greenish black, head and neck purplish black. *Adult male in winter:* similar to summer male, but more highly glossed. *Adult female in summer:* head, neck, and under parts brownish gray, faintly glossed with violet on head and neck and with green on under parts; upper parts darker, wings and tail more glossed with bluish green. *Adult female in winter:* similar to summer female, but paler, more buffy gray anteriorly. *Immature male in first winter:* like adult male, but feathers largely tipped with grayish brown. *Young:* like winter females, but feathers with different texture and without gloss. *Male:* length (skins) 8.40–9.75, wing 4.73–5.27, tail 3.62–4.22, bill .83–.93. *Female:* length (skins) 7.80–8.70, wing 4.56–4.71, tail 3.43–3.65, bill .75–.82." (Bailey) *Nest:* In trees or bushes, made of sticks, dry grass, weed stalks, etc., more or less mixed with mud, and lined with rootlets and hair. *Eggs:* 4 to 6, gray or green heavily blotched, streaked and spotted with browns and lavender (Plate 89, *B*).

Distribution.—*General:* Breeds from central British Columbia, southern Alberta, and Manitoba south to Lower California, New Mexico, and Texas. Winters south to Central America. *In Oregon:* Common permanent resident throughout State.

Brewer's Blackbird is among the most common of Oregon birds and can be found in small numbers in all parts of the State. It is particularly fond of the open country and shows a marked preference for the pastures and fields of cultivated farms. It is tame and unsuspicious and shares with such species as the Meadowlark and Robin almost universal distribution as well as fondness for the vicinity of human habitations. It is a rare farmstead, indeed, that does not have its quota of these shining blackbirds with white or straw-colored eyes. We have records for every county, but the species is most abundant in the farming sections. The numbers increase markedly in late February and begin to decrease in

Plate 89, *A*. Female Red-wing shading young. (Photo by Ira N. Gabrielson.)

Plate 89, *B*. Nest and eggs of Brewer's Blackbird on ground. (Photo by Alex Walker.)

September. The bird is present through the winter in small flocks composed mostly of males.

Albinos or partial albinos are comparatively common. The latter often present most curious combinations of albinism and normal plumage, some of them being piebald white, others having the wings or the tail, sometimes both, partially or entirely white.

The nests, built either on the ground (Plate 89, *B*) or in low bushes, are bulky affairs resembling somewhat the nests of some of the jays. Our own and other notes, covering a great many nests, reveal completed sets of eggs from May 1 to June 24, though we have one record of a nest containing newly hatched young as late as July 17. Two broods are frequently raised, the first small flocks of fledglings appearing in most sections of the State during the last ten days of May. These flocks gradually unite to form larger flocks until the species becomes a conspicuous element in the great blackbird swarms. In western Oregon, it is frequently associated with the Red-winged Blackbirds, although mixed flocks remain comparatively small.

Nevada Cowbird:
Molothrus ater artemisiae Grinnell

Description.—"*Adult male:* Head, neck, and chest uniform brown; rest of plumage glossy black with green and purple reflections. *Adult female:* smaller than male, streaked brownish gray, darker above, lighter on throat. *Young male:* upper parts dull grayish brown or dark brown, feathers bordered with pale buffy or grayish brown and whitish; under parts broadly streaked with brownish, dull buffy, or whitish. *Young female:* like young male, but paler, under parts mainly dull buffy, streaked with grayish brown." (Bailey) *Size:* Length (skins) 7–8, wing 3.82–4.62, tail 2.56–3.13, bill .59–.77. *Nest:* None, eggs laid in nests of smaller birds. *Eggs:* White, the entire surface more or less covered with brownish specks and blotches.

Distribution.—*General:* Breeds from British Columbia, Mackenzie, and Manitoba south to southern Nevada, Utah, and Colorado and east to Dakotas and Minnesota. Winters south to Mexico and Texas. *In Oregon:* In eastern Oregon, widely distributed but not common summer resident, noted in most counties but most abundant in Harney and Malheur. In western Oregon, rare straggler reported from Lincoln and western Lane Counties.

The Nevada Cowbird cannot be considered a common species anywhere in Oregon. It is most often seen in the valleys of the big counties of the southeastern part of the State, where it frequents the open pasture and hay lands of the valley floor, mingling with the livestock and associating with Brewer's Blackbirds or Red-wings. In addition to Lake, Harney, Klamath, and Malheur Counties, from which we have numerous records, it has been noted from Wallowa, Union, Sherman, Wasco, Baker, Wheeler, and Umatilla Counties. It arrives about the first of May (earliest date,

April 21, Umatilla County) and remains until September (latest date, September 28, Klamath County). During May and June, it is usually seen in small groups of two or three birds, but later in the year it mingles with the summer and fall flocks of blackbirds. In these great swarms it is far outnumbered by the Yellow-heads, Red-wings, or Brewer's Blackbirds. It is difficult to distinguish it in these mixed flocks, and consequently fall records are comparatively scarce.

In western Oregon, it can be considered as only a straggler. Bretherton reported it from Newport, March 29, 1897, in manuscript, to the Biological Survey, and Overton Dowell, Jr., twice took specimens at Mercer Lake in western Lane County (August 18, 1925, and July 5, 1930).

Little has been written regarding this species as an Oregon bird. It seems to have been entirely overlooked by the earlier naturalists, or perhaps it has become more abundant in recent years. It was first recorded from the State by Woodcock (1902), who listed it from Baker County. Miller (1904) found it in Wheeler County. Jewett (1909c) included it in his list of Baker County birds. Peck (1911a) reported it in his notes on the northern part of Malheur County. Walker (1917b) found young at the mouth of the Deschutes River, July 28, 1914. Willett (1919) recorded it as a breeding species at Malheur Lake, and Dickey and Van Rossem (1922b) also noted it as a Harney County bird. The manuscript records of the Biological Survey contain many notes by Preble, Bailey, Streator, and others giving it as an uncommon, common, and at times even abundant, summer resident of the three southeastern counties, Malheur, Harney, and Lake. Our own notes also indicate that these three and Klamath are the Oregon counties favored by this bird.

Much has been written about the parasitic habits of the cowbird. The lady of the species has certainly solved the question of raising a family with the least possible trouble to herself by the simple expedient of laying the egg or eggs in the nest of some other small bird. As the cowbird's eggs hatch in 10 days, the shortest incubation period of any of our common passerine birds, the young birds usually have one or more day's start on the legitimate nestlings in competition for the food brought by the parent birds. Friedmann (1929) published a very exhaustive study of the cowbird group, in the course of which he listed 195 species of birds as victimized by *Molothrus ater* in its various forms. These victims naturally cover a wide diversity of groups, but sparrows, warblers, vireos, and blackbirds are those most commonly imposed upon. Little has been learned regarding the species parasitized in Oregon, owing to lack of resident ornithologists in the territory that the cowbird frequents. Jewett has records of three Nevada Savannah Sparrows' nests at Malheur Lake, each of which contained one cowbird's egg. These are our only definite notes.

Tanagers: *Family Thraupidae*

Western Tanager:
Piranga ludoviciana (Wilson)

Description.—"Upper mandible with a tooth-like projection on cutting edge. *Adult male in summer:* head and neck bright orange or red; rest of under parts bright yellow; upper parts black, with yellow rump and wing patches. *Adult female in summer:* upper parts olive green, back and scapulars grayish; wing bars dull yellowish; under parts pale grayish yellow, becoming sulphur yellow on under tail coverts; anterior part of head sometimes tinged with red. *Adult male in winter:* like summer female, but with head yellow or slightly tinged with red, more or less obscured on occiput and hind neck with olive green or dusky tips to feathers; feathers of back usually more or less distinctly edged with yellowish olive; tertials broadly tipped with white or pale yellow; tail feathers more or less tipped with white. *Young male in first autumn:* like adult female, but clearer yellow below and rump yellower. *Young female in first autumn:* like adult female, but duller; upper parts more brownish olive, under parts washed with brownish olive; wing bars narrower, and buffy. *Young male, first plumage:* upper parts olive green; wings blackish, with yellow wing bars; tail with outer webs of feathers edged with olive green; throat and chest grayish, chest tinged with yellow and streaked; chin and under tail coverts yellow; rest of under parts white. *Male:* length (skins) 6.20–6.95, wing 3.71–3.83, tail 2.64–2.98, bill .57–.62. *Female:* length (skins) 6.30–6.90, wing 3.54–3.88, tail 2.68–2.89, bill .53–.63." (Bailey) *Nest:* A somewhat flimsy structure of twigs and grass, sometimes lined with rootlets and hair and placed on a horizontal limb within 20 or 30 feet of the ground. *Eggs:* 3 or 4, bluish green, spotted with brown (Plate 90, *A*).

Distribution.—*General:* Breeds from northern British Columbia, Mackenzie, and southwestern South Dakota south to mountains of western Texas, southern Arizona, and Lower California. Winters in Mexico and Central America. *In Oregon:* Common summer resident and breeding species of forested sections.

Mearns (1879), who reported the Western Tanager at Fort Klamath, was the first to list it for Oregon, and nearly every subsequent writer has had some comment to make on this bird with its brilliant coat and distinctive voice that is a common summer resident and breeding species of the forested areas of the State. It arrives in late April (earliest date, April 11, Josephine County) and remains until September (latest date, September 28, Klamath County). It begins to build its flimsy nest (Plate 90, *A*) soon after its arrival in April and deposits the eggs in May or June. John Hooper Bowles (1902) gave June 4 and 28 as outside limits of egg dates, but Patterson (ms.) listed sets taken from May 13 to June 27, inclusive, in the southern Cascades.

In migration, the Western Tanagers excite a great deal of comment, particularly when unusual weather conditions force them to stop over. In late May 1920 we were together in Harney County when a sudden heavy snowfall forced down a multitude of migrating birds, many of which remained for several days. It was curious to walk through the sagebrush and see the topmost stalks flame-tipped with the brilliant

Plate 90, *A*. Nest and eggs of Western Tanager. (Photo by Alex Walker.)

Plate 90, *B*. Nest and eggs of Willow Goldfinch. Nest built of cotton placed on clothesline for birds. (Photo by Alex Walker.)

yellow, red, and black of these birds. Along with them were numbers of Hermit Warblers and Gray Flycatchers, certainly a combination odd enough to intrigue anyone's interest.

Grosbeaks, Finches, Sparrows, and Buntings: *Family Fringillidae*

Black-headed Grosbeak: *Hedymeles melanocephalus melanocephalus* (Swainson)

Description.—"*Adult male.—Under parts cinnamon brown brightening to lemon yellow on belly and under wing coverts;* upper parts mainly black, with cinnamon brown collar and rump, and sometimes brown stripes back of eye, through middle of crown, and on back; wings and tail black, wings with two white bars and white patch at base of quills, tail with white corners. *Winter male:* lighter brown on upper parts. *Adult female:* upper parts blackish brown, streaked with pale brownish or buffy; collar buffy white; wing bar white; under parts dull buffy, yellowish on belly, flanks, and sometimes breast; sides streaked; under wing coverts lemon yellow. *Winter female:* with buffy or brown stronger; lateral crown stripe streaked with black. *Young:* much like adult female, but under parts paler, without yellow on belly; back spotted; crown stripes uniform blackish brown. *Male:* length (skins) 6.60–7.70, wing 3.72–4.30, tail 2.79–3.38, bill .60–.80. *Female:* length (skins) 6.15–7.80, wing 3.72–4.12, tail 2.70–3.40, bill .61–.78." (Bailey) *Nest:* A flimsy platform of twigs and weeds, in trees or bushes (Plate 91, *A*). *Eggs:* 3 or 4, bluish white, heavily spotted with brown.

Distribution.—*General:* Breeds from southern British Columbia south through California to Lower California. Winters in Mexico. *In Oregon:* Common summer resident and breeding bird of valleys of entire State, least common along northern coast but present in small numbers.

This showy bird, the Black-headed Grosbeak (Plate 91), which replaces the Rose-breasted Grosbeak from the Great Plains westward, is widely distributed in Oregon. It was first reported from the State by Bendire (1877), who considered it rare at Camp Harney, as did Merrill (1888) at Fort Klamath. Since that time many writers have mentioned it for various parts of the State. It is perhaps most abundant or at least most conspicuous in the Rogue River Valley and in the shrub- and tree-filled canyons of eastern Oregon, although we have found it to be a common bird along the Columbia River. When out of song it is less easily detected in the tall trees and dense undergrowth. On the coast we have records for Curry, western Lane, and Tillamook Counties but regard it as much less common than inland. In addition to these records, Dr. A. K. Fisher (ms. notes) found it both at Astoria and Tillamook in 1897, and Overton Dowell, Jr., (ms., in Biological Survey records) reported it from Mercer in western Lane County. It arrives in May (earliest date, April 27,

Plate 91, *A*. Female Black-headed Grosbeak at nest with young. (Photo by Wm. L. Finley and H. T. Bohlman.)

Plate 91, *B*. Male Black-headed Grosbeak feeding young. (Photo by Wm. L. Finley and H. T. Bohlman.)

Yamhill County) and remains until late August (latest date, September 28, Multnomah County).

The rollicking song of the Black-headed Grosbeak is most frequently heard in the cottonwood and willow-filled stream bottoms. There the birds carry on their courtship, the showy males chasing each other or driving the duller-colored females through the trees and over the tops of the bushes, and there they build the flimsy structure that answers for a nest when the brief courtship period is ended. The eggs are laid in May and June, dates for those containing fresh eggs running from May 12 to July 4.

Lazuli Bunting:
Passerina amoena (Say)

Description.—"*Adult male: Upper parts bright turquoise blue*, changing to greenish blue, darker and duller on middle of back; wings with two white bars; *breast and sometimes sides brownish;* belly white. *Adult female:* upper parts grayish brown, tinged with blue on rump; back sometimes streaked; wing bars dingy; anterior lower parts pale buffy, deeper on chest, fading to white on belly and lower tail coverts. *Young:* like female, but without blue tinge on rump, and chest and sides usually streaked. *Male:* length (skins) 5.01–5.54, wing 2.78–3.01, tail 2.07–2.27, bill .39–.41. *Female:* length (skins) 4.91–5.38, wing 2.59–2.83, tail 2.00–2.31, bill .36–.41" (Bailey) *Nest:* A cup of plant fiber and grasses usually woven into a low bush or weed. *Eggs:* 3 or 4, bluish white.

Distribution.—*General:* Breeds from southern British Columbia, Alberta, and Saskatchewan south to Lower California and central western Texas. Winters in Mexico. *In Oregon:* Common summer resident and breeder in valleys of entire State, least abundant along coast.

Ever since Baird (Baird, Cassin, and Lawrence 1858) first listed it from Oregon, at The Dalles, the brightly colored little Lazuli Bunting has attracted the attention of ornithologists, who have recorded it many times. A study of our notes and those of the Biological Survey show it to be a common summer resident of all of eastern Oregon, except the highest mountains, and an equally abundant resident of the Rogue, Umpqua, and Willamette River Valleys west of the Cascades. Along the coast it is much less abundant, although it becomes noticeably more common along the Coquille River and the streams of Curry County southward.

It is a bright-colored little inhabitant of the rose thickets and willow growths—sitting on the topmost twig to utter its pleasing song. It usually arrives in May (earliest date, April 24, Douglas County) and remains until early September (latest date, September 9, Multnomah County), being present in numbers only from May to early September. After mid-June it becomes much less evident, due to the cessation of the song period and to the ranker growth of vegetation that serves as cover for its feeding operations.

The eggs are laid about mid-June, the dates for three nests located by

Jewett being June 17 and 20 (Multnomah County) and June 18 (Umatilla County). Patterson (ms.) gave dates of May 10 to June 8 for the southern Cascades.

Western Evening Grosbeak:
Hesperiphona vespertina brooksi Grinnell

Description.—"Bill large, swollen, depth at base greater than length of bird toe with claw, wing long, pointed, more than five times as long as tarsus; tail short, emarginate; feet small and weak; tarsus little if any longer than culmen. *Adult male:* forehead and superciliary bright yellow; crown, wings, and tail black, wings with large white patches; rest of upper parts olive, grading through yellowish green to yellow on rump; under parts greenish yellow, becoming lemon yellow on under wing and tail coverts. *Adult female:* prevailing color yellowish or yellowish brown; throat bordered by dusky; whitish patch on wings. *Young:* similar to female, but duller and markings less defined. *Male:* length (skins) 6.70–7.30, wing 4.18–4.59, tail 2.50–2.87, bill .78–.89, width of bill at base .49–.60. *Female:* length (skins) 6.50–7.30, wing 4.10–4.40, tail 2.40–2.78, bill .74–.83, width of bill at base .51–.57." (Bailey) *Nest:* A slight structure 15 to 50 feet from the ground, usually in a conifer, composed of sticks and roots, lined with finer roots. *Eggs:* 3 or 4, clear green, blotched with brown.

Distribution.—*General:* Breeds in mountains from central British Columbia and Montana, south to Sierras of California and mountains of Arizona and New Mexico. Winters in lowlands of its breeding area. *In Oregon:* Common permanent resident that spends summer in mountains and may appear in any section during winter. We have records for practically every county except those lying along Columbia between The Dalles and Umatilla.

The Western Evening Grosbeak, with its yellow and black plumage and heavy pale-green bill, is not an uncommon sight anywhere in Oregon. The first published record we can find for the State is in Audubon's Ornithological Biography (1838), in which he listed it as abundant at The Dalles, May 27, 1836. Since that time, many writers have referred to it in various sections of the State, so that from the standpoint of literature it is one of our better known birds. In the winter and spring, the birds are most abundant in the lowlands, although we have records in Multnomah County for every month. While in the towns and cities, the birds feed extensively on mountain-ash, box-elder and maple seeds, often re-
feed extensively on mountain-ash, boelder and maple seeds, often remaining in a given spot as long as the food supply holds out and then moving to another locality. In the summer, they are found in the mountains, their characteristic metallic cry identifying them, either far overhead or when feeding in the trees about the edges of mountain meadows.

In common with the crossbills and other species that feed largely on coniferous seeds, the grosbeaks can often be found about the salt logs, eating the salt with evident relish. When feeding, they are tame and unsuspicious, usually allowing a close approach if no sudden movements are made. This, together with the bizarre appearance of the huge bills, always occasions comment when a flock invades a district from which they have been absent for several years.

We have no records of eggs being taken in Oregon, but there is no question that the birds breed throughout the higher ranges, as they are present all summer long in goodly numbers. At Lick Creek Ranger Station on the Wallowa National Forest, Jewett shot a female, July 16, 1926, that contained one well-developed egg and two smaller ones. On July 25 in the same year, on the west base of Mount McLoughlin on the Rogue River National Forest, Gabrielson saw a pair coaxing a single youngster to fly.

California Purple Finch:
Carpodacus purpureus californicus Baird

Description.—"*Adult male:* Upper parts dark dull madder pink, wine purple on head and paler, more pinkish on rump; back streaked; under parts lighter rose pink and fading to *unstreaked white on middle of belly and under tail coverts;* sides and flanks usually strongly washed with brownish and broadly streaked with darker; tail much shorter than wing, *deeply emarginate*. *Adult female:* upper parts olivaceous, heavily streaked with brown; under parts whitish, narrowly streaked; side of head with white stripe crossing brown of ear coverts and side of throat. *Young:* similar to female, but colors duller and markings less distinct, edgings of wing feathers more buffy or tawny. *Male:* length (skins) 5.20–6.10, wing 3.03–3.20, tail 2.28–2.43, bill .42–.49. *Female:* length (skins) 5.20–5.84, wing 2.95–3.10, tail 2.10–2.33, bill .41–.49." (Bailey) *Nest:* A thin, flat platform of roots and grass, placed on a horizontal limb. *Eggs:* 2 to 4, greenish or bluish, finely speckled with black and brown on the large end.

Distribution.—*General:* Breeds from southern British Columbia south to Lower California west of Cascades and Sierra Nevadas. *In Oregon:* Permanent resident west of Cascades, less common to eastern edge of timber on Cascades.

The California Purple Finch is one of the most common and universally distributed finches in western Oregon, where it is a permanent resident. It is largely associated in the minds of most ornithologists with the coniferous timber, where it spends a great deal of time. During the midsummer, as well as in the coldest part of the winter, flocks are to be found silently hopping about in the willows and alders of the stream bottoms. The dull-red males are comparatively scarce, there usually being three or four females and streaked young to every full-plumaged male. These finches share fondness for salt with the crossbills, siskins, and grosbeaks, mixed companies of which often feed about the salt troughs.

Although abundant in western Oregon, the California Purple Finch is not found regularly east of the Cascades. Gabrielson took a number of specimens at Friend, Wasco County, in June 1919, along the eastern edge of the timber on the Cascades, and Henshaw (1880) reported a single October bird from The Dalles (the first record). Merrill (1888) took a specimen at Fort Klamath on March 1. Miller (1904) reported taking specimens in Wheeler County in 1899, the only record we have for the Blue Mountain area.

In the Cascades, the species is found mingled with Cassin's Purple Finch. In the higher parts of the range, Cassin's is the more abundant, but lower down the reverse is true.

We have few actual nesting records for the State, although newly fledged young are a common sight beginning in early June. On May 24, 1931, Braly took two sets of five eggs each near Klamath Falls, which is one of the localities on the eastern slope of the Cascades where the species is found. The nests were made of stems, roots, fine grass, and mosses, and were lined with wool.

Cassin's Purple Finch:
Carpodacus cassini Baird

Description.—"*Adult male:* Top of head with ***squarish patch*** of bright crimson; rump dull rose pink; back and scapulars dull pinkish brown, sharply streaked with dark brown; under parts pale pink fading to ***unstreaked*** white on belly; ***lower tail coverts usually conspicuously streaked with dusky;*** wing feathers edged with reddish; tail much shorter than wing, deeply emarginate. *Adult female:* whole body sharply streaked with dusky; ground color of upper parts olive gray; of under parts white. *Young:* similar to female, but streaks of lower parts narrower and wing edgings more ochraceous. *Male:* length (skins) 5.39–6.29, wing 3.52–3.80, tail 2.34–2.71, bill .47–.51. *Female:* length (skins) 5.55–6.05, wing 3.42–3.60, bill .49–.50." (Bailey) *Nest:* A thin platform of rootlets and grass, usually on a horizontal branch of a small conifer. *Eggs:* 2 to 4, white, finely speckled, particularly about the larger end, with black and brown.

Distribution.—*General:* Breeds in Boreal Zones from British Columbia, Montana, Wyoming, Lower California, Arizona, and New Mexico. Winters in adjacent lowlands. *In Oregon:* Permanent resident of higher parts of Blue, Steens, and Warner Mountains, Hart Mountain, Cascades, and Siskiyous at least as far as Josephine County, according to Peck (1917). Winters on lower slopes of these ranges.

Bendire (Brewer 1875) first found Cassin's Purple Finch in this State at Camp Harney. Mearns (1879) found it at Fort Klamath, and Henshaw (1880) at The Dalles. Our field notes and those of other members of the Biological Survey show it to be a regular permanent resident of all the principal ranges of Oregon, except the Coast Ranges. It is particularly abundant in the Cascades, the Blue Mountains, and the Warner Mountains, where it is a conspicuous element in the avifauna from the yellow pine up to timber line. It is found along the eastern slope of the Cascades in Wasco, Deschutes, and Klamath Counties, where it mingles with the California Purple Finch along the lower edge of the timber. The sharply defined and much brighter crown patch distinguishes the male bird from the California Purple Finch, and the darker brown streaks of the back and the lack of olive-green wash above distinguish the females and young from the latter form.

Although the streaked newly fledged young are a familiar sight, the only definite breeding records for the State that have come to our attention are a set of eggs taken May 24, 1924, by Patterson (ms.) and a set of three eggs taken May 25, 1931, near Bly, Klamath County, by Braly.

Common House Finch:
Carpodacus mexicanus frontalis (Say)

DESCRIPTION.—"*Adult male:* Forehead, superciliary, and rump rose pink, orange red, or scarlet; rest of upper parts brownish gray, sometimes washed with reddish; *back not distinctly streaked;* throat and breast reddish; *belly whitish, sharply and closely streaked with brown;* tail not decidedly shorter than wing, nearly even; pale grayish instead of reddish. *Adult female:* upper parts grayish brown, indistinctly streaked; under parts white, broadly streaked. *Young:* similar to female, but back more distinctly streaked, under parts more narrowly and less distinctly streaked; wing coverts tipped with buffy. *Male:* length (skins) 4.80–6.10, wing 2.99–3.33, tail 2.14–2.60, bill .38–.50. *Female:* length (skins) 5.00–5.63, wing 2.77–3.05, tail 2.00–2.40, bill .39–.43." (Bailey) *Nest:* A compact mass of dried grass stems and other plant material, placed in trees, bushes, or about houses. *Eggs:* 3 to 6, bluish white, sparingly speckled with black.

DISTRIBUTION.—*General:* From Oregon, Idaho, and Wyoming south through California and New Mexico into Lower California and Mexico. *In Oregon:* Common permanent resident of all valleys of eastern Oregon and of Jackson, Josephine, Curry, and Douglas Counties west of Cascades. Casual elsewhere in western Oregon.

THE ROLLICKING WARBLE of the Common House Finch, or California Linnet, is constantly heard about the towns and farmsteads of eastern Oregon and also in the valleys of the Rogue and Umpqua Rivers in the western part of the State. In the Umpqua Valley, the bird reaches its normal northern limit in western Oregon—although there is a skin of a straggler in the Jewett collection (female, No. 7177) taken March 21, 1932, at Forest Grove—but east of the Cascades it extends beyond the northern boundary of the State into Washington. This species is not found at all in the higher mountains in Oregon but is confined to the lower valleys. It chooses the same sort of homesites as does the English Sparrow and often competes successfully with that ubiquitous foreigner. Ranchers generally prefer the finches, for, although their nests are as dirty as those of the sparrows and their theft of chicken feed as great, at least they entertain with one of the finest songs given by any bird about the farmyard.

Bendire (1877) first listed this species from Oregon, where he found it at Camp Harney. Miller (1904) found it in Wheeler County in 1899, Peck (1911a) in Malheur County, and Walker (1917b) and Willett (1919) in central Oregon. Prill listed it from Warner Valley (1922a), but its presence on the west side of the Cascades was not recognized in print until Gabrielson (1931) listed it from Jackson and Josephine Counties.

Except during the breeding season, which extends from April to June (April 10 to June 5, according to Patterson ms.), the birds roam the country in small flocks, consisting of four or five streaked birds to one adult male. They frequently sit in long rows on fences or telephone wires and behave somewhat like goldfinches or siskins under the same conditions.

Alaska Pine Grosbeak: *Pinicola enucleator alascensis* Ridgway

Description.—"*Adult male:* Body mainly red, pinkish in winter, fading to gray on belly; *back with centers of feathers strikingly dark brownish;* wings with two white bars, whitish tips, and edgings; *bill short and turgid,* upper mandible only slightly longer than lower. *Adult female:* top and sides of head and upper tail coverts tawny yellow, *dark centers of feathers of back distinctly brownish. Male:* length (skins) 8.60–9.69, wing 4.41–5.00, tail 3.34–4.03, bill .55–.60. *Female:* length (skins) 7.69–8.70, wing 4.48–4.73, tail 3.46–3.84, bill .57–.61." (Bailey) *Nest:* A loosely built structure of twigs or rootlets, in coniferous trees. *Eggs:* Probably 3 or 4, greenish or bluish, spotted with brown and black.

Distribution.—*General:* Breeds in high mountains and Boreal zones from northwestern Alaska and northwestern Mackenzie to British Columbia. Winters south into the Northern States from Minnesota to Oregon and Washington. *In Oregon:* Irregular winter visitor to eastern Oregon.

The Alaska Pine Grosbeak is the commoner wintering form of Pine Grosbeak in eastern Oregon, 14 of the 17 available specimens belonging to this subspecies. These birds have been taken from Wallowa County south to Malheur, Harney, and Klamath Counties, and they may be expected to appear in any community during the winter months. They are present between November (earliest date, November 19, Crook County) and March (latest date, March 1, Wallowa County).

Bendire (1877) first recorded the bird from Camp Harney, and Shelton (1917) listed three winter specimens from Sisters. Alex Walker took a number of Pine Grosbeaks in northern Malheur County in the winter of 1919–1920, one of which has been identified as *Pinicola enucleator flammula.* As this is the only record for the State and as we have some of the skins from this flock that are clearly *alascensis,* both by coloration and measurements, we are inclined to question the identification.

While in Oregon, the birds are tame and unsuspicuous, usually allowing a close approach as they feed on buds or dried fruits. The soft-gray females and young males, the latter more or less washed with yellow on the head, far outnumber the rosy males, and observers should look carefully for these duller-colored birds.

Rocky Mountain Pine Grosbeak: *Pinicola enucleator montana* Ridgway

Description.—"*Adult male:* Light [carmine] red, head slightly tinged with yellow and pink, and changing to ash gray on scapulars, belly, flanks, and under tail coverts;

plumage everywhere gray beneath the surface, giving an effect of immaturity; *scapulars and feathers of the central back with only faint trace of dusky centers;* wings and tail dusky, feathers tipped and edged with whitish. *Adult female:* general color clear ash gray, bright tawny yellow on top and sides of head, back of neck, and middle of breast; tail with faint yellow wash on upper coverts. *Young:* like female, but brownish gray, with brownish and grayish edgings to wings and tail. *Male:* length (skins) 8.00–8.55, wing 4.72–4.86, tail 3.67–4.00, bill .61–.68. *Female:* length (skins) 8.00–8.30, wing 4.65–4.69, tail 3.48–3.50." (Bailey) *Nest:* A flimsy affair of rootlets in a conifer. *Eggs:* As with the Alaska Pine Grosbeak.

Distribution.—*General:* Breeds on higher summits of Rocky Mountains from west central Alberta, British Columbia, Idaho, and Montana to northern New Mexico. Winters mostly to south and east. *In Oregon:* Probably breeds in higher parts of Wallowa Mountains. Winters sparingly in extreme eastern part of State.

Jewett (1916a) recorded two specimens of the Rocky Mountain Pine Grosbeak taken on Cliff River in the Wallowa Mountains, September 9, 1915, that were badly worn and were probably breeding birds. There are three more specimens in his collection, one from Fort Warner (Lake County, November 3), one from Crane (Harney County, January 7), and the third from La Grande (Union County, January 25), that are identical with the breeding birds from the Rockies in Montana and Colorado. One taken March 1, 1919, in Wallowa County and listed by Gabrielson (1924a) as this subspecies is, with more adequate comparative material available, found to be *alascensis*. In habits and behavior, the two birds are quite similar, and it is impossible to separate them on field identifications. We have, therefore, confined our records to actual specimens taken.

Hepburn's Rosy Finch:
Leucosticte tephrocotis littoralis Baird

Description.—"Similar to the gray-crowned, ***but gray of crown*** spreading down over sides of head, sometimes covering all but black frontal patch. *Male:* length (skins) 6.04–6.80, wing 4.00–4.32, tail 2.36–2.75, bill .43–.49. *Female:* length (skins) 6.08–6.47, wing 3.94–4.10, bill .45–.49." (Bailey) *Nest:* Dry grass and roots, in rock crevices. *Eggs:* Usually 3 or 4, white.

Distribution.—*General:* Breeds above timber line on mountains from Alaska peninsula south to Three Sisters in central Oregon. Winters widely over adjoining lowlands. *In Oregon:* Breeds on Hood, Jefferson, Three Sisters, probably Mount McLoughlin, and possibly such peaks as Mount Washington and Three-fingered Jack. Winters abundantly but irregularly over eastern Oregon.

The most abundant wintering Rosy Finch in the State is Hepburn's Rosy Finch. It gathers into huge flocks that swirl along the rocky hillsides of eastern Oregon like leaves in a storm. These winter flocks are restless, except when actually feeding. They whirl up in spiral flights, then alight for a few seconds, only to start off again with little apparent reason. Usually they alight on the ground, sometimes on buildings, once in a great while in trees or bushes, and we have seen the telephone and fence wires decorated with them for a considerable space. Gabrielson found flocks of them in stunted bushes and trees near Yakima, Washington, in January 1934 and collected three birds from the group. When feeding, the birds are tame and unsuspicious and allow a fairly close approach before they take wing to circle and whirl over the countryside, usually to return to about the same spot.

The species was first reported from Oregon by Bendire (Brewer 1875), who collected numerous specimens at Camp Harney. Most of the rather numerous subsequent citations refer back to these Bendire specimens. We have collected specimens in winter in Wallowa, Baker, Union, Umatilla, Grant, Lake, and Malheur Counties, and there is no reason to believe the species will not be found in most of the remaining eastern Oregon counties.

Vernon Bailey, Jewett, and Alex Walker were among the members of a Biological Survey and Oregon State Game Commission party that collected on the Three Sisters, on several dates between July 11 and 17, 1914, the first breeding birds taken in the State. Shelton (1917) listed this Rosy Finch as a breeding bird of the area, apparently on the strength of the above specimens in the Oregon Game Commission Collection. Gabrielson saw numerous birds and collected an adult male on Park Ridge just north of Mount Jefferson on June 4, 1926, and has seen both adults and young on Mount Hood on numerous occasions. Vernon Bailey recorded in manuscript notes that he saw a flock of 20 above timber line on Mount McLoughlin between August 23 and 30, 1916. This is the southernmost record for the species in the Oregon Cascades. Like the Gray-crowned Rosy Finch, it lives in alpine surroundings during the summer months, usually selecting the vicinity of some glacier or snow field for its highland home.

Gray-crowned Rosy Finch:
Leucosticte tephrocotis tephrocotis (Swainson)

DESCRIPTION.—"*Adult male in summer:* Bill black, crown black bordered behind and on sides with gray, the gray not spreading down over sides of head; general body color *deep chestnut brown*, lighter, and with blackish mesial streaks on back; belly, rump, upper tail coverts, wings, and tail more or less tinged with pink. *Adult male in winter:* bill yellow, tipped with blackish; brown feathers edged with whitish; black of crown restricted. *Adult female:* like male, with the same seasonal changes, but averaging paler and duller. *Young:* plain brownish, without black or gray on head, or rosy tail coverts. *Male:* length (skins) 5.70–6.81, wing 4.00–4.40, tail 2.42–2.80, bill .42–.48. *Female:* length (skins) 5.60–6.50, wing 3.80–4.19, tail 2.39–2.78, bill .43–.56." (Bailey) *Nest:* Of dry grass and roots, in crevices of rocks. *Eggs:* Usually 3 or 4, white.

DISTRIBUTION.—*General:* Breeds above timber line and in Arctic-Alpine Zone from eastern Alaska, Yukon, and western Alberta south to Montana and Wallowa Mountains of northeastern Oregon. Winters west to Cascades and east to Great Plains. *In Oregon:* Breeds only in highest parts of Wallowa Range from peaks in vicinity of Steamboat Lake to those at head of Big Sheep Creek and Imnaha River. Winters irregularly over adjoining lowlands.

THE BEAUTIFUL little Gray-crowned Rosy Finch was first reported from Oregon by Bendire (Brewer 1875), who took a specimen, January 17, 1875, near Camp Harney. Jewett (1909c) recorded birds taken in Baker County in March 1906, and Grinnell (1913) listed the species from Harney County. It was not definitely established as a breeding bird until 1923, when Jewett collected adult and young birds on July 23 on the head of Big Sheep Creek. A month later (August 21) Gabrielson watched an adult feeding at least three partly grown nestlings in an inaccessible cranny near the summit of Brown Mountain above Minam Lake. These two records mark the eastern and western extremes of the breeding range as we now know it. Since that time, we have found it breeding at numerous intervening points and have collected fledgling young on several of the peaks. In addition to our records, the files of the Biological Survey contain a record by Young and Bailey of Rosy Finches seen in the Wallowa Mountains between August 24 and September 17 that undoubtedly belong to this race.

In winter the birds scatter out over the adjoining low country, usually mingling with the more abundant Hepburn's Rosy Finch, which they closely resemble. In addition to Bendire's and Grinnell's records for wintering birds, we have specimens taken in Baker, Grant, Wallowa, and Lake Counties. The few wintering individuals of this form taken by us would seem to indicate that most of our breeding birds winter toward the east.

The habits of this small finch have made it a species of peculiar interest to ornithologists. It seeks the cold and austere heights for its summer home and there, about the perpetual snow and ice, builds its nests in crevices and crannies in the rocks and forages for food on the surface of the snow fields and glaciers. The rosy finches probably antedated human use of the principles of refrigeration by many thousands of years as they feasted on chilled insects that had fallen benumbed on failure of their endeavors to cross the frozen areas.

Black Rosy Finch:
Leucosticte atrata Ridgway

DESCRIPTION.—"*Adult male in summer:* Crown black, set in gray, which does not extend over sides of head; *body blackish* or deep clove brown; feathers of belly and sides tipped with peach-blossom pink; feathers of hind neck, back, and scapulars with more or less distinct brownish or buffy edgings; rump and patch on wings peach-blossom pink. *Adult male in winter:* similar, but bill yellowish, tipped with dusky, the brownish edgings to scapulars and interscapulars broader, feathers of under parts more or less edged with grayish, and pink markings of a softer, more rosy hue. *Immature male:* like adult male, but pink markings paler, mainly replaced on wings by buffy white. *Adult female:* much duller than the male, under parts grayish brown, upper parts brownish, and pink paler and restricted or replaced by whitish. *Immature female:* like adult female, but duller and browner, feathers conspicuously edged with brownish and buffy. *Male:* length (skins) 5.90–6.28, wing 4.21–4.27, tail 2.62–2.75, bill .41–.48. *Female:* length (skins) 5.60–6.18, wing 3.89–4.19, tail 2.38–2.58, bill .45–.47." (Bailey) *Nest and eggs:* Same as for other Rosy Finches.

DISTRIBUTION.—*General:* Breeds or is summer resident of Wallowa Mountains of Oregon, Salmon River Mountains of Idaho, Uinta Mountains in Utah, and ranges of western Wyoming. Winters south to Utah, Colorado, and New Mexico. *In Oregon:* Included on basis of two specimens only.

THE BLACK ROSY FINCH is included in the Oregon list solely on the basis of two specimens in the Jewett collection, taken July 22 and 23, 1923, on the head of Big Sheep Creek in the Wallowa Mountains, one of which is recorded in the *Condor* (Jewett 1924d). They were with the much more abundant Gray-crowned species at the time.

Common Redpoll:
Acanthis linaria linaria (Linnaeus)

DESCRIPTION.—"*Adult male in breeding plumage:* Chin patch and feathers around bill blackish; crown crimson; throat, sides and rump more or less washed with pink or crimson; rest of under parts white, sides streaked with dusky; upper parts streaked, dark brown and buffy, lighter but *streaked on rump*, rump washed with pink; bill horn color, dusky at tip. *Adult male in winter plumage:* much lighter, wing bands more or less buffy, pink paler; bill light yellow, black at tip. *Adult female:* similar to the male, but pink of under parts replaced by buffy or whitish; seasonal difference same as in male. *Young:* like adults, but without pink or red, crown streaked and sides and wing bands more or less buffy. *Male:* length (skins) 4.31–5.32, wing 2.78–3.01, tail 1.91–2.29, bill .31–.38. *Female:* length (skins) 4.29–5.43, wing 2.76–3.00, tail 1.99–2.30, bill .30–.39." (Bailey) *Nest:* A bulky mass of twigs, straw, or feathers, in bushes or small trees. *Eggs:* 2 to 5, pale bluish green, specked about the larger end with brown and black.

DISTRIBUTION.—*General:* Breeds from northwestern Alaska, northern Mackenzie, and northern Quebec south to Alberta, Manitoba, and Islands in Gulf of St. Lawrence and also through northern Europe and Asia. Winters south to Oregon, California, Colorado, Kansas, Indiana, Ohio, Alabama, and South Carolina. *In Oregon:* Extremely erratic winter visitor that may appear anywhere in State but is most frequently found in eastern Oregon.

THIS ERRATIC VISITOR from the north, the Common Redpoll, was first reported from the State by Bendire (Brewer 1875), who took winter specimens at Camp Harney. Mearns (1879) recorded it from Fort Klamath (May 9, 1878), and Merrill (1888) considered it common there during the winter. It was not noted again until Woodcock (1902) took specimens from a flock of about 150 birds on January 20, 1900, near Corvallis.

Shelton (1917) listed it as a rare visitor to Lane County. Neither of us took any Oregon specimens until January 26, 1933, when Jewett was fortunate enough to encounter a considerable flock at Wallowa, Wallowa County.

The Redpolls resemble wintering goldfinches and pine siskins in habits, notes, and general outline so much that they can easily be overlooked except at close range. Observers in eastern Oregon are apt to find this northerner during the winter months about willow patches or isolated trees and bushes on the hillsides.

Northern Pine Siskin:
Spinus pinus pinus (Wilson)

Description.—"Similar to *Astragalinus* [goldfinch], but plumage streaked gray and brown, without yellow or black except for yellow patches on wings and tail. *Adults:* whole body finely streaked with brown, on brownish ground above, on whitish below; *basal portions of secondaries and tail feathers sulphur yellow. Young:* upper parts mustard yellow, tinged with brownish olive, feathers streaked, except on belly; wing bands and patches brown. *Male:* length (skins) 4.20–4.85, wing 2.72–3.00, tail 1.57–1.83, bill .38–.44. *Female:* length (skins) 4.23–5.14, wing 2.63–2.97, tail 1.60–1.81, bill .39–.47." (Bailey) *Nest:* A slight platform of twigs and plant fibers, lined with rootlets and hair. *Eggs:* 3 or 4, pale greenish blue, speckled with brown and black, largely around the large end.

Distribution.—*General:* Breeds from Alaska, Mackenzie, Manitoba, and Quebec south through mountains to southern California and southern New Mexico and to Minnesota, Michigan, New Hampshire, Maine, and in eastern mountains to North Carolina. Winters over most of United States. *In Oregon:* Common permanent resident of timbered parts. Likely to appear in any locality in winter and spring.

The Northern Pine Siskin, a tiny finch with brown-streaked plumage tinted here and there with yellow, is a familiar sight in the wooded sections of the State where it is found as a common permanent resident. Like many other finches that frequent the coniferous forests, it is somewhat erratic in that it appears in immense numbers in some seasons and is entirely absent or greatly restricted in the same community in subsequent seasons. It can be found, however, in limited numbers generally throughout the State in the wooded areas and is likely to appear in any small planting of trees, even in the sagebrush section in winter or early spring when its wandering movements are at their height.

Both the call note and the flight behavior of the Pine Siskins are reminiscent of the goldfinches. In addition to their high-pitched alarm note or flight note, they have a peculiar wheezing note that is given both as they take wing and as they travel through the air. The flocks of goldfinches are usually larger, and the Pine Siskins mingle with them and leave the coniferous timber to feed in the weed patches with their brighter cousins.

The Pine Siskin was first listed as an Oregon bird by Bendire (Brewer 1875) who took a specimen, December 14, 1874, at Camp Harney. Since that time it has been mentioned many times in the ornithological literature of the State. There are comparatively few nesting records, due perhaps more to lack of egg collectors than to scarcity of birds. Keller (1891a) wrote as follows regarding nesting near Salem:

In this section it begins to carry building material about the 15th or latter part of April and fresh eggs may be found as early as May 1. It generally nests in fir trees, but nests have been found in both maple and oak trees. They are placed from eight to twenty-five feet from the ground. A set of three eggs before me was taken May 7, 1889. The nest was placed on the end of a fir bough, eight feet up, and composed of fir twigs and grass, and lined with hair. The eggs are pale greenish-blue in color, sparingly spotted near the larger end with reddish-brown and pale lilac, and average .63 x .49 in size. Three eggs seem to be the standard number in a set here for out of several taken (among which two sets were incubated) none of them contained over three eggs.

Stryker (1894) found a nest at Milwaukie, containing 4 eggs, that was 40 feet up in a fir tree, but he did not give the date. Neither of us has found a nest, although we have both taken fledglings barely able to fly. This siskin is one of the commonest of the resident species of the coniferous timber, and special efforts directed toward finding its nest would, without doubt, result in success in almost any section of the State.

Pale Goldfinch:
Spinus tristis pallidus Mearns

Description.—"*Adult male in summer:* Whole body canary yellow, in sharp contrast to black crown, wings, and tail; wings with white bars and tail feathers with white patches. *Adult female in summer:* upper parts olive brown, sometimes tinged with green or gray; wings and tail dull blackish brown; white markings duller; under parts grayish white, more or less tinged with yellow. *Adult male in winter:* similar to female in summer, but wings and tail black, broadly and clearly marked with white. *Adult female in winter:* similar to summer plumage, but more tinged with brownish, white markings broader and more tinged with buffy. *Young:* similar to winter adults, but browner, wing markings and general suffusion cinnamon; shoulder patch mixed with black instead of unicolored as in the male. *Male:* length (skins) 4.30–5.09, wing 2.81–3.08, tail 1.72–2.05, bill .38–.43. *Female:* length (skins) 4.42–5.00, wing 2.71–2.92, tail 1.70–2.03, bill .39–.44." (Bailey) *Nest:* A neat cup of plant fibers, lined with thistle down and other similar material. *Eggs:* 3 to 5, plain bluish or bluish white.

Distribution.—*General:* Breeds from southeastern British Columbia and Manitoba south to central Nevada and Colorado. Winters south into Mexico. *In Oregon:* Common permanent resident east of Cascades.

The Pale Goldfinch is a common permanent resident of the lower valleys east of the Cascade Mountains. It is most conspicuous in the valleys around the base of the Blue Mountains and those along the Columbia and Snake Rivers, although it is found in all other parts of the State. The first mention of this bird in literature that can definitely be assigned to this subspecies is that of Bendire (1877), who reported finding it near Camp Harney, May 5, 1876. Since that time numerous writers have mentioned it in various parts of the State.

The Pale Goldfinch differs little in general appearance from the Willow Goldfinch in the western part of the State in the summer plumage, except that a series shows the yellow to be slightly paler. In the winter plumage, however, there is a distinct difference between the two forms. The eastern Oregon bird is then much paler, and the predominant color tone of its back is olive or olive gray in contrast to the brown tint found in specimens taken west of the Cascades.

Regardless of subspecies, the behavior of the goldfinches is similar. They are birds of the open, feeding by choice in thistle patches, on dandelion heads, or on other composites, taking a great variety of other seeds. They remain in flocks long after many other species have established nests. It is late June or early July before the birds take up breeding activities seriously. Their wavelike flight, cheery calls, and bright plumage, combined with the fact that they do feed and live largely in the open, make them familiar to most people in the territory where they are found.

Willow Goldfinch:
Spinus tristis salicamans Grinnell

Description.—"*Adult male in summer:* Except for shorter wings and tail scarcely distinguishable from *tristis* [*pallidus*]; black cap, if anything, not so extended and yellow not so intense; the white edgings on wings worn off so there is scarcely a trace of white left. *Adult female in summer:* much darker than female of *tristis* [*pallidus*], dull greenish yellow on throat instead of bright yellowish green. *Young:* dark colored. *Adult male in winter:* similar to *tristis* [*pallidus*], but *browner* and with much *broader wing markings;* back dark olive brown; sides and flanks shaded with brown; throat bright yellow, shading to dull green on breast and to pure white on belly. *Adult female in winter:* similar to male, but wings, tail, and throat duller; bill dusky. *Male:* length (skins) 4.08–4.82, wing 2.60–2.89, tail 1.70–1.82, bill .39–.42. *Female:* length (skins) 4.28–4.70, wing 2.63–2.72, tail 1.70–1.79, bill .39–.42." (Bailey) *Nest and eggs:* Same as for *S. t. pallidus* (Plate 90, *B*).

Distribution.—*General:* Breeds from British Columbia south to Lower California west of Cascades and Sierra Nevadas. *In Oregon:* Common permanent resident west of Cascades.

The Willow Goldfinch is a common breeding goldfinch of western Oregon and is equally common during the remainder of the year. It is particularly abundant in the open valleys such as the Rogue, Umpqua, and Willamette Valleys. In habits and behavior, it is identical with the goldfinches throughout the United States. Like its eastern Oregon relative, it nests late. Records of numerous fresh or slightly incubated eggs vary from June 15 to July 6.

The first published record of this bird came a number of years after that of the eastern Oregon form, when Anthony (1886) first listed it, stating that it was common in Washington County. Since that time it has appeared in numerous published lists referring to that part of the State. It remains in the State in winter more abundantly than does its eastern Oregon cousin and is one of the birds familiar to bird lovers in the territory west of the Cascades.

Green-backed Goldfinch:
Spinus psaltria hesperophilus (Oberholser)

DESCRIPTION.—"*Adult male:* Ear coverts, and entire upper parts, including wings and tail, black, wings with broad white edgings, tail with most of its feathers extensively white basally; under parts canary yellow. *Adult female:* upper parts plain dull olive green; under parts light greenish yellow; head without black; wings and tail as in male, but black duller, and white more restricted, sometimes obsolete on tail. *Young:* similar to female, but tinged with buffy, and wing coverts tipped with buff. *Immature:* crown black, rest of upper parts grading from olive green to solid black on ear coverts and back; under parts yellow. *Size:* wing 2.46, tail 1.70, bill .35." (Bailey) *Nest and eggs:* Like those of the two preceding species.

DISTRIBUTION.—*General:* Breeds from Columbia River in Oregon west of Cascades and from Utah south into Mexico and winters from northern California into Mexico. *In Oregon:* Permanent resident of valleys west of Cascades, more abundant in summer.

THE GREEN-BACKED GOLDFINCH much resembles the Willow Goldfinch in flight and notes, but it is smaller and in addition to the black cap and wings has a dark-green back. It seems to have been overlooked by most ornithologists who have studied Oregon birds. Merrill (1888) listed it as common near Ashland in August. It was not again mentioned until Woodcock (1902) reported it from four localities, all in the Willamette Valley. Shelton (1917) stated that it was common in west-central Oregon, but it did not again appear in published literature until our *Birds of the Portland Area* (Jewett and Gabrielson 1929). Despite these meager published references, the species is a common summer resident and less common winter resident of the valleys of the State to the Columbia River at Portland. We have records or specimens from practically all of the counties lying in the Willamette Valley, as well as from Douglas, Jackson, and Josephine in southern Oregon. We have not noted it in the coast counties, except Coos, where Gabrielson found it to be fairly common in June (1920). It remains in smaller numbers throughout the Willamette Valley, as well as in southern Oregon.

There are only a few records for this bird in eastern Oregon—a specimen in the Biological Survey collection from Riverside, Malheur County, taken July 20, 1916, by Sheldon, and records in Klamath County by Gabrielson on May 17 and 18 (1920) and September 8 (1929). Patterson (ms.) has taken eggs near Ashland on extreme dates of May 30 and June 21.

Sitka Crossbill:
Loxia curvirostra sitkensis Grinnell

Description.—"*Adult male:* Dull red, generally brighter on rump; gray showing through on under parts; feathers of back indistinctly streaked; wings and tail plain dusky. *Adult females:* olivaceous, often shading to bright yellow. *Young:* streaked, on olive gray ground. *Young male:* mixed with yellow and red before reaching adult stage." (Bailey) *Size:* Length (skins) 4.50–5.20, wing 3.18–3.40, tail 1.73–1.98, bill .55–.61. *Nest:* A flat platform of twigs and shreds of bark, lined with horsehair and fine rootlets. *Eggs:* Usually 4, greenish, spotted with brown and gray.

Distribution.—*General:* From vicinity of Sitka south along coast to central California. *In Oregon:* Permanent resident from summit of Cascades west to Pacific.

The small-billed Sitka Crossbill is an abundant resident of the coniferous forests in the western half of the State. Newberry (1857) published what is undoubtedly our first record for this subspecies as now known. He found it common in the upper Willamette Valley. Since his time many writers have noted its presence. In any locality it may be very erratic, appearing one season and then remaining absent for several years. The birds nest at almost any season, apparently, where an abundant crop of coniferous seed is ready for harvest. Generally they are more regular along the coast than in inland localities. Yachats and Netarts for many years had a regular quota of crossbills present at every season. Then, unaccountably, the birds disappeared from those spots for one entire season or longer.

Out of a representative collection of Oregon crossbills of over one hundred skins, there is only one specimen of this small-billed smaller bird from eastern Oregon. It was taken at Stanley Ranger Station on the Wallowa National Forest, July 22, 1920 (Gabrielson Collection No. 110). All the other numerous eastern Oregon skins are undoubtedly *Loxia curvirostra bendirei*.

These are the gypsies of the bird world, who know no laws of regularity. They wander north, south, east, or west, and up and down the mountains with no apparent correlation with the seasons. This is probably due to their specialized feeding habits that make them largely dependent on coniferous seed. Their curiously crossed bills can open a cone with surprising dexterity and deftly extract the seed from between the scales. Few American birds are more highly specialized. Stomach examinations made by the Biological Survey revealed that 96.47 per cent of the contents of 195 winter stomachs and 68.34 per cent of the contents of 41 summer stomachs was seed of various conifers. Beetles, Hymenoptera, and miscellaneous insects comprised the main part of the summer insect food. At times when feeding on or near the ground, the birds are unsuspicious, allowing a close approach apparently without noticing the intruder. Their fondness for salt has been noticed and commented upon by many writers, and stock-salting stations in our mountains are favored spots that are visited regularly.

Crossbills are difficult to observe at close range as they often fly from the top of one high conifer to another, far above ground. When feeding quietly in such lofty situations, their presence can be detected only by the steady rain of seed coats and wings as they shell out the seeds. When they take flight in straggling flocks, it is usually to the accompaniment of a wheezy call note that is uttered at irregular intervals during the flight. The note, once learned, is so characteristic that passing flocks can frequently be more readily detected by ear than by eye. The birds are of little or no economic importance but contribute much of interest to the nature lover because of their curiously specialized bills and uncertain ways.

Bendire's Crossbill:
Loxia curvirostra bendirei Ridgway

DESCRIPTION.—Same as *L. c. sitkensis* but larger. *Size:* Length (skins) 5.32–6.23, wing 3.30–3.82, tail 1.70–2.25, bill .64–.82. *Nest and eggs:* Same as for *L. c. sitkensis*.

DISTRIBUTION.—*General:* Breeds in mountains from British Columbia, Montana, Wyoming, and Colorado to and including Cascades and Sierra Nevadas, of Washington, Oregon, and California. *In Oregon:* Permanent resident of eastern slope of Cascades, wooded portions of Lake and Klamath Counties, and all timbered parts of Blue Mountain area. Appears in western Oregon only as straggler.

BENDIRE'S CROSSBILL, with its comparatively huge bill, was first recorded by Bendire (Brewer 1875), who found it near Camp Harney. It is a common permanent resident of the eastern part of the State, where it is as abundant and erratic as *sitkensis* is in the western part of the State. It is possible to find newly fledged young at almost any season of the year, although our only actual nesting record is of a nest found by Jewett at Sisters in July 1914. The female was observed on July 21 carrying nesting material to a site 90 feet up in a yellow-pine tree, and the nest and one egg were taken on July 26.

There are two birds in our series taken at Netarts, February 8 and 11, 1915 (Jewett Collection Nos. 1110 and 1111), that seem clearly to belong to this race. This is not surprising, as such erratic wanderers are apt to appear at any point. Aside from these two birds and the single one from Wallowa mentioned under *sitkensis*, our specimens fit well into the concept of the range of the two subspecies as outlined. Curiously enough, birds from the territory south of Bend have bills that average the largest, although there are individuals from the Blue Mountains with huge mandibles. This huge-billed bird from the country between Bend and Klamath Falls early attracted the attention of Ridgway, who published (1884c) a subspecies based on birds from Fort Klamath that was the original description of this form.

White-winged Crossbill:
Loxia leucoptera Gmelin

DESCRIPTION.—Similar to the Sitka Crossbill but with white bars on the wings. The red a brighter color, especially on the rump in the males. *Size:* Length 6.00–6.10. *Nest and eggs:* Same as for other crossbills.

DISTRIBUTION.—*General:* Breeds in the Boreal zone from the limit of trees in northwest Alaska, northern Mackenzie, northern Manitoba and northern Quebec south to southern British Columbia and Mt. Rainier, Washington, southern Alberta to New York, New Hampshire, Maine, and Nova Scotia. *In Oregon:* Occurs only as a straggler.

THE WHITE-WINGED CROSSBILL is known as a bird of Oregon from the record of Alden H. Miller, who collected two males and saw the third in the firs and spruces of a subalpine meadow on the upper Lostine River in Wallowa County on July 12, 1938. There is also a sight record by Anthony (1886) in Washington County.

Green-tailed Towhee:
Oberholseria chlorura (Audubon)

DESCRIPTION.—"Bill small, conical; wing rather long and pointed; tail long, rounded; tarsus long, nearly a third the length of wing; hind claw longer than its toe. (Structurally intermediate between *Zonotrichia* and *Pipilo.*) *Adult male: top of head bright rufous;* throat white; upper parts olive gray, *becoming bright olive green on wings and tail;* malar stripe and middle of belly white; edge of wing, under wing coverts, and axillars bright yellow. *Adult female:* usually slightly duller. *Young:* olive grayish, streaked with dusky; lower parts dingy white, chest and sides streaked with dusky; wings and tail like adults, but wing bars brownish buffy. *Male:* length (skins) 6.21–7.05, wing 3.01–3.28, tail 3.14–3.43, bill .48–.51. *Female:* length (skins) 6.52–7.10, wing 2.80–3.10, tail 2.93–3.33, bill .45–.51." (Bailey) *Nest:* On or near the ground in small bushes, woven of grass and stems and lined with hair. *Eggs:* 4, whitish, speckled with reddish brown.

DISTRIBUTION.—*General:* Breeds from central Oregon and south-central Montana to southern California, southeastern New Mexico, and central-west Texas. Winters south into Mexico. *In Oregon:* Common summer resident of edge of yellow-pine districts of eastern Oregon westward to summit of Cascades and in southern Oregon through higher parts of Siskiyous, at least to vicinity of Oregon Mountain, near where Redwood Highway crosses summit.

THE GREEN-TAILED TOWHEE is a bird of the rank sagebrush of the higher valleys and is usually found most abundantly where the yellow pine and sagebrush meet and intermingle. It is, however, common in the Steens Mountains and similar desert ranges where there is no yellow pine and extends its range westward to and beyond the summit of the Cascades. Since Bendire (1877) first listed the bird from Oregon it has attracted the attention of every ornithologist to visit its haunts. We have found it commonly in Malheur, Harney, Lake, Klamath, Deschutes, Crook, Baker, Grant, and Wheeler Counties, and less frequently in Lane, Jackson,

Josephine, and eastern Clackamas. It arrives in May (earliest date, April 27, Malheur County) and remains until September (latest date, September 23, Jackson County). The westernmost records we have are at Welches, below the west base of Mount Hood (John Carter), May 13, 1933, Mackenzie Bridge (Shelton), Mosquito Ranger Station, Jackson County, July 27, 1926 (Gabrielson Collection No. 1518), and Bolan Mountain, Josephine County, August 18, 1933 (Jewett Collection No. 7953).

The species breeds in late May and June. Jewett's only records are two nests that he discovered on Hart Mountain, July 13, 1931 (4 eggs), and July 25, 1932 (4 eggs). Both were in low bushes within a few inches of the ground, and the former was lined with porcupine hair. Patterson (ms.) reported nests May 23 and 27, and June 6, 1923, in southern Oregon.

The trim, alert Green-tailed Towhee is a somewhat shy bird, although its ringing song and catlike call notes are familiar sounds of the sage country. When in song it will usually be found perched on the topmost twig of a bush or low tree, from which vantage point it is quick to depart when an intruder approaches.

Nevada Towhee:
Pipilo maculatus curtatus Grinnell

Description.—"*Adult male:* Head, neck, and chest black; back black, more or less mixed with olive gray; belly white; flanks reddish brown; wings and tail with *extensive white markings;* wing bars and white edgings of primaries sometimes forming a conspicuous patch, and scapulars heavily streaked with white; white on outer tail feather covering more than half exposed portion beyond coverts (1.30–1.70). *Adult female:* Black, replaced by dull olive brown; back streaked with black; throat and chest grayish brown; white markings obscured. *Young:* streaked with black over brownish ground above, buffy below; lighter in female; markings of wings and tail as in adult, more or less restricted on wings." (Bailey) *Size:* Length (skins) 7.12–8.16, wing 3.22–3.60, tail 3.60–4.21, bill .48–.60, white spot in outer tail feather 1.02–1.25. *Nest:* A substantial structure of twigs, leaves, and grass, lined with grass or rootlets and placed on the ground or in brush piles and low bushes. *Eggs:* 4 or 5, pale greenish or bluish, finely speckled with brown and lavender, especially on larger end.

Distribution.—*General:* Breeds from central British Columbia to eastern Oregon, Nevada, and northeastern California. Winters south to southern California. *In Oregon:* Fairly common breeding species and less common winter resident that we have found in every county in eastern Oregon from eastern base of Cascades to Idaho line. (See Figure 18.)

The Nevada Towhee has appeared in literature under a variety of names as the conception of subspecies has shifted about, the distinction becoming more finely drawn with each succeeding change. It is a safe assumption, however, that resident birds from the eastern half of the State that we have found in every county from the eastern base of the Cascades to the Idaho line belong to this race as it is now defined.

Under the name *P. m. oregonus*, Newberry (1857) listed the birds of the

Deschutes Basin, Suckley (Cooper and Suckley 1860) included them from Fort Dalles, and Baird (Baird, Cassin, and Lawrence 1858) listed a specimen from Fort Dalles, Columbia River, May 27, 1835. If this last-mentioned bird really came from The Dalles, it is undoubtedly the first skin of this race ever taken in Oregon. In 1875 Bendire (Brewer 1875) listed his Camp Harney birds as *P. arcticus* but in 1877 (Bendire 1877) used the name *P. megalonyx* for the same birds, a name that Mearns (1879) used for Fort Klamath birds. Merrill (1888) listed Fort Klamath birds as *P. m. oregonus*. Miller (1904) used the same name for Wheeler County birds, but Peck (1911a) switched to *arcticus* for Malheur County birds. Beginning with Jewett's (1909c) list of Baker County birds, the name *P. m. montanus* was used generally until the separation of the present form by Grinnell (1911). These various records are cited to show the confusion caused by the constant shifting of subspecific concepts. All apply to the same resident group of birds—with the possible exception of stragglers of other races that might reach eastern Oregon.

Although we have records for every month, the species becomes much more abundant about March 15 and decreases greatly in numbers in early October. We have found no nests of this form, but young of the year are usually flying by mid-June, which would place the general nesting period in mid-May. Bendire (1877), however, reported taking a nest with two eggs from a low bush in the Blue Mountains above Camp Harney, June 15, 1875, the only actually published breeding record for this subspecies that we have been able to find for the State.

The Nevada Towhee is in our experience a rather shy bird—in marked contrast to the dooryard habit of the western Oregon form. It flits nervously through the willows or sagebrush well ahead of an intruder, occasionally stopping to perch for an instant on some conspicuous twig.

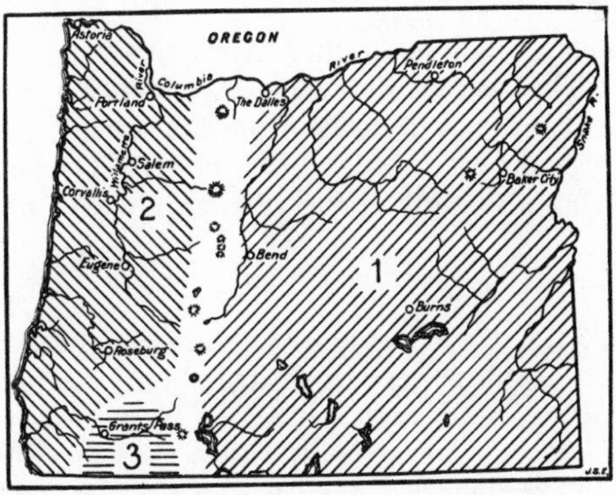

FIGURE 18.—Distribution of three forms of towhees in Oregon: 1, Nevada Towhee (*Pipilo maculatus curtatus*); 2, Oregon Towhee (*P. m. oregonus*); 3, Sacramento Towhee (*P. m. falcinellus*).

Oregon Towhee:
Pipilo maculatus oregonus Bell

DESCRIPTION.—"*Adult male: Upper parts mainly black, white markings inconspicuous;* streaks on back mainly obsolete or concealed; wing bars reduced to disconnected round white spots, white of outer tail feather reduced to 'thumb mark,' less than an inch in length, outer web mainly black; rufous of sides very dark. *Adult female:* black replaced by dark sooty brown or sooty black, indistinctly streaked with black; rufous of sides deep. *Young:* Darker and more uniform than young *megalonyx;* throat and chest sooty, not streaked. *Male:* length (skins) 7.08–8.18, wing 3.22–3.47, tail 3.42–3.87, bill .54–.59. *Female:* length (skins) 6.95–8.00, wing 3.03–3.38, tail 3.31–3.85, bill .52–.58." (Bailey) *Nest and eggs:* As for *P. m. curtatus*.

DISTRIBUTION.—*General:* Breeds in southwestern British Columbia west of Cascades to west-central Oregon. *In Oregon:* Common permanent resident of western Oregon from Cascades to Pacific, south to and including Umpqua Valley. Straggles southward into Rogue River Valley in winter. (See Figure 18.)

THIS IS ONE of the most common permanent resident birds in western Oregon, where every rose thicket and evergreen blackberry patch has its pair of Oregon Towhees. They are present throughout the year so commonly that it is unusual to walk along the bottom lands at any season without seeing a handsome black and white and reddish fellow flirting his tail nervously as he glides to a landing around a clump of bushes or hops about in the thickets.

Johnson (1880) published the first record for Oregon that we can with certainty ascribe to this race. He found it commonly at Portland, Salem, and Forest Grove, a status that continues to the present. Every writer on western Oregon birds since his time has listed it as one of the common subspecies. Between Roseburg and Grants Pass, intergradations of this form and *P. m. falcinellus* occurs. We have one typical *oregonus* from Roseburg, February 1, 1929 (Gabrielson Collection No. 1790), a second from Oakland, August 12, 1934 (Gabrielson Collection No. 2905), and a third from Winona, Josephine County, April 12, 1921 (Gabrielson Collection No. 357). The last mentioned was probably a belated wintering bird from farther north, as all others from that vicinity are *falcinellus*.

The eggs are usually laid in May. Our nesting dates extend from May 3 to June 25, although young of the year are always on the wing before the latter date.

Sacramento Towhee:
Pipilo maculatus falcinellus Swarth

DESCRIPTION.—Similar to *Pipilo maculatus curtatus* but has slightly longer hind claw, decidedly darker brown on sides and crissum, and black areas more intensely and glossy black. Similar to *Pipilo maculatus megalonyx* but has weaker foot, shorter hind claw, somewhat greater extent of white markings, and olivaceous or grayish rump. (Adapted from Swarth 1913.) *Size:* Length (skins) 7.00–8.40, wing 3.30–3.46, tail 3.75–4.00, exposed culmen .51–.59, hind toe and claw .71–.81, length of white spot in outer tail feather .98–1.20. *Nest and eggs:* Similar to those of *P. m. curtatus*.

Distribution.—*General:* Breeds from Jackson County, Oregon, south through interior of California to Tulare County. *In Oregon:* Permanent resident and breeding bird of Jackson and Josephine Counties. (See Figure 18.)

The Sacramento Towhee, which is distinguished most readily from *P. m. oregonus* by the much greater amount of white on the wings and tail, is the resident breeding form of the chaparral thickets of the Rogue River Valley, where it is an abundant and permanent resident, with habits and behavior much like the Oregon Towhee. As nothing had been published regarding the birds of the Rogue River Valley until Gabrielson's (1931) list appeared in the *Condor*, his was the first published reference to the Sacramento Towhee as an Oregon bird. We have numerous specimens from that valley taken throughout the year.

Curiously enough Woodcock (1902) recorded a bird taken at Corvallis, January 20, 1899, as *P. m. arcticus*, that an examination shows to be identical with birds from Grants Pass and Medford. It is evidently a bird that had wandered northward after the breeding season and is the only specimen we have seen from north of Grants Pass.

Patterson (ms.) furnished dates of numerous nests at Ashland between May 2 and June 14, which are the only definite nesting dates we have found for this form.

Oregon Brown Towhee:
Pipilo fuscus bullatus Grinnell and Swarth

Description.—"*Adults: Entire upper parts plain dull grayish brown, slightly deeper on head;* throat light rufous, usually marked with dusky; middle of belly whitish or dull buffy, sides grayish brown; under tail coverts reddish brown. *Young:* like adults, but browner, wing bars and edgings pale brownish; under parts dull buffy, deepening to tawny on throat and belly, and grayish brown along sides; anterior lower parts streaked. *Male:* length (skins) 8.35–9.50, wing 3.75–4.08, tail 4.22–4.55, bill .56–.65. *Female:* length (skins) 8.24–8.60, wing 3.57–3.88, tail 4.14–4.38, bill .56–.63." (Bailey) *Nest:* In bushes and trees, usually within a few feet of the ground, made of inner bark, twigs, and weed stems and lined with plant stems, wool, and hair. *Eggs:* 4 or 5, pale blue, spotted with purplish brown.

Distribution.—*General:* Valleys of Rogue and Umpqua Rivers in southern Oregon. *In Oregon:* Permanent resident of chaparral thickets of Douglas, Jackson, and Josephine Counties.

The Oregon Brown Towhee is a characteristic bird of the bushy hillsides in the interior valleys of Douglas, Jackson, and Josephine Counties. There in the lowlands between the Coast and Cascade Ranges in the Umpqua and Rogue watersheds its characteristic metallic alarm note can be heard throughout the year. Woodcock (1902) mentioned taking one specimen and seeing others near Corvallis, which not only constitutes the first published record for the State but is also the only record for the Willamette Valley. We have not seen this specimen, but it is unlikely that so good an observer as Woodcock would confuse this big Brown Towhee with anything else. Bowles (1910) listed it from Josephine County, and Grinnell (1912) recorded it from southern Oregon.

Patterson (ms.) has found numerous nests about Ashland and Pinehurst with extreme dates of May 2 and 20.

Western Savannah Sparrow:
Passerculus sandwichensis alaudinus Bonaparte

DESCRIPTION.—"Similar to *sandwichensis*, but smaller and averaging grayer, superciliary stripe often white. *Male:* length (skins) 4.50–5.58, wing 2.56–3.06, tail 1.80–2.25, bill .38–.43. *Female:* length (skins) 4.50–5.20, wing 2.56–2.87, tail 1.76–2.10, bill .38–.45." (Bailey) *Nest:* A depression in the ground, lined with dried grass. *Eggs:* 3 to 6, dull white or brownish, spotted with brown.

DISTRIBUTION.—*General:* Breeds from Arctic Coast of Alaska and Mackenzie to British Columbia and Alberta. Winters south into Mexico and Lower California. *In Oregon:* This subspecies, as now restricted, occurs only as migrant and winter resident but is found throughout State, particularly in September and October.

THE WESTERN SAVANNAH SPARROW is the abundant Savannah Sparrow in the fall months throughout the State. It is common in the summit meadows of the Cascades as well as throughout the valleys of both eastern and western Oregon, and it mingles with *P. s. sandwichensis* on the coast. In the spring it is not a conspicuous part of the Savannah Sparrow population as it appears on its northward flight with the breeding forms that in the fall leave for the south before *alaudinus* appears in numbers. Our earliest fall date is September 15; our latest spring date, May 9. We have many specimens taken between these extremes in every section of the State.

The occasional wintering birds we have taken in the Willamette Valley, particularly in Portland, have all been of this race. There has been so much confusion of names between this migrant and the breeding *nevadensis* that it is impossible to satisfactorily assign the references in literature in many instances. All eastern Oregon breeding records should now be considered *nevadensis*, whereas migration records might be either. Because of the ease of confusing this and other races of the Savannah Sparrow we are basing our statements and discussions entirely on our collected birds. As our collecting has of necessity been on the hit-or-miss order, as opportunity offered, more systematic future work may change our present concept of the relations of these races.

Aleutian Savannah Sparrow:
Passerculus sandwichensis sandwichensis (Gmelin)

Description.—"*Adults: Crown stripe and superciliary well marked*, and superciliary usually decidedly yellow; upper parts grayish brown, *heavily streaked with black*, the streaks in sharp contrast to feather edgings of whitish, grayish, or buffy; under parts white, sometimes, especially in fall and winter, tinged with buffy on sides and chest; sides of throat, chest, sides, and flanks streaked with *blackish;* longer *under tail coverts with concealed streaks*. *Young:* similar, but light streaks of upper parts buffy, dark streaks of lower parts less defined, superciliary usually without yellow, and finely streaked with dusky. *Male:* length (skins) 4.93–5.75, wing 2.92–3.14, tail 2.00–2.20, bill .44–.50. *Female:* length (skins) 4.88–5.74, wing 2.70–3.06, tail 1.85–2.10, bill .44–.50." (Bailey) *Nest and eggs:* Same as for *P. s. alaudinus*.

Distribution.—*General:* Breeds in Unalaska and adjacent islands. Winters eastward and southward along coast to central California. *In Oregon:* Rather uncommon migrant resident. Most common along coast, although there are records inland as far as Klamath and Crook Counties.

The big Aleutian Savannah Sparrow is easily distinguished in the hand from all other forms and can usually be detected in the field by its much larger size. It appears in September (earliest date, September 27) and remains until November (latest date, November 5), and in the spring is present from April (earliest date, March 24) until May (latest date, May 20). The first record from the State, that of Henshaw (1880), who took birds on Crooked River in September, is also the farthest inland of two records from east of the Cascades. The second one is Merrill's (1888), from Fort Klamath. Woodcock (1902) listed it from Salem, Beaverton, and Corvallis, and Walker (1924) recorded a specimen from Netarts—the first coast record, although at present we find it to be much more regular in its appearance there than elsewhere in the State.

We have specimens from Netarts, Ocean Park, Port Orford, and Otter Crest along the coast and from Corvallis and Portland inland. In addition, we have four specimens, two from Eagle Point, Jackson County (Gabrielson), and one each from Gearhart and Netarts (Jewett Collection), that must be placed here unless *P. a. anthinus* is recognized, in which case, according to Swarth, these four records belong in that form.

Nevada Savannah Sparrow:
Passerculus sandwichensis nevadensis Grinnell

Description.—Whole lower surface pure white, with narrow blackish streaking on sides of throat, pectoral region, and flanks; sides and top of head with whitish ground, upon which the black streaking is sharply defined; anterior part of superciliary stripe pale canary yellow; whole back, wings, and tail with feathers centrally fuscous or dull blackish and with conspicuous edgings of either whitish or pale-clay color, or both; outer web and tip of outermost rectrix white, and next three inner rectrices outwardly margined and tipped with white but successively more narrowly. Similar to *P. s. alaudinus* and *savanna* but much paler throughout in all plumages, the white replacing the buff, making the black streaks more conspicuously contrasted. (Adapted from Grinnell 1910.) *Size:* Length (skins) 4.50–5.55, wing 2.65–2.88, tail 1.85–2.08, exposed culmen .36–.42. *Nest and eggs:* Same as for *P. s. alaudinus*.

Distribution.—*General:* Breeds in Great Basin from southern British Columbia, eastern Oregon, and northeastern California east to North Dakota and Colorado and south to southern California, southern Nevada, and northern New Mexico. Winters south into Mexico. *In Oregon:* Breeding form east of Cascades.

The Nevada Savannah Sparrow is a common but inconspicuous breeding species throughout the valleys of eastern Oregon. It arrives in April (earliest date, April 7, Wallowa County) and remains until August (latest date, August 20). It builds its nest of dried grass in a depression in the ground and deposits its eggs during May and June. Our dates for full sets of eggs range from May 19 to June 19, but we have been able to put all too little time on gathering nesting data. In April and May, during the courtship and nest-building period, the inconspicuously marked males give their wheezy little song from the top of a weed stalk or from convenient fence posts about the pastures. The breeding form seems to disappear early, as our latest specimen was taken August 20. We have a representative series of fall Savannah Sparrows taken in September and October in their territory, but all prove to be northern forms.

There has been much confusion in the names of Savannah Sparrows so that it is difficult to assign accurately all references in literature to the forms now accepted as valid. Bendire's (1877) records of breeding birds from Camp Harney certainly apply to *nevadensis*. Likewise the records of Mearns (1879) and Merrill (1888) from Fort Klamath belong under this subspecies. Willett (1919) listed it as a breeding bird at Malheur Lake, and Gabrielson (1924a) considered it a common resident of Wallowa County.

Brook's Savannah Sparrow:
Passerculus sandwichensis brooksi Bishop

Description.—Smaller, but slightly darker and browner than *P. s. nevadensis*. *Size:* Wing 2.62, tail 1.83, bill .39. *Nest and eggs:* Same as those of *P. s. alaudinus* (Plate 92, *A*).

Distribution.—*General:* Breeds in western Washington and Oregon. Winters south into California. *In Oregon:* Breeding form throughout Willamette Valley and in coast counties, at least as far south as Coos County.

After long study and consideration of our series of breeding Savannah Sparrows from the Willamette Valley and the coast counties we are forced to the conclusion that Brook's Savannah Sparrow is a valid race, despite its omission from the 1931 A. O. U. Check-List. That list recognized no breeding Savannah Sparrows in Oregon west of the Cascades, and we cannot correlate our birds with any of the forms listed. They are most like *P. a. nevadensis* but are smaller and darker in comparable plumages, and the young birds have distinctly more yellow tones in their plumages.

Since its original description by Bishop this form has appeared in Oregon literature only twice. Walker (1924) listed it from Tillamook, and we included it in *Birds of the Portland Area* (Jewett and Gabrielson 1929), where it is a common summer bird in the river-bottom pastures. We have one straggler, a bird taken at Sparks Lake, Deschutes County, on September 7, that is our only specimen from outside the breeding area, although this Savannah Sparrow undoubtedly passes through the Umpqua and Rogue River Valleys in migration. It happens, however, that our specimens from this territory are of other forms.

While in Oregon, Brook's Savannah Sparrow is characteristically a bird of the open grasslands, where it is a common but inconspicuous summer resident. It appears in April and remains until late September (earliest date, April 1; latest, October 7, both Multnomah County). Its insectlike song, given from a fence post or the top of a weed stalk, attracts little more attention than does the dull-colored, mouselike bird itself, which is overlooked by most people. Breeding records are scarce, but a set of five eggs was taken by Alex Walker at Tillamook on May 26, 1928.

Bryant's Sparrow:
Passerculus sandwichensis bryanti Ridgway

Description.—"Like *sandwichensis*, but darker and browner, with under parts more heavily streaked with black, and in winter plumage, chest, and sides strongly tinged with brownish buff. *Male:* length (skins) 4.53–5.00, wing 2.51–2.80, tail 1.74–2.00, bill .40–.45. *Female:* length (skins) 4.40–4.65, wing 2.47–2.69, tail 1.70–1.92, bill .40–.43." (Bailey) *Nest and eggs:* Same as for other Savannah Sparrows.

Distribution.—*General:* Breeds from southwestern Oregon along coast to San Luis Obispo County, California. Winters southward along coast. *In Oregon:* Found sparingly as summer resident of coastal marshes of Curry County south to California line.

Bryant's Sparrow was first detected in Oregon by Dr. Louis B. Bishop, when he collected specimens at Wedderburn, July 2 and 3, 1929 (Jewett 1930a). Since that time Jewett has collected two adults and two young birds at the mouth of Pistol River (July 11, 1934) that are undoubtedly of this race. This establishes beyond question this form as a summer resident of the extreme southwestern corner of the State.

Plate 92, *A.* Nest and eggs of Brook's Savannah Sparrow. (Photo by Alex Walker.)

Plate 92, *B.* Nest and eggs of Western Vesper Sparrow. (Photo by Alex Walker.)

Western Grasshopper Sparrow:
Ammodramus savannarum bimaculatus Swainson

Description.—"*Adults in summer: under parts buffy on throat and sides*, unmarked; *upper parts reddish brown*, black, gray, and buffy; crown with median buffy stripe between two blackish stripes; nuchal patch ash gray, marked with reddish brown; feathers of back with black eye spots niched with reddish brown; edge of wing yellow; tail double rounded and feathers sharp pointed. *Adults in winter:* brighter colored, chest and sides sometimes indistinctly streaked with brown. *Young:* with little or no reddish brown on upper parts, the feathers being more conspicuously bordered with buffy and whitish; median crown stripe more ashy; lower parts entirely dull buffy whitish, chest distinctly streaked with dusky. *Male:* length (skins) 4.20–5.10, wing 2.25–2.61, tail 1.69–2.02, bill .40–.46. *Female:* length (skins) 4.40–4.85, wing 2.39–2.51, tail 1.82–2.00, bill .40–.44." (Bailey) *Nest:* Of dried grasses, more or less arched over, placed on ground. *Eggs:* 3 to 5, white, spotted with brown, black, or lilac on larger end.

Distribution.—*General:* Breeds from southeastern British Columbia, Montana, North Dakota, and Minnesota south to southern California and southern Texas. Winters from central California and southern Texas south into Mexico. *In Oregon:* Known from one specimen.

Woodcock (1902) listed the Western Grasshopper Sparrow from the Willamette Valley on the authority of Ellis F. Hadley, who called it a "rare migrant," at Dayton and stated that the Warner and Cooke's collection contained a specimen taken May 4, 1888. We have gone over the above collection without finding such a specimen, and Dr. Cooke has no recollection of it. Under the circumstances we do not believe that this constitutes a valid record for the bird in western Oregon. We would look for the bird in the foothill country around the Blue Mountains rather than in the wooded country of the western part of the State, and the Western Grasshopper Sparrow is undoubtedly a more or less regular migrant there, though it has been detected but once. There is a specimen in the Biological Survey collection taken at Robinette, Baker County, June 22, 1916, by H. H. Sheldon that is the only record for the State. This is not surprising when the limited amount of work done in this district is considered. The elusive habits of the bird render it difficult to see, and the weak insectlike song is not likely to attract much attention to its author.

Oregon Vesper Sparrow:
Pooecetes gramineus affinis (Miller)

Description.—"Like *confinis*, but smaller, bill more slender, coloration browner; ground color of upper parts buffy brown rather than grayish brown, and all the light areas of the plumage, including under side of wings, suffused with pinkish buff. *Male:* length (skins) 5.17–5.55, wing 2.90–3.15, tail 2.08–2.38, bill .40–.45. *Female:* length (skins) 5.04–5.65, wing 2.85–3.00, tail 2.20–2.27, bill .40–.46." (Bailey) *Nest and eggs:* Same as for *P. g. confinis*.

DISTRIBUTION.—*General:* Breeds from southern British Columbia south to southern Oregon west of Cascades. Winters south to Lower California. *In Oregon:* Common summer resident west of Cascades from March to September.

THE SMALLER and browner (as compared to *P. g. confinis*) Oregon Vesper Sparrow is an abundant summer resident of the Willamette Valley and a somewhat less common resident in the other valleys west of the Cascades (earliest record, February 22, Jackson County; latest, October 9, Yamhill County). It was not recognized until 1888 when Miller described it, using birds from Salem as the type, but Anthony's (1886) records for Washington County are clearly the first published Oregon reference that pertain to the form. It is less common in the coastal valleys but can be looked for in open meadow and farm lands where it frequents the fence rows and pasture lands.

We have only two definite nesting records, although it is a common summer species. Gabrielson took a set of four eggs in June 1921, on Powell Valley road east of Portland, and Jewett has one from Government Island taken by Dick Bartlett. A little careful search in any farming district would undoubtedly furnish many other nesting records, but this is another of the numerous things that remains undone for lack of time.

Western Vesper Sparrow:
Pooecetes gramineus confinis Baird

DESCRIPTION.—"Upper parts brownish gray narrowly streaked with dusky; *bend of wing reddish brown; outer tail feathers partly white;* under parts dull white, more or less tinged with pale buffy; streaked along sides of throat and across chest. *Male:* length (skins) 5.50–6.25, wing 3.12–3.41, tail 2.49–2.70, bill .43–.46. *Female:* length (skins) 5.21–6.00, wing 3.00–3.30, tail 2.27–2.68, bill .41–.49." (Bailey) *Nest:* Slight depression in the ground, lined with grass. *Eggs:* 3 to 6, greenish white, spotted and streaked with brown and lavender (Plate 92, *B*).

DISTRIBUTION.—*General:* Breeds from British Columbia, Alberta, and Saskatchewan southeast of Cascades to California, Arizona, and Texas. Winters south into Mexico. *In Oregon:* Common summer resident of area east of Cascades.

AS WITH so many other variable birds in Oregon, the forms of the Vesper Sparrow are divided by the Cascades, and the present one, the Western Vesper Sparrow, is the subspecies that is a common summer resident to the east. Its beautiful vesper song is a striking and characteristic sound of the evening throughout that part of the State, where it becomes abundant in early April (earliest date, March 23, Klamath County) and remains a common roadside bird until September (latest date, September 20, Lake County). Such inconspicuously colored sparrows as this one greatly confuse beginners in the study of birds. Each species, however, has certain characteristic marks that serve to identify it with certainty. The Western Vesper Sparrow is the only nesting sparrow of the open low valleys that displays white outer tail feathers in flight, which together with the rufous patch on the bend of the wing serve to distinguish it from all others in the State.

Jewett has found nests containing fresh eggs in Guano Valley (Lake County) on May 24 and Hay Creek (Jefferson County) on June 20, Braly (ms.) took eggs in Klamath County on May 18 and 25, and Bendire (Brewer 1875) recorded a nest and eggs at Camp Harney, May 27, 1875, which was not only the first published nesting record for the State, but also the first record of the species for the State. Subsequent writers have listed it from many localities. These published references, the manuscript notes in the Biological Survey, and our own rather voluminous records show it to be one of the characteristic breeding birds.

Western Lark Sparrow:
Chondestes grammacus strigatus Swainson

Description.—"*Adults: Sides of head with chestnut patch and black and white streaks;* crown chestnut, with white or buffy median stripe; rest of upper parts brownish gray, the back streaked with blackish; *tail blackish brown with white corners*, all but middle feathers tipped with white; under parts white, with a small black central spot on breast. *Young:* without chestnut patch or black and white streaks on head; entire upper parts buffy or brownish, streaked; chest with wedge-shaped blackish streaks. *Male:* length (skins) 5.60–6.60, wing 3.20–3.62, tail 2.52–3.00, bill .41–.54. *Female:* length (skins) 5.50–6.75, wing 3.12–3.51, tail 2.40–2.81, bill .42–.51." (Bailey) *Nest:* On ground or in bushes or low trees, a somewhat flimsy structure of dried grasses and plant stems. *Eggs:* 3 to 6, white, strikingly lined and speckled, especially on the large end, with black and brown (Plate 93, *A*).

Distribution.—*General:* Breeds from southern British Columbia and southern Saskatchewan south to Mexico and east to Great Plains. Winters south to Central America. *In Oregon:* Common summer resident of all of eastern Oregon, except higher mountains. Equally abundant in valleys of Jackson and Josephine Counties. Less common in Umpqua Valley, straggling occasionally northward into Willamette Valley.

The Western Lark Sparrow is easily identified by the brown head markings, the brown spot in the center of the breast, and the white tips to the tail feathers that become conspicuous when the tail is spread fanwise in flight, a mannerism characteristic of the species. This sparrow has a curious distribution in Oregon. It is an abundant roadside bird of the valleys east of the Cascades, is equally numerous in the Rogue River Valley, and is noted frequently but not commonly in the Umpqua Valley. It becomes common the last ten days of March (earliest date, February 22, Jackson County) and remains until about September 15.

The first published Oregon record was by Baird (Baird, Cassin, and Lawrence 1858), who reported it from The Dalles, May 21, 1856. Many subsequent writers have listed it. Johnson (1880) stated that it was a tolerably common breeder in the Willamette Valley, a condition that certainly does not prevail at present, although Jewett saw one near

Plate 93, *A*. Nest and eggs of Western Lark Sparrow. (Photo by Ira N. Gabrielson.)

Plate 93, *B*. Shufeldt's Junco on nest. (Photo by Wm. L. and Irene Finley.)

Goshen, Lane County, July 22, 1927. Woodcock (1902) considered it an uncommon summer resident and breeder at Corvallis, where he found three June nests, all in apple trees at heights of from 4 to 8 feet from the ground. He also recorded Ellis F. Hadley's report of it as a "not uncommon summer resident" at Dayton. Johnson A. Neff (ms.) reported it from Corvallis, April 1, 1925, the most northern recent record we have for the Willamette Valley. The species appears regularly in the Biological Survey manuscript notes for the eastern and southern sections of the State. One record by Sheldon is of a nest containing five fresh eggs from Homestead, Baker County, June 9, 1916. Patterson reported eggs from May 14 to 27. A few stragglers stay behind and possibly winter in southern Oregon, as we have scattered records for the Rogue River Valley as late as December 14.

Desert Sparrow:
Amphispiza bilineata deserticola Ridgway

Description.—"*Adults:* Lores and throat patch black; sides of head dark gray with two white stripes, under parts mainly white; upper parts plain grayish brown; tail, except middle feathers, marked with white. *Young:* without distinct black markings; throat white often marked with gray; chest streaked; wing coverts and edges of tertials light buffy brown. *Male:* length (skins) 4.90–5.45, wing 2.52–2.78, tail 2.40–2.69, bill .39–.42. *Female:* length (skins) 4.80–5.20, wing 2.45–2.60, tail 2.32–2.49, bill .36–.41." (Bailey) *Nest:* In shrubs, made of grass and plant stems and lined with feathers, hair, and wool. *Eggs:* 3 or 4, bluish white.

Distribution.—*General:* Breeds from northeastern California, northern Nevada, Utah, and Colorado south into Mexico. Winters from southern United States southward. *In Oregon:* Known only from two records as rare straggler.

This southern bird, the Desert Sparrow, has straggled into Oregon twice, both times in Harney County. Jewett (1913b) recorded two specimens taken on Wright's Point, June 24 and 25, 1908, by William L. Finley and Herman T. Bohlman. These skins are now in Finley's possession. The other record is of a skin (Jewett Collection No. 2065) taken by Jewett, July 15, 1912, at Silver Lake, in Harney County, not many miles from the spot where the first birds were taken. Although both of us have spent a great deal of time in the sagebrush country of the southeastern part of the State we have failed to detect this species in recent years.

Northern Sage Sparrow:
Amphispiza nevadensis nevadensis (Ridgway)

Description.—"*Adults: Sides of throat with a series of narrow blackish* streaks, but no continuous stripe; chest with black spot; sides and flanks faintly tinged with light brown; rest of under parts whitish; upper parts light grayish brown, back usually streaked narrowly but clearly; outer web of lateral tail feather white. *Young:* like adults but upper parts and chest streaked, and wings with two buffy bands. *Male:* length (skins) 5.50–6.20, wing 3.05–3.20, tail 2.78–3.09, bill .37–.41. *Female:* length (skins) 5.40–6.20, wing 2.85–3.15, tail 2.65–2.98, bill .37–.41." (Bailey) *Nest:* In low bushes and brush, largely of strips of sagebrush bark and fine grasses. *Eggs:* 3 or 4, greenish to grayish white, speckled around larger end with brown.

DISTRIBUTION.—*General:* Breeds in Great Basin from central Washington, central Idaho, southwestern Montana, and western Colorado south to southern Nevada, Utah, and northern New Mexico. Winters south into Mexico. *In Oregon:* Common summer resident and breeding species of sagebrush areas of eastern Oregon. May occasionally winter along Columbia River, as we have one record for January 14 at Umatilla. One record only for western Oregon.

TO THINK of the Northern Sage Sparrow brings to mind the sage-covered sand areas of northern Morrow County, the Fort Rock and Silver Lake area of northern Lake County, and the great valleys of the Silvies and Blitzen Rivers of Harney County, for this is typically a sagebrush bird, its soft coloration blending into the gray landscape so perfectly that it is difficult to detect so long as it remains motionless. Its habit of mounting the topmost twig of a sagebrush, however, to sing its tinkling little refrain, twitching its long black tail all the while, offers an opportunity to view this little desert dweller to good advantage. In common with most other brush-inhabiting species, it has an almost uncanny ability to slip from one bush to another, keeping out of sight of an intruder as it does so.

It nests in the sagebrush areas, usually building on the ground at the base of a sage plant or on a low elevation in the bushes, where it lays three or four eggs in a neat nest of shredded sagebrush bark and grass. Dates on which nests containing fresh eggs have been found vary from April 5 to May 23, depending somewhat on the elevation. The earliest dates are for the sage areas along the Columbia River near Boardman, and the later nests are found on the high sage plateaus of the southeastern part of the State. A. J. Knoblock found a nest containing five young, March 29, 1934, in the area south of Boardman. That season was one that will long be remembered as the year almost without a winter. Wild flowers were in abundant bloom in late January, and this pair of sage sparrows evidently took advantage of the abnormal temperature conditions to nest at least a month ahead of time.

There is one straggler recorded from Portland, where on February 18 and 19, 1914, Jewett watched one from a distance of less than 20 feet in the Sellwood district. An east wind had been blowing for several days—a condition that often caused a drift of eastern Oregon birds down the Columbia to the vicinity of Portland. This record and one on January 14 near Umatilla indicate that the birds winter at least rarely.

The Sage Sparrow has been known from Oregon since Bendire (Brewer 1875) found it breeding near Camp Harney, although little has been written about it. Peck (1911a) found it common in northern Malheur, Walker (1917b) listed it from central Oregon, Willett (1919) considered it common at Malheur Lake, and we listed the Portland straggler in our *Birds of the Portland Area* (Jewett and Gabrielson 1929). These are all the references to it in Oregon ornithological literature.

Our own notes show that we have found it regularly and abundantly in Lake, Morrow, and Harney Counties—the counties containing the great sagebrush areas of Oregon, where one knowing the bird would expect to find it—and less commonly in Malheur, Deschutes, Klamath, Wasco, Jefferson, Crook, and Umatilla Counties, with the one straggler to Multnomah referred to above. It arrives in March and remains until October (earliest date, March 17; latest, October 20, both Lake County). More continuous observation will undoubtedly reveal it in other eastern Oregon counties.

Slate-colored Junco:
Junco hyemalis hyemalis (Linnaeus)

DESCRIPTION.—"*Adults: Whole body, except white belly, dark slaty gray*, often blackish on head in male and washed with brownish in immature male and female, when the sides are also washed with pinkish brown; *two pairs* of outer tail feathers white; bill in life pinkish white or flesh-color. *Young in first plumage:* streaked on brown upper parts, and buffy white under parts, wings with brownish band. *Male:* length (skins) 5.44–6.23, wing 3.02–3.24, tail 2.49–2.80, bill .40–.46. *Female:* length (skins) 5.22–6.10, wing 2.78–3.08, tail 2.45–2.64, bill .39–.46." (Bailey) *Nest:* On the ground or close to it, composed of dried grass and rootlets and lined with similar material. *Eggs:* 4 or 5, white to buffy, speckled with brown.

DISTRIBUTION.—*General:* Breeds from northern Alaska, Mackenzie, Manitoba, and central Quebec south to southern Yukon, Alberta, Minnesota, Michigan, and Pennsylvania. Winters south to Gulf coast. *In Oregon:* Appears as irregular fall migrant or winter resident mostly in eastern Oregon but occasionally in western part of State.

THE FIRST RECORD of the Slate-colored Junco in Oregon is that of Woodcock (1902), who saw one, November 23, 1899, at Corvallis and collected a specimen there, January 13, 1900. There is a skin now in the Jewett collection taken at Netarts by Mrs. R. C. Nielson in the winter of 1916, and Gabrielson has one taken at Portland, January 1, 1928, which was recorded in our *Birds of the Portland Area* (Jewett and Gabrielson 1929) as Cassiar Junco (*J. h. connectens*), a form no longer recognized in the A. O. U. Check-List. These are the only specimens available from the area west of the Cascades. In eastern Oregon we have found these juncos much more frequently. Jewett (1916a) recorded the first one from Miller's Ranch, near the mouth of the Deschutes River, April 12, 1915, and we now have additional skins from the following localities: La Grande, Nyssa, Ontario, Hart Mountain, Klamath Falls, Maupin, Little Summit

Prairie (eastern Crook County), Jack Creek, Adel, and northern Lake County, northeast of Silver Lake. It is found from October (earliest date, September 16, Lake County) to March (latest date, April 12, Wasco County). The localities where these juncos have been found are widely scattered, indicating that continuous observation would reveal the species almost everywhere in the eastern part of the State.

While in Oregon, the birds are usually found in company with the more abundant Shufeldt's Juncos and can be distinguished from them easily by their larger size and the absence of black on the head and pink on the flank. Their behavior is like that of the other species—the flocks, often mixed with other sparrows, feeding together in the weed patches or working through the brush patches and displaying the conspicuous white outer tail feathers as they flit nervously from bush to bush ahead of an observer. When disturbed from the ground the birds often seek shelter in the coniferous trees where they may remain unseen, although their presence is known from the twittering alarm note uttered at frequent intervals.

Oregon Junco:
Junco oreganus oreganus (Townsend)

Description.—"*Adult male:* Head, neck, and chest black or dark slaty, the black chest pattern outlined on the white of the under parts as a black convex; *middle of back dark brown;* sides deep pinkish brown; three outer tail feathers with white, outside pair wholly white. *Adult female:* black of male replaced by slaty; crown and hind neck washed with brown, and rest of upper parts brownish; sides and flanks duller; bill in life pinkish, tipped with dusky, and iris dark brown or claret color. *In winter:* colors stronger, and feathers of chest tipped with whitish. *Young:* streaked, on brown above, buffy below. *Male*: length (skins) 5.50–6.07, wing 2.86–3.08, tail 2.43–2.69, bill .41–.45. *Female:* length (skins) 5.17–5.79, wing 2.78–2.86, tail 2.34–2.46, bill .41–.45." (Bailey) *Nest:* On the ground, made of dried grass and lined with vegetable fiber and hair. *Eggs:* 4 or 5, white, speckled about large end with brown.

Distribution.—*General:* Breeds from Yakutat Bay, Alaska, to Queen Charlotte Islands and Vancouver Island. Winters southward along coast to California. *In Oregon:* Uncommon winter visitor in Willamette Valley and on coast.

As the Oregon Junco is now understood, it is the breeding bird of the coast of southern Alaska and British Columbia that winters south in small numbers in Oregon from October to March (earliest date, October 12; latest, March 18, both Tillamook County), being most abundant on the northern part of the coast. It is a darker and much redder bird in winter than is the much more abundant Shufeldt's Junco, and it can, under favorable light conditions, be distinguished in the field. Under usual conditions, however, this subspecies cannot be distinguished by field observations alone, and we are basing our statements regarding it on collected specimens. We have skins from Tillamook and Lincoln Counties and from numerous points in the Willamette Valley and consider the species most regular along the coast south to and including Lincoln County.

At one time all of the breeding juncos of this territory were called *J. o. oregonus*, and this has made it impossible to correctly determine the proper allocation of old records. Anthony (1886) recorded it as abundant in Washington County, but this record obviously applies largely to *J. o. shufeldti*, although the present form undoubtedly occurred there sparingly in his time just as it does now. Mearns' (1879) and Merrill's (1888) breeding records from Klamath County are undoubtedly referable to *J. o. thurberi*, and Bendire's breeding records from Camp Harney to *J. o. shufeldti*. Bowles' (1901b) eggs recorded from Waldo, Josephine County, also are properly referable to *J. o. thurberi*. Of the winter records, the majority of those west of the Cascades and also those east of that range undoubtedly are now to be considered *J. o. shufeldti*, although a number of this form occurs.

Shufeldt's Junco:
Junco oreganus shufeldti Coale

Description.—"Similar to *oreganus*, but head and neck blackish *slate* instead of jet black, *back dull brown* and sides pinkish brown. *Male:* length (skins) 5.55–6.20, wing 3.00–3.22, tail 2.62–2.84, bill .42–.46. *Female:* length (skins) 5.40–5.92, wing 2.82–3.08, tail 2.30–2.71, bill .41–.43." (Bailey) *Nest and eggs:* Same as those of *J. o. oreganus* (Plate 94).

Distribution.—*General:* Breeds from central British Columbia to Alberta and south to Oregon. Winters south to Mexico. *In Oregon:* Breeds from Columbia River to Umpqua Valley and south in Cascades to vicinity of Three Sisters and eastward in Blue Mountains to Idaho line. Winters throughout State.

Shufeldt's Junco (Plate 93, *B*) is the common junco of the State except in the southern part. It breeds throughout the wooded sections of western Oregon and in the Blue Mountains in suitable locations. Bendire (1877) listed juncos as breeding birds on Canyon Mountain, the first Oregon record that can unquestionably be referred to this form, although of many later notes, the majority undoubtedly refer to this species. The present name, *J. o. shufeldti*, was first used by Bohlman (1903) in referring to Oregon birds, and Miller (1904) recorded juncos under this name from Wheeler County. Since that time there have been numerous records. The summer birds from the northern Cascades are undoubtedly this form, gradually merging into *J. o. thurberi* in the vicinity of the Three Sisters, in eastern Lane County. In the Umpqua Valley the same intergradation occurs.

The nests are usually neatly woven of grass and rootlets and are built

Plate 94. Nest and eggs of Shufeldt's Junco. (Photo by Alex Walker.)

on or close to the ground at the base of a shrub or under an overhanging bank along a creek or trail (Plate 94). Breeding extends over a long period. Our records contain dates for fresh eggs from May 1 to July 18.

After the nesting season the birds roam the country in small family flocks that gradually merge into larger groups that sometimes number into the hundreds. The birds fly close to the ground, straggling along a few at a time unless flushed by some sudden disturbance. Once an observer has learned their characteristic flight note and sharp alarm note, he will hear them much more frequently than he will see them. If the flock is alarmed, the birds make a quick dash to a thick tree where they remain motionless, save for nervous twitchings of their tails, until the danger is past, and then the chattering note is again heard for some little time before the birds venture to return to their feeding place.

Montana Junco:
Junco oreganus montanus Ridgway

Description.—"*Adult male:* Head, neck, and chest slate color; back dull light brown; sides pale pinkish; belly white; outer tail feathers largely white. *Adult female:* similar, but duller, and brown of back extending up over crown. *Adults in winter:* plumage softer. *Young in first winter:* similar to winter adults, but duller, feathers edged largely with brownish. *Male:* length (skins) 5.49–6.00, wing 3.02–3.28, tail 2.58–2.78, bill .39–.44. *Female:* length (skins) 5.25–5.69, wing 2.88–3.03, tail 2.35–2.65, bill .39–.44." (Bailey) *Nest and eggs:* Similar to those of *J. o. thurberi*.

Distribution.—*General:* Breeds in Canadian Zone from southern Alberta south to Idaho and northwestern Montana. Winters south to Mexico. *In Oregon:* Known only as winter resident of Wallowa, Umatilla, Union, Malheur, Baker, and Grant Counties.

Although the latest A. O. U. Check-List includes this subspecies, the Montana Junco, as a breeding bird for eastern Oregon, we have so far been unable to confirm this statement. All our breeding birds from the northeastern corner of the State are much more nearly like *J. o. shufeldti*. We do have numerous winter specimens of this gray-sided bird from the mountains of northeastern Oregon, however, and they are easily distinguished in the hand from the much more common pink-sided *shufeldti*. We are therefore listing this as a wintering species only for the Blue Mountain area, where it is a regular winter resident at least as far south as Ontario and the John Day Valley. It probably will be found farther to the south, particularly in Harney County, when more adequate collecting is carried out. The species is present from October (earliest date, September 1, Baker County) until March (latest date, April 15, Deschutes County). In addition to our own numerous records from the Blue Mountains, there are skins in the Biological Survey collection from Bend (Deschutes County), April 15, 1915; Millers (Wasco County), April 10,

1915; Cord (Malheur County), October 11, 1911; and Cornucopia (Baker County), September 1, 1915. There is a record in the Biological Survey files of a bird from Corvallis, April 2, 1900, identified by Oberholser, but we can find no other trace of it. The specimen may have been one of Woodcock's skins, as he was active there at that time.

The Montana Junco was first recorded for Oregon by Oberholser (1922b), who listed both summer and winter specimens from about the territory given above. He now considers the summer birds to be *shufeldti*, however, a conclusion with which we agree. The only other published record is Gabrielson's (1924a) statement that it is a winter resident of Wallowa County.

Thurber's Junco:
Junco oreganus thurberi Anthony

Description.—"Similar to *oreganus*, but wings and tail longer; head, throat, and breast deep black, *sharply contrasting with light brown of back;* sides buffy rather than pink; young resembling *oreganus*, but upper parts lighter. *Male:* length (skins) 5.32–5.95, wing 2.94–3.12, tail 2.48–2.68, bill .40–.46. *Female:* length (skins) 5.00–5.67, wing 2.82–2.94, tail 2.38–2.56, bill .41–.43." (Bailey) *Nest and eggs:* Same as for *J. o. oreganus*.

Distribution.—*General:* Breeds from southern Oregon south through Sierra Nevada and Coast Ranges to San Diego County, California. Winters south to Lower California. *In Oregon:* Breeds from Three Sisters and Umpqua Valley south through Siskiyous and east through Klamath and Lake Counties to eastern edge of yellow pine in mountains of Lake County. Winters through same area, often mixed with *J. o. shufeldti*.

This paler form, Thurber's Junco, is the breeding subspecies of junco in eastern Lane, Douglas, Coos, Josephine, Jackson, Klamath, Lake, southeastern Deschutes, and probably Curry Counties. In habits and behavior, it is identical with the other forms and can be distinguished from *J. o. shufeldti* only by careful comparison of specimens in the hand. Mearns' (1879) breeding records for Klamath County are referable to this form as now defined and constitute the first recognizable reference to it. It nests in May and June, Patterson (ms.) reporting nests from April 25 to July 7.

Western Tree Sparrow:
Spizella arborea ochracea Brewster

Description.—"*Adults:* Bill yellow in adults; crown, stripe behind eye, and patch on sides of chest rufous, crown often, especially in winter, with ashy median stripe, or rufous obscured by grayish edges to feathers; middle of back buffy, streaked with black and rusty; wings with two conspicuous white bars; under parts grayish, *chest with small dusky spot*. *Young:* streaked beneath. *Male:* length (skins) 5.61–6.00, wing 2.87–3.24, tail 2.59–2.88, bill .38–.41. *Female:* length (skins) 5.41–5.69, wing 2.87–3.10, tail 2.60–2.70, bill .35–.39." (Bailey) *Nest:* On ground or in low bushes, of dried grass and feathers. *Eggs:* 3 to 5, pale greenish blue to brownish, speckled with warm brown.

DISTRIBUTION.—*General:* Breeds from Bering Sea and Point Barrow east to Anderson River and south in mountains to British Columbia. Winters south to New Mexico and Texas. *In Oregon:* Irregular winter resident.

WE DO NOT consider the Western Tree Sparrow an abundant bird in Oregon, nor do published records for the State indicate that others have found it in great numbers. It is an irregular winter resident that reaches Oregon in October (earliest record, October 23, Lake County) and remains until March (our latest record, March 14, Baker County). Bendire (Brewer 1875) reported it at Camp Harney between November 14 and December 5, listed it as moderately abundant there as a winter bird (Bendire 1877), and recorded a specimen seen there on February 5, 1875 (Bendire 1888b). Henshaw (1879) recorded it from The Dalles. After Bendire's (1888) publication it was not again mentioned in Oregon literature until Woodcock (1902) in his list of the birds of the State quoted Bendire's (1877) record but added nothing to it. Grinnell (1902a) published a record from Newport of a bird taken, April 9, 1901, by B. J. Bretherton, not only the latest date for the species in the State but also the only authentic record from west of the Cascades. The next published mention of the species in Oregon ornithological literature was Gabrielson's record from Wallowa County.

This brings us down to our own information, which is meager enough. In view of the infrequent appearance of this sparrow, we list the following records, all substantiated by specimens collected: Two specimens, Hermiston (December 10, 1916, Jewett); two specimens, Enterprise (February 18, 1919, Jewett and Gabrielson); one specimen, Adel, Lake County (October 23, 1926, Gabrielson); three specimens, Ontario (two December 15, 1926; one January 4, 1927, Jewett); and one specimen, Keating, Baker County (March 14, 1929, Jewett).

Almost invariably these birds are found in Oregon about small willow patches, either about springs or creek bottoms. They are usually solitary birds, or at most occur in groups of three or four, and are neither as noisy nor as abundant as the Tree Sparrows of the Eastern States. Their quiet ways render them difficult of detection, and it is possible that they often escape notice and are in fact more abundant than the above records indicate.

Western Chipping Sparrow: *Spizella passerina arizonae* Coues

DESCRIPTION.—"*Adults in summer:* Bill black; top of head rufous, sometimes with indication of ashy median line and dark streaking; *forehead blackish*, cut by median white line; superciliary stripe white or grayish, bordered below by narrow *black eye stripe;* back brownish or pale buffy, streaked with black; rump and upper tail coverts gray; sides of head *dull gray;* under parts white or ashy. *Adults in winter:* similar, but colors duller and darker, tinged with brown on lower parts, black on forehead obscure or wanting, crown usually streaked with dusky, bill brown. *Young:* top of head brownish streaked with blackish; superciliary buffy, streaked; breast streaked; tarsus less than twice as long as bill. *Male:* length (skins) 4.82–5.43, wing 2.64–3.00, tail 2.11–2.57, bill .36–.41. *Female:* length (skins) 4.87–5.26, wing 2.62–2.98, tail 2.12–2.42, bill .35–.40." (Bailey) *Nest:* A neat cup of grass, lined with horse hair and usually close to the ground. *Eggs:* 3 to 5, greenish blue, speckled, largely at big end, with black and brown.

DISTRIBUTION.—*General:* Breeds from southern British Columbia and central Alberta south to Mexico. Winters south far into Mexico. *In Oregon:* Abundant summer resident.

THE WESTERN CHIPPING SPARROW, with its dull-red cap and prominent white line over the eye, is one of our most abundant summer resident birds and is one of the familiar lawn birds of the valley towns throughout the State, where it may be found hopping about in the grass, collecting insects and seeds to feed the youngsters in the hair-lined nest built in some low-hanging bough. It is equally abundant and unsuspicious about the mountain meadows of the Cascades and in the parklike vistas of the yellow-pine forests of the Blue Mountains, where it is present at all but the highest elevations. Its monotonous little song and hair-lined nests are both well known to the small boys, who are often familiar with the "horse hair" bird, before they ever learn the name "Chipping Sparrow." It arrives in early April (earliest date, March 9, Washington County) and remains until September (latest date, October 11, Lake County). It nests usually in June. Egg dates vary from May 1 to July 3, although nests with young have been found as late as July 17.

It was first made known from Oregon by Baird (Baird, Cassin, and Lawrence 1858), who reported it from The Dalles, May 2, 1855, and since that time has had a place in every list of Oregon birds. Our own notes, as well as the Biological Survey files, are filled with records from every county in the State. Willett (1919) commented on seeing several hundred Western Chipping Sparrows in the sagebrush near Malheur Lake on May 14. This was evidently one of those interrupted migrating movements that occasionally causes the sagebrush to blossom out in unexpected colors. We have neither of us happened to see such a migration of Chipping Sparrows but have noted it in connection with other species.

Brewer's Sparrow:
Spizella breweri breweri Cassin

DESCRIPTION.—"*Adults: Entire upper parts streaked with black* on grayish brown ground; under parts soiled grayish. *In winter:* similar but more buffy. *Young:* like adults, but chest and sides streaked, streaks of upper parts broader and less sharply defined, and wings with two distinct bands. *Male:* length (skins) 4.74–5.13, wing

2.37–2.59, tail 2.26–2.44, bill .34–.35. *Female:* length (skins) 4.60–5.19, wing 2.20–2.59, tail 2.26–2.50, bill .34–.36." (Bailey) *Nest:* A compact cup of fine grass, lined with horse hair and placed in a thick sagebrush. *Eggs:* 3 or 4, greenish blue, speckled about the larger end with brown.

DISTRIBUTION.—*General:* Breeds from southeastern British Columbia, Alberta, Montana, and Nebraska south, practically to Mexican boundary. *In Oregon:* Abundant summer resident of sagebrush areas of eastern Oregon.

BREWER'S SPARROW, the little gray sagebrush counterpart of the Chipping Sparrow, is equally as abundant as its more brightly colored cousin, although it sticks persistently to its chosen home. In fact, sagebrush and Brewer's Sparrows are almost synonymous in our experience. Even in isolated patches of sage, high on warm southern exposures in the Blue Mountains, Brewer's Sparrow will be found singing his monotonous little song, and a few moments search, if it be late June, will almost as certainly disclose a cup-shaped nest of dried grasses and fine vegetable fiber skillfully woven into some thick sage top as a receptacle for three or four beautiful greenish-blue eggs wreathed about the larger end with spots and flecks of brown. Bendire (Brewer 1875) took three sets of eggs near Camp Harney, May 29, 1875, which is not only the first nesting record for the State but also the first mention of the species in Oregon ornithological literature. Since then it has been frequently recorded until we now know it as an abundant summer resident and breeding species of every county east of the Cascades that arrives in April (earliest date, April 9, Sherman County) and remains until September (latest date, September 26, Harney County).

The normal nesting season is June, and we have found the greatest number of nests (15) between June 10 and 21. Our earliest date is May 18, near Lakeview, and a nest containing newly hatched young was found as late as July 22, near Crane, by Vernon Bailey and R. H. Becker, of the Biological Survey. Patterson (ms.) took eggs from May 5 to 25.

Harris's Sparrow:
Zonotrichia querula (Nuttall)

DESCRIPTION.—"*Adults:* Top of head and throat solid black, black streaking down over middle of breast; rest of under parts white; sides and flanks buffy brown, streaked with darker brown; upper parts brown; back and scapulars streaked with blackish; wings with two white bars. *Young, first plumage* (described by Preble): upper parts blackish, feathers edged with buffy and brown; wing quills edged with buffy and brown; tail feathers edged and tipped with whitish; sides of head and under parts buffy; malar stripe conspicuous; chest and sides streaked with black. *Male:* length (skins) 6.46–7.33, wing 3.43–3.60, tail 3.14–3.38, bill .50–.52. *Female:* length (skins) 6.66–6.95, wing 3.15–3.35, tail 3.04–3.16, bill .48–.51." (Bailey) *Nest:* Built chiefly of grass, leaves, and weed stalks, with a lining of finer grass (no hair, feathers, or plant down), usually situated in mossy hummocks among stunted spruce trees, under some sort of low shrub and on a sheltered exposure. *Eggs:* 3 to 5, usually 4, ovate, with ground color of pale glaucous-green, the markings, which vary in intensity but not hue, taking the form of splotches, spots, and scrawls of pecan brown, usually distributed over the whole egg. (Adapted from Semple and Sutton.)

DISTRIBUTION.—*General:* Breeds in territory west of Hudson Bay from Fort Churchill to Artillery Lake in Mackenzie. Winters from Kansas and Missouri to Texas. *In Oregon:* Rare winter straggler, of which there are only two records.

THE NORMAL RANGE of Harris's Sparrow is east of the Rockies, and this big handsome bird can be considered only an accidental visitor to Oregon. Dawson (1914b) recorded two birds taken at Medford, February 1 and 2, 1912, by G. F. Hamlin, that are now in the Jewett collection. The only other record is of two birds that spent several weeks in January and February 1932 about the bird-feeding station at the home of Mrs. L. J. Merrill, at Hillsboro, and became very tame (Plate 95, *A*). They were viewed at close range for some time by Gabrielson, who first saw them on January 24, 1932, and who is thoroughly familiar with the species in the Missouri Valley.

White-crowned Sparrow:
Zonotrichia leucophrys leucophrys (Forster)

DESCRIPTION.—"*Adult male:* Top and sides of head striped with black and white, white median stripe usually as wide as adjoining black stripes; *lores black*, white superciliary stripe not extending forward of eye; *edge of wing white;* under parts plain gray; back with fore parts gray; rump brown. *Adult female:* like male and sometimes indistinguishable, but usually with median crown stripe narrower and grayer. *Young:* like adults, but head stripes brown and buffy instead of black and white; under parts buffy, and chest, sides of throat, and sides streaked. *Male:* length (skins) 5.84–6.74, wing 2.98–3.28, tail 2.68–3.23, bill .43–.47. *Female:* length (skins) 6.00–6.63, wing 2.89–3.17, tail 2.69–3.00, bill .41–.47." (Bailey) *Nest:* On the ground or in low bushes, made of fine twigs, rootlets, and grasses. *Eggs:* 3 to 5, pale greenish blue, spotted with warm brown.

DISTRIBUTION.—*General:* Breeds in high parts of Rocky Mountains of British Columbia, higher ranges of Oregon (east of Cascades), and California east to Wyoming and New Mexico, and from tree limit in eastern Canada southward to central Manitoba and southern Quebec. Winters south into Mexico. *In Oregon:* Regular summer resident and breeding species of higher mountains from summit of Cascades eastward.

THERE ARE THREE subspecies of the White-crowned Sparrow found within the State, two of which are breeding forms and the third an abundant migrant. *Z. l. leucophrys* is the breeding bird along the higher summits of the Cascades, through the Wallowa Mountains, the Steens Mountains, Hart Mountain, in Lake County, and other similar ranges. It is most abundant at about the 7,000-foot level, frequenting the willow and aspen thickets about the boreal lakes and streams. It arrives in April (earliest date, April 29, Wallowa County) and remains until September (latest date, September 19, Harney County).

Plate 95, *A*. Harris's Sparrow. (Photo by Mrs. L. J. Merrill.)

Plate 95, *B*. Puget Sound Sparrow. (Photo by Wm. L. and Irene Finley.)

The earlier records of these three forms are so confused that it is difficult properly to segregate them. Bendire's (1877) breeding records of Gambel's Sparrow at Camp Harney undoubtedly apply to the present form, and perhaps Suckley's (Cooper and Suckley 1860) records from The Dalles likewise belong in this race. Mearns (1879) found that birds from Fort Klamath were typical *leucophrys*, and Shelton (1917) reported the breeding birds at Crescent Lake and Diamond Peak as this form. Woodcock's (1902) records received from correspondents show that there was much confusion at that time among those having ornithological interest as to the exact status of these three forms. The only way to interpret his records now is by arbitrary geographical designation, and such determination cannot be considered accurate. We feel that the only wise course is to ignore them entirely so far as making subspecific determinations is concerned. Gabrielson (1924a) recorded the birds as breeding about Stanley Ranger Station and the higher lakes of the Wallowas. We have numerous summer specimens in breeding plumages from the Steens, Hart Mountain, and the Wallowas and find the species to be at present a common breeding one in these ranges. It is much less common in the Cascades. In migration it may be looked for in the migrating hordes of Gambel's Sparrows that are found in every weed patch in eastern Oregon in April and again in early September.

Gambel's Sparrow:
Zonotrichia leucophrys gambeli (Nuttall)

Description.—"Similar to *leucophrys*, but lores not black, white superciliary stripe reaching to bill. *Male:* length (skins) 5.85–6.48, wing 3.00–3.28, tail 2.58–2.92, bill .39–.44. *Female:* length (skins) 5.73–6.43, wing 2.90–3.25, tail 2.64–2.93, bill .39–.43." (Bailey) *Nest and eggs:* Similar to those of *Z. l. leucophrys*.

Distribution.—*General:* Breeds from limit of trees in northwestern Alaska and northern Mackenzie south to central Montana and west to coast of southwestern Alaska and southeastern British Columbia. Winters south into Mexico. *In Oregon:* Abundant spring and fall migrant east of Cascades and much less common in western Oregon. Regular but not common winter resident in lower valleys. Arrives in September and remains until late April.

Gambel's Sparrow is most abundant in September and October (earliest date, September 13, Wheeler County) and again in April (latest date, May 20, Lake County) when the great migratory movements are under way. During migration it forms a dominant element everywhere in the sparrow swarms that infest the fence rows and weed patches. It remains regularly in much smaller numbers through the winter, being most abundant at this season in Malheur, Umatilla, Wasco, and Klamath Counties. It is much less common in western Oregon but may be looked for in April. Braly took specimens at Portland, April 29, 1928, and at other dates.

Puget Sound Sparrow:
Zonotrichia leucophrys pugetensis Grinnell

DESCRIPTION.—"*Adults:* Like *leucophrys*, but lores not black and superciliary stripe extending to bill; median crown stripe usually narrower than lateral stripes, edge of wing yellow, and adults with *upper parts brown* instead of gray, streakings dark brown or blackish, and *under parts brownish gray*. *Young:* ground color of upper parts light buffy olive; under parts pale yellowish." (Description of *nuttalli*, Bailey.) *Size:* wing 2.92, tail 2.84, bill .42. *Nest and eggs:* Same as those of *Z. l. leucophrys* (Plate 96).

DISTRIBUTION.—*General:* Breeds in Pacific Coast belt from Vancouver Island and southern British Columbia south to Mendocino County, California. Winters south to southern California. *In Oregon:* Common summer resident and breeding species and less common but regular winter resident from Cascades to Pacific.

THE PUGET SOUND SPARROW (Plate 95, *B*), or Nuttall's Sparrow, as it was formerly known, is one of the common breeding species of western Oregon from the Cascades to the Pacific. Johnson (1880), who reported Gambel's Sparrow as a common breeder in the Willamette Valley, published the first record that can definitely be referred to this form, although some of Suckley's (Cooper and Suckley 1860) records from The Dalles may have been of this subspecies. Since that date there have been many published records of it, particularly from western Oregon. It is most abundant from about April 1 to October 1 but is a regular resident of the entire western district during the winter also. At that season it withdraws from the mountains and is more common in the valleys of southern Oregon than in those to the north, although it may be found in limited numbers almost anywhere in the western part of the State. In summer it is one of the common birds of the fence rows and dooryards, where its cheery whistled song is heard not only through the day but often into the night. It is one of the most persistent night singers, in fact, among our resident birds and causes much inquiry as to the identity of the nocturnal vocalist.

The nests are usually placed near the ground on low bushes and contain eggs in May or June. Our earliest date for eggs is May 5 and our latest, June 6, although we have records of newly hatched young as late as June 28.

The Puget Sound Sparrows are essentially ground birds, feeding in the thickets or weed patches or close enough to their edges to make a quick dash for the safety of their shelters to escape danger. During migration they frequent weedy fence rows, feeding along the roadsides so abundantly that an early morning drive along country roads is a continual passage through small brown forms dashing for the sheltering weeds and shrubbery. Many other sparrows and often numerous Audubon's Warblers are intermingled in these migrating companies, although the present form and the Golden-crowned Sparrows are by far the most numerous.

Plate 96. Nest and eggs of Puget Sound Sparrow. (Photo by Alex Walker.)

Golden-crowned Sparrow:
Zonotrichia coronata (Pallas)

Description.—"*Adults: Crown inclosed by black stripes, with median stripe yellow in front, ash gray behind;* rest of upper part olive brown, streaked on back with blackish brown; rump and tail plain, wing with two white bands; under parts gray; sides and flanks washed with brown. *Young:* similar, but black crown stripes replaced by brown streaked with black, and median stripe dull brownish yellow flecked or streaked with dusky, the ash gray wanting; upper parts washed with brownish; under parts soiled whitish. *Male:* length (skins) 5.93–7.13, wing 2.99–3.28, tail 2.89–3.28, bill .44–.52. *Female:* length (skins) 6.15–6.65, wing 2.90–3.17, tail 2.71–3.25, bill .45–.50." (Bailey) *Nest:* Built on ground, usually among matted thickets of alders, made of sticks and rootlets and lined with fine grasses. *Eggs:* Usually 5, ovate, with a variable ground color from pale greenish blue to vinaceous buff, minutely spotted with reddish brown, more so at the large end.

Distribution.—*General:* Breeds from central Alaska southeast to central British Columbia. Winters south to southern California. *In Oregon:* Abundant migrant and less common but regular winter resident of western Oregon. Regular but far less abundant migrant in eastern Oregon, where it is casual in winter.

The Golden-crowned Sparrow was first listed from Oregon by Baird (Baird, Cassin, and Lawrence 1858) on the basis of a specimen taken at Fort Dalles, May 11, 1855. Suckley (Cooper and Suckley 1860) erroneously believed it to be breeding at Fort Dalles, but Mearns (1879) and Merrill (1888), both of whom detected it at Fort Klamath, correctly designated it as a migrant species. Since that time it has been mentioned in numerous reports on Oregon birds.

This large, handsome sparrow, with its gleaming golden head, arrives from the North in September (our earliest date, September 10, Klamath County) and remains until May (latest date, May 25, Lane County). In western Oregon it is an exceedingly abundant migrant and a regular winter resident of the fence rows, blackberry thickets, and weed patches. It is most abundant in September and October in the fall and in April and early May in the spring. East of the mountains it is a much less abundant, although regular, migrant that in our experience is most common in September and October, during which months we have records from Klamath, Lake, Umatilla, and Wasco Counties. We have only one winter record for the section east of the Cascades, a single bird noted by Jewett near Vale, Malheur County, January 18, 1917. In the spring we have so far noted it much less commonly, and it appears in our records only in early May in Umatilla and Klamath Counties. This is perhaps due as much to lack of time spent in this section during the spring season as to scarcity of birds. At any rate it is one of the numerous points on which much more detailed observation is needed.

While in Oregon, the Golden-crowned Sparrows behave much as do the Puget Sound Sparrows, which at times they outnumber. During both spring and fall migration the two species will be found feeding amicably together in the thickets and weed patches of the river bottoms or along the fence rows of the cultivated lands.

White-throated Sparrow: *Zonotrichia albicollis* (Gmelin)

Description.—"*Adult male: Throat pure white* sharply contrasted with gray of breast; head striped with black and white; superciliary yellow from bill to eyes; edge of wing yellow; back and scapulars rusty brown streaked with blackish; rump olivaceous or brownish. *Adult female:* sometimes indistinguishable from male, but usually with coloration of head and under parts decidedly duller, crown stripe tinged with brown and buffy. *Young in first winter:* like adult female, but duller, crown stripes browner. *Young:* throat not distinctly whitish, and stripes on head brown and buffy instead of black and white; yellow in front of eyes more or less distinct; under parts brownish white, streaked, except on belly. *Male:* length (skins) 6.12–6.56, wing 2.85–3.04, tail 2.80–3.00, bill .42–.48. *Female:* length (skins) 5.91–6.30, wing 2.74–2.88, tail 2.68–2.90, bill .44–.46." (Bailey) *Nest:* On the ground or in low bushes, made of grass, moss, strips of bark, and rootlets. *Eggs:* 4 or 5, white, finely and uniformly speckled or heavily blotched with brown.

Distribution.—*General:* Breeds from northern Mackenzie, Manitoba, Quebec, and Newfoundland, to Alberta, Montana, Minnesota, Wisconsin, Ontario, and Pennsylvania. Winters from Missouri and Ohio Valleys south. *In Oregon:* Casual straggler in both spring and fall.

This essentially eastern bird, the White-throated Sparrow, straggles more or less irregularly into Oregon, though considering the few collectors in the State a surprising number of specimens have been taken. Henshaw (1880) reported two individuals seen and one taken on the Columbia River about 40 miles from The Dalles sometime during 1877 or 1878, and Beckham (1887) also reported this specimen. Walker (1914c, 1924) recorded taking a male, April 27, 1913, at Mulino, Clackamas County, and a second specimen at Blaine, Tillamook County, October 25, 1923. Cantwell took a bird at Philomath, Benton County, March 14, 1919, that is now in the Biological Survey collection. The latest specimen known to us was taken by Carl Richardson at Prospect, Jackson County, October 13, 1933. In addition to these actual specimens, Dr. E. Raymond Driver (letter to W. A. Eliot, November 9, 1932) reported having White-throated Sparrows at his feeding station at Central Point, December 28, 1927, October 10, 1928, October 6, 1929, November 2, 1930, and October 6 and November 9, 1932. In view of these records it is evident that this soft-plumaged sparrow may be looked for anywhere in the State in both spring and fall migration. With an increased number of competent observers it will probably be found to be a regular, though rare, straggler.

Alberta Fox Sparrow:
Passerella iliaca altivagans Riley

Description.—(Type specimen in fresh fall plumage.) "Upper parts generally mummy brown, most ruddy on dorsum, dullest on rump. Feathers of dorsum with dark centers, giving an obscurely streaked effect. Sides of neck washed with grayish. Upper tail coverts auburn, with narrow edgings of paler brown; exposed portion of rectrices auburn. Under parts white, chin, throat and abdomen nearly immaculate, elsewhere marked with triangular spots, varying in color from some the same shade as the back, to others suffused with blackish. Exposed portion of wing coverts and remiges auburn, like tail. Median and greater wing coverts slightly tipped with whitish, forming two ill-defined bars." (Swarth 1920.) Wing 3.07–3.37, tail 2.70–3.15, bill .39–.45. *Nest:* On ground or in bushes, made of moss and leaves. *Eggs:* 3 or 4, bluish green or gray, speckled and blotched with brown and lilac.

Distribution.—*General:* Breeds in interior of British Columbia and Alberta. Winters in California, chiefly west of desert divides.

Riley (1911) listed the Alberta Fox Sparrow from Fort Klamath, and Swarth (1920) recorded a specimen of Jewett's from Government Island as belonging to this race. We have at the present time the following specimens from Oregon: Government Island (December 15, 1912, Jewett); Millers, Wasco County (April 11, 1915, Alex Walker, now in Jewett Coll.); Prineville (October 27, 1924, W. E. Sherwood, now in Jewett Coll.); Mosquito Ranger Station, Jackson County (September 29, 1926, Gabrielson); and Hart Mountain, Lake County (September 14, 1928, Jewett). This wide scattering of records indicates that these birds move in a broad belt southward through Oregon on their way to their California wintering grounds.

The Fox Sparrows that appear in Oregon, particularly in migration, are so variable and represent so many closely related subspecies that any attempt to separate them in the field is hopeless. The breeding birds of the Cascades, Siskiyous, and eastern Oregon ranges represent the "slate-colored" group of forms, whereas the majority of the migrants in western Oregon are the rich brown forms from the Alaska and British Columbia coast.

We are giving the measurements of wing, tail, and bill in the various races, although differences in size are often too slight to be of practical use. All of the races measure approximately 6 to 7 inches in length—the birds being among our larger sparrows. We have indicated distribution and localities of the various forms solely on the basis of collected specimens, as we have no faith in our own sight records or those of other observers.

The large dark-colored Fox Sparrows are normally birds of the brush and weed patches and are often shy and elusive while in the State. They feed largely on the ground, scratching vigorously to uncover the seeds on which they habitually feed. They are abundant migrants and common winter residents of western Oregon. The relative abundance and breeding ranges of our summer forms are discussed under each form.

Shumagin Fox Sparrow:
Passerella iliaca unalaschcensis (Gmelin)

DESCRIPTION.—"*Upper parts reddish brown, more or less mixed with slaty gray,* becoming dark brown or foxy on rump, wings, and tail; under parts white, thickly marked with triangular spots of dark brown *converging on breast. Male:* length (skins) 6.50–6.70, wing 3.28–3.39, tail 2.88–2.98, bill .49–.50. *Female:* length (skins) 6.20–6.68, wing 3.14–3.19, tail 2.71–2.80, bill .50–.52." (Bailey) *Nest and eggs:* As for *P. i. altivagans*.

DISTRIBUTION.—*General:* Breeds on base of Alaskan Peninsula, Shumagin Islands, and Unalaska. Winters south to California. *In Oregon:* Rare straggler in migration.

THERE ARE ONLY three specimens of the Shumagin Fox Sparrow from this State known to us. One (Calif. Acad. Sci. Coll.) was taken at Portland, November 7, 1912, and recorded by Swarth (1920). The other (Jewett Coll. No. 2194) was taken near Bend, April 20, 1919. The species undoubtedly occurs more frequently than these two records indicate, the lack of specimens being due to a scarcity of collectors rather than of birds. Walker (1926) published a record of a bird taken at Blaine, February 1, 1923. Older records of Bendire, Merrill, and Anthony of this form cannot certainly be identified with the present known conception of any race and are therefore considered only as recording migrants of the dark Alaska forms through the State.

Kodiak Fox Sparrow:
Passerella iliaca insularis Ridgway

DESCRIPTION.—"Like *unalaschcensis* but back warm sepia brown, spots on chest large and deep brown, under tail coverts strongly tinged with buff." (Bailey) *Size:* Wing 3.05–3.37, tail 2.78–3.07, bill .46–.50. *Nest and eggs:* Similar to those of *P. i. altivagans*.

DISTRIBUTION.—*General:* Breeds on Kodiak Island. Winters in coast district south to Los Angeles County, California. *In Oregon:* One of rarer migrants from the north, so far as our collections show.

WE HAVE THREE Oregon specimens of the Kodiak Fox Sparrow taken as follows: Eagle Creek, Clackamas County (February 16, 1907, Jewett); Portland (December 14, 1924, Gabrielson); and near Pinehurst, Jackson County (March 22, 1925, Jewett). We find two notations in the Biological Survey records of a specimen identified by Oberholser taken at Corvallis, April 30, 1901, and there is a specimen in the Biological Survey collection taken near the west base of Mount Jefferson, October 4, 1897, by J. A. Loring.

Valdez Fox Sparrow:
Passerella iliaca sinuosa Grinnell

DESCRIPTION.—Like the last two but bill relatively longer and more slender; intermediate in color, being more reddish than in *P. i. unalaschcensis* and less so than *P. i. insularis*. (Adapted from Swarth.) *Size:* Wing 3.05–3.29, tail 2.68–2.98, bill .43–.50. *Nest and eggs:* Similar to those of *P. i. altivagans*.

DISTRIBUTION.—*General:* Breeds in vicinity of Prince William Sound, Middleton Island, and on Kenai Peninsula. Winters south to northern Lower California. *In Oregon:* Winters commonly west of Cascades, being most abundant form in Willamette Valley and along western slope of Cascades.

THE VALDEZ FOX SPARROW is the common form that winters along the western base of the Cascades and through the Willamette, Umpqua, and Rogue River Valleys. It arrives in October (earliest date, September 23) and remains until March (latest date, April 30). Some 33 specimens, either in the Biological Survey collections or our own, from the following localities outline its range while within Oregon: Portland, Mount Hood, Estacada, Corvallis, Salem, Philomath, Grants Pass, Pinehurst, Mosquito Ranger Station (Jackson County), and Brownsboro, in the interior valleys and along the Cascades, and Mercer and Netarts (single specimens each) on the coast. In addition there is a single bird from Warm Springs, April 30, 1915, collected by Alex Walker, now in the Jewett collection, that was recorded erroneously we believe as from Millers at the mouth of the Deschutes by Walker (1917b).

Earlier records of fox sparrows are so confused that it is impossible to separate them, but the records of Woodcock, Anthony, and Johnson from the Willamette Valley in some cases most certainly refer to this form. Jewett (1916b) published the first definite record for Oregon, when he recorded the Netarts bird taken January 6, 1913, and Walker (1917b) referred to a specimen he took, April 30, 1915, that we believe to be the Warm Springs bird mentioned above, although he located it at Millers. The above records show this race to be the common wintering form in western Oregon except along the coast, where it is much less common than either *fuliginosa* or *townsendi*.

Yakutat Fox Sparrow:
Passerella iliaca annectens Ridgway

DESCRIPTION.—"Similar to *insularis*, but smaller, especially the bill, and coloration slightly browner." (Bailey) *Size:* Wing 3.13–3.25, tail 2.63–2.96, bill .43–.49. *Nest and eggs:* As in *P. i. altivagans*.

DISTRIBUTION.—*General:* Breeds in coast district of Alaska in vicinity of Yakutat Bay. Winters south along coast to Los Angeles. *In Oregon:* Winters along coast and inland to Portland but is one of less common forms.

THE YAKUTAT FOX SPARROW again is one of the less common wintering forms that undoubtedly winters in small numbers throughout western

Oregon, a supposition that will probably be revealed as a fact by more consistent collecting than we have been able to carry out. Swarth (1920) listed specimens from Logan and Beaverton. Aside from these, we have seven skins, three from Portland (February 22, 1921, and April 5, 1925, Gabrielson; December 14, 1924, Jewett), three from Netarts (one, January 13, 1924, Gabrielson; two, December 30, 1926, Jewett) and one from Tillamook (December 19, 1923, Jewett).

Townsend's Fox Sparrow:
Passerella iliaca townsendi (Audubon)

Description.—"Similar to *P. i. annectens* but coloration darker and more castaneous brown, and spots on chest, etc., larger; above deep vandyke brown, duller (more sooty) on pileum, more reddish (inclining to burnt umber or dark chestnut-brown) on upper tail-coverts and tail; sides of head deep sooty brown, the lores dotted, the auricular region finely streaked, with dull whitish; general color of under parts white, but everywhere spotted or streaked with deep chestnut-brown or vandyke brown, the spots mostly of triangular (deltoid and cuneate) form, very heavy and more or less confluent on chest, smaller on throat and breast; sides and flanks almost uniform deep brown, the latter tinged with buffy or pale tawny; under tail-coverts deep olive or olive-brown, broadly margined with buffy or pale fulvous." (Ridgway 1901.) *Size:* Length (skins) 6.10–7.17, wing 2.95–3.27, tail 2.61–3.04, exposed culmen .40–.49. *Nest and eggs:* Same as for *P. i. altivagans*.

Distribution.—*General:* Breeds in coast district of Alaska from Glacier Bay south to Forrester Island and Queen Charlotte Islands. Winters south to Santa Cruz County, California. *In Oregon:* Winters in western Oregon.

The dark-colored Townsend's Fox Sparrow is slightly more reddish in tone and slightly paler than the Sooty Fox Sparrow. It is somewhat less common on the Oregon coast and decidedly less abundant inland than that species. The earlier records are confused between these two dark forms, and so far as we can discern the first authentic record for this subspecies was that of Swarth (1920) when he listed birds (many of them from Jewett's collection from Portland), from Mercer, Grants Pass, and Netarts. In addition to these localities, Jewett has birds from Florence, in western Lane County, and there are numerous specimens from Tillamook County. Like *fuliginosa*, it is decidedly more abundant on the coastal slope than inland, evidently preferring the dense salal thickets to the more open brushlands farther from the coast. It arrives from the north in October (earliest date, October 12) and remains until March (latest date, April 12).

Sooty Fox Sparrow:
Passerella iliaca fuliginosa Ridgway

Description.—The darkest and most heavily marked of the races. The spots on the breast are dull and sooty with little reddish color. (Adapted from Swarth.) *Size:*

Wing 3.09–3.27, tail 2.90–3.06, bill .43–.47. *Nest and eggs:* Similar to those of *P. i. altivagans*.

Distribution.—*General:* Breeds on mainland of southeastern Alaska, British Columbia, Vancouver, Washington, and northwestern Washington. Winters south to central California. *In Oregon:* Common winter resident of entire coast and inland to Portland and Willamette Valley.

The Sooty Fox Sparrow was first recorded from Oregon by Swarth (1920), who listed Jewett's specimen from Marshfield taken on November 26, 1917. It is the common wintering form on the coast and next to *sinuosa* the most common in the Willamette Valley. One collected by D. D. Streeter, Jr., October 12, 1909, at Empire, and now in the Biological Survey collection, furnished the earliest fall date of which we have a record. The latest spring date is of a specimen in the Carnegie Museum taken at Salem, April 24, 1909, by M. E. Peck. There are numerous skins in the Carnegie Museum collection taken at Beaverton in February, March, and April, 1890, by Anthony, and skins from Blaine, Clackamas County, and Tillamook have been identified for Alex Walker by the Biological Survey. In our own collection we have numerous specimens taken at Netarts, Tillamook, Blaine, Devils Lake, Marshfield, Powers, and Gold Beach on the coast and several from the vicinity of Portland.

While in Oregon, this bird is a skulker, frequenting the salal thickets on the coast and the heaviest brush patches when in the vicinity of Portland. The only exception to this behavior we have noted was on December 17 and 18, 1924, when a wet and exceedingly heavy snow had blanketed all the salal slopes in Tillamook County. The snow remained for two days, and during that time the beaches and pasture lands swarmed with Fox Sparrows and Hermit Thrushes that had been driven from their accustomed haunts by the storm. As soon as the snow melted they vanished again into the dense tangles of vines and shrubs that adorn the hillsides in this country of abundant rainfall.

Slate-colored Fox Sparrow:
Passerella iliaca schistacea Baird

Description.—"*Upper parts plain slaty or brownish gray*, becoming rusty on wings, upper tail coverts, and tail; under parts with *chest spots smaller, more scattered;* tail longer than wing, *bill thick*. *Male:* length (skins) 6.23–7.16, wing 3.08–3.43, tail 2.88–3.43, bill .44–.50. *Female:* length (skins) 6.02–6.58, wing 3.02–3.21, bill .45–.50." (Bailey) *Nest:* In bushes and trees, made of plant fiber, grass, and hair. *Eggs:* 3 or 4, greenish, marked with purple and brown.

Distribution.—*General:* Breeds in mountains of Great Basin from southeastern British Columbia south to Nevada and eastern Wyoming. Winters south to Arizona, New Mexico, and southern California. *In Oregon:* Breeds in Blue Mountain area of eastern Oregon and southward through Malheur County to Nevada line on higher ranges. (See Figure 19)

Bendire (1877) published from Camp Harney the first breeding record for this pale Slate-colored Fox Sparrow. Later the same writer (1889c) described the nest and eggs from Grant and Harney Counties and also included Fall River, Deschutes County, a locality in the range ascribed to *P. i. fulva*, which was described much later. Likewise, Shelton's (1917) breeding records for Diamond Peak belong under *fulva*. Many later records have been published by us and others that outline the breeding range as described above. The species arrives in April (earliest date, April 3, Umatilla County) and remains until September (latest date, September 15, Harney County).

This is one of the most musical of Oregon breeding birds, its loud clear song ringing out continually from the brush patches that it loves. There is something haunting about the melody, a quality found elsewhere among our summer resident songsters only in the thrushes. The eggs are laid in June, our three records being June 19, 20, and 22. The June 20th nest, located at Lick Creek Ranger Station by Jewett, contained three slightly incubated eggs. The June 22d nest, found near Anthony, Baker County, by Jewett, contained one egg, and one egg was discovered in the ovary of the female dead on the nest. The June 19th, 1930, record was of a nest built in the sagebrush that contained four eggs. It was found by us while traveling together on the Battle Creek Ranch in extreme southern Malheur County.

Warner Mountains Fox Sparrow: *Passerella iliaca fulva* Swarth

Description.—Coloration about as in *P. i. schistacea* but with somewhat larger bill. (Adapted from Swarth.) *Size:* Wing 3.09–3.33, tail 3.06–3.35, bill .43–.54. *Nest and eggs:* As in *P. i. schistacea.*

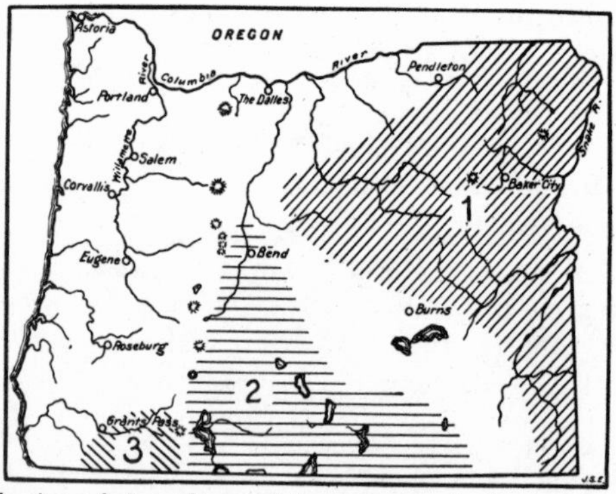

Figure 19.—Distribution of three forms of fox sparrows in Oregon: 1, Slate-colored Fox Sparrow (*Passerella iliaca schistacea*); 2, Warner Mountains Fox Sparrow (*P. i. fulva*); 3, Yosemite Fox Sparrow (*P. i. mariposae*).

Distribution.—*General:* Breeds in south-central Oregon and northeastern California. Winters south into Lower California. *In Oregon:* Breeds in higher sage-covered ranges of southern Harney and Lake Counties and through yellow-pine area of western Lake and all of Klamath County and from there northward along eastern slope of Cascades to Columbia River. (See Figure 19.)

The Warner Mountains Fox Sparrow is the breeding form of Fox Sparrow in south-central Oregon first described by Swarth (1920), who at that time listed specimens from nine Oregon localities. It is a common and characteristic bird of the Steens, Hart, and Warner Mountains and a very abundant inhabitant of the *Ceanothus* thickets of the yellow-pine belt from Keno to the vicinity of Sisters. North of there it becomes less common but is still present to the breaks of the Columbia River south of Bend during May and June. It arrives in April and remains until October (earliest date, March 25; latest, October 18, both Wasco County).

In the early morning one may stop a car anywhere in the yellow pine and be almost certain to hear the rich full song of this soft-plumaged chorister, but the bird itself is difficult to see if one moves about, as it keeps ahead by flitting from one bush to another. By remaining motionless for a time one has a better chance, as the quarry, forgetting the intruder, mounts to the topmost twig of the bush to pour out its song.

On May 18, 1924, Jewett collected a set of three eggs in the Warner Mountains. This nest was located in the lower stems of a dense willow clump. A second nest, found May 25, 1927, on Hart Mountain, was ready for eggs, though surrounded by snow a foot in depth.

Yosemite Fox Sparrow:
Passerella iliaca mariposae Swarth

Description.—A member of the gray group, with a longer tail and a heavier bill than the other gray races in Oregon. (Adapted from Swarth.) *Size:* Wing 3.02–3.32, tail 3.21–3.42, bill .45–.52. *Nest and eggs:* Similar to those of *P. i. schistacea.*

Distribution.—*General:* Breeds from Siskiyous and western slope of Cascades of southern Oregon south to Inyo County, California. Winters in southern California. *In Oregon:* Breeds on western slope of Cascades in Jackson County and in Siskiyous of Jackson and Josephine Counties. (See Figure 19.)

This breeding form of Fox Sparrow, the Yosemite Fox Sparrow, was first recorded by Gabrielson (1923c), who found it common on Robinson's Butte and adjacent points on the western slope of the Cascades in Jackson County, June 13, 1921. An adult male collected at the time was variously identified as *mariposae* and *mariposae X fulva* by different authorities. Subsequently Gabrielson found summer resident Fox Sparrows in the Oregon Siskiyous from Ashland Butte to Greyback Mountain, but no opportunity to collect specimens occurred until July 11, 1933, when the authors were together camped on the Oregon-California line on the summit of the Siskiyous in the vicinity of Little Greyback Mountain and collected several specimens that have been identified by Swarth as typical *mariposae*.

Lincoln's Sparrow:
Melospiza lincolni lincolni (Audubon)

Description.—"*Adults:* Upper parts dark brown and olive, finely and sharply streaked with black; crown with light median stripe; malar region, chest, and sides buffy; sides and *broad buffy chest band narrowly streaked with black*. *Young:* colors more suffused and streaks less sharply defined. *Male:* length (skins) 4.88–5.76, wing 2.26–2.62, tail 2.07–2.44, bill .41–.47. *Female:* length (skins) 4.54–5.43, wing 2.15–2.45, tail 2.01–2.34, bill .38–.46." (Bailey) *Nest:* A cup of grass on the ground. *Eggs:* 4 or 5, greenish white, wreathed about the larger end with brown and gray.

Distribution.—*General:* Breeds from interior Alaska, southern Mackenzie, Manitoba, Quebec, and Newfoundland south to Nova Scotia, New York, Ontario, and Minnesota and in western mountains to southern California and northern New Mexico. Winters south to Central America. *In Oregon:* Common breeding species in higher part of Cascades and Blue Mountains and common migrant through eastern Oregon.

Lincoln's Sparrow is a breeding bird of the open meadows of the higher ranges, where it frequents the straggling growth of willows along the small streams. Except when in song it is an inconspicuous member of the avian population, but its long clear vibrant notes call it to everyone's attention in the courthsip period. Viewed from the back, it is easily mistaken for a song sparrow, but from the front the distinct buffy band across a white breast finely marked with black is distinctive.

Bendire (1877) first listed this species as an Oregon bird, finding it an abundant migrant and occasional breeding species in the vicinity of Camp Harney. Merrill (1888) collected a single specimen at Fort Klamath on March 14 but remarked that it became common later. Woodcock's (1902) records do not distinguish between this subspecies and *M. l. gracilis*, though it is quite probable that his records from Dayton, Salem, and Corvallis were the latter.

We have found it to be a common migrant that can be expected in eastern Oregon in April, May, and September, in company with other migrating sparrows. It is a particularly common breeding species in all higher parts of the Wallowa Mountains in Wallowa and Baker Counties, where it probably attains its greatest abundance in this State. It is less common through Grant, Union, Harney, and Wheeler Counties but is found there at least occasionally. It arrives in April (earliest date, March 14, Klamath County) and remains until October (latest date, November 26, Coos County). We have only two definite breeding records. M. E. Peck (ms. files, Biological Survey) found a pair feeding young at Meacham, Union County, July 29, 1915, and Jewett located a nest containing three newly hatched young and one egg about to hatch near Lick Creek Ranger Station, Wallowa National Forest, July 17, 1926.

Lincoln's Sparrow occasionally strays to western Oregon in migration, as there is a skin in Jewett's collection from Carlton, Yamhill County, taken May 2, 1921, that is certainly this form. There is also an immature male from Bolan Lake, Josephine County, taken August 19, 1933, that probably was hatched in the vicinity of the lake. These two constitute our only records for this form west of the Cascades.

Forbush's Sparrow: *Melospiza lincolni gracilis* (Kittlitz)

Description.—"Similar to *lincolni*, but superciliary stripe and upper parts more strongly olivaceous, and dark streaks, especially on back and upper tail coverts coarser, blacker, and more numerous. *Wing:* 2.35, tail 2.23." (Bailey) *Nest and eggs:* Similar to those of *M. l. lincolni*.

Distribution.—*General:* Breeds from Prince William Sound to Sitkan district, Alaska. Winters south to Lower California and Central America. *In Oregon:* Appears only as uncommon migrant, of which we have seven specimens.

Forbush's Sparrow, the northern breeding form, distinguished from typical *M. l. lincolni* by the much wider black stripes that give it a much darker coloration, is found as a rather inconspicuous migrant throughout western Oregon. Its small size and resemblance to a song sparrow, together with the fact that it is usually associated with the swarms of migrating sparrows, make it rather difficult to detect. Careful and continuous collecting during April, May, and October will reveal it in most localities in western Oregon where it frequents the weed patches and brushy bottoms in company with the hordes of *Zonotrichia* and other migrating sparrows. We have specimens from Portland (October 11 and 12, May 5), Rickreall (December 14), Marshfield (November 26), and Medford (April 23). There is also a skin in the Biological Survey collection taken at Ashland, May 6, 1914, by Goldman. The only reference to this form in Oregon literature that we have found is our own record in the *Birds of the Portland Area* (Jewett and Gabrielson 1929) where we recorded our specimens from Portland as listed above.

Mountain Song Sparrow: *Melospiza melodia fallax* (Baird)

Description.—"Upper parts grayish streaked with black and brown; wings and tail brown; under parts white, chest and sides streaked with brown, streaks more or less confluent on breast. *Male:* length (skins) 5.58–6.49, wing 2.58–2.91, tail 2.50–3.02, bill .44–.55. *Female:* length (skins) 5.35–6.34, wing 2.46–2.75, tail 2.46–2.86, bill .41–.50." (Bailey) *Nest:* A compact cup, woven of grass, in low bushes or on the ground. *Eggs:* 4 or 5, greenish white, spotted with reddish brown.

Distribution.—*General:* Breeds from western Montana to northeastern Oregon and south to Utah, southern Nevada, and northern New Mexico. Winters south into Mexico. *In Oregon:* Breeds in Blue Mountains from Snake River Canyon west to and including Grande Ronde Valley and south into Baker County, and probably also in northern Malheur, Grant, and Wheeler Counties and into eastern Umatilla County. Winters south into Nevada and California. (See Figure 20.)

The Mountain Song Sparrow, a big pale race of song sparrows, is the breeding bird of the northeastern section of Oregon, including Wallowa, Union, and Baker Counties, and merges into *fisherella* in eastern Umatilla, Wheeler, Grant, and northern Harney and Malheur Counties. Birds breeding in the mountainous sections just south of the Malheur River might be either this form or *fisherella*. Winter specimens from the southeastern part of the State may be either form. Two birds from Warner Valley in the Gabrielson collection (Crump Lake, September 9, 1929, and Adel, October 23, 1926) are the farthest west specimens we have. There has been so much confusion among the races of song sparrows in this State that it is almost impossible to untangle them without seeing the specimens on which the numerous publications were based. Bendire (1877) published winter records from Camp Harney as this race, and as it still is found in winter in this territory we have no hesitation in accepting this as the first Oregon record referable to this particular form.

We have no actual nesting records on this race in our own notes, but Cantwell (ms. notes, Biological Survey) reported a nest containing fresh eggs at Paradise, Wallowa County, June 10, 1919, and commented that young had been noted on the wing two days earlier.

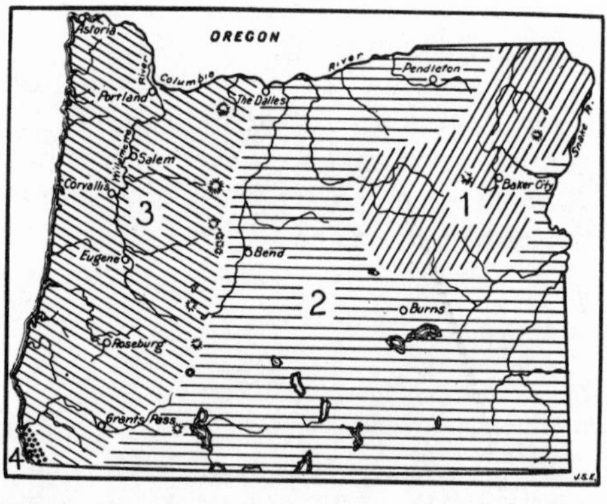

Figure 20.—Distribution of breeding song sparrows in Oregon: 1, Mountain Song Sparrow (*Melospiza melodia fallax*); 2, Modoc Song Sparrow (*M. m. fisherella*); 3, Rusty Song Sparrow (*M. m. morphna*); 4, Mendocino Song Sparrow (*M. m. cleonensis*).

Modoc Song Sparrow:
Melospiza melodia fisherella Oberholser

DESCRIPTION.—Similar to *M. m. fallax* but darker and in all of its markings, the pale browns being replaced by darker shaded tending toward blackish. *Size:* Length (skins) 4.50–5.50, wing 2.48–2.85, tail 2.32–2.93, bill .41–.47. *Nest and eggs:* Similar to those of *M. m. fallax.*

DISTRIBUTION.—*General:* Breeds from southeastern Oregon, northwestern Nevada, and southwestern Idaho south through eastern California to Owens and Shasta Valley. Winters south to California. *In Oregon:* Breeds through most of Malheur (except perhaps some of higher peaks), Harney, Lake, and Klamath Counties north to Columbia River along eastern slope of Cascades and around base of Blue Mountains following lower valleys sometimes well back into range. Winters throughout same area. (See Figure 20.)

THE MODOC SONG SPARROW is the breeding form of the sagebrush areas of the State. It follows the base of the Blue Mountains around from the south and west to Pendleton and extends into the mountain valleys along their western and southern flanks, typical birds being found even to central Baker County. To the west the birds extend over the summit of the Cascades into the Rogue River Valley in more or less typical form that rapidly intergrades into *morphna.*

The first record that can be certainly referred to this race is of Bendire's (Brewer 1875) nest and eggs taken between Camp Harney and Malheur Lake, May 29, 1875, and published under the name *M. m. guttata*, a name no longer in use. Mearns (1879) and Merrill (1888) listed it from Fort Klamath, and since that time it has been recorded from various sections of the State. We have notes of nests containing fresh eggs from May 2 to June 12 inclusive, dates that doubtless could be greatly extended by more intensive field work.

Merrill's Song Sparrow:
Melospiza melodia merrilli Brewster

DESCRIPTION.—"Similar to *morphna*, but with smaller bill and ground color of upper parts lighter and more ashy; dark markings—especially on back—blacker and more sharply defined; the white of under parts clearer and more extended. *Male:* length (skins) 5.65–6.40, wing 2.56–2.75, tail 2.51–2.83, bill .45–.51. *Female:* length (skins) 5.48–6.21, wing 2.50–2.68, tail 2.40–2.76, bill .44–.50." (Bailey) *Nest and eggs:* Same as those of *M. m. fallax.*

DISTRIBUTION.—*General:* Breeds in Idaho and eastern Washington. Winters through eastern Oregon to California, Arizona, and New Mexico. *In Oregon:* Wintering bird only. May be expected in almost any section.

ALTHOUGH Jewett (1909c) referred the song sparrow of Baker County to this race, and Walker (1917) did the same for the birds of central Oregon, the present restrictions on the range of this form entirely eliminate

Merrill's Song Sparrow as an Oregon breeding bird and make the above records apply to *fallax* and *fisherella*. Our *Birds of the Portland Area* (Jewett and Gabrielson 1929), in which we listed two specimens from the Portland district (taken December 24, 1922, and October 28, 1923), is the first publication of the race from Oregon known to us that is based on specimens. Jewett has since taken two at Portland (April 5 and October 6) and one at Seaside (February 4). The Biological Survey collection contains a late spring bird from Warm Springs, Wasco County (May 5, 1915), also taken by Jewett, and other birds taken by Cantwell, Jewett, Bailey, or others at Willows, Gilliam County (April 6, 1915), Millers, Sherman County (April 12 and 17, 1915), Philomath, Benton County (March 13, 1919), Parkdale, Hood River County (April 1, 2, and 3, 1919), and Klamath Falls (no date). There is also a pale bird in the Gabrielson collection, taken at Portland (January 8, 1922), that has been identified as *M. m. inexpectata* Riley by Oberholser, and there are two identical birds in Jewett's possession taken at Prineville (October 10 and 24) that should probably be included here. *Inexpectata* was not recognized in the last A. O. U. Check-List, and no comparative material is available to us to place them otherwise.

Yakutat Song Sparrow:
Melospiza melodia caurina Ridgway

Description.—"Similar to *M. c. rufina* but with decidedly longer and more slender bill and grayer coloration; the superciliary stripe, middle portion of auricular region, sides of neck, hindneck, and edges of interscapulars decidedly gray, in more or less strong contrast with the brown markings; streaks on chest, etc. [and sides and flanks] dark seal brown, and ground color of flanks olive-grayish." (Ridgway 1901.) *Size:* Length (skins) 5.70–6.50, wing 2.65–2.90, tail 2.46–2.82, exposed culmen .50–.56. *Nest and eggs:* Same as those of *M. m. fallax.*

Distribution.—*General:* Breeds on coast of southeastern Alaska from Yakutat Bay to Lituya Bay. Winters along coast south to San Francisco. *In Oregon:* Rather rare winter straggler to coast.

The Yakutat Song Sparrow, a big dark-colored bird, can easily be distinguished from its brown companions when it appears on the Oregon coast. In our rather limited acquaintance with it we have found that while in the State it stays almost entirely in the driftwood on the beach or frequents the rocky points loved by the Black Turnstones. The first authentic Oregon specimen was taken at Netarts, April 14, 1914, and a second one was obtained the following day at the same place by Walker. These were first recorded by Shelton (1915). Gabrielson (1923c) listed a bird taken at Cannon Beach, Clatsop County, February 8, 1922, as *M. m. kenaiensis* on an identification by Oberholser. Subsequent comparison with good series of breeding birds from Alaska and also a re-check by

Oberholser indicates that the bird belongs in the present race and therefore the record of *M. m. kenaiensis* for Oregon should be eliminated. The last Oregon specimen known to us was taken by Walker, February 18, 1934, in Tillamook County.

Rusty Song Sparrow: *Melospiza melodia morphna* Oberholser

Description.—"*Adults:* Upper parts rusty olive, the rusty brown and black streaks obscured; chest widely marked with heavy dark rufous streaks; flanks olivaceous instead of tawny. *Young:* back dark brown streaked with blackish; under parts whitish or buffy grayish; chest and sides buffy or brownish streaked with sooty brown. *Male:* length (skins) 5.69–6.46, wing 2.55–2.81, tail 2.39–2.87, bill .47–.54. *Female:* length (skins) 5.58–6.19, wing 2.45–2.70, tail 2.28–2.67, bill .45–.52." (Bailey) *Nest and eggs:* Similar to those of *M. m. fallax.* (See Plate 97.)

Distribution.—*General:* Breeds from southern Alaska to southern Oregon. Winters south to southern California. *In Oregon:* Breeding form from west slope of Cascades to Pacific and from Columbia River south to Rogue River Valley to, but not including, southern Curry County. Winters throughout its breeding range and southward into California. (See Figure 20.)

The first record definitely identifiable as *morphna* from Oregon was that of Johnson (1880) from Forest Grove, Salem, and East Portland, but since then this form has appeared many times in Oregon literature and the cheerful brown-coated Rusty Song Sparrow is one of the most common and best known birds in the western part of the State. Every willow thicket and every brush patch along the stream bottoms holds its quota of song sparrows, and even the blackberry patches on the hillsides at considerable distances from water are almost certain to shelter at least a pair. In late summer and through the winter "Rusty" is a conspicuous element in the wintering flocks of sparrows that are found in the weed patches and along the fence rows. Although most birds sing only during the breeding season, this one is a most persistent songster, often tuning up on bright winter mornings as well as at most unexpected times and places in the songless summer season.

The species breeds abundantly through a long season. Nests with fresh eggs have been found from April 15 to July 10. The nests are usually built within a foot or two of the ground in thick bushes and normally contain four eggs.

The birds of the Rogue River Valley are a puzzling lot. Superficially they resemble *merrilli*, the breeding bird from northeastern Washington and northern Idaho, and many of our specimens have been so labeled by various taxonomists who have seen them. To call these birds *merrilli* is to cause needless confusion in an already badly tangled group, for genetically they certainly are not the same and geographically they are widely

Plate 97, *A*. Young Rusty Song Sparrows in nest. (Photo by Wm. L. Finley and H. T. Bohlman.)

Plate 97, *B*. Nest and eggs of Rusty Song Sparrow. (Photo by Alex Walker.)

separated by divergent breeding forms. The concept of subspecies is one of geographical variation that somehow cannot well be correlated with discontinuous ranges. Our breeding birds are clearly intermediate between *morphna* and *fisherella* and, all things considered, are probably on the average somewhat more like *fisherella*. To give them a distinct name would not help the situation, for the differences from either of the above recognized races are so slight that the practical effect would be to create two zones of intergradation between even less distinguishable forms. From the standpoint of practical working ornithologists this would be a useless multiplication of poorly distinguished forms, and even from a strictly scientific standpoint the activities of some of the experts on subspecific determinations has been carried to such extremes that we wonder at times if it has not become a game for scientific dabblers rather than serious scientific work. We frankly prefer to recognize areas of intergradation where intermediates may be found, and breeding birds from the Rogue River Valley may be so classed, the majority tending somewhat more toward *fisherella* than *morphna*. Many wintering birds, however, are *morphna* in this area.

Mendocino Song Sparrow:
Melospiza melodia cleonensis McGregor

Description.—General color of upper parts deep rusty olive, conspicuously and broadly streaked on the upper surface with dark rusty brown, or chestnut, and fuscous black; the pileum with a narrow median stripe of smoke gray, the superciliary stripe, lores, and auricular region smoke gray; under parts white, streaked on sides of throat, chest, and abdomen with dark rusty brown or chestnut, the streaks fuscous black medially; sides, flanks, and crissum strongly fulvous. Similar to *Melospiza melodia samuelis* in size and proportions, but averaging slightly smaller with large legs and feet. *Size:* Length (skins) 4.76–5.88, wing 2.15–2.51, tail 2.08–2.48, exposed culmen .41–.50. *Nest and eggs:* Same as those of *M. m. fallax.*

Distribution.—*General:* Breeds from Oregon line through coastal belt of Del Norte and Humboldt Counties to Mendocino County, California. *In Oregon:* Breeds only on coast of Curry County, about mouth of Pistol River, and south to California line. Winters in same territory. (See Figure 20.)

The Mendocino Song Sparrow, the coastal race from California, is the breeding bird of a narrow strip of country extending for approximately 25 miles along the southwestern Oregon coast. Numerous specimens that we have collected in this district both winter and summer prove to be this form, although in winter the much darker *morphna* is also found.

Alaska Longspur:
Calcarius lapponicus alascensis Ridgway

Description.—"Inner web of outer tail feather chiefly dusky. *Adult male in summer: fore parts black*, contrasting strikingly with white of belly and white or buffy line from eye to hind neck; *hind neck deep rufous;* back streaked black, brown, buffy, and whitish; wings dusky, with brown and whitish edgings; tail chiefly blackish brown. *Adult male in winter:* black area and rufous nape patch greatly restricted, and more or less obscured by white or brownish tips to feathers; sides of head mainly light brownish. *Adult female in summer:* like winter male but smaller, markings sharper, black of chest more restricted, and hind neck streaked with blackish. *Adult female in winter:* similar to summer female, but browner and less sharply streaked above; hind neck often without trace of rufous; under parts dingy white, chest markings only suggested. *Young:* upper parts tawny buff, broadly streaked with black except for wings and tail; under parts pale buffy, throat, chest, and sides broadly streaked with black. *Male:* length (skins) 5.75–6.55, wing 3.59–3.92, tail 2.30–2.68, bill .41–.49. *Female:* length (skins) 5.34–6.25, wing 3.39–3.67, tail 2.19–2.48, bill .40–.47." (Bailey) *Nest:* A ground nest of dried grasses and feathers. *Eggs:* 3 to 6, white, speckled with brown.

Distribution.—*General:* Breeds in northern Alaska, including islands of Bering Sea, and east to mouth of Mackenzie River. Winters south to Oregon, Nevada, Colorado, and Kansas. *In Oregon:* Rare winter straggler.

The Alaska Longspur must be listed as one of the winter visitors that reaches Oregon so infrequently as to become a rare straggler. Bendire (Brewer 1875) reported one specimen taken near Camp Harney, December 14, 1874, and stated later (Bendire 1877) that a few wintered at Camp Harney. Woodcock (1902) quoted Bendire's record but could add nothing to it. Shelton (1917) recorded an immature male taken on the coast near Siltcoos Lake, October 15, 1915, by Overton Dowell, Jr.—certainly an unusual record—and Jewett (1926a) listed a single specimen taken at Mikkalo, Gilliam County, December 28, 1924, by R. T. Jackson and presented to him in the flesh. We are unable to add any more data regarding this species as an Oregon bird, but we do suggest that observers in the open country east of the Cascades keep a sharp lookout for it with the purpose of adding to our knowledge of its distribution and regularity of occurrence.

Eastern Snow Bunting:
Plectrophenax nivalis nivalis (Linnaeus)

Description.—"Under mandible thicker than upper, gonys very short, nostrils concealed by plumules; wing nearly five times as long as tarsus; tail emarginate, about two-thirds hidden by coverts; hind claw about as long as its toe, curved. *Adult male in summer:* white, with black on bill, middle of back, scapulars, greater part of primaries, and four to six middle tail feathers. *Adult male in winter:* washed with rusty on upper parts, sides of head, and chest; bill yellow, with dusky tip. *Adult female in summer:* upper parts broadly streaked with black; wing and tail with black of male replaced by blackish brown; wing with much less white. *Adult female in winter:* like summer female, but upper parts more or less stained with rusty brown and feathers of back more edged with buffy. *Young:* under parts dull whitish; upper parts gray; wings and tail mainly dusky and brown; white of wing much restricted. *Male:* length (skins) 5.85–7.21, wing 4.19–4.58, tail 2.40–2.91, bill .38–.45. *Female:*

length (skins) 5.95–6.62, wing 3.90–4.10, tail 2.39–2.62, bill .38–.43." (Bailey) *Nest:* A ground nest of dried grasses and feathers. *Eggs:* 4 or 5, white or tinted with green or purple and speckled on larger end with brown.

DISTRIBUTION.—*General:* Breeds in Arctic regions south to northern point of mainland in Alaska and Quebec. Winters south into northern United States. Casual farther south. *In Oregon:* Irregular winter visitor to eastern Oregon that has straggled to coast.

THE EASTERN SNOW BUNTING, whitest of all the numerous sparrows that are found in Oregon, is an irregular winter visitor to the State. It arrives in November (earliest date, November 17, Malheur County) and remains until March (latest date, March 10, Wallowa County). It was first reported by Bendire (1877) from Camp Harney. Woodcock (1902) listed this same Bendire record and also a statement of B. J. Bretherton that he took two or three specimens every winter at Yaquina Bay. Our own records and published notes are the only other sources of information regarding its status in the State. In some winters it is quite common, particularly in the Wallowa Valley, from which we have a number of records and specimens. We have also seen it in Malheur and Harney Counties, and when adequate winter collecting is done it most certainly will be found much more frequently than our records indicate in eastern Oregon, in the counties bordering the Blue Mountains and thence to the south of the Columbia River. For western Oregon, Jewett (1913a) recorded a single specimen taken by Murie at Netarts, Tillamook County, December 31, 1912, and Walker took one at the same place, October 27, 1934.

While in Oregon, the Snow Bunting's behavior is similar to that of the Horned Larks and Rosy Finches. The birds feed in the stubble fields and open grasslands in flocks that sometimes attain considerable size. We have seen them in mixed flocks with Horned Larks but more frequently by themselves. Their flight behavior is quite characteristic: When the birds—feeding on the weed seeds, waste grain in stubble fields, or summer fallow—are alarmed they take off in irregular flocks that whirl about in the air for a few moments and then frequently return to the same spot from which they had alighted or to a nearby place. This characteristic behavior and their very marked plumage will be certain to identify the birds without difficulty.

Hypothetical List

Certain birds have been listed for Oregon on evidence or information that for various reasons is not now considered sufficient. For example, several species of southern sea birds have long been credited to Oregon on the basis of birds collected by Townsend over one hundred years ago. Nothing has occurred since that time to confirm these species as belonging within the present limits of the State, and present-day ornithologists generally discredit these as North American records. Such questionable records as we have found are listed here until more definite and convincing information can be obtained.

Flat-billed Albatross:
Thalassogeron chrysostomus (Forster)

THIS BIRD is included in Oregon bird lists solely on the statement of Townsend (1839), whose specimens are supposed to have been taken off the Oregon coast. This record, as well as those of several other southern birds, is considered too indefinite and uncertain to be considered authentic, and the bird was excluded from the last A. O. U. Check-List. It has usually appeared as Yellow-nosed Albatross *Thalassogeron culminatus* (Gould) and is confused with another southern albatross, neither of which belongs in an Oregon list of birds.

American Sooty Albatross:
Phoebetria palpebrata auduboni Nichols and Murphy

THIS ALBATROSS appears as an Oregon bird exactly as the previous one—on the sole basis of some of Townsend's (1839) specimens reputed to have been taken off the coast of Oregon.

Black-vented Shearwater:
Puffinus opisthomelas Coues

THIS SPECIES ranges north occasionally to Washington and British Columbia but has never to our knowledge been taken off the Oregon coast. In company with Braly (Gabrielson, Jewett, and Braly 1930) we saw small, white-bellied shearwaters off Newport, Lincoln County, that were probably of this species, but we did not get close enough to take specimens, and the bird has not yet been identified definitely from Oregon. Because of the similarity of this form to other white-breasted shearwaters, we do not deem it advisable to add the bird to the Oregon list on the basis of sight records.

Slender-billed Fulmar:
Priocella antarctica (Stephens)

THIS IS another one of Townsend's Pacific Ocean specimens that has been credited to Oregon but that present-day ornithologists feel is not a satisfactory record of North American occurrence.

Giant Fulmar:
Macronectes giganteus (Gmelin)

THERE IS a specimen of this bird in the National Museum collected by Townsend (1839), labeled "Off the Columbia River." A bird so indefinitely labeled is not regarded as a satisfactory North American record.

Leach's Petrel:
Oceanodroma leucorhoa leucorhoa (Vieillot)

THIS PETREL is credited to Oregon on the strength of Woodcock's (1902) statements, based on information furnished by Bernard J. Bretherton and Ellis F. Hadley, that it occurred in Yaquina Bay and at Tillamook. There is no evidence to indicate that this northern race, as at present understood, has occurred in Oregon, as our breeding birds are now referable to *O. l. beali*.

Ashy Petrel:
Oceanodroma homochroa (Coues)

THIS SPECIES is credited to Oregon on the basis of Woodcock's (1902) statements recording it from Yaquina Bay on information furnished by Bernard J. Bretherton. In view of the fact that the Forked-tailed Petrel, which is a common breeding bird on the Oregon coast, is not mentioned in Woodcock's list and that there are no other records of this southern breeding bird this far north, we are placing the species in the hypothetical list.

Greater Snow Goose:
Chen hyperborea atlantica Kennard

THE GREATER SNOW GOOSE was reported by Bernard J. Bretherton as common in the fall of 1899 on Yaquina Bay. The statement is recorded by Woodcock (1902). There is no other record of this eastern bird in western Oregon, and it is undoubtedly a plain case of confusion between the two forms of Snow Goose. The Lesser Snow Goose is even today a common migrant in Oregon and occasionally congregates on the coastal bays of the State.

Red-legged Black Duck:
Anas rubripes rubripes Brewster

This northern and eastern species, which does not come regularly far west of the Mississippi, was reported by Law (1887) from Sauvies Island, Oregon. We have not been able to trace any specimens on which this record was based, and in view of the absence of any other reference to the bird, we are placing it on the hypothetical list.

Red-bellied Hawk:
Buteo lineatus elegans Cassin

This bird was recorded by Johnson (1880) as occurring in East Portland, Forest Grove, and Salem; and Bendire (1892) listed eggs from Camp Harney. Other than this we have no record of this species from Oregon and are inclined to doubt the correctness of the identifications. We are placing it in the hypothetical list therefore until further information is available.

Richardson's Pigeon Hawk:
Falco columbarius richardsoni Ridgway

Recorded by Bendire (1877, 1892) and Brooks (1896), this species as now understood, is not an Oregon bird, its place on our list having been taken by the Western Pigeon Hawk.

Northern White-tailed Ptarmigan:
Lagopus leucurus leucurus (Richardson)

All of the records of this bird in Oregon can be traced back to statements of early explorers that it occurred in the Mount Hood and Mount Jefferson regions. So far as we know, it has never been taken in the State. The present southern range of the species is in the Washington Cascades just south of Mount Rainier. We are therefore placing it in the hypothetical list.

Greater Prairie Chicken:
Tympanuchus cupido americanus (Reichenbach)

Bonaparte (1828) reported the Prairie Chicken from Oregon, and Woodcock (1902) published the statement of Ellis F. Hadley that one was killed in October 1892, near Dayton. There is no other record of this bird in the State, and we are placing it in the hypothetical list, as it is almost certainly a case of mistaken identity. Eastern Oregon records of the Prairie Chicken undoubtedly refer to the Columbian Sharp-tailed Grouse.

California Quail:
Lophortyx californica californica (Shaw)

The California Quail has long been considered one of the birds of Oregon. It has been reported by many observers. We have collected quails extensively, both in the areas where they are naturally found as well as in districts where they have been introduced. Every specimen that we have taken or seen in Oregon has proved to be the Valley Quail. The only actual specimen of the California Quail is one collected by Newberry (1857) and labeled, "Willamette Valley, Oregon." This specimen is now in the National Museum and has been determined by Dr. Alexander Wetmore as true *L. c. californica*. In view of the indefiniteness of the labels on many of Newberry's specimens and in view of the further fact that he collected many birds in California while on this trip, we believe that this bird was taken farther south than the present boundaries of the State of Oregon and are therefore placing the form in the hypothetical list.

Whooping Crane:
Grus americana (Linnaeus)

This bird has been occasionally referred to in Oregon literature since Townsend listed it in 1839, stating it was found in the territory of Oregon. Brackett (1844) said that it bred in the State, and Anthony (1886) recorded it as rare at Beaverton. In view of the absence of records of this species from the western country we are inclined to view these as mistaken identifications and are placing the bird in the hypothetical list.

American Oyster-catcher:
Haematopus palliatus palliatus Temminck

This bird has no place in the Oregon fauna. The listing of the species under this name is surely a mistaken identification. We are therefore placing it in the hypothetical list.

European Turnstone:
Arenaria interpres interpres (Linnaeus)

This old-world form was listed as an Oregon bird by Woodcock (1902) on the authority of A. W. Anthony. The Ruddy Turnstone is a regular migrant on the Oregon coast, and we believe this to be purely a case of mistaken identity.

Semipalmated Sandpiper:
Ereunetes pusillus (Linnaeus)

Townsend (1839) listed this bird as found in the territory of Oregon. It is occasionally reported for British Columbia and Washington, and we have collected extensive series of Western Sandpipers in the hopes of obtaining this very similar bird. To date we have not been successful.

Long-tailed Jaeger:
Stercorarius longicaudus Vieillot

Woodcock (1902) recorded this bird in the Oregon list on Anthony's statement that it occurred off the coast. There is every reason to believe that this is correct, but despite rather extensive collecting offshore and along the beaches we have never succeeded in obtaining this species. Neither are there any existing specimens so far as we have been able to learn. It should eventually be taken.

Gull-billed Tern:
Gelochelidon nilotica aranea (Wilson)

This is another case of mistaken identity. The bird was listed for Oregon by Woodcock (1902) on the statement of Bernard J. Bretherton that it was a very common fall migrant on Yaquina Bay. The bird was undoubtedly confused with the Arctic or some other migrating tern.

Temminck's Murrelet:
Synthliboramphus wumizusume (Temminck)

Woodcock (1902) listed this Asiatic species on the strength of statements by Bernard J. Bretherton. It has no place in Oregon bird literature and has long ago been discarded from North American lists.

Morcom's Hummingbird:
Atthis heloisa morcomi Ridgway

Prill (1922a) recorded this species in his list of birds collected in Lake County, Oregon, a positive case of mistaken identity. The bird is now regarded as identical with *Atthis heloisa heloisa*.

Nuttall's Woodpecker:
Dryobates nuttalli (Gambel)

Newberry (1857) is reported to have taken one of these birds in the Umpqua Valley in August 1855. We have not been able to trace the specimen, and in view of the indefinite labeling of a number of the specimens taken on this expedition, we are inclined to doubt the correctness of the locality record. We have hunted assiduously in southern Oregon for this small bird without success. It should therefore appear in this list as a hypothetical record until specimens are taken. This is not entirely impossible as the bird ranges north in California well toward the Oregon line.

Cassin's Kingbird:
Tyrannus vociferans Swainson

Bendire (1895) recorded this species from Beaverton, Oregon, on the strength of statements by A. W. Anthony. Prill (1922a) recorded it from the Warner Valley. There is no question but that these records refer to the Arkansas Kingbird, which is an abundant species in the Warner Valley and a regular straggler in western Oregon.

Black Phoebe:
Sayornis nigricans nigricans (Swainson)

This is another one of the birds recorded from Oregon from the Umpqua Valley by Newberry (1857). Johnson (1880) recorded a bird from Salem in July 1879. We have not been able to trace satisfactorily these records of this southern bird and are therefore placing it in the hypothetical list. It may possibly be taken in the State at some future date.

Yellow-billed Magpie:
Pica nuttalli (Audubon)

Stone (1892) referred to a record of this bird from the Columbia River from the Townsend collection. There is no other indication that the species has ever appeared in Oregon. We are therefore placing it in the hypothetical list.

Nicasio Wren:
Thryomanes bewicki marinensis Grinnell

This subspecies is recorded in the last A. O. U. Check-List as occurring from the southwestern coast of Oregon to Marin County, California. We do not know the basis for this statement and have never obtained specimens within the State limits definitely referable to this form.

Eastern Ruby-crowned Kinglet:
Corthylio calendula calendula (Linnaeus)

Bishop (1926) listed this bird from the State on the basis of a few rather poorly defined specimens. In our extensive series we have no birds that are not either the Western Ruby-crowned Kinglet or the Sitka Kinglet.

Magnolia Warbler:
Dendroica magnolia (Wilson)

Finley (1907d) stated that William Warner reported one bird from Salem, Oregon, in January 1907. Inquiry of Mr. Finley brought no recollection to him of this particularly uncertain record, and in view of the date and lack of substantiating records, we unhesitatingly place this in the hypothetical list.

Bicolored Red-wing:
Agelaius phoeniceus californicus Nelson

The Bicolored Red-wing has been reported frequently from Oregon, beginning with Bendire (Brewer 1875), who stated that it was found breeding in Camp Harney. Following his records, Mearns (1879) stated that it was abundant at Fort Klamath. Johnson (1880) and Anthony (1886) listed it as an abundant summer resident of the Willamette Valley, but the supposed specimens of the Bicolored Red-wing in the Johnson collection in the museum at the University of Washington have been examined and prove to be *A. p. caurinus*. We have not been able, in spite of diligent collecting, to find this species in this State. We occasionally get a bird with little or none of the buffy edging to the wing coverts but that otherwise has the characteristics of either the Northwestern Red-wing or the Nevada Red-wing, and we therefore believe the above records to be cases of mistaken identity. The two subspecies of red-wing just mentioned are abundant breeders throughout the State and, with the exception of a small colony of Tricolored Red-wings in Klamath County, are the only members of this genus now breeding in Oregon.

Kodiak Pine Grosbeak:
Pinicola enucleator flammula Homeyer

This bird has been credited to Oregon on the basis of one skin taken by Alex Walker near Ironside, Malheur County, on December 17, 1919. We have not seen this particular bird, but others taken by Walker at the same time and from the same flocks prove to be *P. e. alascensis*. We are therefore placing this form in the hypothetical list, as we know of no specimens from anywhere south of the Olympic Peninsula.

Baird's Sparrow:
Ammodramus bairdi (Audubon)

THIS BIRD has been admitted to the Oregon lists on Bendire's (1877) statement that he took a supposed nest with four eggs at Camp Harney on May 24, 1876. In view of the fact that this is a bird of the Great Plains country and has never been taken in our section of the West, we are placing it in the hypothetical list.

Western Field Sparrow:
Spizella pusilla arenacea Chadbourne

THIS IS another species that is in the Oregon list on the basis of Ellis F. Hadley's statements (Woodcock 1902), who found a nest containing three eggs, June 14, 1900, near Dayton. In view of the fact that no specimens of the bird were taken and of the further fact that this species has never been taken west of the Rockies, we are placing it in the hypothetical list.

Bibliography

ANONYMOUS.
1874. Possibly a new bird from Oregon. Forest and Stream 3: 68.
1897. Notes from Oregon. Dwarf Hermit Thrush. Bull. Wilson Orn. Ch. 13: 19.

ABBOTT, GERARD ALAN.
1915. Abbott's collection of North American warblers' eggs. Oologist 32: 129–130.

ALDRICH, ELMER C.
1939. Notes on the salt-feeding habits of the Red Crossbill. Condor 41: 172–173.

ALLEN, JOEL ASAPH.
1876a. Breeding of the Canada Goose in trees. Bull. Nuttall Orn. Club 1: 50.
1876b. *Anser rossii* in Oregon. Bull. Nuttall Orn. Club 1: 52.
1892. The North American species of the genus *Colaptes*, considered with special reference to the relationships of *C. auratus* and *C. cafer*. Bull. Amer. Mus. Nat. Hist. 4: 21–44 (see 31).
1899. Republication of descriptions of new species and subspecies of North American birds. Auk 16: 338–350 (see 348, 349).
1900. The little Black Rail. Auk 17: 1–8 (see 4–5).
1906. The name of the Western Sandpiper. Auk 23: 97–98.
1908. Shaw's 'The China or Denny Pheasant in Oregon'. Auk 25: 241–242.
1909. The habitat groups of North American birds in the American Museum of Natural History. Auk 26: 165–174; illus. (see 171).

———, and BREWSTER, WILLIAM.
1883. Lists of birds observed in the vicinity of Colorado Springs, Colorado, during March, April, and May, 1882. Bull. Nuttall Orn. Club 8: 151–161, 189–198 (see 192).

AMERICAN ORNITHOLOGISTS' UNION COMMITTEE.
1891. Third supplement to the American Ornithologists' Union check-list of North American birds. Auk 8: 83–90 (see 85).
1895. Seventh supplement to the American Ornithologists' Union check-list of North American birds. Auk 12: 163–169 (see 165).
1916. Changes in the American Ornithologists' Union check-list of North American birds proposed since the publication of the sixteenth supplement. Auk 33: 425–431 (see 426, 427).
1931. Check-list of North American birds . . . constituting the "Systema Avium" for North America north of Mexico. 4th ed. 526 pp. Lancaster, Pa.

ANDRUS, FRED H.
1893. A nest (plum) full. Oologist 10: 300.
1894. Hutton's Vireo. Oologist 11: 287–288.
1896. Unusual nesting of American Merganser. Nidologist 3: 72–73.

A[NTHONY], A[LFRED] W[EBSTER].
1884a. The Oregon Jay (*Perisoreus obscurus*). Orn. and Ool. 9: 69.
1884b. Breeding habits of the Rufous Hummingbird (*Selasphorus rufus*). Orn. and Ool. 9: 91–93.
1885a. Cassin's Vireo (*Lanivireo solitarius cassini*). Orn. and Ool. 10: 47.
1885b. The Oregon Snowbird (*Junco oregonus*). Orn. and Ool. 10: 133.
1886. Field notes on the birds of Washington County, Oregon. Auk 3: 161–172.
1889. New birds from Lower California, Mexico. Calif. Acad. Sci. Proc. (Second Series) 2: 73–82.
1890a. The nests and eggs of Townsend's Junco (*Junco townsendi*) and San Pedro Partridge (*Oreortyx pictus confinis*). Zoe 1: 5–6.
1890b. Notice of a supposed new vireo from Oregon. Zoe 1: 307–308.
1891a. Secondary migration of birds. Zoe 1: 379–381.
1891b. Oregon's imported songsters. Zoe 2: 6–11.

A[NTHONY], A[LFRED] W[EBSTER]—Continued.
1893. *Salpinctes obsoletus* in Washington and Oregon. Auk 10: 87.
1895. Nests without eggs. Nidiologist 2: 66–67.
1899. Hybrid Grouse. Auk 16: 180–181.
1900. [Brewer's Blackbirds along Columbia River Valley.] Condor 2: 29.
1903a. Migration of Richardson's Grouse. Auk 20: 24–27.
1903b. Nesting of the Townsend Solitaire. Condor 5: 10–12, illus.
1911. Notes on some species from eastern Oregon. Auk 28: 274–275.
1912. Eastern Oregon notes. Auk 29: 253–254.
1921. Strange behavior of a Bullock's Oriole. Auk 38: 277.
1923. Predatory Brewer Blackbirds. Condor 25: 106.

APPLEGATE, ELMER I.
1905a. Robin notes. Condor 7: 83.
1905b. [Bird life in the Klamath region.] Condor 7: 114.

AUDUBON, JOHN JAMES.
1831–1839. Ornithological biography, or an account of the habits of the birds of the United States of America [etc.]. 5 vols. Edinburgh.
1840–1844. The birds of America, from drawings made in the United States and their territories. 7 vols. Philadelphia.

BACON, GEORGE R.
1877. General notes. Zoology. Notes on some Oregon birds. Amer. Nat. 11: 44.

BAILEY, FLORENCE [AUGUSTA] MERRIAM (see also MERRIAM, FLORENCE [AUGUSTA]).
1902. Handbook of birds of the Western United States [etc.]. 512 pp., illus. Boston and New York. (Rev. edition, 590 pp., illus. 1921.)
1916a. A home in the forest. Bird-Lore 18: 229–233.
1916b. Notable birds of McKenzie Bridge. Oreg. Sportsman 4: 96–98.
1917. Birds of the humid coast. Condor 19: 8–13, 46–54, 95–101.
1928. Birds of New Mexico. 807 pp., illus. New Mexico Dept. of Game and Fish.

BAILEY, VERNON [ORLANDO].
1900. Where the grebe skins come from. Bird-Lore 2: 34.
1936. The mammals and life zones of Oregon. U. S. Dept. Agr., Biol. Surv., North Amer. Fauna 55, 416 pp.

BAIRD, SPENCER FULLERTON.
1852. An expedition to the valley of the Great Salt Lake of Utah . . . by Howard Stansbury. Appendix C. Zoology. Birds, pp. 314–335 (see 316, 328–330). Philadelphia.

———; BREWER, THOMAS MAYO; and RIDGWAY, ROBERT.
1874. History of North American birds. Land birds. 3 vols. Boston.
1884. . . . The water birds of North America. 2 vols. Boston.

———; CASSIN, JOHN; and LAWRENCE, GEORGE NEWBOLD.
1858. Reports of explorations and surveys, to ascertain . . . route for a railroad from the Mississippi River to the Pacific Ocean, made . . . in 1853–6. Vol. IX. Part II. General report upon the zoology of the several Pacific Railroad routes. Birds. 1005 pp. Washington.

BANGS, OUTRAM.
1900. A review of the Three-toed Woodpeckers of North America. Auk 17: 126–142.

BARBER, OLIVER.
1934. A Coos Bay screech owl. Bird-Lore 36: 364–365.

BARNEKOFF, IRENE.
1917. Gulls at Bandon, Oregon. Bird-Lore 19: 224–226.

BARNSTON, GEORGE.
1860. Abridged sketch of the life of Mr. David Douglas, botanist, with a few details of his travels and discoveries. Canad. Nat. and Geol. 5: 120–132, 200–208, 267–278, 329–349 (see 208).

BATCHELDER, CHARLES FOSTER.
1889. An undescribed subspecies of *Dryobates pubescens*. Auk 6: 253–255.

BAYNARD, OSCAR EDWARD.
1912. Food of herons and ibises. Wilson Bull. (n.s. 19) 24: 167–169.

BEAL, FOSTER ELLENBOROUGH LASCELLES.
1907. Birds of California in relation to the fruit industry. Part I. U. S. Dept. Agr., Biol. Surv. Bull. 30: 100 pp., illus. (see 113–134).
1910. Birds of California in relation to the fruit industry. Part II. U. S. Dept. Agr., Biol. Surv. Bull. 34: 96 pp., illus.
1911. Food of the woodpeckers of the United States. U. S. Dept. Agr., Biol. Surv. Bull. 37: 64 pp., illus.
1912. Food of our more important flycatchers. U. S. Dept. Agr., Biol. Surv. Bull. 44: 67 pp., illus.
1918. Food habits of the swallows, a family of valuable native birds. U. S. Dept. Agr. Bull. 619: 28 pp., illus.

BEAN, A. M., and MURIE, OLAUS JOHAN.
1914. Bird-Lore's fourteenth Christmas census. Forest Grove, Ore. (along Gale's Creek, and in the hills 800 feet). Bird-Lore 16: 49.

BECKHAM, CHARLES WICKLIFFE.
1887. Additional notes on the birds of Pueblo County, Colorado. Auk 4: 120–125 (see 122).

BEEBE, CHARLES WILLIAM.
1918–1922. A monograph of the pheasants. 4 vols., illus. London.
1926. Pheasants, their lives and homes. 2 vols., illus. Garden City, N. Y.

BELDING, LYMAN.
1889. The small thrushes of California. Calif. Acad. Sci. Proc. (second series) 2: 57–72.
1890. Land birds of the Pacific District. Calif. Acad. Sci., Occas. Papers, 274 pp.
1891. Notices of some California birds. Zoe 2: 97–100 (see 100).

BELL, JOHN.
1852. On the *Pipilo oregonus* as distinguished from the *Pipilo arcticus* of Swainson. Ann. Lyc. Nat. Hist. New York 5: 6–8. (Read Nov. 27, 1848.)

BENDIRE, CHARLES EMIL (see also BREWER, 1875, and EDITOR, 1882).
1876. Notes on the breeding habits of Clarke's Crow (*Picicorvus columbianus*), with an account of its nest and eggs. Bull. Nuttall Orn. Club 1: 44–45.
1877. Notes on some of the birds found in southeastern Oregon, particularly in the vicinity of Camp Harney, from November, 1874, to January, 1877. Boston Soc. Nat. Hist. Proc. 19: 109–149.
1882a. American Long-eared Owl. Orn. and Ool. 6: 81–82.
1882b. Clarke's Crow. Orn. and Ool. 7: 105–107, 113–114.
1882c. Malheur Lake, Oregon. Orn. and Ool. 7: 129–131, 137–138.
1883. Description of the nest and young of the Pygmy Owl (*Glaucidium gnoma*). Bull. Nuttall Orn. Club 8: 242.
1888a. Notes on the habits, nests, and eggs of the genus *Sphyrapicus* Baird. Auk 5: 225–240.
1888b. Notes on the habits, nests and eggs of the genus *Glaucidium* Boie. Auk 5: 366–372.
1889a. Notes on the habits, nests, and eggs of *Dendragapus obscurus fuliginosus*, the Sooty Grouse. Auk 6: 32–39.
1889b. *Sphyrapicus ruber* breeding in coniferous trees. Auk 6: 71.
1889c. Notes on the general habits, nests and eggs of the genus *Passerella*. Auk 6: 107–116.
1889d. *Picicorvus columbianus* (Wils.), Clarke's Nutcracker. Its nest and eggs, etc. Auk 6: 226–236.
1892. Life histories of North American birds, with special reference to their breeding habits and eggs. Smithsonian Contributions to Knowledge 28: 446 pp., illus.; also published as U. S. Nat. Mus. Spec. Bull. 1.
1895a. Life histories of North American birds, from the parrots to the grackles, with special reference to their breeding habits and eggs. Smithsonian Contributions to Knowledge 32: 518 pp., illus.; also published as U. S. Nat. Mus. Spec. Bull 3.
1895b. The Road-runner. Forest and Stream 44: 484.
1895c. The cowbirds. Rept. U. S. Nat. Mus. 1895: 589–624.

Bent, Arthur Cleveland.

1919. Life histories of North American diving birds, order Pygopodes. U. S. Nat. Mus. Bull. 107: 245 pp., illus.

1921. Life histories of North American gulls and terns, order Longipennes. U. S. Nat. Mus. Bull. 113: 345 pp., illus.

1922. Life histories of North American petrels, pelicans, and their allies, order Tubinares and order Steganopodes. U. S. Nat. Mus. Bull. 121: 343 pp., illus.

1923. Life histories of North American wild fowl, order Anseres (Part). U. S. Nat. Mus. Bull. 126: 250 pp., illus.

1925. Life histories of North American wild fowl, order Anseres (Part). U. S. Nat. Mus. Bull. 130: 376 pp., illus.

1926. Life histories of North American marsh birds, orders Odontoglossae, Herodiones, and Paludicolae. U. S. Nat. Mus. Bull. 135: 490 pp., illus.

1927. Life histories of North American shore birds, order Limicolae (Part 1). U. S. Nat. Mus. Bull. 142: 420 pp., illus.

1929. Life histories of North American shore birds, order Limicolae (Part 2). U. S. Nat. Mus. Bull. 146: 412 pp., illus.

1932. Life histories of North American gallinaceous birds, orders Galliformes and Columbiformes. U. S. Nat. Mus. Bull. 162: 490 pp., illus.

Bergtold, William Harry.

1926. Harris's Sparrow in Colorado. Auk 43: 245.

Birtwell, Francis Joseph.

1901. Description of a supposed new subspecies of *Parus* from New Mexico. Auk 18: 165–167.

Bishop, Louis Bennett (see also **Sanford, Bishop, and Van Dyke**).

1900. Descriptions of three new birds from Alaska. Auk 17: 113–120 (see 117).

1915. Description of a new race of Savannah Sparrow and suggestions on some California birds. Condor 17: 185–189.

1921. Description of a new loon. Auk 38: 364–370 (see 369).

1926. The distribution of the races of the Ruby-crowned Kinglet. Condor 28: 183.

Blaisdell, W. O.

1890. Chinese Pheasants in Illinois. Forest and Stream 35: 312.

1894. Foreign birds for America. Forest and Stream 42: 5.

Bohlman, Herman Theodore.

1903. Nesting habits of the Shufeldt Junco. Condor 5: 94–95, illus.

Bonaparte, Charles Lucien.

1827. Supplement to the genera of North American birds, and to the synopsis of the species found within the territory of the United States. Zool. Jour. 3: 49–53 (see 50–51).

1828. The genera of North American birds, and a synopsis of the species found within the territory of the United States; systematically arranged in orders and families. Ann. Lyc. Nat. Hist. New York 2: 7–128, 293–451 (see 57–128, 438). (Read January 24, 1826.)

Bourne, Thomas Lothrop.

1922. Two interesting occurrences of the Alder Flycatcher in Erie County, N. Y. Auk 39: 260–261.

Bowles, Charles Warren.

1901a. [Sets of eggs of Black-throated Gray Warbler and Pileated Woodpecker taken in Oregon.] Condor 3: 105.

1901b. Communications. A boon for oologists. Condor 3: 106.

1902. Notes on the Black-throated Gray Warbler. Condor 4: 82–85.

1910. The California Towhee in Oregon. Condor 12: 204.

1912. An elevated camp. Condor 14: 196–199, illus.

Bowles, John Hooper.

1902. The Louisiana Tanager (*Piranga ludoviciana*). Condor 4: 16.

1907. Two new winter records from Tacoma, Washington. Condor 9: 60.

1911. Notes extending the range of certain birds on the Pacific slope. Auk 28: 169–178.

Bowles, John Hooper—Continued.
1917. The winter migration of 1916–17 in the Northwest. Condor 19: 125–129, illus. (see 127).
1920. Report of J. Hooper Bowles, of Tacoma, Washington. Murrelet 1 (1): 6–7.

———, and Decker, Frank Russel.
1927. Nesting habits of the Townsend's Solitaire. Murrelet 8: 12–13.

Brackett, A. G.
1884. The cranes. Amer. Field 21: 209.

Braly, John Claude (see also Gabrielson, Jewett, and Braly).
1930a. The Cassin Auklet breeding off the coast of Oregon. Condor 32: 302.
1930b. Nesting of the California Pygmy Owl in Oregon. Condor 32: 304.
1931. Nesting of the Pinon Jay in Oregon. Condor 33: 29.
1938. Occurrence of the Marbled Godwit on the coast of Oregon. Condor 40: 88–89.

Bretherton, Bernard J.
1893. Mongolian Pheasants of Oregon. Zoe 4: 225.
1902. The destruction of birds by lighthouses. Osprey (n.s.) 1: 76–78.

Brewer, Thomas Mayo (see also Baird, Brewer, and Ridgway).
1875. Notes on seventy-nine species of birds observed in the neighborhood of Camp Harney, Oregon, compiled from the correspondence of Capt. Charles Bendire, 1st Cavalry U.S.A. Boston Soc. Nat. Hist. Proc. 18: 153–168.
1880. Eggs of *Picus albolarvatus*. Bull. Nuttall Orn. Club 5: 56.

Brewster, William (see also Allen and Brewster).
1882. On Kennicott's Owl and some of its allies, with a description of a proposed new race. Bull. Nuttall Orn. Club 7: 27–33.
1886. Bird migration. Mem. Nuttall Orn. Club 1: 5–22.
1891. Descriptions of seven supposed new North American birds. Auk 8: 139–149.

Brooks, Allan [Cyril].
1914. The races of *Branta canadensis*. Suggested by Swarth's "Study of a collection of geese." Condor 16: 123–124.
1926a. Notes on the status of the Peale Falcon. Condor 28: 77–79.
1926b. From field and study. The present status of the Trumpeter Swan. Condor 28: 129.

———, and Swarth, Harry Schelwaldt.
1925. A distributional list of the birds of British Columbia. Cooper Orn. Club, Pacific Coast Avifauna 17: 1–158, illus., including maps.

Brooks, William Edwin.
1896. Remarks on Richardson's Merlin (*Falco richardsoni*, Ridgway). Ibis (Seventh Series) 2: 226–228, illus.

Brown, Donald E. (see Walker and Brown).

Bryant, Amy Morrish (see Bryant and Bryant).

Bryant, Harold Child (see also Grinnell, Bryant, and Storer).
1914. A survey of the breeding grounds of ducks in California in 1914. Condor 16: 217–239, illus.

———, and Bryant, Amy Morrish.
1915. From field and study. A two hour's acquaintance with a family of Water Ouzels. Condor 17: 98–99.

Bryant, Walter [Pierc] E.
1887. Additions to the ornithology of Guadalupe Island. Bull. Calif. Acad. Sci. 2 (1886–1887): 269–318 (see 304).

Burcham, John Samuel.
1904. From field and study. Notes on the habits of the Water Ouzel (*Cinclus mexicanus*). Condor 6: 50.

Burns, Franklin Lorenzo.
1895. The American Crow (*Corvus americanus*) with special reference to its nest and eggs. Bull. Wilson Orn. Ch. 5: 1–41 (see 12–41).

Butler, Amos William.
1892. Some notes concerning the Evening Grosbeak. Auk 9: 238–247 (see 239).

Campbell, Mamie; Raker, Mary Estelle; Eliot, Willard Ayres; and Raker, William Samuel.
1923. Bird-Lore's twenty-third Christmas census. Portland, Oreg. Bird-Lore 25: 44.

Cartlidge, P. Gregory.
1918. How I mothered a pair of hummingbirds. Bird-Lore 20: 272–276.

Cassin, John (see also Baird, Cassin, and Lawrence).
1852. Monograph of the birds composing the genera *Hydropsalis*, Wagler, and *Antrostomus*, Nuttall. Journ. Acad. Nat. Sci. Phila. (Second Series) 2: 113–124, illus. (see 123).
1853a. Catalogue of the Hirundinidae in the collection of the Academy of Natural Sciences of Philadelphia. Acad. Nat. Sci. Phila. Proc. 6: Not paged; at end of volume.
1853b. Synopsis of the species of Falconidae which inhabit America north of Mexico; with descriptions of new species. Acad. Nat. Sci. Phila. Proc. 6: 450–453.
1856. Illustrations of the birds of California, Texas, Oregon, British and Russian America. Intended to contain descriptions and figures of all North-American birds not given by former American authors, and a general synopsis of North American ornithology 1853 to 1855. 298 pp., illus. Philadelphia.
1863. Notes on the Picidae, with descriptions of new and little known species. Acad. Nat. Sci. Phila. Proc. 15: 194–204, 322–328 (see 328).

Chapman, Frank Michler.
1888. List of additions to the North American avifauna and of eliminations and changes in nomenclature proposed since the publication of the A. O. U. check-list. Auk 5: 393–402 (see 396).
1890. On a collection of birds made by Mr. Clark P. Streator in British Columbia, with field notes by the collector. Bull. Amer. Mus. Nat. Hist. 3: 123–158 (see 134).
1900. A study of the genus *Sturnella*. Bull. Amer. Mus. Nat. Hist. 13: 297–320, illus. (see 317).
1904. A new grouse from California. Bull. Amer. Mus. Nat. Hist. 20: 159–161.
1907. The warblers of North America. 306 pp., illus. New York.
1912. Handbook of birds of eastern North America. Second edition. 530 pp., illus. New York. (Second revised edition 580 pp., illus. New York 1932.)

Clark, Austin Hobart.
1910. The birds collected and observed during the cruise of the United States Fisheries Steamer "Albatross" in the North Pacific Ocean, and in the Bering, Okhotsk, Japan, and Eastern Seas, from April to December, 1906. U. S. Nat. Mus. Proc. 33 (1911): 25–74.

Clark [William] (see Lewis and Clark).

Cleaves, Howard Henderson.
1913. What the American Bird Banding Association has accomplished during 1912. Auk 30: 248–261, illus.

Coale, Henry Kelso.
1915. The present status of the Trumpeter Swan (*Olor buccinator*). Auk 32: 82–90, illus.

Cooke, Clinton T.
1891a. Nesting of the Sooty Grouse. Orn. and Ool. 16: 145–146.
1891b. Nesting of MacGillivray's Warbler. Orn. and Ool. 16: 161–162.

Cooke, Wells Woodbridge.
1897. The birds of Colorado. Colo. Agr. Expt. Sta. Bull. 37, 239 pp. (see 163). (Also issued as Bull. 44, 1898, and Bull. 56, 1900.)
1904a. Distribution and migration of North American warblers. U. S. Dept. Agr., Biol. Surv. Bull. 18, 142 pp.
1904b. The migration of warblers. Second paper. Bird-Lore 6: 21–24, 57–60, illus. (see 23, 59).

COOKE, WELLS WOODBRIDGE—Continued.
1905. The migration of warblers. Eighth, tenth, twelfth, and thirteenth papers. Bird-Lore 7: 32–35, 169–170, 237–239, 275–278, illus. (see 34, 170, 238, 278).
1906. Distribution and migration of North American ducks, geese, and swans. U. S. Dept. Agr., Biol. Surv. Bull. 26, 90 pp.
1908. The migration of flycatchers. Sixth and seventh papers. Bird-Lore 10: 210–212, 258–259, illus.
1909a. The migration of vireos. Third and concluding paper. Bird-Lore 11: 165–168.
1909b. The migration of North American sparrows. First paper. Bird-Lore 11: 254–260.
1910a. The migration of North American sparrows. Bird-Lore 12: 139–141.
1910b. Distribution and migration of North American shorebirds. U. S. Dept. Agr., Biol. Surv. Bull. 35, 100 pp., illus.
1911. The migration of North American sparrows. Ninth, tenth, and twelfth papers. Bird-Lore 13: 83–88, 144–146, 248–249.
1912. The migration of North American sparrows. Fifteenth, sixteenth, and seventeenth papers. Bird-Lore 14: 98–105, 158–161, 218–219.
1913a. The migration of North American sparrows. Twenty-first, twenty-third, twenty-fourth, and twenty-fifth papers. Bird-Lore 15: 104–107, map; 236–240; 301–303; 364–365.
1913b. Distribution and migration of North American herons and their allies. U. S. Dept. Agr., Biol. Surv. Bull. 45, 70 pp., illus.
1914. Distribution and migration of North American rails and their allies. U. S. Dept. Agr. Bull. 128, 50 pp., illus.
1915a. Bird migration. U. S. Dept. Agr. Bull. 185, 48 pp., illus.
1915b. The migration of North American birds. Bird-Lore 17: 378–379.
1915c. Our shorebirds and their future. U. S. Dept. Agr. Yearbook Separate 642, pp. 275–294, illus.
1915d. Distribution and migration of North American gulls and their allies. U. S. Dept. Agr. Bull. 292, 70 pp., illus.

COOPER, JAMES GRAHAM.
1868. Some recent additions to the fauna of California. Calif. Acad. Sci. Proc. 4: 3–13 (see 10).
1869. The fauna of Montana territory. II. Birds. Amer. Nat. 2: 596–600; 3: 31–35 (see 598, 34).
1877. On seventy-five doubtful West-coast birds. Bull. Nuttall Orn. Club 2: 88–97.

———, and SUCKLEY, GEORGE.
1860. Reports of explorations and surveys, to ascertain . . . route for a railroad from the Mississippi River to the Pacific Ocean, 1853–1855. Vol. XII. Book 2. Part III. Zoological report. No. 3. Report upon the birds collected on the survey. Chap. I. Land birds, pp. 140–226, illus. (by Cooper). Chap. II. Water birds, pp. 227–291, illus. (by Suckley).

CORY, CHARLES BARNEY.
1897. How to know the ducks, geese, and swans. 95 pp., illus. Boston.

COTTAM, CLARENCE.
1938. Nesting of an Eastern Kingbird in a deserted Oriole nest. Condor 40: 259.

COUES, ELLIOTT.
1862. Revision of the gulls of North America; based upon specimens in the Museum of the Smithsonian Institution. Acad. Nat. Sci. Phila. Proc. 14 (1863): 291–312 (see 299).
1866. A critical review of the family Procellariidae:—Part III; embracing the Fulmareae. Acad. Nat. Sci. Phila. Proc. 1866: 25–33 (see 32).
1874. Birds of the Northwest [etc.]. Dept. Int., U. S. Geol. Surv. Ter., F. V. Hayden, Geologist-in-charge, Misc. Pub. 3, 791 pp.
1876. General notes. Zoology. Range of the Bay Ibis. Amer. Nat. 10: 48.
1878. Birds of the Colorado valley [etc.]. Dept. Int., U. S. Geol. Surv. Ter., F. V. Hayden, Geologist-in-charge, Misc. Pub. 11, 807 pp., illus.
1897. General notes. Type locality of *Fuligula collaris*. Auk 14: 206–207.
1903. Key to North American birds, . . . Fifth edition, revised. 2 vols. Boston.

CURRIER, EDMONDE SAMUEL.

1926. Coast Wren-tit! A nest I did not find. Murrelet 7: 64.

1928. From field and study. Lewis's Woodpeckers nesting in colonies. Condor 30: 356.

1929a. From field and study. Least Bittern near Portland, Oregon. Condor 31: 78.

1929b. From field and study. Lesser Yellow-legs in Willamette Valley, Oregon. Condor 31: 80.

1936. Anthony's Green Heron near Portland, Oregon. Murrelet 17: 53.

CUSHING, JOHN E., JR.

1938. The status of the Fox Sparrow of southwestern Oregon. Condor 40: 73–76, illus.

DAVIS, W. B.

1899. Odd actions of birds unexplained. Osprey 3: 103–104.

DAWSON, WILLIAM LEON.

1914a. From field and study. A new record for Oregon. Condor 16: 41.

1914b. From field and study. Probable occurrence of the Harris Sparrow in Washington. Condor 16: 93.

DEANE, RUTHVEN.

1880a. Additional cases of albinism and melanism in North American birds. Bull. Nuttall Orn. Club 5: 25–30 (see 27).

1880b. General notes. The Bohemian Waxwing in northern New York. Bull. Nuttall Orn. Club 5: 118.

DEARBORN, NED.

1912. The English Sparrow as a pest. U. S. Dept. Agr. Farmers' Bull. 493, 24 pp., illus.

1914. Bird houses and how to build them. U. S. Dept. Agr. Farmers' Bull. 609, 19 pp., illus.

DECKER, FRANK RUSSEL (see BOWLES and DECKER).

DICE, LEE RAYMOND.

1917. Habits of the magpie in southeastern Washington. Condor 19: 121–124, illus.

DICKEY, DONALD RYDER.

1922. From field and study. Second occurrence of the Yakutat Song Sparrow in California. Condor 24: 65.

———, and VAN ROSSEM, ADRIAN JOSEPH.

1922a. From field and study. The Gray Flycatcher in the White Mountains of California. Condor 24: 137.

1922b. Distribution of *Molothrus ater* in California, with the description of a new race. Condor 24: 206–210.

1923. Description of a new grouse from southern California. Condor 25: 168–169.

1925. A revisionary study of the Western Gull. Condor 27: 162–164.

DIETRICH, ERICH J. (see also WALKER and DIETRICH).

1914. Some notes on Macgillivray's Warbler. Oologist 31: 105–111, illus.

DIXON, JOSEPH (see GRINNELL, DIXON, and LINSDALE).

DOUGLAS, DAVID.

1828. Observations on the *Vultur californianus* of Shaw. Zool. Journ. 4 (1829): 328–330.

1829. Observations on some species of the genera *Tetrao* and *Ortyx*, natives of North America; with descriptions of four new species of the former, and two of the latter genus. [Read Dec. 16, 1828. Published in 1829. Whole vol. dated 1833.] Linn. Soc. London, Trans, 16: 133–149.

1914. Journal kept by David Douglas during his travels in North America 1823–1827. . . . 364 pp., illus. London.

DU BOIS, H. M.

1935. From field and study. Another winter record of the Townsend Warbler in Portland, Oregon. Condor 37: 171.

DUTCHER, WILLIAM.

1905. The Tree Sparrow. Bird-Lore 7: 254–256.

1908. Three new reservations. Bird-Lore 10: 231–232.

Dwight, Jonathan, Jr.

1890. The Horned Larks of North America. Auk 7: 138–158, illus.

1900. The moult of the North American Tetraonidae (quails, partridges and grouse). Auk 17: 34–51, 143–166, illus.

1925. The gulls (Laridae) of the world; Their plumages, moults, variations, relationships and distribution. Bull. Amer. Mus. Nat. Hist. 52: 63–401, illus.

Eaton, Elon Howard.

1910. Birds of New York. New York State Museum Memoir 12. Part 1. Introductory chapters. Water birds and game birds. 501 pp., illus. Albany.

1914. Birds of New York. New York State Museum Memoir 12. Part 2. General chapters. Land birds. 719 pp., illus. Albany.

Eckstrom, Fannie Hardy.

1901. The woodpeckers. 131 pp., illus. Boston.

1902. A description of the adult Black Merlin (*Falco columbarius suckleyi*). Auk 19: 382–385.

[Editor.]

1857. Donations to museum. In September and October, 1856. Acad. Nat. Sci. Phila. Proc. 8 (1856): xviii–xx (see xix).

1882. Gleanings from Bendire's letters. Orn. & Ool. 7: 153–154.

1887. Oregon Chinese Pheasants. Forest and Stream 29: 447.

1890. Chinese Pheasants in America. Forest and Stream 35: 28.

1892. [A letter regarding the introduction of German song birds in Portland, Oregon.] Del. Valley Orn. Club Abstract of Proc. for 1890 and 1891, p. 3.

1905. State reports. Oregon. Bird-Lore 7: 103–108, 336–342, illus.

El Comancho.

1895. Notes of a flying trip. Forest and Stream 44: 392.

Eliot, Willard Ayres (see also Campbell, etc.).

1923. Birds of the Pacific Coast. 211 pp., illus. New York and London.

———; Raker, William Samuel; and Raker, Mary Estelle.

1924. Bird-Lore's twenty-fourth Christmas census. Portland, Oregon. Bird-Lore 26: 49–50.

———; Gilbert, Harold S.; and others.

1934. Bird-Lore's thirty-fourth Christmas census. Portland, Oregon. Bird-Lore 36: 61–62.

Elliot, Daniel Giraud.

1862. Remarks on the species composing the genus *Pediocaetes* Baird. Acad. Nat. Sci. Phila. Proc. 14: 402–404.

1864–65. A monograph of the Tetraoninae—or, family of the grouse. [40] pp., illus. (see text to pls. 3, 8, 14, 25). New York.

1869. The new and heretofore unfigured species of the birds of North America. 2 vols. New York (see vol. 2, text to pls. 42, 58, 59). (Issued 15 parts in 14, 1866–69, with cover-title "The Birds of North America".)

1898. The wild fowl of the United States and British Possessions; or, the swan, geese, ducks, and mergansers of North America. 316 pp., illus. New York.

Emerson, William Otto.

1901. The American Redstart in Oregon. Condor 3: 145.

1906. *Oceanodroma leucorhoa* and its relatives on the Pacific Coast. Condor 8: 53–55 (see 54).

Estabrook, Arthur Howard.

1907. The present status of the English Sparrow problem in America. Auk 24: 129–134 (see 131).

Evermann, Barton Warren.

1919. From field and study. Large set of eggs of the Canada Goose. Condor 21: 126.

Farrell, Thomas G.

1890. Notes. [The Evening Grosbeak in Oregon.] Amer. Field 33: 560.

1891. American swans. Amer. Field 35: 274–275.

Faxon, Walter.
1890. General notes. The Long-billed Marsh Wren, Maryland Yellow-throat, Nashville Warbler, and Great Blue Heron in eastern Massachusetts in winter. Auk 7: 408–410.

Ferris, Reed W.
1933. From field and study. A Grinnell Water-thrush in Oregon. Condor 35: 80.

Finley, Irene (see Finley and Finley).

Finley, William Lovell.
1901. Catching birds with a camera. Condor 3: 137–139, illus.
1902. Among the sea birds of the Oregon coast. Condor 4: 53–57, illus.
1903. Two vireos caught with a camera. Condor 5: 61–64, illus.
1904a. Two Oregon warblers. Condor 6: 31–35, illus.
1904b. The Lutescent Warbler (*Helminthophila celata lutescens*). Condor 6: 131–133, illus.
1904c. The Black-headed Grosbeak (*Zamelodia melanocephala*). Condor 6: 145–148.
1905a. Photographing the aerie of a Western Red-tail. Condor 7: 2–7, illus.
1905b. Hummingbird studies. Condor 7: 59–62, illus.
1905c. A study in bird confidence. Condor 7: 91–94.
1905d. Among the sea birds off the Oregon coast. Parts I and II. Condor 7: 119–127, 161–169. illus.
1906a. Herons at home. Condor 8: 35–40, illus.
1906b. The chickadee at home. Condor 8: 63–67, illus.
1906c. The Barn Owl and its economic value. Condor 8: 83–88, illus.
1907a. Among the gulls on Klamath Lake. Condor 9: 12–16, illus.
1907b. Among the pelicans. Condor 9: 35–41, illus.
1907c. The grebes of southern Oregon. Condor 9: 97–101, illus.
1907d. From field and study. Magnolia Warbler in Oregon. Condor 9: 110.
1907e. Two studies in blue. Condor 9: 121–127, illus.
1907f. American birds studied and photographed from life. 256 pp., illus. New York.
1908a. Life history of the California Condor. Part II. Historical data and range of the condor. Condor 10: 5–10, illus.
1908b. Reports of field agents. Report of William L. Finley. Bird-Lore 10: 291–295, illus.
1909a. Some bird accidents. Condor 11: 181–184, illus.
1909b. The Bush-Tit. Bird-Lore 11: 225–228, illus.
1911. Reports of field agents. Report of William L. Finley. Bird-Lore 13: 347–350.
1912. Reports of field agents. Report of William L. Finley, field agent for the Pacific Coast States. Bird-Lore 14: 415–418, illus.
1915a. The lure of the wild duck. Bird-Lore 17: 75–79, illus.
1915b. With the field-agents. Cruising the Klamath. Bird-Lore 17: 485–491, illus.
1915c. The Bob-white in Oregon. Oreg. Sportsman 3: 25–27.
1918. Reports of field agents. Report of William L. Finley, field agent for the Pacific Coast States. Bird-Lore 20: 467–468, illus.
1923. From field and study. Further indictment of the Brewer Blackbird. Condor 25: 179–180.

———, and Finley, Irene.
1915. With the field agents. Bird-friends in Arizona. Bird-Lore 17: 237–245, illus.
1924. Changing habits of Vaux Swift and Western Martin. Condor 26: 6–9, illus.

Fisher, Albert Kenrick.
1893. The hawks and owls of the United States in their relation to agriculture. U. S. Dept. Agr., Div. Orn. and Mammal. Bull. 3, 210 pp., illus.
1902. Two vanishing game birds. Reprint from U. S. Dept. Agr. Yearbook for 1901, pp. 447–458, illus.
1907. Hawks and owls from the standpoint of the farmer. U. S. Dept. Agr., Biol. Surv. Circ. 61, 18 pp., illus.

Fisher, Walter Kenrick.
1902a. The Oregon Song Sparrow. Condor 4: 36–37.
1902b. Status of *Cyanocitta stelleri carbonacea* Grinnell. Condor 4: 41–44, map.

FISHER, WALTER KENRICK—Continued.
1902c. The Downy Woodpeckers of California. Condor 4: 68–70.
1904. From field and study. Notes on the birds of Hoopa Valley, California. Condor 6: 50–51.

FITCH, HENRY (see STEVENSON and FITCH).

FLEMING, JAMES HENRY.
1924. From field and study. The California Condor in Washington: Another version of an old record. Condor 26: 111–112.

FORBUSH, EDWARD HOWE.
1910. Bob-white. Bird-Lore 12: 255–258, illus.
1911. The Cedar Waxwing. Bird-Lore 13: 55–58, illus.
1925–1929. Birds of Massachusetts and other New England States. 3 vols., illus. Vol. 1, 1925; vol. 2, 1927; vol. 3, 1929. Boston.

FREMONT, JOHN CHARLES.
1850. Oregon and California. The exploring expedition to the Rocky Mountains. 456 pp. Buffalo and Cleveland.

FRENCH, DWIGHT AARON.
1933. Geese rest on Crater Lake. Nature Notes Crater Lake Nat. Park 6 (4): 6–7.

FRIEDMANN, HERBERT.
1929. The cowbirds; a study in the biology of social parasitism. 421 pp., illus. Springfield, Ill., and Baltimore, Md.

GABRIELSON, IRA NOEL (see also JEWETT and GABRIELSON).
1913. Nest life of the Catbird, *Dumetella carolinensis* Linn. Wilson Bull. (n.s. 20) 25: 166–187.
1914. Pied-billed Grebe notes. Wilson Bull. (n.s. 21) 26: 13–15.
1921. From field and study. An addition to the Oregon list of birds. Condor 23: 96.
1922a. The season. Portland (Oregon) region. Bird-Lore 24: 103–104, 160–162, 225–226, 287–288, 355–356.
1922b. Factors contributing to the destruction of birds' nest and eggs. Bird-Lore 24: 136–139.
1922c. From field and study. Some hawks of Harney Valley, Oregon. Condor 24: 33–34.
1923a. From field and study. A winter record of the Spotted Sandpiper for the Olympic Peninsula. Condor 25: 106.
1923b. From field and study. A few notes on some Oregon species of shore birds. Condor 25: 109–110.
1923c. From field and study. Four new bird records for Oregon. Condor 25: 139–140.
1923d. Notes from Portland, Oregon. Murrelet 4 (1): 11.
1923e. The season. Portland (Oregon) region. Bird-Lore 25: 52–53, 135–136, 200–201, 267–268, 331, 407.
1924a. Notes on the birds of Wallowa County, Oregon. Auk 41: 552–565.
1924b. The season. Portland (Oregon) region. Bird-Lore 26: 62, 128–129, 196–197, 275–276, 343–344, 422–423.
1924c. From field and study. Two Oregon water bird records of interest. Condor 26: 230–231.
1924d. Food habits of some winter bird visitants. U. S. Dept. Agr. Bull. 1249, 32 pp., illus.
1925a. General notes. Bird notes from Oregon. Murrelet 6: 61.
1925b. The season. Portland (Oregon) region. Bird-Lore 27: 19, 122–123, 194–195, 269, 345–346, 415.
1926a. The season. Portland (Oregon) region. Bird-Lore 28: 66–67, 145–146, 217–218, 285–286, 352–354.
1926b. General notes. Note on certain birds feeding on wild cherry. Murrelet 7: 63.
1927. The season. [Portland] Oregon region. Bird-Lore 29: 62–63, 135, 282–283, 355–356, 435–436.
1928. The season. Oregon region. Bird-Lore 30: 21–22, 135, 205–206, 279–280, 345–346, 409–410.
1929. The season. Portland (Oregon) region. Bird-Lore 31: 131–132, 208–209, 281–283, 349, 415–416.

GABRIELSON, IRA NOEL (see also JEWETT and GABRIELSON)—Continued.
1930. The season. Portland (Oregon) region. Bird-Lore 32: 144–145, 217, 291–292, 366–367, 439–440.
1931. The birds of the Rogue River Valley, Oregon. Condor 33: 110–121.
1933a. General notes. An Oregon record of the Red-legged Kittiwake (*Rissa brevirostris*). Auk 50: 216.
1933b. General notes. The Harris Sparrow at Hillsboro, Oregon. Murrelet 14: 16.
1933c. General notes. Recent observations on the Oregon coast. Murrelet 14: 16–17.
1934a. General notes. Some Oregon specimens worthy of record. Murrelet 15: 25.
1934b. General notes. The Herring Gull on the Columbia River. Murrelet 15: 25.
1934c. General notes. Monterey Hermit Thrush (*Hylocichla guttata slevini*) from northern California. Murrelet 15: 53.
1935. General notes. Black Pigeon Hawk in eastern Oregon. Murrelet 16: 39–40.

———, and JEWETT, STANLEY GORDON.
1930. White-throated Swift in Oregon. Murrelet 11: 74.
1933. General notes. First record of Pomarine Jaeger for Oregon. Murrelet 14: 15.
1934a. General notes. American Egret in Portland, Oregon. Murrelet 15: 25.
1934b. General notes. Two new birds for Oregon. Murrelet 15: 50–51.

———; JEWETT, STANLEY GORDON; and BRALY, J. C.
1930. Some notes from the Oregon coast. Murrelet 11: 10–12.

GADOW, HANS.
1883. Catalogue of the birds in the British Museum, Vol. VIII. Catalogue of the Passeriformes or perching birds in the collection of the British Museum. Cichlomorphae: Part V, containing the families Paridae and Laniidae * * * and Certhiomorpha [etc.]. 385 pp., illus. (see 34). London.

GAMBEL, WILLIAM.
1848. Ueber die in Oberkalifornien beobachteten Voegel. Archiv fuer Naturgeschichte Jahrg. 14: Bd. I, 82–112.

GAULT, BENJAMIN TRUE.
1884. Nuttall's Woodpecker (*Picus nuttallii*). Amer. Field 21: 305.
1887. *Dryobates nuttallii* (Gamb.) Nuttall's Woodpecker. Bull. Ridgway Orn. Club 2: 78.

GETCHELL, ELLA.
1918a. Notes from field and study. The Black-chinned Hummingbird. Bird-Lore 20: 292–293.
1918b. Notes from field and study. An Oregon oriole. Bird-Lore 20: 355–356.

GILBERT, HAROLD S. (see ELIOT, GILBERT, and others.)

GONZALES, BOYER.
1889. Overland journey—Texas to the Pacific. Orn. & Ool. 14: 161–162.

GORDON, KENNETH.
1932. General notes. Sex of incubating killdeers. Auk 49: 218.
1939. The House Finch in the Willamette Valley, Oregon. Condor 41: 164.

GOSS, NATHANIEL STICKNEY.
1889. Additions to the catalogue of the birds of Kansas, with notes in regard to their habits. Auk 6: 122–124.
1891. History of the birds of Kansas. 693 pp., illus. Topeka.

GOULD, JOHN.
1861. A monograph of the Trochilidae, or family of hummingbirds. 5 vols., illus. London. (See vol. 3, text to pl. 136.) (Originally issued in 25 parts, 1849–1861.)

GREENE, S. H.
1892. The Water Ousel. Forest and Stream 38: 395.
1893. Oregon pheasants and quail. Forest and Stream 40: 385.
1894. Oregon notes. [Mongolian Pheasants plentiful.] Forest and Stream 43: 226.
1895. Oregon notes. Forest and Stream 45: 422, 493.

GRIEPENTROG, ELMER LOWELL.
1929. General notes. Nesting of *Accipiter velox* in the Willamette Valley, Oregon. Murrelet 10: 40–41.
1934a. Late nesting of the Shufeldt's Junco. Oologist 51: 143.
1934b. The nesting of the Calaveras Warbler in the Willamette Valley, Oregon. Oologist 51: 145–146.
1935. The nesting of the Calaveras Warbler in the Willamette Valley, Oregon. Oologist 52: 10.

GRIFFEE, WILLIAM E.
1936. Nesting of the Hooded Merganser at Portland, Oregon. Murrelet 17: 53–54.

GRINNELL, GEORGE BIRD.
1910. American game bird shooting. 558 pp., illus. New York.

GRINNELL, JOSEPH.
1897. New race of *Spinus tristis* from the Pacific Coast. Auk 14: 397.
1900. New races of birds from the Pacific Coast. Condor 2: 127–129.
1901. The Monterey Hermit Thrush. Auk 18: 258–259.
1902a. General notes. Northern visitants to Oregon. Auk 19: 92–93.
1902b. Geographical variation in abrasion. Auk 19: 128–131.
1903. The California Yellow Warbler. Condor 5: 71–73.
1904. The origin and distribution of the Chestnut-backed Chickadee. Auk 21: 364–382, map (see 380).
1905. The Pacific Nighthawk. Condor 7: 170.
1908. The Southern California Chickadee. Condor 10: 29–30.
1909a. A collection of birds from Forty-mile, Yukon Territory, Canada. Condor 11: 202–207 (see 206).
1909b. Birds and mammals of the 1907 Alexander expedition to southeastern Alaska. The birds. Calif. Univ. Pubs., Zool. 5: 181–284.
1910. The Savannah Sparrow of the Great Basin. Calif. Univ. Pubs. Zool. 5: 312–316.
1911. Description of a new Spotted Towhee from the Great Basin. Calif. Univ. Pubs., Zool. 7: 309–311.
1912. From field and study. The Northern Brown Towhee. Condor 14: 199.
1913. *Leucosticte tephrocotis dawsoni*—a new race of Rosy Finch from the Sierra Nevada. Condor 15: 76–79.
1915a. A distributional list of the birds of California. Cooper Orn. Club, Pacific Coast Avifauna 11, 217 pp., illus. (see 176, 179, 180, 187).
1915b. A new subspecies of Screech Owl from California. Auk 32: 59–60.
1917a. The subspecies of *Hesperiphona vespertina*. Condor 19: 17–22 (see 20).
1917b. An invasion of California by the Eastern Goshawk. Condor 19: 70–71.
1918. From field and study. The status of the White-rumped Petrels of the California Coast. Condor 20: 46.
1921. Concerning the status of the supposed two races of the Long-billed Curlew. Condor 23: 21–27 (see 22).
1922. The "Anthony Vireo" not a tenable subspecies. Condor 24: 32–33.
1928. Notes on the systematics of West American birds. III. Condor 30: 185–189.
1938. Ocean waifs and what they mean for distribution. Condor 40: 242–245.

———; BRYANT, HAROLD CHILD; and STORER, TRACY IRWIN.
1918. The game birds of California. 642 pp., illus. Berkeley.

———; DIXON, JOSEPH; and LINSDALE, JEAN MYRON.
1930. Vertebrate natural history of a section of northern California through the Lassen Peak region. Calif. Univ. Pubs., Zool. 35: 594 pp., illus.

———, and STORER, TRACY IRWIN.
1924. Animal life in the Yosemite: An account of the mammals, birds, reptiles, and amphibians in a cross-section of the Sierra Nevada. 752 pp., illus. Berkeley.

———, and SWARTH, HARRY SCHELWALDT.
1926. Systematic review of the Pacific Coast Brown Towhees. Calif. Univ. Pubs., Zool. 21: 427–433.

Gross, Alfred Otto.
1923. The black-crowned Night Heron (*Nycticorax nycticorax naevius*) of Sandy Neck. Auk 40: 1–30, 191–214, illus.

Gurney, John Henry.
1882. Notes on a Catalogue of the Accipitres in the British Museum by R. Bowdler Sharpe (1874). Ibis (Fourth Series) 6: 290–321 (see 297).

Hadley, Ellis F.
1893. Leaving nest eggs. Oologist 10: 254.
1895. The Mountain Partridge in captivity. Oologist 12: 90–92.
1899. Sooty Grouse. Oologist 16: 134–136.
1901. Queer nesting. Oologist 18: 62–63.

Hague, Florence.
1925. From field and study. The Black Swift in Oregon. Condor 27: 70.

Hall, Eugene Raymond.
1925. Pelicans versus fishes in Pyramid Lake. Condor 27: 147–160 (see 149).

Hall, Frank Stevens.
1930. General notes. Great Gray Owl taken in Oregon. Murrelet 11: 74.

Hartlaub, Gustav.
1852. R. Titian Peale's Voegel der "United States Exploring Expedition". Archiv. fuer Naturgeschichte, Jahrg. 18, Bd. I, 93–138.

Hasbrouck, Edwin Marble.
1893. The geographical distribution of the genus *Megascops* in North America. Auk 10: 250–264, 2 maps.

Haskin, Leslie Loren.
1919. Notes from field and study. Townsend's Solitaire. Bird-Lore 21: 242–243.

Hayden, Ferdinand Vandiveer.
1862. On the geology and natural history of the Upper Missouri; with a map. Amer. Phil. Soc. Trans. 12: 218 pp. (see 160).

Heermann, Adolphus L.
1853. Notes on the birds of California, observed during a residence of three years in that country. Journ. Acad. Nat. Sci. Phila. (Second Series) 2: 259–272 (see 260).
1859. Reports of explorations and surveys, to ascertain . . . route for a railroad from the Mississippi River to the Pacific Ocean . . . 1853–6. Vol. X. Report . . . near 32d parallel of north latitude . . . by John G. Parke. Zoological Report No. 1. Report on birds collected on the survey, pp. 9–20, illus., and Report of explorations in California . . . by Lieut. R. S. Williamson. Part IV. Zoological Report No. 2. Report upon birds collected on the survey, pp. 29–80, illus.

Henderson, Junius.
1920. From field and study. The Varied Thrush in Wyoming. Condor 22: 75.

Henninger, Walther Friedrich.
1920. General notes. The Plain Titmouse a new bird for Oregon. Auk 37: 594.

———, and Jones, Lynds.
1909. The Falcones of North America. Wilson Bull. (n.s. 16) 21: 77–94, illus. (see 81, 85).

Henshaw, Henry Wetherbee.
1875. Report upon geographical and geological explorations west of the one hundredth meridian in charge of First Lieut. Geo. M. Wheeler . . . Vol. V, Zoology. Chap. III. Report upon the ornithological collections made in portions of Nevada, Utah, California, Colorado, New Mexico, and Arizona, during the years 1871, 1872, 1873 and 1874, pp. 133–507, illus. (see 258–275).
1878. Additional remarks on *Selasphorus alleni*. Bull. Nuttall Orn. Club 3: 11–15 (see 15).
1879a. Occurrence of Ross's Goose (*Anser rossii*) on the Pacific Coast and inland. Bull. Nuttall Orn. Club 4: 126.
1879b. *Melospiza meloda* and its allies. Bull. Nuttall Orn. Club 4: 155–160.

HENSHAW, HENRY WETHERBEE—Continued.
1880. Ornithological report from observations and collections made in portions of California, Nevada, and Oregon.
Appendix L. Appendix oo. Annual Report of Captain George M. Wheeler, Corps of Engineers, U.S.A., for 1879. Geographical Surveys of the Territory of the United States West of the One Hundredth Meridian in the States and Territories of California, Colorado, Kansas, Nebraska, Nevada, Oregon, Texas, Arizona, Idaho, Montana, New Mexico, Utah, Washington and Wyoming. Annual Report of the Secretary of War for 1879, Vol. II, Pt. 3, 1880, pp. 2260–2313.
Also, Executive Documents of the House of Representatives for the Second Session of the Forty-sixth Congress 1879–80, Vol. V, No. 1, Pt. 2, War Department Annual Reports, 1879, Vol. 2, Engineers, Pt. 3 (Serial No. 1906) February 1880, pp. 2260–2313.
Also, Annual Report upon the Geographical Surveys of the United States West of the One Hundredth Meridian, by George M. Wheeler, First Lieutenant, Corps of Engineers, 1879 (1880), pp. 282–335.
1884. The shore larks of the United States and adjacent territory. Auk 1: 254–268.
1913. Fifty common birds of farm and orchard. U. S. Dept. Agr. Farmers' Bull. 513, 31 pp., illus.
1918. The book of birds. Common birds of town and country and American game birds. Illustrated in natural colors with 250 paintings by Louis Agassiz Fuertes. With chapters . . . by F. H. Kennard, Wells W. Cooke, and George Shiras. 195 pp. Washington, D. C., National Geographic Society.
1919–20. Autobiographical notes. Condor 21: 102–107, 165–171, 177–181, 217–222; and 22: 3–10, 55–60, 95–101 (see 22: 55–56).

HOFFMAN, WALTER JAMES.
1881. Annotated list of the birds of Nevada. Dept. Int., Bull. U. S. Geol. and Geog. Surv. Ter., F. V. Hayden, U. S. Geologist-in-charge, vol. 6 (1881–1882), Bull. 2: 203–256.

HOFFMANN, RALPH.
1924. From field and study. Song of the Gray Flycatcher. Condor 26: 195.
1926a. From field and study. Male American Crossbill feeds female. Condor 28: 48.
1926b. From field and study. Lesser Yellow-legs in western Oregon. Condor 28: 94.
1927. Birds of the Pacific States; containing brief biographies and descriptions of about four hundred species, with especial reference to their appearances in the field. 353 pp., illus. Boston and New York.

HORSFALL, ROBERT BRUCE.
1924. Nesting of American Crossbill in Multnomah County, Oregon. Murrelet 5 (2): 10.

HOWELL, ARTHUR HOLMES.
1932. Florida Bird Life. Florida Dept. Game and Fresh Water Fish and Biol. Surv. U. S. Dept. Agr. 579 pp., illus. New York.

HURLEY, JOHN B.
1926. Birds observed in Idaho, Washington and Oregon. Murrelet 7: 35–36.

JENKINS, HUBERT OLIVER.
1906. Variation in the Hairy Woodpecker (*Dryobates villosus* and subspecies). Auk 23: 161–171 (see 168).

JEWETT, STANLEY GORDON (see also GABRIELSON and JEWETT, and GABRIELSON, JEWETT, and BRALY).
1908. Large sets of *Merula migratoria propinqua;* Western Robin. Oologist 25: 138–139.
1909a. Birds singing on nests. Oologist 26: 12.
1909b. Vaux's Swift nesting in chimneys. Oologist 26: 57.
1909c. Some birds of Baker County, Oregon. Auk 26: 5–9.
1909d. From field and study. Some unusual records from Portland, Oregon. Condor 11: 138–139.
1910. General notes. Northwestern Saw-whet and Snowy Owls in Oregon. Auk 27: 340.
1912a. Four spring days on Government Island. Oologist 29: 366.

Jewett, Stanley Gordon (see also Gabrielson and Jewett, and Gabrielson, Jewett, and Braly)—Continued.

1912b. General notes. Another Saw-whet Owl from Oregon. Auk 29: 102.

1912c. General notes. Western records of the Catbird (*Dumetella carolinensis*). Auk 29: 106.

1913a. From field and study. Two stragglers on the Oregon coast. Condor 15: 226.

1913b. From field and study. Three new birds from eastern Oregon. Condor 15: 229.

1913c. General notes. A correction. Auk 30: 117.

1914a. From field and study. Two birds new to Oregon. Condor 16: 93.

1914b. Bird notes from Netarts Bay, Oregon. Condor 16: 107–115, illus.

1916a. New and interesting bird records from Oregon. Condor 18: 21–22.

1916b. Notes on some land birds of Tillamook County, Oregon. Condor 18: 74–80.

1916c. Nesting of the Crossbill (*Loxia curvirostra minor*) in Crook County, Oregon. Auk 33: 201.

1919. From field and study. Gray Gyrfalcon taken in Oregon. Condor 21: 123.

1921a. From field and study. Range of the Plain Titmouse in Oregon. Condor 23: 33.

1921b. Additional notes on the water and shore birds of Netarts Bay, Oregon. Condor 23: 91–93, illus.

1922a. A day (any January day) in the field at Portland, Oregon. Murrelet 3 (1): 18–19.

1922b. From field and study. Waterfowl caught in fish nets. Condor 24: 95.

1922c. From field and study. Townsend Solitaire on the Oregon coast. Condor 24: 97.

1923a. From field and study. An early fall record of the Hepburn Rosy Finch. Condor 25: 32.

1923b. From field and study. The Horned Puffin on the coast of Oregon. Condor 25: 138.

1924a. From field and study. Additional records of the European Widgeon in Oregon. Condor 26: 32.

1924b. From field and study. Three Oregon stragglers. Condor 26: 35.

1924c. From field and study. An intelligent crow. Condor 26: 72.

1924d. From field and study. Additional records of Alpine birds in Oregon. Condor 26: 78.

1924e. From field and study. The Red-eyed Vireo as a bird of Oregon. Condor 26: 227.

1924f. From field and study. The pipit nesting in Oregon. Condor 26: 230.

1925. The Pacific Harlequin Duck breeding in Oregon. Condor 27: 241.

1926a. From field and study. Notes on some unusual Oregon birds. Condor 28: 41.

1926b. From field and study. The Prairie Falcon in the Willamette Valley, Oregon. Condor 28: 98.

1926c. From field and study. The Ferruginous Rough-leg nesting in Oregon. Condor 28: 245–246.

1927. Netarts Bay, Oregon, re-visited in 1926. Murrelet 8: 3–4.

1928a. From field and study. Assistant parentage among birds. Condor 30: 127–128.

1928b. From field and study. The Little Green Heron in Oregon. Condor 30: 129.

1928c. From field and study. The Flammulated Screech Owl in Oregon. Condor 30: 164.

1928d. From field and study. Bird notes from Oregon. Condor 30: 356–358.

1929a. Allen Hummingbird in Oregon. Condor 31: 226.

1929b. Limicolae of the State of Oregon. Auk 46: 214–222.

1930a. General notes. The Bryant Marsh Sparrow in Oregon. Murrelet 11: 73.

1930b. General notes. A cross-billed bluebird. Murrelet 11: 74.

1930c. From field and study. An extension of the range of the Band-tailed Pigeon and of the Lead-colored Bush-tit in Oregon. Condor 32: 72.

1930d. From field and study. The cardinal in Oregon. Condor 32: 301.

1930e. General notes. Upland Plover (*Bartramia longicauda*) in Oregon. Auk 47: 78.

1931a. The season. Portland (Oregon) region. Bird-Lore 33: 21–23, 136–137, 203–205, 276–277, 340–341, 415–417.

1931b. From field and study. Upland Plover apparently established in Oregon. Condor 33: 245.

1931c. From field and study. Nesting of the Pacific Harlequin Duck in Oregon. Condor 33: 255.

1932a. The season. Portland (Oregon) region. Bird-Lore 34: 20–21, 149–151, 214–216, 279–280, 348–349, 406–408.

JEWETT, STANLEY GORDON (see also GABRIELSON and JEWETT, and GABRIELSON, JEWETT, and BRALY)—Continued.

1932b. From field and study. The White-cheeked Goose in Oregon. Condor 34: 136.

1932c. From field and study. Winter occurrence of the Townsend Warbler at Portland, Oregon. Condor 34: 190.

1933. General notes. White-tailed Kite in Oregon. Murrelet 14: 79.

1934a. The season. Portland (Oregon) region. Bird-Lore 36: 120–121, 188–189, 251–252, 315–316, 377–378.

1934b. Nesting of the Orange-crowned Warbler in Oregon. Condor 36: 242.

1934c. The Anthony Green Heron again in northern Oregon. Condor 36: 246.

1934d. General notes. The mystery of the Marbled Murrelet deepens. Murrelet 15: 24.

1934e. General notes. Two Oregon stragglers. Murrelet 15: 51.

1935a. General notes. A Red Phalarope disaster. Murrelet 16: 15–16.

1935b. General notes. The Prairie Falcon at Portland, Oregon. Murrelet 16: 16.

1935c. The season. Portland (Oregon) region. Bird-Lore 37: 146–147, 230.

1935d. The Man-o'-war-bird off the Oregon coast. Condor 37: 212–213.

1936a. Bird notes from Harney County, Oregon, during May 1934. Murrelet 17: 41–47.

1936b. Malheur Lake—Greatest of wildfowl refuges. Outdoor America NS (No. 11) 1: 6–7.

1937a. The Western Mockingbird in Oregon. Condor 39: 91–92

1937b. A northern record for the Gray Titmouse in Oregon. Condor 39: 125.

1939a. Additional notes on the Black Pigeon Hawk. Condor 41: 84–85.

1939b. A Pacific Kittiwake comes inland. Condor 41: 170.

———, and GABRIELSON, IRA NOEL.

1929. Birds of the Portland area, Oregon. Cooper Orn. Club, Pacific Coast Avifauna 19, 54 pp., illus. Berkeley, Calif.

1933. General notes. The New Zealand Shearwater, *Thyellodroma bulleri* (Salvin) off the Columbia River, Oregon. Auk 50: 91.

JOHNSON, HENRY C.

1900. In the breeding home of Clarke's Nutcracker (*Nucifraga columbianus*). Condor 2: 49–52, illus.

JOHNSON, O. B.

1880. List of the birds of the Willamette Valley, Oregon. Amer. Nat. 14: 485–491, 635–641.

JOHNSON, ROBERT ANTHONY.

1927. The Ruffed Grouse in winter. Auk 44: 319–321, illus.

JONES, LYNDS (see also HENNINGER and JONES).

1900. The horizons. Wilson Bull. (n.s. 7, No. 4) 12 (No. 33): 10–38 (see 19–20).

1907. Birds from a car window again. Wilson Bull. (n.s. 14) 19: 109–113.

JUDD, SYLVESTER DWIGHT.

1901a. The food of nestling birds. U. S. Dept. Agr. Yearbook Separate 194, pp. 411–436, illus.

1901b. The relation of sparrows to agriculture. U. S. Dept. Agr., Biol. Surv. Bull. 15, 98 pp., illus.

1905a. The bobwhite and other quails of the United States in their economic relations. U. S. Dept. Agr., Biol. Surv. Bull. 21, 66 pp., illus.

1905b. The grouse and wild turkeys of the United States and their economic value. U. S. Dept. Agr., Biol. Surv. Bull. 24, 55 pp., illus.

K.

1895. In eastern Oregon. Forest and Stream 44: 393.

KAEDING, HENRY BARROILHET.

1899. The genus *Junco* in California. Bull. Cooper Orn. Club 1: 79–81 (see 80).

KALMBACH, EDWIN RICHARD.

1914. Birds in relation to the alfalfa weevil. U. S. Dept. Agr. Bull. 107, 64 pp., illus.

1918. The crow and its relation to man. U. S. Dept. Agr. Bull. 621, 92 pp., illus.

1920. The crow in its relation to agriculture. U. S. Dept. Agr. Farmers' Bull. 1102, 20 pp., illus.

1927. The magpie in relation to agriculture. U.S. Dept. Agr. Tech. Bull. 24, 30 pp., illus.

KALMBACH, EDWIN RICHARD, and MCATEE, WALDO LEE.
1926. Homes for birds. U. S. Dept. Agr. Farmers' Bull. 1456, 22 pp., illus.

KELLER, CLYDE L.
1890a. [Western Meadow lark?] Orn. and Ool. 15: 15.
1890b. Who will furnish the incubator? Orn. and Ool. 15: 184.
1891a. Nesting of *Spinus pinus* in the North-west. Oologist 8: 31.
1891b. Notes on Wright's Flycatcher (*Empidonax obscurus*). Oologist 8: 103–104.
1891c. Nesting of the Chestnut-backed Chickadee. Oologist 8: 147.
1891d. Nest and eggs of the Rufous Hummingbird (*Trochilus rufus*). Oologist 8: 157–158.
1891e. Gambel's White-crowned Sparrow (*Zonotrichia gambeli*). Oologist 8: 178–179.
1891f. Thanksgiving notes from the far West. Oologist 8: 239.
1891g. Birds and their value. Orn. and Ool. 16: 130.
1892a. Bird notes from Oregon. Oologist 9: 128.
1892b. Habits and nesting of the Violet-green Swallow. Orn. and Ool. 17: 23.
1892c. Birds singing on their nests. Orn. and Ool. 17: 62.
1893. Birds as pets. One way of taming them. Oologist 10: 22–23.

KELLOGG, LOUISE.
1911. A collection of winter birds from Trinity and Shasta Counties, California. Condor 13: 118–121.

KERRY, MORTIMER.
1874. Zoology of the Northwestern Territories. The Anserinae and Cygninae. Forest and Stream 3: 129–130.

KNIGHT, ORA WILLIS.
1908. The birds of Maine [etc.]. 693 pp., illus. (see 446). Bangor, Me.

KOENIG-WARTHAUSEN, RICHARD.
1868. Bemerkungen ueber die Fortpflanzung einiger Caprimulgiden. Jour. fuer Ornith. 16: 361–368 (see 373–379).

L., J. F.
1890a. The Chinese Pheasant. Forest and Stream 33: 471.
1890b. Chinese Pheasants. Forest and Stream 35: 431.

LAW, GEORGE.
1887. The game birds of Oregon. Amer. Field 28: 174–175.

LAW, JOHN EUGENE.
1925. With the bird banders. Among the banding stations. Condor 27: 79–80.

LAWRENCE, GEORGE NEWBOLD (see also BAIRD, CASSIN, and LAWRENCE).
1852. Ornitholgical notes. Ann. Lyc. Nat. Hist. New York 5: 220–223 (see 222).
1864. Descriptions of new species of birds of the families Caerebidae, Tanagridae, Icteridae and Scolopacidae. Acad. Nat. Sci. Phila. Proc. 16: 106–108.

LEWIS, MERIWETHER, and CLARK, [WILLIAM].
1814. History of the expedition under the command of Captains Lewis and Clark, to the sources of the Missouri, thence across the Rocky Mountains and down the river Columbia to the Pacific Ocean. Performed during the years 1804–5–6. By order of the Government of the United States. 2 vols. Paul Allen edition. Philadelphia.

LINCOLN, FREDERICK CHARLES.
1924a. Banding notes on the migration of the Pintail. Condor 26: 88–90.
1924b. Returns from banded birds, 1920 to 1923. U. S. Dept. Agr. Bull. 1268, 56 pp., illus.
1926a. Bird banding—in progress and prospect. Auk 43: 153–161.
1926b. The migration of the Cackling Goose. Condor 28: 153–157, illus.
1927. Returns from banded birds, 1923 to 1926. U. S. Dept. Agr. Tech. Bull. 32, 96 pp., illus.
1928. From field and study. Banded Pintail recovered in British Honduras. Condor 30: 359.
1932. General notes. The Black Duck in Oregon. Auk 49: 344.

LINSDALE, JEAN MYRON (see GRINNELL, DIXON, and LINSDALE).

[Lloyd, Hoyes].
1925. Additional returns from birds banded in 1924. Canad. Field-Nat. 39: 206–209 (see 207).
1926–1932. Official Canadian record of bird-banding. Canad. Field-Nat. 40 (1926), 106–110 (see 106); 43 (1929), 86–91 (see 90); 44 (1930), 72–76 (see 76); 45 (1931), 44–48 and 150–154 (see 46, 151); 46 (1932), 70–74 (see 71, 72).

Loomis, Leverett Mills.
1901. General notes. Birds observed during a steamer voyage from San Francisco to Victoria, British Columbia,—September 8, 1898. Auk 18: 201 (see 71, 72).

Lord, William Rogers.
1902a. A first book upon the birds of Oregon and Washington; a pocket guide and pupil's assistant in a study of the more common land birds and a few of the shore and water birds of these States. 304 pp., illus. Portland.
1902b. The Western Evening Grosbeak. Bird-Lore 4: 9–11, illus.

McAtee, Waldo Lee (see also Kalmbach and McAtee).
1905. The Horned Larks and their relation to agriculture. U. S. Dept. Agr., Biol. Surv. Bull. 23, 37 pp., illus.
1908. Food habits of the Grosbeaks. U. S. Dept. Agr., Biol. Surv. Bull. 32, 92 pp., illus.
1911a. Local names of waterfowl and other birds. Forest and Stream 77: 172–174, 196.
1911b. Our vanishing shorebirds. U. S. Dept. Agr., Biol. Surv. Circ. 79, 9 pp., illus.
1911c. Woodpeckers in relation to trees and tree products. U. S. Dept. Agr., Biol. Surv. Bull. 39, 99 pp., illus.
1911d. Our grosbeaks and their value to agriculture. U. S. Dept. Agr. Farmers' Bull. 456, 14 pp., illus.
1915. Eleven important wild-duck foods. U. S. Dept. Agr. Bull. 205, 25 pp., illus.
1917. Propagation of wild-duck foods. U. S. Dept. Agr. Bull. 465, 40 pp., illus.
1918. Food habits of the mallard ducks of the United States. U. S. Dept. Agr. Bull. 720, 36 pp., illus.
1923. Local names of migratory game birds. U. S. Dept. Agr. Misc. Circ. 13, 96 pp., illus.
1927. Propagation of game birds. U. S. Dept. Agr. Farmers' Bull. 1521, 57 pp., illus.

McCabe, Elinor Bolles (see McCabe and McCabe).

McCabe, Thomas Tonkin, and McCabe, Elinor Bolles.
1932. Preliminary studies of Western Hermit Thrushes. Condor 34: 26–40 (see 38).

———, and Miller, Alden Holmes.
1933. Geographic variation in the Northern Water-thrushes. Condor 35: 192–197.

McCamant, Tom.
1918. My back-yard feeding station. Bird-Lore 20: 183–184.
1919. The Western Robin. Bird-Lore 21: 131–132.

McGregor, Richard Crittenden.
1899. Description of a new California Song Sparrow. Bull. Cooper Orn. Club 1: 35.

McNamee, Clay.
1890a. The Chinese or Mongolian Pheasant in Idaho. Oologist 7: 88.
1890b. Ichthy-ornithological. Voracious mountain trout. Oologist 7: 138.

Macoun, James Melville (see Macoun and Macoun).

Macoun, John, and Macoun, James Meville.
1909. Catalogue of Canadian Birds. Canada Dept. of Mines, Geol. Surv. Branch. 761 pp. (see 219, 309, 337, 413, 675).

Mailliard, Joseph.
1922. Status of the Crested Jays on the northwestern coast of California. Condor 24: 127–133, map.
1927. The birds and mammals of Modoc County, California. Calif. Acad. Sci. Proc., Fourth Series 16: 261–359 (see 279, 283, 339).

[Martin, John W.].
1900. [Nesting building of juncos and Western Meadowlark in Oregon.] Condor 2: 71.

MAY, JOHN BICHARD.
1935. The hawks of North America. Their field identification and feeding habits. 140 pp., illus. New York.

MEARNS, EDGAR ALEXANDER.
1879. A partial list of the birds of Fort Klamath, Oregon, collected by Lieutenant Willis Wittich, U.S.A., with annotations and additions by the collector. Bull. Nuttall Orn. Club 4: 161–166, 194–199.
1892. A study of the Sparrow Hawks (subgenus *Tinnunculus*) of America, with especial reference to the continental species (*Falco sparverius* Linn.) Auk 9: 252–270 (see 258).

MEINERTZHAGEN, RICHARD.
1925. The distribution of the Phalaropes. Ibis (Twelfth Series) 1: 325–344, illus. (see 336, 342).

MERCER, W. A.
1886. [Supply of game in Steen Mountain, Oregon.] Forest and Stream 26: 68.

MERRIAM, CLINTON HART.
1873. Sixth annual report of the U. S. Geol. Surv. of the territories embracing portions of Montana, Idaho, Wyoming and Utah; . . . for the year 1872, by F. V. Hayden. Part III. Special reports on zoology and botany. Report on the mammals and birds of the expedition. pp. 661–715 (see 693–699).
1891. Results of a biological reconnaissance of Idaho, south of latitude 45° and east of the thirty-eighth meridian, made during the summer of 1890, with annotated lists of the animals and birds and descriptions of new species. U. S. Dept. Agr., Orn. and Mammal., North American Fauna 5, 130 pp., illus.
1899. Results of a biological survey of Mount Shasta, California. U. S. Dept. Agr., Biol. Surv., North Amer. Fauna 16, 179 pp., illus.

MERRIAM, FLORENCE A[UGUSTA] (see also BAILEY, FLORENCE [AUGUSTA] MERRIAM).
1899. Clark's Crows and Oregon Jays on Mount Hood. Bird-Lore 1: 46–48, 72–76, illus.

MERRILL, JAMES CUSHING.
1888. Notes on the birds of Fort Klamath, Oregon. With remarks on certain species by William Brewster. Auk 5: 139–146, 251–262, 357–366.
1897. Notes on the birds of Fort Sherman, Idaho. Auk 14: 347–357 (see 353–355).

MERRILL, L. J. (MRS.).
1929. Notes from field and study. A Song Sparrow with a sweet tooth. Bird-Lore 31: 191–192.

MILLER, ALDEN HOLMES (see also MCCABE and MILLER).
1931. Systematic revision and natural history of the American shrikes (*Lanius*). Calif. Univ. Pubs., Zool. 38: 11–242, illus.
1933. From field and study. The inner abdominal feather region in brooding woodpeckers. Condor 35: 78–79.
1938. A summer record of the White-winged Crossbill in Oregon. Condor 40: 226.
1939a. The breeding Leucostictes of the Wallowa Mountains, Oregon. Condor 41: 34–35.
1939b. Status of the breeding Lincoln's Sparrows of Oregon. Auk 56: 342–343.

MILLER, GERRITT SMITH, JR.
1888. Description of an apparently new *Poocaetes gramineus affinis*, subsp. nov. from Oregon. Auk 5: 404–405.
1891. General notes. The first plumage of *Otocoris alpestris strigata* Hensh. Auk 8: 314.

MILLER, LOYE HOLMES.
1904. The birds of John Day region, Oregon. Condor 6: 100–106.
1924a. Anomalies in the distribution of fossil gulls. Condor 26: 173–174.
1924b. *Branta dickeyi* from the McKittrick Pleistocene. Condor 26: 178–180, illus.

MORRIS, ROBERT T.
1892. A bit of grouse hunter's lore. Forest and Stream 39: 49.

MULTNOMAH.
1879. Albinoes. Forest and Stream 13: 907.

MUNRO, JOHN ALEXANDER.
1922. The Band-tailed Pigeon in British Columbia. Canad. Field-Nat. 36: 1–4.

MURIE, OLAUS JOHAN (see also BEAN and MURIE).
1913. From field and study. Unusual nesting site of the mallard. Condor 15: 176–178, illus.

MURPHY, ROBERT CUSHMAN (see NICHOLS and MURPHY).

NAUMBURG, ELSIE MARGARET BINGER.
1926. The bird fauna of North America in relation to its distribution in South America. Auk 43: 485–492 (see 490).

NEFF, JOHNSON ANDREW.
1933. From field and study. The Tri-colored Red-wing in Oregon. Condor 35: 234–235.

NEHRLING, HENRY.
1885. Die Buschmeise. (*Psaltriparus minimus* Bonap. Least Tit, Bush Tit.) Monatss. Deut. Ver. Schutze Vogelwelt 10: 21–25.

NELSON, ARNOLD LARS.
1934. Some early summer food preferences of the American Raven in southeastern Oregon. Condor 36: 10–15.

NELSON, EDWARD WILLIAM.
1900. Description of a new subspecies of *Meleagris gallopavo* and proposed changes in the nomenclature of certain North American birds. Auk 17: 120–126.
1904. A revision of the North American mainland species of *Myiarchus*. Biol. Soc. Wash. Proc. 17: 21–50 (see 33–35).
1913. The Alaska Longspur. Bird-Lore 15: 202–205, illus.

NELSON, MILTON O.
1915. Notes from field and study. A familiar Winter Wren. Bird-Lore 17: 135.

NEWBERRY, JOHN STRONG.
1857. Reports of explorations and surveys, to ascertain . . . route for a railroad from the Mississippi River to the Pacific Ocean . . . 1854–55. Vol. VI. Part IV. Zoological Report. No. 2. Report upon the zoology of the route. Chapter II. Report upon the birds. pp. 73–110, illus.

NEWTON, ROXEY.
1888. The Ruffed Grouse. Amer. Field 29: 126.

NICHOLS, JOHN TREADWELL.
1909. Notes on Pacific Coast shore birds. Bird-Lore 11: 10–11, illus.
———, and MURPHY, ROBERT CUSHMAN.
1914. A review of the genus *Phoebetria*. Auk 31: 526–534, illus.

N[ORRIS], J[OSEPH] P[ARKER].
1882a. A series of eggs of *Oroscoptes* [sic] *montanus*. Orn. and Ool. 13: 162.
1888b. Nesting of *Otocoris alpestris strigata*. Orn. and Ool. 13: 162–163.
1889c. A series of eggs of *Sitta pygmaea*. Orn. and Ool. 13: 173–174.
1890. A remarkable set of eggs of the Mountain Chickadee. Orn. and Ool. 15: 71.

NUTTALL, THOMAS.
1834. A manual of the ornithology of the United States and of Canada. The water birds. 627 pp., illus. Boston.
1840. A manual of the ornithology of the United States and of Canada. The land birds, 2d ed., with additions. 832 pp., illus. Boston.

OATES, EUGENE WILLIAM.
1902. Catalogue of the collection of birds' eggs in the British Museum (natural history). Vol. II. Carinatae (Charadriiformes-Strigiformes). 400 pp., illus. (see 201).
———, and REID, SAVILE GRAY.
1903. Catalogue of the collection of birds' eggs in the British Museum (natural history). Vol. III. Carinatae (Psittaciformes-Passeriformes). 349 pp., illus. (see 231). London.

OBERHOLSER, HARRY CHURCH.
1897. Critical remarks on *Cistothorus palustris* (Wils.) and its western allies. Auk 14: 186–196 (see 193).
1898. A revision of the wrens of the genus *Thryomanes sclater*. U. S. Nat. Mus. Proc. 21: 421–450 (see 427, 440, 441).
1899a. Description of a new *Hylocichla*. Auk 16: 23–25.
1899b. Description of a new *Geothlypis*. Auk 16: 256–258.
1902. A review of the larks of the genus *Otocoris*. U. S. Nat. Mus. Proc. 24: 801–883 (see 817–839).
1903a. A review of the genus *Catherpes*. Auk 20: 196–198.
1903b. A synopsis of the genus *Psaltriparus*. Auk 20: 198–201 (see 200).
1904. A revision of the American Great Horned Owls. U. S. Nat. Mus. Proc. 27: 27, 177–192 (see 183, 186, 187, 191).
1905. The forms of *Vermivora celata* (Say). Auk 22: 242–247.
1906. The North American eagles and their economic relations. U. S. Dept. Agr., Biol. Surv. Bull. 27, 31 pp., illus.
1911a. Description of a new *Melospiza* from California. Biol. Soc. Wash. Proc. 24: 251–252.
1911b. A revision of the forms of the Hairy Woodpecker (*Dryobates villosus* [Linnaeus]). U. S. Nat. Mus. Proc. 40: 595–621 (see 610–616).
1917a. Description of a new subspecies of *Perisoreus obscurus*. Biol. Soc. Wash. Proc. 30: 185–187.
1917b. Notes on North American Birds. II. *Loxia curvirostra bendirei* Ridgway. Auk 34: 328–329.
1918a. The migration of North American birds. Second Series. VII. Magpies. Bird-Lore 20: 415.
1918b. Notes on North American Birds. V. *Passerella iliaca altivagans* Riley. Auk 35: 186–187.
1918c. Notes on the subspecies of *Numenius americanus* Bechstein. Auk 35: 188–195.
1919a. Notes on the wrens of the genus *Nannus billberg*. U. S. Nat. Mus. Proc. 55: 223–236 (see 235, 236).
1919b. The migration of North American birds. Second Series. VIII. Ravens. Bird-Lore 21: 23–24.
1919c. The migration of North American birds. Second Series. XI. Canada Jay, Oregon Jay, Clarke's Nutcracker, and Pinon Jay. Bird-Lore 21: 354–355.
1920a. A synopsis of the genus *Thryomanes*. Wilson Bull. (n.s. 27) 32: 18–28.
1920b. From field and study. *Empidonax griseus* in Oregon. Condor 22: 37.
1920c. *Empidonax griseus* in Nevada. Auk 37: 133.
1921. The migration of North American birds. Second Series. XV. Yellow-headed Blackbird and meadowlarks. Bird-Lore 23: 78–82.
1922a. Notes on North American birds. XI. Auk 39: 72–78.
1922b. General notes. *Junco oreganus montanus* in Oregon. Auk 39: 421.
1922c. The migration of North American birds. Second Series. XVIII. Red-winged Blackbirds. Bird-Lore 24: 86–88.
1923. Notes on the forms of the genus *Oreortyx* Baird. Auk 40: 80–84.
1924. The migration of North American birds. Second Series. XXVI. Broad-tailed, Rufous, and Allen's Hummingbirds. Bird-Lore 26: 398–399.
1928a. The migration of North American birds. Second Series. XXXVI. Pileated and Ant-eating Woodpeckers. Bird-Lore 30: 112–113.
1928b. The migration of North American birds. Second Series. XXXVIII. Williamson's Sapsucker and White-headed Woodpecker. Bird-Lore 30: 388.
1930a. The migration of North American birds. Second Series. XLII. Hairy and Downy Woodpeckers. Bird-Lore 32: 120–123.
1930b. Notes on a collection of birds from Arizona and New Mexico. Cleveland Mus. Nat. Hist. Sci. Pubs. 1: 83–124 (see 96, 101, 111).
1932. Descriptions of new birds from Oregon, chiefly from the Warner Valley region. Cleveland Mus. Nat. Hist. Sci. Pubs. 4: 1–12.

OGILVIE-GRANT, WILLIAM ROBERT (see also SHARPE and OGILVIE-GRANT).
1912. Catalogue of the collection of birds' eggs in the British Museum (natural history). Vol. V. Carinatae (Passeriformes completed), 547 pp., illus. (see 61, 121, 283). London.

OSGOOD, WILFRED HUDSON.
1899. *Chamaea fasciata* and its subspecies. Biol. Soc. Wash. Proc. 13: 41–42.
1901. New subspecies of North American birds. Auk 18: 179–185 (see 182–184).

OVER, WILLIAM HENRY, and THOMS, CRAIG SHARP.
1921. Birds of South Dakota. S. Dak. State Geol. and Nat. Hist. Surv. Bull 9, 142 pp., illus. (see 49).

OVUM.
1875. Birds' nests and eggs. Oologist (Willard's) 1: 34.
1876. Birds' eggs and nests. Oologist (Willard's) 2: 11.

PARKER, SAMUEL (REV.).
1844. Journal of an exploring tour beyond the Rocky Mountains, under the direction of the A. B. C. F. M. [performed in the years 1835, '36, and '37] containing a description of the geography, geology, climate, productions of the country, and the numbers, manners, and customs of the natives; with a map of Oregon Territory. 4th ed. 416 pp., map. Ithaca. (See 219–221.)

P[EARSON], THOMAS GILBERT.
1911. Klamath Lake Reservation. Bird-Lore 13: 331.
1912. Report of the Secretary. Egret protection. Bird-Lore 14: 386.
1913. The Green Heron. Bird-Lore 15: 198–201, illus.
1919. Least Bittern. Bird-Lore 21: 198–201, illus.

PECK, GEORGE DELRANE.
1896. Notes on the warblers of western Oregon. Wilson Orn. Chap. Bull. 11: 6–7.
1904. The Cal[ifornia] Vulture in Douglas Co[unty]. Oregon. Oologist 21: 55.
1913. Winter notes. Salem, Oregon. Oologist 30: 51.
1916. Oregon birds. Oologist 33: 122.
1917a. Shufeldt's Junco. Oologist 34: 93.
1917b. Purple Finch. Oologist 34: 103.
1934. In defense of Mr. Crow. Oologist 51: 139.

PECK, MORTON EATON.
1911a. Summer birds of Willow Creek Valley, Malheur County, Oregon. Condor 13: 63–69.
1911b. From field and study. Pinyon Jay at Salem, Oregon. Condor 13: 75.

PETERS, JAMES LEE.
1931. Check-list of birds of the world. Vol. 1, 345 pp. Cambridge, Mass.

PHILLIPS, JOHN CHARLES.
1922–1926. A natural history of the ducks. 4 vols., illus. Boston.
1928. Wild birds introduced or transplanted in North America. U. S. Dept. Agr. Tech. Bull. 61, 64 pp.

PICKWELL, GAYLE.
1930. The sex of the incubating Killdeer. Auk 47: 499–506, illus.

PIPES, WADE H.
1894. Western Warbling Vireo. The Oologist 11: 13.

POOLE, CECIL A.
1923. Bird-Lore's twenty-third Christmas census. Monmouth, Oregon. Bird-Lore 25: 44.
1924. Bird-Lore's twenty-fourth Christmas census. Monmouth, Oregon. Bird-Lore 26: 49.

POPE, ARTHUR L.
1891. Interesting notes from Oregon. Oologist 8: 163.
1893a. The Sooty Grouse, *Dendragapus obscurus fuliginosus*. Oologist 10: 48–49.
1893b. Notes from Yamhill County, Oregon. Oologist 10: 203–204.
1894. Queer nidification of the Sooty Grouse. Nidiologist 1: 167.

PREBLE, EDWARD ALEXANDER.
1908. A biological investigation of the Athabaska-Mackenzie region. U. S. Dept. Agr., Biol. Surv., North Amer. Fauna 27, 574 pp., illus.

PRILL, ALBERT GREGORY.
1891a. Western Horned Owl (*Bubo virginianus subarcticus*). Oologist 8: 10.
1891b. Some early winter birds of Linn County, Oregon. Oologist 8: 63–64.
1891c. Ring Pheasant [*Phasianus torquatus* (Gmel.)]. Oologist 8: 118–119.
1891d. American Dipper (*Cinclus mexicanus*). Oologist 8: 120–121.
1891e. Western Robin. No. 761a, *Merula migratoria propinqua* Ridgw. Oologist 8: 216–217.
1891f. Russet-backed Thrush. No. 758, *Turdus ustulatus* (Nutt.). Oologist 8: 237–238.
1891g. Bird nesting in November. Oologist 8: 241.
1892a. Western Blue bird. No. 767, *Sialia mexicana* (Swains.). Oologist 9: 36–37.
1892b. Myrtle Warbler, *Dendroica coronata* (Linn.) No. 655. Oologist 9: 128.
1893a. Band-tailed Pigeon, *Columbidae* [sic] *fasciata*. Oologist 10: 113–114.
1893b. A day in the woods. Oologist 10: 282–283.
1895a. Winter birds of Linn County, Oregon. Oologist 12: 47–49.
1895b. The Ring Pheasant. (*Phasianus torquatus*.) Nidiologist 2: 97–98.
1900. Queer nesting. Oologist 17: 156.
1901. A visit to Otter Rock, Pacific Ocean. "Among the sea birds". Osprey 5: 133–134, illus.
1922a. Nesting birds of Lake County, Oregon. (With special reference to Warner Valley.) Wilson Bull. (n.s. 29) 34: 131–140, illus.
1922b. Nesting of the Sandhill Crane, Warner Valley, Oregon. Wilson Bull. (n.s. 29) 34: 169–171.
1924. Nesting birds of Lake County, Oregon. Wilson Bull. (n.s. 31) 36: 24–25.
1928. General notes. Some Oregon records. Wilson Bull. (n.s. 35) 40: 112.
1931. General notes. A land migration of coots. Wilson Bull. (n.s. 38) 43: 148–149.

RAKER, MARY ESTELLE (see also CAMPBELL, etc., and ELIOT, etc., 1924).
1918. The Bohemian Waxwing in Oregon. Bird-Lore 20: 187–188.

RAKER, WILLIAM SAMUEL (see CAMPBELL, etc., and ELIOT, etc., 1924).

RANDLE, FAYE.
1919. A pocket sanctuary. Bird-Lore 21: 219–223.

RATHBUN, SAMUEL FREDERICK.
1917. Description of a new subspecies of the Western Meadowlark. Auk 34: 68–70.

REID, SAVILE GRAY (see OATES and REID).

RHOADS, SAMUEL NICHOLSON.
1893. The *Vireo huttoni* group, with description of a new race from Vancouver Island. Auk 10: 238–241 (see 239).
1894. The birds observed in British Columbia and Washington during spring and summer, 1892. Acad. Nat. Sci. Phila. Proc. 1893: 21–65 (see 52).

RICHARDSON, JOHN (see SWAINSON and RICHARDSON).

RIDGWAY, ROBERT (see also BAIRD, BREWER, and RIDGWAY).
1873a. The grouse and quails of North America. Discussed in relation to their variation with habitat. Forest and Stream 1: 289–290.
1873b. Revision of the Falconine genera, *Micrastur*, *Geranospiza* and *Rupornis*, and the Strigine genus, *Glaucidium*. Boston Soc. Nat. Hist. Proc. 16 (1873–1874): 73–106 (see 95).
1875. A monograph of the genus Leucosticte Swainson; or Gray-crowned Purple Finches. Dept. Int. Bull. U. S. Geol. and Geog. Surv. Ter., F. V. Hayden, U. S. Geologist-in-charge, vol. 1 (1874 and 1875), Bull. 2.—Second Series Art. I: 51–82 (see 75).
1878. Studies of the American Herodiones. Part I. Synopsis of the American genera of Ardeidae and Ciconiidae; including descriptions of three new genera and a monograph of the American species of the genus *Ardea*, Linn. Dept. Int. Bull. U. S. Geol. and Geog. Surv. Ter., F. V. Hayden, U. S. Geologist-in-charge, vol. 4, Bull 1, Art. IX: 219–251, illus. (see 243).
1879. Descriptions of new species and races of American birds, including a synopsis of the genus *Tyrannus*, Cuvier. U. S. Nat. Mus. (1878) 1: 466–486 (see 485).
1880. Catalogue of Trochilidae in the collection of the United States National Museum. U. S. Nat. Mus. Proc. 3: 308–320 (see 314).

RIDGWAY, ROBERT (see also BAIRD, BREWER, and RIDGWAY)—Continued.
1882. Descriptions of some new North American birds. U. S. Nat. Mus. Proc. 5: 343–346 (see 344).
1884a. [Comments on *Phalacrocorax resplendens*.] Auk 1: 165.
1884b. Descriptions of some new North American birds. Biol. Soc. Wash. Proc. 2: 89–95 (see 93).
1884c. A review of the American Crossbills (*Loxia*) of the *L. curvirostra* type. Biol. Soc. Wash. Proc. 2: 101–107 (see 102–103).
1885. Note on the *Anser leucopareius* of Brandt. U. S. Nat. Mus. Proc. 8: 21–22.
1888. Description of a new *Psaltriparus* from southern Arizona. U. S. Nat. Mus. Proc. (1887) 10: 697.
1891. The hummingbirds. U. S. Nat. Mus. Rept. for 1890, pp. 253–383, illus.
1894a. On geographical variation in *Sialia mexicana* Swainson. Auk 11: 145–160.
1894b. Geographical, versus sexual, variation in *Oreortyx pictus*. Auk 11: 193–197.
1898. New species, etc., of American birds.—II. Fringillidae (continued). Auk 15: 319–324 (see 320).
1901. New birds of the families Tanagridae and Icteridae. Wash. Acad. Sci. Proc. 3: 149–155 (see 154).
1901–1919. Birds of North and Middle America. U. S. Nat. Mus. Bull. 50, Parts I-VIII.
1926. From field and study. As to the type of *Falco peregrinus pealei*. Condor 28: 240.

RILEY, JOSEPH HARVEY.
1911. Descriptions of three new birds from Canada. Biol. Soc. Wash. Proc. 24: 233–235 (see 235).

ROBERTS, THOMAS SADLER.
1932. The birds of Minnesota. 2 vols., illus. Minneapolis.

ROBERTSON, JOHN MCBRAIR.
1928a. From field and study. Some returns of banded mallards. Condor 30: 321.
1928b. From field and study. Returns of banded gulls. Condor 30: 354–355, map.

ROCKWELL, CLEVELAND.
1878. A tough young night hawk. Forest and Stream 11: 46.

ROCKWELL, ROBERT BLANCHARD.
1908. [Nesting habits of the Arkansas Kingbird.] Oologist 25: 136–137.
1909. The use of magpies' nests by other birds. Condor 11: 90–92, illus.

ROWAN, WILLIAM.
1931. The riddle of migration. 151 pp., illus. Baltimore.

S., O. O.
1892. The Ousel in Oregon. Forest and Stream 38: 319.

S., W. A.
1890. About swans. Amer. Field 34: 391–392.

SALVADORI, [PALEOTTI, ADELARDO], T[OMMASO].
1895. Catalogue of the birds in the British Museum, Vol. XXVII. Catalogue of the Chenomorphae (Palamedeae, Phoenicopteri, Anseres), Crypturi, and Ratitae. 636 pp. (see 252). London.

SALVIN, OSBERT (see SAUNDERS and SALVIN).

SANFORD, LEONARD CUTLER; BISHOP, LOUIS BENNETT; and VAN DYKE, THEODORE STRONG.
1903. The water-fowl family. 598 pp., illus. (see 96, 115, 134, 249, 291, 334, 342, 349, 424, 426, 429, 503, 524, and 526). New York and London.

SAUNDERS, ARETAS ANDREWS.
1921. A distribution list of the birds of Montana, with notes on the migration and nesting of the better known species. Cooper Orn. Club, Pacific Coast Avifauna 14: 194 pp., illus.
1929. Bird song. N. Y. State Mus. Handbook 7, 202 pp., illus. The University of the State of New York. Albany.
1935. A guide to bird songs; descriptions and diagrams of the songs and singing habits of the land birds of northeastern United States. 285 pp. New York.

SAUNDERS, HOWARD, and SALVIN, OSBERT.
1896. Catalogue of the birds in the British Museum, Vol. XXV. Catalogue of the Gaviae and Tubinares [etc.]. 475 pp., illus. (see 332). London.

SAUNDERS, WILLIAM EDWIN.
1902. Canadian hummingbirds. Ottawa Nat. 16: 97–103 (see 100).

SCHEFFER, THEO. H.
1934. Some food resources of our waterfowl in the Pacific Northwest. Murrelet 15: 63–68, illus.

SCLATER, PHILIP LUTLEY.
1856. Synopsis Avium Tanagrinarum—A descriptive catalogue of the known species of tanagers. Zool. Soc. London, Proc. 1856: 108–132 (see 131).
1857. Notes on the birds in the Museum of the Academy of Natural Sciences of Philadelphia, and other collections in the United States of America. Zool. Soc. London, Proc. 1857: 1–8 (see 8).
1859. A synopsis of the thrushes (Turdidae) of the New World. Zool. Soc. London, Proc. 1859: 321–347 (see 325–326).
1883. A review of the species of the family Icteridae—Pt. II. Icterinae. Ibis (Fifth Series) 1: 352–374 (see 355).
1912. A history of the birds of Colorado. 576 pp., illus. London.

SCOTT, WILLIAM EARLE DODGE.
1883. On the avi-fauna of Pinal County, with remarks on some birds of Pima and Gila Counties, Arizona. (With annotations by J. A. Allen.) Auk 5: 159–168 (see 164).

SEMPLE, JOHN BONNER, and SUTTON, GEORGE MIKSCH.
1932. Nesting of Harris's Sparrow (*Zonotrichia querula*) at Churchill, Manitoba. Auk 49: 166–183, illus.

SHARPE, R[ICHARD] BOWLDER.
1885. Catalogue of the birds in the British Museum, Vol. X. Catalogue of the Passeriformes or perching birds in the collection of the British Museum. Tringilliformes: Part 1 [etc.]. 682 pp., illus. London.

———, and OGILVIE-GRANT, W[ILLIAM] R[OBERT].
1898. Catalogue of the birds in the British Museum, Vol. XXVI. Catalogue of the Plataleae, Herodiones, Steganopodes, Pygopodes, Aleae, and Impennes [etc.]. 687 pp., illus. (see 36). London.

SHAW, WILLIAM THOMAS (see also TAYLOR and SHAW).
1908. The China or Denny Pheasant in Oregon, with notes on the native grouse of the Pacific Northwest. 24 pp., illus. Philadelphia and London.
1923. From field and study. Bobolinks in Oregon. Condor 25: 66–67.
1924. From field and study. The Sabine Gull in Oregon and on the Lower Yukon. Condor 26: 108.

SHELTON, ALFRED COOPER.
1915. From field and study. Yakutat Song Sparrow in Oregon. Condor 17: 60.
1917. A distributional list of the land birds of west central Oregon. Univ. Oreg. Bull. n.s. 14 (4), 51 pp., illus.

SHERWOOD, WILLIAM E.
1924. From field and study. Dotted Canyon Wren in Oregon. Condor 26: 112.
1927a. From field and study. An English Sparrow deceived. Condor 29: 162.
1927b. From field and study. Feeding habits of Lewis Woodpecker. Condor 29: 171.

SHUFELDT, ROBERT WILSON.
1890. A skeleton of the Ivory-bill. Forest and Stream 35: 431.
1891. Tertiary fossils of North American birds. Auk 8: 365–368.
1913. Contributions to avian paleontology. Auk 30: 29–39.

SISKIYOU.
1890. [Habits of the Chinese Pheasant.] Amer. Field 33: 199.

SKINNER, MILTON PHILO.
1917. The birds of Molly Island, Yellowstone National Park. Condor 19: 177–182, illus.
1925. The birds of Yellowstone National Park. Roosevelt Wild Life Bull., Syracuse Univ., N. Y. State College of Forestry 3 (1), 192 pp., illus.

SLOANAKER, JOSEPH LYDAY.
1925. From field and study. Notes from Spokane. Condor 27: 73–74.

STANNARD, EARL.
1909. From field and study. Winter observations in Oregon. Condor 11: 68.

STEELE, RAY CALDWELL.
1922a. Depredations of ducks. Murrelet 3 (2): 6.
1922b. Oregon notes. Murrelet 3 (3): 3–4.
1923a. Fact and comment. [A Gadwall and a white goose killed at Tule Lake, Oregon.] Murrelet 4 (1): 14.
1923b. European Widgeon in western Oregon. Murrelet 4 (3): 17.
1924. Emperor Goose in Oregon. Murrelet 5 (1): 11.

STEJNEGER, LEONHARD [HESS].
1882. Outlines of a monograph of the Cygninae. U. S. Nat. Mus. Proc. 5: 174–221 (see 215–218).
1884. Analecta ornithologica. IX. [*Priocella tenuirostris* (Aud.) not a bird of Bering Sea or the Arctic Ocean.] Auk 1: 233–234.

STEVENSON, JAMES.
1934. Comments upon systematics of Pacific Coast jays of the genus *Cyanocitta*. Condor 36: 72–78.

———, and FITCH, HENRY.
1933. From field and study. Bird notes from southwestern Oregon. Condor 35: 167–168.

STONE, WITMER.
1891. Catalogue of the owls in the collection of the Academy of Natural Sciences of Philadelphia. Acad. Nat. Sci. Phila. Proc. 1890: 124–131 (see 130).
1892. Catalogue of the Corvidae, Paradiseidae and Oriolidae in the collection of the Academy of Natural Sciences of Philadelphia. Acad. Nat. Sci. Phila. Proc. 1891: 441–450 (see 442).
1906. A bibliography and nomenclator of the ornithological works of John James Audubon. Auk 23: 298–312 (see 307, 308).
1913. The Catbird. Bird-Lore 15: 327–330 (see 329).
1915. General notes. Type locality of Lewis's Woodpecker and Clarke's Nutcracker. Auk 32: 371–372.
1930. General notes. Townsend's Oregon Tubinares. Auk 47: 414–415.
1931. General notes. In re "Townsend's Oregon Tubinares". Auk 48: 106–109.

STORER, TRACY IRWIN (see GRINNELL, BRYANT, and STORER; and GRINNELL and STORER).

STOVER, A. J.
1912. Notes from field and study. Northern Pileated Woodpecker at Corvallis, Oregon. Bird-Lore 14: 297.
1913a. Bird-Lore's thirteenth bird census. Corvallis, Oregon. Bird-Lore 15: 44–45.
1913b. General notes. The night song of Nuttall's Sparrow. Auk 30: 584–585.

STRONG, W. A.
1917. Speed cop shoots bald eagle and is arrested. Oologist 34: 113.

STRYKER, GUY.
1894. My first set of Pine Siskins. Oologist 11: 185–186.
1897. Great Gray Owl. Oreg. Nat. 4: 19.

STUHR, F. A.
1896. Field notes. Three albino crows. Nidologist 4: 21.

SUCKLEY, GEORGE (see COOPER and SUCKLEY).

SUTTON, GEORGE MIKSCH (see SEMPLE and SUTTON).

SWAINSON, WILLIAM, and RICHARDSON, JOHN.
1831. Fauna boreali-Americana; or the zoology of the northern parts of British America . . . Part II. The birds. 524 pp., illus. (see 2, 4, 6, 315, 316, 349, 359, 400, 402, 465). London.

SWALLOW, C. W.
1890. Notes on the winter birds of Clatsop County, Oregon. Orn. and Ool. 15: 67–68.
1891. General notes. Bird notes from Clatrop [sic] County, Oregon. Auk 8: 396–397.

SWARTH, HARRY SCHELWALDT (see also BROOKS and SWARTH; and GRINNELL and SWARTH).
1913. A revision of the California forms of *Pipilo maculatus* Swainson, with description of a new subspecies. Condor 15: 167–175, map.
1914a. A distributional list of the birds of Arizona. Cooper Orn. Club, Pacific Coast Avifauna 10, 133 pp., colored map of life zones.
1914b. The California forms of the genus *Psaltriparus*. Auk 31: 499–526, map (see 501, 509, 511, 516).
1914c. A study of the status of certain island forms of the genus *Salpinctes*. Condor 16: 211–217 (see 217).
1917a. Geographical variation in *Sphyrapicus thyroideus*. Condor 19: 62–65 (see 65).
1917b. A revision of the Marsh Wrens of California. Auk 34: 308–318, map.
1918. The distribution of the subspecies of the Brown Towhee (*Pipilo crissalis*). Condor 20: 117–121, illus. (see 119, 120).
1920. Revision of the avian genus *Passerella* with special reference to the distribution and migration of the races in California. Calif. Univ. Pubs., Zool. 21: 75–224, illus. (see 120, 131, 135, 140, 155, 158, 185, 192, 198, 200).
1922. Birds and mammals of the Stikine River region of northern British Columbia and southeastern Alaska. Calif. Univ. Pubs., Zool. 24: 125–314, illus.
1923. The systematic status of some northwestern song sparrows. Condor 25: 214–223 (see 214, 215, 221, 222).
1924. Birds and mammals of the Skeena River region of northern British Columbia. Calif. Univ. Pubs., Zool. 24: 315–394, illus.

TAVERNER, PERCY ALGERNON.
1926. Birds of western Canada. Canada Dept. Mines, Victoria Mem. Mus. Bull. 41, 380 pp., illus. Ottawa.
1931. A study of *Branta canadensis* (Linnaeus) the Canada Goose. Canada Nat. Mus. Bull. 67: 28–40.
1934. Birds of Canada. Canada Dept. Mines. Canada Nat. Mus. Bull. 72 (Biol. Ser. 19): 445 pp., illus. Ottawa.

TAYLOR, HENRY REED.
1905. From field and study. The nest and eggs of the Vaux Swift. Condor 7: 177, 179, illus.

TAYLOR, WALTER PENN.
1923. Doctor Suckley on the magpie versus livestock. Auk 40: 126.
1925. The breeding and wintering of the Pallid Horned Lark in Washington State. Auk 42: 349–353.

———, and SHAW, WILLIAM THOMAS.
1927. Mammals and birds of Mount Rainier National Park. U. S. Dept. Int. 249 pp., illus.

TELFORD, HARRY.
1916. From field and study. White-winged Scoter in Klamath County, Oregon. Condor 18: 35.

THAYER, GERALD HENDERSON.
1909. Concealing coloration in the animal kingdom; an exposition of the laws of disguise through color and pattern: being a summary of Abbott H. Thayer's discoveries. 260 pp., illus. New York.

THOMPSON, HARRIET W.
1913. Bird-Lore's thirteenth bird census. Eugene, Oregon. Bird-Lore 15: 44.

THOMS, CRAIG SHARP (see OVER and THOMS).

TOWNSEND, CHARLES WENDELL.
1909. The use of the wings and feet by diving birds. Auk 26: 234–248 (see 242).

TOWNSEND, JOHN KIRK.
1837. Description of twelve new species of birds, chiefly from the vicinity of the Columbia River. [Read Nov. 15, 1836.] Jour. Acad. Nat. Sci. Phila. 7: 187–193.
1839. Narrative of a journey across the Rocky Mountains to the Columbia River, and a visit to the Sandwich Islands, Chili, etc., with a scientific appendix. 352 pp. Philadelphia.

TOWNSEND, MANLEY BACON.
1917. Nesting habits of the Cliff Swallow. Bird-Lore 19: 252–257, illus. (see 253).

VAN DYKE, THEODORE STRONG (see SANFORD, BISHOP, and VAN DYKE).

VAN ROSSEM, ADRIAAN JOSEPH (see also DICKEY and VAN ROSSEM).
1926. The California forms of *Agelaius phoeniceus* (Linnaeus). Condor 28: 215–230, illus.
1928. General notes. A northern race of the Mountain Chickadee. Auk 45: 104–105.
1929. The races of *Sitta pygmaea* Vigors. Biol. Soc. Wash. Proc. 42: 175–177 (see 176).

WALKER, ALEXANDER.
1912a. Unusual nesting site of Brewer's Blackbird. Oologist 29: 317–318.
1912b. Northern Red-breasted Sapsucker. Oologist 29: 395–397.
1914a. From field and study. Mallard nesting in tree. Condor 16: 93.
1914b. From field and study. Nesting of the Gray Flycatcher in Oregon. Condor 16: 94.
1914c. From field and study. White-throated Sparrow in Oregon. Condor 16: 183.
1915. Albinos. Oologist 32: 66.
1916. Another unusual nesting site of Brewer's Blackbird. Oologist 33: 177.
1917a. Nest of Brewer's Blackbird on the ground at Mailno [=Mulino] Ore. [photo.] Oologist 34: 40.
1917b. Some birds of central Oregon. Condor 19: 131–140, illus.
1918. From field and study. Corrections. Condor 20: 44.
1921. From field and study. A record for the Emperor Goose in Oregon. Condor 23: 65.
1923. From field and study. The European Widgeon in Oregon. Condor 25: 70.
1924. Notes on some birds from Tillamook County, Oregon. Condor 26: 180–182.
1926. From field and study. Additional notes on the birds of Tillamook County, Oregon. Condor 28: 181–182.
1927. From field and study. Additional records of the Prairie Falcon in the Willamette Valley, Oregon. Condor 29: 118.
1934a. From field and study. Nuttall Poor-will on the Oregon coast. Condor 36: 178.
1934b. From field and study. The black-chinned Hummingbird in Oregon. Condor 36: 252.
1935. From field and study. The Snowy Egret in Oregon. Condor 37: 80.

———, and BROWN, DONALD E.
1914. Bird-Lore's fourteenth Christmas census. Mulino, Oregon. Bird-Lore 16: 49.

———, and DIETRICH, ERICH J.
1913. Bird-Lore's thirteenth bird census. Mulino, Oregon. (Ten miles south of Oregon City.) Bird-Lore 15: 44.

WARD, HENRY LEVI.
1906. Notes of the Herring Gull and the Caspian Tern (*Larus argentatus* and *Sterna caspia*). Wis. Nat. Hist. Soc. Bull. (New Series) 4: 113–134, illus. (see 126).

WETMORE, [FRANK] ALEXANDER.
1915. Mortality among waterfowl around Great Salt Lake, Utah. U. S. Dept. Agr. Bull. 217, 10 pp., illus.
1918. The duck sickness in Utah. U. S. Dept. Agr. Bull. 672, 26 pp., illus.
1919. Lead poisoning in waterfowl. U. S. Dept. Agr. Bull. 793, 12 pp., illus.
1921. Wild ducks and duck foods of the Bear River marshes, Utah. U. S. Dept. Agr. Bull. 936, 20 pp., illus.
1923. Migration records from wild ducks and other birds banded in the Salt Lake Valley, Utah. U. S. Dept. Agr. Bull. 1145, 16 pp., illus.

WETMORE, [FRANK] ALEXANDER—Continued.
1924. Food and economic relations of North American grebes. U. S. Dept. Agr. Bull. 1196, 24 pp., illus.
1925. Food of American phalaropes, avocets, and stilts. U. S. Dept. Agr. Bull. 1359, 20 pp., illus.
1926. The migration of birds. 217 pp., illus. Cambridge.
1927. Our migrant shorebirds in southern South America. U. S. Dept. Agr. Tech. Bull. 26, 24 pp., illus.
1928. From field and study. The Short-tailed Albatross in Oregon. Condor 30: 191.

WHITE, HARRY GORDON.
1890. Geographical variation of eggs. Orn. and Ool. 15: 1–4.

WILCOX, TIMOTHY ERASTUS.
1885. General notes. Introduced game birds in Oregon and Idaho. Auk 2: 315.

WILCOX, W. A.
1891. Japanese pheasants in Oregon. Forest and Stream 35: 491.

WILLETT, GEORGE.
1919. Bird notes from southeastern Oregon and northeastern California. Condor 21: 194–207, illus.
1933. A revised list of the birds of southwestern California. Cooper Orn. Club, Pacific Coast Avifauna 21, 204 pp. (see 106).

WITHERBY, HARRY FORBES [Editor], and others.
1920. A practical handbook of British birds. Vol. 1, 522 pp. London.

WOOD, CASEY ALBERT.
1923. A letter from T. M. Brewer to Osbert Salvin. Condor 25: 100–101.
1924. The Starling family at home and abroad. Condor 26: 123–136, illus.

WOOD, WILLIAM.
1881. California Pigmy Owl (*Glaucidium gnoma*) life size. Orn. and Ool. 6: 33–35, 47–48, illus. (see 34).

WOODCOCK, ARTHUR ROY.
1902. An annotated list of the birds of Oregon. Oreg. Agr. Expt. Sta. Bull. 68, 119 pp., illus.

Index

A CATALOGUE OF SELECTED DOVER BOOKS IN ALL FIELDS OF INTEREST

A CATALOGUE OF SELECTED DOVER BOOKS IN ALL FIELDS OF INTEREST

WHAT IS SCIENCE?, *N. Campbell*
The role of experiment and measurement, the function of mathematics, the nature of scientific laws, the difference between laws and theories, the limitations of science, and many similarly provocative topics are treated clearly and without technicalities by an eminent scientist. "Still an excellent introduction to scientific philosophy," H. Margenau in *Physics Today*. "A first-rate primer . . . deserves a wide audience," *Scientific American*. 192pp. 5⅜ x 8.
S43 Paperbound $1.25

THE NATURE OF LIGHT AND COLOUR IN THE OPEN AIR, *M. Minnaert*
Why are shadows sometimes blue, sometimes green, or other colors depending on the light and surroundings? What causes mirages? Why do multiple suns and moons appear in the sky? Professor Minnaert explains these unusual phenomena and hundreds of others in simple, easy-to-understand terms based on optical laws and the properties of light and color. No mathematics is required but artists, scientists, students, and everyone fascinated by these "tricks" of nature will find thousands of useful and amazing pieces of information. Hundreds of observational experiments are suggested which require no special equipment. 200 illustrations; 42 photos. xvi + 362pp. 5⅜ x 8.
T196 Paperbound $2.00

THE STRANGE STORY OF THE QUANTUM, AN ACCOUNT FOR THE GENERAL READER OF THE GROWTH OF IDEAS UNDERLYING OUR PRESENT ATOMIC KNOWLEDGE, *B. Hoffmann*
Presents lucidly and expertly, with barest amount of mathematics, the problems and theories which led to modern quantum physics. Dr. Hoffmann begins with the closing years of the 19th century, when certain trifling discrepancies were noticed, and with illuminating analogies and examples takes you through the brilliant concepts of Planck, Einstein, Pauli, Broglie, Bohr, Schroedinger, Heisenberg, Dirac, Sommerfeld, Feynman, etc. This edition includes a new, long postscript carrying the story through 1958. "Of the books attempting an account of the history and contents of our modern atomic physics which have come to my attention, this is the best," H. Margenau, Yale University, in *American Journal of Physics*. 32 tables and line illustrations. Index. 275pp. 5⅜ x 8.
T518 Paperbound $2.00

GREAT IDEAS OF MODERN MATHEMATICS: THEIR NATURE AND USE, *Jagjit Singh*
Reader with only high school math will understand main mathematical ideas of modern physics, astronomy, genetics, psychology, evolution, etc. better than many who use them as tools, but comprehend little of their basic structure. Author uses his wide knowledge of non-mathematical fields in brilliant exposition of differential equations, matrices, group theory, logic, statistics, problems of mathematical foundations, imaginary numbers, vectors, etc. Original publication. 2 appendixes. 2 indexes. 65 ills. 322pp. 5⅜ x 8.
T587 Paperbound $2.00

SHAKESPEARE AS A DRAMATIC ARTIST, *Richard G. Moulton*
Analyses of *Merchant of Venice, Richard III, King Lear, The Tempest,* and other plays show Shakespeare's skill at integrating story plots, blending light and serious moods, use of such themes as judgment by appearances, antithesis of outer and inner life, repeated use of such characters as court fool, and other important elements. "Only notable book on Shakespeare's handling of plot . . . one of the most valuable of all books on Shakespeare," Eric Bentley. Introduction by Eric Bentley. Appendix. Indexes. xviii + 443pp. 5⅜ x 8.
T1546 Paperbound $2.50

THE ENGLISH AND SCOTTISH POPULAR BALLADS, *Francis James Child*
A great work of American scholarship, which established and exhausted a whole field of literary inquiry. "Child" ballads are those 305 ballads and their numerous variants preserved orally from medieval, Renaissance and earlier times. Every known variant (sometimes several dozen) of these ballads known at the time is given here. Child's commentary traces these ballads' origins, investigates references in literature, relates them to parallel literary traditions of other countries. This edition also includes "Professor Child and the Ballad," an essay by Prof. Walter Morris Hart. Biographical sketch by G. L. Kittredge. Appendixes. Total of lxvii + 2694pp. 6½ x 9¼.
T1409—T1413 Five volume set, Paperbound $13.75

WORLD DRAMA, *edited by B. H. Clark*
The dramatic activity of a score of ages and eras—all in two handy, compact volumes. More than one-third of this material is unavailable in any other current edition! In all, there are 46 plays from the ancient and the modern worlds: Greece, Rome, Medieval Europe, France, Germany, Italy, England, Russia, Scandinavia, India, China, Japan, etc.; classic authors such as Aeschylus, Sophocles, Euripides, Aristophanes, Plautus, Marlowe, Jonson, Farquhar, Goldsmith, Cervantes, Molière, Dumas, Goethe, Schiller, Ibsen. A creative collection that avoids hackneyed material to include only completely first-rate plays which are relatively little known or difficult to obtain. "The most comprehensive collection of important plays from all literature available in English," *Saturday Review.* Vol. I: Ancient Greece and Rome, China, Japan, Medieval Europe, England. Vol. II: Modern Europe. Introduction. Reading lists. Total of 1,364pp. 5⅜ x 8. T57, T59 Two volume set, paperbound $6.00

HISTORY OF PHILOSOPHY, *Julián Marías*
One-volume history of philosophy by a contemporary Spanish philosopher. Major, perhaps the most important post-war philosophical history. Strong coverage of recent and still-living philosophers (in many cases the only coverage of these figures available at this level) such as Bergson, Jaspers, Buber, Marcel, Sartre, Whitehead, Russell and Boas; full coverage of Spanish philosophers (particularly the pre-W.W. II School of Madrid) such as Suárez, Sanz del Río, Santayana, Unamuno and Ortega. Thoroughly organized, lucidly written for self-study as well as for the classroom. Translated by S. Appelbaum and C. C. Strowbridge. Bibliography. Index. xix + 505pp. 5⅜ x 8½.
T1739 Paperbound $2.75

DICTIONARY OF AMERICAN PORTRAITS, *edited by Hayward and Blanche Cirker, and the staff of Dover Publications, Inc.*

Reference work and pictorial archive, entirely unique, containing over 4,000 portraits of important Americans who made their impact on American life before approximately 1905. Probably the largest archive of American portraiture ever assembled. The product of many years of investigation and collection, compiled and selected with the assistance of noted authorities in many fields. The work contains a wide representation of figures including Presidents, signers of the Declaration of Independence, diplomats, inventors, businessmen, great men of science and the arts, military figures, Indian leaders, society figures, famous sports figures, pioneers, criminals and their victims, and dozens of other categories. Artist and/or engraver of each portrait supplied where known. List of sources of pictures. Bibliography. Index. 4,045 portraits. xiv + 756pp. 9½ x 12¾. T1823 Clothbound $30.00

HEAVENS ON EARTH: UTOPIAN COMMUNITIES IN AMERICA, 1680-1880, *Mark Holloway*

The history of one of young America's strangest adventures: the establishment of strictly regulated communities that strove for a "utopian" existence through adherence to a variety of fascinating and eccentric religious, economic, or social beliefs. The account is entertaining and absorbing as it covers the high intentions, organization, property and buildings, industry and amusements, clothing, beliefs concerning sex, money, and women's rights, reasons for failure, character of the leaders, etc. for virtually every major community that was established: Brook Farm, New Harmony, the Shaker settlements, Oneida, the Fourierist phalanxes, dozens of others. As interesting to the layman as to the historian and the sociologist. Revised (1960) edition. New bibliography. Map. 14 illustrations. xvi + 246pp. 5⅜ x 8½. T1593 Paperbound $1.85

INCIDENTS OF TRAVEL IN YUCATAN, *John L. Stephens*

One of the first white men to penetrate interior of Yucatan tells the thrilling story of his discoveries of 44 cities, remains of once-powerful Maya civilization. Compelling text combines narrative power with historical significance as it takes you through heat, dust, storms of Yucatan; native festivals with brutal bull fights; great ruined temples atop man-made mounds. Countless idols, sculptures, tombs, examples of Mayan taste for rich ornamentation, from gateways to personal trinkets, accurately illustrated, discussed in text. Will appeal to those interested in ancient civilizations, and those who like stories of exploration, discovery, adventure. Republication of last (1843) edition. 124 illustrations by English artist, F. Catherwood. Appendix on Mayan architecture, chronology. Total of xxviii + 927pp.

T926, T927 Two volume set, paperbound $4.50

FIGURE DRAWING, *Richard G. Hatton*

One of the few anatomy texts to approach figure drawing from the point of view of the draftsman. Providing wealth of information on anatomy, musculature, etc., but stressing problems of rendering difficult curves and planes of human face and form. Illustrated with 377 figures (with as many as 10 different views of the same subject), showing undraped figures, details of faces, hands, fingers, feet, legs, arms, etc. in dozens of life positions. Index. xi +350pp. 5⅜ x 8. T1377 Paperbound $2.50

It's Fun to Make Things From Scrap Materials, *Evelyn Glantz Hershoff*
What use are empty spools, tin cans, bottle tops? What can be made from rubber bands, clothes pins, paper clips, and buttons? This book provides simply worded instructions and large diagrams showing you how to make cookie cutters, toy trucks, paper turkeys, Halloween masks, telephone sets, aprons, linoleum block- and spatter prints — in all 399 projects! Many are easy enough for young children to figure out for themselves; some challenging enough to entertain adults; all are remarkably ingenious ways to make things from materials that cost pennies or less! Formerly "Scrap Fun for Everyone." Index. 214 illustrations. 373pp. 5⅜ x 8½. Paperbound $1.50

Symbolic Logic and The Game of Logic, *Lewis Carroll*
"Symbolic Logic" is not concerned with modern symbolic logic, but is instead a collection of over 380 problems posed with charm and imagination, using the syllogism and a fascinating diagrammatic method of drawing conclusions. In "The Game of Logic" Carroll's whimsical imagination devises a logical game played with 2 diagrams and counters (included) to manipulate hundreds of tricky syllogisms. The final section, "Hit or Miss" is a lagniappe of 101 additional puzzles in the delightful Carroll manner. Until this reprint edition, both of these books were rarities costing up to $15 each. Symbolic Logic: Index. xxxi + 199pp. The Game of Logic: 96pp. 2 vols. bound as one. 5⅜ x 8. Paperbound $2.00

Mathematical Puzzles of Sam Loyd, Part I
selected and edited by M. Gardner
Choice puzzles by the greatest American puzzle creator and innovator. Selected from his famous collection, "Cyclopedia of Puzzles," they retain the unique style and historical flavor of the originals. There are posers based on arithmetic, algebra, probability, game theory, route tracing, topology, counter and sliding block, operations research, geometrical dissection. Includes the famous "14-15" puzzle which was a national craze, and his "Horse of a Different Color" which sold millions of copies. 117 of his most ingenious puzzles in all. 120 line drawings and diagrams. Solutions. Selected references. xx + 167pp. 5⅜ x 8. Paperbound $1.00

String Figures and How to Make Them, *Caroline Furness Jayne*
107 string figures plus variations selected from the best primitive and modern examples developed by Navajo, Apache, pygmies of Africa, Eskimo, in Europe, Australia, China, etc. The most readily understandable, easy-to-follow book in English on perennially popular recreation. Crystal-clear exposition; step-by-step diagrams. Everyone from kindergarten children to adults looking for unusual diversion will be endlessly amused. Index. Bibliography. Introduction by A. C. Haddon. 17 full-page plates, 960 illustrations. xxiii + 401pp. 5⅜ x 8½. Paperbound $2.00

Paper Folding for Beginners, *W. D. Murray and F. J. Rigney*
A delightful introduction to the varied and entertaining Japanese art of origami (paper folding), with a full, crystal-clear text that anticipates every difficulty; over 275 clearly labeled diagrams of all important stages in creation. You get results at each stage, since complex figures are logically developed from simpler ones. 43 different pieces are explained: sailboats, frogs, roosters, etc. 6 photographic plates. 279 diagrams. 95pp. 5⅝ x 8⅜. Paperbound $1.00

PRINCIPLES OF ART HISTORY,
H. Wölfflin
Analyzing such terms as "baroque," "classic," "neoclassic," "primitive," "picturesque," and 164 different works by artists like Botticelli, van Cleve, Dürer, Hobbema, Holbein, Hals, Rembrandt, Titian, Brueghel, Vermeer, and many others, the author establishes the classifications of art history and style on a firm, concrete basis. This classic of art criticism shows what really occurred between the 14th-century primitives and the sophistication of the 18th century in terms of basic attitudes and philosophies. "A remarkable lesson in the art of seeing," *Sat. Rev. of Literature*. Translated from the 7th German edition. 150 illustrations. 254pp. 6⅛ x 9¼. Paperbound $2.00

PRIMITIVE ART,
Franz Boas
This authoritative and exhaustive work by a great American anthropologist covers the entire gamut of primitive art. Pottery, leatherwork, metal work, stone work, wood, basketry, are treated in detail. Theories of primitive art, historical depth in art history, technical virtuosity, unconscious levels of patterning, symbolism, styles, literature, music, dance, etc. A must book for the interested layman, the anthropologist, artist, handicrafter (hundreds of unusual motifs), and the historian. Over 900 illustrations (50 ceramic vessels, 12 totem poles, etc.). 376pp. 5⅜ x 8. Paperbound $2.25

THE GENTLEMAN AND CABINET MAKER'S DIRECTOR,
Thomas Chippendale
A reprint of the 1762 catalogue of furniture designs that went on to influence generations of English and Colonial and Early Republic American furniture makers. The 200 plates, most of them full-page sized, show Chippendale's designs for French (Louis XV), Gothic, and Chinese-manner chairs, sofas, canopy and dome beds, cornices, chamber organs, cabinets, shaving tables, commodes, picture frames, frets, candle stands, chimney pieces, decorations, etc. The drawings are all elegant and highly detailed; many include construction diagrams and elevations. A supplement of 24 photographs shows surviving pieces of original and Chippendale-style pieces of furniture. Brief biography of Chippendale by N. I. Bienenstock, editor of *Furniture World*. Reproduced from the 1762 edition. 200 plates, plus 19 photographic plates. vi + 249pp. 9⅛ x 12¼. Paperbound $3.50

AMERICAN ANTIQUE FURNITURE: A BOOK FOR AMATEURS,
Edgar G. Miller, Jr.
Standard introduction and practical guide to identification of valuable American antique furniture. 2115 illustrations, mostly photographs taken by the author in 148 private homes, are arranged in chronological order in extensive chapters on chairs, sofas, chests, desks, bedsteads, mirrors, tables, clocks, and other articles. Focus is on furniture accessible to the collector, including simpler pieces and a larger than usual coverage of Empire style. Introductory chapters identify structural elements, characteristics of various styles, how to avoid fakes, etc. "We are frequently asked to name some book on American furniture that will meet the requirements of the novice collector, the beginning dealer, and . . . the general public. . . . We believe Mr. Miller's two volumes more completely satisfy this specification than any other work," *Antiques*. Appendix. Index. Total of vi + 1106pp. 7⅞ x 10¾.
Two volume set, paperbound $7.50

THE BAD CHILD'S BOOK OF BEASTS, MORE BEASTS FOR WORSE CHILDREN, and A MORAL ALPHABET, *H. Belloc*

Hardly and anthology of humorous verse has appeared in the last 50 years without at least a couple of these famous nonsense verses. But one must see the entire volumes — with all the delightful original illustrations by Sir Basil Blackwood — to appreciate fully Belloc's charming and witty verses that play so subacidly on the platitudes of life and morals that beset his day — and ours. A great humor classic. Three books in one. Total of 157pp. 5⅜ x 8.

Paperbound $1.00

THE DEVIL'S DICTIONARY, *Ambrose Bierce*

Sardonic and irreverent barbs puncturing the pomposities and absurdities of American politics, business, religion, literature, and arts, by the country's greatest satirist in the classic tradition. Epigrammatic as Shaw, piercing as Swift, American as Mark Twain, Will Rogers, and Fred Allen, Bierce will always remain the favorite of a small coterie of enthusiasts, and of writers and speakers whom he supplies with "some of the most gorgeous witticisms of the English language" (H. L. Mencken). Over 1000 entries in alphabetical order. 144pp. 5⅜ x 8. Paperbound $1.00

THE COMPLETE NONSENSE OF EDWARD LEAR.

This is the only complete edition of this master of gentle madness available at a popular price. *A Book of Nonsense, Nonsense Songs, More Nonsense Songs and Stories* in their entirety with all the old favorites that have delighted children and adults for years. The Dong With A Luminous Nose, The Jumblies, The Owl and the Pussycat, and hundreds of other bits of wonderful nonsense. 214 limericks, 3 sets of Nonsense Botany, 5 Nonsense Alphabets, 546 drawings by Lear himself, and much more. 320pp. 5⅜ x 8. Paperbound $1.00

THE WIT AND HUMOR OF OSCAR WILDE, *ed. by Alvin Redman*

Wilde at his most brilliant, in 1000 epigrams exposing weaknesses and hypocrisies of "civilized" society. Divided into 49 categories—sin, wealth, women, America, etc.—to aid writers, speakers. Includes excerpts from his trials, books, plays, criticism. Formerly "The Epigrams of Oscar Wilde." Introduction by Vyvyan Holland, Wilde's only living son. Introductory essay by editor. 260pp. 5⅜ x 8.

Paperbound $1.00

A CHILD'S PRIMER OF NATURAL HISTORY, *Oliver Herford*

Scarcely an anthology of whimsy and humor has appeared in the last 50 years without a contribution from Oliver Herford. Yet the works from which these examples are drawn have been almost impossible to obtain! Here at last are Herford's improbable definitions of a menagerie of familiar and weird animals, each verse illustrated by the author's own drawings. 24 drawings in 2 colors; 24 additional drawings. vii + 95pp. 6½ x 6. Paperbound $1.00

THE BROWNIES: THEIR BOOK, *Palmer Cox*

The book that made the Brownies a household word. Generations of readers have enjoyed the antics, predicaments and adventures of these jovial sprites, who emerge from the forest at night to play or to come to the aid of a deserving human. Delightful illustrations by the author decorate nearly every page. 24 short verse tales with 266 illustrations. 155pp. 6⅝ x 9¼.

Paperbound $1.50

THE PRINCIPLES OF PSYCHOLOGY,
William James

The full long-course, unabridged, of one of the great classics of Western literature and science. Wonderfully lucid descriptions of human mental activity, the stream of thought, consciousness, time perception, memory, imagination, emotions, reason, abnormal phenomena, and similar topics. Original contributions are integrated with the work of such men as Berkeley, Binet, Mills, Darwin, Hume, Kant, Royce, Schopenhauer, Spinoza, Locke, Descartes, Galton, Wundt, Lotze, Herbart, Fechner, and scores of others. All contrasting interpretations of mental phenomena are examined in detail—introspective analysis, philosophical interpretation, and experimental research. "A classic," *Journal of Consulting Psychology*. "The main lines are as valid as ever," *Psychoanalytical Quarterly*. "Standard reading... a classic of interpretation," *Psychiatric Quarterly*. 94 illustrations. 1408pp. 5⅜ x 8.

Vol. 1 Paperbound $2.50, Vol. 2 Paperbound $2.50,
The set $5.00

VISUAL ILLUSIONS: THEIR CAUSES, CHARACTERISTICS AND APPLICATIONS,
M. Luckiesh

"Seeing is deceiving," asserts the author of this introduction to virtually every type of optical illusion known. The text both describes and explains the principles involved in color illusions, figure-ground, distance illusions, etc. 100 photographs, drawings and diagrams prove how easy it is to fool the sense: circles that aren't round, parallel lines that seem to bend, stationary figures that seem to move as you stare at them – illustration after illustration strains our credulity at what we see. Fascinating book from many points of view, from applications for artists, in camouflage, etc. to the psychology of vision. New introduction by William Ittleson, Dept. of Psychology, Queens College. Index. Bibliography. xxi + 252pp. 5⅜ x 8½. Paperbound $1.50

FADS AND FALLACIES IN THE NAME OF SCIENCE,
Martin Gardner

This is the standard account of various cults, quack systems, and delusions which have masqueraded as science: hollow earth fanatics. Reich and orgone sex energy, dianetics, Atlantis, multiple moons, Forteanism, flying saucers, medical fallacies like iridiagnosis, zone therapy, etc. A new chapter has been added on Bridey Murphy, psionics, and other recent manifestations in this field. This is a fair, reasoned appraisal of eccentric theory which provides excellent inoculation against cleverly masked nonsense. "Should be read by everyone, scientist and non-scientist alike," R. T. Birge, Prof. Emeritus of Physics, Univ. of California; Former President, American Physical Society. Index. x + 365pp. 5⅜ x 8. Paperbound $1.85

ILLUSIONS AND DELUSIONS OF THE SUPERNATURAL AND THE OCCULT,
D. H. Rawcliffe

Holds up to rational examination hundreds of persistent delusions including crystal gazing, automatic writing, table turning, mediumistic trances, mental healing, stigmata, lycanthropy, live burial, the Indian Rope Trick, spiritualism, dowsing, telepathy, clairvoyance, ghosts, ESP, etc. The author explains and exposes the mental and physical deceptions involved, making this not only an exposé of supernatural phenomena, but a valuable exposition of characteristic types of abnormal psychology. Originally titled "The Psychology of the Occult." 14 illustrations. Index. 551pp. 5⅜ x 8. Paperbound $2.25

SOCIAL THOUGHT FROM LORE TO SCIENCE,
H. E. Barnes and H. Becker
An immense survey of sociological thought and ways of viewing, studying, planning, and reforming society from earliest times to the present. Includes thought on society of preliterate peoples, ancient non-Western cultures, and every great movement in Europe, America, and modern Japan. Analyzes hundreds of great thinkers: Plato, Augustine, Bodin, Vico, Montesquieu, Herder, Comte, Marx, etc. Weighs the contributions of utopians, sophists, fascists and communists; economists, jurists, philosophers, ecclesiastics, and every 19th and 20th century school of scientific sociology, anthropology, and social psychology throughout the world. Combines topical, chronological, and regional approaches, treating the evolution of social thought as a process rather than as a series of mere topics. "Impressive accuracy, competence, and discrimination . . . easily the best single survey," *Nation.* Thoroughly revised, with new material up to 1960. 2 indexes. Over 2200 bibliographical notes. Three volume set. Total of 1586pp. 5⅜ x 8.
Vol. 1 Paperbound $2.75, Vol. 2 Paperbound $2.75, Vol. 3 Paperbound $2.50
The set $8.00

A HISTORY OF HISTORICAL WRITING, *Harry Elmer Barnes*
Virtually the only adequate survey of the whole course of historical writing in a single volume. Surveys developments from the beginnings of historiography in the ancient Near East and the Classical World, up through the Cold War. Covers major historians in detail, shows interrelationship with cultural background, makes clear individual contributions, evaluates and estimates importance; also enormously rich upon minor authors and thinkers who are usually passed over. Packed with scholarship and learning, clear, easily written. Indispensable to every student of history. Revised and enlarged up to 1961. Index and bibliography. xv + 442pp. 5⅜ x 8½. Paperbound $2.50

JOHANN SEBASTIAN BACH, *Philipp Spitta*
The complete and unabridged text of the definitive study of Bach. Written some 70 years ago, it is still unsurpassed for its coverage of nearly all aspects of Bach's life and work. There could hardly be a finer non-technical introduction to Bach's music than the detailed, lucid analyses which Spitta provides for hundreds of individual pieces. 26 solid pages are devoted to the B minor mass, for example, and 30 pages to the glorious St. Matthew Passion. This monumental set also includes a major analysis of the music of the 18th century: Buxtehude, Pachelbel, etc. "Unchallenged as the last word on one of the supreme geniuses of music," John Barkham, *Saturday Review Syndicate.* Total of 1819pp. Heavy cloth binding. 5⅜ x 8.
Two volume set, clothbound $13.50

BEETHOVEN AND HIS NINE SYMPHONIES, *George Grove*
In this modern middle-level classic of musicology Grove not only analyzes all nine of Beethoven's symphonies very thoroughly in terms of their musical structure, but also discusses the circumstances under which they were written, Beethoven's stylistic development, and much other background material. This is an extremely rich book, yet very easily followed; it is highly recommended to anyone seriously interested in music. Over 250 musical passages. Index. viii + 407pp. 5⅜ x 8. Paperbound $2.00

HEAR ME TALKIN' TO YA, *edited by Nat Shapiro and Nat Hentoff*
In their own words, Louis Armstrong, King Oliver, Fletcher Henderson, Bunk Johnson, Bix Beiderbecke, Billy Holiday, Fats Waller, Jelly Roll Morton, Duke Ellington, and many others comment on the origins of jazz in New Orleans and its growth in Chicago's South Side, Kansas City's jam sessions, Depression Harlem, and the modernism of the West Coast schools. Taken from taped conversations, letters, magazine articles, other first-hand sources. Editors' introduction. xvi + 429pp. 5⅜ x 8½. T1726 Paperbound $2.00

THE JOURNAL OF HENRY D. THOREAU
A 25-year record by the great American observer and critic, as complete a record of a great man's inner life as is anywhere available. Thoreau's Journals served him as raw material for his formal pieces, as a place where he could develop his ideas, as an outlet for his interests in wild life and plants, in writing as an art, in classics of literature, Walt Whitman and other contemporaries, in politics, slavery, individual's relation to the State, etc. The Journals present a portrait of a remarkable man, and are an observant social history. Unabridged republication of 1906 edition, Bradford Torrey and Francis H. Allen, editors. Illustrations. Total of 1888pp. 8⅜ x 12¼.
T312, T313 Two volume set, clothbound $25.00

A SHAKESPEARIAN GRAMMAR, *E. A. Abbott*
Basic reference to Shakespeare and his contemporaries, explaining through thousands of quotations from Shakespeare, Jonson, Beaumont and Fletcher, North's *Plutarch* and other sources the grammatical usage differing from the modern. First published in 1870 and written by a scholar who spent much of his life isolating principles of Elizabethan language, the book is unlikely ever to be superseded. Indexes. xxiv + 511pp. 5⅜ x 8½. T1582 Paperbound $2.75

FOLK-LORE OF SHAKESPEARE, *T. F. Thistelton Dyer*
Classic study, drawing from Shakespeare a large body of references to supernatural beliefs, terminology of falconry and hunting, games and sports, good luck charms, marriage customs, folk medicines, superstitions about plants, animals, birds, argot of the underworld, sexual slang of London, proverbs, drinking customs, weather lore, and much else. From full compilation comes a mirror of the 17th-century popular mind. Index. ix + 526pp. 5⅜ x 8½.
T1614 Paperbound $2.75

THE NEW VARIORUM SHAKESPEARE, *edited by H. H. Furness*
By far the richest editions of the plays ever produced in any country or language. Each volume contains complete text (usually First Folio) of the play, all variants in Quarto and other Folio texts, editorial changes by every major editor to Furness's own time (1900), footnotes to obscure references or language, extensive quotes from literature of Shakespearian criticism, essays on plot sources (often reprinting sources in full), and much more.

HAMLET, *edited by H. H. Furness*
Total of xxvi + 905pp. 5⅜ x 8½.
T1004, T1005 Two volume set, paperbound $5.25

TWELFTH NIGHT, *edited by H. H. Furness*
Index. xxii + 434pp. 5⅜ x 8½. T1189 Paperbound $2.75

LA BOHEME BY GIACOMO PUCCINI,
translated and introduced by Ellen H. Bleiler
Complete handbook for the operagoer, with everything needed for full enjoyment except the musical score itself. Complete Italian libretto, with new, modern English line-by-line translation—the only libretto printing all repeats; biography of Puccini; the librettists; background to the opera, Murger's La Boheme, etc.; circumstances of composition and performances; plot summary; and pictorial section of 73 illustrations showing Puccini, famous singers and performances, etc. Large clear type for easy reading. 124pp. 5⅜ x 8½.
T404 Paperbound $1.00

ANTONIO STRADIVARI: HIS LIFE AND WORK (1644-1737),
W. Henry Hill, Arthur F. Hill, and Alfred E. Hill
Still the only book that really delves into life and art of the incomparable Italian craftsman, maker of the finest musical instruments in the world today. The authors, expert violin-makers themselves, discuss Stradivari's ancestry, his construction and finishing techniques, distinguished characteristics of many of his instruments and their locations. Included, too, is story of introduction of his instruments into France, England, first revelation of their supreme merit, and information on his labels, number of instruments made, prices, mystery of ingredients of his varnish, tone of pre-1684 Stradivari violin and changes between 1684 and 1690. An extremely interesting, informative account for all music lovers, from craftsman to concert-goer. Republication of original (1902) edition. New introduction by Sydney Beck, Head of Rare Book and Manuscript Collections, Music Division, New York Public Library. Analytical index by Rembert Wurlitzer. Appendixes. 68 illustrations. 30 full-page plates. 4 in color. xxvi + 315pp. 5⅜ x 8½. T425 Paperbound $2.25

MUSICAL AUTOGRAPHS FROM MONTEVERDI TO HINDEMITH,
Emanuel Winternitz
For beauty, for intrinsic interest, for perspective on the composer's personality, for subtleties of phrasing, shading, emphasis indicated in the autograph but suppressed in the printed score, the mss. of musical composition are fascinating documents which repay close study in many different ways. This 2-volume work reprints facsimiles of mss. by virtually every major composer, and many minor figures—196 examples in all. A full text points out what can be learned from mss., analyzes each sample. Index. Bibliography. 18 figures. 196 plates. Total of 170pp. of text. 7⅞ x 10¾.
T1312, T1313 Two volume set, paperbound $4.00

J. S. BACH,
Albert Schweitzer
One of the few great full-length studies of Bach's life and work, and the study upon which Schweitzer's renown as a musicologist rests. On first appearance (1911), revolutionized Bach performance. The only writer on Bach to be musicologist, performing musician, and student of history, theology and philosophy, Schweitzer contributes particularly full sections on history of German Protestant church music, theories on motivic pictorial representations in vocal music, and practical suggestions for performance. Translated by Ernest Newman. Indexes. 5 illustrations. 650 musical examples. Total of xix + 928pp. 5⅜ x 8½. T1631, T1632 Two volume set, paperbound $4.50

THE METHODS OF ETHICS, *Henry Sidgwick*
Propounding no organized system of its own, study subjects every major methodological approach to ethics to rigorous, objective analysis. Study discusses and relates ethical thought of Plato, Aristotle, Bentham, Clarke, Butler, Hobbes, Hume, Mill, Spencer, Kant, and dozens of others. Sidgwick retains conclusions from each system which follow from ethical premises, rejecting the faulty. Considered by many in the field to be among the most important treatises on ethical philosophy. Appendix. Index. xlvii + 528pp. 5⅜ x 8½.
T1608 Paperbound $2.50

TEUTONIC MYTHOLOGY, *Jakob Grimm*
A milestone in Western culture; the work which established on a modern basis the study of history of religions and comparative religions. 4-volume work assembles and interprets everything available on religious and folkloristic beliefs of Germanic people (including Scandinavians, Anglo-Saxons, etc.). Assembling material from such sources as Tacitus, surviving Old Norse and Icelandic texts, archeological remains, folktales, surviving superstitions, comparative traditions, linguistic analysis, etc. Grimm explores pagan deities, heroes, folklore of nature, religious practices, and every other area of pagan German belief. To this day, the unrivaled, definitive, exhaustive study. Translated by J. S. Stallybrass from 4th (1883) German edition. Indexes. Total of lxxvii + 1887pp. 5⅜ x 8½.
T1602, T1603, T1604, T1605 Four volume set, paperbound $10.00

THE I CHING, *translated by James Legge*
Called "The Book of Changes" in English, this is one of the Five Classics edited by Confucius, basic and central to Chinese thought. Explains perhaps the most complex system of divination known, founded on the theory that all things happening at any one time have characteristic features which can be isolated and related. Significant in Oriental studies, in history of religions and philosophy, and also to Jungian psychoanalysis and other areas of modern European thought. Index. Appendixes. 6 plates. xxi + 448pp. 5⅜ x 8½.
T1062 Paperbound $2.75

HISTORY OF ANCIENT PHILOSOPHY, *W. Windelband*
One of the clearest, most accurate comprehensive surveys of Greek and Roman philosophy. Discusses ancient philosophy in general, intellectual life in Greece in the 7th and 6th centuries B.C., Thales, Anaximander, Anaximenes, Heraclitus, the Eleatics, Empedocles, Anaxagoras, Leucippus, the Pythagoreans, the Sophists, Socrates, Democritus (20 pages), Plato (50 pages), Aristotle (70 pages), the Peripatetics, Stoics, Epicureans, Sceptics, Neo-platonists, Christian Apologists, etc. 2nd German edition translated by H. E. Cushman. xv + 393pp. 5⅜ x 8.
T357 Paperbound $2.25

THE PALACE OF PLEASURE, *William Painter*
Elizabethan versions of Italian and French novels from *The Decameron*, Cinthio, Straparola, Queen Margaret of Navarre, and other continental sources — the very work that provided Shakespeare and dozens of his contemporaries with many of their plots and sub-plots and, therefore, justly considered one of the most influential books in all English literature. It is also a book that any reader will still enjoy. Total of cviii + 1,224pp.
T1691, T1692, T1693 Three volume set, paperbound $6.75

Fables of Aesop,
according to Sir Roger L'Estrange, with 50 drawings by Alexander Calder
Republication of rare 1931 Paris edition (limited to 665 copies) of 200 fables by Aesop in the 1692 L'Estrange translation. Illustrated with 50 highly imaginative, witty and occasionally ribald line drawings by the inventor of "mobiles" and "stabiles." "Fifty wonderfully inventive Alexander Calder drawings, impertinent as any of the artist's wire sculptures, make a delightful, modern counterpoint to the thoroughly moral tales," *Saturday Review*. 124pp. 6½ x 9¼. Paperbound $1.25

Drawings of Rembrandt
One of the earliest and best collections of Rembrandt drawings—the Lippmann-Hofstede de Groot facsimiles (1888)—is here reproduced in entirety. Collection contains 550 faithfully reproduced drawings in inks, chalks, and silverpoint; some, hasty sketches recorded on a handy scrap of paper; others, studies for well-known oil paintings. Edited, with scholarly commentary by Seymour Slive, Harvard University. "In large matters of appearance, size (9 x 12-inch page), paper color and weight, uniformity of plate texture, typography and printing, these two volumes could scarcely be improved," *Arts and Architecture*. "Altogether commendable . . . among the year's best," *New York Times*. Editor's introduction, notes. 3 indexes, 2 concordances. Total of lxxix + 552pp. 9⅛ x 12¼. Two volume set, paperbound $6.00
Two volume set, clothbound $12.50

The Early Work of Aubrey Beardsley
Together with *The Later Work*, the standard source for the most important Beardsley drawings. Edited by John Lane, *Early Work* contains 157 full-page plates including Burne-Jones style work, the *Morte d'Arthur* series, cover designs and illustrations from *The Studio* and other magazines, theatre posters, "Kiss of Judas," "Seigfried," portraits of himself, Emile Zola, and Verdi, and illustrations for Wilde's play *Salome*. 2 color plates. Introduction by H. C. Marillier. xii + 175pp. 8⅛ x 11. Paperbound $2.50
Clothbound $8.50

The Later Work of Aubrey Beardsley
Edited by John Lane, collection contains 174 full-page plates including *Savoy* and *Yellow Book* illustrations, book plates, "The Wagnerites," "La Dame aux Camellias," selections from *Lysistrata*, illustrations to *Das Rheingold, Venus and Tannhauser*, and the "Rape of the Lock" series. 2 color plates. xiv + 174pp. 8⅛ x 11. Paperbound $2.50
Clothbound $8.50

Prices subject to change without notice.

Available at your book dealer or write for free catalogue to Dept. Adsci, Dover Publications, Inc., 180 Varick St., N.Y., N.Y. 10014. Dover publishes more than 150 books each year on science, elementary and advanced mathematics, biology, music, art, literary history, social sciences and other areas.